W9-DEU-519

WITHDRAWN

American Literary Scholarship
1985

American Literary Scholarship

An Annual / 1985

Edited by J. Albert Robbins

Essays by Philip F. Gura, Rita K. Gollin, Kent P. Ljungquist, Brian Higgins, Jerome Loving, Louis J. Budd, Robert L. Gale, Hugh Witemeyer, Karl F. Zender, Michael S. Reynolds, William J. Scheick, David J. Nordloh, John J. Murphy, Louis Owens, Jerome Klinkowitz, Timothy A. Hunt, Lee Bartlett, Walter J. Meserve, John M. Reilly, Michael J. Hoffman, F. Lyra, Marc Chénetier, Rolf Meyn, Keiko Beppu, Mona Pers

Duke University Press Durham North Carolina 1987

© 1987 Duke University Press. Library of Congress Catalog Card number 65-19450. ISBN
0-8223-0720-0. Printed in the United States of
America by Heritage Printers, Inc.

Foreword

Almost every year sees some resignations and replacements but this year's turnover is the largest I can remember—11 out of 20 chapter authors. If we gave service ribbons for longest service to *ALS* the most decorated veteran this year would be Louis Budd, with four years reviewing 19th-century fiction and the past 10 years reviewing Mark Twain scholarship. A close second is Robert L. Gale with a full decade of work on Henry James. John M. Reilly has seven on Black Literature; Karl F. Zender, six on Faulkner; Lee Bartlett, six on poetry, 1940s to the present; Jerome Loving, five on Whitman and Dickinson; and with four or less Rita Gollin, Hugh Witemeyer, Louis Owens, and David J. Nordloh. Altogether, a total of 63 service years.

On behalf of the many who use and depend upon *American Literary Scholarship*, I thank these scholars who have invested substantial time and effort—often precious summer months—to keeping us informed.

The new contributors to next year's volume (*ALS 1986*) are, for Hawthorne, Claudia D. Johnson (Univ. of Alabama); for Whitman and Dickinson, Vivian R. Pollak (Univ. of Washington, Seattle); for Twain, a former contributor, Hamlin Hill (Texas A&M Univ.); for James, Richard A. Hocks (Univ. of Missouri); for Pound and Eliot, Reed Way Dasenbrock (New Mexico State Univ.); for Faulkner, M. Thomas Inge (Randolph-Macon College); for Fitzgerald and Hemingway, Gerry Brenner (Univ. of Montana); for Fiction: 1930s to the 1960s, Virginia Spencer Carr (Georgia State University); for Poetry: 1900 to the 1940s, our former contributor, Linda W. Wagner-Martin (Michigan State Univ.); for Poetry: 1940s to the Present, Richard J. Calhoun (Clemson Univ.). There will be no chapter on Black Literature in next year's volume. Despite an extensive search, the co-editors have not yet found a successor for John M. Reilley, who contributed so long and so well on that topic.

I leave for separate mention our new co-editor, former contributor David J. Nordloh (Indiana University), who will edit *ALS 1986*. He has a range of credentials as textual and general editor of a selected

edition of W. D. Howells, chairman of the Committee on Scholarly
Editions, bibliographer, and, as our readers may have noted, author
for the past three years of the 19th-Century Literature chapter.
Which brings us to a correlative matter: Nordloh's replacement
in Chapter 12. We are delighted to welcome back James L. Woodress
(University of California, Davis), founding editor of this series in the
early 1960s. But Jim has not been totally absent. We have meanwhile
had his good counsel and judgment on many occasions.

The essay on Italian scholarship for 1985 did not reach us in time
to be included. The essay for 1986 will be provided by Professor Massimo Bacigalupo of the University of Genoa. The Japanese essay for
1986 will be done by Professor Hiroko Sato of the Tokyo Woman's
Christian University.

Though we have acknowledged the help of others from time to
time we have not, I think, tried to tie them all into one bundle. Here
at home I am grateful for the assistance and backing of our Department of English and our chairperson, Mary A. Burgan. Our secre-
tarial staff is invaluable and skilled with both typewriter and word
processor. The department also helps us with postage and telephone
service. The Indiana University Library is an indispensable resource.
We are indebted for aid in many forms to Dr. Anthony W. Shipps,
our English Subject Librarian, and to Ann B. Beltran and her able
Reference Department staff, to whom we often turn for computer
searches and help with bibliographical snags. Dean Morton Lowen-
grub and his office of Research and Graduate Development have assisted us with the timely help of grants-in-aid for such larger expenses
as indexing and library searching.

We are grateful to Professor James L. Harner (Bowling Green
State University, Ohio), chairman of Festschriften and Other Collections Section of the *MLA International Bibliography*, who every
year sends us book leads from here and abroad on American literature.
We thus hear of elusive materials we would otherwise miss.

Eileen M. Mackesy, Director of the MLA Center for Bibliographical Services, continues to help us with facsimile printouts each year
of material in the *MLA International Bibliography* in progress.

We are grateful to Sims Kline, editor of *Literary Criticism Register*, for copies of that useful guide to recent books and periodical essays on American literature.

The able editorial staff of Duke University Press consistently
achieves excellent house editing and management of editing and pro-

duction to insure volumes with high standards of accuracy and professional design for the *ALS* series.

We urge scholars to send review copies of their 1986 books and
articles to the 1986 editor, Professor David J. Nordloh, Department
of English, Indiana University, Bloomington, IN 47405.

❀   ❀   ❀   ❀

The recent announcement, simultaneously, of *two* new histories
of American literature suggests that the Spiller-Thorpe *Literary History of the United State* (LHUS), first published in 1948, is at last
obsolete. Although there has been little advance publicity, most
specialists are aware of the new works now being written: *The Columbia History of American Literature* (general editor, Emory Elliott), and the *Cambridge History of American Literature* (general
editor, Sacvan Bercovitch). The former, I have been told, is to be in
one large volume; the latter, a set of volumes on periods and genres.
The new projects have triggered two essays in *American Literature*
this year on literary historiography: Annette Kolodny, "The Integrity
of Memory: Creating a New Literary History of the United States"
(57:291–307) and William C. Spengemann, "American Things/Liter-
ary Things: The Problem of American Literary History" (57:456–81).

J. Albert Robbins

Indiana University

Table of Contents

Foreword   v

Key to Abbreviations   xi

Part I

1. Emerson, Thoreau, and   3   Philip F. Gura
   Transcendentalism

2. Hawthorne   25   Rita K. Gollin

3. Poe   43   Kent P. Ljungquist

4. Melville   57   Brian Higgins

5. Whitman and Dickinson   69   Jerome Loving

6. Mark Twain   89   Louis J. Budd

7. Henry James   103   Robert L. Gale

8. Pound and Eliot   123   Hugh Witemeyer

9. Faulkner   147   Karl F. Zender

10. Fitzgerald and Hemingway   169   Michael S. Reynolds

Part II

11. Literature to 1800   189   William J. Scheick

12. 19th-Century Literature   205   David J. Nordloh

13. Fiction: 1900 to the 1930s   229   John J. Murphy

14. Fiction: The 1930s to the   253   Louis Owens
    1960s

15. Fiction: The 1960s to the   277   Jerome Klinkowitz
    Present

16. Poetry: 1900 to the 1940s   301   *Timothy A. Hunt*

17. Poetry: The 1940s to the   323   *Lee Bartlett*
        Present

18. Drama   347   *Walter J. Meserve*

19. Black Literature   367   *John M. Reilly*

20. Themes, Topics, Criticism   415   *Michael J. Hoffman*

21. Foreign Scholarship   443   *F. Lyra, Marc Chénetier,*
                                            Rolf Meyn, Keiko Beppu,
                                            Mona Pers

22. General Reference Works   501   *J. Albert Robbins*

    Author Index   505

    Subject Index   526

Key to Abbreviations

Festschriften, Essay Collections, and Books
Discussed in More Than One Chapter

Adultery in the American Novel /
Donald J. Greiner, *Adultery in the
American Novel: Updike, James,
and Hawthorne* (So. Car.)
After Strange Texts / Gregory S.
Jay and David L. Miller, eds.,
*After Strange Texts: The Role of
Theory in the Study of Literature*
(Alabama)
Amalgamation / James Kinney,
*Amalgamation: Race, Sex, and
Rhetoric in the Nineteenth-Century
American Novel* (Greenwood)
American Apocalypses / Douglas
Robinson, *American Apocalypses:
The Image of the End of the
World in American Literature*
(Hopkins)
American Poetry / Roland
Hagenbüchle, ed., *American
Poetry Between Tradition and
Modernism, 1865–1914* (Regens-
burg, W. Ger., Friedrich Pustet,
1984). Papers from poetry
sessions, European Assn. for
American Studies, Paris, 1982
*The American Renaissance
Reconsidered* / Walter Benn
Michaels and Donald E. Pease,
eds., *The American Renaissance
Reconsidered: Selected Papers
from the English Institute, 1982–
83* (Hopkins)
*American Romanticism and the
Marketplace* / Michael J. Gilmore,
*American Romanticism and the
Marketplace* (Chicago)
Black and White Women / Monrose
C. Gwin, *Black and White Women
of the Old South* (Tenn.)

Black Feminist Criticism / Barbara
Christian, *Black Feminist Criti-
cism: Perspectives on Black
Women Writers* (New York:
Pergamon)
Conjuring / Marjorie Pryse and
Hortense J. Spillers, eds.,
*Conjuring: Black Women, Fiction,
and Literary Tradition* (Indiana)
*Contemporary American Women
Writers* / Catherine Rainwater
and William J. Scheick, eds.,
*Contemporary American Women
Writers: Narrative Strategies*
(Kentucky)
Fictions in Autobiography / Paul
John Eakin, *Fictions in Auto-
biography: Studies in the Art of
Self-Invention* (Princeton)
*Fifteen American Authors Before
1900* / Earl N. Harbert and
Robert A. Rees, eds., *Fifteen
American Authors Before 1900:
Bibliographic Essays on Research
and Criticism*, rev. ed. (Wisconsin,
1984)
The Form of the Unfinished /
Balachandra Rajan, *The Form of
the Unfinished: English Poetics
from Spenser to Pound* (Princeton)
From Fact to Fiction / Shelley Fisher
Fishkin, *From Fact to Fiction:
Journalism & Imaginative Writing
in America* (Hopkins)
Hard Facts / Philip Fisher, *Hard
Facts: Setting and Form in the
American Novel* (Oxford)
The Haunted Dusk / Howard Kerr,
John W. Crowley, and Charles L.
Crow, eds., *The Haunted Dusk:*

American Supernatural Fiction,
1870–1920 (Georgia, 1983)
Hopkins Among the Poets / Richard F.
Giles, ed., *Hopkins Among the*
Poets: Studies in Modern Responses
to Gerard Manley Hopkins
(Hamilton, Ont.: International
Hopkins Assn.)
In Hawthorne's Shadow / Samuel
Chase Coale, *In Hawthorne's*
Shadow: American Romance from
Melville to Mailer (Kentucky)
Interface / Daniel Royot, ed., *Inter-*
face: Essays on History, Myth, and
Art in American Literature
(Montpellier, France: Université
Paul Valéry)
Intertextuality / Michel Gresset and
Noel Polk, eds., *Intertextuality*
in Faulkner (Miss.)
Joseph Conrad and American
Writers / Robert Secor and Debra
Moddelmog, *Joseph Conrad and*
American Writers: A Bibliographi-
cal Study of Affinities, Influences
and Relations (Greenwood)
Language and Power / Cheris
Kramarae, Muriel Schulz, William
M. O'Barr, eds., *Language and*
Power (Beverly Hills, Calif.,
Sage Publications, 1984)
Making a Difference / Gayle Greene
and Coppelia Kahn, eds., *Making*
a Difference: Feminist Literary
Criticism (Methuen)
A Master's Due / William J. Cooper,
Jr., et al., eds., *A Master's Due:*
Essays in Honor of David Herbert
Donald (LSU)
The Maze in the Mind / Donald
Gutierrez, *The Maze in the Mind*
and the World: Labyrinths in
Modern Literature (Whitson)
Metamorphoses of the Raven / Jeffer-
son Humphries, *Metamorphoses*
of the Raven: Literary Over-
determinedness in France and the
South since Poe (LSU)
Money and Fiction / John Vernon,
Money and Fiction: Literary
Realism in the Nineteenth and

Early Twentieth Centuries
(Cornell, 1984)
Mythos und Aufklärung / Dieter
Meindl et al., eds., *Mythos und*
Aufklärung in der amerikanischen
Literatur / *Myth and Enlighten-*
ment in American Literature,
Zu Ehren von Hans-Joachim Lang
(Erlangen)
Naturalism in American Fiction /
John J. Conder, *Naturalism in*
American Fiction: The Classic
Phase (Kentucky, 1984)
New Essays / Matthew J. Bruccoli,
ed., *New Essays on* The Great
Gatsby (Cambridge)
Nineteenth-Century American Poetry /
A. Robert Lee, ed., *Nineteenth-*
Century American Poetry (Vision)
The Poetics of Protest / George
Goodin, *The Poetics of Protest:*
Literary Form and Political Imagi-
nation in the Victim-of-Society
Novel (So. Ill.)
Rage and Celebration / Sigmund Ro,
Rage and Celebration: Essays on
Contemporary Afro-American
Writing (Atlantic Highlands, N.J.:
Humanities Press, 1984)
Regionalism and the Female
Imagination / Emily Toth, ed.,
Regionalism and the Female
Imagination (New York: Human
Sciences Press)
The Rhetoric of American Romance /
Evan Carton, *The Rhetoric of*
American Romance: Dialectic and
Identity in Emerson, Dickinson,
Poe, and Hawthorne (Hopkins)
The Sacred Game / Albert J. Von
Frank, *The Sacred Game:*
Provincialism and Frontier
Consciousness in American
Literature, 1630–1860
(Cambridge)
Shakespeare and Southern Writers /
Philip C. Kolin, ed., *Shakespeare*
and Southern Writers: A Study
in Influence (Miss.)
The Simple Life / David E. Shi,
The Simple Life: Plain Living and

Key to Abbreviations

High Thinking in American Culture (Oxford)
The Slave's Narrative, Charles T. Davis and Henry Louis Gates, Jr., eds. (Oxford)
The Southern Belle / Kathryn Lee Seidel, *The Southern Belle in the American Novel* (Florida)
Toward the End / John Gerlach, *Toward the End: Closure and*

Structure in the American Short Story (Alabama)
W. E. B. Du Bois / William L. Andrews, ed., *Critical Essays on W. E. B. Du Bois* (Hall)
Women Writers of the Contemporary South / Peggy Whitman Prenshaw, ed., *Women Writers of the Contemporary South* (Miss.)

Periodicals, Annuals, Series

ABBW / *AB Bookman's Weekly*
Aevum
Agenda
AI / *American Imago*
AL / *American Literature*
ALASH / *Acta Litteraria Academiae Scientiarum Hungaricae*
ALR / *American Literary Realism, 1870–1910*
ALS / *American Literary Scholarship*
ALUB / *Annales Littéraires de l'Université de Besançon*
AmerP / *American Poetry*
AmerS / *American Studies*
AmerSS / *American Studies in Scandinavia*
Amst / *Amerikastudien*
AmTh / *American Theatre*
Anais
AN&Q / *American Notes and Queries*
Anglia: Zeitschrift für Englische Philologie
Antaeus
APR / *American Poetry Review*
AQ / *American Quarterly*
ArAA / *Arbeiten aus Anglistik und Amerikanistik*
ArQ / *Arizona Quarterly*
Artes, Tidskrift för litterature, konst och musik (Stockholm)
ASch / *American Scholar*
ATQ / *American Transcendental Quarterly*
AuLS / *Australian Literary Studies*
AUSBSPM / *Annales Universitatis Scientiarum Budapestiensis, Sectio Philologica Moderna*
BALF / *Black American Literature Forum*

BB / *Bulletin of Bibliography*
BIS / *Browning Institute Studies*
BJRL / *Bulletin of the John Rylands Univ. Library of Manchester*
Boundary / *Boundary 2*
BRH / *Bulletin of Research in the Humanities*
Caliban (Toulouse, France)
Callaloo: A Black South Journal of Arts and Letters
CCC / *College Composition and Communication*
CEA / *CEA Critic*
CentR / *The Centennial Review*
CHA / *Cuadernos Hispanoamericanos*
ChH / *Church History*
ChildL / *Children's Literature, An International Journal*
ChiR / *Chicago Review*
CJ / *Classical Journal*
CL / *Comparative Literature*
CLAJ / *College Language Assn. Journal*
CLAQ / *Children's Literature Assn. Quarterly*
ClioI / *CLIO: A Journal of Literature, History, and the Philosophy of History*
CLQ / *Colby Library Quarterly*
CLS / *Comparative Literature Studies*
CML / *Classical and Modern Literature*
CollL / *College Literature*
Confrontation: A Literary Journal of Long Island University
Conjunctions
ConL / *Contemporary Literature*
Costerus: Essays in English and American Language and Literature

CP / *Concerning Poetry*
CRAA / Centre de Recherche sur
l'Amérique Anglophone
(Université de Grenoble III)
*Credences: A Journal of Twentieth
Century Poetry and Poetics*
CRevAS / *Canadian Review of
American Studies*
Crit / *Critique: Studies in Modern
Fiction*
CritI / *Critical Inquiry*
*Criticism: A Quarterly for Literature
and the Arts*
CritQ / *Critical Quarterly*
CS / *Concord Saunterer*
CSE / Center for Scholarly Editions
Currents (Providence, R.I.)
CVE / *Cahiers Victoriens et
Edouardiens* (Montpellier, France)
DCLB / *Dartmouth College Library
Bulletin*
DeltaES / *Delta: Revue de Centre
d'Etudes et de Recherche sur
les Ecrivains du Sud aux Etats-
Unis* (Montpellier, France)
DGQ / *Dramatist Guild Quarterly*
DicS / *Dickinson Studies*
DLB / Dictionary of Literary
Biography (Gale)
DQ / *Denver Quarterly*
DR / *Dalhousie Review*
DrN / *Dreiser Newsletter*
EA / *Etudes Anglaises*
EAL / *Early American Literature*
E&S / *Essays and Studies* (London)
EAS / *Essays in Arts and Science*
EAST / *Englisch Amerikanische
Studien*
ECS / *Eighteenth-Century Studies*
EdWN / *Edith Wharton Newsletter*
EigoS / *Eigo Seinen* (Tokyo)
EIHC / *Essex Institute Historical
Collections*
EJ / *English Journal*
ELH [formerly *Journal of English
Literary History*]
ELN / *English Language Notes*
ELWIU / *Essays in Literature*
(Western Ill. Univ.)
*English: The Journal of the English
Assn.* (London)

ES / *English Studies*
ESA / *English Studies in Africa: A
Journal of the Humanities*
ESC / *English Studies in Canada*
*ESQ: A Journal of the American
Renaissance*
Expl / *Explicator*
Fabula (Univ. de Lille, France)
*Field: Contemporary Poetry and
Poetics*
FilmC / *Film Criticism*
FJ / *Faulkner Journal* (Ohio
Northern Univ.)
FSt / *Feminist Studies*
GaR / *Georgia Review*
Genre
GRAAT / Groupe de Recherches
Anglo-Américaines de Tours
(Université François-Rabelais)
Grand Street
GRENA / Groups d'Etudes et de
Recherches Nord-Américaines
(Aix: Université de Provence)
HC / *Hollins Critic*
HemR / *Hemingway Review*
HJ / *Higginson Journal*
HJR / *Henry James Review*
HLB / *Harvard Library Bulletin*
HSN / *Hawthorne Society Newsletter*
IAT / *Izvestiia Akademii Nauk
Turkmenskoi SSR, Serii
Obshchestvennykh Nauk*
IFR / *International Fiction Review*
*Insula: Revista de Letras y Ciencias
Humanas*
IonC / *Index on Censorship*
IowaR / *Iowa Review*
Ironwood
JAC / *Journal of American Culture*
(Bowling Green State Univ., Ohio)
JAmS / *Journal of American Studies*
JEthS / *Journal of Ethical Studies*
JHI / *Journal of the History of Ideas*
JLN / *Jack London Newsletter*
JML / *Journal of Modern Literature*
JNH / *Journal of Negro History*
JNT / *Journal of Narrative Technique*
JoPL / *Journal of Popular Literature*
(Bowling Green State Univ., Ohio)
JPC / *Journal of Popular Culture*
JQ / *Journalism Quarterly*
JSSE / *Journal of the Short Story in*

Key to Abbreviations

English [formerly *Cahiers de
la Nouvelle*] (Angers, France)
KAL / *Kyushu American Literature*
Kalki: *Studies in James Branch Cabell*
KR / *Kenyon Review*
L&M / *Literature & Medicine*
L&P / *Literature and Psychology*
Lang&S / *Language and Style*
LangQ / *The USF Language
Quarterly* (Univ. of South Florida)
LCUT / *Library Chronicle of the
Univ. of Texas*
LFQ / *Literature/Film Quarterly*
LHRev / *Langston Hughes Review*
LJHum / *Lamar Journal of the
Humanities*
LOS / *Literary Onomastics Studies*
LWU / *Literatur in Wissenschaft und
Unterricht*
MarkhamR / *Markham Review*
MD / *Modern Drama*
Menckeniana: *A Quarterly Review*
MFS / *Modern Fiction Studies*
MHLS / *Mid-Hudson Language
Studies*
Midamerica: *The Yearbook of the
Society for the Study of
Midwestern Literature*
Midstream: *A Quarterly Jewish
Review*
MissQ / *Mississippi Quarterly*
MLN [formerly *Modern Language
Notes*]
MLQ / *Modern Language Quarterly*
MLS / *Modern Language Studies*
MMN / *Marianne Moore Newsletter*
Monatshefte
Mosaic: *A Journal for the Inter-
disciplinary Study of Literature*
MP / *Modern Philology*
MQR / *Michigan Quarterly Review*
MR / *Massachusetts Review*
MSE / *Massachusetts Studies in
English*
MSEx / *Melville Society Extracts*
MSI / *Moody Street Irregulars: A
Jack Kerouac Newsletter*
MSpr / *Moderna Språk*
MTJ / *Mark Twain Journal*
MTSB / *Mark Twain Society Bulletin*
Nabokovian
N&Q / *Notes and Queries*

NCF / *Nineteenth-Century Fiction*
NCHR / *North Carolina Historical
Review*
NConL / *Notes on Contemporary
Literature*
NDQ / *North Dakota Quarterly*
Neohelicon: *Acta Comparationis
Universarum*
NEQ / *New England Quarterly*
NER / *New England Review &
Bread Loaf Quarterly*
NLH / *New Literary History: A
Journal of Theory and
Interpretation*
NMAL: *Notes on Modern American
Literature*
NMW / *Notes on Mississippi Writers*
NOR / *New Orleans Review*
Novel: *A Forum on Fiction*
NYRB / *New York Review of Books*
NYTBR / *New York Times Book
Review*
Obsidian: *Black Literature in Review*
OhR / *Ohio Review*
OL / *Orbis Litterarum: International
Review of Literary Studies*
ON / *The Old Northwest*
PAAS / *Proceedings of the American
Antiquarian Society*
PaH / *Pennsylvania History*
Paideuma: *A Journal Devoted to
Ezra Pound Scholarship*
ParisR / *Paris Review*
Parnassus: *Poetry in Review*
PBSA / *Papers of the Bibliographical
Society of America*
PCP / *Pacific Coast Philology*
PE&W / *Philosophy East and West*
PerfAJ / *Performing Arts Journal*
PLL / *Papers on Language and
Literature*
Ploughshares
PMHB / *Pennsylvania Magazine of
History and Biography*
PMHS / *Proceedings of the
Massachusetts Historical Society*
PMLA: *Publications of the Modern
Language Assn.*
PMPA / *Publications of the Missouri
Philological Assn.*
PNotes / *Pynchon Notes*
PoeS / *Poe Studies*

Poesis: A Journal of Criticism
POMPA / *Publications of the Mississippi Philological Assn.*
PoT / *Poetics Today* (Jerusalem)
PR / *Partisan Review*
Prospects: An Annual Journal of American Cultural Studies
Proteus (Shippensburg Univ.)
PRR / *Journal of Pre-Raphaelite Studies*
PQ / *Philological Quarterly*
PSt / *Prose Studies*
PULC / *Princeton University Library Chronicle*
QL / *La Quinzaine Littéraire*
RALS / *Resources for American Literary Study*
RANAM / *Recherches Anglaises et Américaines*
R&L / *Religion and Literature*
Raritan, A Quarterly Review
RBPH / *Revue Belge de Philologie et d'Histoire*
Renascence: Essays on Value in Literature
RFEA / *Revue Française d'Etudes Américaines* (Paris)
SAF / *Studies in American Fiction*
Sage: A Scholarly Journal on Black Women (Georgia State Univ.)
Sagetrieb: A Journal Devoted to Poets in the Pound-H.D.-Williams Tradition
SALit / *Chu-Shikoku Studies in American Literature*
Salmagundi
SAQ / *South Atlantic Quarterly*
SAR / *Studies in the American Renaissance*
SB / *Studies in Bibliography*
SBJ / *Saul Bellow Journal*
Scotia: American-Canadian Journal of Scottish Studies
SCR / *South Carolina Review*
SDR / *South Dakota Review*
SELit / *Studies in English Literature* (Tokyo)
SHR / *Southern Humanities Review*
Signs: Journal of Women in Culture and Society
SinN / *Sin Nombre*
SIR / *Studies in Romanticism*

SJS / *San Jose Studies*
SLitI / *Studies in the Literary Imagination*
SLJ / *Southern Literary Journal*
SLRJ / *St. Louis University Research Journal of the Graduate School of Arts and Sciences*
SN / *Studia Neophilologica*
SNNTS / *Studies in the Novel* (North Texas State Univ.)
SoAR / *South Atlantic Review*
SoQ / *Southern Quarterly*
SoR / *Southern Review*
SoSt / *Southern Studies*
Soundings: An Interdisciplinary Journal
SPELL / *Swiss Papers in English Language and Literature*
Sphinx: A Magazine of Literature and Society
SR / *Sewanee Review*
SSF / *Studies in Short Fiction*
Standpunte
StQ / *Steinbeck Quarterly*
Style
SubStance: A Review of Theory and Literary Criticism
Sulfur
TCL / *Twentieth-Century Literature*
TDR / *Drama Review*
Theater
ThHS / *Theatre History Studies*
ThoreauQ / *Thoreau Quarterly*
Thought
ThS / *Theatre Survey*
TJ / *Theatre Journal*
TkR / *Tamkang Review: A Quarterly of Comparative Studies between Chinese and Foreign Literatures*
TriQ / *TriQuarterly*
TSL / *Tennessee Studies in Literature*
TSLL / *Texas Studies in Literature and Language*
TSWL / *Tulsa Studies in Women's Literature*
Turner Studies: His Art and Epoch, 1775–1851 (London)
TUSAS / *Twayne United States Authors Series*
TWN / *Thomas Wolfe Newsletter*
Vinduet (Oslo, Norway)
VLit / *Voprosy Literatury*

VMU / Vestnik Moskovskogo
  Universiteta. Seriia 9, Filologiia
VP / Victorian Poetry
VQR / Virginia Quarterly Review
WAL / Western American Literature
WCWR / William Carlos Williams
  Review
WE / Winesburg Eagle: The
  Official Publication of the
  Sherwood Anderson Society
WHR / Western Humanities Review
WiF / William Faulkner: Materials,
  Studies, and Criticism (Tokyo)
WIRS / Western Illinois Regional
  Studies
WLT / World Literature Today
WLWE / World Literature Written
  in English

WMQ / William and Mary Quarterly
WMR / William and Mary Review
WQ / Wilson Quarterly
WS / Women's Studies
WSJ / Wallace Stevens Journal
WVUPP / West Virginia Univ.
  Philological Papers
WWQR / Walt Whitman Quarterly
  Review
WWS / Western Writers Series
  (Boise State Univ.)
Yeats: An Annual Publication of
  Critical and Textual Studies
YES / Yearbook of English Studies
YR / Yale Review
YULG / Yale University Library
  Gazette

Publishers

Alabama / University: Univ. of
  Alabama Press
Algonquin / Algonquin Books of
  Chapel Hill (N.C.)
Allen & Unwin (London)
AMS Press (New York)
Archon / Hamden, Conn: Archon
  Books
Ardis / Ann Arbor, Mich.: Ardis
  Publications
Arizona / Tucson: Univ. of Arizona
  Press
Atheneum / New York: Atheneum
  Publishers
Avon / New York: Avon Books
Barnes and Noble (Totowa, N.J.)
Beacon / Boston: Beacon Press
Belknap / Cambridge, Mass.: Belknap
  Press of Harvard Univ. Press
Bowling Green / Bowling Green,
  Ohio: Bowling Green State Univ.,
  Popular Press
Brownstone Books (Madison, Ind.)
Bucknell / Lewisburg, Pa.: Bucknell
  Univ. Press
Calif. / Berkeley: Univ. of California
  Press
Cambridge / Cambridge and New
  York: Cambridge Univ. Press
Carcanet / New York: Carcanet Press

Carl Winter (Heidelberg)
Chatto and Windus (London)
Chelsea House (New York)
Chicago / Chicago: Univ. of Chicago
  Press
Clarendon / Oxford: Clarendon Press
Columbia / New York: Columbia
  Univ. Press
Cornell / Ithaca, N.Y.: Cornell Univ.
  Press
Croom Helm (London)
Delaware / Newark: Univ. of
  Delaware Press
Dell / New York: Dell Publishing Co.
Doubleday / New York: Doubleday
  and Co.
Erlangen / Universitätsbund
  Erlangen-Nürnberg
Fairleigh Dickinson / Madison, N.J.:
  Fairleigh Dickinson Univ. Press
Feminist Press of City University of
  New York
Florida / Gainesville: Univ. Presses
  of Florida
Fortress Press (Philadelphia)
Gale / Detroit: Gale Research Co.
Georgia / Athens: Univ. of Georgia
  Press
Gordian / New York: Gordian Press
Göteborg Sweden: Acta Universitatis
  Gothoburgensis

Greenwood / Westport, Conn.:
Greenwood Press
Grove / New York: Grove Press
Hall / Boston: G. K. Hall & Co.
Harper / New York: Harper and Row
Harvester / Brighton, Sussex:
Harvester Press
Hill & Wang (New York)
Hopkins / Baltimore: Johns Hopkins
Univ. Press
Houghton Mifflin / Boston: Houghton
Mifflin Co.
Hum. Res. Center / Austin: Ransom
Humanities Research Center,
Univ. of Texas
Illinois / Urbana: Univ. of Illinois
Press
Indiana / Bloomington: Indiana Univ.
Press
Iowa State / Ames: Iowa State Univ.
Press
Kansas / Lawrence, Kan.: Univ. Press
of Kansas
Kent State / Kent, Ohio: Kent State
Univ. Press
Kentucky / Lexington: Univ. Press of
Kentucky
Knopf / New York: Alfred A. Knopf
Libraries Unlimited (Littleton, Colo.)
Library of America (New York)
Little, Brown / Boston: Little, Brown
& Co.
Longman / Harlow, Essex, U.K.,
Longman Group
Longman / White Plains, N.Y.:
Longman
LSU / Baton Rouge: Louisiana State
Univ. Press
McFarland / Jefferson, N.C.:
McFarland & Co.
Macmillan (New York)
Manchester / Manchester: Manchester
Univ. Press
Mass. / Amherst: Univ. of
Massachusetts Press
Max Reinhardt (London)
Methuen (London)
Michigan / Ann Arbor: Univ. of
Michigan Press
Minnesota / Minneapolis: Univ. of
Minnesota Press

Miss. / Jackson: Univ. Press of
Mississippi
Missouri / Columbia: Univ. of
Missouri Press
MLA / New York: Modern Language
Assn.
Mysterious Press (New York)
NAL / New York: New American
Library
Natl. Poetry Found. / Orono, Me.:
National Poetry Foundation
Nebraska / Lincoln: Univ. of
Nebraska Press
New Directions / New York: New
Directions Publishing Corp.
New England / Hanover, N.H.:
Univ. Press of New England
N. Mex. / Albuquerque: Univ. of
New Mexico Press
No. Car. / Chapel Hill: Univ. of
North Carolina Press
Northwestern / Evanston, Ill.:
Northwestern Univ. Press
Norton / New York: W. W. Norton
& Co.
NYU / New York: New York Univ.
Press
Odense / Odense, Denmark: Odense
Univ. Press
Ohio / Athens: Ohio Univ. Press
Ohio State / Columbus: Ohio State
Univ. Press.
Oklahoma / Norman: Univ. of
Oklahoma Press
Oslo / Oslo: Universitetsforlaget
Oxford / New York: Oxford Univ.
Press
Pantheon / New York: Pantheon
Books
Paulist Press (Mahwah, N.J.)
Penn. / Philadelphia: Univ. of
Pennsylvania Press
Penn. State / University Park:
Pennsylvania State Univ. Press
Persea / New York: Persea Books
Peter Lang / New York: Peter Lang
Publishing Co.
Pittsburgh / Pittsburgh: Univ. of
Pittsburgh Press
Polity Press (Oxford, U.K.)
Princeton / Princeton, N.J.:
Princeton Univ. Press

Proscenium / Newark, Del.:
Proscenium Press
Purdue / West Lafayette, Ind.:
Purdue Univ. Press
Research Publishing (Washington,
D.C.)
Routledge / London: Routledge and
Kegan Paul
Rowman & Allanheld (Totowa, N.J.)
Rutgers / New Brunswick, N.J.:
Rutgers Univ. Press
St. Martin's / New York: St. Martin's
Press
Salem / Englewood Cliffs, N.J.:
Salem Press
Scarecrow / Metuchen, N.J.:
Scarecrow Press
Schenkman Books (Cambridge, Mass.)
Scholars' Facsimiles / Delmar, N.Y.:
Scholars' Facsimiles and Reprints
Scribner's / New York: Charles
Scribner's Sons
Secker & Warburg (London)
Seejay / Columbia, S.C.: Seejay Press
Shoe String / Hamden, Conn.: Shoe
String Press
Simon & Schuster (New York)
Smith / New York: The Smith
SMU / Dallas: Southern Methodist
Univ. Press
SUNY / Albany: State Univ. of
New York Press
Syracuse / Syracuse, N.Y.: Syracuse
Univ. Press
Taylor / Dallas: Taylor Publishing Co.

TCG / New York: Theatre
Communications Group
Tenn. / Knoxville: Univ. of
Tennessee Press
Toronto / Univ. of Toronto Press
Turkey Press (Santa Barbara, Calif.)
Twayne / Boston: Twayne Publishers
(G. K. Hall & Co.)
UMI / Ann Arbor, Mich.: University
Microfilms International
UMI Research Press (Ann Arbor,
Mich.)
Ungar / New York: Frederick
Ungar Publishing Co.
Univ. Press / Lanham, Md.: Univ.
Press of America
Univ. Pubs. / Frederick, Md.:
University Publications of America
Uppsala / Acta Universitatis
Uppsaliensis
Viking / New York: Viking Press
Virginia / Charlottesville: Univ.
Press of Virginia
Vision / London: Vision Press
Wadsworth / Belmont, Calif.:
Wadsworth Publishing Co.
Weidenfeld and Nicholson (New
York)
Wesleyan / Middletown, Conn.:
Wesleyan Univ. Press
Whitston / Troy, N.Y.: Whitston
Publishing Co.
Yale / New Haven, Conn.: Yale
Univ. Press
York / Toronto, Ont.: York Publishing

Part I

1. Emerson, Thoreau, and Transcendentalism

Philip F. Gura

In comparison to the extraordinary number and quality of the items I surveyed last year in my inaugural essay, this year's offering seems more nearly like what one should expect (and so allowed me to catch my breath). No book-length editions appeared, although there was some interesting primary material on Margaret Fuller and George Ripley made available for the first time. No book on Emerson either, although the Concord sage was well served in several engaging essays; and his friend Thoreau, while seeming to fare better with three lengthy studies devoted to him, also was more provocatively treated in the many essays devoted to his work. Thus, while I cannot say that I was disappointed by what was published on the Transcendentalists in 1985, for me it was a year which provided more insight into the rhythms of scholarly publishing: when there is not much that is extraordinarily good, one is forced to discriminate more carefully to declare what in fact is worth reading, and as a result to see more clearly how inferior other work is. Still, as I hope the reader will see from this year's review, Transcendentalist ground remains to be worked, and if Sharon Cameron's book on Thoreau is any indication, in the future more and more the tools scholars bring to this task will have been forged in schools of critical theory. I leave it to each reader to decide if this means that there is in fact more day to dawn as the morning star of the theoreticians rises even over Henry's *Journal.*

i. Bibliographies, Editions, General Studies

The only major bibliography of the year is invaluable. In *Emerson: An Annotated Secondary Bibliography* (Pittsburgh) Robert E. Burkholder and Joel Myerson have provided 5,659 entries on critical and biographical studies (and 182 more of a miscellaneous nature) of the Concord sage, covering the years from 1816 to 1879; hitherto all Emerson scholars are in their debt. A project of a different order but very satisfactorily completed is Robert Sattelmeyer's essay-review, "Study Nature and Know Thyself: Recent Thoreau Criticism" (*ESQ* 31:190–208). The author assesses nine books on Thoreau published since 1981 (all of which have been or will be reviewed in *ALS*) which address, among other subjects, Thoreau's place in his culture and ours, his reputation over time, his career as a man of letters, his development as a writer, and his practice as a naturalist. But even if these topics now are satisfactorily addressed, Sattelmeyer reminds us, all is not yet done: "it also is necessary to preserve some sense of the distinctiveness of the cultural moment that [Thoreau] both epitomized and excoriated in his writing," a project seemingly made to order for the "new" literary historians. In "Making the Emerson Text Adequate: Problems, Approaches, and Revisions" (*CRevAS* 16:205–19), John Stephen Martin treats four volumes in a similar attempt to direct scholars to the most fertile scholarly or critical ground, in this case in Emerson's fields. *The* problem in Emerson studies, Martin claims, "is in making the available texts of Emerson—both 'public' and 'private'—adequate for an explanation of Emerson's transmutation of the pressures of life into art that is universal and enduring," seemingly not an overly startling suggestion. But Martin's investigation of the books under his eye does indeed yield some valuable suggestions for future scholarship and is well worth one's time, particularly because of his sensitivity to psychological issues raised in the *Journals*. In "The Legacy of Emerson's Journals" (*RALS* 13:1–9) David Robinson, before reviewing the last two volumes of the Harvard edition of this masterwork, discusses how the needs of scholars as well as of general readers have been met by the editors of this monumental undertaking. And this year the *Concord Saunterer* (18, i:1–50) issued a cumulative index to its contents since its inception in 1966. As all Thoreauvians know, this journal is a treasure trove of useful information, and thus this tool is much welcomed.

Some interesting manuscript material on Emerson was made more readily available. In "Elizabeth of Concord: Selected Letters of Elizabeth Sherman Hoar (1814–1878) to the Emersons, Family, and the Emerson Circle (Part II)" (*SAR*, pp. 95–156), Elizabeth Maxfield-Miller prints 84 letters written between 1821 and 1839. Her introduction to this significant body of primary material appeared in last year's *SAR*; a third installment next year will carry the correspondence through Hoar's death. Karen Kalinevitch, in "Emerson on Friendship: An Unpublished Manuscript" (*SAR*, pp. 47–61), prints a manuscript which, from evidence in Emerson's journals, she believes was written in the 1830s and which thus predates by several years his famous essay on the same subject. Wesley T. Mott provides another interesting Emerson item in "From Natural Religion to Transcendentalism: An Edition of Emerson's Sermon No. 43" (*SAR*, pp. 1–32). In this sermon, which Emerson delivered a score of times between 1829 and 1838, one can study the way Emerson moved from the Unitarian camp to the more open fields of Transcendentalism; in particular it displays his attempt to merge the rigorous piety of the Puritan tradition with the Idealism of Berkeley, which led Emerson to redefine revelation as a direct experience of God. In "Emerson and Cape Ann" (*EIHC* 121:257–68) Marshall W. S. Swan documents Emerson's visits to the North Shore in the 1840s for lecture engagements and for recreation in the decade following, and discusses his continued interest in the region through the 1870s. Finally, in "Fire and Smoke: Emerson's Letter to Whitman" (*MLN* 15, ii: 3–7) George Monteiro reviews all relevant evidence surrounding Emerson's famous 21 July 1855 letter to Whitman and concludes that Emerson did not in fact consider the author of *Leaves of Grass* as *the* poet for whom he had called a decade earlier. Monteiro argues that here and elsewhere Emerson carefully weighed his words to avoid that judgment, a fact clearly reflected in other of his correspondence about Whitman and his book in the years immediately after 1855.

There was not much new primary material on Thoreau, but other Transcendentalists fared a bit better. In "An Overlooked Early Review of Thoreau's Writings" (*CS* 18, ii:49–55) Thomas Blanding reprints a lengthy review of *A Week, Walden, Excursions,* and *The Maine Woods* which appeared in *The Church Monthly*'s October 1864 issue; it is worth reading to learn what a New England Episcopalian journal had to say about Thoreau and his work. Marlene A. Ogden and Clifton Keller published *Walden: A Concordance* (Garland), a useful book for those who wish to pursue the kinds of studies such tools make possible. Much more likely to forward scholarship on Transcendentalism is an item like Sterling F. Delano's "Calendar of Meetings of the 'Boston Religious Union of Associationists,' 1847–1850" (*SAR*, pp. 187–268). Numbering among its members W. H. Channing, John Sullivan Dwight, George Ripley, and Elizabeth

Peabody, this little-studied "group of dedicated and high-minded individuals," as Delano calls them, were committed to "the utopian cause of introducing 'upon the planet earth an Era of Universal Unity.' " This "calendar" offers detailed descriptions of what happened at the Association's meetings and is grist for the mill of any scholar who wishes to trace into the 1850s the religious dimensions of the Transcendentalist movement. Another valuable source for a similarly little-studied phenomenon, in this case the *Harbinger's* relocation to New York City after the disastrous fire at Brook Farm, is Joel Myerson's "New Light on George Ripley and the *Harbinger's* New York Years" (*HLB* 33:313–35). Myerson publishes 12 letters from Ripley to Dwight, sent between October 1847 and December 1848, in which Ripley, who by that time had relinquished the journal's editorship to Parke Godwin, complained of the many problems, fiscal and otherwise, which plagued the *Harbinger* in its last years.

In her "Letters of Elizabeth Palmer Peabody and Others Concerning a Problem at 13 West Street" (*EIHC* 121:21–43) Pauline S. Grearson discusses the personal difficulties between Peabody and Caroline Hinckley, who had been left in charge of Peabody's bookstore in 1851 while the owner was traveling. The accompanying letters (from Hinckley to Peabody and to her brother, as well as from Mary Peabody Mann to this same sibling) speak to the general management of the store, problems with Miss Hinckley's personal work habits, and her fiscal indebtedness to Peabody. They offer a fascinating glimpse of both the solicitude and high-handedness of a "feminist" to an obviously weak protégé. Frank Shuffleton makes available another important primary document in his "Margaret Fuller at the Greene Street School: The Journal of Evelina Metcalf" (*SAR*, pp. 29–46). Detailing both the daily routine at and the frequent visitors to the Providence school in the month of June 1837, Metcalf's journal is the fourth such item we have by students taught by Fuller after she left Bronson Alcott's Temple School and the first to be printed in the same form in which it was kept. Another significant Fuller item is Robert D. Habich's "Margaret Fuller's Journal for October 1842" (*HLB* 33:280–91), in which Fuller's main concern is the marriage between her good friend Anna Barker and Samuel Gray Ward, with whom Fuller herself seemed to be in love. Needless to say, because of the searching personal nature of many of the passages, Emerson, W. H. Channing, and James Freeman Clarke did not excerpt much from this journal in their *Memoirs* of the Countess d'Ossoli. Finally, Richard L. Herrnstadt, in his "Alcott in Iowa: Two Letters of Mary Newbury Adams and Five Letters of A. Bronson Alcott" (*SAR*, pp. 323–32), publishes some documents which relate to Alcott's visits to Dubuque in the 1870s.

Several studies of American church history that contain chapters on the Transcendentalists deserve notice. In particular it was a good year for those interested in the religious background to Transcendentalism's earliest manifestations. In *The Unitarians and the Universalists* (Greenwood) David Robinson contributes a 200-page commentary on these two groups, followed by a valuable biographical dictionary of Unitarian and Universalist leaders. Although he has only 12 pages on the Transcendentalist controversy per se, his general history of the Unitarians is valuable for quick reference, particularly for those interested, say, in the Free Religion movement. Robinson also published *William Ellery Channing: Selected Writings* (Paulist Press). In addition to nine selections from Channing covering the years 1815 to 1842 (including such pieces as "Unitarian Christianity," "Likeness to God," and "Self-Culture" but not, surprisingly, his essay on Milton), he offers a useful 37-page introduction to this spiritual godfather to the Transcendentalists.

Likely to be much more influential than either of these two works, though, is Sydney E. Ahlstrom and Jonathan S. Carey's *An American Reformation: A Documentary History of Unitarian Christianity* (Wesleyan), a massive anthology which in church history circles should do for its subject what Perry Miller's *The Transcendentalists: An Anthology* (1950) did for its. Students of American literature will be most interested in section 5, "The Challenge of Emerson and Transcendentalism," which contains generous excerpts from Frederic Henry Hedge, Henry Ware, Jr., George E. Ellis, and Andrews Norton. Ahlstrom also contributed a chapter on "Ralph Waldo Emerson and the American Transcendentalists" to the second volume of *Nineteenth Century Religious Thought in the West*, eds. Ninian Smart et al. (Cambridge; pp. 29–68). The essay is a rich condensation of Ahlstrom's lifelong consideration of 19th-century American church history and makes us lament all the more his death in the summer of 1984, while this essay was in press. I also should add that all three of the volumes under this title should be of interest to serious scholars of American civilization and its relation to the various religious traditions of the West. Most of the major European figures and movements which affected American Transcendentalism are treated at essay length.

A much more wide-ranging study than the above four, Bruce Kuklick's *Churchmen and Philosophers: From Jonathan Edwards to John Dewey* (Yale) should be perused for its brief discussions of James Marsh and Vermont Transcendentalism as well as of William Torrey Harris and the St. Louis Hegelians. On Emerson and his immediate circle, though, Kuklick has little new to say. Finally, in "Horace Bushnell's 'The Age of Homespun' and Transcendental Symbolism" (*ATQ* 55:5–18) Theodore Hovet argues that in Bushnell's hands the use of symbol occasionally became more than a mere tool for moral instruction. Closely reading this address, delivered in Litchfield, Connecticut, in 1851, Hovet points out Bushnell's elaborate use of metaphor as he settled on the image of weaving to discuss the great economic and technological changes which had occurred in the past century, and particularly their effect on the family and the relationship between the sexes. If this essay does not greatly advance our understanding of Bushnell's theory of symbolism, it provides proof that in Bushnell one can indeed sometimes find the Transcendentalist in spite of himself.

Several general studies of American literature and culture included chapters on Transcendentalists. As one might expect, anyone who writes a book with the title *The Simple Life: Plain Living and High Thinking in American Culture* (Oxford) cannot avoid this group. Thus in his chapter on "Transcendental Simplicity" David Shi discusses how Emerson, Thoreau, Alcott, and others "grafted a romantic naturalism onto the tough and springy root of Puritan moralism" and then, with the approach of the Civil War, came to believe that this trial might serve to regenerate a people grown morally flabby. A generalist's study, the book holds few surprises for scholars of Transcendentalism, but it is enjoyable reading in this, another flabby, age. So, too, is Albert J. Von Frank's *The Sacred Game: Provincialism and Frontier Consciousness in American Literature* (Cambridge), and much more worth the specialist's time. Claiming that "provincial conditions were not the special case in America before the Civil War but, in fact, quite the ordinary context for artistic expression," Von Frank draws our attention to, among other things, "the elegaic note supplied in American literature by the frontier consciousness of defeated conservatives." He ranges from the Colonial period (with chapters on Anne Bradstreet and Timothy Dwight) through the mid-19th century; his chapters on Fuller and Emerson should be of most interest to readers of this essay. He sees Emerson, for example, as one who used his provincial position constructively, as "an opportunity to return to something better and more fundamental" based on the specialness of American nature. In contrast, Fuller never could come to terms with America's provincial conditions, yet, ironically, her struggle against this "major irritant" in fact helped her to produce her strongest work.

In *The Rhetoric of American Romance* Evan Carton defines romance as "a specific and urgent kind of rhetorical performance, a self-consciously dialectical enactment of critical and philosophical concerns about the relation of words to things and the nature of the self," and places Emerson squarely in this tradition. His second chapter, "Originality and the Self," will be of most use to Emersonians, but the entire study is worth reading for its thought-provoking redefinition of the category of "romance," which hitherto we have associated primarily with novelists. Written by someone obviously at home in critical theory, it illustrates what good can come when such training is linked to an equally strong commitment to intellectual history.

In "Spenser and the Transcendentalists" (*ATQ* 55:29–39) Joann Peck Krieg traces this poet's reception among Emerson, Alcott, Thoreau, and others. Among other things, she is interested in why Emerson, who in the mid-1830s had numbered Spenser among the great, never gave a proposed lecture on the poet; she suggests that Alcott, who viewed him more as a devotional and moral writer, may have tempered his friend's more intuitive response to the man and his work. Finally, readers of *ALS* should look through *The American Renaissance Reconsidered*. None of the essays in this volume focuses directly on Emerson, Thoreau, or Transcendentalism, but several are of tangential interest, particularly Eric J. Sundquist's "Slavery, Revolution, and the American Renaissance" (pp. 1–33) and Jonathan Arac's "F. O. Matthiessen: Authorizing an American Renaissance" (pp. 90–112).

ii. Emerson

There were no book-length treatments of Emerson, but he was amply discussed in several strong essays. In "Mulberry Leaves and Satin: Emerson's Theory of the Creative Process" (*SAR*, pp. 79–94) Merton

M. Sealts, Jr., discusses Emerson's view of the creative process beginning with his important lectures on "The Philosophy of History," delivered after he published *Nature* but before the "American Scholar" address. Sealts believes that his later productions (like the address before the graduating class of the Harvard Divinity School in 1838) are all rooted in the ground he broke therein and feed specifically on his notion that the spirit manifests itself in material forms. Thus for Emerson, Sealts claims, literature becomes the conversion of action into thought, and thence to utterance. Equally challenging in a quite different way is Robert M. Greenberg's "Shooting the Gulf: Emerson's Sense of Experience" (*ESQ* 31:211–29), in which he attempts to redress what he considers the usual limited view of Emerson by focusing on the modernity of his espousal of a unitary self even as he found his own self in fragmentary disarray. Greenberg regards Emerson as "an explorer of the flux of individual consciousness," that is, of the relativism of human perception and the epistemological questions which flow from this fact. To Emerson, then, experience is an oscillation or fluctuation between polarities as man constantly struggles to assert unity but as well always fails to attain it. This essay is well worth considering, particularly in light of critical theorists who remind us of the final instability of any statements we strongly believe to be unequivocally coherent. Emerson, it seems, was very sensitive to the anomaly of this situation.

Another rewarding essay which speaks to this same problem but from yet another vantage in intellectual history is Anthony J. Cascardi's "The Logic of Moods: An Essay on Emerson and Rousseau" (*SIR* 24:223–37). Cascardi claims that Emerson rejected the Kantian notion that knowledge must recognize limits, for he regarded such limitations as failures of human perception, even as he understood that such disappointments in fact characterized his own experience. Thus he was "driven to seek the basis of our relationship to the world *in* experience," Cascardi argues, "and not in our knowledge of it." Emerson's plea for experience, he continues, resembles Rousseau's sensualism; the bulk of the essay is an extended discussion of "moods," which, Cascardi claims, "function as a regulative principle of experience" in Emerson, as they similarly do for Rousseau in his *Reveries of the Solitary Walker*. Coupled with his fine essay on Kant and Emerson published in 1984, this effort marks Cascardi as one of our most astute commentators on the relationship of Emerson to earlier philosophical discourse on the Continent in the late 18th and early 19th centuries.

Two essays dealt specifically with Emerson's poetic theory and practice. In "Essaying the Poet: Emerson's Poetic Theory and Practice" (*MLS* 15, ii:9–23) Mutlu Konuk Blasing discusses Emerson's verse in relation to the poetic theory proposed in his various essays and concludes that the poems and essays have "different yet complementary intentions." Because the poems are "formal constructs meant to parallel the correspondence of the orders of nature and the Spirit," critics should not treat them, nor expect them to read like, the essays. Blasing concludes that "Emerson's concept of poetry as the language of law—or even as language *as* law—makes clear that his idea of poetry is much more restrictive than what critics have termed the musical or inspired speech of his essays." In " 'Frolic Architecture': Music and Metamorphosis in Emerson's Poetry" (*Nineteenth-Century American Poetry*, pp. 100–117) Brian Harding reads a large sampling of Emerson's verse, beginning with "The Snow-Storm," and argues that in many of his most challenging poems Emerson "attempted to express an idea of poetry that combined (through metaphor) the apparently irreconcilable qualities of architecture and music," another way of saying that he urged man "to find meaning *in* the flux of experience rather than in escape from it." Like Blasing's essay, Harding's will be rewarding to those who seek a handle when considering the relation between Emerson's theory of language and the art he produced through its principles.

Another aspect of Emerson's aesthetic is discussed in Gayle L. Smith's "Emerson and the Luminist Painters: A Study of their Styles" (*AQ* 37:193–215). In this rewarding essay she compares the formal, compositional features of Luminist painting to the linguistic features which characterize Emerson's prose style and concludes that Emerson "developed a style that in many ways defies the common-sense limits of discursive prose and dynamically suggests the contemplative mind apprehending the One in the Many, the eternal in the momentary, and the subject and object in one another"—in other words, he did in words what people like Fitz Hugh Lane and Martin Johnson Heade did in paint. If we couple this with John Conron's essay on Thoreau's *A Week* as a Luminist landscape (see *ALS 1980*), we finally can speak *concretely* about Luminism as a manifestation of the Transcendental impulse in mid-19th-century American culture, a notion forwarded as long ago as 1969 by Barbara Novak in her *American Painting of the Nineteenth Century* but about which she and others after her have spoken only impressionistically.

In "Emerson's Prose Style: Following Nature with Language" (*ATQ* 56:19–30) Smith comes at the question of Emerson's distinctive prose from another angle. Studying "Self-Reliance," "The Poet," and "Experience," she argues that in Emerson's prose the "essential, functional, temporal, spatial, and causal distinctions dissolve in a vision characterized by a continuously metamorphosing identity that is created and recreated . . . by the interchange between subject and object, seer and seen, artist and the world." Thus to Emerson language did not "follow" the action of nature but suggested the action of the Reason responding to it. In yet a third offering, "Reading Emerson on the Right Side of the Brain" (*MLS* 15, ii:24–31), Smith discusses how Emerson's observation that "our common sense perceptions may blind us to the scenes around us every day" is akin to what Betty Edwards argues in her *Drawing on the Right Side of the Brain* (1979), a book with something of a cult following a few years ago. Smith marvels that Emerson "tried, and with amazing frequency it appears, succeeded in conveying the experience of this unmediated 'right-brained' perception with language, the instrument of the 'left-brain.'" Despite its trendy title, this essay is primarily about Emerson's notion of perception; the weakest of Smith's essays, it, like her other efforts, still displays a gift for close reading, even if it does not contribute as much as her other work does to our understanding of the mechanics and the philosophical underpinnings of Emerson's prose.

Ian F. A. Bell, in "The Hard Currency of Words: Emerson's Fiscal Metaphor in *Nature*" (*ELH* 52:733–53), comes to his scholarly task asking a quite different set of questions, but his investigation is equally rewarding and a good example of rehabilitated intellectual history. Bell astutely links Emerson's concern with debased language to national debates over currency and paper money in Jacksonian America. The Second National Bank is the central villain, he argues, for through its policies power and wealth became divorced from the arena of actual production and instead were centered in the "paper" world of banks, corporations, and the stock market; that is, they were *abstracted* from the means of production. "The debates about money during the period surrounding the composition of *Nature*," Bell notes, "registered a coalition of a series of social and aesthetic questions concerning the nature of symbolism, its material referents, and its consequent role in redefined understandings about the nature of power and liberty within the new conditions instigated by corporate industry." Read alongside the essays in Michael T. Gilmore's *American Romanticism and the Marketplace* (see below), Bell's essay provides more evidence of how important ideology is to our understanding of the Transcendentalists and their works, and how influenced they were by economic forces ultimately beyond their control.

Intellectual and cultural history also informs "The Soldier and the Scholar: Emerson's Warring Heroes" (*JAmS* 19:165–97), in which Edward Stessel proposes that by the 1860s the soldier had become a more important image in Emerson's writings than the scholar, who had dominated his earlier essays, which in turn may account for the different (some would say the weaker) intellectual temper of Emerson's post-Civil War writing. This essay is a solid addition to the literature which treats the effect of slavery and the sectional crisis on Emerson's thought. In "Emerson, Napoleon, and the Concept of the Representative" (*ESQ* 31:230–42) Mark Patterson offers a much more speculative essay which provides another view of Emerson's heroes. A detailed and nuanced examination of Emerson's notion of the representative man (with particular emphasis on his interest in Napoleon), this essay turns on Patterson's reading of "representative" as "acting for" rather than "standing for." By 1851, he argues, the theory of *representation* outlined in *Nature* has turned to a theory of the *representative*, that is, from the matter of "agency" to the "agent." We misunderstand Emerson, Patterson continues, if we read the representative man as a "great" man whose identity arises from the universality of his acts. Rather, "the representative man is such because he can be put to use as an agent rather than exist as an autonomous model man." Thus the individual himself constitutes or empowers representative men, so that finally, as Emerson was well aware, "all representation is self-representation." Though its general argument sometimes gets caught in the coils of its own language, this still is a first-rate essay.

Other essays address more limited themes. In "A Comparative Study of Emerson's 'Friendship' and Whitman's *Calamus*" (*ATQ* 55:49–61) M. Wynn Thomas argues that both Emerson and Whitman have a very high regard for friendship, even as Whitman's concept of it, partaking at times of the homosexual, can never be the same as Emerson's more intellectualized understanding. Enough said. A little more weighty is John S. Martin's "The Other Side of Concord: A Critique of Emerson in Hawthorne's 'Old Manse'" (*NEQ* 58:453–58), in which he proposes that in the introductory chapter to this collection of stories, Hawthorne is consciously parodying certain of the key premises of *Nature* because he felt that Emerson's idealism was "all too easy and automatic." In " 'Monadnoc': Emerson's Quotidian Apocalypse" (*ESQ* 31:149–63) Richard A. Grusin suggests that in this poem Emerson has distilled 10 years of apocalyptic thought. Between the poem's germination in the 1839 journals and its inclusion in *Poems* (1846), Grusin argues, Emerson's meditations on the relationship of the poet to nature had resulted in "an altered understanding of the Orphic doctrine of poetic apocalypse." Thus the vision he presents in 'Monadnoc' is not a redemptive one of a new and better world but rather "a momentary glimpse of the transience of this one." The author has bitten off just what he wanted to chew, and the result is a solid and thoughtful reading of this lovely poem. An equally good essay is Timothy Morris' "The Free-Rhyming Poetry of Emerson and Dickinson" (*ELWIU* 12:225–40). Combining strong close readings of, among other of Emerson's poems, "Merlin I" and "Merlin II" with an analysis of Emerson's poetic theory, Morris goes on to argue that Dickinson's greatest debt to Emerson lies in her adaptation of his "short lines of irregular meter" and "asymmetrical rhyme-schemes" to her own purposes in some 23 or more "complete and substantial free-rhyming poems" written in the early 1860s. Although all readers will not go as far as Morris to claim that this free-rhyming genre influenced everyone from Whitman to Eliot, what he says about Dickinson is of interest.

Two Emersonian source studies are worth mentioning. In "Emerson and *Fraser's* on Coleridge's *Aids to Reflection*" (*ATQ* 57:15–19) J. Lasley Dameron discusses an essay by John Abraham Heraud, "Some Account of Coleridge's Philosophy," which appeared in an 1832 issue of *Fraser's*, a journal which Emerson frequently read. Dameron thinks that this piece is particularly significant because it presented the rudiments of Coleridge's transcendental thought and in particular focused on what would be so important to Emerson four years later—the proposition "that sense experiences are valid cognitive manifestations of a harmonious and divinely ordained universe." And in "The Anti-Slavery Background of Emerson's 'Ode Inscribed to W. H. Channing'" (*SAR*, pp. 63–77) Len Gougeon claims that this poem was written in direct response to the funeral of the abolitionist

Charles Turner Torrey, which, Gougeon proves, Emerson in fact attended and at which Channing was the main speaker. This experience appears to have confirmed Emerson's moderate antislavery stance against the more radical "no union" position espoused by Channing at the funeral as well as by others in the antislavery movement. "The work as a whole," Gougeon concludes, after offering a detailed reading of the poem in light of the above propositions, "clearly confirms Emerson's unswerving commitment at this time to the value and efficacy of his more poetic role in social reform." This essay is a fine example of the importance of first-rate literary detective work.

Finally, in "Right Men in the Right Places: The Meeting of Ralph Waldo Emerson and John Muir" (*WHR* 39:165–72) Arlen J. Hansen reviews the circumstances which led to the famous encounter between America's 70-year-old man of letters and the then-unknown 33-year-old naturalist, a meeting engineered in part by their mutual friend, Mrs. Jeanne C. Carr. As much as Muir's discovery of the writings of Thoreau, this encounter was formative for Muir's later career; concomitantly, Hansen argues, in Muir Emerson recognized a kindred spirit who demonstrated that Emerson's "principal notions would be carried on, in eminently capable hands."

iii. Thoreau

There were three book-length studies and a festschrift devoted to the Concord saunterer. Sharon Cameron's *Writing Nature: Henry Thoreau's "Journal"* (Oxford) is the most ambitious but is not as powerful as her previous books on Melville and Dickinson. Starting with the fact that Thoreau "came to think of the *Journal* as his central literary enterprise," Cameron claims that one of the primary questions it raises is "how part of a phenomenon is related to the whole of that phenomenon or another phenomenon," or, more specifically, how Thoreau's daily observations of natural facts relate to his understanding of the total natural world. She suggests that the *Journal* is a particularly challenging and rewarding text because he addresses this issue not by anthropomorphizing nature but rather insisting on its "infinite self-referentiality." Cameron also examines "what it means for an author to designate the work he kept 'private'" as his "principal" work, for if the *Journal* was indeed Thoreau's main literary enterprise, this confounds "the distinction between the private and the public on which our determinations about how to treat discourse conventionally depend." The *Journal*, she claims, finally shows Thoreau separated from the nature he loves. Because nature "has no fixed meanings, there would be no way to settle man's relation to it and no way, as well, to discuss it as central"; instead, he must be content to draw in words mere tangents to its elusive sphericity. She concludes that the "greatest problem posed by the *Journal* is our wish not to be assaulted by its ideas as these are at once fearful and familiar: that meaning is not circumscribed; that we cannot excerpt it; that nature remains alien; that, notwithstanding, we continue to see it."

As one might guess from the above synopsis, however inadequate, of a complex book, *Writing Nature* raises important issues about Thoreau as a writer which not many others have yet considered. Obviously Cameron finds the *Journal* a literary production which directly addresses questions now being posed by critical theorists, and her book can be added to the essays on Thoreau by John Carlos Rowe (*ALS 1983*, p. 36), Eric Sundquist (*ALS 1979*, p. 14), and Walter Benn Michaels (*ALS 1977*, p. 14) as examples of what light—some might say haze—can be cast on Thoreau's works by scholars working from new critical positions. It is thus ironic that the man whom Emerson described as never being honored by any parts of the "academy," in all likelihood because "these learned bodies feared the satire of his presence," now has been fully appropriated by precisely such individuals. Cameron's book will be cited because it is the first lengthy treatment of its subject by someone who is deeply involved with the implications of the new critical theory, but I suspect that many Thoreau scholars will find it more problematic than satisfying, particularly because Cameron makes little effort to link her idea to the observations of other scholars who have treated his notion of language and its relation to nature, be it in his *Journal* or in his public works.

Willard H. Bonner's *Harp on the Shore: Thoreau and the Sea* (SUNY) is a much more conventional and predictable work, useful primarily to orient readers to a book like *Cape Cod* and whose contents are more suited to presentation in essay form. Bonner argues that "the maritime world rendered Thoreau enormous enrichment in mind and art, extending beyond vivid rhetorical devices to such philosophical concepts as 1) his notion of man's struggle to attain individuality and identity, 2) his notion of Homeric or Edenic man, and 3) his notion that some middle ground was best where men can and should stand between such things as the natural and the civilized." The book ably demonstrates these things and thus does not disappoint, even if it hardly provides any news about Thoreau's beliefs. In *Henry Thoreau and John Muir among the Indians* (Archon) Richard Fleck gives us three essays—on Thoreau's interest in the Indians, on Muir's interest in Thoreau, and on Muir's interest in Indians and Eskimos. There are no surprises here for those who know Robert F. Sayre's *Thoreau and the American Indians* (see *ALS 1977*), but it is interesting to learn the extent of Muir's indebtedness to Thoreau. Indeed, graduate students who seek an interesting project should turn to the set of Thoreau's works owned and heavily annotated by Muir, which now is in the possession of the University of the Pacific. The second of Fleck's essays, "John Muir's Homage to Henry David Thoreau," can also be found in the *Pacific Historian* (29:55–64). This same issue contains Edmund Schofield's "John Muir's Yankee Friends and Mentors: The New England Connection" (29:65–89), in which Schofield discusses, among other things, the influence of New England Transcendentalism generally on Muir, whom we are wont to associate primarily with California.

Rita K. Gollin and James B. Scholes edited *Thoreau Among Others* (State Univ. College of Arts and Sciences at Geneseo, N. Y., 1983), the proceedings of a conference held in October 1982 to honor the eminent Thoreauvian Walter Harding upon his retirement. I wish that I could say the volume is a treasure trove of information and insight, as are all of Harding's works on Thoreau, but I believe it is fair to say that most of the contributions are what one would call "occasional" pieces and even as such vary in merit. Here I list those which might be of some use to scholars: Michael Meyer, "Thoreau, Abolitionists, and Reformers" (pp. 16–26), Elizabeth Hall Witherell's "Thoreau and the Women in His Life and Art" (pp. 74–84), Harding's own "Thoreau and Children" (pp. 86–101), and Joel Myerson's "Thoreau and the Transcendentalists" (pp. 102–22).

Take it all around, as Huck Finn might say, Thoreau fared better in the many essays devoted to him, and particularly in those which treat *Walden*. One of the stronger general essays is Philip Abbott's "Henry David Thoreau, the State of Nature, and the Redemption of Liberalism" (*Jour. of Politics* 47:183–208). In an attempt to find a "structural and thematic base that underlies his directly political writings" Abbott studies *A Week, Walden,* and *Cape Cod*, books in which Thoreau outlines and discusses, Abbott contends, a state of nature from which a new communitarian spirit can arise. But despite the fact that Thoreau often sought and evaluated the potential for utopia, his political theorizing always was limited by his "inability to transcend permanently his own sense of personal crisis," a frequent theme in his writings. Thus because the stability and coherence of his self was so fragile, Abbott argues, Thoreau could not move from moral outrage to extended commitment to institutional change, a sobering thought to those who persist in considering him a fountainhead of American radicalism. In " 'Walking' from England to America: Re-Viewing Thoreau's Romanticism" (*NEQ* 58:221–41) Lorrie Smith discusses an equally problematic subject in Thoreau criticism, the complexity of his relationship to European Romantics. This is an important essay which links Thoreau to the second generation of English Romantics—specifically to Keats and Shelley—rather than merely to Wordsworth, and which makes us realize that we short-change ourselves if we take Thoreau's hyperbolic affirmations of his Americanness at face value. Discussing parts of *Walden* and "Walking" in relation to Shelley's "Defence of Poetry" and Keats's "To Autumn," Smith demonstrates how Thoreau moves beyond "a Wordsworthian effort to recollect and reconstruct experience" into both "a Shelleyan acceptance of evanescence and immersion in wildness and a Keatsian understanding of revelation tied to seasonal, diurnal time."

It is instructive to read Richard J. Schneider's "Thoreau and Nineteenth-Century Landscape Painting" (*ESQ* 31:67–88) right after Gayle Smith's essay on Emerson and Luminism (see above). Schneider points out that in almost all Thoreau's extended descriptions of landscape he employs organizational principles based on color and spatial relations common to painting. Comparing Thoreau's aesthetic ideas and goals to those of the Hudson River School, the Luminists, and the American Impressionists, Schneider concludes that Thoreau had an essentially visual approach to nature and commonly used the principles of composition found in contemporary landscape painting in his descriptive prose; but, unlike Smith, he does not demonstrate this in the very syntax of the writer's language. Thus his essay is another of those which treat the relation between 19th-century American art and literature in a way more tantalizing than convincing. Walter Hesford's "Coming Down the Pages of Nature: Thoreau on Language and Nature" (*ELWIU* 12:85–95) is an ambitious essay whose subject is akin to Cameron's (see above). Beginning with Thoreau's question in *A Week*—"Is not Nature, rightly read, that of which she is commonly taken to be the symbol?"—Hesford asks what he considers an allied question—whether "we can read nature—or write about reading it—without being distant from it," or, in the jargon of the critical theorists, "absent from its real presence"—and then discusses how Thoreau, who placed reading and writing *within* nature and thus "naturalized" the phenomenon of literature, reformed or extended the venerable tradition of nature writing. Anyone interested in this piece probably would do better to come to it after reading Cameron's more lucid treatment of allied themes. More rewarding is Robert Sattelmeyer and Richard A. Hocks's "Thoreau and Coleridge's *Theory of Life*" (*SAR*, pp. 269–84), which directly addresses the question of the relation of Thoreau's scientific study to his literary work. The authors discuss at length Thoreau's reading in and excerpts from an important book which only recently has found its proper home in the Coleridge canon. They demonstrate how it provided Thoreau with a theoretical basis for natural science which harmonized with those parts of Coleridge's thought which fed the Romantic impulse generally and that of the Transcendentalists in America specifically.

Four essays deal with Thoreau's currency among our contemporaries. In " 'Into the Bladelike Arms of God': The Quest for Meaning through Symbolic Language in Thoreau and Annie Dillard" (*DQ* 20:103–16) Mary Davidson McConahay compares the general structural metaphors in *Walden* and *Pilgrim at Tinker Creek*. There are no surprises about Thoreau, but the essay should move Thoreauvians who know Dillard only as a name to read her fine book. A similar effort, Herbert Nibbelink's "Thoreau and Wendell Berry: Bachelor and Husband of Nature (*SAQ* 84:127–40), reads Berry's works in light of Thoreau's. Nibbelink concludes that Berry is much less naive, because he knows how much of the natural world already has been irrecoverably lost. And William Doreski, in "A Dull, Uncertain, Blundering Purpose: Robert Lowell's Sonnets on Thoreau" (*ThoreauQ* 16:69–74), discusses two poems about Thoreau in Lowell's *History* (1973) and concludes that both Thoreau and Lowell "commit themselves to the subjective vision in full realization of its potential and its limitations," thus accounting for the latter's respect for Thoreau's example and work. And Gigliola Nocera, in "Henry David Thoreau et il neotranscendentalismo di John Cage" (*Le forme et la storia* 4[1983]:83–115), discusses several of Cage's works in relation to the ideas of an intellectual and aesthetic predecessor who obviously greatly influences him.

Walden drew out one of the strongest efforts of the year, "*Walden* and the 'Curse of Trade,' " a chapter in Michael T. Gilmore's *American Romanticism and the Marketplace*, a book which in its entirety should interest *ALS* readers, even if some of its chapters have appeared elsewhere (see, for example, *ALS 1982*, p. 11). A sophisticated treatment of how Thoreau's struggle to publish his work also influenced his notion of symbolism, this essay demonstrates as well that Thoreau's analysis of "commodification" has "certain affinities with the Marxist critique of capitalism." Thoreau, Gilmore writes, "sees the exchange process as emptying the world of its concrete reality and not only converting objects into dollars but causing their 'it-ness' or being to disappear"; this fact, of course, is related to how the *literary* symbol operates, for it, too, is "both what it is and the token of something else." The similarity here to Ian F. A. Bell's essay (see above) should be obvious, and, like the former, this chapter is a delight—highly intelligent and eminently readable—and all to the purpose of showing the complexity of Thoreau's relation to the marketplace. The first two chapters of *Walden*—indeed, the whole book—are illuminated by the sharply focused ideological light Gilmore shines through this essay.

Equally delightful, if not quite as far-ranging, is Robert A. Gross's "The Great Bean Field Hoax: Thoreau and the Agricultural Reformers" (*VQR* 61:483–97), which, like Bell's essay, is profitably read alongside Gilmore's chapter on *Walden*. Gross demonstrates that "The Bean-Field" chapter of *Walden* is a spoof on contemporary agricultural reformers who urged farmers to maximize production on their acreage. By writing a tall tale of man and beans in that chapter, Thoreau sought, Gross contends, to "turn the sober literature of agricultural improvement, with its spiritually deadening obsession with crop rotations, manures, turnips, and tools, upside down." Informed by the knowledge of the social and cultural historian, this essay, for all its lightheartedness, is a valuable contribution to our understanding both of Thoreau's satire and of agricultural reform in mid-19th-century New England. Another valuable piece, one which in particular shows how important a single overlooked fact can be, is Sargent Bush, Jr.'s, "The End and Means in *Walden*: Thoreau's Use of the Catechism" (*ESQ* 31:1–10). Bush shows that two direct allusions to the Westminster Shorter Catechism in *Walden*'s opening chapters lead directly to Thoreau's main thematic concerns in the book as a whole. In the "Economy" chapter, we remember, Thoreau asks "What is the chief end of man?", and in the second chapter answers his query at the end of the famous passage in which he tells readers why he went to live in the woods—"to glorify God and enjoy him forever." This is a nicely measured essay in which Bush demonstrates how *Walden* attempts to answer the Catechism's question through Thoreau's example to his townspeople that God must be rediscovered daily in their own lives. One enjoys the lack of pretension in this essay: Bush understands that *Walden* could have been written without these references and still been successful, but by including them Thoreau put a finer edge on his criticism of his contemporaries, most of whom would have immediately recognized the allusions.

Another essay which easily could be pretentious but blessedly is not is Henry Golemba's "The Voices of *Walden*" (*ESQ* 31:243–51). Golemba is interested in those passages in *Walden* in which parody is preeminent, thus making the text "multi-vocal." A sophisticated treatment of how parody functions—particularly of how it allows the author "greater license in that he can make his primary text even more extreme, knowing its extreme statement will be balanced by its parody"—this essay demonstrates how parody "provided Thoreau with a rhetorical strategy by which his style and expression could sound free, expansive, and undogmatic, while simultaneously remaining true to his profoundest beliefs." It is particularly convincing because Golemba has combined it with some good textual work, tracing how Thoreau refined his use of parody in the various manuscript versions of his masterpiece. Of a lesser order is Cheryl B. Torsney's "Learning the Language of the Railroad in *Walden*" (*ATQ* 55:19–28), in which she details how Thoreau uses the railroad metaphorically, like the pond, as a symbol of transcendence: just as the pond reflects the route to the Oversoul, so the railroad provides a link to society—both are mediators of sorts. Because in *Walden* the railroad is a metonym for language and communication—it transports meaning—Torsney reads the famous railroad-cut passage as a demonstration of the unification in Thoreau's mind of the railroad and nature, civilization and the natural order. This essay is fine as far as it goes but at times seems a bit contrived, as though it were an elaborate exercise. Finally, Michel Granger, in "Le Paysage intermediaire de Henry D. Thoreau" (*RFEA* 10:359–71), discusses the ideological and psychological dimensions of Thoreau's descriptions of landscape in *Walden* and other works, and finds that he is most committed to writing about a middle ground which allows him, at least metaphorically, to enjoy nature and culture, and so to resolve certain contrary tendencies in his very nature. The essential characteristic of his composite landscape, Granger argues, "tient à son appartenance à ce qu'on pourrait appeler la caté-gorie de l'intermédiaire, qui met en relation les contraires, les extrêmes, tout en les maintenant distincts, qui articule les différences et les symbolise." Although as I summarize the essay, it may sound like an elaboration of Leo Marx, in fact Granger, particularly as he speaks of the psychological importance of such a landscape to Thoreau, is well worth perusing.

The Maine Woods and Cape Cod gathered one essay each. In " 'Ktaadn': Thoreau in the Wilderness of Words" (ESQ 31:137–48) John Tallmadge claims that those who find the famous "Contact!" passage seemingly aberrant have missed Thoreau's main point there-in, to make more apparent the "troubling interdependency of nature and language." As Thoreau climbs to the center of the wilderness, Tallmadge argues, he falls back on a "direct unmediated experience" of what nature is, because he knows that language cannot adequately describe his emotions at that moment. "By causing the collapse of his own linguistic apparatus" as he calls for "Contact!", Thoreau, Tallmadge writes, "has momentarily returned, in a psychological as well as a physical sense, to the state of nature." Tallmadge sees the passage as indicative of a self-critical mode which would become crucially important to Thoreau in Walden. This essay is a welcome addition to the literature which treats Thoreau's notion of language and its relation to nature, and particularly so because it focuses on a book which has not drawn a lot of attention in this regard. In "From Walden Out" (ThoreauQ 16:75–85) Sherman Paul stresses how in Cape Cod Thoreau's views are unsettled because he does not know what to expect of the vast seascape he explores. "What is remarkable" in this book, Paul writes, "is Thoreau's respect for the accidental," his view of a universe in which human purpose "fails, or if it succeeds does so in some unfathomable fashion." As an injunction to take Cape Cod seriously, this essay is well worth one's time; it is not, how-ever, a systematic study of the book.

Kenneth V. Egan's "Thoreau's Pastoral Vision in 'Walking' " (ATQ 57:21–30) finds in Thoreau's essay a movement from the village to the heart of nature, a reenactment of the Fall, each day, thus making a pastoral vision essential to the race's regeneration. I do not think anyone will deny that the essay can be read in this way. In "Thoreau, Garrison, and Dymond: Unbending Firmness of Mind" (AL 57:309–17) James Duban speculates, seemingly with good reason, that Jonathan Dymond's *Essays on the Principles of Morality* (1829) may have had a significant influence on Thoreau's "Resistance to Civil Government." Thoreau had encountered this book in Edward Tyrell Channing's writing class at Harvard; Duban succinctly indicates how similar some of Thoreau's notions in his famous essay are to the thoughts of this London linen draper and Quaker, whose writings also were known to Garrison. Though not fully conclusive, this essay is a provocative source study. Much less solid is "Thoreau's Poem 'Sympathy': His 'Gentle Boy' Identified" (*CS* 18, ii:20–27). Herein Mary E. Pitts suggests that the poem's subject is Thoreau himself. In the poem, she writes, Thoreau "first acknowledges and accepts the change which the years have brought in the onset of mystical states, from being spontaneously 'dealt with by superior powers' in youth to deliberately seeking and attempting to initiate the experiences in his adulthood." Well, perhaps. And, finally, in "Thoreau's Friend Ricketson: What Manner of Man?" (*CS* 18, ii:1–19) Don Mortland presents as good a biographical portrait as we have of Thoreau's New Bedford friend and admirer.

iv. Other Transcendentalists

Robert D. Habich has done a valuable service in his *Transcendentalism and the "Western Messenger": A History of the Magazine and Its Contributors* (Fairleigh Dickinson), for now we have a study comparable to Joel Myerson's fine one on the *Dial* (see *ALS 1980*) which treats what in effect was the first Transcendentalist periodical, founded in Cincinnati in 1835. As Habich rightly claims in his introduction, "In the magazine, and in the activities and viewpoints of those who conducted it, lies a contemporary, seriatim definition of the nascent Transcendentalist movement in America." Habich's goals herein—to reconstruct the internal and external history of the journal and to "see what that history can tell us about American literary and religious life during the 1830s and 40s, especially the interaction of Unitarianism and Transcendentalism"—have been admirably met, making this a book to be owned by all serious students of Transcendentalism.

Bryan F. LeBeau published a monograph on Frederic Henry Hedge, one of the key figures in the early years of the Transcendentalist, and thereafter in the Unitarian, movement. His *Frederic Henry Hedge: Nineteenth Century American Transcendentalist* (Pittsburgh

Theological Monographs, n.s. 16) primarily focuses on Hedge's continuing importance to the Unitarians, for he was one of the few among them who attempted to provide a more or less systematic theology, particularly in his *Reason in Religion* (1865). LeBeau makes the point that, although Hedge remained within the bosom of the Unitarian church, he always remained loyal to Transcendentalism as a critical method. Unlike others among his friends and contemporaries (Emerson, say, or Theodore Parker), he did not succumb to secularism or extreme individualism but rather became a "leading spokesman for the moderate mainstream of American Transcendentalism, an area yet to be explored." This solid study is aimed at those who have regarded Hedge as the most disappointing or disappointed Transcendentalist (see, for example, Joel Myerson's essay on Hedge, reviewed in *ALS 1975*, p. 14); LeBeau shows that such views are too often based on comments about him by his more radical critics. A synopsis of LeBeau's arguments can be found in his "Frederic Henry Hedge and the 'Eminent Orthodox Divines' of American Transcendentalism" (*ATQ* 57:3–14).

Margaret Fuller received two assessments in addition to the one by Von Frank (see above), which far and away is the most interesting. In *Niagara Falls: Icon of the American Sublime* (Cambridge) Elizabeth McKinsey discusses Fuller's trip to the West in 1843 as a search "for the roots of American culture" as well as an "exploration of primitive human nature," and notes how for Fuller Niagara Falls became a symbol of the future potential of the West. Those interested in this subject will do better to turn to the pages on Fuller in Annette Kolodny's *The Land Before Her* (see *ALS* 1984), but everyone should purchase McKinsey's book for its beauty: its graphics and design are splendid, and it is as well an interesting study of its primary subject. Carolyn Hlus offered "Margaret Fuller, Transcendentalist: A Reassessment" (*CRevAS* 16:1–13) to remind us that Fuller was first and foremost a major member of the Transcendentalist circle. She made her major contributions to American intellectual history, Hlus argues, as a teacher, a parlor lecturer, and an editor who adhered to basic Transcendentalist tenets as they then were being articulated, particularly Swedenborgian correspondence and the primacy of the individual soul. Hlus's reminder is timely, but her elaboration is not overly novel and, I would guess, hardly necessary for most readers of this chapter of *ALS*.

University of North Carolina, Chapel Hill

2. Hawthorne

Rita K. Gollin

Most of this year's books and essays continue the emphases of the last few years—on Hawthorne as a self-aware writer, ambivalent and ambiguous, concealing while revealing himself through his narrators and his characters, drawing on but altering generic conventions, and incorporating materials from a wide range of sources. None of the changes suggests a trend, though there is a slight upswing of attention to Emerson, midcentury marketplace values, and the genre of romance; and (partly in consequence) "The Custom-House" is examined more closely than ever. The year's work includes book-length studies, parts of books, a collection of critical essays, and other studies ranging in length from brief notes in the *Hawthorne Society Newsletter* to longer essays in periodicals of all kinds, covering the entire gamut of quality and approach. But there is absolutely no doubt about the year's major publishing event: at long last, we have the first two of the projected five volumes of Hawthorne's letters.

i. Primary Materials

The Letters, 1813–43 and *The Letters, 1843–53* (Ohio State)—Volumes XV and XVI in the Centenary Edition—do credit to the editors, Thomas Woodson, L. Neal Smith, and Norman Holmes Pearson. Woodson's 83–page introduction to both volumes (which total over 1,500 pages) clearly identifies Hawthorne's major correspondents and his relationships with them: like the "Chronology of Nathaniel Hawthorne's Life to 1853" which follows, it is a tool for biographical study and a contribution in itself. The annotations identify quotations and allusions, provide succinct information on such matters as the plays Hawthorne attended and the logistics of his travels, and illuminate such important events as his dismissal from the Custom House. In sum, the textual apparatus makes it possible to accomplish in a few hours what formerly would have required days of effort. Obviously, what is most important is that we now have trustworthy texts of the letters themselves—eventually to include "every known surviving letter by Hawthorne for which the text is available, and letters by others in which he had a hand." During their decades of preparation, all the editors have shared their transcripts, enabling scholars to supplement and correct what had already been published. But confronting all of the letters in sequence and in their entirety (including a few recent discoveries) makes Hawthorne come freshly alive. Though relatively few of his early letters have survived, we can readily see which traits continue from childhood on, and follow the emerging concerns of his maturity. Even a brief note to a publisher or an admirer contributes to our understanding of the self-examining writer. No Hawthorne scholar can do without these two volumes—or the three to come.

A recently discovered letter from Hawthorne to Calvin Stowe is presented by Kenneth Walter Cameron in a pamphlet entitled *Hawthorne Among Connecticut Congregationalists: The Odyssey of a Letter* (Hartford: Watkinson Lib.). After reading the interpretation of *The Marble Faun* as a psychomachia prepared by Stowe's sister-in-law Martha Tyler, Hawthorne told Stowe that her delicate appreciation made "up for the deficiencies of the author." The courteous remark was taken to be an endorsement, and the religious "key" to the novel's allegory was published in *The New Englander*.

Another recent discovery is Hawthorne's "Northern Volunteers: From a Journal" (*HSN* 11, i:1–2), an unequivocally pro-Union sketch about his trip to Civil War Virginia that appeared in *The Monitor* in June 1862. In his introductory note Thomas Woodson briefly compares Hawthorne's report with those of his companions Edward Dicey and Nathaniel Parker Willis, and includes a paragraph from "Chiefly About War Matters" that "alludes to some of the same matters."

ii. General Studies

One book, sections of others, and a few essays range across Hawthorne's entire career. I have serious problems with the central theses of both Agnes McNeill Donohue's *Hawthorne: Calvin's Ironic Stepchild* (Kent State) and Samuel Coale's *In Hawthorne's Shadow: American Romance from Melville to Mailer* (Kentucky). Donohue boldly if unconvincingly argues that Hawthorne's irony was "ordained by Calvin's damnatory theology," while his European years "emasculated" his art "of its primal terror and stress." It is all too easy to identify question-begging and misstatement: "Hester, Dimmesdale, and Chillingworth must be damned in order to humanize the elf-child Pearl"; Hawthorne thought death "is the only consummation devoutly to be wished": his widowed mother "retired to her room in the Manning household and remained a recluse until her death"; "the basic tenets of Calvin . . . were never tried until [Hawthorne's] seven years in Europe"; "he was snared by Sophia Peabody (who lived next door . . .)"—and all this before page 10. But the more serious problems are that Donohue approaches Hawthorne's moral beliefs as if they came in some unmediated form from Calvin; and oversimplifications of Calvin frequently distort the text—e.g., "Hilda and Kenyon, then, are to be judged by the standards of Calvin—they have barely escaped with their lives from the Roman Catholic church, the whore of Babylon, the Antichrist." Coale regards Hawthorne as the progenitor of a "distinctly Manichean" romantic tradition of radical dualism, assuming that his statements about evil in the human heart mean that he thought the heart is evil. Hawthorne did have dark thoughts about earthly mysteries, but that does not mean he thought the world is without moral or religious value, nor that the only internal conflicts he anatomized were Manichean. Hawthorne worried about the functions of language as expression and as evasion; but why call that Manichean? As a single example of the implications for close reading, Coale says the Minister's black veil "possesses the people and the minister and becomes the dark idol of their devil worship. . . ." It is true that Hawthorne's literary heirs have necessarily grappled with his theory and practice of romance; but the Manichean label obfuscates instead of clarifying the writers' common concerns.

The second half of Evan Carton's *The Rhetoric of American Romance* interprets Hawthorne's career as a "struggle with the pressures and implications of romance." Conceiving of romance as a "rhetorical performance" which addresses central problems about reality and truth, Carton analyzes interrelationships of art and history, past and present, concealment and revelation, and self-presentation in Hawthorne's four completed novels and their prefaces, and examines the "Legends of the Province-House" as they prefigure later concerns and interrelationships. Readings of familiar passages are usually challenging (though occasionally inexact, reductive, or equivocal—e.g., Alice Vane's address to Edward Randolph's portrait is a "witch's curse," or "Donatello falls with the man he kills, now *his* model . . .").

Carton wrestles with such central issues as Hawthorne's anxieties about his enterprise and the repeated conjunctions in his fiction of "putative opposites" (hate and love, the Maules and the Pyncheons).

In *American Romanticism and the Marketplace* (Chicago) Michael T. Gilmore says Hawthorne, Emerson, Thoreau, and Melville had to choose between speaking the truth to a small elite and disguising the truth to reach a wider audience. He says Melville addressed that conflict in "Hawthorne and His Mosses," hoping Hawthorne would win the recognition he deserved yet doubting that the public could appreciate his dark truths. Gilmore's readings of Hawthorne are audacious and consistent, even when not entirely convincing. Thus he interprets "Rappaccini's Daughter" as "a version of Hawthorne's literary circumstances in 1844 and an allegory of the common reader's inability to read him rightly": Beatrice is Hawthorne; Giovanni is the common reader; Rappaccini is the Transcendental intellectual writer and Baglioni the ordinary pen and ink man; and the poison represents Hawthorne's "difficulty in selling" and, beneath that, the growth of capitalism. But his more typical discussion of *The Scarlet Letter* astutely comments on the author's and characters' concerns about public self-display and the problems of clear and truthful communication. Hawthorne's story anatomized his own options: he could be true to himself but remain on the fringes of society (like Hester), or dissemble (like Dimmesdale) to win the approval of the multitude. To enter *The House of the Seven Gables*, Gilmore addresses the problem of wearing a false smile—as Judge Pyncheon always does, as Hepzibah attempts when opening her cent shop, and as Hawthorne attempts in contriving a happy ending. As in the case of the corpse that Holgrave is reluctant to reveal, Gilmore is attuned to concealed problems.

Carolyn L. Karcher in "Philanthropy and the Occult in the Fiction of Hawthorne, Brownson, and Melville," in *The Haunted Dusk* (pp. 67–97), discusses Hawthorne, Brownson, and Melville as "chief originators" of a literary subgenre—satire of the pseudosciences. She approaches "The Hall of Fantasy," "The Procession of Life," and other sketches of the '40s as anti-reform satires, then says the spiritualist craze of the '50s helped popularize and shape the subgenre. Treating the interpenetration of occultism and radical social protest as a persistent cultural pattern, Karcher discusses *The Blithedale Romance* in that light, then draws interesting comparisons to Brownson's statements in *Spirit-Rapper: An Autobiography* and Melville's in *The Confidence-Man*.

Tom Quirk in "Hawthorne's Last Tales and 'The Custom-House' " (*ESQ* 30:221–31) discusses four of the five stories written after the *Mosses* as ways of working out solutions to particular literary problems, solutions reaffirmed in "the Custom-House." "Main-street" criticizes mechanical manipulation of narrative, "Feathertop" criticizes inauthentic characters and undiscerning critics, "The Snow-Image" contrasts sympathetic response with "practical demands of stubborn materialists," and "The Great Stone Face" works out deeper problems of aesthetic response through Ernest, whose discerning sensibility and sympathetic imagination establish him as both the ideal artist and the ideal reader. The approach is fresh and stimulating, particularly the treatment of "The Great Stone Face" and "The Custom-House" as "companion pieces."

"Romance, Character, and the Bounds of Sense," by John Burt (*Raritan* 5:74–89), focuses on Hawthorne and particularly on "The Custom-House" to define and assess the dilemma of the American romancer. Moments of imaginative transcendence are also baffling impasses, at once liberating and problematic, with interpretation "excruciatingly undecidable" for the author as well as his characters. Burt provocatively compares the romancer's imaginative power to political fanaticism, saying the claim to liberty undoes itself (as with the Maules), and "doubts about whether imaginative power will validate or destroy the work are at the same time doubts about whether private authority will destroy or empower democracy."

Hawthorne's treatment of women remains a lively topic. In "Gender, Hawthorne, and Literary Criticism" (*Mosaic* 18:91–100) David Stineback argues that a "new critical" approach cannot adequately cope with Hawthorne's complex and ambivalent attitudes about women, unusually sympathetic given the sexual politics of his time, which the "failures" of Hester, Zenobia, and Martha of "The Shaker Bridal" call into question. Critics must take into account the gender of the writer, the characters, and themselves. That is true; but gender does not explain the differences between my readings and Stineback's. Understanding "The Shaker Bridal" (for example) requires accuracy about the Shaker beliefs Hawthorne appropriated and about his text. He is not parodying the Shakers' beliefs in the millennium; their attitudes toward sexuality are not primarily "an attack on female reproduction"; and Martha does not "all but" die: she dies. In "Thwarted Nature: Nathaniel Hawthorne as Feminist," in *American Novelists Revisited* (Hall, 1982), Nina Baym begins by defining the

limitations of prior feminist and "prefeminist" criticism of Hawthorne's woman characters, then argues that they "represent desirable
and valuable qualities lacking in the male protagonist." In depicting
men's mistreatment of women, Hawthorne indicts patriarchal society,
including himself. Repeatedly, as in "The Birthmark" and "Rappaccini's Daughter," a self-centered man rejects sexual union with a
woman, harming them both; and Baym attributes authorial disclaim-
ers to Hawthorne's guilty awareness that his art expressed "deformed
sexuality, for its obsessive fantasy is that of doing harm to a woman."
Whether accepted or rejected, the women of *The Blithedale Romance*
and *The Marble Faun* are degraded and victimized by men's fantasies. Baym attributes the triumph of *The Scarlet Letter* to its celebration of Hester, particularly as a mother: through Hester, Hawthorne expressed the hope that women might eventually "heal the
split in the male psyche" between sex and love.

In "Hawthorne in France (1963–1985)" (*HSN* 11, ii:1–3) Roger
Asselineau discusses the small body of criticism of Hawthorne in
France (by Jean Normand, Violet Sachs, and Julian Green), explaining that the French prefer the luxuriance of a Poe, Melville, or Faulkner, and find Puritanism repugnant. Yet Asselineau notes that interest
in Hawthorne is manifested by translations of his first three novels
and *A Wonder Book* and several collections of tales.

iii. Novels

The Scarlet Letter always receives more attention than any other
novel, but this year the disparity is greater than usual. One of the
year's best essays and the most surprising influence study is Larry J.
Reynolds' "*The Scarlet Letter* and Revolutions Abroad" (*AL* 57:44–
67). Reynolds reads the novel in the context of the quickly crushed
European revolutions of 1848, which reaffirmed Hawthorne's skepticism about revolutions (evident since "My Kinsman, Major Molineux"). He accounts for apparent inconsistencies in the treatment of
Hester and Dimmesdale by saying they are criticized to the extent
that they become "radicalized." More surprisingly, he suggests that
contemporary allusions to the French Revolution illuminate the
novel's scaffold scenes and Hawthorne's self-presentation as decapitated surveyor in "The Custom-House"; and he suggests that the
English civil war underlies the novel's dates of 1642 to 1647 (with
Dimmesdale recalling the decapitated King Charles). Reynolds pro-

poses a specific source for the romance, a book Hawthorne read while writing it: Lamartine's popular *History of the Girondists*, which sympathized with the decapitated king and used a scaffold as setting and structural device.

New Essays on The Scarlet Letter, edited by Michael J. Colacurcio (Cambridge), is one of the first three in a new series of critical guides to major works of American fiction intended for undergraduates, though its four essays assume a relatively sophisticated audience. The introduction provides comments on the novel's composition and its critical reception, though an undergraduate might welcome more precise information (about Hawthorne's political ouster, for example), and the undergraduate and the professor might be equally puzzled by some of the remarks (e.g., Matthiessen "explains that Hawthorne's 'variety of symbolic reference,' epitomized by the 'device of multiple choice,' can be called 'allegory' only in defiance of the authority of Coleridge"). In commenting on recent criticism, Colacurcio encourages all readers to enter Hawthorne's novel "by studying the various word-worlds in which his signs have life."

The first of the new essays, Michael Davitt Bell's "Arts of Deception: Hawthorne, 'Romance,' and *The Scarlet Letter*" (pp. 29–56), interprets Hawthorne's comments about romance in "The Custom-House" (and other prefaces) as wily attempts to conceal his subversive purpose: he presents "unconscious fantasy in the *disguise* of socially respectable reality." Bell thinks Hawthorne drew disingenuous distinctions between the novel and the romance because imaginative fiction was considered unwholesome, "revolutionary, or at least antisocial," and he wanted his romance to seem harmless. Though some of his assumptions are open to question (e.g., that the "neutral territory" passage was designed to distract "attention from the real issue" of what the romancer does), Bell assiduously analyzes the writer's pose as an editor. The duplicity of the preface is an "appropriate gateway" to the romance itself, with Hester and Dimmesdale likened to their creator as "artists, manipulating appearances," mediating between "their own subversive impulses" and society's "orthodox expectations." (Similar issues are raised by Burt's essay, discussed in section **ii.**)

David Van Leer in "Hester's Labyrinth: Transcendental Rhetoric in Puritan Boston" (pp. 57–100) focuses on Hawthorne's conflation of Puritan and Transcendental vocabulary and concepts in *The Scarlet Letter*. The narrator offers Romantic "translations" of traditional

Puritan ideas, sometimes ironically echoing Emerson (as in the phrase about Hester's "labyrinth of mind" or the "inmost Me" passage in "The Custom-House"). Coping with apparent contradictions between the narrator's roles as editor/historian and romancer, Van Leer says the novel repeatedly undermines itself by displaying the impossibility of clearly understanding language and symbols. After exploring the materialistic implications of the concept of sympathy, he concludes that Hawthorne was attacking "a false objectification of the ineffable," a confusion of the materiality of language and the apparent materiality of spirit. If Van Leer is sometimes on thin ice (e.g., he says the preface contains "the re-creation of the Old General's triumph at Ticonderoga" and that Dimmesdale senses "Pearl is more nearly the result of his semen than of his sin"), the essay is challenging.

Colacurcio's essay, " 'The Woman's Own Choice': Sex, Metaphor, and the Puritan 'Sources' of *The Scarlet Letter*" (pp. 101–35), argues that Hawthorne drew on the theological politics and sexual language of Winthrop's *History of New England* to probe "the power of sexual figures to structure religious ideology and confuse natural experience." Whether or not Hawthorne was as attentive a reader and as ironic a deployer of Puritan texts as Colacurcio contends, he illuminates the historical moment of Hester's adultery by suggesting two reasons why Hawthorne decided to call Bellingham "Governor" of Boston in June 1642. The 50-year-old widower had lost the election the month before partly because he had simply declared himself married to a young woman of 20; and in judging a case of sexual abuse, he had taken a legalistic rather than a humane approach. As instances of "an exuberant life of Puritan sexual metaphor" (which might have "obscured rather than redeemed their own sexual life"), Colacurcio discusses the Puritans' rhetoric of sacred love, their assumption that Anne Hutchinson's heresy was a form of sexual libertinism, and Winthrop's 1645 speech about the "quasi-marital nature of 'liberty' and 'authority.' "

In the final new essay, "His Folly, Her Weakness: Demystified Adultery in *The Scarlet Letter*" (pp. 137–59), Carol Bensick clearly sets Hawthorne's work in the context of the European novel of adultery: the mainstream perpetuates social institutions while showing their toll, she says, but Hawthorne also questions the institutions. In writing about an incompatible marriage he differs from the "consensus that the most important betrayal is the sexual one": both Hester and Chillingworth are seen to be victims of their mutually exclusive yet socially conditioned expectations of marriage. Among other deviations from the generic tradition, Hawthorne's adulteress survives and her child finds happiness. *Anna Karenina* is Tolstoy's "retort" to Hawthorne, his demonstration that adulterers always come to bad ends.

Assuming too rigid a genre distinction in "Hawthorne's Genres: The Letter of the Law *Appliquée*" (pp. 69–84) in *After Strange Texts*, Peggy Kamuf says Hawthorne called *The Scarlet Letter* a romance because "he did not want to be mistaken for a female scribbler of novels." But her main concern is the interesting relationship between "the text of the letter and the letter of the law," particularly in the scaffold scenes. Dimmesdale and the community assume the meteor has transcendent meaning though their interpretations are opposed; interpretation of the Minister's revelation divides the community. Hester's "display" is her legal punishment but also manifests the "duplicity within the law itself," the "complicity between the outlaw and the law." She is " 'woman' presented in social spectacle," moved to feminist speculation about obviating such repression.

Kent Bales's "Pictures, Signs, and Stereotypes in Hawthorne's Meditations on the Origins of American Culture" (pp. 35–44) is the best of the four papers on Hawthorne in *The Origins and Originality of American Culture* (Budapest: Akademiai Kiado, 1984). (A second essay on *The Scarlet Letter* simply says Hawthorne's novel is a more challenging study of Puritanism than Miller's *The Crucible*; and the collection includes a rambling commentary on Hawthorne's artists and a schematic definition of *The House of the Seven Gables* as a romance.) Bales discusses *The Scarlet Letter* as Hawthorne's "most deliberate and sustained study of the transformation of the old into the new," his meditation about the persistent Puritan past and the dynamics of cultural change. He exhibited himself in "The Custom-House" as—like Hester—a victim of Puritan beliefs who tries (with limited success) to effect change, though the complexity of subject matter and narration precludes simple analysis. The novel's three scaffold scenes assert the Puritan belief system while pitting it against alternatives (e.g., Hester as adulteress but also the Virgin Mary and Anne Hutchinson). The reader must repeatedly move between competing interpretive systems (as when pondering the "happy ending" convention of Pearl's marriage). Hester herself harbors alternative systems of belief, though her final concern about purity, like her tombstone, affirms the values of her "oppressors."

Luther H. Martin in "Hawthorne's *The Scarlet Letter*: A is for Alchemy?" (*ATQ* 58:31–42) offers an alchemical reading of the story, beginning with Chillingworth's role as alchemist: he presides over an alchemical wedding of Hester and Dimmesdale and over their "mercurial child of gold," Martin claims. The red of Hester, the white of Dimmesdale, and Chillingworth's black constitute the "chromatic trichotomy of alchemical transformation"; and the main characters are transformed by Hester's A, identified as the "red-gold philosopher's stone." Martin also thinks alchemical transformation serves as a metaphor for art in "The Custom-House": the writer's imagination is alchemical; his artful transformation of real predicaments is an alchemical process. The reading is consistent and interesting if not convincing. In "*The Scarlet Letter*: A Political Reading" (*Prospects* 9:49–70) the late Ellen Moers argues that the novel's central issue is publicity: Hawthorne treated Boston as the "hated smalltown America" which opposed deviants, and the "true ending" of his story is Pearl's expatriation. Other questionable assertions are generated by the "political reading": e.g., that Dimmesdale's moral struggle is not with God but his community; that he "thoroughly despises the town, which is so thoroughly duped"; and that his "final encounter with the town," his election sermon, is his "political apotheosis." In "Hawthorne's Reflexive Imagination: *The Scarlet Letter* as Compositional Allegory" (*ATQ* 56:55–63), overingenuity interferes with Richard C. Freed's attempt to demonstrate that the novel is about the compositional process from conception to completion—with Pearl as the work in progress, and Hester, Dimmesdale, and Chillingworth as the "authors." Although in "The Custom-House" Hawthorne wrote a fiction about recovering the ability to write fiction, that does not mean the book as a whole represents the stages of his subsequent development. The notion of a psychomachia produces distortions— e.g., Dimmesdale's texts are lively "because they are about the passion of creation—about Pearl"; or the crowd's festive mood at the conclusion reflects Hawthorne's own change from hostility to ambivalence about society. Freed is sympathetically responsive to the novel as mystifying self-revelation, but his mistake about the sequence of composition is only one of the grounds for challenging his thesis about the writer's evolution.

In "The Germ Theory of *The Scarlet Letter*" (*HSN* 11, i:11–13)
Hershel Parker raises important issues about the chronology of the
book's composition, correcting those critics who took at face value
what James T. Fields said over two decades after the fact—that he had
read the "germ" of the story in manuscript and convinced Hawthorne
to "elaborate" it for separate publication rather than as part of a collection. Fields "had nothing to do with its reaching the length it did,"
Parker says, citing correspondence between the writer and the publisher, "although he had everything to do with its being published as
a novel." Clearly, the manuscript Fields first saw contained the opening of Hawthorne's story, not a short version of it; and Parker corrects
critics like Branch (who thought imperfections in *The Scarlet Letter*
resulted from Hawthorne's "hurried efforts" to provide text for Fields)
and Nissenbaum (who thought the preface was written after the text
was in print).

Only one essay and a note are devoted to *The House of the Seven
Gables*, but both are sound and interesting. Walter Benn Michaels in
"Property and Real Estate" in *The American Renaissance Reconsidered* (pp. 156–82) discusses problems of "inalienability" in *The
House of the Seven Gables* in the context of 19th-century property
rights as well as Hawthorne's assumptions about both individual integrity and the province of romance. He moves from Hawthorne's
prefatory statements about romance—his castle in the air that infringes
on no one's property rights—to fundamentals of 19th-century property
law and the rights to oneself inherent in Stowe's treatment of slavery
and in Hawthorne's presentation of Alice Pyncheon—the "alienable"
victim of her father's greed, Matthew Maule's potency, and belief in
her own inviolability. Michaels addresses specific social issues such as
the economic prospects of young men like Holgrave (though not
others equally relevant, such as those involved in the final move to
Judge Pyncheon's house or Uncle Venner's entitlement to house-
room). A brief note by Dr. Fred S. Rosen (*HSN* 11, i:13) identifies
"The Pyncheon Malady" as hereditary angioneurotic edema, "a genetic disease inherited as a dominant trait" whose symptoms include
laryngeal edema and bloody foam emerging from the mouth at the
time of death, whose symptoms Hawthorne might have observed in
members of the Ropes family of Salem.

James McIntosh's is the soundest of the three essays on *The Blithedale Romance*. Concentrating on Coverdale in "The Instability of

Belief in *The Blithedale Romance*" (*Prospects* 9:71–114), McIntosh examines the novel as Hawthorne's considered response to fundamental tenets of Puritanism and Transcendentalism, and to midcentury erosions of authority and social discontinuities. Coverdale is intellectually and morally disoriented in a disintegrating world, his baffled concern evidence of "intelligent tentativeness." He is not sustained by religious or cultural orthodoxy, or comforted like Emerson by symbolic readings of nature. He is split from the world, as his feelings of cloddishness and confusion indicate, except that both are chaotic; and the image of mossy logs shows that nature cannot provide him with uplifting spiritual emblems. Hawthorne produced a fundamentally desperate novel, McIntosh says, though a "strange sense of freedom accompanies its despair." C. J. Wershoven in "Doubles and Devils at Blithedale" (*ATQ* 58:43–54) regards Westervelt's "milieu" and Blithedale as essentially alike. She sees Blithedale as "a farcical distortion of the real world," its hopes of reform thwarted when Priscilla "brings in worldly temptation" and Zenobia rightly shrinks before her threat, her "sickness." According to Wershoven, Priscilla is Zenobia's worldly twin, Westervelt is Hollingsworth's, and Moodie is Coverdale's; she thinks Zenobia veils herself to win Hollingsworth but eventually recognizes him as the devil; and she thinks Coverdale becomes in the end "all earthy substance" yet says he lives in a dreamworld. But Wershoven rightly reads the Veiled Lady "tableau" as a criticism of the romantic American ideal of marriage and recognizes that all the novel's characters remain fragmented. A single sentence from John Dolis' "Hawthorne's *Blithedale*: Narrative Ethos and Absence" (*ArAA* 10:156–64) will demonstrate the wit and—for the uninitiated—the impenetrability of his poststructural treatment of Coverdale's limitations: "Entirely proscribed by an alien context, his narration fails to inscribe him as his own author(ity): he is, rather, its (k)not—the thread that comes undone."

As her title suggests, Carol Hanbery MacKay in "Hawthorne, Sophia, and Hilda as Copyists: Duplication and Transformation in *The Marble Faun*" (*BIS* 12[1984]:93–120) correlates Hawthorne's incorporation of passages from his notebooks into his romance, his wife's edition of his notebooks for posthumous publication, and Hilda's copying of paintings. MacKay recognizes that "the differences may make it seem equivocating to call Hawthorne and Sophia copyists," but it *is* equivocating to use the same term for such different

kinds of appropriation. MacKay does not come to grips with basic
epistemological issues, and she uses the idea of copying so loosely
that it includes Miriam's resemblance to the portrait of Beatrice Cenci
and Donatello's recollections of the model's death. It is inaccurate to
say that Hawthorne and Sophia were obsessed with the idea of copying, that Sophia wavered between copying and creating, or that
Hawthorne was engaging in "self-worship" through Hilda. Nonetheless, it is true that the role of copying is a central concern of *The
Marble Faun.* Lou Thompson in "The Contagion of Guilt and the
Women in Hawthorne's *The Marble Faun*" (*LJHum* 10[1984]:39–45)
sees "no fundamental difference between Hilda and Miriam" as
sinners and sufferers despite their "polar natures." His concern about
the women's bond of sorrow is seen to be part of a broader inquiry into
the contaminating effects of sin and the peculiar confraternity of
guilt.

Two essays cope with the unfinished romances. In "Continuity and
Indeterminacy in Hawthorne's Unfinished Romances," (*ESC* 11:311–
33) Kristin Brady demonstrates that the American Claimant and
Elixir of Life manuscripts all insist on the need to live in the present:
pursuit of an Edenic past or a perfect future proves destructive. In
each case, reader and writer "strive toward a meaning while failing
always to reach it," though the central ideas and ironic closure can be
inferred. Even Brady's asides are provocative, as when she notes that
Hawthorne was writing the Claimant manuscripts while *David Cop-
perfield* was being serialized. Drawing on Iser, she observes that
excessive indeterminacy both strains and challenges the reader, who
is drawn into Hawthorne's "present" consciousness by his comments
on difficulties in writing about past, present, and future. In "*Septimius
Felton*: 'The whole thing lies in the blossom of an herb' " (*MarkhamR*
14:15–20) Judy R. Smith discusses Hawthorne's profound ambivalence about female sexuality: Sybil Dacy is killed by the beautiful
fungus symbolic of her dangerous attraction, the fair Rose is not a
viable sexual partner, and Septimius is "left going to seed." Some
images are overread and the rhetoric is often overheated: vines throt-
tling pine trees are said to "lure" the trees; Sybil "deceptively invites
Septimius into the apparently warm, fragrant, juicy interiors of her
femininity." Smith is right in showing how plant images powerfully
convey sexual anxieties and right to note that the narrative itself
is described as an entangling vine; but it is not a deadly vine, and I

do not think Hawthorne concludes that "men and women are critically injured by the inevitable sexual thwarting that defines their interaction."

iv. Short Works

Hawthorne (like Irving and Poe) rates a chapter to himself in Eugene Current-García's *The American Short Story Before 1850: A Critical History* (*Twayne*, pp. 42–58). The brief chapter begins by discussing the role of the short story in Hawthorne's career, then goes on to consider his presumed and announced intentions, the circumstances of publication of particular stories and collections, and their critical reception. Current-García summarizes Hawthorne's contributions to the development of the American short story—particularly his psychological probing, his use of the past, his ambivalence, and his anatomization of sexual relationships—and provides some commentary on representative stories.

Contrasting with this 17-page chapter about all of Hawthorne's stories is a book of 167 pages about a single story. In *La Nouvelle Beatrice: Renaissance and Romance in "Rappaccini's Daughter"* (Rutgers) Carol Marie Bensick examines Hawthorne's story in its historical context, offering bold if not always convincing readings that range from small matters (Lisabetta is "evidently . . . a dabbler in folk remedies, perhaps a midwife" who "would be hard pressed to disprove an accusation of witchcraft") to the startling central hypothesis that what has poisoned Beatrice and Giovanni is syphilis. She argues that the narrator presents the story as an allegory, with Beatrice figuring as religious faith, while the author himself shows that Transcendental idealism is an inadequate guide to experience. She also argues that in addressing such 19th-century concerns as the validity of sense information, Hawthorne drew on disputes between Paracelsans and Galenists, Neoplatonists and Aristotelians in 16th-century Padua. The story is thus seen to be about the split between science and faith in both periods. (For Michael J. Gilmore's very different reading, see section **ii**.)

Three critics take different approaches to the perennially interesting topic of Hawthorne and art. Stephanie Fay's "Lights from Dark Corners: Works of Art in 'The Prophetic Pictures' and 'The Artist of the Beautiful' " (*SAF* 13:15–29) studies the relationship of the tales' artists to their works, subjects, and audiences. Each artist is "deluded, unsympathetic, and complacent," yet produces "a work whose im-

portance the narratives endorse." A few readings are questionable
(e.g., the narrator's approval of Owen's butterfly is "slowly undermined"), but Fay raises interesting questions (e.g., about the painter's
venture into the wilderness he does not "copy"); and her speculations
about "inadequate" artist and "sufficient" work are relevant to Hawthorne's ambivalence about himself and his fictions. In "A Show of
Hands in 'The Artist of the Beautiful'" (*SSF* 22:455–60) John L.
Idol, Jr., discusses the way hands in "The Artist of the Beautiful"
develop the contrasting characters and suggests that Hawthorne was
applying the theories in the British physiologist Charles Bell's 1834
book *The Hand: Its Mechanism and Vital Endowments, as Evincing
Design and Illustrating the Power, Wisdom, and Goodness of God,*
specifically that the hands express individual mind and will, and that
human progress occurs in three stages—ministering to individual
necessity, laboring for society, then finally (as with Owen) actuating
spiritual yearnings. Patricia Dunlavy Valenti in "The Frozen Art or
the Ethereal Domain: Hawthorne's Concept of Sculpture" (*SSF*
22:323–30) sees a central paradox in Hawthorne's attitudes toward
sculpture, as expressed in the short stories as well as in the notebooks
and *The Marble Faun*: he had misgivings about marble statues, which
forfeit vitality, but he used a snow-maiden, a mechanical butterfly,
and a figurehead conceived in love to affirm that accepting earthly
mutability can release "the spirit for timeless enjoyment." Valenti is
not directly concerned about Hawthorne's attitudes on technical issues such as the relation of clay model to finished marble, but she
recognizes that he used statues of various kinds (the Man of Adamant
among them) to articulate his beliefs about the transient and the
eternal.

The year's work includes a short essay on each of two stories and
notes on two others. Rosemary F. Franklin in "'The Minister's Black
Veil': A Parable" (*ATQ* 56:55–63) takes the subtitle as a key to the
motives and expectations of both Hooper and Hawthorne. She dis-
cusses the Book of Isaiah as a probable source, then points out that
Hooper was committing the sin he dramatized and that he could be
faulted for arrogance in testing his congregation's spiritual condition.
Even more convincingly, she suggests that the subtitle with its New
Testament reverberations conveys Hawthorne's expectation that few
readers would adequately understand him. Max L. Autrey argues in
"'My Kinsman, Major Molineux': Hawthorne's Allegory of the Urban
Movement" (*CollL* 12:211–21) that the story's "underlying socio-

logical study" of the movement from agrarian to urban life combines
three other "allegorical views"—about the loss of Eden, the American
Revolution, and the transition from childhood to adulthood. Despite
occasional inaccuracies (e.g., Robin "threatens" the old gentleman,
abandons his cudgel, and rejects the "urban church"; the pillared
mansion is the Major's residence; and the kindly gentleman "insists"
that Robin postpone his return home), Autrey does well to focus on
Hawthorne's imagery of urban life. In "The Conquest of Canaan:
Suppression of Merry Mount" (NCF 40:345–54) Thomas Pribeck explores the implications of Endicott's accusation that Blackstone was
a "priest of Baal." Since Baal was a pagan fertility god and the fertility
goddess Asherah was worshiped at sacred poles near his altars, the
accusation recalls the Israelites' struggles against idolatry. The de-
pravities of Merry Mount recall the licentiousness of Canaan fertility
cults, and Endicott is "a leader of the new Children of Israel in the
New England wilderness." In "'Gold-Gathering Expedition[s]': Three
Possible Sources for 'Peter Goldthwaite's Treasure'" (HSN 11, ii:13–
15) Margaret B. Moore presents interesting suggestions about contemporary events that might have nurtured Hawthorne's imagination.
He might well have known about Salemites who went south in
search of gold in 1828 and in 1830; and he might have known that the
Mormon founder Joseph Smith visited Salem in 1836 in a fruitless
search for treasure reportedly hidden in a Salem house.

Two studies focus on Hawthorne's narrators, and another on the
narrative frame of a children's book. Elizabeth McKinsey discusses a
relatively unexamined sketch, "My Visit to Niagara," as "a dramatization of the dilemma of expectation and disappointment and its solution by the Romantic artist." Her 10-page section entitled "'Blessed
were the wanderers of old'—Hawthorne's Recovery of the Sublime
Experience" (pp. 191–200) in *Niagara Falls: Icon of the American
Sublime* (Cambridge) focuses on the narrator. His inflated expectations lead to an initial disappointment with the Falls, but he gradually
achieves a personal response to their sublimity. He can then write
about the experience and so both relive it and share it. In "The Other
Side of Concord: A Critique of Emerson in Hawthorne's 'The Old
Manse'" (NEQ 58:453–58) John S. Martin postulates a remarkably
sly narrator who "happen[s] across" the study where Emerson had
written "Nature" and then from its window "conveniently" spots the
Concord River, where the white water lily springs from mud even if
it "chooses to ignore it." Even those who do not entirely accept this

subtext can agree that Emerson and the limits of idealism were on Hawthorne's mind when he wrote the essay. Finally, the title of Elizabeth Peck's note—"Hawthorne's Nonsexist Narrative Framework: The Real Wonder of *A Wonder Book*" (*CLAQ* 10:116–19)—sums up her conclusion. (See the following section for a study of "The Paradise of Children.")

v. Hawthorne and Others

Studies of Hawthorne's sources and his influence go back to Greek myth and forward to major 19th- and 20th-century writers. (Several source and influence studies are included in the previous three sections.) In "Hawthorne's Pandora, Milton's Eve, and the Fortunate Fall" (*ESQ* 31:164–72) Martin K. Doudna discusses "The Paradise of Children" as Hawthorne's version of the temptation and fall in *Paradise Lost*, pointing out the many precise parallels with Milton and the signal differences: Hawthorne changed Adam and Eve into children, placed them in a Greek myth, and clarified the paradox of the Fortunate Fall for his young readers. Doudna points out how Hawthorne differed from Hesiod and subsequent retellings of the Pandora myth: the adults become children, with Epimetheus an active character but Pandora a far more attractive and enterprising one, and Milton-derived details are added. Hawthorne thus produced a Christian version of the pagan story of sin and temptation as a children's story with "adult dimensions."

In reassessing a relationship originally suggested by Poe, Thomas Baginski gives a strong *no* to the question in his title, "Was Hawthorne a Puritan Tieck? Aspects of Nature Imagery in Hawthorne's *Tales* and Tieck's *Marchen*" (*LWU* 18:175–91). The two writers' divergent worldviews account for differences in their nature imagery. Because Hawthorne assumed a polarity of man and nature and connected images to ideas, he used similes and presented subjective transformations of perceived reality; because Tieck assumed an original unity of man and nature, he preferred metaphors and attempted to restore "the original unity of all being" through sensual (particularly auditory) imagery.

Edward Stokes in *Hawthorne's Influence on Dickens and George Eliot* (St. Lucia: Univ. of Queensland Press) fulfills the promise of his title, summarizing previous scholarship and going well beyond it. He shows Dickens' indebtedness to *The Scarlet Letter* and *The House of the Seven Gables,* particularly in *Bleak House* (with Lady Dedlock combining traits of Hester and Dimmesdale and Tulkinghorn resembling Chillingworth), and *Hard Times* (where Sissy resembles Phoebe and the antithesis of head of heart seems a cheapening of Hawthorne's psychology); but he also traces Hawthorne's influence on later novels. Stokes demonstrates that the influence on Eliot was more pervasive, as when he compares Hetty Sorrel and Hester Prynne as dark-haired adulteresses and Donnithorne and Dimmesdale as hypocrites. Hester is also seen behind Maggie Tulliver and Silas Marner; and Stokes painstakingly, modestly, and convincingly produces "a great deal of solid evidence of Hawthorne's influence in *Scenes of Clerical Life, Adam Bede, The Mill on the Floss, Silas Marner, Romola, Felix Holt,* and *Middlemarch.*"

In *Adultery in the American Novel* Donald J. Greiner addresses the question of how John Updike has "synthesized and adapted" his predecessors' fictions. Greiner summarizes Updike's criticism of Hawthorne and compares the two writers' fictions about erotic desire and sexual transgression, trying to distinguish their underlying moral beliefs. There is some misreading (e.g., Dimmesdale "sullies his Election Day Sermon" by his "exclamation that he is . . . a prophet serving God") and some overgeneralizing (e.g., "once sexuality in women is admitted, adultery follows"). But the slender study makes interesting distinctions about the moral concerns that govern Updike's, James's, and Hawthorne's sympathetic treatments of adultery.

In *Joseph Conrad and American Writers: A Bibliographical Study of Affinities, Influences, and Relations* (Greenwood) Robert Secor and Debra Moddelmog include a reference to Hawthorne in *Lord Jim* and over two dozen biographical and critical studies that compare Conrad and Hawthorne, a few of them suggesting the possibility of influence.

Probably the most unusual comparison of the year occurs in Harold Schechter's "'The Bosom Serpent': Folklore and Popular Art" (*GaR* 39:93–108). Schecter compares Hawthorne's tale with Ridley Scott's *Alien* as an instance of how serious art transforms and popular art simply transmits folk motifs: *Alien* is without intellectual pretensions, but closer to its source than Hawthorne's sketch. As this study of a minor tale and the rest of the year's work indicates, the art of Nathaniel Hawthorne continues to be a vital concern for a wide range of scholars and critics.

State University of New York, Geneseo

3. Poe

Kent P. Ljungquist

In last year's chapter I noted a disconcerting division in Poe studies, a radical split between theoretically minded criticism and historically oriented scholarship. This trend continued in 1985. Source and influence studies continue to turn up small but interesting discoveries, but sometimes without any acknowledgment of the theoretical concerns that have complicated the study of literary influence. On the other hand, theoretical analyses of Poe have proliferated, but all too often these discussions display an indifference to Poe as a figure in his social, cultural, and literary milieu. In some theoretical studies a neglect of previous scholarship on Poe has led to either repetition of old claims or outright inaccuracies. In the best studies covered in this year's survey, one observes an attention to Poe as a writer of his own time balanced by critical and theoretical perspectives of our own. Discussions by Dana Brand, Craig Howes, and Tobin Siebers demonstrate, in exemplary fashion, that such a balance can be struck. Such examples show, moreover, that historicists and theorists can learn from one another.

i. Texts and Bibliographical Studies

Only an individual who has devoted his career to Poe scholarship could have produced the copiously annotated edition of *The Brevities: Pinakidia, Marginalia, Fifty Suggestions, and Other Works* (Gordian). From Burton R. Pollin's informative notes on the miscellaneous filler items that Poe contributed to various magazines, one receives edification on a number of issues: the complex history of the Redfield edition; Poe's distaste for the "mannerist" style of Southey, Bulwer, and Hawthorne; his distinction between the song and the poem; a 1,500-word attack on Eugene Sue's *The Wandering Jew*, still in manuscript at the Huntington Library; several uncollected reviews in *Burton's Gentleman's Magazine*; and Poe's sustained admiration for the poetry of Alexander Pope. A dogged pursuit of information on sources and on connections to tales and poems has produced a series of notes that should provide a firm foundation on which Pollin and other scholars will build future studies.

The textual policy followed for this "edition," however, is perplexing. Despite extant manuscripts of several portions of the "Marginalia," Pollin chooses to print published versions. Poe's intended changes accompany only the installments in the 1844–46 *Democratic Review*, but even in this case Pollin follows the printed texts for his "edition." For other manuscript materials, some of which contain substantive variants from published texts, Pollin provides no collations. There is a list of "Typographical Variants and Errors," most of which correct faulty spellings for foreign words, but even with access to the manuscripts of the *Democratic Review*, he sometimes refuses to emend (e.g., "auto da fe" is not emended to "auto-da-fé"). The textual policy for this edition could be termed inconsistent or idiosyncratic; it follows no established or normative policy, a problem especially evident when Pollin acknowledges: "No attempt . . . is made to differentiate between a clear author's error and a typesetter's error, though some of the latter can be seen" (p. xli).

Other irregularities may prove bothersome to some readers, as when problems in documentation obtrude: N. Bryllion Fagin is referred to as H. B. Fagin; the editor of the Boston *Transcript* was Cornelia Walter, not Walters; a reference to David K. Jackson's 1933 article in *AL* is botched (p. 5); John Black, translator of Schlegel, becomes James (p. 13); Mary Hewitt is temporarily confused with Mary Howitt (p. 173); an article in *Ex Libris* (1940) is mentioned without its author, the late John C. French; and an article by Dwight Thomas receives mention without bibliographical information (p. 168). Since Pollin devotes considerable attention to Poe's word coinages, Fred R. Shapiro's addition to that compilation ["Poe's Early Usage of the Word *Linguistic*," *N&Q* 32:351] can receive convenient mention here, a usage appearing in an 1846 "Marginalia" entry.

All Poe scholars will probably want to consult the relevant section of the *Bibliography of American Literature*, volume 7 (Yale, [1983], pp. 115–54), completed after Jacob Blanck's death by Virginia L. Smyers and Michael Winship. The compilers helpfully correct some of the errors in the Heartman-Canny bibliography.

Two additions to 19th-century secondary bibliography on Poe appeared in 1985, and a third piece dealt with his exploits as a public speaker. In "The Richmond *Compiler* and Poe in 1845: Two Hostile Notices" (*PoeS* 18:6–7) Pollin notes that a newspaper previously supportive of Poe published a negative review of the 1845 *Tales* and predicted, somewhat prematurely, the end of his literary career. In "Two Critical Notices on Poe in *Southern Punch*" (*PoeS* 18:21–22) Edward J. Piacentino reprints two pieces by John W. Overall, editor of a weekly humorous magazine that praised Poe in 1863. Commenting on Poe's 19th-century reception, Muktar Ali Isani in "Poe and 'The Raven': Some Recollections" (*PoeS* 18:7–9) reprints an interview from the 1905 *Los Angeles Times*, an anonymous reminiscence of Poe's reading "The Raven."

Of the two bibliographical projects on Poe completed by Benjamin Franklin Fisher IV, his contribution to *Research Guide to Biography and Publishing* (Research Publishing, pp. 922–26), edited by Walton Beacham, provides more general information. Via terse annotations, he offers evaluative comments on a selected group of biographical and critical sources. Despite some typographical errors and an omitted coauthor for one article, Fisher's contribution to Walter Albert's Edgar Award-winning *Detective and Mystery Fiction: An International Bibliography of Secondary Sources* (Brownstone Books, pp. 588–601) provides an inclusive listing of secondary works, including some interesting 19th-century items that focus on Poe's pioneering achievements in a unique genre. Previously compiled by Fisher, "Fugitive Poe References: A Bibliography"(*PoeS* 18:9–12) fell into the hands of Richard Kopley, who offers a helpful checklist of items touching on Poe, but not directly focused on him. In place of its annual bibliographical survey, *Poe Studies* (17 [1984]:1–40) devoted an entire issue to an "Index to the Bibliographies of Poe Criticism and Scholarship Appearing in *Poe Studies* 1969–1983," keyed to entries and annotations in all previous bibliographical installments of that journal. Together with Michael Burduck's topical index appearing last year (see *ALS 1984*, p. 53), the scholar now has easy access to items appearing in *Poe Studies* in the last decade and one half.

Frederick S. Frank attached to his special Poe issue of *Sphinx* (4:277–301) a fairly inclusive annotated bibliography on Poe's Gothicism. Individual entries derive nearly verbatim from his *Guide to the Gothic: An Annotated Bibliography of Criticism* (Scarecrow [1984], pp. 243–61). Those consulting only the *Sphinx* issue will miss some Poe-related items, such as Richard P. Benton's introduction to the 1972 *ESQ* Gothic symposium and G. Richard Thompson's intro-

duction to *Romantic Gothic Tales* (1979). Other omissions are curious: Frank cites Clark Griffith on "Poe and the Gothic" in *Papers on
Poe* (1972), but not related items in the same volume; similarly, he
cites Thompson's essay on "Usher" in *Ruined Eden of the Present*
(1981), but not Patrick Quinn's response in the same volume.

ii. Sources and Influences

Drawing on Thomas Ollive Mabbott's collected materials, specifically
Poe's manuscript excerpts from Milton and Shakespeare, Pollin has
assembled "Shakespeare in the Works of Poe" (*SAR*, pp. 157–86), a
compilation of quotations from and allusions to Shakespeare in Poe's
oeuvre. Intending his listings as resources for further investigation
rather than as final statements on his chosen subject, Pollin does note
the "parallel chains" of development in individual tales and *Macbeth*.
Curiously, he does not cite Richard Wilbur's 1982 essay dealing partially with that subject (*ALS 1982*, pp. 45–46). Nor does he mention
Kermit Vanderbilt's 1968 essay on "The Masque of the Red Death"
after claiming that connections between Poe's tale and *The Tempest*
have received almost no mention. Pollin, nevertheless, has provided
a useful scholarly tool with other potential applications, such as to
associations with contemporaries like Elizabeth Oakes Smith, who
several times characterized Poe as "a Hamlet-like man."

Also drawing on suggestions by Mabbott, Kenneth W. Graham's
" 'Inconnue Dans Les Annales de La Terre': Beckford's Benign and
Demonic Influence on Poe" (*Sphinx* 4:226–40) suggests that William
Beckford's works appealed to Poe in two different ways. Incorporating
allusions to Beckford in the landscape tales, Poe may have been stirred
by the British author's accounts of the mysteries of genius and creativity. On the other hand, the impact of *Vathek* may account for
demonic dimensions in Poe's works, notably "Ligeia," "Masque," and
"Usher." Graham may neglect ways in which creative genius links
inextricably with demonic experience, as I argued in a previous essay on "Uses of the Daemon in Selected Works of Poe" (*ALS 1982*,
pp. 47–48). Nevertheless, Graham's essay adds to our knowledge of
Poe's use of evocative settings as well as of specific sources.

Other studies treat Poe's sources with considerably less amplitude.
In a tidy note ("Another Source for 'The Black Cat,'" *PoeS* 18:25)
E. Kate Stewart calls our attention to a story entitled "The Black Cat"
in the short-lived *Baltimore Monument* (1836). In addition to similar

settings and attention to occult matters, the identically titled tales share the theme of love's transformation into hatred. In "A Possible Source in Dickens for Poe's 'Imp of the Perverse'" (*PoeS* 18:25) Adeline R. Tintner adds to previous studies of the Poe-Dickens relationship by noting use of the words "imp" and "perverse" in *Oliver Twist*. In a densely packed note ("Empedocles in *Eureka*: Addenda," *PoeS* 18:24–25) David Ketterer responds to Peter C. Page's 1978 article on Poe's cosmological treatise (*ALS* 1978, pp. 40–41). Noting Poe's possible direct access to translated fragments of Empedocles' *Nature*, Ketterer points to five similarities between the ancient philosopher's view of the cosmic cycle and that of Poe, affinities suggesting a serious rather than satiric context for *Eureka*. Two notes from 1984 deal with what Poe may, or may not, have gleaned from his sources. In "The Greek Joke in Poe's 'Bon-Bon'" (*AL* 56 [1984]:580–83) Anthony Kemp suggests, contrary to Mabbott's claims, that the Greek passage in the conversation between Poe's title character and the devil represents a graphic pun playing upon the unreliability of linguistic signification. In "Mrs. Osgood's 'The Life-Voyage' and 'Annabel Lee'" (*PoeS* 17[1984]:23) John E. Reilly attempts to refute the thesis advanced by Buford Jones and myself that Frances Sargent Osgood's "The Life-Voyage" provided a probable source for Poe's 1849 poem (see *ALS 1983*, p. 48). Reilly claims that Osgood's poem, subtitled "A Ballad," is not a ballad in the "traditional" sense.

Poe's influence on American authors received sparse attention in 1985. Taking his title from an essay by V. S. Pritchett, Alan Gribben, in "'That Pair of Spiritual Derelicts': The Poe-Twain Relationship" (*PoeS* 18:17–21), provides an inventory of the half-dozen studies on Poe and Twain, then examines the latter's scattered comments on the former. The most interesting comment, a previously unpublished opinion from the Mark Twain Papers on "The Murders in the Rue Morgue," may open up fresh lines of inquiry. Among the affinities Gribben finds worthy of further exploration are the authors' shared interest in practical jokes, premature burials, and psychological doubles. Offering general comments on recent scholarship that finds Twain's work more Gothic and Poe's more ironic, Gribben concludes that these two major artists have more in common than previously acknowledged. The publication of *The Journals of Thornton Wilder* (Yale), edited by Donald Gallup, may lead to study of Poe's influence on another American author. Wilder's 1950–51 Charles Eliot Norton

Lectures at Harvard contained fairly detailed treatments of Poe, with *Eureka* singled out for special praise (pp. 102–05, 195–200). Excerpts from these journals received advance publication in the *New Criterion* (4:6–23). "The Half-Rusted Helmet: Julian Hawthorne's Poe and Flann O'Brien's Joyce" (*ELWIU* 12:97–109), by Andrew Horn, an essay that deals with fun had at Poe's expense in Julian Hawthorne's "My Adventure With Edgar Allan Poe" (1891), discusses how fiction can serve to settle scores with previous or competing authors. Horn locates an antecedent for such treatment in Nathaniel Hawthorne's "P's Correspondence," a connection with Poe first developed by the late Arlin Turner.

One of three studies dealing with Poe's impact abroad focuses on his illustrators. Richard Kopley's "Early Illustrations of *Pym*'s 'Shrouded Human Figure,'" in *Scope of the Fantastic* (Greenwood, pp. 155–70), supplements Pollin's previous work on the same subject (*ALS 1982*, p. 45). Kopley's survey of English, French, German, Italian, and Danish illustrations suggests their anticipation of scholarly interpretations of Poe's white figure. Two essays by Thomas C. Carlson explore Poe's impact in Romania, a country with a strong Romance language tradition, and therefore a place where French translations of Poe asserted significant influence. In "The Reception of Edgar Allan Poe in Romania" (*MissQ* 38:441–46) Carlson traces that influence on writers from the 1860s to the present. His companion study, "Romanian Translations of 'The Raven'" (*PoeS* 18:22–24), singles out Titu Maiorescu, an ardent Poe defender who championed "The Raven" in 1867, an event that augured a debate on the problems of translating Poe and a series of actual translations listed chronologically by Carlson. (On the issue of translation, see the discussion of Jefferson Humphries, below.)

iii. General Topics

Two veteran scholars offer solid, if unspectacular, general treatments of Poe. Eugene Current-García's discussion of Poe in *The American Short Story Before 1850: A Critical History* (Twayne, pp. 59–83) reflects the author's strong grounding in literary history. Noting parallels between Poe's Folio Club project and Irving's *Tales of a Traveller*, Current-García traces complementary developments of the tale in the hands of Poe and Hawthorne. Theories of irony and the grotesque play a significant role in his discussion of Poe's tonalities, evidenced by detection of undercurrents of mockery and satire in the "serious" tales. His roughly chronological survey concludes with a "Critical Reappraisal of Poe's Literary Achievements Since 1950," an unexceptionable discussion of scholarly and popular opinion. The Poe chapter by Robert D. Jacobs in the *History of Southern Literature* (LSU, pp. 127–35) provides a realistic assessment of Poe's strengths and weaknesses as well as a balanced view of his contributions to Southern letters. As might be expected from his previous studies of Poe, Jacobs offers particularly astute comments on Byronic influence, Poe's aesthetic credo, and his journalistic career. Novice students of Poe would find much reliable material in small compass in these two chapters by Current-García and Jacobs.

Turning from Jacobs' cautious, eminently readable discussion of Poe's role in southern literature to that by Jefferson Humphries in *Metamorphoses of the Raven* (LSU), one may encounter shock as well as confusion. Humphries has assumed a large undertaking, a study of the affinities among writers in the American South and their counterparts in late 19th-century and modern France. Despite much abstruse terminology, what promises to be an ambitious exercise in comparative cultural and literary analysis reduces itself to a commonplace: the Southern and French obsession with defeat and the grotesque. For biographical information on Poe, Humphries relies on the not always accurate *The Tell-Tale Heart* by Julian Symons. No articles on Poe appear in the bibliography, and the most recent book cited is David Ketterer's *The Rationale of Deception in Poe* (1979). Even secondary literature that touches on the complex issue of translation, supposedly the main focus of Humphries' study, receives little attention. (For a sampling of such discussions, see Thomas C. Carlson's articles mentioned above and *ALS 1984*, p. 56.) Humphries' discussion of Poe's southern characteristics (pp. 26–27) is brief and simplistic, and his marshaling of factual material faulty. For example, he suggests that Poe undercuts the concept of verisimilitude, despite the high praise for such techniques in an 1836 magazine review of *Robinson Crusoe*. Moreover, Baudelaire drew on articles by John R. Thompson (not John M., as Humphries claims); and Valéry has not been the "only serious writer" to praise *Eureka*. (For one example to the contrary, see the discussion of Thornton Wilder, above.)

As in Humphries' monograph, rhetorical concerns play a significant role in Evan Carton's discussion of Poe in *The Rhetoric of American Romance*. Carton defines romance as a rhetorical performance, a

dialectical enactment of philosophical concerns about signification
and selfhood. After this definition, the binary oppositions indeed proliferate as Carton explores the tensions in Poe's tales (perception vs.
illusion; reason vs. madness; life vs. death; integration vs. dissolution). Carton has read widely in critical theory and 19th-century
German philosophy. One comes away from his book, nevertheless,
with a sense that few key questions about Poe's works have been resolved. After all, Poe, who could speak so unequivocally about a
range of concerns in his magazine reviews, did not always leave such
issues in a state of philosophical irresolution. Carton, moreover, has
not always done sufficient homework in the secondary literature.
Analyzing "Ligeia" as a send-up of Transcendentalism, he cites
neither Clark Griffith's indispensable essay on that subject (1954 and
subsequently reprinted) nor Ottavio Casale's several studies of Poe's
responses to Emerson and his Concord brethren.

Louis Renza's contribution to *The American Renaissance Reconsidered* (pp. 58–89) begins with some outdated statements about
Poe's importance in the American literary canon, then provides a survey of criticism from F. O. Mathiessen to Harold Bloom and John T.
Irwin as if very little scholarship had intervened. "Poe's Secret Autobiography" approaches autobiography in Paul de Man's sense as a
figure of reading rather than as a genre of writing. Renza, more specifically, sees Poe reading his own texts as he imagines their being
misread by others. Without mentioning any biographical facts, Renza
approaches the tales as "autobiographical cryptograms," stories with
all surface and no depth that disclose their "autobiographical subtext"
through a self-alienating act of reading. All the puns mentioned by
Renza (the play on Poe's name in "Siope," the play on Dupin's name,
Arnheim as an anagram of "near him") have been anticipated by
previous critics. Much of the theoretical material cited by Renza
appears, in reprinted form, in Bloom's edited collection, *Modern
Critical Views: Edgar Allan Poe* (Chelsea House). Bloom's introduction, which originally appeared in the 1984 *New York Review of
Books*, keeps enthusiasm for Poe firmly under control. Bloom includes
previously published essays by Clark Griffith (cited above), Richard
Wilbur, Daniel Hoffman, John T. Irwin, and Shoshana Felman.

A more cogent argument than Renza's for Poe's centrality in the
American Renaissance appears in Douglas Robinson's *American
Apocalypses* (Hopkins). Robinson has not only consulted relevant
works in critical theory but has also immersed himself in biblical

interpretation, religious commentary, and secondary scholarship on a range of American authors. Although he joins together Emerson and Poe as our "seminal apocalyptists," his primary focus falls clearly on the latter, discussed in every chapter in part two of the book. Informed by a lucid distinction between literal and allegorical interpretations of the apocalypse, Robinson's approach supersedes that of David Ketterer in *New Worlds for Old* (*ALS 1975*, pp. 40–41). Allowing Poe his visionary metaphysics, Robinson relates the ending of *Pym* to the New Testament imagery of the white shadow. (See the discussion of Michael Williams' essay on "Shadow.—A Parable" and of my own article on *Pym*, below.) In one of the most subtle analyses of Poe's narrative thus far, Robinson suggests that its enigmatic conclusion points not to the transcendental beyond but to that line of deferral at which transfiguration as well as the reader's interpretation begins. In subsequent chapters Robinson extends his suggestive discussion of figuration to "Usher" and "Ligeia." In a related study, "Beyond 'Gothic Flummery': A Cosmoramic View of Poe's Symbolism and Ideas" (*Sphinx* 4:241–49), Edward W. R. Pitcher attempts to say something of general significance in a brief space, but his points are obvious: Poe's narrators, to be distinguished from the author, are types of the artist. Pitcher makes an intriguing case for the significance of a series of linked symbolic images (sea, lake, and river), but scrutiny of image clusters, the kind of study that paid off so handsomely in Stanley Kunitz's analysis of Keats, deserves a more sustained treatment in the case of Poe.

Two essays attempt to establish a nexus between Poe's poetic creations and his critical practice. Robert von Hallberg, contributing a chapter on Poe to *Nineteenth-Century American Poetry* (Barnes & Noble, pp. 80–99), tries to account for the special breed of "poet-critics" who resist the dominant literary tradition in the name of independence. Referring to Poe as a "tinkerer among poets," von Hallberg rehashes old arguments about his alleged extremism and provincialism. A more intriguing approach distinguishes Sara E. Selby's "The Music of Mr. Poe" (*POMPA*, pp. 52–57), which suggests that accusations about Poe's excessive musicality do not sufficiently acknowledge the close 19th-century connection between the song and the poem. Unfortunately, the essay compromises its suggestive argument by its incompleteness. Selby cites the "Marginalia" entry of 1849, but she does not attend to the longish review of George Pope Morris' *American Melodies* from which Poe extracted this entry. Nor does she cite Burton Pollin's 1972 essay on "Eldorado" as a song of the West. (See the discussion in Pollin's *Brevities*, pp. 337ff.)

The title of Ross Chambers' "Narratorial Authority and 'The Purloined Letter,'" chapter 3 in his *Story and Situation: Narrative Seduction and the Power of Fiction* (Minnesota, pp. 50–72), may suggest a focus on one work, but his concerns are more wide-ranging. In particular, he investigates Poe's tale as an example of the potentially "seductive" program of fiction. A story that purports merely to divulge information uses duplicity and self-reference to promote a relational, rather than informational, concept of discourse. The combination of concealment and disclosure in Dupin's personality point to his "artistic" superiority to the Minister, a status that transcends his explicit pronouncements.

In contrast to the self-enclosed "systems" and technical terminologies of Chambers, Carton, and Humphries, the jargon-free approaches of Dana Brand and Tobin Siebers carry a welcome freshness and clarity. In "Reconstructing the 'Flaneur': Poe's Invention of the Detective Story" (*Genre* 18:36–56) Brand takes as his point of departure Walter Benjamin's essay on "The Flaneur." Tracing Poe's transition from "The Man of the Crowd" to the detective stories, he singles out the "flaneur," an urban spectator who aspired to "read" the city as an accessible text. Brand, moreover, establishes Poe's exposure to this tradition in the Theophrastan character books of the 17th century and in the writings of La Bruyère, Dickens, and Willis. "The Man of the Crowd" posits the requirement for an urban interpreter, a need answered in the detective stories by the appearance of Dupin, a master of urban observation through his expert scrutiny of key "texts." Curiously, Brand does not cite J. Gerald Kennedy's essay on "Poe's Deluded Detectives," the first study to relate "The Man of the Crowd" to detective fiction (*ALS 1975*, pp. 41–42). In *The Romantic Fantastic* (Cornell, 1984) Siebers deals more with Hawthorne and European authors than with Poe. Nevertheless, his use of anthropological theories of the victim and the marginal personality lead to fascinating perspectives on "The Man of the Crowd" and "Usher." Suggesting that the supernatural need not be deemed a mere literary category, he argues for an inextricable, and perhaps salutary, connection between literature and superstition. Confronting the banishment of faith and superstition by Enlightenment rationalism, such Romantic authors as Poe pursued a unique and strange quest. Seeking belief in an age that equated superstition with untruth, Romantic fantasists found recourse in lies, hoaxes, and madness, modes of self-mystification and self-destruction. In their attentiveness to history as well as literary history, both Brand and Siebers give their theoretical perpectives clarity, texture, and definition.

The last general study to be mentioned, George Zayed's *The Genius of Edgar Allan Poe* (Schenkman) makes no pretense to originality. In 17 short chapters the author pursues two goals: (1) demonstrating Poe's genius; and (2) accounting for the difference in Poe's reception in America and abroad. Ironically, his comments on Poe's morbid obsessions serve to sustain some of the myths he sets out to demolish.

iv. Individual Works

One of the few studies in 1985 to deal with Poe's poetry, Dwayne Thorpe's "Poe and the Revision of 'Tamerlane'" (*PoeS* 18:1–5) scrutinizes, in a careful, scholarly manner, the complex history of a poem sometimes dismissed as an adolescent experiment or a total botch. "Tamerlane," in Thorpe's view, represents Poe's initial treatment of one of his more significant themes: the conflict of mortality with the ideal. Excision of Byronic elements, moreover, enhanced the skill with which Poe presented this theme. Thorpe's most valid claim, one that underscores the poem's interplay between heavenly vision and earthly reality, points to the 1829 version's greater emphasis on time and fate. Thorpe's study concludes by noting suggestive parallels between Tamerlane and the troubled narrators of Poe's tales.

One of the most stimulating studies of the year, Craig Howes's "Burke, Poe, and 'Usher': The Sublime and Rising Woman" (*ESQ* 13:173–89), deals with the sources of terror in Poe's classic tale via the aesthetics of Edmund Burke. Poe, like Burke, makes a sharp distinction between the power of sublimity and the highly feminine notion of beauty. Such a rigid bifurcation rules out the possibility that women can play a role in the dynamics associated with the sublime. The consequence for Roderick Usher, the last of his line and living with his sister, is his horrifying confrontation with historical and sexual imperatives intensified by 19th-century social conventions. In what Howes terms Poe's psychologically astute portrayal of his main character's dilemma, Usher projects his anxiety onto his surroundings, only to have the supposedly weak Madeline rise to "possess" him. Poe's juxtaposition of death, fear, and melancholy with women, beauty, and poetry suggests that he never granted the "feminine" a truly salutary psychological or social power. Howes's treatment of the issue of incest may be the most thoughtful and balanced we have had thus far on "Usher," a less sensationalized discussion than that offered by William Patrick Day's monograph, *In the Circles of Fear and Desire: A Study of Gothic Fantasy* (Chicago, pp. 129–31). In comparison with Howes's novel analysis, the other study of Usher to appear this year, Leonard W. Engel's "The Journey from Reason to Madness: Edgar Allan Poe's 'The Fall of the House of Usher' " (*EAS* 14:23–31) appears to repeat previous claims, a sense of déjà vu compounded by Engel's "Identity and Enclosure in Edgar Allan Poe's 'William Wilson' " (*CLAJ* 29:91–99).

Of the two studies of the sea tales, one investigates the ending of *Pym*. My " 'Speculative Mythology' and the Titan Myth in Poe's *Pym* and Melville's *Pierre*" (*Sphinx* 4:250–57) begins by discussing the pervasiveness of versions of the Titan myth in the early 19th century. I call attention to a possible mythic analogue for the ending of *Pym*, a description by Francis Wilford of a churning, boiling, milky-white ocean presided over by figures of gigantic size. The ending of *Pym*, moreover, has a parallel in the "Enceladus" chapter of *Pierre*, an analogous treatment of mythic decline. Gary Scharnhorst's "Another Night-Sea Journey: Poe's 'MS. Found in a Bottle' " (*SSF* 22:203–08) surveys a psychological seascape in which Poe's seaman (a pun on "semen," according to the author) voyages within a womb.

Noting a trend in American Romantic studies, Michael Williams, in "Poe's 'Shadow.—A Parable' and the Problem of Language" (*AL* 57:622–32), shows how post-structuralist investigations have focused on texts that probe the problems of signification. As Williams contended in previous studies of "The Gold Bug" and "Some Words with a Mummy," Poe's recurrent subject is language itself (see *ALS 1982*, p. 51, and *ALS 1983*, p. 57). With "parable" defined as a "dark saying" whose significance is consumed in obscurity, Poe's shadows suggest a disjunction between signifier and signified, a loss of authoritative meaning. (For an alternative view of Poe's shadow imagery, see the discussion of Douglas Robinson, above.)

According to Williams, Poe retained an acute awareness of the role of the reader in construing, or misconstruing, a text as it became dis-

placed over time. In "The Accomplice in 'The Tell-Tale Heart'"
(*SSF* 22:471–75) Paul Witherington uses a reader-centered approach
to implicate Poe's voyeuristic audience in the crime described by his
narrator. Poe broaches, according to Witherington, a perplexing challenge to distinguish those who commit crime from those who like to
hear about it. The puzzle for readers of "The Masque of the Red
Death," according to Nicholas Ruddick ("The Hoax of the Red
Death: Poe as Allegorist," *Sphinx* 4:268–76), is the conflict between
Poe's expressed disdain for allegory and allegorical interpretations
of the tale. Relying on the theoretical work of Angus Fletcher but not
quite following his conflation of allegory and symbolism, Ruddick
claims that Poe intended "Masque" as "a trap for allegorical exegetes."
One has the uneasy sense that Ruddick, using traditional modes of
allegorical interpretation, has derived a few comments about en-
coding devices from literary theory to flesh out a "new" reading of the
tale.

Of three remaining studies that focus on minor tales, two draw
upon knowledge of 19th-century science. Elmar Schenkel's "Disease
and Vision: Perspectives on Poe's 'The Sphinx'" (*SAF* 13:89–92) cites
information from the fields of optics and medicine to suggest that
Poe's tale probes the nature of vision. Knowledge of physics and
chemistry leads to Christian Kock's new reading of a tale explicitly
about the apocalypse ("The Irony of Oxygen in Poe's 'Eiros and
Charmion,'" *SSF* 22:317–21). Kock contends that we misread the tale
if we assume the earth's destruction by an external force. Rather, if
read with proper and sufficient irony, the tale suggests that fear is the
real cause of extinction. Such a reading, Kock concludes, connects this
tale more meaningfully to the theme of "Usher," a point made more
skillfully by James Gargano in a 1982 essay. (See *ALS 1982*, pp. 52–53,
and Douglas Robinson's discussion of the apocalypse, above.) Of the
various contributors to the Poe issue of *Sphinx*, Martin Roth ("Poe's
'Three Sundays in a Week,'" 4:258–67) offers surprising substance
in dealing with a text that appears to promise little. In an attempt to
connect this slight tale to Poe's cosmology, Roth notes numerous oppositions: actuality and imagination; speech and thought; action and
intention; present and future. To these paired contrasts, supposedly
suggesting the forces of attraction and repulsion in the universe, one
might add the humorous incongruity between weakness ("faible")
and strength ("forté"). (Pollin notes this pairing in his edition of

The Brevities [p. 147] discussed above.) Despite Poe's wordplay and letter play, this comic tale reflects the tensions exerted just before the end of things, an appropriate place to conclude my discussion of Roth's intriguing essay—and this year's Poe chapter.

Worcester Polytechnic Institute

4. Melville

Brian Higgins

Two new reference works and a collection of essays on teaching *Moby-Dick* appeared in 1985. In other scholarship and criticism no dominant trend was apparent, though the European influence continued to make itself felt. Meanwhile, the "recognition" of Melville took new forms. During May "Herman Melville Week" was celebrated in New York City, as Melville was inducted into the American Poets Corner in the Cathedral of St. John the Divine. The same week a documentary on Melville's life and works, *Herman Melville, Damned in Paradise*, narrated by John Huston and featuring interviews with a score of Melvilleans, including Leon Howard, Jay Leyda, Henry A. Murray, and Robert Penn Warren, was presented on PBS television.

i. Concordances, Indexes, and Bibliographies

Larry Edward Wegener's *A Concordance to Herman Melville's Pierre; or, The Ambiguities* (2 vols., Garland), keyed to the Northwestern-Newberry edition, will facilitate detailed study of the words in *Pierre*—or at least most of them. With no explanation, Wegener omits 168 words from the body of the concordance and lists them in an appendix of "Deleted Words," with frequencies but without page or line references. The concordance is marred, too, by Wegener's preface, which begins with outright errors (Wegener creates a new and wordier version of Melville's well-known allusion to "Krakens" in his letter of mid-November 1851 to Hawthorne; Pierre is identified as Melville's narrator), then mistakenly attempts to demonstrate ways in which the volumes can be used to defend Melville's artistry. Wegener's critical judgments throughout are questionable at best.

Gail Coffler's *Melville's Classical Allusions: A Comprehensive Index and Glossary* (Greenwood), keyed to the Northwestern-Newberry edition or to alternate editions for volumes yet to appear in the

Northwestern-Newberry, contains, besides its master index of classical allusions in Melville's works, an alphabetized index and a sequential list of classical allusions in each work; an alphabetized index and
a chronological list of classical allusions in Melville's letters and his
1849 and 1856–57 journals; a list of allusions by categories, such as
geography, history, and myth; and a glossary, which identifies the
allusions. The indexes and lists should provide a useful starting point
for the further exploration of Melville's classicism Coffler wishes to
stimulate. The glossary, which will probably be the part of the book
most frequently consulted, is not always as handy, however, as might
be expected: entries do not always contain pertinent information, and
not all allusions are identified. Coffler's lists for *Pierre*, for example,
include the phrase "Ephesian matron allegorized"; the glossary identifies only "Ephesus" and "Ephesian letters." The reader of *Pierre* unfamiliar with Petronius' *Satyricon* will need to go elsewhere, to Henry
A. Murray's notes in his Hendricks House edition, for example, to
discover the story of the Ephesian matron and its relevance to the
Pamphlet.

Reviewers began making comparisons between Melville and Conrad in the late 1890s. *Joseph Conrad and American Writers* includes
a 19-page annotated bibliography of commentary on similarities between the two writers and Conrad's possible indebtedness to Melville, in reviews (1896–1929), in biographies and criticism, and in
dissertations.

ii. Biography

Three of this year's most interesting pieces concern members of Melville's family. Stanton Garner's "The Picaresque Career of Thomas
Melvill, Junior" (*MSEx* 60[1984]:1–10 and *MSEx* 62:1,4–10) offers
some new and some uncollected information about Thomas' young
manhood in France, his earliest years in Pittsfield, and his old age in
Galena. (As Garner notes, "the insistent influence of the life of the
uncle on the imagination of the nephew," demonstrated in detail by
Merton Sealts, "gives the subject a special importance and, even,
urgency.") What Garner brings to light here are Thomas' "patterns
of associating with important persons and of being tainted by corruption," beginning in France and continued in Pittsfield and Galena.
Jay Leyda's "From the New *Log*: The Year 1821" (*MSEx* 62:1–4) includes letters by Thomas, his brother Allan (Melville's father), and

their father, Major Melvill, from the forthcoming new edition of *The Melville Log*, which shed additional light on Thomas' strained relations with Allan and his financial predicament in 1821, when for several months he was imprisoned for debt. "Allan Melvill's By-Blow" by Henry A. Murray, Harvey Myerson, and Eugene Taylor (*MSEx* 61:1–6) reprints and analyzes the letter from Thomas to Lemuel Shaw (first published by Amy Puett Emmers, see *ALS 1977*, pp. 49–50) regarding two women who called at the Melvill house in Boston, making claims on the estate of Melville's father shortly after his death in January 1832. (Charles Olson apparently first discovered the letter and subsequently passed it on to Murray about the time he was preparing the Hendricks House edition of *Pierre*.) Like Emmers, Murray and his collaborators infer from the letter that "Mrs. A.M.A." was Allan's illegitimate daughter; they go on to identify the two women as aunt and niece, Ann Bent and Ann M. Allen (importers of English and French goods in Boston), and Miss Allen as the daughter of Martha Bethuel Allen, Ann Bent's sister. (Emmers had inferred from the letter, reasonably enough, that the two women were mother and daughter.) The inference that Miss A.M.A. was Allan Melvill's illegitimate daughter seems to be the correct one; and the identifications provided by Murray, Myerson, and Taylor are plausible and almost wholly convincing. Room for caution remains, however (as Hershel Parker and I point out in our chapter on *Pierre* in the forthcoming Garland *Companion to Melville Studies*, ed. John Bryant).

Robert K. Wallace's "The 'sultry creator of Captain Ahab': Herman Melville and J. M. W. Turner" (*Turner Studies* 5,ii:2–19) is valuable for what it adds to our knowledge of Melville's opportunities to study and discuss European masterpieces, ancient and modern, during his visit to London and Europe in the fall of 1849, when, according to Wallace, his study of painting "reached its full maturity." The first half of the essay focuses on Melville's meetings with several of the literati he encountered in London, particularly Samuel Rogers, on his new acquaintances' interest in painting and knowledge of Turner, and on the works he saw at London and European galleries and especially at Rogers' house, where he "had the rare opportunity—for a New Yorker in the 1840s—of comparing Turner and the Old Masters side by side." In the second half of the essay Wallace maintains that numerous chapters in *Moby-Dick* embody Melville's knowledge of Turner; more specifically he argues (not altogether convincingly) that two reviews of Turner's Royal Academy Exhibition in 1845 (one by Thackeray), in addition to a passage in Ruskin, influenced Melville's description of the painting in the Spouter-Inn at the beginning of chapter 3.

The attractive, lavishly illustrated "Companion Guide" to the documentary *Herman Melville, Damned in Paradise*, produced by The Film Company and broadcast on PBS television, contains short, well-informed essays on "Melville at Sea," "Melville and His Times," "Melville and New York City," and other topics, by Patricia Ward.

iii. General Studies

In the most ambitious of this year's general studies, "Melville as Novelist: The German Example" (*SAF* 13:31–44), Gustaaf Van Cromphout usefully shows the affinities between Melville's unconventional novelistic practices (in such works as *Mardi, Moby-Dick, Pierre,* and *The Confidence-Man*) and both the German Romantic novel and novelistic theory (propagating "the encyclopedic-dynamic-ironic mode") expounded by writers such as Herder, Novalis, Jean Paul, and Schlegel. Much as Melville's works seem to demonstrate that he had absorbed German literary ideas, however, one cannot, in the absence of external evidence, confidently claim that Melville consciously assimilated German influences, as Van Cromphout appears to do when he writes that it was "in his attempts to express 'totality' that he found the German novel so helpful a precedent." In the other general essays Richard D. Sharp gives a pedestrian and unilluminating survey of Melville's views on war and pacifism in *Mardi, White-Jacket,* and *Moby-Dick* ("War and Pacifism in the Novels of Herman Melville," *CLAJ* 29:57–81), while Stuart M. Frank tries to make much of little in " 'Cheer'ly Man': Chanteying in *Omoo* and *Moby-Dick*" (*NEQ* 58:68–82), arguing that "the singing of chanteys is of strategic value to the articulation and development" of Melville's themes. Marty Roth's "Melville and Madness" (*ArQ* 41:119–30) tells us little about either.

iv. Miscellaneous

Two more important items from Melville's library surfaced this year. "Herman at Christie's: On the Block—Again" (*MSEx* 63:10–12) gives Christie's detailed catalog description of his copies of Dante and Hazlitt's *Criticisms on Art*, with reproductions of two marked and annotated pages from "Paradise" and the title page of the Hazlitt. "The Results from Christie's" (*MSEx* 64:10) reports the results of the auction and reproduces the first page of "Hell" and facing page, both annotated.

In "Expanding the Influence: Faulkner and Four Melville Tales" (*SoAR* 50:81–92) Ronald Wesley Hoag cites verbal and thematic parallels which suggest that in *Light in August* Faulkner may have been influenced by the endings of "Bartleby," "Benito Cereno," "The Bell-Tower," and *Billy Budd*. Faulkner named Melville as one of the four greatest influences on his work, as Hoag reminds us; he contends that Faulkner "knew more Melville and knew it earlier than has yet been credited."

v. *Mardi* to *White-Jacket*

The year's most substantial essay on the earlier works is Watson Branch's "The Etiology of *Mardi*" (*PQ* 64:317–36), a study of the book's composition. In place of the three stages of composition proposed by Merrell R. Davis in his 1952 book on *Mardi*, Branch discovers five, his stages differing considerably in some respects from Davis'. Contrary to Davis (and Elizabeth S. Foster in the "Historical Note" to the Northwestern-Newberry edition of *Mardi*), Branch speculates, for example, that most of the chapters describing the voyage around the contemporary world were written before May 1848 and that only the sections based on current events were inserted later. Prominent in Branch's hypothesis is his contention that "the whole Taji-Hautia-Yillah romance is the *last* stage . . . in the composition of *Mardi* rather than the second stage, as has been argued or assumed by scholars who have discussed the growth of the manuscript." Branch's argument is closely reasoned, and his conclusions, though necessarily speculative, fit with what we know of Melville's piecemeal methods of composition. They also correspond with Hershel Parker's and Harrison Hayford's hypotheses (*ALS 1969*, pp. 33–34, and *ALS 1978*, pp. 49–50) that a major character or major characters were introduced at a late stage or relatively late stages in the composition of *Redburn* and *Moby-Dick* and written into chapters composed earlier. Like Hayford's, Branch's hypothesis, if correct, explains many of the discontinuities and inconsistencies in the published book.

Brian Saunders, in "Facing the Fire at Home: Redburn's 'Inland

Imagination'" (*SNNTS* 17:355–70), observes perceptively that in
Redburn Melville is not simply tracing "childhood features from
memory"—he is also "tracing memory itself back to the original im-
pressionabilities of a young mind," reaching "toward the often unconscious determinants of an event's emotional impact," patterning
autobiographic elements "to define and advance his perception of
psychic design." Though Saunders does not make the connection,
Redburn in this respect is an unheralded forerunner of *Pierre*, a book
with which it has seldom been linked. Concerned with "the layered,
psychological depth of the speaker," with "what is fixed and repetitive" in Redburn's character, Saunders cogently analyzes the "primary
influence" of Redburn's father and his stories, Redburn's attempt "to
conflate the outer progression of his 'first voyage' with an inner re-
gression to his earliest assumptions," and Redburn's "millenial vision
of America," which "reasserts" his "earliest ideals of father and fireside security"—though he fails to show how the rest of the Liverpool
chapters—and their social awareness—relate to Redburn's regressive
patterns.

   In "The Holy Guide-Book and the Sword of the Lord: How Melville Used the Bible in *Redburn* and *White-Jacket*" (*SNNTS* 17:241–
54) Kris Lackey usefully identifies biblical quotations and allusions
but breaks little new ground in examining the ways in which both
narrators "invoke the teachings of Jesus in their condemnations of
inhumanity." Lackey finds that Redburn's piety is consolatory and
escapist, whereas in White Jacket's hands the New Testament is "a
revolutionary's manifesto"—he "translates his observations into biblical metaphor to incite action." Much of Roger C. Press's commentary
on Redburn and Harry Bolton in "The Unicorn and the Eagle: The
Old World and the New World in Melville's *Redburn*" (*ArQ* 41:169–
82) is also routine. Press finds that Redburn and Bolton are not consistently representatives of the New and Old Worlds and that the
book does not always maintain a clear contrast between dynamic
New World and decadent Old World.

vi. *Moby-Dick* and *Pierre*

Approaches to Teaching Melville's Moby-Dick, ed. Martin Bickman,
is a welcome addition to the MLA's *Approaches to Teaching Masterpieces of World Literature* series, a collection of essays designed as
"a sourcebook of material, information, and ideas" on teaching *Moby-*

Dick to undergraduates and "intended to serve nonspecialists as well as specialists, inexperienced as well as experienced teachers." It contains a concise, well-informed bibliographical section by Bickman ("Materials"), followed by two overlapping sections ("Approaching the Text" and "The Classroom Situation"), 14 essays in all, focused on teaching *Moby-Dick* and encompassing a variety of pedagogical aims and methods, as well as reflecting most of the critical approaches to the book in the decades since the Revival. The high standard of the essays in the first section by Millicent Bell ("The Indeterminate *Moby-Dick*") and Robert Milder ("*Moby-Dick:* The Rationale of Narrative Form") is not sustained throughout the collection, but the essays are lively and informative and cheerfully promote interpretations and "structures for teaching" which others "can adapt, modify, or completely reverse." The collection will be helpful primarily to those who are new or relatively new to teaching *Moby-Dick*, but even old Melville hands are likely to come across ideas they will want to incorporate in their teaching.

In "The Word and the Thing: *Moby-Dick* and the Limits of Language" (*ESQ* 31:260–71) Gayle L. Smith writes perceptively about Ishmael's "deviation from ordinary language patterns," particularly the great number of "negated negatives" he employs—phrases like "not seldom," "not unattended," and "not disincline"—and about "the peculiar demands they make on the reader." Ishmael's "multilayered" constructions, Smith finds, "suggest how much is not directly understandable, not neatly this or that," frequently revealing "a mind unwilling to adopt either pole in a situation, opting instead to suggest that an infinite, if unnamed, continuum lies between the named poles." His linguistic choices, Smith suggests, reflect his need "to go beyond the common forms and structures of language to contemplate and express the complex reality he has experienced," in contrast to Ahab's, which "reflect a rigid, correspondential notion of language, a faith that meaning and reality somehow inhere in language itself."

Concern with language and identity is central to Ramón Saldívar's "The Apotheosis of Subjectivity: Performative and Constative in Melville's *Moby-Dick*" (in his *Figural Language in the Novel: The Flowers of Speech from Cervantes to Joyce* [Princeton], pp. 110–55). According to Saldívar, Ishmael "would re-establish identity through a circular process of recollection and storytelling; Ahab would establish it through a linear process of pursuit and command." Differentiating between Ishmael's and Ahab's language in terms of speech

act theory, Saldívar finds that "Ishmael's words reporting his encounter with the world and Ahab's words conceiving that encounter
function constatively and performatively," though he concludes that
for Ahab "the performance is insufficient without the necessary constative moment; and for Ishmael, while the constative is valid in its
own right, it is incomplete without the moment of performance as
narrative." In *Moby-Dick*, Saldívar argues, "the referentiality of the
issue of identity is thus suspended between two modes: the performative mode, which would define it as activity, and the constative mode,
which would define it as a matter of knowledge." So brief a summary
does little to suggest the complexity of Saldívar's argument, which
also draws on deconstructionist theories. Saldívar is at times illuminating; more often his readings struck me as dubious (e.g., his discussion
of Ahab's statement "Ahab is for ever Ahab," where he omits the
sentence "I am the Fates' lieutenant" from his quotation of Ahab's
speech, decides that it is "not entirely clear" under whose orders
Ahab acts, and interprets the passage—an important one in his argument—as Ahab's "declaration of independence").

Also concerned with Melville's language—or languages—Carolyn
Porter in "Melville's Realism" (*NOR* 12:5–14) draws on Mikhail
Bakhtin to propose *Moby-Dick* as an example of "dialogical realism,"
in which Melville "incorporates extraliterary genres and languages
whose authority is at once undermined and exploited." Porter supports this reading largely by skewed accounts of "The Affadavit" (in
which, she maintains, Ishmael's "dialogized language functions, paradoxically, to authorize the reader's acceptance of certain ideas, while
it simultaneously de-authorizes the conventional voices of authority
in his society") and "The Advocate" (where his "dialogical language
is responsible for destabilizing both meaning and authority").

Arnold M. Hartstein's "Myth and History in *Moby-Dick*" (*ATQ*
57:31–43) proposes another distinction between Ishmael and Ahab.
Ahab's role in a 19th-century world "undergoing vast spiritual
change" is that of the mythic hero who "seeks to confirm the existence
of a divine and moral sanction to nature and history." In contrast,
Ishmael, like many of the authors of the 19th century, attempts "to
shape a comprehensive but resilient vision, one that accommodates
the disjunction between nature and moral order." Hartstein's viable
propositions yield little fresh insight in the accompanying discussion
of the two characters. Freda E. Yeager's "The Dark Ishmael and the
First Weaver in *Moby-Dick*" (*ArQ* 41:152–68) muddles the relation-

ship between younger, *Pequod* crewman Ishmael and older, narrator Ishmael with "a study of the imagery of weaving" and "The Town-Ho's Story." Gene Bluestein proposes in "Ahab's Sin" (*ArQ* 41:101–16) that Melville "gives us a Protestant, existential theory of tragedy, expressed within the frame of Emerson's esthetic rather than in Aristotelian terms," with no apparent awareness of the long history of commentary on the nature of Ahab's tragedy and its relation to Emersonian thought.

In this year's one piece on *Pierre*, Daryl E. Jones finds a link between the central conceit in Plinlimmon's pamphlet and two extended passages concerning chronometers in Fenimore Cooper's *Jack Tier*, passages which embody that novel's "fundamental theme, illustrating clearly the relation between moral absolutes and practical expedients that must be understood if one is to survive the perils of this life"— though, as Jones cautiously admits, in the absence of conclusive evidence that Melville actually read *Jack Tier* the case for borrowing remains circumstantial (" 'Chronometricals and Horologicals': A Possible Source in Cooper's *Jack Tier*," *ATQ* 58:55–61).

vii. Stories

The year's crop of essays on the tales was undistinguished. After last year's perceptive essay on Sir Thomas Browne's influence on *Mardi* and *Moby-Dick* (*ALS 1984*, pp. 67–68), Brian Foley's "Dickens Revised: 'Bartleby' and *Bleak House*" (*ELWIU* 12:241–50) was disappointing, adding one or two interesting parallels to those which other critics have noted between "Bartleby" and *Bleak House* but in general straining too hard to show that Melville was "reworking a considerable portion" of *Bleak House* and both mocking and satirizing Dickens in the process. Michael Murphy's mildly ingenious " 'Bartleby, the Scrivener': A Simple Reading" (*ArQ* 41:143–51) argues, with little close attention to the text, that "Bartleby" is a story with only one character—the lawyer. According to Murphy, Bartleby "is simply an aspect of The Lawyer's character, long suppressed"; Ginger Nut, Nippers, and Turkey "are other facets of his personality or stages in his career," while even "personages with 'walk-on' parts like The Grubman, The Turnkey, and The Landlord are not separate characters, but parts of The Lawyer." Thomas Pribek argues plausibly (if unsurprisingly) that in the passages describing his "doctrine of assumptions" the lawyer is viewing himself ironically, seeing his reasoning as a travesty of rational argument ("An Assumption of Naïveté: The Tone of Melville's Lawyer," *ArQ* 41:131–42). Pribek overestimates, however, both the change that has taken place in the lawyer between his experiences with Bartleby and his telling of the story and the lawyer's recognition of his own "self-bias." Walter Evans' weakly argued "Hawthorne and 'Bartleby the Scrivener' " (*ATQ* 57:45–58) gives a distorted account of the relationship between Melville and Hawthorne. According to Evans, the lawyer represents "certain of Melville's strongest personal impressions of Hawthorne," while Bartleby reflects or caricatures "various aspects of Melville's personality and behavior, especially as they relate to Hawthorne."

Charles Swann's "Whodunnit? Or, Who Did What? *Benito Cereno* and the Politics of Narrative Structure" (*American Studies in Transition*, ed. David E. Nye and Christen Kold Thomsen, Odense, pp. 199–234) makes profitable use of comments by Raymond Chandler to illuminate Melville's achievement in structuring the mystery story in "Benito Cereno." He is less successful in his attempt, again using Chandler, to relate the tale's "serious political meanings" to "the form of the mystery story"; his contention that "many of the conventional critical problems have to be reformulated" when the tale is "located within the genre" of the mystery story leads to no startling revelations.

Largely on the basis of the epigraphs to the eighth sketch of "The Encantadas," Carol Moses concludes, in "Hunilla and Oberlus: Ambiguous Companions" (*SSF* 22:339–42), that Hunilla may be either "a temptress whose story is a total fabrication" or a "religious figure"— an ambiguity continued in the portrayal of Oberlus, who "represents both God and Satan." Darryl Hattenhauer's discussion of ways in which Melville creates and subverts impressions of timelessness and changelessness in "The Encantadas" is no more convincing ("Ambiguities of Time in Melville's 'The Encantadas,'" *ATQ* 56:5–17). Carol P. Hovanec points out common 19th-century elements of the "sublime" in Melville's description of the landscape in "The Tartarus of Maids" ("Melville as Artist of the Sublime: Design in 'The Tartarus of Maids,'" *MHLS* 8:41–51) but has little to support her claim that Melville uses the story "to make a powerful statement about the use and misuse of art as well as the terrible dangers inherent in unrestrictive progress." Edgar A. Dryden's "From the Piazza to the Enchanted Isles: Melville's Textual Rovings" (*After Strange Texts*, pp. 46–68) argues that in "The Piazza" "haunting presences from Hawthorne's prefaces," particularly the preface to *Mosses from an Old Manse*, and from Melville's own earlier works, especially "Hawthorne and His Mosses," blend with other literary echoes and allusions "to disturb the clarity and meaning of the narrative voice," for "almost every statement is qualified, twisted, or redirected by the other voices that speak through it." The intrusive "voices" often seem more the product of Dryden's own labored ingenuity than genuine "presences" in the text, and his discussion of sources and allusions, of "questions of authority and originality and the related problem of representation" in "The Encantadas" is similarly labored.

viii. The Confidence-Man

According to P. L. Hirsch, part of *The Confidence-Man* functions "as a tribute to the past, an oblique farewell to Melville's earlier expectations about the artist's magical capacity" ("Melville's Ambivalence toward the Writer's 'Wizardry': Allusions to Theurgic Magic in *The Confidence-Man*," *ESQ* 31:100–115). During the course of the 1850s, in Hirsch's view, Melville "came to think of the writer's magic less and less as a positive force" and to believe "that the artist's spell on his reader was evil and his deceit a demonic labyrinth which, as truth-teller, he was obliged to depict." Allusions to "theurgy, or spiritual magic" in *The Confidence-Man* "underline the dubious distinction between white magic and black, emphasizing a writer's tragic kinship to the devil," while "at the same time, they acknowledge the beauty and hope of the magian legacy which sustains him." The argument is fascinating, but Hirsch fails to demonstrate convincingly that Melville is indeed alluding to "the writer's magian heritage" or even, in most instances that she cites, to writers or writing at all. The general agreement among critics, cited by Hirsch, that in *The Confidence-Man* the title character "represents the writer" and that "fiction is shown to be an untrustworthy diabolical contest between reader and writer" is an invention of her own.

In "Shakespeare and the Conclusion of Melville's *The Confidence-Man*" (*ATQ* 55:41–47) Vincent F. Petronella finds similarities of language, characterization, and theme between scenes in *Macbeth* and the last chapter of *The Confidence-Man*; in particular he sees resemblances between the roles of the Old Man of Act II, scene iv, and Melville's old man. The "similarities" are not compelling.

ix. Poetry and *Billy Budd, Sailor*

A. Robert Lee, in " 'Eminently adapted for unpopularity'? Melville's Poetry" (*Nineteenth-Century American Poetry*, pp. 118–45), provides a gracefully written introduction to Melville's poetry, its place in his career, and its relation to his prose works, with attention to "the *kind* of poetry" he wrote in *Battle-Pieces, Clarel, John Marr*, and *Timoleon*. More specialized, Gail Coffler's "Form as Resolution: Classical Elements in Melville's *Battle-Pieces*" (*American Poetry*, pp. 105–21) finds in Melville's Civil War poems such classical elements as restraint, simplicity, and harmony, and claims as Melville's "special gift" the "dual vision which allowed him to distinguish between the actual and the ideal and to see how they were one." While Coffler manages to illustrate duality in the poems, her analyses stop short of showing how in Melville's vision the actual and the ideal "were one."

In "Melville and Charles F. Briggs: *Working a Passage* to *Billy Budd*" (*ELN* 22:48–54) John Bryant finds not only "another instance of the theme of the tragically dutiful sailor" in Briggs's work but also parallels to Claggart (in a malevolent chief mate) and to Billy (in an old Norwegian ship's carpenter) which suggest to him that Melville "may have had his old friend's book in mind when he composed *Billy Budd*," though "no objective evidence of his having read *Working a Passage* is available." Eric Henderson's "Vices of the Intellect in *Billy Budd*" (*ESC* 11:40–52) makes yet another case against Captain Vere, rehashing a good deal of what has been said before while citing correspondences between Vere and Claggart and arguing that "Claggart's irrational or demonic self seeks the destruction of Billy's innocence while Vere's irrational self in the disguise of the 'disciplinarian' accomplishes this destruction." Lastly, Joe K. Law's " 'We Have Ventured to Tidy up Vere': The Adapters' Dialogue in *Billy Budd*" (*TCL* 31:297–314) examines ways in which Vere's role in E. M. Forster and Eric Crozier's libretto "differs radically" from his role in Melville's story.

University of Illinois at Chicago

5. Whitman and Dickinson

Jerome Loving

The televised typewriters continue to turn out material on these two poets—Derridean echoes, feminist feints, psychoanalytical forays, bogus editions, and opaque "literary" studies of language instead of literature. Like food processors, they slice up the works into "texts" to discover endless tidbits of meaning(s). During the last five years in which I have been writing this chapter (and before), the image of American literature has changed. It used to be that the "canonized" voices represented the best of what was "subversive" in us; now there is the fashionable notion that American literature is slightly more than "what gets taught"—"Ideology" from R. W. Emerson to F. O. Matthiessen. It's all exciting if unnerving, but it is also time to get out of the kitchen. In departing from *ALS* I am also departing from the practice of a general introduction by reviewing a book under the rubric of both poets, the Polish scholar Agnieszka Salska's *Walt Whitman and Emily Dickinson: Poetry of the Central Consciousness* (Penn.), because its integrative rather than parallel structure defies the usual classification or division of treatment. Salska sets out to chart—in Northrop Frye's phrase—"the structure of each poet's imagination" with regard to Emerson's concept of a central consciousness. Seeing a kind of "objective correlative" in Whitman's poetry, she argues that Whitman's marriage of mind and matter, thought and object, involves an Emersonian return "to natural innocence, to the unfallen condition of language and of man." For Dickinson, on the other hand, language does not offer a metonymic sense of oneness with the universe but a confrontation with experience that leaves the poet with a feeling of fragmentation—or, as she told Higginson, "bare and charred." The feminist subtext to this comparison of a one-dimensional Whitman with a multivalent Dickinson is that the male poet is writing out of the ideology of a logocentric universe, while

Preparation of this chapter was facilitated by the research assistance of Susan Roberson Moon.

the female poet is writing out of a sense of true aesthetics because for her language has no clear referents. "Writing poems became for her," Salska argues, "not a quest for saving the truth, which it still was for Emerson and Whitman, but radically, itself the very act of salvation." Margaret Homans made the same argument using Emerson as her straight man (*ALS 1980*, pp. 83–84), but the problem with both readings is that what's true for Dickinson is not necessarily false for the male poet. It is difficult to distinguish between Salska's Whitman of "Song of Myself" and the poet of such later poems as the "Calamus" sequence and "As I Ebb'd with the Ocean of Life" precisely because her discussion is based upon the assumption that Whitman is always confident his words are "connecting." Never mind those "peals of distant ironical laughter" the poet receives at "every word" he has written in "As I Ebb'd" or even the "stunned" condition of the narrator "on the verge of the usual mistake" in "Song of Myself." God gave language to Adam, the precursor of all male poets, and so Whitman is not subject (or privy) to the tensions of a true aesthetic sense. All this is to say that while Salska reveals a high appreciation for Whitman in her learned treatment, her study is nevertheless unbalanced because of its implicit preference for Dickinson as the more interesting poet.

i. Whitman

a. **Bibliography, Editing.** The *Walt Whitman Quarterly Review* continues to provide a reliable and up-to-date bibliography, but an especially helpful compilation this year is found in William White's "Walt Whitman: A Bibliographical Checklist" (*WWQR* 3,i:28–47). His accurate and detailed descriptions of the early editions of *Leaves of Grass* are especially welcome. Collectors and students of Whitman should also see Walter H. Eitner's account of a "remarkably personal" copy of a later edition in "A Unique Copy of *Leaves of Grass, 1882*" (*WWQR* 1[1983],i:40–44); Wayne W. Westbrook, "The Case of Dr. Bowen: An Unknown Whitman Letter Recommending an Army Doctor" (*WWQR* 1[1983],ii:26–29); Ed Folsom, "The Mystical Ornithologist and the Iowa Tufthunter: Two Unpublished Whitman Letters and Some Identifications" (*WWQR* 1[1983],i:18–29); W. T. Bandy, "An Unknown 'Washington' Letter by Walt Whitman" (*WWQR* 2,iii:23–27); and Harold Aspiz, "Another Early Review of *Democratic Vistas*" (*WWQR* 2,iv:31–35).

b. **Biography.**   After years of work on what has obviously been a labor of true love, Florence Bernstein Freedman has produced *William Douglas O'Connor: Walt Whitman's Chosen Knight* (Ohio). While we may still wonder exactly who chose whom in this unique literary relationship, we can nevertheless appreciate Freedman's unstinting efforts to bring to life the whole story of this remarkable Irish-American. For the first time O'Connor is presented not in the shadow of his "Good Gray Poet" (as he was in my *Walt Whitman's Champion, ALS 1977,* pp. 67–68) but in his own right as a minor but mighty literary man of his day. Clearly written and well-researched, the biography unearths some new information on Whitman, such as the role of William Thayer (copublisher of the 1860 *Leaves*) in the Whitman-O'Connor circle during the war years and beyond. Although Freedman tends to exaggerate O'Connor's importance at Whitman's expense, her study is on the whole balanced and insightful. For "facts" the future biographer of Whitman will want to avoid David Cavitch's *My Soul and I: The Inner Life of Walt Whitman* (Beacon), another study involving O'Connor and a psychobiography that is poorly researched and careless with the material it has collected. Otherwise, this Freudian approach to the connection between Whitman's family life and his fictional life, or poetry, is interesting and provocative. *Leaves of Grass,* Cavitch argues, is a psychological reworking of Whitman's childhood between a dominating father and a possessive mother. In his re-creation the poet becomes the powerful product of "the loving fusion of contrary parts of himself." The rest of the scenario has the poet winning out over his father by becoming "a great tender mother-man" by the third edition, but then relapsing and having to reenact the family drama in his relationship with O'Connor and his wife, Nelly. Here basic information is either skewed or overlooked to make the story work. O'Connor may have "loved" Whitman, but there is no evidence of homosexuality in this radically heterosexual man who carried on extramarital affairs and may have had his death complicated by syphilis. Nor is there any firm evidence that Mrs. O'Connor was expressing in her letters to Whitman more than the sentiment of the romantic convention characteristic of the Victorian era in America. Cavitch simply took a good idea too far, or ultimately in the wrong direction. He has, however, opened an important door for other critics better versed in the wealth of Whitman scholarship.

Several pieces of minor importance round out the biographical section for Whitman this year. In his discussion of Whitman's and Emer-

son's involvement in the Boston abolition movement of 1860–61, Len
Gougeon in "Whitman, Emerson, and 'The Ballad of the Abolition
Blunder-Buss' " (*WWQR* 3,ii:21–27) produces two political cartoons,
one of which uses Whitman in an effort to embarrass Emerson. It
presents Emerson atop his Pegasus as the animal munches on
" 'Leaves of Grass' by Walt Whitman." The sketches appeared shortly
after Emerson had been booed off the stage of the Tremont Temple
while attempting to deliver an abolitionist address. Linking him to
Whitman was a way of undermining his credibility with regard to
the antislavery movement. In "Whitman Viewed by Two Southern
Gentlemen" (*WWQR* 3,i:16–21) W. T. Bandy finds similar evidence
of Whitman's growing notoriety by the time of the Civil War (indeed,
by the war's end he would be fired from his government job allegedly
for being the author of an indecent book). *The Southern Field and
Fireside* of 9 June 1860 upheld the "standards of the evening lamp"
with two attacks upon Whitman—by John R. Thompson, editor of the
Southern Literary Messenger during Poe's editorship, and Paul Hamilton Hayne, South Carolina poet. The ultimate effect of the third contribution in this area of Whitman's tarnished image in the 1860s is
to produce the menu for Whitman's 70th birthday party in Camden,
New Jersey (Louis Szathmary, "The Culinary Walt Whitman,"
WWQR 3,ii:28–33), but it also presents a wartime sketch by Edwin
Forbes, the American artist who accompanied the Army of the Po-
tomac and made drawings for *Frank Leslie's Illustrated Newspaper*.
Entitled "Fall in for soup," the sketch depicts in a line of soldiers a
figure resembling Whitman. No date for the publication of the sketch
is provided, but more than likely it was late in the war when Whitman
had become known around Washington, D.C., as the "wound dresser"
because of his work in its military hospitals. Leslie's purpose may have
been to soften the harsh image of the "barbaric yawper" whose book,
as E. P. Whipple quipped to Emerson, had every leaf "except the
fig leaf." It would take much more than Emerson's famous endorsement of 21 July 1855 to gain Whitman public acceptance. Even James
Elliot Cabot, Emerson's close friend and literary executor, demurred
from Emerson's solitary support of Whitman and his "free & brave
thought"—according to Len Gougeon, who reprints Cabot's letter to
Emerson "for the first time" ("Whitman's *Leaves of Grass*: Another
Contemporary View," *WWQR* 1[1983]i:37–39). That distinction,
however, belongs to Eleanor M. Tilton (*ALS 1979*, p. 68), who reprinted with that letter another to suggest that even those who did

defend Whitman sometimes did it sarcastically (see in her article the letter to Emerson by a "wood-Choper by profession"). Throughout the 19th century in this country Whitman would continue to be an occasional target of such derision; see, for example, Harold Aspiz, "Whitman in *The Southern Literary Messenger*" (*WWQR* 1[1983]i:44–45), and W. T. Bandy, "An Unknown Whitman Parody" (*WWQR* 2,iv:45–46).

c. **Criticism: General.** The reader taking up Shelley Fisher Fishkin's chapter on Whitman in *From Fact to Fiction: Journalism & Imaginative Writing in America* (Hopkins) might think she was arguing the obvious, but the essay is original in showing how this particular aspect of the famous foreground taught Whitman to think for himself. It also taught him to become "both in and out of the game" he reported back in neo-Emersonian tropes. As a result, Fishkin observes in her perceptive reading of "Song of Myself," there is in the poem "this mixture of sympathy and objective detachment, the ability to merge with the lives of others and to extricate oneself from the merge [*sic*], that characterizes the poet's relation to the world" he envisions. What was once familiar as mere "fact" became the "fiction" of a symbiotic relationship between writer and reader in *Leaves of Grass.* If the chapter has a weakness, it is its failure to view the poet's accomplishment in its Transcendentalist context and the neglect of one or two of the standard works on Whitman's journalism—such as Thomas L. Brasher's study of Whitman as editor of the *Brooklyn Daily Eagle* (*ALS 1970,* pp. 57–58). One might say that the essay is short on "journalism" and long on "imaginative writing."

In "The Federal Mother: Whitman as Revolutionary Son" (*Prospects* 10:423–41) Betsy Erkkila presents an intriguing argument for Whitman and "Ideology." The poet drew his inspiration and metaphors not out of his understanding of Emersonian self-reliance but from the "democratic culture" that began with the familial image of sons seeking to save mothers and daughters from abusive fathers. In this "relocation of authority in the individual rather than the state" of King George, the revolutionary fathers were frequently portrayed as being united by the "harmonizing and equalizing female figure of power." It was out of his commitment to the ideals of the American Revolution, projected as a potent female genius, that Whitman discovered his identity as a poet. The feminist aspect of the "political poet" is weak, but the argument is otherwise richly documented and

eloquently executed. It is, admittedly, an argument for "Ideology,"
however, and not one for ideology inverted by the "mystical experience" of the romantically American self-begotten self—that idealistic
and imaginative voyager from Washington Irving to (even) Clifford
Irving who wakes us up to the inherent fiction in most American
"facts." The same can be said for Whitman's linguistic source in nation instead of nature (every son instead of Emerson) in Erkkila's
"Walt Whitman: The Politics of Language" (*AmerS* 24[1984]:21–34).
According to Erkkila, Whitman saw the connection between American language and American polity, but she goes on to make an original
argument for Whitman's use of French (the language of revolution
against the English) and—more important—shows him using it earlier
than has been generally thought and not as clumsily as has been
maintained: "Whitman's French usage cannot be faulted. The French
words add to the rhythmic and tonal quality of the verse, at the same
time that they whisper of hidden delights and half-formed erotic
fantasies in the dream-state." The article concludes with the political
poet who anticipated contemporary efforts at linguistic reform along
"less radically and sexually biased" lines, but I prefer her earlier explanation in *Walt Whitman Among the French* (*ALS 1980*, p. 78)
that by his use of French Whitman was trying to liberate himself and
America from the deeply rooted Puritan sensibility about sex he
associated with his father and the fatherland of England.

Walt Whitman: Here and Now (Greenwood), ed. Joann P. Krieg,
should have been called "Walt Whitman: Then and There" because
the Hofstra Whitman conference it records was held five years ago—
on the 125th anniversary of the first *Leaves of Grass*. As far as I can
tell, none of the essays has been updated, and the only statement
more recent than 1980 is William White's bibliographical essay, which
observes that in the four years following the conference there have
appeared 373 articles, 144 book reviews, 23 books, 29 doctoral dissertations, and nine new editions of Whitman's writings. Many of the
conference pieces have already been published, directly or indirectly,
in books on the poet—in Justin Kaplan's *Walt Whitman: A Life*
(*ALS 1980*, pp. 70–71), Harold Aspiz's *Walt Whitman: The Body
Beautiful* (*ALS 1980*, pp. 71–72), my own *Emerson, Whitman, and
the American Muse* (*ALS 1982*, p. 85), and David Cavitch's *My
Soul and I* (reviewed above). Other arguments, such as Alan Helms's
for Whitman's concealment of his homosexual themes (*ALS 1984*,
p. 91), have appeared elsewhere in slightly different forms. In ad-

dition to being outdated, the collection is uneven in quality. Probably half of the contributions should have been forgotten as conference papers, but Joseph Cady's *"Drum Taps* and Nineteenth Century Male Homosexual Literature" offers a new angle on an old theme. Cady argues that the war allowed Whitman a convention for expressing homosexual sentiments, mainly through the motif of "soldier-comradeship" and the elegy. Another essay, possibly the best in the volume, is M. J. Killingsworth, "Walt Whitman's Pose and the Ethics of Sexual Liberation," which sees Whitman as a sexual romantic caught between the movements of libertinism and Victorian prudery.

Tenney Nathanson borrows from Jacques Derrida (*Of Grammatology*) in "Whitman's Tropes of Light and Flood: Language of Representation in the Early Editions of *Leaves of Grass*" (*ESQ* 31:116–34), observing that Whitman's speech-based prose goes beyond mere representation to achieve a coherence of presence—or what Emerson described in "The Poet" as reattaching the part to the whole. Natalie Harris is perhaps making reference to the critical opacity characterized by Nathanson's essay in "Whitman's Kinetic Criticism" (*AmerP* 2:19–33). She discusses the 1855 Preface, *Democratic Vistas*, and "A Backward Glance O'er Travel'd Roads" to argue that the poet—and in this case Whitman—is the best kind of critic because he avoids the "hermeticism of intricate system building," which tends to denaturize literature, and writes a criticism that is in itself the very literature the deconstructionists and other literary theorists *think* they are writing. Unfortunately, it is never that clear what the author means exactly by Whitman's "kinetic criticism." Also lacking in lucidity is Robert Paul Lamb in "Prophet and Idolater: Walt Whitman in 1855 and 1860" (*SAQ* 84:419–34). In arguing for the poet's movement from self-reliance to what is essentially God-reliance, Lamb leaps over the 1856 edition and its important nuances in the poet's progress. When the essay is not accepting at face value questionable generalizations in recent biographies, it is engaging in its own fictions which lead to facile readings of the poetry.

d. **Criticism: Individual Works.**   Coverage in this area ranges from Whitman's newspaper days to *Specimen Days*. In " 'Whitman's Literary Intemperance': *Franklin Evans*, or The Power of Love" (*WWQR* 2,iii:17–22) Anne Dalke finds in Whitman's 1842 novel a structure which functions as "a parody of the judgmental nature of the typical temperance tract, for which Whitman substitutes in-

stead a call for compassion." Whitman would have liked her argument, for in his old age he kept quiet about the serialized tale and
when confronted with it by Horace Traubel told him he had written
it with the help of a bottle of port. He would have preferred that his
literary executors concentrate their efforts on such unpublished works
as the posthumously published *Words* and *The Primer of Words*. In
"Dating Whitman's Language Studies" (*WWQR* 1[1983],ii:1–7)
James Perrin Warren argues against considerable evidence but persuasively that these language studies began as early as 1855 or at least
between the compositions of the first and second editions of *Leaves of
Grass*. Also using the early notebooks is R. S. Mishra in "'The Sleepers,'
and Some Whitman Notes" (*WWQR* 1[1983],i:30–36), who argues
for a Whitmanesque concept of friendship that sees through "the
necessary distinctions of the day" (i.e., those between homosexual and
heterosexual affection); pages 32 and 33 are reversed. This idea is also
found in Michael Rainer's "Uroboric Incest in Whitman's 'The
Sleepers'" (*WWQR* 1[1983],ii:8–13). Using as a gloss the post-
Jungian concept of the "Uroboros" (snake with tail in its mouth),
he attempts to explain the unity of the poet's nocturnal vision. All
differences (and difficulties) vanish, including those of race, nationality, sex, and education, as the poet is reunited with the collective
unconscious.

M. Jimmie Killingsworth advances his work on placing the poet
more clearly within the context of 19th-century American attitudes
toward sex in "Sentimentality and Homosexuality in Whitman's
'Calamus'" (*ESQ* 29[1983]:144–53). He sees Whitman using the
language of heterosexual love, or romantic hyperbole, to express
homosexual attitudes. Whatever the message, the supposedly spontaneous and confessional poems in "Calamus" were penned "with a
considerable degree of artistic attachment"—according to M. Wynn
Thomas in "Whitman's Achievements in the Personal Style in *Calamus*" (*WWQR* 1[1983],iii:36–47). The argument is carefully laid out
and supported with ample evidence, but it finally proves what has
been implicit in most arguments for the confessional theme: that
Whitman was able to sustain the emotional level while reworking the
language. It was a personal style rendered ultimately public, learned
in "Calamus" perhaps but definitely mastered in "When Lilacs Last
in the Dooryard Bloom'd." The principal vehicle for the pluralized
emotion, of course, is Lincoln, the "western fallen star" of American
democracy. This is not the conclusion of Jeffrey Steele in "Poetic

Grief-Work in Whitman's 'Lilacs'," (*WWQR* 2,iii:10–16), but he does find in his Freudian analysis a movement of mourning in which the unnamed subject of the poem becomes the "emblem and centre" of death's democratic release. The poet's "grief-work" consists of a series of operations which ultimately reappropriate the world now tinged with death and place it "within the context of an ongoing life-process."

Ever since Richard Chase branded Whitman a "speechmaker" in "Passage to India," many critics (myself included) have faulted the poem for its lack of romantic spontaneity and aesthetic open-endedness. In response to this trend, Harsharan Singh Ahluwalia in "A Reading of Whitman's 'Passage to India'" (*WWQR* 1[1983],i:9–17) defends the poem not on the grounds of "freshness" or "craft-manship" but on the ideological ones that its rich imagery strategically involves the reader "in the prophecy of the poem." The "true son of God," this poet of "Passage" promises to justify by his accomplishments on the spiritual plane the deeds of the scientists and inventors on the material plane and thus restore to mankind "the lost paradisal state." In other words, the poem's 19th-century preoccupation with the Transcendentalist connection between the technological and the spiritual is its merit, but—according to Martin K. Doudna in "'The Essential Ultimate Me': Whitman's Achievement in 'Passage to India'" (*WWQR* 2,iii:1–9)—this is precisely the reason for its critical unpopularity in the late 20th century, one in which there has occurred a shift from "a history-of-ideas approach to an aesthetic" appreciation. We thus prefer "Song of Myself" and generally the poems of the first three editions because Whitman advanced Emersonianism by contradicting it, by providing new questions instead of old answers. The latter pointed to the "Ultimate Me"—"a mysticism difficult for the twentieth century to follow." But if we take seriously Whitman's pronouncements in the poem, Doudna writes from the University of Hawaii at Hilo, "we may return to it and find in it the powerful expression of an idea that has at least as much value for our age as it had for his." Once again, the poem must be defended on teleological grounds, a dubious move indeed, for to include it in the canon of the poet's best work is to move in the direction of Sacvan Bercovitch's statement that the whole of *Leaves of Grass* is a "text-proof of America's errand into the future" ("The Rites of Assent: Rhetoric, Ritual, and the Ideology of American Consensus" in *The American Self: Myth, Ideology, and Popular Culture* [N. Mex., 1981], ed. Sam B.

Girgus, pp. 5–42). "None of our classic writers," Bercovitch writes, "conceived of imaginative perspectives other than those implicit in the vision of America. Their works are characterized by an *unmediated* relation between the facts of American life and the ideals of American free enterprise."

e. Affinities and Influences. The ideological Whitman is perhaps better left back in the 19th century with the Whitmaniacs his "prophecies" spawned. Most of their screeds are properly buried in Traubel's *The Conservator* (1890–1919), but one near-disciple who used the ideology in the manner Bercovitch suggests was Hamlin Garland. Kenneth M. Price's "Hamlin Garland's 'The Evolution of American Thought': A Missing Link in the History of Whitman Criticism" (*WWQR* 3,ii:1–20) reprints the chapter on Whitman in Garland's ambitious and never-completed treatise (ca. 1886–87) to suggest not only how the future novelist saw Whitman as both culminating and anticipating the "evolution" of American thought in literature but that Whitman's paradoxical view of romantic individualism softened the deterministic influences on Garland in *Main-Travelled Roads* (1891). Perceptively, Price chooses as one of his examples the soldier in "The Return of a Private." While presented as a victim of economic naturalism, he is nevertheless allowed a certain dignity in his defeat. As Garland wrote in the story, "Here was the epic figure which Whitman has in mind, and which he calls the 'common American Soldier.'" The ideology may not always mesh with the naturalism—as earlier in the story the common soldier is described as crawling home "like some minute, wingless variety of fly," but the contrast merely underscores Price's argument for Whitman's influence on the composition of *Main-Travelled Roads*—surely something of "a backward glance." The open or main-traveled road also contained an analeptic look for Jorge Luis Borges, according to Joseph J. Benevento in "What Borges Learned from Whitman: The Open Road and Its Forking Paths" (*WWQR* 2,iv:21–30). Whitman gave Borges the sense of the "composite persona," which included not only the poetic self and the reader but the persona that encompasses everybody else.

Continuing the investigation of "Calamus" is M. Wynn Thomas in "A Comparative Study of Emerson's 'Friendship' and Whitman's 'Calamus'" (*ATQ* 55:49–61). He warns against seeing Emerson as an advocate of coldness and Whitman as an apostle of physical passion. Rather, he argues, "their branching differences can frequently be traced to a single trunk, and that trunk itself, upon investigation, turns into the labyrinthine difference of the elaborate root-systems of their thought." In other words, there is something of the "Calamus" passion in "Friendship" with respect to the author's underlying desire to communicate the impossible. There is really no difference between the two writers in Dana Brand's "The Escape from Solipsism: William James's Reformulation of Emerson and Whitman" (*ESQ* 31:38–48), an essay that focuses ultimately on James's address at the Emerson centenary in Concord. The American philosopher used Whitman's hurrahing for the universe as a scapegoat for what he disapproved of in Emerson's attempt in the early essays to overcome the Cartesian dualism in a quest for a prelapsarian unity of body and soul. James was more indebted to Whitman than he realized in 1903, but then every writer and thinker has unacknowledged sources, even Shakespeare—especially Shakespeare! Whitman himself, for example, would be somewhat surprised to learn from S. Krishnamoorthy Aithal in "The Origin of Whitman's 'Out of the Cradle Endlessly Rocking' " (*AN&Q* 23:109–11) that the source for the poem is the "well-known story relating to Valmiki, the author of the famous Indian epic *The Ramayana*." According to this piece of guesswork, Whitman's poem makes only "modifications" on the original tale. For Michael Vande Berg in " 'Taking All the Hints to Use Them': The Sources of 'Out of the Cradle Endlessly Rocking' " (*WWQR* 2,iv:1–20) there are three particular, if minor, sources: two ornithological studies and an essay which figuratively applied the mockingbird to poets. As is the case with most (or some) source studies, this one is informative, suggestive, but also mechanical and finally reductive in its failure to address the question of the writer's literary synthesis.

A number of parallel studies appeared but in the interest of chapter space their allusions will have to be limited to title—which in most cases are descriptive enough to serve as partial annotations: Guy Rotella, "Cummings' 'kind)' and Whitman's Astronomer" (*ConP* 18:39–46); Ed Folsom, "Arthur Lundkvist's Swedish Ode to Whitman" (*WWQR* 3,ii:33–35); and Hank Lazer, "Louis Simpson and Walt Whitman: Destroying the Teacher" (*WWQR* 1[1983],iii:1–21). The comparisons also extend to the world of painting. In "The Luminist Walt Whitman" (*AmerP* 2:2–16) Stephen Adams juxtaposes Whitman's poetry with the work of the luminist painters, an offshoot of the Hudson River School that flourished between 1850 and 1880. And finally, we have two more linkings of Whitman's celestial imagery and Vincent Van Gogh's "Starry Night." Hope B. Werness' article is more interesting for what it presents on Van Gogh's use of the stars than it is for the connection she makes to Whitman ("Whitman and Van Gogh: Starry Nights and Other Similarities," *WWQR* 2,iv:35–41), but Jean Schwind in "Van Gogh's 'Starry Night' and Whitman: A Study in Source" (*WWQR* 3,i:1–15) makes one of the strongest cases I have read. Although this piece is also more about Van Gogh than Whitman, it is successful in tracing the painter's visual and verbal references to Whitman in such poems as "Passage to India" and "The Prayer of Columbus."

ii. Dickinson

a. **Bibliography, Editing.**   William White continues to serve Dickinson checklists as well as those for Whitman—in *DicS* (56:53–59) and in *HJ* (42:23–31), where there appears "a current bibliography mostly 1984, including Japan." Of more interest if also disappointing is *Emily Dickinson: Selected Letters* (Harvard), ed. Thomas H. Johnson. It contains approximately 270 of the 1,046 letters originally presented in Harvard's three-volume edition in 1958. No effort, however, has been made to update the original introduction and annotations. Hence, we have in 1985 as well as in 1958 the statement that the poet "did not live in history and held no view of it, past or current." The portrait is that of a Lady Poet for All-Male Seasons who is oblivious to questions of gender and genocide. Saying that war was a mere "annoyance" to Dickinson, the editor (and we have to wonder who that is—Johnson or the Harvard University Press) conveniently omits Letter 245, which is dramatic evidence of the impact the war had on Dickinson. The volume also fails to reflect the recent discoveries of poems published during the poet's lifetime and the implications of this information on the question of whether she actively sought publication. Also missing from this commercial (if selected) *issue* are several letters giving evidence of Dickinson's having read major American authors, including those alluding to Emerson (Letters 30 and 481), Hawthorne (60), Poe (622), and Thoreau (692). While it is possibly convenient to have a one-volume selected edition, it is unfortunate that an effort was not made to bring the editorial apparatus up to date.

b. **Biography.**   In "A Glimpse of Dickinson at Work" (*AL* 57:483–85) Gary Scharnhorst edits a letter published in the Boston *Women's Journal* of 26 March 1900 by Louise Norcross in which she writes that her cousin composed in the pantry "while she skimmed the milk," often reciting her verses between—we would assume—her kitchen duties. One wonders, however, whether Scharnhorst's discovery is of Dickinson at work or Norcross at work fourteen years after the poet's death. The Norcross cousins (Loo and Fanny), though favorites of Dickinson, were a little "crack'd" themselves, finding in their poet-chef a surrogate for the early departure of their parents. Before granting Mabel Loomis Todd access to Dickinson's letters to them for her 1894 edition, Louise subjected the correspondence to a heavy censorship. Hence, we should treat with caution what might well be a distorted or exaggerated accounting of the truth. Also embellished to some extent is Betsy Erkkila's account in "Emily Dickinson on Her Own Terms" (*WQ* 9,ii:98–109) of how it was Helen Hunt Jackson rather than Thomas Wentworth Higginson who first recognized Dickinson's poetic genius. In fact, Higginson introduced Jackson to Dickinson. The *other* poet from Amherst may have been more impressed with Dickinson's work, but such a comparison is really useless. Despite his Victorian myopia when it came to poetry, Higginson nevertheless saw enough talent—and before Jackson—to keep up a correspondence with the poet for almost a quarter century, during which time he read many of her poems and advised her as best he could. And according to Larry R. Olpin, "In Defense of the Colonel, Thomas Wentworth Higginson" (*HJ* 42:3–14), the colonel was a better judge of poetry—of Dickinson's poetry—than he has been credited as being. Most of the article is a rehash of Higginson's life and times, and finally the argument is no more convincing (or useful) than Erkkila's. Higginson simply does not measure up to either male or female expectations of the 20th century because he failed to recognize fully (can we really blame him?) what is essentially modern poetry.

Another aspect of the biography we would like to insist upon in the 20th century is that the poet wore only white after 30—as the bridesmaid instead of the bride of experience. In this way we engage Dickinson in our hermeneutical fiction. Yet if white was the uniform of the day, there had to be a practical reason as well, and to this end we hear more about the domestic side of the poet's life from Kathryn Whitford in "Why Emily Dickinson Wore White" (*DicS* 55,i:12–

18). The poet wore white because it was the easiest color to maintain before the advent of modern vat colors that better resist fading. And not only, so the legend goes, did she wear white but she also had or desired a flesh-and-blood lover. The latest candidate for this demanding role, according to love-letter editor Polly Longsworth (*ALS 1984*, p. 94), is the poet's cousin (" 'Was Mr. Dudley Dear?': Emily Dickinson and John Langdon Dudley," *MR* 26:360–72). The argument is more successful in discrediting Charles Wadsworth as "lover" and "master" than it is in warranting further consideration of Dudley.

c. **Criticism: General.**   Two studies that employ philosophy and language theory in their analyses are Evan Carton's *The Rhetoric of American Romance* and E. Miller Budick's *Emily Dickinson and the Life of Language: A Study in Symbolic Poetics* (LSU). Carton uses the Hegelian dialect to examine the nature of the American romance and finds in Emerson what William James found when he prepared his centennial address—that the Concord "Philosopher" contradicted himself in *Nature* when he attempted to define the dialectic between empirical and transcendent reason. He finds "self-parody" embedded in the endeavor that is ultimately converted into power. Emerson, of course, was *not* a philosopher but a writer whose thought thrived upon the paradoxes of language, but Carton's general inquiry is epistomological rather than aesthetic. Dickinson, really a post-American romantic who was more aware of the quotidian consequence of language than Emerson, is presented as a ready example of the power of self-parody. Carton's readings of her poems are both original and refreshing because he is one of the first to examine Dickinson's ars poetica in the light of Hegel's dialectic (which she could not have read, but then neither could Whitman have read Darwin before writing the first *Leaves of Grass*). Almost as thoughtful is Budick, who studies Dickinson's "paradoxical condemnation and celebration of symbolic perception." The poet rejects conventional symbology both sacramental and idealist in order to forge a poetic of her own. Dickinson's symbolism does not revel in a synecdochic/Christian connection, nor does it fully transcend in the idealist scenario; rather, it retains its early consciousness while also reaching out beyond the phenomenal world. As in Carton, the study of literature is secondary to the study of language and its relation to knowledge; yet Budick's individual readings are not quite as useful or interesting as Carton's. Her study is more important as an investigation of symbolic poetics.

Two other books appearing this year are Jane Donahue Eberwein's *Dickinson: Strategies of Limitation* (Mass.) and Greg Johnson's *Emily Dickinson: Perception and the Poet's Quest* (Alabama). According to Eberwein, Dickinson's "strategy" (and I think we ought to give this word a vacation) was to exploit her sense of cosmic smallness by expanding her "circumference" or inner space to the limits of death and immortality. The thesis resembles in part Carton's idea and to a greater extent Suzanne Juhasz's in *The Undiscovered Continent* (*ALS 1983*, pp. 91–92), at least in feminist applications of the strategic retreat. Dickinson's art, Eberwein argues, thrived upon constriction—what she calls the "magic prison" of liberation. Unfortunately, the study is not well organized, probably because there wasn't enough of an idea—however interesting—for a book-length study. Also not well organized or clearly focused is Johnson in *Perception and the Poet's Quest*. Like Eberwein, Johnson has published a couple of sound articles on the poet recently, but his book (which incorporates them) didn't have enough to talk about either. It purports to define Dickinson's "central place in the thrust of American Romanticism toward a unity of mind," but unlike Joann Diehl's placement of Dickinson within the English romantic tradition (*ALS 1981*, pp. 87–88), Johnson's treatise is sometimes inexact in its terms and vapid in its argument. The only truly clear and original idea about perception to emerge is the concept of "ratio," which Johnson introduced previously in a short article (*ALS 1980*, p. 85). Eberwein's and Johnson's books are probably two examples of publishing perishable goods instead of perishing for the lack of publishing.

Margaret Homans continues to build on the thesis of her important book (*ALS 1980*, pp. 67, 83–84), but I cannot be as sanguine about " 'Syllables of Velvet': Dickinson, Rossetti, and the Rhetorics of Sexuality" (*FSt* 11:569–93). She argues that Dickinson inverts the Petrarchan love lyric and its 19th-century successor the lyric of male romantic desire to produce a rhetoric of female sexuality. This is one in which there is no male/female, subject/object convention of desire but instead a female palace of "pleasure" in which the "painful plot of desire is replaced by a plotless and joyous intersubjectivity." Applying Luce Irigaray's observation that the female lacks the ability of representation because she has no "visible sex organ" to her thesis about Dickinson's ambiguous use of language, Homans observes that the female poet must resort to the vague language of touch. All this devolves into Derridean echoes about language as "infinitely circular

and self-referential" and a discussion of imagery pertaining to the
"lips" of the labia. Play on the word is applied to readings of the
poetry (from labia lips to those which articulate syllables) to suggest
a kind of orgiastic "intersubjective communion" of females enjoying
their freedom from referentiality and hence as passive objects of male
sexual desire. Left out of the analysis is Dickinson's famous "Granite
lip!" which might have saved a potentially valuable reading from such
Lacanian excess. The missing word in the article is "Renunciation,"
the theme of Juhasz's "Tea and Revolution: Emily Dickinson Popu-
lates the Mind" (*ELWIU* 12:145–50). Juhasz, who has a penchant for
journalistic headlines in her titles (see her *Feminist Critics Read
Emily Dickinson* [*ALS 1983*, pp. 89–92]), operates on the at least
questionable premise that renunciation "is at the heart of Dickinson's
agenda for becoming a poet." That is to say, she felt the need "to
renounce her social self, because it was seen by society to be at odds
with her creative or poet [*sic*] self (by implication, more 'masculine')."
Like Homans, Juhasz sees this renunciation as becoming a kind of
"psychomachiac" withdrawal in which the poet "could take back or
repossess what she had ostensibly given up: having it, however, on
her own terms." The poem centrally involved in this assessment is
"The Soul Selects Her Own Society," one that does not implicitly
overlook Dickinson's generic use of the feminine pronoun. And yet we
have to ask what serious writer ever succeeded without selecting *their*
own "society"? To privilege Dickinson in this regard is simply to en-
list her poetic success in a political cause—one that would see Dickinson as having a feminist text when it is at the very best a subtext.

Dickinson didn't have to work in a customhouse or as a copyist in
Washington, D.C., in order to be a writer. She had a sinecure on
Main Street that allowed this "Nobody" to be anybody in the poems—
this last point from Sister Charlotte Downey in "Emily Dickinson's
Appeal for a Child Audience," (*DicS* 55, i:21–31). The piece is well
illustrated with examples of Dickinson's childlike persona, not only
in her "nature" poems but in ones such as "Because I Could Not Stop
for Death." It was a matter not only of "role" but of "voice," according to Lucy Brashear in "Emily Dickinson's Dramatic Monologues"
(*ATQ* 56:65–67) and Frank D. Rashid in "Emily Dickinson's Voice
of Endings" (*ESQ* 31:23–27). The first is useful for its emphasis on the
dramatic immediacy of Dickinson's poetic voice, but its six categories
remind me of those of Higginson and Todd in the first three editions
of Dickinson's poems. Attention to the poet's cricket imagery might

sound as reductive, but Rashid's discussion of their use further suggests the rich texture of Dickinson's poetry. The crickets are contrasted with her bee imagery, which suggests the spring and summer of life—whereas the sound of crickets comes at night and at the end of summer, long after "Summer's full."

d. Criticism: Individual Works. With the unacknowledged help from Derrida's long two-level essay about Maurice Blanchot's *L'arret de mort* in *Deconstruction and Criticism*, B. N. Raina finds a "rich ambiguity" in "Dickinson's 'Because I Could Not Stop for Death'" (*Expl* 43,iii:11–12). It means that death both *came* to her and that death *stopped* for her, but whatever that means is not made clear. On the imagery of death in Dickinson, Katrina Bachinger answers George Monteiro (*ALS 1984*, p. 98) by looking for the meaning of Dickinson's fly in theology rather than folklore ("Dickinson's 'I Heard a Fly Buzz,'" *Expl* 43,iii:12–15). Meanwhile, Monteiro moves on to an explication of "I Taste a Liquor Never Brewed" (*Expl* 43,iii:16–17) and discovers an allusion to "chamomile the plant and especially to the tea brewed from the plant." Hence, the poet's "little Tippler" not only remains true to the teetotaler's pledge but literally drinks "a liquor never brewed" since the "tea" is "unprocessed from the *manzanilla* (chamomile) plant." In "'Devil's Wine': A Re-examination of Emily Dickinson's #214" (*AN&Q* 23:78–80) Anne French Dalke finds a source for the poem in Emerson's "The Poet." Dickinson was satirizing his optimism about nature's being "'God's wine,' but in Dickinson's satire, it seems more the devil's." In other words, for Dickinson (as a female poet) "poetry provide[d] not an analogy but rather a challenge to the conventional religious experience" (Emerson?); the rest of the argument will be familiar to anyone keeping up with Dickinson scholarship in the last five years. And one who hasn't been reading the journals is Norma M. Fitzgerald in "Dickinson's 'I Took Power in My Hand'" (*Expl* 43:20–21), who thinks only seven poems were published in the poet's lifetime.

e. Affinities and Influences. The line between this category and the previous one is not clear this year because studies of particular poems also involve an argument for a parallel or source. This is the case of Timothy Morris' "The Free-rhyming Poetry of Emerson and Dickinson" (*ELWIU* 12:225–40), a sound discussion of Emerson's prosody and its underlying theory as well as an argument for an important

difference between Emerson and Dickinson in terms of how form reflects meaning. Morris argues that "In Winter—in My Room" represents Dickinson's late repudiation of the aesthetics behind Emerson's
free-rhyming poetry. In "Dickinson's 'Red Sea'" (*Expl* 43:18–20)
Barton Levi St. Armand challenges Wendy Martin's reading (*ALS
1983*, p. 95) of "'Red Sea,' indeed! Talk Not to Me" as an antipatri-
archial retelling of the Moses story. He calls it "a dramatic monologue
spoken neither by a reconciled Moses nor an ecologically-minded
Miriam, but by the God who is the romantic poet, the true transforming power above and beyond all meretricious questions of gender."
We may have a clash of ideologies here. Finally, there is Lois A.
Cuddy in "Shelley's Glorious Titan: Reflection on Emily Dickinson's
Self-Image and Achievement" (*DicS* 55, i:32–40). She sees the Shelley
of E. J. Trelawny (a portrait in which the poet's promiscuous sexuality
and marital experimentation are ignored and his qualities of independence, isolation, and loneliness are highlighted) as a model for Dickinson as she contemplated her career as an "independent artist." There
are several misconceptions or at least undocumented assertions in this
farfetched argument, but the following statement ought to exemplify
its histrionic nature: "Baking bread and cookies by day, Emily Dickinson remained shackled (if also protected) by her New England
spinster existence, yet by the candlelight of a Promethean flame she
created verse that speaks clearly today."

iii. Conclusion

Almost completely missing from Whitman and Dickinson scholarship
this year and in years past are (1) a feminist argument for Whitman
and (2) an "ideological" one for Dickinson. Perhaps in an era in which
the literary message is largely viewed as political instead of personal
it is time to get Whitman back into the closet (so to speak) and
Dickinson out of the house. Feminist studies already abound for
Dickinson, who more often than not employs the generic male pronoun; and yet Whitman, who found a prostitute as worthy as a president, is dismissed in this area probably because he loved his mother
and motherhood too much. Overlooked are the female writers—Kate
Chopin comes to mind as one of the richest recipients—who took
something from Whitman's work that is distinctly feminine and
feminist. Dickinson, on the other hand, may not have prayed to the
same "Eclipse" her family and the rest of America worshiped, but she

did write at the height of her powers as a poet: "Perhaps you laugh at me! Perhaps the whole United States are laughing at me too! *I* can't stop for that! *My* business is to love." Isn't this "Ideology"? Isn't the poet expressing her sense of destiny which is bound up with the America that *ought* to be listening to the sounds she hears? Since both approaches—feminism and "Ideology"—exhibit the deconstructionist desire to empty literature of myth, it seems odd that their applications should be so sharply divided between two of America's greatest poets—a male and a female. In view of all we hear these days about "opening up the canon" and "looking for the text in either the class or the grass," it seems appropriate to probe these enigmas in poets who were in their turn candidly private and clandestinely public. To my mind, only two scholars have even scratched the surface of these respective areas—Betsy Erkkila in "The Federal Mother" (reviewed above) and Shira Wolosky in *Emily Dickinson: A Voice of War* (*ALS 1984*, pp. 96–97).

Texas A&M University

6. Mark Twain

Louis J. Budd

It was a flood tide with the (continuing) ado over *Adventures of Huckleberry Finn* swelled by the sesquicentennial of Twain's birth, which outperformed Halley's Comet. The fact long known to scholars that Twain once subsidized a black student in the Yale Law School became prime-time news. A clay-animation movie about his own "adventures" was reviewed in *USA Today* and the *New York Times*. David Carkeet's ingenious *I Been There Before: A Novel* (Harper) brought him back to earth for several lively months. Eventually *Soviet Life* (Nov. 1985) reacted with "Mark Twain / Why We Love Him, Too." By the end of the year a few sour notes sounded from a kind of hangover. But Twainians can look back on a great party and will need 1986 for catching up with the worthwhile books and articles, more than this chapter can itemize.

i. Biography

Even so, space must be borrowed to recall Everett Emerson's *The Authentic Mark Twain: A Literary Biography of Samuel L. Clemens* (Penn., 1984), overlooked here because I had so quickly put it to private use. Clear and substantial (330 pp.), it emerges as the book to recommend for a dependable survey of both primary and secondary materials. Emerson, who excels at discussing the major texts while weaving in the minor or almost forgotten pieces, focuses on their "intersection" with Twain's personality, career, and "somewhat imperfect sense of the literary marketplace." Reviewers in Emerson's own marketplace have quarreled most with the tactic that climaxes in his chapter entitled "The Disappearance of Mark Twain," which hinges on his preference for the free-swinging, irreverent, chance-taking, and protean humorist of the earlier years and, to a lesser degree, for Twain's comedy over his dark weightiness. While always free of idolatry, Emerson's reasoned and reasonable approach earns the right to conclude that "it is easy to become an admirer" of Twain's writings.

Edgar M. Branch's masterful *Men Call Me Lucky: Mark Twain and the "Pennsylvania"* (Miami Univ., Ohio: Friends of the Library Society) recovers an amazing fineness of detail and thus adds a rich vividness to the week that Clemens spent in Memphis watching his brother Henry die. Branch's "The Pilot and the Writer" (*MTJ* 23,ii: 28–43) again does an amazing job—he *is* a lightning scholar!—of recovering the facts; here they establish Clemens' ability and high standing in the steamboat trade. With similar patience William Baker ("Mark Twain and the Shrewd Ohio Audiences," *ALR* 18:14–30) combed three daily newspapers between 1865 and 1885 to weave a useful composite of Twain's reception as a lecturer and personality. More narrowly, Miriam Shillingsburg's "From Ballarat to Bendigo with Mark Twain" (*AuLS* 12:116–19) follows him into semifrontier towns reminiscent of Virginia City. In "Susy Clemens's Shakespeare: An Addition to the Twain Library Books in the HRHRC" (*LCUT* 27[1984]:95–103) Alan Gribben, the world-class expert on Twain's reading, follows up a gift of a set of the plays and inventively builds it into its own minidrama of emotions and events in a close-knit family.

Though Twain's private life is fascinating in itself, biographers like to merge it with his writings. In *The Making of Mark Twain* (Houghton Mifflin) John Lauber, who goes up only to the marriage in 1870, stays alert not just to the earliest sketches but to the works that came much later. So far as we can judge from the (commercially) limited notes, he did little fresh research, and he refrains from offering a psychic map or some other guide to the secret of Twain's genius. However, he uses all the standard sources to conduct a sensible, balanced, and graceful account occasionally enriched by a shrewd intuition about his subject's feelings or motives. His slips on minor fact are too few to dampen my wish that his biography will attract many a general reader.

The Mark Twain Book, written and published by Oliver and Goldena Howard [New London, Mo.], is much more intriguing for its hunter's stew of local lore, commonsense inferences, precision on such details as a tumblebug, and casualness toward the academic stockpile. With cheerful nostalgia the Howards can explain how boys made skates or slingshots during the 1840s. Living on the spot, they managed to dig up further records about John Marshall Clemens and other members of the family or to build an argument that young Sam could handle at least a simple musical score. Not even a veteran scholar, supported by the NEH for a year, could have moved in and produced *The Mark Twain Book*, which will show up in any further analyses of the Florida-Hannibal years.

While Kenneth E. Eble has high standing among scholars, he did not aim at them with *Old Clemens and W. D. H.: The Story of a Remarkable Friendship* (LSU). Its culminating chapter suggests it was inspired by friendship as a practicing ideal needed today more than ever. In fact, without growing didactic, Eble implies a set of social-ethical values, both in how we judge character and why we choose our level of discourse, which sometimes should favor subjects of broad appeal posed in terms useful beyond a professional subset. Avoiding all condescension, he treats the Howells-Twain camaraderie as productive for them as human beings as well as writers. Biographically he helps us understand Twain better by clarifying the reasons for his loyalty to Howells, the qualities that in turn attracted his crony, and the dynamics of an intimacy that rode through several crises. Eble set out, admittedly, to find harmonies, and bitter realists may wish for more angst, for a few clouds with strontium 90 at the core. But they should settle for a humane, humanizing, and humanistic study.

If only because of Edith Salsbury's *Susy and Mark Twain* (1965), the sketch of his character that his oldest daughter started at age 13 was already familiar. Charles Neider has now edited the complete, uninterrupted text as *Papa: An Intimate Biography of Mark Twain* (Doubleday) and has speculated about her personality in a long introduction. The more Susy emerges from her father's shadow, the more clearly we will perceive him also.

ii. Editions

Among the commercial reprints, at least *The Signet Classic Book of Mark Twain's Short Stories* (NAL) rates a mention. Justin Kaplan aimed to make its 670 pages a true cross section, though he could not resist borrowing parts of the travel books. P. M. Zall, with increasingly loose criteria of authenticity after passing 1910, might claim to reprint primary texts in *Mark Twain Laughing: Humorous Anecdotes by and about Samuel L. Clemens* (Tenn.). While fairly knowledgeable, Zall specializes in this kind of anthology more than Twain's work.

Essentially *Mark Twain Laughing* offers pleasant reminders of punch
lines that might come in handy.

Waiting for the Iowa/California *Huckleberry Finn* is easier now
that the text edited for it by Walter Blair and Victor Fischer has appeared, both paperback and hardcover, in the Mark Twain Library
(Calif.). In fact, this edition may be handier for the classroom and
most other uses. It has a fully responsive yet brief introduction, surely
enough explanatory notes, five maps, and—most significantly—all the
original illustrations. Scooping the Iowa/California evidence, we can
already learn that, despite minor flaws and some brief skips by the
compositor, the first printing of *Huckleberry Finn* served its readers
well except for omitting the raftsmen's passage, which the Mark
Twain Library restores to its rightful niche. How any publisher could
top this volume I can't foresee.

Its own publisher, ironically, might quibble on behalf of the
Pennyroyal-California Edition. Also printing the text established by
the Mark Twain Project, it adds a brief, urbane foreword by Henry
Nash Smith and—its big selling point—woodcuts by Barry Moser, who
grates on my sense of the novel's characters and moods. On the basis
of price, however, John Seelye challenges both volumes. For a loss-
leader $1.95, the Penguin Classics paperback, though admitting the
raftsmen's passage no further than an appendix, supplies a dependable text—curiously, the first British printing. Charles Neider doubtless felt combative when he projected his edition (Doubleday). While
giving that passage full entry, he cut 9,000 words from the final eight
chapters. I predict less of a market for it than for Twain's *Burlesque
Hamlet*, even in the paperback presumably to come.

iii. General Interpretations

The New Mark Twain Handbook (Garland) asserts that "few" books
and articles published since 1957 "contribute new ideas" or even "add
information to what is already known." If true, such a judgment
means that the revised *Handbook* could not matter much at best.
Actually, a thorough review would be discussing mostly the original
version. Instead of starting over, E. Hudson Long and J. R. LeMaster
merely pieced in some of the later scholarship. They end up with
strange proportions such as six paragraphs for Edward Wagen-
knecht's critical biography but only one for Kaplan's (a "credible
job") or with contradictory passages (e.g., on whether Twain wrote

the Quintus Curtius Snodgrass letters). More valuable as a basic tool is L. Terry Oggel and William Nelles' *Index to Volumes 1–21 of the "Mark Twain Journal," 1936–1983* (*MTJ*), which includes the precursor *Mark Twain Quarterly*.

More valuable as a currently synoptic view is the special Autumn issue (vol. 13) of *Studies in American Fiction* that James Nagel engineered. For it Everett Emerson's "The Strange Disappearance of Mark Twain" (pp. 143–55), a "by product" of his book, traces the subsiding eruptions of a westerner who settled into domesticity back East. In "Mark Twain's Bad Women" (pp. 157–68) Susan K. Harris contends persuasively that *The Gilded Age* kills off Laura Hawkins because she perverted her conventional "role as household angel," that *Pudd'nhead Wilson* makes Roxy another "trickster" whose sex disqualifies her for heroism, and that Twain could approve only of the "good" woman whose conduct reassured males that altruism struggles on despite their own behavior. Stan Poole's "In Search of the Missing Link: Mark Twain and Darwinism" (pp. 201–15) defends sensitively the thesis that he accepted the theory of biological evolution as "a source of stimulating ideas" for "expressing his own varied response to life" yet never adapted it into a "unified vision" nor let it overwhelm "his deep compassion and moral conviction." With "Mark Twain: A Man for All Regions" (pp. 239–46) Leland Krauth tots up the claims made on behalf of four formative sectionalisms before concluding that Twain, at varying times, embodied each of them within an encompassing archetype, the self-made man in an upwardly mobile society. My "Hiding Out in Public: Mark Twain as a Speaker" (pp. 129–41) examines his craftiness in talking about himself, particularly as a southerner.

The pick of the litter—that is, the special issue of *SAF*—may be Alan Gribben's "Those Other Thematic Patterns in Mark Twain's Writings" (pp. 185–200). Imaginative yet based in the teeming oeuvre rather than just the favored pieces, it traces a "fascination with the painful, the ghastly, the grotesque" or, as a practical motive, the adeptness at "gratifying his readers' need for comedy while catering to their less wholesome appetites." Reminding us that Twain's work also echoed many reassuring values, Gribben decides that its multivalence, its synthesis of "mirth and tears," is what makes his fiction so appealing to modern taste. But that taste shows a jagged spread in *Mark Twain: A Sumptuous Variety* (Barnes & Noble), ed. Robert Giddings, whose introduction outclasses most of the nine essays. The contributors, perhaps scrambling against a deadline, rush into and enlarge any possible openings. At least William Kaufman's "The Comedic Stance: Sam Clemens, His Masquerade" discusses interestingly the seesaw of impulses that tipped toward rage, leaving *Pudd'nhead Wilson* as the last work in which the humorist engagingly managed a weighty theme.

Too brief to rank as major, the section in *History of Southern Literature* (LSU, pp. 233–40) by Louis D. Rubin, Jr., has august balance. While one of the few critics who avoids denigrating *The Adventures of Tom Sawyer* on behalf of greatness to come, he celebrates *Huckleberry Finn* as the first modern southern novel. For a special issue focused on humor Alan Gribben outdid his essay on thematic patterns. "The Importance of Mark Twain" (*AQ* 37:30–49) revitalizes the big question of what lastingly distinguishes him among many hundreds of competitors. Having stressed three answers, Gribben concludes that Twain has grown into "one of our few symbolic means of maintaining the crucial continuity between our past cultural heritage and our present-day attitudes." Valuable because it discovers a central yet undeveloped approach, James Grove's "Mark Twain and the Endangered Family" (*AL* 57:377–94) first shows that sentimental regard for domesticity often "subverted" his themes, starting with the *The Gilded Age*. After Grove next develops richly the commonplace that the family can prove a hindrance or a disappointing refuge for lively boys, he has laid the basis for finding that Twain's fiction holds "multi-layered attempts to cope with, understand, and perhaps escape the always alluring domestic world which both soothed and wounded him." A needed analysis that leaves the field still open is the Twain chapter in Shelley Fisher Fishkin's *From Fact to Fiction: Journalism & Imaginative Writing in America* (Hopkins). She works from an idealized notion of 19th-century newspapers. More specifically, she fails to benefit from Branch and Robert H. Hirst's magisterial *Early Tales and Sketches* or some of Branch's beautifully concrete articles.

Though the emphasis falls on *The Man Who Loved Children* (1940), Jonathan Arac's "The Struggle for the Cultural Heritage: Christina Stead Refunctions Charles Dickens and Mark Twain" (*Cultural Critique* 2:171–89) provocatively argues that the modern novel, having invoked two heroes of "Popular Leftist humanism," in effect "shatters them as false idols" even while drawing upon their strengths. My "Mark Twain: Still in Bed but Wide-Awake" (*Amst*

30:177–85) speculates about some nonpolitical yet usable images carried up to the present through a line of white-suited impersonators. A more ambitious yet orotund analysis by a political scientist, "Mark Twain as Democratic Educator: Rebel with an Innocent Eye," a chapter in *Thought and Character: The Rhetoric of Democratic Education* (Iowa State), treats him as a platform sage worthy of comparison with Ralph Waldo Emerson and William James. To Frederick J. Antczak that sage, despite his late indulgence in celebrity, taught his audiences to practice critical, creative judgment. Though likewise spongy on details, Thomas J. Richardson, with "Is Shakespeare Dead? Mark Twain's Irreverent Question," pp. 63–82 in *Shakespeare and Southern Writers*, again demonstrates how doggedly Twain could hold on to some misfiring project.

iv. Individual Works through 1885

Monotonous as it is to keep praising Edgar M. Branch, his "Fact and Fiction in the Blind Lead Episode of *Roughing It*" (*Nev. Hist. Soc. Quar.* 28:234–48) sets a model for research, which here cuts through the complexities of old mining laws. Then he does an Olympic-level backflip. Just when we have learned always to mistrust Twain's autobiography, Branch proves that one of its shakiest yarns stands solidly on fact. As usual, Branch, having braced his scholarly tunnels, goes on to literary analysis. Quicker to launch ideas than to scrounge for facts, Neil Schmitz in "Mark Twain, Henry James and Jacksonian Dreaming" (*Criticism* 27:155–73) pairs *The Gilded Age* with *Roderick Hudson* as anatomizing the "hyperbole of the male hysteric" that drove the antebellum speculators; redoubling his own bets, he not only makes John Marshall Clemens a forerunner of Colonel Sellers ("old Young America") but ignores Twain's lifelong habit of dreaming big.

In a section of *Fast Talk & Flush Times: The Confidence Man as a Literary Convention* (Missouri) the high-rolling William Lenz, having explicated both Sellers and Senator Dilworthy as con men and having annexed *Huckleberry Finn* as showing an "entire society" dominated by their "methods and ethics," expands to assert that for Twain they reveal the "bankruptcy of the twin traditions of sentimental and humorous consolation that inform" his "contemporary culture." With a lower pitch and a welcome caution toward terms, Lyall Powers' "Mark Twain and the Future of the Picaresque" (in

Giddings) separates the picaro from the "quixotic" with a healthy
payoff for *Tom Sawyer*—and less so for *Huckleberry Finn* and none
at all for *A Connecticut Yankee in King Arthur's Court*. John S. Whitley's "Kid Stuff: Mark Twain's Boys" (in Giddings) lowers the pitch
further to point out that both *Tom Sawyer* and *The Prince and the
Pauper*, as books for children, clearly headed for a happy ending
from the start. Admirers of the earlier novel will be relieved to hear
that it aroused at least one essay solely on its own—Fred G. See's
"Tom Sawyer and Children's Literature" (*ELWIU* 12:251–71). Without proposing a mere compromise, he mediates between the old school
critics who still expound a "boy-book" and the recent theorists who
draw gloomy social and cultural themes from it. Tom does not capitu-
late to adult values; on the other hand, he has learned to respect and
use the powers of sequential logic though he will continue to challenge it with fantasy. See's crowded and bold analysis, backed by
erudition, deserves to be judged firsthand instead of by my précis.

But John E. Bassett offers to demote the novel in a fresh way.
For "Tom, Huck and the Young Pilot: Twain's Quest for Authority"
(*MissQ* 39:3–19) he decided "to consider *Tom Sawyer*, the first sixteen chapters of *Huckleberry Finn*, and to some extent 'Old Times on
the Mississippi' as a single text written between 1872 and 1876, overlapping in fact *The Gilded Age* both temporally and thematically."
After testing this new work in various ways, Bassett rides it to the
insight that Twain learned a "strategy of childhood worlds or distant
imagined pasts not bound to contemporary readers' anxieties but allowing the flexibility of romance with the authority of moral fable."
That caveat of "to some extent" about "Old Times" did prove necessary, though my opinion may be swayed by how Branch's interpretation in "The Pilot and the Writer" anchors itself in research. As for
recovering the facts, the ultimate model has to be *The Grangerford-
Shepherdson Feud by Mark Twain*, constructed by Branch (again!)
and Robert H. Hirst. They dredged up a staggering amount about
nonentities in the hinterlands of 130 years ago in order to compare
how Twain reshaped his versions of a now memorable episode. The
only reasonable complaint is that their booklet was born as a rarity,
as a keepsake for the Friends of the Bancroft Library.

The opposite problem of glut, swelled by the popular media, cut
the visibility of out-of-the-way writing about *Huckleberry Finn* during the accumulating sweep of a two-year centennial. Inevitably
Reader's Digest fielded an article, and *People* magazine sketched

Huck's life. An issue of *Nemo: The Classic Comics Library* (sent to me by M. Thomas Inge) compiled an informed, informative tribute. Both masscult and higher-brow magazines tended to feature the past bannings of the novel or else the recent indictments for racism. The most knowledgeable editors lined up critics like Justin Kaplan and Leo Marx. The most hostile editor lined up a jeering attack on the amount and the subtlety of the academic commentary—J. C. Furnas' "The Crowded Raft: *Huckleberry Finn* & Its Critics" (*ASch* 54:517–24).

Because four symposia drew the spotlight, W. R. Irwin's "Mark Twain and Sigmund Freud on the Discontents of Civilization" (*IowaR* 14,ii[1984]:30–47) may get overlooked, though it capably expounds *Huckleberry Finn* as an "uneasy peace" between the "blessings and the unwelcome demands" of life within society. Because Anthony J. Berrett's title arouses skepticism, "The Influence of *Hamlet* on *Huckleberry Finn* (*ALR* 18:196–207) may get passed over, though, as background for his thesis, it supplies an enlightening history of burlesques of the play. But scholars will come to "Twain's 'Nigger' Jim: The Tragic Face Behind the Minstrel Mask" (*MTJ* 23,i:10–17) because Thomas A. Tenney has quickly convinced them to keep up with his journal. While granting that Twain achieved greater humaneness than a white peer, Bernard W. Bell shrewdly points out that even black readers often identify better with Huck than with Jim. Unsurprisingly, he deprecates the closing episode, which is defended with sophistication by Joseph Sawicki's "Authority/Author-ity: Representation and Fictionality in *Huckleberry Finn*" (*MFS* 31:691–702) and Douglas Anderson's "*Huckleberry Finn* and Emerson's 'Concord Hymn'" (*NCF* 40:43–60). Since both articles ran in eminent journals they will fortunately reach their clienteles, perhaps fairly divergent since the two titles promise quite different nutrition. In spite of a seductive title, Thomas C. Richardson's "Sir Walter Scott and Mark Twain: The Real Story" (*Scotia* 9:28–40) deserves mention primarily just because the journal is scarce. Within the genre of the historical novel as defined by George Lukács he elicits parallels between Jeanie Deans and Huck.

None of three relevant essays in that Autumn issue (vol. 13, no. 2) of *SAF* happened to focus on the now notorious ending. Roger Asselineau's "A Transcendentalist Poet Named Huckleberry Finn" (pp. 217–26) offers a highly allusive appreciation. George Monteiro's "Narrative Law and Narrative Lies in *Adventures of Huckleberry*

Finn" (pp. 227–37) argues neatly that one of its major devices is the "interplay of lying as play and playing as lie." But with "The Modernist Ordeal of Huckleberry Finn" (pp. 169–83) Everett Carter sallies forth to measure Twain's intentions against critical fashions and the sociopolitical trends they follow. He insists that the novel's genius lies not in its alienation but in its "representativeness"; as a "realistic comic epic in prose" it "consistently criticizes the ills of its society with a healing sense of the possibilities of improvement" and "summarizes most of the basic commitments of its culture." Carter admirably combines such generalities with a disciplined search of the text, pointing out, for instance, that Huck stays an incurable do-gooder beneath his truancy and also that he lives by the sturdy common sense Americans like to claim. However, John Seelye's 20-page introduction for the Penguin Classics, which will lure readers because of his own repute, explicitly challenges the novel's allegiance to realism as he highlights its similarities to Scott, Dickens, and even Cooper.

During 1985 separately published essays had to compete furthermore with the past, refurbished handsomely in *Huck Finn among the Critics: A Centennial Selection* (Univ. Pubs.). Its editor, M. Thomas Inge, starting from three reviews in 1885, chose the soundest along with the best-known criticism. Through his taste anyway, the first hundred years turned out far better than a Tower of Babel. Characteristic for Inge, the one new article he includes is Perry Frank's "*Adventures of Huckleberry Finn* on Film" (pp. 293–313). Given those results so far, elitists may care little about her report, but they could benefit from wondering why the novel has frustrated Hollywood so consistently. Inge's anthology rounds off with 150 pages of "An Annotated Checklist of Criticism, 1884–1984" by Thomas A. Tenney, who improves on his own previous, meticulous work. Despite the end-date stated, he comes up into 1985—and to a summary of an ABC-TV "Nightline" debate.

I am baffled how to cover briefly yet effectively the 25 essays in *One Hundred Years of "Huckleberry Finn": The Boy, His Book and American Culture* (Missouri), eds. Robert Sattelmeyer and J. Donald Crowley. As in those movies about the air force, should I shoot down one of our own to prove this is a serious affair? Should I assert an amused superiority like Furnas or like deaf Tom Nash with his verdict on Hannibal in 1902, his whispered shout at the train station, "Same damned fools, Sam"? Or should I buy insurance against getting skewered myself and declare (from a Lincoln anecdote) that each essay is as good as the next and a damn sight better too? I'd like to single out the Old Guard, but in a youth culture that registers as a sneer; besides, the dean might push early retirement for anybody crowned as a Grand Old Man. On the other hand, it's tricky to praise anybody as "promising" who was born before, say, 1960. Yet, while cramming in too much of his dissertation, David Sewell's "We Ain't All Trying to Talk Alike: Varieties of Language in *Huckleberry Finn*" does push on brilliantly from the insights about the uses of the vernacular that have satisfied critics for the past 20 years.

The obvious point is that *One Hundred Years of "Huckleberry Finn"* runs a gamut of approaches far wider than the editors' five groupings. In itself their collection outlines the post-Inge era. It contains new gleaners of fact and fearless hawks of idea (e.g., Tom is the "true protagonist"). Less plentifully than it would have a generation ago, it serves up both psychological and sociopolitical critics. Though a few sections treat Huck as a set of handy masks, he is praised predominantly as a complex, rounded character. The few fanciers of comedy as the central mode are overshadowed by the readings aimed at the heart of darkest Arkansaw; the few voices that discuss a boy-book fade under the insistence on themes that many adults cannot comprehend. Some essays follow up a certain kind of passage or motif while many more hunt for the grand design. Though two or three of the essays explain the novel primarily from within its own era, two or three times as many emphasize a modernist alienation (pace Carter) while occasionally allowing a relief through absurdist humor. Critics committed to literary history keep trying to learn from links with Twain's other work and even other writers, but it emerges most often as an isolated monument. Sattelmeyer and Crowley accepted (or got) just one feminist gloss, and the hottest metacritics rarely thicken the footnotes, perhaps because the project had a long adolescence. Fortunately, one essay deals with translations (here, Japanese), not a central but a rewarding subject. *One Hundred Years of "Huckleberry Finn"* is already turning up in other footnotes, but only a hands-on contact can do justice to its variety, admirably edited and nicely produced.

Not planned to compete for centennial allure, *New Essays on Adventures of Huckleberry Finn* (Cambridge) helps initiate a series that hopes to prosper beyond campuses. As volume editor, I contracted to survey the critical history since 1885, and the four essays were chosen for a spread of perspectives. Michael Bell's "Mark Twain, 'Realism,' and *Huckleberry Finn*" (pp. 35–59) questions, like Seelye, the novel's claim to mimesis or even its concern for giving the hero a set of ethical motives. Intrepidly reengaging its language, Janet Holmgren McKay's " 'An Art So High': Style in *Adventures of Huckleberry Finn*" (pp. 61–81) analyzes more closely than ever before its movement from sentence to sentence, from word to word. Lee Clark Mitchell's " 'Nobody but Our Gang Warn't Around': The Authority of Language in *Huckleberry Finn*" (pp. 83–106) discusses not linguistic craft but the way that words give order to experience while, in turn, humankind is patterned by the verbal system it has invented. After starting with language now conceived as a strategy, Steven Mailloux's "Reading *Huckleberry Finn*: The Rhetoric of Performed Ideology" (pp. 107–33) broadens intellectual beliefs to mean both a sociopolitical gestalt and the context of evolving critical practice. In that context three of the four essays felt called to cope with the ending, for which the "Evasion" has become an ironic term.

v. Individual Works after 1885

The temptation to fold the tent quickly after the *Huckleberry Finn* circus is compounded by Douglas Robinson's "Revising the American Dream," an intricate chapter in his *American Apocalypses* which erects its framework on Harold Bloom reinforced by Kenneth Burke. He starts from the idea that *A Connecticut Yankee* vacillated between a paradisal return and a march toward cataclysm and soon reaches the principle that magic and science are "ultimately similar dream tools" (which still leaves me worried more about one nuclear accident than about 1,001 astrologers). Likewise, he expounds Hank Morgan's final delirium as teaching that "all dream and all realities—and all apocalypses, real or dreamed—are illusions that do not pretend to deceive." By contrast, Jeff E. Biddle's "Veblen, Twain and the Connecticut Yankee: A Note" (*Hist. of Pol. Econ.* 17:97–107) discusses luminously whether Hank's career confronted questions that even maverick economists had not yet perceived. And studying Mary Boewe's factual, packed "Twain on Lecky: Some Marginalia at Quarry Farm" (*MTSB* 8,i:1–6) is like getting back to one's carrel. Having discovered new jottings in one of Twain's favorite books, she makes them especially pertinent to *A Connecticut Yankee*.

By Susan K. Gillman and Robert L. Patten, "Dickens: Doubles:: Twain: Twins" (*NCF* 39:441–58) is highly suggestive, though it ig-

nores the writings that Twain completed after 1895. It works toward
the conclusion that his belief in a definable self had long kept weak-
ening until *Pudd'nhead Wilson* "exposed the artist's own illusions:
the illusion of authorial control, of intentionality, of omniscience, of
ironic distance." Meanwhile, Gillman and Patten have tended to lift
him from a historical into an aesthetic reality; for example, the white
master "is as much imposed upon as are his slaves." Firmly assuming
that the owners had the easier life, James Kinney's "Nurture not Nature: *Pudd'nhead Wilson*" in *Amalgamation: Race, Sex, and Rhetoric
in the Nineteenth-Century American Novel* (Greenwood), which
analyzes 60 preceding plots, finds in false Tom the "central proposition" that racial categories "are 'a fiction of law and custom'"; overall, *Pudd'nhead Wilson* surpasses most earlier novels about mis-
cegenation "in its irony and complexity."

Doubly interesting because a political scientist takes up a novel
much ignored, Dennis J. Mahoney's "The Hero Abroad: Toward an
Interpretation of *Tom Sawyer Abroad*," in *Natural Right and Political
Right: Essays in Honor of Harry V. Jaffa* (Durham, N.C.: Carolina
Academic Press, 1984), ed. Thomas B. Silver and Peter W. Schramm,
leads us to ponder the social values supporting Tom as "hero of middle America." A brave feminist, Christina Zwarg, breaks the record
of respect for a work that a lone ranger has tried to defend now and
then. "Woman as Force in Twain's *Joan of Arc*: The Unwordable
Fascination" (*Criticism* 27:57–72) builds upon startling assertions
such as that his hagiography was "neither a sentimental nor transcendent attempt to inscribe the innocent female into history" but
instead examined how Joan, present "as representative woman, has
been written out of history by the very act of inscription." Also an
up-to-date metacritic, Zwarg concludes that *Joan of Arc* is a "meta-
romance, designed to shake our faith in the work of historian, poet,
and storyteller alike."

Twain's two years in Vienna make an unexpected blip. In "Mark
Twain's Philosemitism: 'Concerning the Jews'" (*MTJ* 23,ii:18–25)
Sholom J. Kahn knowledgeably covers backgrounds before emphasizing the "skill and biting wit" with which Twain "distilled a complex
argument" into a "masterpiece of essayistic and satiric form"—which
was again reprinted as a booklet, this time by the Running Press
(Philadelphia). But Carl Dolmetsch's "Mark Twain and the Viennese
Anti-Semites: New Light on 'Concerning the Jews'" (*MTJ* 23,ii:10–
17) renders previous commentary obsolete with a first-rate, even

classic job of research. Digging up cartoons (one of which makes a splendid cover for this issue of *MTJ*), interviews, and sly rumors, he marshals definitive evidence that Twain had wandered into a web of Christian-Jewish tensions. Therefore—though Dolmetsch may ride topicality too hard—the essay gives a "measured riposte to personal anti-Semitic slanders" laid upon Twain in and by the local press. We can never be so naive again about his sojourn in Vienna. We now know that Walter Grünzweig could have probed deeper with "Comanches in the Austrian Parliament: Austria as a Metaphor for Mark Twain's Disillusionment with Democracy" (*MTJ* 23,ii:3–9). Still, we can benefit from speculations that the events behind "Stirring Times in Austria" colored Twain's judgments about the political process back home.

While nobody centered on any version of "The Mysterious Stranger," Douglas Robinson's chapter did conclude with it. Its growing visibility is affirmed by Lou Willett Stanek; "Twain's Farewell to His Art: A New Version of *The Mysterious Stranger*" (*Top of the News* [Chicago] 41:177–79) aims to interest "scholarly adolescents" in doing their papers about "No.44" or else interest their teachers in assigning such a topic. Robert Giddings' "Mark Twain and King Leopold of the Belgians" (in Giddings) makes the first—and maybe last—attempt to prove artistic triumph for *King Leopold's Soliloquy*. At least Giddings' readers will get capably tutored in the historical sources.

vi. An Exit

I give up writing this chapter with cheerful regret. Regret because I had to pass over some worthwhile essays (especially in Sattelmeyer and Crowley) from a bumper crop. Cheerful because it was the liveliest year ever for Twainians. Cheerful also because Hamlin Hill finds this chapter important enough to take it over again in *ALS 1986*.

Duke University

7. Henry James

Robert L. Gale

James continues to intrigue the critics. Almost a hundred books, chapters, and articles concerning him have appeared since my last report. Comparison and influence studies lead the way. And *The American, The Portrait of a Lady, The Bostonians* (including the film version), *What Maisie Knew*, "The Turn of the Screw," the three major-phase novels, and his criticism and *Autobiography* have proved especially challenging. His short fiction has been somewhat slighted.

i. Editions, Letters, Bibliographies, Biographical Studies

The Library of America (Viking) has issued its second volume of James's novels, reprinting *Washington Square, The Portrait of a Lady*, and *The Bostonians*, with chronology; brief textual and explanatory notes are provided by William T. Stafford. The texts reprinted are, respectively, the two-volume Macmillan (1881), the one-volume Houghton (1882 [1881]), and the three-volume Macmillan (1886). Like its predecessors, this Library of America volume is a beautiful bargain. Aziz Maqbool has edited the third volume of *The Tales of Henry James* (Clarendon, 1984), with introduction, ten 1875–79 stories, textual variants, and informative appendixes. Christof Wegelin's edition of *Tales of Henry James* (Norton, 1984) reprints nine stories by James, together with his pertinent notebook, prefatory, and epistolary comments. Wegelin also includes 16 conservative critical essays and snippets (all but one previously published). Mention should be made of Adeline R. Tintner's essay, "Edel's Henry IV" (*ALR*: 17[1984]:264–76), on the last volume of James's letters, as edited by Leon Edel. Tintner reviews James's life and friendships, his reading, comments on his own fiction, and how World War I hurt him. Tintner

I acknowledge with gratitude the valuable assistance of Michael Schneider. And I thank again this year Sims Kline, editor of *Literary Criticism Register*, for his continued generosity.—R.L.G.

in "Henry James and Stark Young: The Correct Version of the Legendary Letter" (*AL* 57:318–21) discusses the letter from James
(dated 14 September 1913) in which he sends "the young man from
Texas" two lists of his recommended works: she indicates minor errors in the 1920, 1951, and 1984 published versions, and prints the correct one. And Tintner in "Henry James and the First World War: The
Release from Repression," pp. 169–84 in *Literature and War: Reflections and Refractions*, ed. Elizabeth W. Trahan (Monterey Institute
of International Studies), discusses the extent of James's 1914–16
activities and writings, and how both provided a release from his lifelong repression by enabling him not only to express his being thrilled
by war but also to nurse handsome wounded soldiers.

The big biographical item of the year is Leon Edel's *Henry James:
A Life* (Harper). It will be recalled that Edel revised his 2,195-page,
five-volume, prizewinning life of James (1953–72), calling the two-
volume 1977 result "definitive." Now we have the Harper finale—
a beautiful, illustrated, 740-page volume, updated, condensed (with
Catharine Carver's help), partly rewritten, easier to handle, and
quicker-paced than the previous efforts. There are eight titled parts,
each with three to six titled chapters and titled subsections. The present book makes use of our new openness as well as new secondary
material (much on sex, but also on Alice James, Edith Wharton, and
Urbain Mengin), thus possibly clarifying some of the psychoanalysis
which was more conjectural earlier. (See Edel, "Biography and the
Sexual Revolution—Why Curiosity Is No Longer Vulgar" [*NYTBR*,24
Nov., pp. 13–14].) To me, the best part here—in addition to the glit-
tering beauty of the retouched portrait of "the Master"—is Edel's
revelation of "a new and prime source for 'The Turn of the Screw.'"
On the debit side, Edel's footnotes and bibliography remain sketchy;
further, we are referred to the original five volumes for notes (which
are also sketchy). Also the index, though annotated usefully, is incomplete. (To find the new "Turn of the Screw" source, don't look under that title but under Taylor, Tom.) More problematic are Edel's
unshakable belief that James's fiction is almost always autobiographical and Edel's taking of everything in James's life—including his
symbiotic sibship with William James, Constance Fenimore Wool-
son's death, and his friendship with Hendrik Andersen—down into
psychosexual depths. For details, whether integrated or casual, the
five-volume original biography is still the best. (Early short reviews

of *Henry James: A Life* are laudatory, but see Millicent Bell's review, *NYTBR*, 24 Nov., p. 12.)

Katherine Weissbourd's *Growing Up in the James Family: Henry James, Sr., as Son and Father* (UMI Research Press) applies E. H. Erikson's concepts of identity and sponsorship to the relationship of James's father and James's brother William. Of interest to us is her fascinating biography of the James family from 1790 to 1860. The future novelist takes a backseat here but does appear, is quoted, and is analyzed. Weissbourd theorizes that the James siblings "internalized the values which their father portrayed." Alfred Habegger's "Precocious Incest: First Novels by Louisa May Alcott and Henry James" (*MR* 26:233–52) discusses "the antagonistic subterranean relationship between Alcott and James." Alcott wrote pseudonymous thrillers featuring father-lovers "to detoxify . . . oppressive" spouse images. James met and spoke to her about *Moods* (her first adult novel [1865]), then in a review harshly criticized its character-combination of "precocious little girls" and "not less unprofitable middle-aged lover[s]," and yet "absorb[ed such] character-types in his own narratives"—notably but not exclusively *Watch and Ward*, "a nice-guys-finish-first daydream" darkened later into such nightmares as the relationship of Gilbert Osmond, no nice guy, to Isabel Archer in *The Portrait of a Lady*. George Monteiro in "Henry James and Mrs. [Charles] Roundell's Book" (*N&Q* n.s.32:365–66) publishes a gracious 1889 letter from James to Houghton Mifflin in which he recommends (unsuccessfully) that the American publisher reissue his friend Julia Tollemache Roundell's book (published in London) on the Azores. Dean Flower in "Henry James in Northampton: The View from Prospect House" (*MR* 26:217–32) reviews James's gradually mellowing impressions of New England and includes copies of eight portrait photographs of James taken in 1905 by Katherine Elizabeth Mc-Clellan, Smith College photographer.

ii. Sources, Parallels, Influences

In "A Portrait of Isabel Archer: Correggio's *Virgin Adoring the Christ Child* in Henry James's *The Portrait of a Lady*" (*CEA* 47,iv:39–50) Gerald Eager rightly notes that Henrietta Stackpole's love of Correggio's painting, made much of in *The Portrait of a Lady*, reflects her friend Isabel Archer's "ingenuous" nature more than Henrietta's attributes. Good too is Eager's equating Pansy Osmond with the Infant in the same picture. Less persuasive is his assigning Isabel's shadowy chapter 42 vigil the "tonalities" of Correggio, or comparing the meager landscape background in Correggio's painting to Isabel's Roman ruins environment, or irrelevantly comparing Gilbert Osmond to Raphael's portrait of Pope Leo X. Eager's best stroke is his observing that dying Ralph Touchett's last word, "adored," both "summariz[es] . . . the portrait of the lady in the novel" and "evokes . . . the devotional image by Correggio." The farfetched thesis of Courtney Johnson's "Was There a Real Model for the Portrait in James's *The Sacred Fount?*" (*CentR* 28[1984]–29:105–21) is that perhaps James saw—was it in Paris?—*The Portrait of the Jester Calabazas* by Diego Velázquez, of a man who has a half-insane, half-sage face and holds an androgynous miniature possibly resembling a larger harlequin mask; further, that all of this could have prompted some of the ambiguity surrounding James's portrait of the man with the mask in *The Sacred Fount.*

Masayuki Akiyama's "James and Nanboku: A Comparative Study of Supernatural Stories in the West and East" (*CLS* 22:43–52) compares three James ghost stories with Japanese playwright-novelist Nanboku Tsuruya's 1825 *Tōkaidō*, a Kabuki play.

Peter Brooks's *The Melodramatic Imagination: Balzac, Henry James, Melodrama, and the Mode of Excess*, published some years ago (see *ALS 1976*, pp. 98–99), has been reissued (Columbia). Unusually noteworthy are Brooks's comments on *The American, The Golden Bowl*, "The Turn of the Screw," and *The Wings of the Dove*: James dramatizes "pure and polar concepts" of morality, and stresses "the manichaeistic struggle of good and evil."

Ross Posnock in his *Henry James and the Problem of Robert Browning* (Georgia) theorizes that James was so disturbed by the "puzzling . . . discontinuity between Browning's public and private selves" that he tried to solve the problem by periodically rewriting Browning. James did so in "The Lesson of the Master" (based partly on Browning's *The Inn Album*), "The Private Life," *The Wings of the Dove* (echoing *In a Balcony*), *The Golden Bowl* (shades of *Fifine at the Fair*), and "The Novel in *The Ring and the Book*" (which "sketches his audacious project to rewrite Browning's masterpiece as a Jamesian novel"). Posnock analyzes James's public and private comments on Browning, whose influence on James was unique, through being both literary and face-to-face. By "rewriting," he "seeks to

mitigate his personal anxiety about the older writer and pays tribute
to the suggestiveness of his poetic achievement." William E. Buckler
in the beginning of his *Poetry and Truth in Robert Browning's* The
Ring and the Book (NYU) reworks part of a fine earlier essay (see
ALS 1984, p. 130).

John Halperin's "Trollope, James, and 'The Retribution of Time' "
(*SHR* 19:301–08) first points out plot parallels between Anthony Trollope's *Sir Henry Hotspur of Humblethwaite* (1870) and James's later
Washington Square, and then notes differences in the way "two great
writers handle a novelistic situation in outline so essentially similar."
Trollope presents a "pathetic incident" in an action which stops; James
portrays characters in an open-ended plot. Trollope is concerned with
what happens; James, in how things happen.

Elizabeth Langland in *Society in the Novel* (No. Car., 1984) sees
George Eliot as influencing James to make his characters "move . . .
inward," so that at their best "they . . . see beyond a particular socially
determined correctness to a larger 'rightness.' "

The Literary Notebooks of Thomas Hardy, 2 vols., ed. Lennart A.
Björk (NYU), contain comments by Hardy on James and Balzac,
Stevenson, and Hawthorne; one fine footnote also traces the evolution
of Hardy's "attitude" toward James from "negative" to "milder."

Source-hunter A. R. Tintner is still on safari. Her "Henry James,
The Scapegoat, and the William Holman Hunts" (*PRR* 6:34–41)
shows that Hunt's painting *The Scapegoat* long terrified James and
provides a metaphor in *The Golden Bowl*. She also discusses James's
relationship with Hunt and his wife. Four letters by James to the
latter are published here. Tintner in "Henry James' Tribute to a Victorian Novelist: Mrs. Oliphant" (*ABBW* 22 April:3016, 3018, 3020,
3022, 3024, 3026, 3028) shows that Mrs. Harvey in James's story
"Broken Wings" is partly based on Margaret Wilson Oliphant, whose
works James deplored but whose pluck he admired. Tintner's "The
Disappearing Furniture in Maupassant's 'Qui Sait?' " (*HJR* 6:3–7)
sees in Guy de Maupassant's 1890 story "Qui Sait?" a source for the
"passive animism" of Mrs. Gereth's holdings as they move to Ricks
and back to Poynton in *The Spoils of Poynton*. Tintner in "Roth's
'Pain' and James's 'Obscure Hurt' " (*Midstream* 31:58–60) shows that
The Anatomy Lesson, book three of Philip Roth's Zuckerman trilogy,
echoes elements from James's *Autobiography*.

Neil Schmitz in "Mark Twain, Henry James, and Jacksonian
Dreaming" (*Criticism* 27:155–73) argues that "[t]he writers who

come of age during the Reconstruction, notably Mark Twain and
Henry James, refuse to take the romantic question in the Jacksonian
text seriously, and when they represent the [Jacksonian] style in their
fiction the expression is invariably lunatic."

Daniel J. Schneider's "James and Conrad: The Psychological
Premises" (*HJR* 6:32–38) contends that the closest link between
James and Joseph Conrad is "their shared convictions regarding the
deep motives of human nature," namely that we "create" ideal self-
images and rationalize to "maintain" them, we seek security, and we
wonder what prompts our choices. Schneider offers much proof from
both writers: Fleda Vetch (*The Spoils of Poynton*) is a "rationalizing
idealist"; the main characters in *The Golden Bowl* finally want peace;
Lambert Strether (*The Ambassadors*) acts on a "dynamogenic" belief
in illusion; etc.

Douglas Keesey contrasts aspects of James's argument with H. G.
Wells in "So Much Life with (So to Speak) So Little Living: The
Literary Side of the James-Wells Debate" (*HJR* 6:80–88). Keesey
stresses the two novelists' opposed philosophies concerning style and
concludes that "each side . . . makes good sense." Richard Hauer
Costa's revised *H. G. Wells* (TEAS) usefully summarizes the whole
argument.

Robert Gregory reasons in "Porpoise-iveness Without Porpoise:
Why Nabokov Called James a Fish" (*HJR* 6:52–59) that in spite of
disliking and parodying James, and differing from him, Vladimir
Nabokov "thought of him as a rival and wrote sometimes with the
purpose of battling him." Gregory's curious title derives from Im-
manuel Kant, James's imagery, and a letter from Nabokov to Edmund
Wilson.

Patricia C. Willis' " 'Tell Me, Tell Me' and Henry James" (*MMN*
7[1983]:44–45) discusses some lines in Marianne Moore's 1960 poem
"Tell Me, Tell Me" which come from James's *Autobiography*.

Motivated by James Agee and his "religious estimation of silence,"
J. A. Ward in *American Silences* (LSU) develops his earlier comments
on Jamesian silence (see *ALS 1982*, pp. 124–25) as part of his contrast
of 19th-century writers' "use [of] fantasy and myth to suggest an
eternal silence remote from commonplace experience" with 20th-
century writers' treatment of silence in its realistic social context.
Ward briefly considers James in conjunction with Edgar Allan Poe,
Herman Melville, and Henry Adams here.

Donald J. Greiner's *Adultery in the American Novel: Updike,*

James, and Hawthorne (So. Car.) concentrates on John Updike's fiction and opinions; but he also considers Nathaniel Hawthorne, particularly *The Scarlet Letter* and *The Marble Faun*, and James, mainly *The Golden Bowl*, and to a lesser extent *The Portrait of a Lady*, "A London Life," *What Maisie Knew*, and *The Wings of the Dove*. Greiner concludes that "Hawthorne may stress the moral order, James the social, and Updike the individual, but all three consider sexual transgression the consummate obstacle to the peaceful marriage and thus the most attractive material for fiction." More specifically, Greiner comments on James thus: "Of all the nineteenth-century American novelists, he understood best that marriage is more contract than sacrament and that contracts are written to be broken." It is of interest that Updike sees James as "the benchmark for novelists who aspire to greatness."

David Leon Higdon in "Henry James and Lillian Hellman: An Unnoted Source" (*HJR* 6:134–35) observes that details of Horace Gliddens' death in Hellman's *The Little Foxes* are reminiscent of the old Marquis de Bellegarde's death in James's *The American*.

Lyall H. Powers shows in "Henry James and James Baldwin: The Complex Figure" (*MFS* 30[1984]:651–67) that Baldwin's frequent comments on and echoes of James "constitute a virtual invitation from Baldwin to think of Henry James as we read his [Baldwin's] work, especially *Another Country*."

In *The Visual Arts, Pictorialism, and the Novel: James, Lawrence, and Woolf* (Princeton) Marianna Torgovnick integrates comments on her three modernist (i.e., 1880–1940) and painterly novelists. James, for whom only "Impressionism [among art movements] is crucial," is the "most conservative." She discusses the use by all three writers of the visual arts on a continuum which includes decorative (as seen in *Roderick Hudson* and *The Tragic Muse*), biographically motivated, ideological (including iconographical), and interpretive (including perceptual or psychological, and also hermeneutic—especially as seen in *The Portrait of a Lady*, *The Ambassadors*, and *The Golden Bowl*). Innovative is Torgovnick's conflating of picture-viewing and text-reading, both in response to pictorial stimuli.

One of the finest "parallels" studies ever done involving James is Ralph F. Bogardus' lavishly illustrated *Pictures and Texts: Henry James, A. L. Coburn, and New Ways of Seeing in Literary Culture* (UMI Research Press, 1984), which explains how James became "director, scenarist, and editor" of Alvin Langdon Coburn's New York

Edition photographs, all reprinted here. Bogardus discusses James's chronic dislike of illustrations for fiction in general, and his own in particular—and with well-documented reasons: pictures limit tonal effects, reduce imaginative quality, and conflict with verbal pictorialism. James more gracefully tolerated having his travel books illustrated. Especially fine is Bogardus' treatment of James's 1893 *Picture and Text*. Less pertinent to James is Bogardus' tracing of the history of photography as it relates to painting and elitist Victorian culture. James was ambivalent on photography as art, resented being "exposed," at first liked photographs mainly as documents, but evolved beyond literary realism to the modernist position through his appreciation of the artistry of such photographers as Coburn. Bogardus considers this genius's career and relates his New York Edition masterpieces to James's texts and ideas therein.

Steve Vineberg begins "The Responsibility of the Adapter: *The Bostonians* on Film" (*ArQ* 41:223–30) by suggesting that adapters of novels to film ought to realize that they can wreck readers' enjoyment both before and after their moviegoing; contends that director James Ivory and screenwriter Ruth Prawer Jhabvala turned James's *The Europeans*, "an explosively funny novel, . . . into a solemn costume drama, a graveyard"; and criticizes their film of *The Bostonians* as resembling "a community production of a Restoration comedy" and "a 1920s college musical-comedy," with Olive Chancellor and Basil Ransom reductively presented as "the Wicked Witch and Prince Charming."

iii. Criticism: General

Millicent Bell's "Henry James, Meaning and Unmeaning" (*Raritan* 4[1984]:29–46) shows that formalist James perhaps questioned form, that his fictive points of view often betray a tug between interpretation and indeterminacy, that he teases us both by holding out the possibility of valid interpretation of his fiction and also by "reprov[ing]" those "who insist on reducing . . . mystification to . . . certainty."

The best work of the year on James, I say, is *Henry James and the Problem of Audience: An International Act* by Anne T. Margolis (UMI Research Press). This attractive book offers readable astuteness, extensive documentation (including unpublished letters between James and his agent), and a detailed index. Its thesis is that "the master," long both rightly "canonized" and wrongly castigated as purposely aloof, wanted to sell well, tried to compete with women "scribblers" and other commercial successes, compromised to the extent of adapting some of "the conventional themes and devices of popular fiction," and associated honestly with "the emerging English-speaking avant-garde." Yet James always reserved the right to create his own audience, criticize its shortcomings, "challenge . . . genteel prescriptions," and prove by his own example—"part writer, part actor, and part magician"—that writing is an art not a trade. Margolis blends commentary on James's writings and discussions of the English-speaking book business, his theatrical ventures, his self-revealing major-phase characters, and his unconsciously confessional "retrospective" Prefaces.

"'The Salt That Saves': Fiction and History in the Late Work of Henry James," pp. 299–319 in *Mythos und Aufklärung*, is Heinz Ickstadt's intriguing title for an essay the thesis of which is that "history" connoted three related, tension-producing things to James: an "ensemble . . . of collectively remembered . . . forms and objects," a present time eclipsing "continuities," and a process of "creating order." In a triple response, the writer preserves, is puzzled, and builds. Ickstadt proves his points by using Jamesian evidence solely from *The Golden Bowl*, later fiction, and reminiscence. James dramatizes would-be societal equilibration in the face of the entropy of civilization. For one example among several, *The Golden Bowl* offers a "quasi-utopian projection of the gentry myth celebrating the power of the imagination to transform society," but later *The Ivory Tower* is James's "radical negation" of that myth.

Tony Tanner's *Henry James: The Writer and His Work* (Mass.) is a reprint in book form of his introduction to James in three pamphlets (Longman, 1979–81). Chapter 1 concerns the "complex fate" of Americans in Europe; chapter 2, James in London; and chapter 3, literary production at Rye. Tanner seems harsh on Robert Acton in *The Europeans* and Nick Dormer in *The Tragic Muse*, noteworthy on *Washington Square* and *What Maisie Knew*, too laudatory concerning *Confidence, The Other House, The Awkward Age*, and *The Sacred Fount*, superb on James's *Hawthorne, The Portrait of a Lady*, and *The Bostonians*, thin on *The Princess Casamassima*, "The Turn of the Screw," and *The American Scene*, and spellbinding on the major-phase novels. Tanner writes tenderly of James's "declining years," "his avowed homoeroticism," and "a central, abiding paradox in James's life—a desire to have experience without involvement," that is, his dilemma of empathy vs. detachment, curiosity vs. reticence, and inquisitiveness vs. decorum. Tanner rather slights James's short fiction.

Mary Ann Caws in *Reading Frames in Modern Fiction* (Princeton) theorizes that in the best narratives (from Jane Austen through Marcel Proust) certain passages stand out, that such passages permit another genre to intrude, and that in modernist fiction (including James's) framing calls attention to itself rather than to what is framed. In *The Ambassadors* framing devices help to pictorialize; in *The Wings of the Dove* melodrama threatens the frame; in *The Golden Bowl* rhetorical devices play with the frame. Caws also uses other Jamesian texts.

Ian F. A. Bell, editor of *Henry James: Fiction as History* (Barnes and Noble), feels that James's "over-complication" has been wrongly "valoriz[ed]," even imprisoned by "a precious and wrongly sensitized [critical] rhetoric." Hence Bell's collection of eight essays by more sociohistorically democratic critics. First off, Bell himself relates commercial expansion, hard money, and credit (the background economic concerns in *Washington Square*) to characterization. Next, David Howard considers a reversal in "The Papers": Grub Street writers have plenty of intelligence and wit, easily enough to avenge themselves on supposedly superior publicity-seekers. Millicent Bell reads "The Turn of the Screw" not mainly to define ghosts but as an uneasy story by a narrator whose "see-saw" perceptions, deductions, and judgments eventuate in "indeterminacy." Nicola Bradbury contrasts the final words in *The Wings of the Dove* (an "ellipsis of future . . . and past") and *The Ambassadors* ("fixity of time and place"): thus James balances closure and "Derrida's *difference*" to "celebrat[e] . . . absence as a positive joy." Maud Ellmann suggests that in *The Ambassadors* James shows the ruin of power (Mrs. Newsome) by her representatives, who "mock mimesis," get loose from her, and represent each other. Stuart Culver sees James of the prefaces as less either craftsman or autobiographer, and more as "entrepreneur reasserting his property rights over his texts," now revised into partly "new commodities." Ellman Crasnow images James as a complex Janus, not "a simple binarism" but the "god of doorways," through which the artist moves between "oppositional structure[s]" in his fiction to "economy in . . . non-fictional work." Richard Godden shows that shifts in the fictive depiction of manners (by James and others) parallel the shift between our time of economic "expansion and accumulation" (1850–

1900) and our time of producing "profit to support that accumulation" (1900–1930). These eight essays are difficult, prolix, and at times precious.

"Henry James and the Seal of Love," pp. 209–26 in *Biblical Patterns in Modern Literature*, ed. David H. Hirsch and Nehama Aschkenasy (Scholars Press, 1984), is a shortened version of Hirsch's earlier essay of the same title (see *ALS 1983*, pp. 119–20). Its thesis is that in James, as in much other Western literature of his time, "*eros* is not only divorced from *agapé*, it is wed to *thanatos*," and that often in James "the sickness of love turns into the sickness of death."

Merla Wolk in "The Sweet-Shop Window, the House of Fiction and the Jamesian Artist" (*AI* 42:269–95) explicates Jamesian window imagery and symbolism: windows separate the artist (figurative here) from objects beyond them all to deprive, exclude; protect, give visual access; and distance, link visually. Wolk also defines "the dilemma of the developing artist and . . . its solution." She theorizes (relying mainly on *What Maisie Knew*) that the emerging artist suffers "conflict over other-self boundaries" but once mature protects himself (since he needs "safe space") by constructing walls of syntactical thickness for his many-windowed house of fiction.

The general thesis of Jenni Calder's "Cash and the Sex Nexus," in *Sexuality and the Victorian Novel*, ed. Don Richard Cox (*TSL* 27 [1984]:40–53), is that in many Victorian novels "[m]arriage was valued more as a social and economic institution than as a personal or sexual union." Starting with George Meredith, then moving forward in time to others, Calder concludes with James, who, she notes with striking obviousness, "discourses not of sexuality but of social sexual relations," and that "he never questions that the sex nexus is the cash nexus." Her evidence comes from *What Maisie Knew, The Wings of the Dove*, and *The Golden Bowl*. Vern Wagner in "Henry James: Money and Sex" (PR 93:216–31) asserts that James "uses money and sex as the primary impelling forces in human behavior." Wagner's clearest but not his only evidence comes from *What Maisie Knew*. Believing that "the association between antique collecting and male homosexuality is a virtual cliché," Judith Weissman in "Antique Secrets in Henry James" (*PR* 93:196–215) theorizes that James depicts his main antique collectors as "weak, nonathletic, aesthetic types," adding that their "homosexuality . . . is shadowy." She skirts the case of James's most vigorous collector, the late Mr. Gereth of *The Spoils of Poynton*, by merely noting that "we never see" him.

Her opening assertion that Oscar Wilde's novel *The Picture of Dorian Gray* and "some of Henry James's novels are the first in English in in which antiques are important" rests on firmer ground, as does her follow-up conflation of "antique collecting and the breakdown of the family and the community."

In "Reflections on Holland in the Works of Henry James" (*HJR* 6:39–45) Enny de Boer Eshuis discusses "James's treatment of Holland and the Dutch" in travel writing, art critiques, five novels, and a short story. James ambivalently saw Holland as both peaceful and imagination-numbing; he began by stereotyping the Dutch but later imaginatively sketched their homeland as temporary haven, relief, sanctuary.

Relying on James's New York Edition and his autobiographical volumes, Charles Caramello in "The Author's Taste, Or, Unturning the Screw" (*DR* 64[1984]:36–45) suggests a paradox: James sought to make a given body of his writing both "a flawless essence" and a demonstration of literary art as an "undying process."

Of general interest is Robert O. Preyer's "Breaking Out: The English Assimilation of Continental Thought in Nineteenth-Century Rome" (*BIS* 12[1984]:53–72), which serves Jamesians by showing that Isabel Archer (of *The Portrait of a Lady*) soothes her suffering in Rome through awareness that the Eternal City offers "root room for the psyche" by dramatizing "an alternative time sense." The entire essay is a grand historical parade, showing that Rome unblocks repressions, renews the spirit, integrates feeling and thought, inspires expression, and especially disturbs the conventional time sense by letting the rowdy present jostle the monumental past.

iv. Criticism: Individual Novels

Stuart Johnson starts (and ends) his "Germinal James: The Lesson of the Apprentice" (*MFS* 31:233–47) with the celebrated but naive distinction made by Cynthia Ozick (see "The Lesson of the Master," *NYRB*, 12 Aug. 1982, pp. 20–21) between enticing life in the early James and off-putting art in the late James. Johnson explains that even in the early *Watch and Ward*, James shows that its hero "chooses life— love, marriage, and family—and [still] finds that life is not immediately available but must be fabricated."

Ian Bell's " 'This Exchange of Epigrams': Commodity and Style in *Washington Square*" (*JAmS* 19:49–68) cites James's detailed references to time and place in *Washington Square* to show that James—far from having little historical sense, as often alleged—not only hints at "the development of the bourgeois temperament" but also presents Austin Sloper's resistance to encroaching commercial "turbulence." Bell is gracious in commenting on James's "competing" (i.e., careless) time and place references, concluding that a playful "historical relativism [is thus] exhibited." (For more on *Washington Square*, see Ian Bell, above.)

Robert K. Martin's thesis in *"The Bostonians:* James's Dystopian View of Social Reform" (*Mosaic* 18:107–13) is that James was skeptical concerning "the idealism that underlies utopian thought," since he was radically opposed to "German Idealism and American Transcendentalism, both of which he considered inadequate as means to deal with the reality of the age." Reformers try to impose their will on others seeking to preserve unique identities, and hence "confuse . . . personal rights and group rights." In "The Politics of Temporality in James's *The Bostonians*" (*NCF* 40:187–215) Susan L. Mizruchi connects "sociopolitical and artistic themes" in *The Bostonians* by suggesting that in it "power and politics . . . are implicated in the very processes of talk and narration." In the work, one can dominate self and others by "establish[ing] one's own sense of time and one's own version of history." Concentrating on eight characters and the narrator, Mizruchi shows that their "relations to time" are of "social significance." In "James's Rhetorical Arena: The Metaphor of Battle in *The Bostonians*" (*TSLL* 27:270–83) Janet A. Gabler with subtle re-revisionistic logic concludes that James "undercut[s]" Olive Chancellor's rhetoric concerning "a woman's true destiny," "agree[s] with [Basil] Ransom's view of the woman's role," and "creates a narrator who openly criticizes Ransom . . . so smugly and pretentiously" that he should not be taken seriously. Further, Verena Tarrant is viewed as the "presiding . . . judge" over the two principals' "rhetorical struggle." Millicent Bell in "The Bostonian Story" (*PR* 52:109–19) believes that the film adaptors badly altered *The Bostonians*, which she sees as a "comic satire" with "a plot of pure fairy tale," by "preserv[ing] . . . *both* romance and tragedy . . . keep[ing] *both* Basil [Ransom] as fairy-tale hero and Olive [Chancellor] as tragic heroine." Bell writes much about New England "female bonding" and feels that the movie wrongly "makes our [mere] suspicion of Olive's lesbianism a certainty." But the best part of this essay is its commentary on James's attitude toward marriage ("a threat . . . to human potential"), especially after his parents' death in 1882. (For more on the filmic *Bostonians*, see Steve Vineberg, above.)

John Budd in "*The Spoils of Poynton*: The Revisions and the Critics" (*MSE* 10:1–11) tactfully corrects some 10 prematurely opinionated critics of Fletch Vetch and Owen Gereth by surveying textual changes in *The Spoils of Poynton* from its *Atlantic Monthly* serial form (1896) to book versions published by Heinemann (1897) and Houghton Mifflin (also 1897) to "the best text extant," that of the New York Edition (1908). Budd's conclusion: "James clarifies his intention in many instances with simplification of language and at other times with elaboration of description," his intention being to make his hero and heroine more mature, moral, emotional, and loving. Budd neatly calls Owen "more . . . a weapon than . . . a participant" in the battle for the spoils.

In "L'Image de Venise dans *The Wings of the Dove*" (*ALUB*) Hubert Teyssandier discusses the interrelationship between rich, doomed Milly Theale's Venice in *The Wings of the Dove*, and the theatricality, picturesqueness, and symbolism of that splendid, corrupt city of water, palaces, canals, squares, cafés, and poetry. Three plates add to the value of Teyssandier's analysis. What did Milly Theale die of? Caroline G. Mercer and Sarah D. Wangensteen in " 'Consumption, heart-disease, or whatever': *The Wings of the Dove*" (*Jour. of the Hist. of Medicine and Allied Sciences* 40:259–85) theorize that it was of chlorosis (the green sickness, *mal d'amour, morbus virgineus*). They summarize the medical literature on this puzzling illness, perhaps psychopathologic in origin and now eradicated possibly by a healthier social environment. More important for Jamesians is Mercer and Wangensteen's handling of Miss Theale's symptoms, and the diagnosis and advice of her physician Sir Luke Strett, shown here to be modeled on Alice James's physician Sir Andrew Clark and on James's friend Dr. William Wilberforce Baldwin. (For more on *The Wings of the Dove*, see Nicola Bradbury, above.) Jeffrey Meyers in *Disease and the Novel, 1880–1960* (St. Martin's) might have considered Milly Theale, but instead merely touches on the heroines of "Daisy Miller" and "The Turn of the Screw."

Alan W. Bellringer's sensible book entitled simply *The Ambassadors* (Allen & Unwin, 1984) considers the general biographical and cultural background of James's *Ambassadors*, its form, its "evolution," its plot, interpretations of it, and critical responses to it. Hubert Teyssandier in "De Balzac à James: La Vision de Paris dans *The Ambassadors* (1903)" (*CVE* 21:51–62) shows that James in sorrow modifies the exactitude of enthusiastic Balzac to show more impressionistically, à la Manet and Renoir, that the fin de siècle Seine tragically separates not only the Right Bank and the Left but also the historical, elegant old and the predatory, hypocritical new, with individual residences—including rooms, furnishings, studios, balconies, and gardens—of Parisians and expatriates defining their occupants. In "The 'Drama of Discrimination': Style as Plot in *The Ambassadors*" (*Lang&S* 18:46–63) Mary Cross hypersubtly views hero Lambert Strether as "the editor of his experience" and "his story a much-amended manuscript," in which "language is the prominent action . . . , its stylized patterns a context where peripeteia is a word; narrative is syntax; and meaning, an event." (For more on *The Ambassadors*, see Maud Ellman, above.)

In his "Philosophy, Interpretation and *The Golden Bowl*," pp. 211–28 in *Philosophy and Literature*, ed. A. Phillips Griffiths (Cambridge, 1984), Peter Jones identifies "the moral dimensions of . . . *The Golden Bowl*" (to be truly moral one must be smart, be expressive, avoid passivity, be decisive, and transcend egotism to think of others); relates James's fictive presentation of arguable philosophy to his prefatory comments (accept dangers, be free rather than easy, and appreciate the most those novels which invite us to practice gaining knowledge by experiencing ideas); and incidentally shows that William James, even while labeling his brother's novels musty and indirect, philosophized regularly on the relativity of knowledge and beliefs, which relativity those very novels challenge us to ponder. Mark Reynolds in "Counting the Crisis: The Infirmity of Art and *The Golden Bowl*" (*HJR* 6:15–26) reasons that just as marriage and bowl-buying in *The Golden Bowl* are "social contracts" involving "price and faith," so James makes a contract with his readers by asking them not only to have faith that "the complexities inherent in experience appear to be contained" in controlled fiction but also to pay "the price exacted for its effect."

Susan M. Griffin in "Seeing Double: Reflections of the Self in James's *The Sense of the Past*" (*MLQ* 45[1984]:48–60) reasons that *The Sense of the Past* does not dramatize withdrawal—either James's or his hero's—but rather offers the hero a present-exaggerating past in which to "work out *new* patterns for solving old problems."

v. Criticism: Individual Tales

Tamar Yacobi's jargon-filled "Hero or Heroine? *Daisy Miller* and the
Focus of Interest in Narrative" (*Style* 19:1–35) refines on Meir
Sternberg's theory concerning focus of interest to move from his text
to her context. Yacobi focuses on "Daisy Miller," first contrasting
early Daisy-stressing reader response and recent Winterbourne-
stressing reader response, and then arbitrating such "divergence in
centering" to "coordinat[e]" both "actual" and "implied reader," and
"interpretation" and "communication."

In "The Use of Stupidity as a Narrative Device: The Gullible
Teller in James's 'Louisa Pallant'" (*JNT* 15:69–74) A. R. Tintner
interprets "Louisa Pallant" as a story told by a "gullible narrator" who
fails to see that Linda Pallant's mother, Louisa, is not remorsefully
telling the truth about her daughter to save the narrator's nephew
but is lying about her so that she will catch a better husband. Tintner
in "Henry James' Two Ways of Seeing" (*ABBW* 21 January:363, 368,
370, 372, 374) contrasts the profound, "binocular" vision of the narrator of "John Delavoy" and the superficial, "monocular" way his
editor looks at things. By 1898, when "John Delavoy" was published,
James preferred in-depth perceiving to panoramic, "Impressionist"
seeing.

"Reading 'The Figure in the Carpet': Henry James and Wolfgang
Iser" (*ESA* 27[1984]:107–21) by M. A. Williams is a model of academic scholarship: it summarizes previous published research, considers the text, and offers something new. Here Williams, following
The Act of Reading by phenomenologist Wolfgang Iser (see *ALS
1979*, pp. 453–54) but freely noting "his failure[s]," argues that "the
'figure in the carpet' is neither maliciously concealed nor frustratingly
non-existent. Instead, it is to be traced out through the very act of
reading which engages the responsive consciousness with the text."

George Bishop's "Shattered Notions of Mastery: Henry James's
'Glasses'" (*Criticism* 27:347–62) discusses Mrs. Meldrum's age in
the short story "Glasses," puns on "spectacles," narrative "embarrass-
ment[s]," but mainly "blunders" by the narrator.

Edel in *Henry James: A Life* (see section i, above) offers as a
source for "The Turn of the Screw" Tom Taylor's *Temptation*, serialized in *Frank Leslie's New York Journal* in 1855, and with characters
named Peter Quin and Miles, a brother-sister combination (the little
boy of which dies), and a house on Harley Street. David S. Miall's es-

say "Designed Horror: James's Vision of Evil in *The Turn of the Screw*" (*NCF* 39[1984]:305–27) argues that "James intended us to take the ghosts seriously but that this does not commit us to [accept] the reality of the supernatural," since James here offers us the "truth . . . of the emotions" and shows us "an evil . . . operative and undefeated." Miall discusses a real-life haunted house story, reported in the 1898 *Proceedings of the Society for Psychical Research.* The case resembles "The Turn of the Screw" in eight specified ways. But James turned one harmless ghost into two malevolent Bly ghosts. He creates "evil" in his story by rejecting scientific explanations and instead "endow[ing] . . . his ghosts with intentions—at least in the eyes of the governess" and their ambience with symbolism, and also by conveying "the uncanny . . . by coincidences and repetitions." In a letter to the editor captioned "The Governess and the Ghosts" (*PMLA* 100:96–97) Peter G. Beidler demonstrates that Frederic W. H. Myers, "a founding member" of the Society for Psychical Research and a friend of James, "thought the governess was a generally reliable narrator of a story about ghosts." Beidler quotes from an 1898 Myers letter. (For more on "The Turn of the Screw," see Millicent Bell, above.)

In "The Right Way with Reality: James's 'The Real Right Thing'" (*HJR* 6:8–14) J. P. Telotte argues that the ghost "apparently" warning George Withermore not to write dead Ashton Doyne's biography may be hardly less "real" than Doyne's literary remains. Further, is it "right" for Withermore to use them? Often such evidence "troublingly eludes our usual . . . representations."

In "The Archaeology of Ancient Rome: Sexual Metaphor in 'The Beast in the Jungle'" (*HJR* 6:27–31) James Ellis notes that John Marcher thought he and May Bartram met in Rome whereas they did so at Pompeii, and then argues that Rome may be equated with Marcher's Caligula-like mad egotism and Pompeii with May's offer of "life rediscovered," along with the joy of sex. (Why not this? May reminds Marcher of Roman energy, while he reminds her of Pompeiian death.)

vi. Criticism: Specific Nonfictional Works

Susan Carlson in *Women of Grace: James's Plays and the Comedy of Manners* (UMI Research Press) defines elements of post-Restoration British comedy of manners; discusses the role of female characters,

who have "superior social understanding from the compromised positions society's double standard puts them in," featured in works by
a dozen or so playwrights from 1890 to 1915 (and a little beyond);
and places "James's dramatic women . . . in the company of other
comic heroines who share their social prowess and social visions."
Carlson shows that James's plays are often part of a tradition (not
favored now) of dramatizing the close relationship between "social
grace and social good." Especially fine is her treatment of James's
Tenants, The Reprobate, Disengaged, Guy Domville, The High Bid
(her favorite), and *The Outcry.*

Bruce Redford's "Keeping Story out of History: Henry James's
Biographical *tour de force*" (*AL* 57:215–25) shows that James, though
aware that William Wetmore Story had neither a great mind nor any
great adventures, wrote a commendable two-volume biography of
the man in 1903. James did so by being evocative and discursive, by
using "diversion, indirection, and decentralization," and by abandoning biographical data and instead stressing the Rome of old days and
friends.

Jean Kimball combines titanic labor and attractive modesty in "A
Classified Subject Index to Henry James's Critical Prefaces to the
New York Edition (Collected in *The Art of the Novel*)" (*HJR* 6:89–
133). This useful index is divided into four categories, each with subdivisions, thus: 1. Allusions (a. Artists and Writers, b. Historical Persons and Events, c. Periodicals, d. Places, e. Works of Other Writers);
2. Analogies and Comparisons; 3. Henry James (a. The Novels and
Tales, b. Personal Information and Commentary); and 4. Terms and
Concepts. Do you need to know, for example, where James in his
Prefaces mentions Balzac, Black Death, *Punch*, Ireland, *Uncle Tom's
Cabin*, The New York Edition, the international theme, or *ficelles*?
Answers to these queries and hundreds of others may be found in
Kimball's index.

The best of recent St. Martin's Press books on James is Vivien
Jones's informative *James the Critic*. Jones treats the Master's evolving interrelationships with American, British, and French critics
and novelists, especially Matthew Arnold, Honoré de Balzac, Walter
Besant, Alphonse Daudet, Gustave Flaubert, William Dean Howells,
Guy de Maupassant, Charles Augustin Sainte-Beuve, George Sand,
G. B. Shaw, Robert Louis Stevenson, H. G. Wells, and Émile Zola.
James moved from American "prescriptive . . . idealism" to an appreciation of French "aesthetic awareness" and realism (though docu-

mentary Naturalism was, in his view, a dead end), and then to British moralism (toward British pandering to the public, Shavian socialism, and Wellsian sloppiness, however, he was "consistently dismissive"). The last chapter concerns James's Prefaces, "the first English attempt at anything like a poetics of fiction." The Prefaces hint at their author's unconscious preference for formalism over mimesis even as they reconstruct creativity, show "rationale and method" interacting, discuss specific fictive techniques, and point up certain "weaknesses inherent in all James's criticism." Jones closes by explaining James's "legacy": James questioned the "mimetic assumptions" of "traditional realism," shared the modernists' "concern with perception," and saw in form both a source of meaning and an obligation to morality. He was such a watershed figure that his eclecticism is inevitably inconsistent at times. But he remains both "a model and a quarry."

In "Henry James Criticism: A Case Study in Critical Inquiry" (*NCF* 40:327–44) Elizabeth Coleman tries to counter common notions concerning James as a critic. She bitterly theorizes that since his "central critical value was what he called life," he overpraised certain writers for immersing themselves in life while undervaluing others because they were too detached "from a spontaneous, immediate, and felt relation to life." Coleman finds James's own dissociation of reality and craft ironic, especially as unconsciously revealed in "The Art of Fiction." She much prefers "A Humble Remonstrance," the rejoinder by Robert Louis Stevenson, who, contra James, calls on the critic simply to discern the artist's freely determined purposes. In "Henry James's 'The Art of Fiction': Word, Self, Experience" (*PQ* 64:225–38) Matthew Little interconnects Hippolyte Taine's *On Intelligence* (1868, rev. ed. 1872), William James's use of it, and Henry James's own theories as to "the nature of human consciousness and the organic [and growing] wholeness of the work of fiction." All are imaged by James as a "huge spider-web . . . catching . . . air-borne particle[s]." Sensibility, experience, literary form, and literary content are inseparable in the writer's creative process.

Carol Holly in "The British Reception of Henry James's Autobiographies" (*AL* 57:570–87) discusses critical approaches to *A Small Boy and Others* and then *Notes of a Son and Brother* in many 1913–14 British reviews. The reviewers intrigued James's coterie of readers by praising his experimental techniques in autobiography: his use of narrative innovations, centering the point of view in the "reminiscing consciousness," and nonchronological ordering of memories. The reviewers read the two volumes as history, as art, and as both, and also as an interweaving of memoir and autobiography. Most preferred the second volume, for moving away from "mental analysis" toward warm portraiture. The three main points of James Olney's "Psychology, Memory, and Autobiography: William and Henry James" (*HJR* 6:46–51) are that Henry practiced in his autobiographical volumes what William theorized about concerning remembrance, that memory is creative, and that Henry's "subject"—both in autobiography (served by memory) and in fiction (served by imagination)—is consciousness.

University of Pittsburgh

8. Pound and Eliot

Hugh Witemeyer

i. Pound

Ezra Pound was born 30 October 1885. At least 12 centenary celebrations of that event took place this year in Rapallo, Italy; Cambridge, England; Cogolin, France; the University of Heidelberg; the
University of Maine at Orono; Yale University; Rutgers University;
Hamilton College; the University of Alabama; Hailey, Idaho; San
Jose State University; and Kansai University, Japan. Special Pound
issues of the *Iowa Review, Field* (Oberlin, Ohio), and *Los Cuadernos del Norte* (Oviedo, Spain) were published; and the proceedings
of a 1984 conference on *Ezra Pound a Venezia*, ed. Rosella Mamoli
Zorzi (Florence: Leo S. Olschki), also appeared. Massimo Bacigalupo
describes the Venice conference in *Paideuma* 14:125–28, and his
catalog of the 1985 Rapallo festivities, featuring a speech by Donald
Davie, has already been published as *Ezra Pound: un poeta a Rapallo*
(Genoa: San Marco dei Giustiniani). More spinoffs from this vortex
of activity are doubtless on the way.

a. **Text and Biography.** The major textual work of the year is *Pound/
Lewis: The Letters of Ezra Pound and Wyndham Lewis*, ed. Timothy
Materer (New Directions). This volume contains 252 items of corre-
spondence exchanged by "WynDAMN" and "Ezroar" between 1914
and 1957. Materer provides an informative introduction and selective
annotations. Item 183 appears also as "Letter to Wyndham Lewis"
(*Paideuma* 14:97–101). Meanwhile, "*Pound/Ford*: Addenda and
Corrections" by Brita Lindberg-Seyersted and Archie Henderson
(*Paideuma* 14:117–24) updates that excellent volume in the New Directions series.

Other correspondence appears for the first time this year. *At the
Circulo de Recreo with Ezra Pound: A Letter from Ezra Pound to
Viola Baxter, May 9, 1906*, ed. Donald Gallup (New Haven: Beinecke
Library, Yale University), is an annotated facsimile edition of a let-

ter from Spain describing incidents later recalled in Canto 81 ("Eso es luto, *haw!*"). *Agenda* (23,iii–iv:136) prints a photocopy of a 1917 letter to C. F. G. Masterman in which Pound offers his services to the British war effort. George Bornstein unearths "Eight Letters from Ezra Pound to Parker Tyler in the 1930s" (*MQR* 24:1–17), interesting for their comments on the contemporary literary scene. In "The Pound/de Angulo Connection" (*Paideuma* 14:52–77) Lee Bartlett reproduces 25 letters written by Ezra and Dorothy Pound to anthropologist Jaime de Angulo (1887–1950) and his wife between 1949 and 1954. Finally, *Dear Ez: Letters from William Carlos Williams to Ezra Pound*, ed. Mary Ellen Solt (Bloomington, Ind.: Frederic Brewer), contains seven letters written to Pound in St. Elizabeths between 1946 and 1951.

Pound's unpublished manuscript of December 1928 on "The Music of Beowulf" (see Gallup, E6g) is printed in the *Yale Literary Magazine* (150,i[1982]:88–91). The status of such manuscript material under the new U.S. Copyright Law is clarified by Peggy L. Fox in "Copyright for Scholars" (*Paideuma* 14:129–34). This essay is required reading for Pound scholars uncertain about permissions and fees.

The major biographical work of the year is James J. Wilhelm's *The American Roots of Ezra Pound* (Garland), parts of which appear as "Pound's Four Fascinating Grandparents" (*Paideuma* 14:377–84). Readable and well-researched, though rather casually documented, this biography of the first 23 years of the poet's life uncovers much new information. Mary Anne Kenner suggests in "A Cameo" (*Paideuma* 14:325–26) that Pound's lifelong interest in cameos may be traceable to a pair of earrings his mother used to wear.

Several recent studies recall Pound's London and Paris years. In *Henri Gaudier and Ezra Pound: A Friendship* (London: Anthony d'Offay, 1982) Richard Cork describes that London relationship. Richard Sieburth's "Ezra Pound (1885–1972)" in *American Writers in Paris, 1920–1939*, ed. Karen Lane Rood (Gale, 1980), lucidly summarizes "the place of Paris within Pound's pattern of exile." In "Ezra Pound in Paris (1921–1924): A Cure of Youthfulness" (*Paideuma* 14:385–93) Philippe Mikriammos assembles colorful anecdotes from previously published sources.

James Laughlin's memoir of "E. P.: A Loving Man" (*AmerP* 2,iii:64–69) should be read as a rebuttal of E. Fuller Torrey's thesis about Pound's "narcissistic" personality (see *ALS 1984*, p. 135). Fur-

ther reminiscences appear in Laughlin's "Three Poems" (*IowaR*
15,ii:3–7), in the notes to his *Stolen and Contaminated Poems* (Turkey Press), and in "Solving the Ezragrams: Pound at 100" (*NYTBR*
10 Nov.:58–59). Torrey's controversial account of Pound's treatment
at St. Elizabeths is sidestepped by psychiatrist Jerome Kavka in
" 'Olson Saved My Life': Ezra Pound" (*Paideuma* 14:7–30). Kavka
prefers to analyze the triangular "group therapy" that went on among
himself, Pound, and Charles Olson during the first three months of
1946. Andrew J. Kappel's diagnosis of Pound as a classic paranoiac
in "Psychiatrists, Paranoia, and the Mind of Ezra Pound" (*L&M*
4:70–85) ends up close to Torrey's diagnosis of narcissism.

Stephen Spender's recollections of Pound are preserved in *Writers
at Work: The* Paris Review *Interviews: Sixth Series,* ed. George Plimpton (Secker & Warburg). Finally, a Tiresian voice speaks in "The
Just Price" by Henry Swabey (*Agenda* 23,iii–iv:144–46). Converted
to Pound's economics in 1935, Swabey believes in them still.

b. **General Studies.** The centenary year called forth a great many
studies. P. N. Furbank's *Pound* (Philadelphia: Open Univ. Press) is
a breezy but not altogether reliable introduction to Pound's *Selected
Poems.* This primer is not to be preferred to Hugh Kenner's classic
The Poetry of Ezra Pound (1951), now reissued in paperback (Nebraska). Kenner discusses the origins of that book and the history of
Pound's reputation in "The Making of the Modernist Canon" (*ChiR*
34[1984],ii:49–61).

Spanish-speaking readers are well-served by four learned and
intelligent discussions of Pound's life and work. These include Jorge
Uscatescu's "Centenario de Ezra Pound" (*CHA* 426:164–79) and
three essays in *Los Cuadernos del Norte* 6,xxxiii: Jesús Pardo's "Ezra
Pound y los Cantos" (pp. 97–101), Andrés Linares' "Notas sobre
Ezra Pound" (pp. 102–03), and Ignacio Gracia Noriega's "Los dias,
las opiniones, y los versos de Ezra Pound" (pp. 104–09). The interplay of critical voices continues in Burton Raffel's *Possum and Ole Ez
in the Public Eye: Contemporaries and Peers on T. S. Eliot and Ezra
Pound, 1892–1972* (Archon). Raffel's "montage of observations" on
the two poets creates a lively dialectic of conflicting opinions.

The intellectual backgrounds and cultural implications of Pound's
modernist poetics attract several studies of high quality. Sanford
Schwartz's *The Matrix of Modernism: Pound, Eliot, and Early Twentieth-Century Thought* (Princeton) views literary modernism in the

context of the philosophical writings of Bergson, William James, Bradley, and Nietzsche. In "Writing 'Frankly': Pound's Rhetoric against Science" (*Boundary* 13[1984]:405–38) Kathryne V. Lindberg argues that Pound and Gourmont share Nietzsche's project of restoring poetic metaphor to scientific language. Alan Robinson's *Symbol to Vortex: Poetry, Painting, and Ideas, 1885–1914* (St. Martin's) argues that Imagism and Vorticism participate in a "shared post-Impressionist ideology" of empathy, animism, and transcendentalism. In the periodicals of the day Robinson finds a new and credible context for the Vorticist critique of Impressionism.

William Skaff links "Pound's Imagism and the Surreal" (*JML* 12:185–210), stressing the function of metaphor and the unconscious in both theories. Elsewhere, the Pound chapter of Theo Hermans' *The Structure of Modernist Poetry* (Croom Helm, 1982) rehearses derivative ideas about Imagism, Vorticism, and the ideogram; while Y. T. Walther's discussion of "Juxtaposition and Its Limitations: An Explanation of Obscurity in Ezra Pound's Poetry" (*TkR* 14[1983–84]: 199–212) arrives at obvious conclusions.

Several studies treat Pound's Vorticism and his interest in the visual arts. Reed Way Dasenbrock's *The Literary Vorticism of Ezra Pound and Wyndham Lewis: Towards the Condition of Painting* (Hopkins) contends that "the painting and sculpture of the Vorticist movement are not so significant as the literature it inspired and influenced." To illustrate his point, Dasenbrock offers perceptive and intelligent readings of *Homage to Sextus Propertius*, *The Cantos*, and Lewis' *Enemy of the Stars*. The ethos of Vorticism interests Charles Altieri in two essays: "Pound's Vorticism as a Renewal of Humanism" (*Boundary* 13[1984]:439–62) and "Modernist Abstraction and Pound's First Cantos: The Ethos for a New Renaissance" (*KR* 7,iv:79–105).

Three solid essays on *Pound's Artists:Ezra Pound and the Visual Arts in London, Paris, and Italy* (London: Tate Gallery Pubns.) grace the catalog of the Kettle's Yard/Tate Gallery exhibition held this year in Cambridge and London. In "Demon Pantechnicon Driver: Pound in the London Vortex, 1908–1920" Richard Humphreys reviews the poet's many Vorticist enterprises, calling special attention to his criticism of London architecture. John Alexander surveys Pound's activities and contacts in "Parenthetical Paris, 1920–1925: Pound, Picabia, Brancusi, and Léger." And in "Ezra Pound and Italian Art" Peter Robinson examines Pound's interest in the artists and patrons of the early Renaissance.

Pound's use of sculpture and architecture as analogues for poetry interests Michael North in several chapters of *The Final Sculpture: Public Monuments and Modern Poets* (Cornell). Pound evokes the spatial arts, North argues, to create a public poetry; but this ambition is undermined by a private aesthetic which increasingly isolates him from a general audience. Also concerned with Pound's alienation of the general public is Balz Engler in "'Go, My Songs, . . . and Defy Opinion': The Modernist Poet and his Audience" (*ES* 66:316–25). The poems of Pound and of Eliot provide many examples of spatial/ temporal "iconicity" to illustrate the argument of two closely related essays by Max Nänny: "The Need for an Iconic Criticism" (*Jour. of Literary Criticism* [Delhi] 1[1984]:29–42) and "Iconic Dimensions in Poetry" (*SPELL* 2:111–35).

According to Marjorie Perloff in *The Dance of the Intellect: Studies in the Poetry of the Pound Tradition* (Cambridge), the "collage, fragmentation, parataxis" of Pound's poetry and prose anticipate "the hybrid texts of our own time." As in *The Poetics of Indeterminacy* (see *ALS 1981*), Perloff situates Pound in a tradition that justifies a certain type of open, nongeneric, and sometimes nonreferential contemporary American writing.

In "Poetry or Doubletalk: Pound and Modernist Poetics" (*CritQ* 27,ii:39–48) John Tucker uses "Information Theory" to characterize Pound's "poetic of minimum redundancy." Donald Hall hears a redundancy in "Pound's Sounds" (*Field* 33:8–13), especially in one particular "sound-figure" that employs monosyllabic caesuras succeeded by a falling rhythm.

Post-structuralist readings with a neo-Marxist slant dominate a collection of essays entitled *Ezra Pound and History*, ed. Marianne Korn (Natl. Poetry Found.). The 12 contributors include Michael André Bernstein, Alan Durant, Martin Kayman, Dennis Brown, Stephen Wilson, Ian F. A. Bell, Alan J. Peacock, John J. Nolde, Lionel Kelly, Mohammad Y. Shaheen, Burton Hatlen, and David Murray. A common theme of the essays is "the seductive and elegant totalitarianism of Pound's text" (Wilson), resulting from his "simple insistence upon meaning being tied to correspondence with a real world" (Durant). In "Poundians Now" (*Paideuma* 14:167–77) Donald Davie attacks post-structuralism and other recent trends in Pound studies for subordinating poetry to ideology.

According to Charles Bernstein in "Pounding Fascism" (*Sulfur* 13:98–103) the "polyvocal textuality" of *The Cantos* undermines

"Pound's fascist ideals." In "The Desert and the Swamp: Enlightenment, Orientalism, and the Jews in Ezra Pound" (*MLQ* 45[1984]: 263–86) Robert Casillo connects Pound's anti-Semitism to the "Enlightenment anti-Semitism" of Voltaire and to 19th-century Orientalism. Casillo analyzes these traditions of cultural prejudice in Lacanian terms of phallocentrism, heliocentrism, and logocentrism. In "Troubadour Love and Usury in Ezra Pound's Writings" (*TSLL* 27:125–53) Casillo deconstructs Pound's antithesis between life-enhancing *amor* and life-denying *usura*. Elsewhere, Stephen Sicari interprets "The Secret of Eleusis, or How Pound Grounds His 'Epic of Judgment'" (*Paideuma* 14:303–21) as a return to the Freudian/Lacanian "infant's pre-linguistic state."

When Reszö Forgacs staged a production in which words by Pound "were choreographed against a background of mime, with some homosexual and nude acts," Hungarian authorities were not amused. The prosecution of this production is described in "Pornography Trial" (*IonC* 14,v:29). For good, clean fun the commissars might try James Laughlin's "E. P.: The Lighter Side" (*Paideuma* 14:367–75). Surveying Pound's "use of the comic as a rhetorical device," Laughlin adduces many different types and instances of his humor.

c. **Relation to Other Writers.**   Ten essays in *Ezra Pound among the Poets*, ed. George Bornstein (Chicago), consider Pound's relation to other writers. Each of the first nine treats Pound's link with one major predecessor or contemporary. The pairings include Pound and Homer (Hugh Kenner), Ovid (Lillian Feder), Li Po (Ronald Bush), Dante (Stuart Y. McDougal), Whitman (myself), Browning (George Bornstein), Yeats (A. Walton Litz), William Carlos Williams (Thomas Parkinson), and T. S. Eliot (Robert Langbaum). The closing essay by Marjorie Perloff surveys Pound's influence upon a selection of later poets. The papers of Bornstein and Parkinson stand out for their excellent use of previously unpublished material.

Hugh Kenner also contributes an essay to *Dante among the Moderns*, ed. Stuart Y. McDougal (No. Car.). "Ezra Pound's *Commedia*" is an imaginative descant on various analogies between *The Divine Comedy* and *The Cantos*. In "Shepard, Pound, and Bertran de Born" (*Paideuma* 14:331–39) John Leigh links Pound's view of De Born to two essays in which William Pierce Shepard, Pound's instructor in

Provençal, praises the troubadour's vigorous personality. In "Pound and Milton" (*Paideuma* 14:341–45) G. Singh argues none too persuasively that "the ethos and essence of [Pound's] thinking is basically akin to Milton's."

Pound's 19th-century affiliations are the subject of several studies. The source of his favorite quotation from Turgenev is identified by H. Hauge in " 'Nothing but Death Is Irrevocable': A Note on Pound's and Eliot's Use of Turgenev" (*Paideuma* 14:347–50). A perceptive account of Pound's responses to Walt Whitman appears in Stephen Tapscott's *American Beauty: William Carlos Williams and the Modernist Whitman* (Columbia, 1984). In "Browning's *Sordello* and the Parables of Modernist Poetics" (*ELH* 52:965–92) Christine Froula argues that "Pound devised in his ideogrammic method a poetics of fragments, gaps, and holes not unlike that of *Sordello*." According to Jonathan Ward in "Pound's Browning and the Issue of 'Historical Sense' " (*BSNotes* 15:10–28), *Sordello* confronted Pound with the central questions of "the nineteenth-century historiographical tradition." That Pound was influenced more by Robert Bridges than by Gerard Manley Hopkins is the argument of my "Pound, Bridges, and Hopkins" in *Hopkins among the Poets: Studies in Modern Responses to Gerard Manley Hopkins*, ed. Richard F. Giles (Hamilton, Ont.: International Hopkins Assn.). Pound's 1922 scrap with George Bernard Shaw over Joyce's *Ulysses* is documented in four of Shaw's *Collected Letters, Volume 3: 1911–1925*, ed. Dan H. Laurence (Max Reinhardt).

Five essays treat Pound's friendship with William Butler Yeats. In "The Order of the Brothers Minor: Pound and Yeats at Stone Cottage 1913–1916" (*Paideuma* 14:395–403) James Longenbach identifies several ways in which Yeats's esoteric interests influenced the work Pound was doing at the time. Colin McDowell and Timothy Materer argue in "Gyre and Vortex: W. B. Yeats and Ezra Pound" (*TCL* 31:343–67) that "both poets were in fact deeply committed to occult studies" and to the use of "esoteric images." In "Pound, Yeats, and the Noh Theater" (*IowaR* 15,ii:34–50) Daniel Albright argues that the two poets saw in the Noh a "Hiberno-Japanese hybrid drama . . . at once extremely physical and extremely disembodied." Balachandra Rajan contrasts Pound's sense of the poetic fragment to that of Yeats in "Its Own Executioner: Yeats and the Fragment" (*Yeats* 3:72–87). Finally, Russell J. Reising's "Yeats, the Rhymers' Club, and

Pound's *Hugh Selwyn Mauberley*" (JML 12:179–82) argues that
"'Siena mi fe'; Disfecemi Maremma'" is indebted to a reading and a
lecture on the Rhymers that Yeats gave in 1910.

A. Walton Litz's "Lawrence, Pound, and Early Modernism" in
D. H. Lawrence: A Centenary Consideration, ed. Peter Balbert and
Phillip L. Marcus (Cornell), argues that the "deep divisions in per-
sonality and artistic ideals" between the two writers "symbolize the
most fundamental divisions in modernist literature." Hilda Doolittle's
personal and literary relationship with Pound figures in a number of
the studies recently devoted to her. Janice S. Robinson's *H. D.: The
Life and Work of an American Poet* (Houghton Mifflin, 1982) and
Barbara Guest's *Herself Defined: The Poet H. D. and Her World*
(Doubleday, 1984) have much to say about Pound, as does Michael
King's "Williams, Pound, H. D.: A Modern Triangle" in *WCW &
Others*, ed. Dave Oliphant and Thomas Zigal (Hum. Res. Center). In
"H. D. and the Origins of Imagism" (*Sagetrieb* 4:73–97) Cyrena N.
Pondrom offers a revisionist history of Imagism and Vorticism, argu-
ing that H. D. was "the catalyst and her poems the model" for both
movements.

Evidence of Robert Duncan's admiration for both H. D. and E. P.
abounds in the Duncan Special Issue of *Sagetrieb* (4:ii–iii). Duncan's
reflections on Pound highlight an excerpt "From the *H. D. Book*, Part
II, Chapter 5" (pp. 39–85) and an "Interview with Robert Duncan"
by Michael André Bernstein and Burton Hatlen (pp. 87–135). In
"Robert Duncan: Talent and the Individual Tradition" (pp. 177–90)
Bernstein compares and contrasts Duncan's poetics with those of
Pound. R. S. Hamilton's "After Strange Gods: Robert Duncan Reading Ezra Pound and H. D." (pp. 225–40) shows how Duncan confirms his own visionary-erotic poetics by singling out similar elements
in Pound's early criticism and late cantos.

Two other contemporary poets acknowledge their indebtedness
to Pound: Charles Wright in "Improvisations on Pound" (*Field*
33:63–70) and "W. S. Merwin on Ezra Pound," ed. Ed Folsom (*IowaR*
15,ii:70–73). Lois Oppenheim's "The Field of Poetic Constitution"
in *The Existential Co-ordinates of the Human Condition*, ed. Anna-
Teresa Tymieniecka (Dordrecht: D. Riedel, 1984), finds a "profound
similarity" between the "esthetic viewpoints" of Pound and French
poet-critic Jacques Garelli. And György Novak's "'Before November
One': Ezra Pound and Tibor Serly" in *Papers in English and American
Studies, Volume 2*, ed. Bálint Rozsnyai and Tibor Fabiny (Szeged,

Hungary: Attila József Univ., 1982, pp. 195–225), offers an interesting account of Pound's collaboration with an important Hungarian composer and conductor.

d. The Shorter Poems. Ten essays are devoted to the shorter poems. Despite its grandiose title, Donald Justice's "The Invention of Free Verse" (*IowaR* 15,ii:8–11) is little more than an appreciation of the metrics of "Cino." Analyses of "The Garden" appear in both "Young Ezra" by William Matthews and "Pound's Garden" by Stanley Plumly (*Field* 33:15–18,19–22). In "Another Note on Ezra Pound's 'Papyrus'" (*Paideuma* 14:103–04) Franz Link concludes that "as a translation and emendation the poem remains a doubtful achievement." Also critical of the literal accuracy of Pound's "devious" translations is Gyung-Ryul Jang in "*Cathay* Reconsidered: Pound as Inventor of Chinese Poetry" (*Paideuma* 14:351–62). In "The Scholar's Attic" (*LCUT* 23[1983]:51–61) Hugh Kenner makes more than he should of the fact that an early draft of "I Vecchii" appears in Pound's copy of *Cathay*.

Propertius meets Bakhtin in Stan Smith's lively essay, "Neither Calliope nor Apollo: Pound's Propertius and the Refusal of Epic" (*English* 34:212–31). Applying Bakhtin's distinction between epic and dialogical modes, Smith argues that the "subversive polyphony" of Pound's *Homage* challenges "the hegemonic discourse of an imperial and patriarchal culture." In "Rambling around Pound's Propertius" (*Field* 33:26–36) James Laughlin senses Pound's "growing dislike of the banking system" behind the mistranslation "Welsh mines and the profit Marus had out of them." And Daniel M. Hooley's "Pound's Propertius, Again" (*MLN* 100:1025–45) seeks to articulate Pound's underlying assumptions about translation.

In "Pound and Mauberley: The Eroding Difference" (*PLL* 21:43–63) Robert Casillo finds in *Hugh Selwyn Mauberley* an overriding phallocentric fear of the vagina dentata ("the *chopped* seas held him") and castration. Especially significant is the fact that the poem ends with the letter *z*, "the castrating letter." This is unquestionably one of the two silliest essays on Pound to appear in the centenary year.

e. The Cantos. Two competent introductions to *The Cantos* appear this year. William Cookson's *A Guide to the Cantos of Ezra Pound* (Persea) comments on the themes and sources of each canto and selectively glosses names, allusions, and foreign language phrases. Before quoting from the *Guide*, scholars should consult the comparable glosses in C. F. Terrell's *A Companion to the Cantos of Ezra Pound* (2 vols., Calif., 1980–84). The latter is more comprehensive and in some instances more authoritative. *Pound's Cantos* by Peter Makin (Allen & Unwin) is a thorough, informed, and sympathetic primer that ranks among the best books on Pound of its kind.

The perennial question of "'Major Form' in Pound's *Cantos*" is raised by the late Ben D. Kimpel and T. C. Duncan Eaves (*IowaR* 15,ii:51–66). Kimpel and Eaves deny that the poem has any "causal sequence," progression, or "structure in the usual sense." In "The Design of the *Cantos*: An Introduction" (*IowaR* 15,ii:12–33) Richard Sieburth argues that the poem abolishes "previous distinctions between lyric and epic, poetry and history, literature and non-literature," and is best defined as "a protracted Action Poem." Implicitly disagreeing with Kimpel, Eaves, and Sieburth, David Gordon in "*The Great Digest*: A Pattern" (*Paideuma* 14:253–57) maintains that the "structural plan" of the poem derives from "the ten gradations of order in *The Great Digest*" of Confucius.

In "Ezra Pound's Tigullio" (*Paideuma* 14:179–209) Massimo Bacigalupo traces the various appearances in the poem of Rapallo, its environs, and its inhabitants. Andrew J. Kappel's "Ezra Pound and the Myth of Venice" (*ClioI* 13[1984]:203–25) argues that Venice was always for Pound a "civilization that maximizes freedom and order." In "The Literal Image: Illustrations in *The Cantos*" (*Paideuma* 14:227–51) John Cayley urges us to see the Chinese ideograms as "purely visual signifiers," used by Pound "without reference to a linguistic sense—etymological, lexical, or contextual." Greg Larkin takes a more conventional approach to the subject in "From Noman to Everyman: Chinese Characters in the *Pisan Cantos*" (*TkR* 11[1981]:307–15).

In the Pound chapter of *The Form of the Unfinished* Balachandra Rajan reads *The Cantos* as an unresolved dialectic between logocentricity and indeterminacy, closure and openness, holistic objective and fragmentary method. Philip Kuberski privileges Rajan's second set of terms in "Ego, Scriptor: Pound's Odyssean Writing" (*Paideuma* 14:31–51), aligning the poem fully with "a post-modernist poetic of the open or indeterminate work." In "A Note on the Ell-Square Pitkin" in Canto 1 (*Paideuma* 14:363) Michael Fournier attributes a monetary significance to the image because "L is also the shape of the British pound sign." This is the other truly silly item on Pound published in 1985.

In "Ezra Pound and the Japanese Cosmogony" (*Paideuma* 14: 259–72) Michele F. Cooper relates a line in Canto 2, "So-shu churned in the sea," to a Japanese creation-myth about a brother and sister who stir the sea with a jeweled spear to form an island. Cantos 2 and 31–41 figure in the wandering, vaguely Freudian argument of David Trotter's *The Making of the Reader: Language and Subjectivity in Modern American, English, and Irish Poetry* (St. Martin's, 1984). Norman Dubie, in "Some Notes: Into the Sere and Yellow" (*Field* 33: 39–45), attempts to establish a specific geographical and historical setting for the bucolic Chinese landscape of Canto 49.

Three essays consider aspects of the *Pisan Cantos*. In "Not of One Bird but of Many: Pound's Janequin" (*Paideuma* 14:211–25) Walter Baumann questions Pound's onomatopoetic interpretation of Jane-quin's "Canzone degli Uccelli." In " 'Atasal' in Canto LXXVI and Ernest Renan on Sufi Mysticism" (*Paideuma* 14:327–29) Matthew Little traces Pound's use of an Arabic term to Renan's *Averroës et l'averroisme* (1852), where it denotes a union with God achieved by unnatural means. In "Alba LXXIX" (*Field* 33:55–59) Carol Muske argues that the woman celebrated in the aubade of Canto 79 is not H. D. but an idealized "Provençal Lady."

In his examination of "History as Metaphor and Metonym: The Frame of Reference in Pound's 'Canto 85' " (*TkR* 14[1983–84]: 173–97) Frank Stevenson finds similar "patterns of historical transcendence and return" in the Chinese and Western materials of the first *Rock-Drill* canto. Two other essays examine Pound's credulous use in Cantos 94 and 97 of the pseudohistorical works of L. A. Waddell. Richard Sawyer's " 'To Know the Histories': L. A. Waddell's Sumer and Akkad" (*Paideuma* 14:79–94) explains Waddell's bizarre pan-Sumerian thesis and its relevance to "the thematic structure of the later cantos." Robert Casillo's "Ezra Pound, L. A. Waddell, and the Aryan Tradition of *The Cantos*" (*MLS* 15:65–81) argues that Pound saw in Waddell's books a "racial interpretation of history" justifying the myth of Aryan supremacy.

Finally, three articles treat very late cantos. In "A Note on 'Crusaders' Bows' " (*Paideuma* 14:105–08) David Gordon explicates a phrase in Canto 99. Peter Stoicheff examines "Pound's Final Personae in *Drafts and Fragments*" (*Paideuma* 14:273–302), distinguishing five different speakers. In " 'To "See Again," ' or the Dangers of

Unlimited Reference"(*Paideuma* 14:109–14) Massimo Bacigalupo corrects Walter Baumann's reading of a line in Canto 116.

As we move toward the second centenary of the poet's birth, the words of Donald Davie in "Pound's Friends" (*London Rev. of Books* 7, 23 May: 19–20) remind us why it is worthwhile to work on *The Cantos*. "Anyone," says Davie, "may be excused for deciding that life is too short for coming to terms with *The Cantos*; but if we make that decision we thereby disqualify ourselves from having any opinion worth listening to, about poetry in English of this century."

ii. Eliot

Although Eliot's centenary will not be celebrated until 1988, recent studies of his work rival in number the books and essays devoted to Pound. Special Eliot issues of *Agenda* and *Southern Review* contain important new material, but the palm for imaginative interpretation goes to David Lodge's delightful novel, *Small World: An Academic Romance* (Secker & Warburg, 1984). This scintillating work of criticism in new composition renews the archetypes of *The Waste Land*.

a. **Text and Biography.** Actual or reconstructed texts of three Eliot lectures are published for the first time. "Tradition and the Practice of Poetry," ed. A. Walton Litz (*SoR* 21:873–88), is a 1936 Dublin address that considers the question of literary nationality and marks an important stage in Eliot's rapprochement with Yeats. A 1944 London talk on "Walt Whitman and Modern Poetry" is reconstructed from notes taken by Donald Gallup, who attended "Mr. Eliot at the Churchill Club" (*SoR* 21:969–73). In a 1952 lecture given in Nice, Eliot uses the archetypal myth of "Scylla and Charybdis" (*Agenda* 23,i–ii:5–21) to describe the poet's struggle with contending forces of language, form, and mode.

The logistical and formal problems of Eliot biography are discussed by one of its ablest practitioners, Lyndall Gordon, in *The Craft of Literary Biography*, ed. Jeffrey Meyers (Macmillan). In "T. S. Eliot and Emily Hale: Some Fresh Evidence" (*ES* 66:432–36) William Baker scrutinizes the personal inscriptions in the books Eliot gave to Miss Hale between 1927 and 1959.

To Roger Sharrock in "Our Health Is the Disease, or the One and the Many" (*Agenda* 23,i–ii:97–102) it seems that biography possesses "the now dominant appeal" in Eliot studies. Certainly many of this year's memoirs respond to the instigations of Michael Hastings' *Tom and Viv* and Peter Ackroyd's *T. S. Eliot* (see *ALS 1984*, p. 144). In "T. S. Eliot: An Expostulation by Way of a Memoir" (*Agenda* 23,i–ii:137–55) E. W. F. Tomlin argues that Eliot had a "balanced and stable character" and "would have made a good town-councillor." In "T. S. Eliot—Man and Poet" (*Agenda* 23,i–ii:156–70) Joseph Chiari adds little to the adulatory portrait in his *T. S. Eliot: A Memoir* (London: Enitharmon Press, 1982).

Several other memoirs stress Eliot's reserve and role-playing. Brand Blanshard recalls the "laconic remarks" and "Mona Lisa smiles" of "Eliot at Oxford" (*SoR* 21:889–98) in 1914–15. In *Recollections: Mainly of Artists and Writers* (Chatto and Windus, 1984) Geoffrey Grigson describes a meeting with Eliot at Alice Harbert's. Dame Rebecca West thought Eliot "was a poseur," but the "element of acting" in his behavior did not bother Stephen Spender; their recollections appear in *Writers at Work: The* Paris Review *Interviews: Sixth Series*, ed. George Plimpton (Secker & Warburg).

Elsewhere, William Empson's reminiscences of Eliot are reprinted in *Using Biography* (Chatto and Windus, 1984). Austin Warren offers "A Survivor's Tribute to T. S. Eliot" (*SoR* 21:1110–17), recalling their London encounters of 1930. "Time in Sever Hall and in the *Quartets*" by Wallace Fowlie (*SoR* 21:957–66) combines recollections of Eliot at Harvard in 1931–32 with a meditation on the theme of time in *Four Quartets*. "Old Possum at Possum House" by Harry Levin (*SoR* 21:1008–11) also recalls the Harvard visit, while "Tom Possum and the Roberts Family" by Janet Adam Smith (*SoR* 21:1057–70) describes Eliot's kindness to her and her children during the 1940s. Peter du Sautoy, Eliot's coworker at Faber and Faber from 1946 to 1965, contributes two disappointingly uninformative memoirs, "T. S. Eliot and Publishing" (*Agenda* 23,i–ii:171–76) and "T. S. Eliot: Personal Reminiscences" (*SoR* 21:947–56).

Christopher Fry's "Recollections of T. S. Eliot" (*SoR* 21:967–68) document Eliot's encouragement of a talented young playwright around 1939–40, while "Eliot in the Theatre" (*SoR* 21:985–86) is the memoir of Sir Alec Guinness, who played Henry Harcourt-Reilly in the original 1949 production of *The Cocktail Party*. In *Customs and Characters: Contemporary Portraits* (Weidenfeld and Nicolson, 1982) Peter Quennell recalls Eliot and John Hayward at Carlyle Mansions in the 1950s. In "A Photographic Memoir, with a Note by James Olney" (*SoR* 21:987–98) Valerie Eliot prints 11 snapshots of her husband taken between 1958 and 1960. Finally, "To Valerie Eliot, a Letter" (*SoR* 21:999) prints the letter of condolence that Robert Lowell sent to Mrs. Eliot in April 1965.

b. **General Studies.**   Also resembling an album of snapshots is Burton Raffel's *Possum and Ole Ez in the Public Eye: Contemporaries and Peers on T. S. Eliot and Ezra Pound, 1892–1972* (Archon). Among these interestingly juxtaposed snippets from letters, diaries, reviews, and the like, Virginia Woolf's remarks on Eliot stand out for their insight.

The year's most impressive new studies of Eliot view his writing in the context of Continental philosophy. In *T. S. Eliot and Hermeneutics: Absence and Interpretation in* The Waste Land (LSU) Harriet Davidson relates Eliot's preconversion poetry and prose to "the hermeneutic existentialism of Heidegger." Eliot's 1916 dissertation on F. H. Bradley, as Davidson reads it, shows the pupil distancing himself from the master and becoming a "good phenomenologist." In "Eliot, Narrative, and the Time of the World" (*NER* 8:98–108) Davidson analyzes Eliot's "use of narrative" in similar terms. For James Longenbach in "Guarding the Horned Gates: History and Interpretation in the Early Poetry of T. S. Eliot" (*ELH* 52:503–27), the existential historicism of Wilhelm Dilthey best clarifies the "interpretive strategies" of Eliot's early work. In *The Matrix of Modernism: Pound, Eliot and Early Twentieth-Century Thought* (Princeton) Sanford Schwartz, like Davidson, revalues the Bradley dissertation, stressing its connections with Meinong and Husserl. Schwartz also clarifies Eliot's affinities with Bergson, William James, and Nietzsche.

Three other general studies of Eliot's modernism are less compelling than those just mentioned. In *Mapping Literary Modernism: Time and Development* (Princeton) Ricardo J. Quinones argues that Eliot rejects the Renaissance-bourgeois conception of time as linear, predictive, and ethical in favor of an archaic-mythological conception of time as discontinuous, innovative, and spiritual. No less given to sweeping generalization is George Watson in his redundantly titled essay, "The Phantom Ghost of Modernism" (*ASch* 54:253–68). Eliot's work also figures in the elusive, vaguely Freudian argument of David Trotter's *The Making of the Reader: Language and Subjectivity in Modern American, English, and Irish Poetry* (St. Martin's, 1984).

The nature of Eliot's poetic language is the main focus of four studies. In *The Form of the Unfinished* Balachandra Rajan reads the "macro-poem" of Eliot's oeuvre in terms of a dialectic between logo-centricity and indeterminacy, design and accident, closure and aper-ture. What Rajan calls Eliot's "language of loss" is also the subject of Heather McClave's "Tongued with Fire: The Primitive Terror and the Word in T. S. Eliot" in *Ineffability: Naming the Unnamable from Dante to Beckett*, ed. Peter S. Hawkins and Anne Howland Schotter (AMS Press, 1984). Likewise concerned with the problem of significa-tion is Alan Weinblatt in "T. S. Eliot: Poet of Adequation" (*SoR* 21: 1118–37). This essay comes from the book Weinblatt published last year (see *ALS 1984*, p. 146). In "Intertextual Eliot" (*SoR* 21:1094–1109) Leonard Unger cites Eliot's poetic use of "the lexicon of journalism" as an example of "non-specific" intertextuality.

According to Ronald Schuchard in "Eliot and the Horrific Mo-ment" (*SoR* 21:1045–56), Eliot practices a poetics not just of loss but of horror. In "The Man and the Mind" (*Agenda* 23,i–ii:82–86) F. T. Prince likewise argues that "the power and fascination of [Eliot's] poetry lie in its use of a subdued rational manner of speaking to deal with the violent irrational forces of human experience." In "Three Readings of T. S. Eliot: Clio, Melpomene, Euterpe" (*Agenda* 23,i–ii: 72–81) Derek Stanford and Julie Whitby offer "a *theory of tempera-ment*" that does not explain anything in particular.

The pursuit of religious understanding led Eliot to explore what Jewel Spears Brooker calls "Substitutes for Christianity in the Poetry of T. S. Eliot" (*SoR* 21:899–913). The "substitute" of Indian philos-ophy is examined in three important essays by Jeffrey M. Perl and Andrew Tuck. In "The Hidden Advantage of Tradition: On the Significance of T. S. Eliot's Indic Studies" (*PE&W* 35,ii:115–32) Perl and Tuck quote abundantly from Eliot's unpublished graduate school notebooks and essays written for his courses in Sanskrit and Oriental philosophy. In "Foreign Metaphysics: The Significance of T. S. Eliot's Philosophical Notebooks" and in "The Language of Theory and the Language of Poetry" (*SoR* 21:79–88,1012–23) Perl and Tuck explain that Eliot preferred Buddhist to Western philosophy because of its "soteriological purpose" and its relativistic, contextual view of truth.

As a rule, studies of Eliot and Indian thought make similar argu-ments without mentioning one another. A partial exception to this rule is *T. S. Eliot, Vedanta, and Buddhism* by P. S. Sri (Vancouver: Univ. of British Columbia Press). In this lively study of "Eliot's overt and covert use of Indian philosophical themes and symbols" Sri cites some of his predecessors and writes better English than most. In

138 Pound and Eliot

Imagery in T. S. Eliot's Poetry (New Delhi: Vikas Pub. House, 1984),
S. B. Srivastava relates Eliot's Dantesque imagery to Hindu and Buddhist mysticism. In *Time and T. S. Eliot: His Poetry, Plays, and Philosophy* (New York: Apt Books) Jitendra Kumar Sharma links Eliot's
conception of time to both Indian philosophy and Western phenom-
enology. In *Yeats and Eliot: Perspectives on India* (New Delhi: Associated Pub. House, 1983) Ramesh Chandra Shah credits Eliot for
his "receptivity and sensitivity to the Indian mechanism of sensibility," but suggests that Yeats experienced "ascent on the metaphysical plane" more fully than Eliot.

Descending from the metaphysical plane, we encounter the earthy
humor of Roy Fuller's "*L'Oncle Tom*: Some Notes and Queries"
(*Agenda* 23,i–ii:41–52), an irreverent parody of picayune scholarship.
Parodies of Eliot himself by F. Giles, John Heath-Stubbs, Peter Dale,
and W. S. Milne appear in *Agenda* (23, i–ii:180–84), while Victor
Purcell's *The Sweeniad* (1957) is republished under the title "*How
Unpleasant to Meet Mr. Eliot*," ed. Sheila Sullivan (Allen & Unwin).

c. Relation to Other Writers. Gareth Reeves discusses the relations
among "T. S. Eliot, Virgil, and Theodor Haecker: Empire and the
Agrarian Ideal" (*Agenda* 23,iii–iv:180–201). Reeves proves that
Eliot's thinking about Virgil's proto-Christian classicism and about
"the agrarian hierarchy of empire" owes a great deal to Haecker's
Virgil, Father of the West, trans. A. W. Wheen (1934). In his essay
on "T. S. Eliot's Metaphysical Dante" in *Dante among the Moderns*
(No. Car.) Stuart Y. McDougal identifies many direct verbal echoes
of Dante in Eliot's published and unpublished work. This essay is
more informative than Ronald Gaskell's meandering and impressionistic "Eliot and Dante" (*Agenda* 23,iii–iv:167–79).

According to Patricia Clements in *Baudelaire and the English
Tradition: Canonization of the Subversive* (Princeton), Eliot's Baudelaire is a deformed Dante, "newly canonized" and assimilated to
"the orthodoxies of classicism, conservatism and Catholicism." Both
Dante and Baudelaire come to Eliot through "The City of Dreadful
Night" (1874), Robert Crawford argues in a well-researched essay
on "James Thomson and T. S. Eliot" (*VP* 23:23–42). Eliot's resistance
to the work of another Victorian predecessor is the subject of Ronald
Bush's "Eliot and Hopkins: Through a Glass Darkly" in *Hopkins
among the Poets*.

Six studies link Eliot with more recent British and Irish authors.

The ninth chapter of *Joseph Conrad and American Writers: A Biblio-graphic Study of Affinities, Influences, and Relations* by Robert Secor and Debra Moddelmog (Greenwood) contains evaluative checklists of Eliot's published remarks about Conrad and of critical studies of Conrad's influence upon the poet. Eliot serves as an important point of reference in two discussions of Yeats, Balachandra Rajan's "Its Own Executioner: Yeats and the Fragment" and M. J. Sidnell's " 'Tara Uprooted': Yeats's *In the Seven Woods* in Relation to Modernism" (*Yeats* 3:72–87, 107–20). Furthermore, Vinod Sena argues in "T. S. Eliot, W. B. Yeats, and Tradition" (*Journal of Literary Criticism* [Delhi, India] 1[1984]:57–62) that Yeats's view of the "relationship between tradition and personality" is "more complete and profound" than Eliot's. In "Forster, Eliot, and the Literary Life" (*TCL* 31:170–75) P. N. Furbank outlines the "tenuous, but actually rather friendly, relationship" between the two men of letters. Finally, Keith Douglas' brief and somewhat abortive contacts with Eliot in 1940–41 are documented in *Keith Douglas: A Prose Miscellany*, ed. Desmond Graham (Carcanet).

Three essays discuss Eliot's connections with modern Hispanic writers. In "Luis Cernuda, Edward Wilson y T. S. Eliot" (*Insula* 432 [1982]:1,10) Rafael Martínez Nadal publishes some of a three-way correspondence in which Wilson tried in 1946–47 to interest Eliot in Cernuda's Spanish translation of Shakespeare's *Troilus and Cressida*. "T. S. Eliot en Cernuda" by Fernando Ortiz (*CHA* 416:95–104) is a more general consideration of "las afinidades entre los dos poetas." K. M. Sibbald's "Jorge Guillén y T. S. Eliot: una coincidencia de cosmovisión" (*SinN* 14[1984],iv:72–84) compares the careers and attitudes of the two poets, calling special attention to their views of the leisured class.

In "Nathaniel Hawthorne and T. S. Eliot's American Connection" (*SoR* 21:924–33) Ronald Bush returns us to Eliot's Yankee heritage. Both writers saw themselves, Bush argues, as observer-aliens, cold and incapable of love but clairvoyant in their grasp of "the secret heart of humanity." Such detachment little suited the taste of Harriet Monroe, who thought it "hopeless to expect an all-round great poem of our time from a man who could not thrill" to the idea of meeting Thomas Edison, as Ann Massa reminds us in "Harriet Monroe and T. S. Eliot: A Curious and Typical Response" (*N&Q* 32:380–82). In "Eliot's Joke" (*Agenda* 23,iii–iv:215–17) Ian F. A. Bell associates Eliot's 1918 proposal of *A Guide to Useless Books* with Pound's 1913 proposal of a "table of opinions" that would expedite the assignment of clichés in book reviews.

Three recent studies assess William Faulkner's borrowings from Eliot. In *The Origins of Faulkner's Art* (Texas, 1984) Judith L. Sensibar traces the influence of "The Love Song of J. Alfred Prufrock" upon Faulkner's early poem *Visions in Spring* and upon *Light in August*. Listening closely to verbal patterns, Masaji Onoe also identifies "Some T. S. Eliot Echoes in Faulkner" in *Faulkner Studies in Japan*, ed. Thomas L. McHaney (Georgia). But there are limits to Eliot's influence, Susie Paul Johnson argues in "*Pylon*: Faulkner's Waste Land" (*MissQ* 38:287–94). The townscape of *Pylon* derives not from Eliot's poem but from Faulkner's direct experience of New Orleans.

In a "Symposium of Poets on T. S. Eliot" (*SoR* 21:1138–63) nine Americans talk about their first encounters with his poetry and about how they see him today. The poets include Stephen Berg, Louise Glück, Donald Hall, Anthony Hecht, Howard Moss, Lisel Mueller, Carol Muske, Robert Pinsky, and Theodore Weiss.

For an offbeat essay on Eliot's literary affinities, one could hardly do better than Wylie Sypher's "Mrs. Post, May I Present Mr. Eliot" (*ASch* 54:250–52). Sypher solemnly elaborates the similarities between *The Waste Land* and *Emily Post's Etiquette*, both published in 1922.

d. The Poems. In "Adolescents Singing Each to Each—When We and Eliot Were Young" (*NYTBR* Oct. 20:3,37) M. L. Rosenthal identifies "the adolescent keys" in Eliot's early work that appealed to readers growing up in the 1930s. Rosenthal might well agree with Hirofumi Iwamatsu's assertion, in "Eliot's Americanism" (*KAL* 25 [1984]:25–33), that Eliot remained "fundamentally an American . . . in his emotional aspect."

In a 1932 essay reprinted this year as "Mr. T. S. Eliot" (*Agenda* 23,i–ii:185–90) Basil Bunting writes well about "the hypnotics of verse" in Eliot's early work. One source of these "hypnotics" may be the type of metaphor analyzed in Midori Matsui's "The Tactics of Difference: Notes toward the Definition of T. S. Eliot's Intentional Metaphor" (*SELit* 61[1984]:269–86). Eliot's modernist metaphors "denigrate natural authority," according to Matsui, by creating surreal or hallucinatory discrepancies between vehicle and tenor. Matsui's incisive discussion is more illuminating than I. E. Glenn's paraphrase of themes in "The Making of the Artist: T. S. Eliot's Early Poetry" (*Standpunte* 37 [1984]:19–33).

Two discussions of "The Love Song of J. Alfred Prufrock" say little that is new. Frederik L. Rusch's essay, "Approaching Literature through the Social Psychology of Erich Fromm" in *Psychological Perspectives on Literature*, ed. Joseph Natoli (Archon, 1984), concludes that Prufrock is "a modern, mass man" who is "bored by his modern, urban society." Stanley Sultan's "Tradition and the Individual Talent in 'Prufrock'" (*JML* 12:77–90) is a tired survey of the poem's sources and affinities.

In "Eliot Misquotes Marlowe: The Ironist Perspective in 'Portrait of a Lady'" (*UWR* 18[1984]:91–94) Eugene McNamara notes that the epigraph of "Portrait of a Lady" collapses two speeches in *The Jew of Malta* into what looks like a monologue. "The Figure of St. Sebastian" by Harvey Gross (*SoR* 21:974–84) identifies both pictorial and theatrical sources for "The Love Song of St. Sebastian" and offers a psychoanalytic reading of homoerotic and sadomasochistic elements. In an essay "On 'Gerontion'" (*SoR* 21:934–46) Denis Donoghue reads the poem as a satire of the "vaunting eloquence" of Edward FitzGerald, Henry Adams, and W. B. Yeats.

Seven studies examine *The Waste Land*. In *Literature of Crisis, 1910–1922* (St. Martin's, 1984) Anne Wright argues that the poem "presents crisis as a continuous present" in both the historical and the grammatical senses of the term. "The Poetic Space of *The Waste Land*" by Robert Franciosi (*AmerP* 2,ii:17–29) is a phenomenological reading indebted to Gaston Bachelard. Max Nänny's "The Waste Land: A Menippean Satire" (*ES* 66:526–35) is a beefed-up version of a previously published Bakhtinian reading of the poem (see *ALS 1983*, pp. 145–46). Thomas E. Helm's "Hermeneutics of Time in T. S. Eliot's *The Waste Land*" (*Jour. of Religion* 65:208–24) presents an Eliot confident of the power of "interpretative retrieval" to recover "the creative word" from buried texts and traditions. In "'Broken Images': Discursive Fragmentation and the Paradigmatic Integrity in the Poetry of T. S. Eliot" (*PoT* 6:399–416) Anthony L. Johnson describes the "paradigmatic dynamics" by which Eliot's reader reconstructs meaning from a text perforated by syntagmatic gaps. But in "A Handful of Words: The Credibility of Language in *The Waste Land*" (*TSLL* 27:154–77) Jonathan Bishop presents an Eliot who calls into doubt "the credibility of discourse" and the adequacy "of all personal centers, psychic or linguistic." Bishop would have little use for the naively referential argument of Allen Walker Read's "The Onomastic Component of T. S. Eliot's *The Waste Land*" (*LOS* 10 [1983]:177–200).

Possible sources of *The Waste Land* and other poems are canvassed by John Heath-Stubbs in "Structure and Source in Eliot's Major Poetry" (*Agenda* 23,i–ii:22–35). "Ash-Wednesday" by Kathleen Raine (*Agenda* 23,i–ii:59–65) finds in Eliot's Lady "the archetype of all that woman signifies of love, consolation, intercession, compassion, protection" and the antithesis of "the liberated woman and the unisex girl in blue jeans." Linda Leavell makes large claims for "Eliot's Ritual Method: *Ash Wednesday*" (*SoR* 21:1000–1007), but she fails to support them with precise definitions and illustrations.

Recent studies of Eliot's last major poem include John E. Booty's *Meditating on* Four Quartets (Cambridge, Mass.: Cowley Pubns., 1983). This Christian commentary is clear, informed, and thankful for "the wealth of inspiration these poems contain." Equally reverential but less substantive are Heather Buck's "T. S. Eliot: A Cable for Posterity" and Alan Massey's "*The Four Quartets*: Eliot's Masterpiece" (*Agenda* 23, i–ii:53–58, 66–71). For trite paraphrase, Douglas Lecroy's "Reality and Art in T. S. Eliot's 'The Four Quartets' " (*SLRJ* 14[1983]: 455–68) is unexcelled.

Two critics who dislike *Four Quartets* are C. H. Sisson in "T. S. Eliot" (*Agenda* 23,i–ii:36–40) and M. L. Rosenthal in "Psychological Pressure in *Four Quartets*" (*SoR* 21:1033–44). Sisson compares the later Eliot to the later Wordsworth, while Rosenthal finds in the sequence too much "guru-wisdom, quietistic religious intonation, and sheer rhetoric." But William M. Burke in "Faith and T. S. Eliot's 'Dry Salvages' " (*Thought* 60:49–57) praises the poem's affirmation of "faith as *fides*, trust, confidence in the purpose of the created universe." In "Eliot's Sestina in 'The Dry Salvages' " (*CollL* 12:277–81) Tahita Fulkerson argues that the modified sestina form in Part II mimes its thematic content. "Prose Rhythm and Oral Tradition" by Peter Dale (*Agenda* 23,i–ii:87–92) analyzes the prosody of a passage in "Little Gidding." Finally, Bernard Sharratt's Marxist revisions of the first two quartets appear in *The Literary Labyrinth: Contemporary Critical Discourses* (Harvester, 1984) as "Learnt Torsions" and "Least Workers."

According to Paul Douglass in "Eliot's Cats: Serious Play behind the Playful Seriousness" (*ChildL* 11[1983]:109–24), the poems in *Old*

Possum's Book have no didactic design, moral or theological, upon us. They are nevertheless serious, as a child is about its play.

e. The Plays.   Eliot's plays attract more attention than usual this year. In " 'Wanna Go Home, Baby?': 'Sweeney Agonistes' " (*Agenda* 23,i–ii:103–10) Jonathan Barker relates the fragmentary drama to *The Waste Land* and "The Hollow Men." Carol H. Smith and Nancy D. Hargrove prefer to view Sweeney as the agonized, guilty forerunner of Eliot's later dramatic protagonists. Smith's "Sweeney and the Jazz Age," Hargrove's "The Symbolism of Sweeney in the Works of T. S. Eliot," and Jonathan Morse's "Sweeney, the Sties of the Irish, and *The Waste Land*" are the only previously unpublished items in *Critical Essays on T. S. Eliot: The Sweeney Motif*, ed. Kinley E. Roby (Hall). Morse relates Sweeney to "the caricature Irishman of the nineteenth century" depicted in the cartoons of Thomas Nast.

T. S. Eliot: Plays: A Selection of Critical Essays, ed. Arnold P. Hinchliffe (St. Martin's), contains excerpts from Eliot's own writings about drama together with 20 reviews and critical discussions of his plays. In "Nietzsche's Theory of Tragedy in the Plays of T. S. Eliot" (*TCL* 31:111–26) Linda Leavell argues that the dramas parallel *The Birth of Tragedy* in their "sense of musical design" and "extensive use of Apollonian and Dionysian themes."

Five recent studies examine *Murder in the Cathedral*. Clifford Davidson's "T. S. Eliot's *Murder in the Cathedral* and the Saint's Play Tradition" (*PLL* 21:152–69) articulates the affinities between Eliot's work and "the medieval drama of the saints." Similarly, Roland Bouyssou argues in "*Murder in the Cathedral*, liturgie de la Croix" (*Caliban* 21[1984]:29–42) that the story of Becket is a figural reenactment of the passion of Christ. Gerald B. Kinneavy's "Becket, the Chorus, and the Redemption of Waiting" (*LangQ* 22[1984],iii–iv:25–29) concentrates upon the birth of awareness within the chorus. According to Monique Lojkine-Morelec in "*Murder in the Cathedral* ou l'exorcisme du désir" (*EA* 37[1984]:41–53), the female chorus can achieve "la transmutation du désir en amour" only by accepting the humiliation of a figurative violation and death. The chorus consists entirely of women, Patricia Mosco Holloway explains in "T. S. Eliot's *Murder in the Cathedral*" (*Expl* 43,ii:35–36), because women, like martyrs, give birth to new life by undergoing a bloody ordeal.

The Cocktail Party is the subject of three studies. In " 'Nothing but Death Is Irrevocable': A Note on Pound's and Eliot's Use of

Turgenev" (*Paideuma* 14:347–50) H. Hauge identifies a source of the play in Turgenev's novel, *The House of Gentlefolks*. In "The Orchestration of Monologues: 'The Cocktail Party' and a Developing Genre" (*Agenda* 23,iii–iv:202–09) Stephen Wade fails to support his thesis that Eliot's use of the monologue represents "a new departure in the genre of the verse drama." And in *The Talking Cure: Literary Representations of Psychoanalysis* (NYU) Jeffrey Berman psychoanalyzes Edward, Celia, Sir Henry ("his choice of profession suggests counterphobic motivation") and Eliot himself ("narcissistic personality disturbances").

"In Argos or in England" by Jean MacVean (*Agenda* 23,i–ii:111–30) is a sympathetic and detailed reading of *The Family Reunion*. But the large claims made by Peter Levi for the poetry of "Eliot's Late Plays" (*Agenda* 23,i–ii:131–36) are not supported with specific illustrations.

f. **The Criticism.** Two useful surveys of unreprinted criticism appear in Robert Craft's *Present Perspectives: Critical Writings* (Knopf, 1984). Craft quotes abundantly from Eliot's periodical reviews of philosophy and prose fiction.

Edward Davenport argues in "Updating Wilhelm Dilthey: Values and Objectivity in Literary Criticism" (*Mosaic* 14[1981],iv:89–105) that Eliot wrongly believed in the possibility of "a value-free criticism." In "Eliot and the Concept of Literary Influence" (*SoR* 21:1071–93) Stanley Sultan attempts to mediate between Eliot's idea of influence and Harold Bloom's. Dismissing Bloom's theory, John Steven Childs in "Eliot, Tradition, and Textuality" (*TSLL* 27:311–23) reinterprets Eliot's idea of tradition in post-structuralist terms of intertextuality. J. P. Riquelme, in "The Modernist Essay: The Case of T. S. Eliot—Poet as Critic" (*SoR* 21:1024–32), reads "Tradition and the Individual Talent" as an example of Wildean "creative criticism."

The Eliot chapter of John Needham's *"The Completest Mode": I. A. Richards and the Continuity of English Literary Criticism* (Columbia, 1982) argues that Eliot's "criticism [has] always been impressionistic," supported by "very little analysis" and no consistent critical principles. In *Mirror Up to Shakespeare*, ed. J. C. Gray (Toronto, 1984), Kenneth Muir accuses "T. S. Eliot's Criticism of Elizabethan Drama" of being excessively literary and insufficiently theatrical. In *The Social Mission of English Criticism, 1848–1932* (Oxford, 1983)

Chris Baldick repeats the false Marxist charge that Eliot's criticism denies "the idea of history as a process." In "T. S. Eliot and the American South" (*SoR* 21:914–23) Cleanth Brooks tries to rehabilitate *After Strange Gods* and *Notes toward a Definition of Culture* by emphasizing their "concern for the older Southern culture" as "a tradition still alive and relatively coherent."

University of New Mexico

9. Faulkner

Karl F. Zender

Returning to writing this review after a two-year vacation has allowed me to approach the task with renewed enthusiasm; nevertheless I have decided (permanently, I believe) to relinquish responsibility for the chapter to someone else. Because of this circumstance, I had hoped to confront a body of work capable of sustaining a gesture—either elegiac or apocalyptic—of closure. Instead I am obliged to end my career with *ALS* by surveying yet another middling year, one displaying much valuable work and many good insights but no earthshaking revelations. Such it seems is life: our most frequent option is neither grief nor nothing but something somewhere in between.

i. Bibliography, Editions, and Manuscripts

The year saw two interrelated developments in the editing and publishing of Faulkner's novels. The first is the appearance of Noel Polk's *An Editorial Handbook for William Faulkner's "The Sound and the Fury"* (Garland), a detailed record of the editorial decisions Polk made in creating the copy-text for the edition of *The Sound and the Fury* published by Random House in 1984 (see *ALS 1984*, p. 157). The second is the publication of *William Faulkner: Novels, 1930–1935* (Library of America). This handsome volume, the first fruit of a landmark agreement with Random House that will lead to the publication of most (if not all) of Faulkner's fiction in the Library of America series, contains the four novels Faulkner wrote between *The Sound and the Fury* and *Absalom, Absalom!* It also contains back matter by Joseph Blotner and Noel Polk of a sort familiar to users of the series: an ample and accurate chronology of Faulkner's life, a note on the texts, and a set of highly selective but useful notes on the novels themselves. The volume reflects a major effort at reediting Faulkner's fiction undertaken by Polk, for, like the 1984 edition of *The Sound and the Fury,* the novels in this volume have been newly edited from Faulkner's manuscripts and typescripts. Evidently Random House intends to replace the current trade editions of these novels with the Polk texts and to have Polk reedit Faulkner's other novels as well. The additional new texts will then presumably be made available to the Library of America for use in their series.

It is fair to ask what assessment of this major editorial project the *Editorial Handbook* and the Library of America volume invite us to reach. The answer, for me at least, is cautiously affirmative. Certainly the sorry condition into which the Vintage edition of *The Sound and the Fury* has been allowed to fall makes Polk's reediting of this novel very welcome; and the *Editorial Handbook* shows convincingly that each of the ways in which the new edition deviates from the 1929 Cape and Smith first edition is the result of a carefully considered and defensible editorial decision. Similarly the changes made in the texts of the novels in the Library of America volume reflect a careful application of the editorial principles stated in the note on the texts (and in more elaborate form in the introduction to the *Editorial Handbook*). Finally, with the exception noted below, the editorial principles themselves seem prudent and reasonable.

Against these reassuring observations, though, should be weighed three reservations. The first is a version of the criticism leveled at the Pennsylvania Edition of *Sister Carrie* by Donald Pizer—that the status of a work of literature as a cultural document means we should favor the published version(s) of a text unless we are confronted with compelling evidence of authorial dissatisfaction. This evidence Faulkner's career by and large fails to provide. The second reservation results from Polk's statement in the Library of America volume that his texts "accept only those revisions on typescript or proof that Faulkner seems to have initiated himself as a response to his own text, not those he made in response to a revision or a correction suggested by an editor" (p. 1021). Although Polk calls this "a very conservative policy," it is radical in the severity of its view of Faulkner's relation with his editors, which was on the whole congenial and cooperative. The third point—more an observation than a reservation—is that in several instances (including *The Sound and the Fury*) the final setting copy of Faulkner's novels has not survived. This means that differences between the last extant typescript version and the published text may as well be the result of changes initiated by Faulkner as of editorial intervention. Hence many of the editorial judgments Polk is obliged to make are less bibliographical than literary in character; they are judgments as to whether the typescript or the published version is more consistent with the meaning of the novel as Polk understands it. Fortunately Polk is a sensitive and tactful reader. But I cannot help wondering what will happen when he is called upon to apply his editorial principles to texts where the differences between typescript and first edition are more extreme than in the novels he has edited thus far. Will he provide us with better versions of these works or simply with different ones? By the time these comments are being read we will have an answer to this question, since Random House published the Polk edition of *Absalom, Absalom!* (a notoriously thorny text) in the fall of 1986.

The publication of previously unpublished work by Faulkner continued in 1985 with the appearance of four items. The first is Louis Daniel Brodsky and Robert W. Hamblin's *Faulkner: A Comprehensive Guide to the Brodsky Collection*, vol. 4: *Battle Cry* (Miss.). This addition to the important Brodsky-Hamblin series reprints an expanded story treatment and a draft screenplay of a never-completed Howard Hawks film on which Faulkner worked in 1943. The book contains a brief, nostalgic essay by Meta Carpenter Wilde and Orin Borsten entitled "Faulkner: Hollywood: 1943"; and an illuminating introduction by Brodsky and Hamblin which locates the film project in Faulkner's career, describes the stages of its development and eventual abandonment, and speculates on the influence of Faulkner's work at Warner Brothers on his later fiction. As with past volumes in the series, *Battle Cry* is scrupulously edited and handsomely produced.

The second and third of the four items are also by Brodsky. "A Textual History of William Faulkner's *The Wishing-Tree* and *The Wishing Tree*" (*SB* 38:330–74) reprints two versions of an important precursor to *The Sound and the Fury* that Faulkner gave to young acquaintances in 1927 and again in 1948. The story was published by Random House in 1967, but because of extensive house editing the published version differs markedly from the versions reprinted here. The third item, " 'Elder Watson in Heaven': Poet Faulkner as Satirist" (*FJ* 1,i:2–7), reprints with commentary a nine-stanza poem almost certainly written in 1921. The fourth and final item, Doreen Fowler and Campbell McCool's "On Suffering: A Letter from William Faulkner" (*AL* 57:650–52), reprints a letter Faulkner wrote in September 1934 to a childhood friend who had lost a daughter. The letter expresses attitudes toward suffering and grief relevant to Faulkner's later fiction.

The year also saw the publication of Patricia E. Sweeney's *William Faulkner's Women Characters: An Annotated Bibliography of Criticism, 1930–1983* (ABC-Clio Information Services). This 497-page book uncomfortably straddles two stools. As its title suggests, the book does not pretend to be a comprehensive bibliography of Faulkner criticism; yet Sweeney includes nearly every work of criticism that mentions Faulkner's female characters, even if only in passing. Hence students interested in studying Faulkner's women will be led down many blind alleys, but without a compensatory assurance that they are seeing everything written on a particular work of fiction. The section of the book on Faulkner's short stories omits several stories ("Mule in the Yard," for example) containing prominent female characters.

It should be noted that the annual Faulkner issue of *MissQ* continues to publish a review of Faulkner criticism similar to this one and that *The Faulkner Newsletter* continues to publish information for book collectors and brief reviews and notes.

ii. Biography

The brief list of contributions to our understanding of Faulkner's life is headed by Michel Gresset's *A Faulkner Chronology* (Miss.). This welcome volume is essentially a chronological log of Faulkner's activities as an artist and as a public man, situated within a brief narrative history of his native region. In the words of Joseph Blotner, Gresset supplies "the facts of gestation, development, and publication of [Faulkner's] work," along with "mini-essays on themes, techniques, and interrelationships as well as aspects of the life." I suspect that the book will be mainly useful as a guide to Blotner's *Faulkner: A Biography.* Anyone who has spent time paging through the two-volume version of this book trying to determine when one event in Faulkner's life happened in relation to another will be grateful to Gresset. I regret, though, Gresset's decision not to cover Faulkner's family life in the log. Failure to mention such matters as Faulkner's startling letter to Hal Smith on the eve of his marriage and Estelle Faulkner's honeymoon suicide attempt can distort our understanding of the genesis of Faulkner's art.

The other two items in this category can be briefly treated. Louis Daniel Brodsky's "Reflections on William Faulkner: An Interview with Albert I. Bezzerides" (*SoR* 21:376–403) reprints a long interview with the screenwriter who was one of Faulkner's closest companions in Hollywood. Of particular interest is Bezzerides' account of his having overheard a violent sexual encounter between Faulkner and his wife during a visit to Rowan Oak in the late 1940s. The final item, Joseph Blotner and Chester A. McLarty's "Faulkner's Last Days" (*AL* 57:641–49), is an expanded account (relative to *Faulkner: A Biography*) of the final days of Faulkner's life. The essay draws on McLarty's insights as Faulkner's physician to make some interesting observations, but it contains no startling new revelations. Mention should also be made of Jane Isbell Haynes's *William Faulkner—His Tippah County Heritage: Lands, Houses, and Businesses, Ripley, Mississippi* (Seejay). I became aware of this book too late to do anything more than note its existence here; readers interested in learning more about it may wish to consult Michael Millgate's review in *MissQ* (Spring 1986).

iii. Criticism: General

a. **Books.**   The year saw the publication of four books on Faulkner and two collections of essays, but before turning to this material I wish to welcome a new addition to Faulkner studies and to regret an absence. The new addition is *The Faulkner Journal* (Ada, Ohio), a biannual publication edited by James B. Carothers and John T. Matthews. Open to all schools of Faulkner criticism, the journal promises to be a welcome addition to Faulkner studies. The absence is Doreen Fowler and Ann J. Abadie's volume of proceedings from the 1984 Faulkner and Yoknapatawpha Conference. Delays in publication gave this book (entitled *Faulkner and Humor*) a 1986 copyright date, so it will be reviewed in next year's *ALS*.

The first of the four books on Faulkner, Robert Harrison's *Aviation Lore in Faulkner* (Philadelphia: John Benjamins), is a fascinating, well-written, and—so far as I can tell—authoritative examination of the topic named in its title. The book begins with a discussion of information and terminology basic to an understanding of flight and with a brief account, based on published materials, of Faulkner's history as an aviator. The body of the book consists of a set of detailed glosses of each of Faulkner's works containing references to airplanes and flight. I came away from the book enlightened about a number of passages that had always puzzled me and impressed by the verisimilitude of Faulkner's depictions of flight. My only complaints are that the typeface is minute and that the choice of a European publisher may mean the book will not receive the attention in America it deserves.

The second of the four books, Robert Dale Parker's *Faulkner and the Novelistic Imagination* (Illinois), is a promising but overly cautious study of how Faulkner withholds and reveals information in *As I Lay Dying, Sanctuary, Light in August*, and *Absalom, Absalom!* At his best—which is quite good—Parker brings a sophisticated awareness of the dynamics of repression and displacement to bear on his analysis of Faulkner's plot structures; but he generally does not pursue his psychological insights as far as he might. A similar observation can be made about Parker's readings of individual novels. His analysis of *As I Lay Dying*, for example, begins with a very strong discussion of the ways Faulkner defamiliarizes his narrative; but rather than pursue the implications of his insights Parker devotes the second half of his chapter to a largely unconvincing attempt to reestablish a naturalistic interpretation of the novel. I suspect that this retreat (as I see it) arises from a discomfort with deconstructive strategies of reading. This discomfort many readers of Faulkner share; but I wish Parker had confronted it in a more productive way—perhaps by examining it as a theme within the fiction itself. Despite my reservations I welcome the appearance of this book, for it marks the entry into Faulkner studies of a subtle critical intelligence.

The third and fourth books can be more briefly treated. Max Putzel's *Genius of Place: William Faulkner's Triumphant Beginnings* (LSU) is an ambitious but idiosyncratic study of the origins of Faulkner's mature fiction. In contrast to Judith Sensibar, with whose *Origins of Faulkner's Art* this book should be compared, Putzel does not believe that Faulkner's poetry had anything to do with his artistic development. This is an odd and unconvincing position to take. But even if we allow Putzel his exclusive emphasis on Faulkner's prose, his book fails to provide the developmental study it promises; nor does it ever answer the question with which it begins, of how Faulkner's "genius of place" provided guidance for his fiction. Yet the book is by no means without merit. It contains a number of interesting readings

and suggestive allusions to other writers, and it is informed throughout by a garrulous but never inauthentic love of literature. The fourth
book, Alan Warren Friedman's *William Faulkner* (Ungar), is an
entry in Ungar's Literature and Life series. Like other books in the
series, Friedman's is directed primarily at students and general
readers. Unlike many student handbooks, *William Faulkner* is intelligently written, sensitive to critical nuance, and informed by a sophisticated notion of the forces governing Faulkner's creativity.

The two collections of essays to appear during 1985 are *Intertextuality in Faulkner*, ed. Michel Gresset and Noel Polk (Miss.), and
Faulkner Studies in Japan, ed. Thomas L. McHaney and comp. Kenzaburo Ohashi and Kiyoyuki Ono (Georgia). *Intertextuality in Faulkner* reprints the proceedings of the Second International Colloquium
on William Faulkner, held at the University of Paris in April 1982. In
addition to an introduction by Gresset the volume contains an interesting general reflection on intertextuality by Kenzaburo Ohashi. This
essay, entitled " 'Motion' and the Intertextuality in Faulkner's Fiction"
(pp. 158–67), calls for an investigation of the ways Faulkner's understanding of intertextuality changed as his career advanced. The other
essays in this volume will be discussed in the appropriate sections
below. *Faulkner Studies in Japan* reprints a number of essays central
to the development of the Japanese interest in Faulkner's fiction; it
also contains an intriguing set of responses to Faulkner by Japanese
authors. Because most of the contents of this volume have appeared
in print before, I merely note its existence here. Finally, notice should
also be taken of *The History of Southern Literature* (LSU); the brief
essay on Faulkner (pp. 333–42) is by Cleanth Brooks.

b. **Articles.** The year saw the publication of seven articles on general topics. The first to be considered here, K. J. Phillips' "Faulkner
in the Garden of Eden" (*SHR* 19:1–19), discusses a wide array of
images of trees in Faulkner's fiction. I sympathize with much of Phillips' argument, but I wish he had broadened his sense of the allusive-
ness of Faulkner's references to trees beyond the Garden of Eden. The
second essay, Virginia V. Hlavsa's "The Mirror, the Lamp, and the
Bed: Faulkner and the Modernists" (*AL* 57:23–43), begins promis-
ingly with an attempt to identify some of the defining characteristics
of modernism but soon turns into a recapitulation and defense of two
earlier essays by Hlavsa. Nothing said in the new essay causes me to

reconsider the judgments I expressed when the earlier essays appeared (see *ALS 1974*, pp. 134–35, and *ALS 1980*, p. 163). Certainly, as Hlavsa says, we misread Faulkner if we ignore his modernist affiliations; but it does not follow that "any explanation of Joe [Christmas]" must take into account Hlavsa's rebus-like series of parallels between the novel, the Gospel According to John, and *The Golden Bough*. I cannot understand why *American Literature* devoted space to this essay.

The third item in this category, Dinnah Pladott's "William Faulkner: The Tragic Dilemma" (*JNT* 15:97–119), also returns to an earlier essay, but as a point of departure for a more comprehensive study. Pladott's essay seeks to apply to Faulkner's career as a whole a distinction between "destructive" and "affirmative" sacrifice she first explored in an essay on *A Fable* (see *ALS 1982*, p. 164). The paradigm she develops provides some insight into *The Sound and the Fury* and *Absalom, Absalom!*, but it comes accompanied by a heavy burden of Aristotelian and Fryean critical baggage. When Pladott speaks of Faulkner "transform[ing] the *pharmakos* rites as well as the Dionysiac *sparagmos* ritual . . . into the psychological terms of giving or withholding love and recognition," one wonders to what extent she is attempting to describe Faulkner's actual artistic development.

The four remaining essays on general themes can be briefly treated. Catalina Montes' "Notes on the Third International Faulkner Colloquium" (*NMW* 17:83–92) and Joseph Blotner's "Faulkner in the Soviet Union" (*MQR* 24:461–76) are both accounts of international symposia—Montes' of the colloquium held in Salamanca in April 1984 and Blotner's of the conference held at the A. M. Gorky Institute in Moscow in June 1984. The summaries of papers in Montes' essay make me look forward eagerly to the promised publication of the proceedings of the colloquium. The two remaining essays are Cleanth Brooks's "Faulkner's 'Motherless' Children" (*WiF* 7,i:1–17) and Calvin S. Brown's "Some Problems in Faulkner: Words, Sources, and Allusions" (*FJ* 1,i:55–56). Brooks's essay examines in a preliminary fashion the large number of motherless or essentially motherless children in Faulkner's fiction. Brown's essay inaugurates a feature in the new *Faulkner Journal* in which selected scholars are invited to pose questions of fact or interpretation about Faulkner's fiction. Some of Brown's questions are answered by James Hinkle and Doreen Fowler in the second issue of the journal.

iv. Criticism: Special Studies

a. **Ideas, Influences, Intellectual Background.** Of the 10 items in this category, eight are influence studies. The most useful of these are Michael Grimwood's "Lyle Saxon's *Father Mississippi* as a Source for Faulkner's 'Old Man' and 'Mississippi' " (*NMW* 17:55–62) and two essays by Martin Bidley, "Faulkner's Variations on Romantic Themes: Blake, Wordsworth, Byron, and Shelley in *Light in August*" (*MissQ* 38:277–86) and "Victorian Vision in Mississippi: Tennysonian Resonances in Faulkner's *Dark House / Light in August*" (*VP* 23: 43–57). All three of these essays focus on specific, provable connections between Faulkner's fiction and earlier literature. Also valuable are three more wide-ranging, speculative studies: John T. Matthews' "Intertextuality and Originality: Hawthorne, Faulkner, Updike" (*Intertextuality in Faulkner*, pp. 144–57) and the relevant sections in Samuel Chase Coale's *In Hawthorne's Shadow* (pp. 66–79) and Jefferson Humphries' *Metamorphoses of the Raven* (pp. 93–114). Matthews' essay uses Faulkner as the crossing point between a look back at Hawthorne and a look forward to Updike; he argues that Faulkner's *As I Lay Dying* and Updike's *A Month of Sundays* are in part rewritings of *The Scarlet Letter*, particularly in their association of writing with sexual transgression. Coale's book is also concerned with the influence of Hawthorne on Faulkner, but more broadly; he sees Faulkner as a detranscendentalized Hawthorne. Finally, Humphries' book is a difficult but intriguing Lacanian study of literary relations between France and the American South. His chapter on Faulkner suffers from underdevelopment. It begins with some astute comments on the lessons Faulkner learned from Mallarmé, but then turns somewhat inconsequently to a discussion of Sartre's reading of Faulkner.

One of the remaining two influence studies, Mary E. Davis' "The Haunted Voice: Echoes of William Faulkner in García Márquez, Fuentes, and Vargas Llosa" (*WLT* 59:531–35), is a brief survey of the influence relationships identified in its title. The other, Timothy Kevin Conley's "Resounding Fury: Faulkner's Shakespeare, Shakespeare's Faulkner" (*Shakespeare and Southern Writers*, pp. 83–124), is a disappointing study of an important topic. The main problems with the essay are structural. Instead of tracing individual Shakespearean references through the canon or examining selected works exhaustively, Conley writes a short history of Faulkner's career, using Shakespearean allusions as a leitmotif. The essay is more than half finished before it reaches *The Sound and the Fury*, and it contains little of interest on the important Shakespeare echoes in the major fiction. The main value of the essay lies in its comments on the influence of Shakespearean comedy on Faulkner's first two novels.

The remaining two items in this category are concerned with the literary and social contexts out of which Faulkner's fiction arose. Jean Rouberol's "Southwestern Humor and Faulkner's View of Man" (*WiF* 7,i:38–46) argues that Faulkner turns the antidemocratic, anti-Jacksonian bias of southwestern humor on its head. The essay contains an odd reading of "Afternoon of a Cow" as a rejection of southwestern humor; Rouberol does not seem to be aware of the story's parodic qualities. In the chapter on Faulkner in *The Southern Belle in the American Novel* (pp. 97–116) Kathryn Lee Seidel devotes considerable attention to Narcissa Benbow and Temple Drake. The chapter contains occasional good comments, but it is often critically naive: Seidel says that Temple becomes a prostitute; she cites *Sartoris* rather than *Flags in the Dust* without saying why; and she treats Faulkner's characters as if they were entirely consistent from one work to another. I am surprised to see a critic who voices feminist sentiments rely so heavily (and so uncritically) on the work of Karen Horney.

b. **Style and Structure.**   Only one study of Faulkner's style appeared during the year, but it is an excellent one. Michael Toolan's "Syntactical Styles as a Means of Characterization in Narrative" (*Style* 19:78–93) uses three passages from *Go Down, Moses* as sample texts for a demonstration of "how variable deployment of a range of syntactic features and patterns serves to further, and in part constitute, narrative characterization." The demonstration is precise, detailed, and quite convincing. Mention should also be made here of Cleanth Brooks's *The Language of the American South* (Georgia). This brief book, a transcript of Brooks's Lamar Memorial Lectures at Mercer University, contains some comments on Faulkner's use of southern language.

c. **Race.**   The year saw no general studies of Faulkner's treatment of racial themes. This situation will soon change dramatically, because the theme of the 1986 Faulkner and Yoknapatawpha Conference was Faulkner and Race.

v. Individual Works to 1929

In a sharp break with tradition, *Flags in the Dust*, not *The Sound and the Fury*, dominated the year's work on the first decade of Faulkner's career. This extraordinary outpouring of work on *Flags* is headed by Arthur F. Kinney's *Critical Essays on William Faulkner: The Sartoris Family* (Hall). This book is the second in a series of collections of critical essays and background materials on Faulkner's major fictional families. (For a review of the first, on the Compson family, see *ALS 1982*, pp. 156–58.) The book contains materials on several of Faulkner's short stories, on the movie script *War Birds*, and on *The Unvanquished*, but I have chosen to discuss it here because most of its contents are either directly or indirectly concerned with *Sartoris / Flags in the Dust*. The book contains 19 critical essays (nine of them new), a selection of early reviews, a set of historical background materials, a selection of materials by Faulkner that presage or discuss the Sartoris fiction, and a collection of materials pertinent to the controversy surrounding the editing of the Random House edition of *Flags in the Dust*.

The overall impression created by this book is mixed. On the one hand, it contains a variety of materials, some not easily accessible elsewhere, relevant to an understanding of the historical backgrounds on which Faulkner drew. Also three of the nine essays published here for the first time—Andrea Dimino's "The Dream of the Present: Time, Creativity, and the Sartoris Family" (pp. 332–61), Bruce Kawin's "*War Birds* and the Politics of Refusal" (pp. 274–89), and François L. Pitavy's "'Anything but Earth': The Disastrous and Necessary Sartoris Game" (pp. 267–73)—are of considerable merit. Kawin's essay is particularly rewarding; it argues for the relevance of the movie script *War Birds* to an understanding of the ways Faulkner's attitudes toward revenge changed in the 1930s. Kawin's argument merits comparison with David Wyatt's important comments on the same topic in *Prodigal Sons* (see *ALS 1980*, p. 149; Wyatt's comments are not reprinted in Kinney).

On the other hand, the book provides substantial grounds for dissatisfaction. Both Kinney's long introduction and his selection of ma-

terials encourage a naively mimetic view of the relation between
Faulkner's Sartoris fiction and its historical and biographical backgrounds. Furthermore, his introduction treats the Sartoris materials
as if they were parts of an internally consistent text, not outgrowths
of a dynamic and changing vision, and it exhibits some disturbing
failures of voice. When Kinney says that Mississippi at the time of the
Civil War "wished only to be left alone, insuring regional peace,
human dignity, individual liberty, and family solidarity" (p. 4), we
have a right to ask whose opinion we are hearing. If, as later comments suggest, it is not Kinney's, then this fact should be made clear.
Finally, two of the newly published essays are too weak to merit inclusion. I have in mind Sherrill Harbison's "Two Sartoris Women:
Faulkner, Femininity, and Changing Times" (pp. 289–302) and
Esther Alexander Terry's "For 'blood and kin and home': Black
Characterization in Faulkner's Sartoris Saga" (pp. 303–17). Harbison's essay is a naive discussion of Faulkner's characters as if they
were real people. Terry's essay is a vitriolic attack on Faulkner for the
way he depicts black characters in the Sartoris fiction. Never once
does Terry suggest that there might be an element of authorial cen-
sure in the depictions of inequality and injustice she discovers in
the fiction (and uses as sticks to beat Faulkner with).

Of the six remaining items on *Flags in the Dust*, only one—Michiyo
Ishii's "Faulkner's Style in *Flags in the Dust*" (*WiF* 6,ii:45–62)—is not
by Philip Cohen. Ishii's essay is a competent study of point of view
and narratorial omniscience. Cohen's annus mirablis consists of the
following items: "The Composition of *Flags in the Dust* and Faulkner's Narrative Technique of Juxtaposition" (*JML* 12:345–54);
"Faulkner's Early Narrative Technique and *Flags in the Dust*" (*SoSt*
24:202–20); "The Last Sartoris: Benbow Sartoris' Birth in *Flags in
the Dust*" (*SLJ* 18:30–39); "*Madame Bovary* and *Flags in the Dust*:
Flaubert's Influence on Faulkner" (*CLS* 22:344–61); and "Textual
Anomalies in Faulkner's *Flags in the Dust*" (*NMW* 17:35–40). All
of these essays and notes apparently derive from Cohen's 1984 University of Delaware dissertation; they are solid, thoughtful pieces of
work. Of particular interest are the study of the influence of *Madame
Bovary* (which should be compared with André Bleikasten's essay in
Intertextuality; see section *vi.*) and the two studies of narrative technique. I wish, though, that Cohen had cited the Random House
edition of the novel along with the manuscript and typescript versions
housed at the University of Virginia. It may be, as Cohen says, that

the Random House edition is unreliable; but it (or the closely related Vintage edition) is all most readers of the novel have, and citing it hardly constitutes a seal of approval.

The short list of items on *The Sound and the Fury* is headed by Stephen M. Ross's "Rev. Shegog's Powerful Voice" (*FJ* 1,i:8–16), a reading of the Shegog sermon in stylistic terms. This is a stimulating essay, especially in its first half, where Ross discusses the "discursive gestures" that generate the power of voice in Faulkner's fiction. These consist of the presentation of voice as a phenomenon in its own right, the separation of voice from speaker and sometimes from speech, and the establishment of a competition between voice and sight resulting in the triumph of voice. The remaining three items are less significant. Paul M. Hedeen's "A Symbolic Center in a Conceptual Country: A Gassian Rubric for *The Sound and the Fury*" (*MFS* 31:623–43) attempts to read *The Sound and the Fury* as a metafiction. There is little here that has not been more persuasively stated by André Bleikasten in *The Most Splendid Failure*, a book Hedeen does not cite. The other two studies—"Gerald Bland's Shadow" (*L&P* 31,iv[1981]:4–12) and "Faulkner's *The Sound and the Fury*: The Incest Theme" (*AI* 42:85–98)—are both by Richard Feldstein. They are Freudian studies of a traditional sort. In the first Feldstein argues that Quentin Compson's obsession with Gerald Bland is the result of homosexual panic; in the second he argues that the Dilsey-Shegog relationship reiterates the incest theme of the earlier sections and that therefore Faulkner's use of third-person point of view in the fourth section does not constitute an act of authorial repression.

vi. Individual Works, 1930–39

The 24 items on the fiction of the 1930s are fairly evenly distributed throughout the period, with every novel the subject of at least one study and no novel the subject of more than six. The five studies devoted to *As I Lay Dying* are of varying merit. Nancy Blake's "The Word as Truth or Delirium: Faulkner's *As I Lay Dying*" (*RBPH* 63: 554–63) is a needlessly difficult Lacanian study of Faulkner's novel. After working my way through a daunting array of undefined terms and orphic pronouncements, I reached the conclusion that Faulkner deconstructs a matriarchal version of the dream of presence in *As I Lay Dying*. In contrast to Blake's essay, C. H. Peake's "The Irreconcilable Dimensions of Faulkner's 'As I Lay Dying'" (*E&S*, pp.

98–110) is a model of clarity and grace. Peake examines four central polarities (inertia-movement, words-doing, rigidity-fluidity, and space-time), all in relation to the novel's frequent images of right-angled relationships. Using these images as a rubric allows Peake to elucidate the oddly oblique, asymmetrical character of the polarities.

The third study, Frederik N. Smith's "Telepathic Diction: Verbal Repetition in *As I Lay Dying*" (*Style* 19:66–77), examines some interesting repetitions of words and phrases. Especially provocative is Smith's comment that the Bundrens rely "upon a system of communication based on stare, glance, or looking away" (p. 74). This observation suggests an interesting connection between *As I Lay Dying* and *Light in August*, a novel in which these forms of communication are extremely important. The fourth study, Kiyoyuki Ono's "Faulkner and History: *As I Lay Dying* and *The Scarlet Letter*" (*WiF* 7,i:18–36), examines the influence of Hawthorne's novel on Faulkner's. Ono argues that Faulkner's allusions to *The Scarlet Letter* provide a sense of history otherwise absent in *As I Lay Dying*. Finally, the year also saw the publication of *William Faulkner's "As I Lay Dying": A Critical Casebook* (Garland), ed. Dianne Cox. Like the other volumes in the Garland Casebook series this book combines an introduction and annotated bibliography by the editor with a collection of critical essays by various hands. Although the book contains no statement of the principle on which the critical essays were selected (nor even any indication of their previous publication history), it appears that Cox has chosen to include only journal articles and chapters from dissertations, not chapters from books. While this is an understandable and defensible decision, it has resulted in a book focused rather narrowly on issues of style and characterization. Beginning students will probably be better advised to start with André Bleikasten's *Faulkner's "As I Lay Dying"* and the relevant chapters in Brooks, Millgate, and Vickery.

Sanctuary was the subject of four strong studies in 1985. André Bleikasten's "Terror and Nausea: Bodies in *Sanctuary*" (*FJ* 1,i:17–29) is a revised version of an essay originally published in *Sud* in 1975; it examines, with its author's characteristic subtlety and panache, *Sanctuary* as a detranscendentalized text. As Bleikasten says, in *Sanctuary* "the physical has ceased to gesture toward the meta-physical, just as it has ceased to reflect the psychological." Hence bodies lack coherence and depth; they are represented synecdochecally, as isolated parts (faces, mouths), or as gestures void of meaning. The second essay on *Sanctuary*, " 'Cet affreux goût d'encre': Emma Bovary's Ghost in *Sanctuary*" (*Intertextuality*, pp. 36–56), is also by Bleikasten. It continues the line of argument of the first essay, arguing that Faulkner's interest in the "black stuff" that emerges from Emma Bovary's mouth begins where Flaubert's ends: Flaubert depicts the death of the concept of the self, but Faulkner depicts the form life takes after this death has occurred. This essay first appeared in English in somewhat different form in *WiF* in 1983 (see *ALS 1983*, p. 164). The other two essays on *Sanctuary* also appeared in *Intertextuality*. Noel Polk's "The Space Between *Sanctuary*" (pp. 16–35) is an intriguing, strongly argued examination of the differences between the original and the revised versions of *Sanctuary*. This essay is especially valuable for its speculations about the psychological significance of the revisions. The other essay, Michel Gresset's "Of Sailboats and Kites: The 'Dying Fall' in Faulkner's *Sanctuary* and Beckett's *Murphy*" (pp. 57–72), examines a number of interesting similarities between the conclusions of Faulkner's and Beckett's novels.

The year's work on *Light in August* includes Martin Bidley's two important influence studies (see section *iv.a*). The four remaining studies of the novel are headed by Eileen T. Bender's "Faulkner as Surrealist: The Persistence of Memory in *Light in August*" (*SLJ* 18: 3–12). Although this essay contains a number of irritating factual errors and misquotations, it makes a good case for the relevance of the surrealist tradition to an understanding of *Light in August*. Also of value is Stephen Hahn's " 'What Leaf-Fring'd Legend Haunts About Thy Shape?': *Light in August* and Southern Pastoral" (*FJ* 1,i:30–40). This essay is an intelligent and carefully reasoned but somewhat jargon-ridden analysis of the ideological implications of pastoral myths of timelessness in *Light in August, I'll Take My Stand*, and Cleanth Brooks's Faulkner criticism. The value of Hahn's discussion of Brooks is limited by his exclusive reliance on *The Hidden God* for evidence; nowhere does he discuss the chapter entitled "Faulkner as Nature Poet" in *William Faulkner: The Yoknapatawpha Country*. Also I wish Hahn had given more emphasis to the ways Faulkner places pastoral timelessness in tension with "motion," to use Faulkner's term for history and change.

The other two studies of *Light in August* can be briefly discussed. Ronald Wesley Hoag's "Ends and Loose Ends: The Triptych Conclusion of *Light in August*" (*MFS* 31:675–90) is a well-written but

somewhat inconsequent study of the triple conclusion of the novel.
It contains a good demonstration of how the first two conclusions
darken the third. Although Debra A. Moddelmog's "Faulkner's The-
ban Saga: *Light in August*" (*SLJ* 18:13–29) ostensibly attempts to
read *Light in August* in relation to Sophocles' Oedipus trilogy, its
true concern seems to be with the ways the novel criticizes patriarchal
values. Moddelmog's argument is sometimes forced, as when she en-
rolls Joanna Burden and Roz Thompson in the roster of Joe Christ-
mas' "fathers," and the single-mindedness of her devotion to individualism is disquieting. The only study of *Pylon* to appear is Susie
Paul Johnson's "*Pylon*: Faulkner's Waste Land" (*MissQ* 38:287–94),
a relentlessly moralistic and antimodern reading of the novel as a
depiction of a technological nightmare. Reflection on Faulkner's
statement in his review of *Test Pilot* of his desire for a modern mythology of speed might have given Johnson pause.

The first of the six essays on *Absalom, Absalom!* to be considered,
Stephen M. Ross's "Oratory and the Dialogical in *Absalom, Absalom!*" (*Intertextuality*, pp. 73–86), draws on Bakhtin's distinction
between the monologic and dialogic imaginations to examine the
way in which the multiple narratorial perspectives of *Absalom, Absalom!* continually threaten to merge into a single "overvoice." When
Ross says that this overvoice "re-presents Sutpen's authority as 'father'
in the novel" he broaches the extremely interesting question of the
relation between Faulkner's style and his political vision. This consistently stimulating essay would have benefited from being considerably longer. Suzanne W. Jones's "*Absalom, Absalom!* and the
Custom of Storytelling: A Reflection of Southern Social and Literary
History" (*SoSt* 24:82–112) resembles Ross's essay in being concerned
with the novel's monologic qualities, but Jones's approach is social
and historical rather than philosophical and rhetorical. Jones exhibits
a good eye for the ways in which the various narratives in the novel
reflect their speakers' social backgrounds. Her use of evidence is
sometimes unsophisticated, as when she discusses the Compson Appendix as if it were part of the original version of *The Sound and the
Fury*. Also of value is the chapter on *Absalom, Absalom!* in Minrose
C. Gwin's *Black and White Women of the Old South* (Tenn., pp. 111–
29). Gwin assigns the relation between Rosa Coldfield and Clytie Sutpen more centrality than it possesses in the novel, but she makes some
good observations about how Rosa's racial views are related to her
sexual repression.

The three remaining items on *Absalom, Absalom!* all appeared in *Intertextuality*. Nancy Blake's "Creation and Procreation: The Voice and the Name, or Biblical Intertextuality in *Absalom, Absalom!*" (pp. 128–43) takes a Lacanian approach to the monologic quality mentioned above. In arguing that "all [the] narrators are simply mouthpieces for a voice that is unique, singular, and indivisible" (p. 130), Blake flattens out one of the central conflicts of the novel. The second item, Olga Scherer's "A Polyphonic Insert: Charles's Letter to Judith" (pp. 168–77), uses a theoretical framework derived from Bakhtin to examine the letter named in its title. Scherer's comments have been largely superseded by David Krause's essay on Bon's Letter (see *ALS 1984*, p. 168). Finally Patrick Samway's "Searching for Jason Richmond Compson: A Question of Echolalia and a Problem of Palimpsest" (pp. 178–209) attempts to determine whether Mr. Compson has an existence independent of Quentin's superheated image of him. Using the ingenious approach of examining words only Mr. Compson uses, Samway concludes that an identifiable character of this name does indeed exist. I quarrel with the very positive view Samway takes of Mr. Compson in *Absalom, Absalom!*

The only item on *The Unvanquished* to appear during 1985, E. O. Hawkins' "Rosa Millard and Ann Franklin" (*SoQ* 23:87–93), reprints an account of a trip to Memphis undertaken by one of Malcolm Franklin's ancestors during the Civil War. The parallels Hawkins draws to Rosa Millard's adventures are not so exact as to compel agreement, but neither are they factitious.

The remaining three items in this section are all on *The Wild Palms*. In a recent review (*SR* 94[1986]:167–80) Calvin S. Brown jokingly dismisses Pamela Rhodes and Richard Godden's "*The Wild Palms*: Degraded Culture, Devalued Texts" (*Intertextuality*, pp. 87–113) by saying that it interprets Faulkner's novel as "a deliberate Marxist tract." In contrast to Brown, I find this essay extremely valuable. The authors' Marxist orientation leads to an occasional odd emphasis, as when they read the Tall Convict's sojourn in the swamp in ideological terms; but the wealth of detail in their essay and the subtlety of its argument opens *The Wild Palms* to interpretation in exciting new ways. I come away from this essay (and from some of my own recent work) convinced that Faulkner engaged in a more searching exploration of the Great Depression than any other American author. Who besides Faulkner, after all, really tried to see whether a modernist aesthetic could encompass a depression subject matter?

The other two studies of *The Wild Palms* are "Forgetting Jerusalem: An Ironical Chart for *The Wild Palms*" (*Intertextuality*, pp.
114–27) by François Pitavy and "Distant Mirrors: The Intertextual
Relationship of Quentin Compson and Harry Wilbourne" (*FJ* 1,i:41–
45) by Gary Harrington. Pitavy's essay is an elegant demonstration
of the inappropriateness of reading Faulkner's allusions to Psalm 137
unironically. It seems to me the danger lies in the opposite direction,
in an excessive deromanticizing of the novel. Harrington's brief essay
examines some of the ways Harry Wilbourne resembles Quentin
Compson. I wish Harrington had extended his insight further, by
looking at how Caddy Compson resembles Charlotte Rittenmeyer and
at how Quentin and Harry are figures of the artist.

vii. Individual Works, 1940–49

The only study exclusively of *The Hamlet* in 1985 appeared in a
delayed issue of *L&P*. In "Making Labove Cast a Shadow: The
Rhetoric of Neurosis" (*L&P* 31,iv[1981]:32–38) Dawn Trouard uses
Otto Fenichel's *The Psychoanalytic Theory of Neurosis* as a basis for
analyzing Labove as an obsessive-compulsive personality. The essay
contains several good observations, but Trouard spends more time
than necessary justifying her approach. Margaret Dunn's "The Illusion of Freedom in *The Hamlet* and *Go Down, Moses*" (*AL* 57:407–
23) examines the theme identified in its title. Dunn points out some
intriguing parallels between *The Hamlet* and *Go Down, Moses*, but
she never explains why Faulkner should wish (or need) to depict
freedom as illusory. The absence of a discussion of this point leaves
me with the impression that Dunn takes the illusoriness of freedom
to be an existential truth—a position she is welcome to hold, of
course, but not one all of her readers will share.

The list of six items exclusively on *Go Down, Moses* is headed
by Patrick McGee's "Gender and Generation in Faulkner's 'The Bear'"
(*FJ* 1,i:46–54). This fine essay recasts the traditional criticism of Isaac
McCaslin in a contemporary idiom. In McGee's terms Ike's failure
consists of his refusal to accept history, gender differentiation, and
reading (in the sense of a never-ending process of deciphering and
creating meaning). Ike cannot accept these aspects of life, McGee
says, because he is dominated by "the dream of an innocent and omni-
potent subjectivity." In contrast to McGee's essay, David Mickelsen's

"The Campfire and the Hearth in *Go Down, Moses*" (*MissQ* 38:311–27) repeats the traditional criticism of Ike in a reductive way. Mickelsen says that the campfire and the hearth symbolize childishness and maturity respectively and that "evil is located . . . in continued allegiance to the flawed, infantile game world represented by the hunt." Mickelsen never explores the possibility that the conflict between campfire and hearth may be irreconcilable, and therefore tragic, or that we may sometimes serve maturity best by acknowledging and expressing our childishness.

The first of the remaining four items on *Go Down, Moses*, John L. Selzer's " 'Go Down, Moses' and *Go Down, Moses*" (SAF 13:89–96), argues that reading "Go Down, Moses" in the context of the novel reveals Gavin Stevens' moral deficiencies in a way that reading the story in isolation does not. Selzer relies at times on a too-simple opposition between intuition and intellect, as when he argues that Gavin Stevens' college education places him in direct opposition to the values of the wilderness. In "The Evolution of Roth Edmonds in *Go Down, Moses*" (*MissQ* 38:295–309) David Paul Ragan studies Roth Edmonds' characterization; he draws on the short story originals of "The Fire and the Hearth" and "Delta Autumn" for some of his evidence and creates a forgiving view of Roth. In "Poker and Semantics: Unravelling the Gordian Knot in Faulkner's 'Was'" (*AL* 57:129–37) Sharon L. Leahy strives valiantly to explain the hands of poker depicted in "Was." As an early warrior in this quest, I sympathize with Leahy's effort; I am not inspired to confidence, though, by her claim that the first hand played is a version of lowball or by her conclusion that Tomey's Terrel has no reason to cheat. Finally, Winifred Frazer's " 'Habet' in *The Bear* [*sic*]" (*NMW* 17:41–43) explores the background in Edward Bulwer-Lytton's *The Last Days of Pompeii* and Henryk Sienkiewicz's *Quo Vadis* of Faulkner's use of the word "habet."

viii. Individual Works, 1950–62

The brief list of studies of the fiction of the last decade of Faulkner's career is headed by Noel Polk and Lawrence Z. Pizzi's The Town: *A Concordance to the Novel* (UMI). This addition to the ongoing series of Faulkner concordances exhibits the same high standards of accuracy and craftsmanship as previous volumes. I regret,

though, the absence of an introduction by an invited scholar, a useful
feature of past volumes in the series. The only study of *A Fable* to
appear during the year, Richard H. King's "*A Fable*: Faulkner's Political Novel?" (*SLJ* 17:3–17), examines the novel's equivocal confrontation with the political dimension of existence. The essay is filled
with shrewd insights, as when King says that "Faulkner's was a politics of privatism" and that gestures of freedom in Faulkner's fiction
entail "a violent wrenching away *from* necessity . . . which is only
momentarily an intervention *in* history." This essay can be read profitably in conjunction with Rhodes and Godden's essay on *The Wild
Palms* (see section *vi*) and with McGee's and Dunn's essays on *Go
Down, Moses* (see section *vii*). Finally, Calvin S. Brown's "Style as
Symbol: The Ending of *The Mansion*" (*WiF* 6,ii:36–44) examines
how stylistic shifts in the conclusion of *The Mansion* reflect Mink's
merger with all humanity.

ix. The Stories

The year saw the appearance of nine items on Faulkner's short stories.
Foremost among these is James B. Carothers' *William Faulkner's
Short Stories* (UMI Research Press), a comprehensive and judicious
study of Faulkner's contributions to the genre. Carothers takes a
balanced approach to the vexed question of the relation of the short
stories to the novels, arguing that the stories must be read both as
autonomous works of art and (when appropriate) as source materials
for the novels. The book's greatest strengths are its analysis of the
various ways the short stories and novels interconnect and its readings of individual stories. Its most serious limitation is that Carothers
devotes an excessive amount of time to fending off wrongheaded interpretations of the short stories and of Faulkner's fiction generally.
Also his interpretation of Faulkner's career as a movement from pessimism to optimism needs substantial qualification if it is to be convincing. A second book-length study, David G. Yellin and Marie
Connors' *Tomorrow and Tomorrow and Tomorrow* (Miss.) is less
concerned with Faulkner's short story "Tomorrow" than with the
transformation of the story into a television play and a motion picture.
The book's bibliography does not list Jack Barbera's essay on the
same subject (see *ALS 1981*, p. 170).

Of the remaining seven items in this category (all studies of individual stories) three are on "That Evening Sun." Ken Bennett's "The Language of the Blues in Faulkner's 'That Evening Sun' " (*MissQ* 38:339–42) demonstrates convincingly that Faulkner's allusions to the blues in the story are not limited to "The St. Louis Blues." The other two studies, Laurence Perrine's " 'That Evening Sun': A Skein of Uncertainties" (*SSF* 22:295–307) and a section on the story in John Gerlach's *Toward the End* (pp. 130–43), both examine the story's epistemology, focusing in particular on the question of whether Nancy's fears for her life are well-founded. Both studies conclude that the story is deliberately ambiguous. This is an understandable position to take; but at times the uncertainties cited by the authors—especially by Perrine—seem more ratiocinative than real. Also I wonder whether emphasizing questions of empirical verification doesn't divert attention from the true interest of the story, which resides, for me at least, in the social, psychological, and political circumstances that encourage Nancy's fear to exist.

Of the four remaining studies the most interesting is Michael Grimwood's " 'Mr. Faulkner' and 'Ernest V. Trueblood' " (*SoR* 21: 361–71). Grimwood argues convincingly that "Afternoon of a Cow" needs to be read reflexively, as an examination of Faulkner's understanding of himself as an artist. I wonder, though, whether the story can carry quite the burden of authorial anxiety that Grimwood loads it with and whether it foreshadows Faulkner's later difficulties with his literary vocation as fully as Grimwood claims. I myself prefer to see in the story a playful, unanxious depiction of two essential dimensions of Faulkner's creativity: the earthy, id-related fantasist called "William Faulkner," and the censorious, superego-related editor called "Ernest V. Trueblood."

The final three items are all of limited value. In "Kinship and Heredity in Faulkner's 'Barn Burning' " (*MissQ* 38:329–37) Jane Hiles argues that Sarty's repudiation of his father's values simply repeats his father's antisocial behavior. Hiles seems to found her argument on the assumption that sons are never supposed to rebel against their fathers—a position which, as the father of fourteen- and sixteen-year-old boys, I find attractive but not entirely tenable. John L. Skinner's " 'A Rose for Emily': Against Interpretation" (*JNT* 15:42–51) heaps a considerable amount of scorn on critics who comment on theme, character, and meaning. Of his own analysis, Skinner says that while "it may seem excessively formalistic . . . it . . . is surely more useful than the pursuit of subjective impressions." I would say in rejoinder that *all* truly useful acts of criticism pursue subjective impressions. Finally, Mary Flowers Braswell's " 'Pardners Alike': William Faulkner's Use of the Pardoner's Tale?" (*ELN* 23:66–70) argues that Chaucer's tale influenced "Lizards in Jamshyd's Courtyard." The resemblances Braswell cites are all predictable.

University of California, Davis

10. Fitzgerald and Hemingway

Michael S. Reynolds

Last year's trend slightly favored feminist attempts to revise our reading of Hemingway. This year the only trend was the norm: great interest in *The Great Gatsby* and *The Sun Also Rises*. Last year Fitzgerald strove to give balance to this chapter. This year Hemingway stole the entire show: four general studies, two new texts, two major biographies. With the exception of a minor paste-up of aphorisms, one chapter in a bibliography, and a spate of *Gatsby* articles, Fitzgerald lost staying power.

i. Bibliography, Texts, and Biography

The only major bibliography—*Joseph Conrad and American Writers* (Greenwood) ed. Robert Secor and Debra Moddelmog—has a chapter devoted to each writer's Conrad connection. Categorized are statements about Conrad in Fitzgerald/Hemingway nonfiction and letters, fictional references to Conrad in their books, plus biographical and critical connections that link Conrad with either American writer. A glance into the remarkable index confirms the book's value. Any connection between either writer and Conrad is indexed two different ways. For example, under Fitzgerald are listed all the Conrad connections to each of Fitzgerald's works; under Conrad are listed all the connections with Fitzgerald to each of Conrad's works.

Another important bibliography is *The Ernest Hemingway Collection of Charles D. Field* prepared by Bonnie D. Cherrin (Stanford University Libraries). Stanford University's recently acquired collection includes Hemingway first editions, most of Hemingway's introductions and forewords, numerous translations, various ephemera, a good selection of critical works, interviews, memoirs, and feature stories. There are also 121 Hemingway letters, including most of his letters to Carlos Baker between 1951 and 1961. Of the 24 manuscripts and documents, most are typed and signed manuscripts of Hemingway's *Esquire* pieces.

The new Hemingway text given most attention was *The Dangerous Summer* (Scribner's). Edited by Michael Pietsch (no credit given), the book represents approximately half of the manuscript Hemingway wrote but could not edit for his commissioned *Life* magazine feature in 1960. Despite reviewers who found the book self-parodic (An inane response. Did they expect him to sound like someone else?), *The Dangerous Summer* is an interesting testament of what was wrong and right with Hemingway at his life's end. The book follows two bullfighters through an author-inflated duel across the Spanish summer. Perversely identifying with the younger bullfighter, Hemingway, the narrator, works imperfectly but steadily on the theme of doubleness which haunts all of his posthumous publications. The people and the places, the look of the Spanish earth, the taste of the wine, the movement of bulls and men in sunlight—all the Hemingway touchstones are included. But the book is about death, about growing old, about losing; it is about these things even though they are mostly left out. It is not all pretty, but it is there, and we must deal with it sensibly.

A more important new Hemingway text was William White's editing of *Dateline: Toronto* (Scribner's), which collects for the first time all of Hemingway's Toronto *Star* journalism, 1920–24: 100 previously unavailable *Star* pieces and 72 others that have been in reprint. Biographers, literary historians, and critics will all profit from a careful reading of these pieces. It is immediately obvious, for example, that Hemingway learned the value and effect of word repetition well before he met Gertrude Stein. The book's comprehensive, 18-page index makes it a scholar's delight.

In comment on the text of Hemingway's "A Clean Well-Lighted Place" ("Counterfeit Hemingway: A Small Scandal in Quotation Marks," *JML* 12:91–108), David Kerner gives a lucid explanation of anti-metronomic dialogue, arguing for its proper usage in Hemingway's "Well-Lighted Place." As Kerner points out, our misunderstanding of Hemingway's legitimate and frequently used device led us to badger Hemingway's publisher to correct what scholars took as a textual error. Kerner convinces me that the text was right all along and should be changed back to its original reading. But Kerner should go easy on Scribner's: the fault was with those of us who argued so fiercely for the change.

Larry Phillips pasted together *F. Scott Fitzgerald on Writing* (Scribner's), a text of sorts: charming paragraphs and one-liners from Fitzgerald's books, essays, and letters that comment on his art. As in last year's companion volume on Hemingway, Phillips has organized the material generically: The Act of Writing, Characters, Publishing, etc. This book has the same pluses and minuses as his Hemingway collection (*ALS 1984*, p. 178). Lack of index will frustrate some; non-chronological organization, others. The sad part is how often Hemingway's name appears, haunting Fitzgerald's adult life. The curious part is that there is not a single letter to Hemingway quoted.

The continuing news in Hemingway circles is, of course, the five biographies appearing or soon to appear (Jeffrey Meyers, Peter Griffin, Michael Reynolds, Kenneth Lynn, James Mellow). Circling about this flotilla are a number of biographical essays of merit and interest. The best biographical essay of the year was Scott Donaldson's "Dos and Hem: A Literary Friendship" (*CentR* 29:163–85). Using letters (published and unpublished), biographies, fiction, and unpublished manuscripts, Donaldson presents an accurate, straightforward picture of the relationship from its Paris beginnings in 1924 to its angry conclusion over the Spanish Civil War. Even better, Donaldson shows how the relationship surfaced in the fiction of both writers to the very ends of their lives.

The other Michael Reynolds (the one who writes essays rather than evaluates them) analyzed the medical history of the Hemingway family—"Hemingway's Home: Depression and Suicide" (*AL* 57:600–610). Using unpublished family letters and other biographies, Reynolds assembled a record of high blood pressure, diabetes, insomnia, paranoia, and severe depression running through three generations of the Hemingway family, and resulting, so far, in four suicides. The essay proves that Hemingway's father suffered from depressions early in the young boy's development, depressions so severe that they altered the Doctor's relationship with his son. Later in his life Hemingway chose to blame his mother for his father's death rather than admit that the suicide might have been the result of a biological trap.

Robert Thornberry's "Hemingway's 'Ce Soir' Interview (1937) and the Battle of Teruel" (*HemR* 5,i:2–8) provides the historical framework for reading Hemingway's interview with the French communist newspaper *Ce Soir* during the Spanish Civil War. Thornberry reprints in translation the entire interview, explaining in footnotes the now obscure references to a war that never was clear at the time. Linda Miller published the second part of her "Gerald Murphy and Ernest Hemingway" (*SAF* 13:1–13), taking the relationship from the Hadley divorce in 1926 through to their last significant meeting in 1932. Once more, Miller has good detail and liberal quotations from Murphy letters; her analysis of the rift between the two men seems sound: Hemingway resented Murphy's paternalism in Hemingway's divorce and was put off by Murphy's "charm and the tendency to hyperbolize." N. Ann Doyle and Neal B. Houston added to our understanding of the later Hemingway with their twice-published article "Letters to Adriana Ivancich" (*LCUT* n.s.30; and reprinted in *HemR* 5,i:14–29). With a good deal of tact, they describe in chronological sequence the 65 Hemingway-Ivancich letters to be found in the Humanities Research Center at the University of Texas. Without quotations (not permitted), the two scholars do an admirable job of synopsizing the 128 pages of Hemingway letters and relating them to his life and art.

The headline story of 1985 was, of course, the publication of two new biographies: Peter Griffin's study *Along with Youth: Hemingway, The Early Years* (Oxford) and Jeffrey Meyers' full-length *Hemingway, A Biography* (Harper). Let me immediately say that my bias is wide and deep. With my newly published (1986) Hemingway biography on the table before me, I have to be prejudiced.

Because the Griffin biography covers exactly the same ground as my book, my dissatisfaction with *Along with Youth* must sound peevish. Well, it is peevish, but not without reasons. I am not dissatisfied because Griffin occasionally puts in cars before they were produced or songs before they were written. I am only a little dissatisfied that he played by a different set of rules than the other four biographers: Griffin quotes liberally from unpublished letters and manuscripts which were forbidden to most of us; he also publishes five stories written before the summer of 1921, which makes the book a necessity until the stories are republished in an authoritative edition. (Note: there are several errors in Griffin's versions of the stories, like the possessive title of "The Ash-Heel's Tendon" and the misspelled name of its detective; the "Cross Road" sketches are not complete.) I am a bit more disturbed by Griffin's casual attitude toward significant dates and names. He has "Fathers and Sons" being published variously in the "late thirties" and in 1935. It was published in 1933. Griffin's opening sentence makes Ernest six when Grandfather Hall died: no, he was five. Griffin has the battle of Caporetto starting one day late. Griffin spells Nick Nerone's name wrong consistently because he is certain that it is right in Hemingway's manuscripts. A bit more irritating are the facts which Griffin did not check, repeating old inaccuracies: Hemingway did not receive the medals from General Diaz; Dr. Hemingway did not spend four months at the Lying-In Hospital in 1908; Hemingway did not read *One Hundred Narrative Poems* his freshman year in high school (see National Union Catalog.)

I also wonder at the numerous bits of new information—some with vague sources; some without source. Griffin says Hemingway read and reread *The Red Badge of Courage* in Oak Park. Yet there is no evidence that I know of that he saw the book in Oak Park. The single library copy did not enter Oak Park until Hemingway's junior year in high school. Griffin says that Dr. Hemingway flunked out of Oberlin College. The source is unpublished Oberlin College records. Griffin says that Dr. Hemingway was high school board chairman in 1913 without giving any source. Having read through the holograph board minutes, I do not recall seeing Dr. Hemingway's name mentioned. Griffin speaks of the picture of Grace Hall in the Madison Square Garden program for her opera debut, but he does not publish the program picture or cite its location. As several of us have been interested in that question, we'd have loved to see the evidence.

What most irritates me with the Griffin biography is its two basic assumptions: (1) any fiction that Hemingway wrote was actually biography; and (2) anything Hemingway put on paper in letters, journalism, or fiction is true. Both of these assumptions are terribly wrong, and the result is a terribly flawed biography. When faced with scant information on Hemingway's World War I experience, Griffin simply lifts great quotes from *A Farewell to Arms* to fill in the gaps. This falsifying tactic is used throughout the biography. Griffin misdates more than one manuscript and willfully misreads others. He takes the barroom talk of out-of-work rummies in a 1930s Hemingway piece called "Crime and Punishment" and transfers their experience to Hemingway's own experience in 1918. Using that principle, one can fashion a terribly exciting life for Hemingway but one that is essentially false. Read the book because you have to, but check everything in it very carefully.

Jeffrey Meyers' *Hemingway, A Biography* is both more and less than what we have needed. Written in two years from scratch (a feat in which the author takes some pride), the book has several strong points. Meyers is good at relating Hemingway's writing thematically to his life. He is good at set pieces: Hemingway and Kipling, for example. He has sound insights on Hemingway's relationship with Pound, Joyce, Stein. He ranges at will over the whole Hemingway canon finding connections that are provocative. Because he relied heavily on interviews, Meyers is best in the post-1940 period where the survivors still had their wits intact. What he does best of all is fill in the supporting cast of characters (Gilbert Seldes, Ward Price, Chink Dorman-Smith), a luxury he is allowed because, like all of us, Meyers knows that the Baker biography is there for the basic chronology. Because he did not spend the required time in the letters and unpublished manuscripts, Meyers repeats some old errors in chronology. He is wonderful on Hemingway's experience at the Greco-Turkish war but sloppy on Hemingway's relationship with Pound. In the index Pound gets three pages, Fitzgerald five pages, Stein seven. Wyndham Lewis, on the other hand, gets five pages and Kipling gets seven. Meyers plays to what he knows best and to what he has found that's fresh: John H. Patterson with four pages and Philip Percival with six. Meyers, like Hemingway, has a wonderful ear for gossip and slander; he also cannot refrain from Freudianizing at obvious points, nor can he resist bedroom peeking: did Hemingway really sleep with Agnes, Adriana, or Valerie? (Do we really care?) The book is quite readable, entertaining, insightful, but it is not a literary biography. We never see Hemingway struggling with his art because Meyers is not interested in that aspect of the artist. He uses the manuscripts only when they cast some light on the biography. In a challenge match, this biography was meant to replace Baker. It doesn't. Nor could it have been written without the Baker biography in place.

Never one to basket his light, Meyers published an interesting account of his Hemingway research ("The Quest for Hemingway" *VQR* 61:584–602) in which he detailed the rich experiences he had while shooting the elephant. In the essay he says: "I made the most interesting find using the Freedom of Information Act to obtain a copy of the FBI file on Hemingway. . . ." He goes on to tell us how he published an article on the file in the *New York Review of Books*. What he does not say is that the FBI file was obtained from me during a visit to my house. I had the file and loaned it to Meyers because I had no immediate use for it. He found immediate use but no immediate need to credit the source.

ii. Influence Studies

Kim Moreland, "The Education of Scott Fitzgerald: Lessons in the Theory of History" (*SHR* 19,i:25–38), explores the impact of Henry Adams on Fitzgerald's first two novels and of Spengler's *Decline of the West* on Fitzgerald's post-1924 writing. Making perceptive biographical connections, Moreland finds a good deal of Henry Adams' character in Thornton Hancock and Anthony Patch and even more of Spengler's pessimism in *Tender Is the Night*, the *Crack-up* essays, and the unfinished *Phillippe, Count of Darkness*.

Adeline Tinter suggests in "The Significance of D'Annunzio in *Across the River and into the Trees*" (*HemR* 5,i:9–13) that the Italian writer's *Notturno* influenced Hemingway in a number of ways. In that journal of the soldier-poet's recovery from war wounds, D'Annunzio is cared for by his illegitimate daughter, Renata; Tinter sees this relationship as a model for Cantwell's relation with his Renata. Her other influences are less convincing, for they could have come from other D'Annunzio sources. Unfortunately, Tintner repeats most of what Nick Gerogiannis told us four years ago ("Hemingway's Poetry: Angry Notes of an Ambivalent Overman" in *Ernest Hemingway: The Papers of a Writer*, ed. Bernard Oldsey [Garland]).

Kathleen Verduin's "Hemingway's Dante: A Note on *Across the River and into the Trees*" (*AL* 57:633–40) states without proving that Hemingway's knowledge of Dante was superficial, and that his use of Dante in the novel is based on a popularized Byronic view of the poet that suited Hemingway's own needs.

W. R. Martin and Warren U. Ober suggest that Frederic Henry's key statement about words one could no longer stand to hear— "sacred, glorious and sacrifice"—is similar to and may derive from a passage in D. H. Lawrence's *Lady Chatterley's Lover* ("Lawrence and Hemingway: The Canceled Great Words," *ArQ* 41:357–61). Their sense of the similarity of the two passages is correct. Their supposition that Hemingway read Lawrence before making his final revisions is also true. But the revisions to this particular passage were made long before Hemingway read *Chatterley*. The manuscript shows the passage was heavily revised in holograph into its present form during the first draft of the manuscript. Suppositions that can be answered by checking the manuscript are, at best, vexing. Martin and Ober do a better job with their "Hemingway and James: 'A Canary

for One' and 'Daisy Miller' " (SSF 22:469–71) in which they note
the points of parallel and argue that Hemingway is using the James
allusion for structural force and pathos.

   In spite of fairly conclusive source studies on "The Snows of Kilimanjaro," Alice Hall Petry suggests that Hemingway very likely
heard and used some of Beryl Markham's African adventures (West
with the Night, 1942) before she published them. In "Voice Out of
Africa: A Possible Oral Source for Hemingway's 'The Snows of Kilimanjaro' " (HemR 4,ii:7–11) Petry does a convincing job of linking
Hemingway and Markham.

   Influence studies flow in two directions as evidenced by the following essays charting Hemingway's impact on younger writers. An
interesting study was published by Peter Hays and Stephanie Tucker,
"No Sanctuary: Hemingway's 'The Killers' and Pinter's The Birthday
Party" (PLL 21:417–24), which establishes Hemingway's influence
on the plot, conflict, characters, setting, and style of Pinter's play. A
much longer, more discursive essay, "The Rules of Magic: Hemingway as Ellison's Ancestor" by Robert O'Meally (SoR 21:751–69), compiles the numerous comments that Ralph Ellison has made about
Hemingway over the last 30 years. The essay gives a coherent chronological account of the black writer's professed debt to Hemingway,
but O'Meally is less convincing when he tries to see the Invisible Man
as "a brownskin cousin of Nick Adams." Bottom line: much better on
Ellison than on Hemingway.

iii. Criticism

a. **Full-Length Studies.**   Without a Fitzgerald book in sight, Hemingway again dominates the critical scene with four books, the value
of which varies wildly. The most balanced of the four is Gregory
Sojka's *Ernest Hemingway: The Angler as Artist* (Peter Lang), which
integrates Hemingway's values, his aesthetics, and his love of fishing.
Drawing on fiction and nonfiction, letters and manuscripts, criticism
and biography, Sojka cogently analyzes how fishing works in Hemingway's professional life and in the lives of his characters: the
aesthetics of angling become a kind of moral philosophy.

   Angel Capellan's *Hemingway and the Hispanic World* (UMI
Research Press) is more emotionally charged than Sojka but less
convincing. The book is useful and detailed on Hemingway's knowl-

edge of Spain, his numerous visits there, and his love of Spanish spectacle and custom. But intent on naturalizing Hemingway into a true Spaniard, Capellan becomes so extreme that few can follow. Capellan wants the central conflict to be between modern times and primeval culture, with Hemingway always opting for the primeval's curative powers. (The absence of references to Jake's wound in Book III of *The Sun* "could be interpreted as evidence of physical regeneration.") The heroic prototype for Hemingway is Don Quixote and the bullfighter, not just sometimes but always. That's the rub. Capellan's insistence that Hemingway is a Spanish writer with Spanish sources and Spanish values will never become accepted doctrine. Throughout there is an hysterical edge to the argument that leaves one puzzled.

One problem with Capellan's book and the Kobler and Grimes books to follow is they are all dissertations revived a decade or more after their defense. Because most dissertations must impress a committee, it is rare that one is fit to print until it has been seriously revised and cleansed of its absolutes. Of these three, Capellan is the most extreme; Grimes merely obsessed; and Kobler perfectly sane. All three are dated, finished in 1977, 1968, and 1974 respectively. Each has attempted to incorporate Hemingway scholarship published during the interim, but it is mostly lip service. The basic theses remain unchanged by the intervening decade's work. Any dissertation so well written that it requires only modest and superficial revision 10 years later is doubly rare. Of these three, only Kobler is the exception.

As with many dissertations, Larry Grimes's *The Religious Design of Hemingway's Early Fiction* (UMI Research Press) pushes ideas to extremes and ignores parts that don't fit. Many of his readings are quite sensitive, and what he has to say about style is well done. But he gets into a morass trying to define Hemingway's "fifth dimension" and trying to make his definitions fit the fiction up to 1929. The book is loaded with jargon out of Rudolph Otto, Johan Huizinga, and Mircea Eliade—philosophically and religiously oriented game theorists. Nothing that has been done in manuscript work since 1968 has apparently changed any of Grimes's original ideas.

J. F. Kobler's *Ernest Hemingway: Journalist and Artist* (UMI Research Press) is the least dated of the three books because it is concerned with style, a Hemingway subject seldom investigated in any depth. Kobler investigates the relationship between Hemingway's journalism and his fiction. Looking at content, ideas, themes, politics, and style, Grimes does a comparative job that sometimes overlaps with Robert O. Stephens' *Hemingway's Nonfiction* (1968) but more frequently complements it. Kobler is particularly useful on the changes in style; in his tabular compilations he has more comparative data than anyone else has given us.

b. **Collections.**   Matthew J. Bruccoli's *New Essays on* The Great Gatsby (Cambridge) was the only collection of new criticism to appear this year. The introduction and five essays (see section **iii.d.**) were all commissioned to be "new" perspectives on a novel whose critical canon is already formidable. Given the task, Bruccoli has assembled a respectable mix: historical overviews, an influence study, stylistic and thematic analyses, and an estimate of the novel's place in the great American novel sweepstakes. Averaging 20 pages each, the essays seem less than "new" and a bit overwritten, a common flaw in commissioned work. Each essay has its fine moments, however, and all are useful. On the other hand, Harold Bloom's edition of old essays, *Ernest Hemingway* (Chelsea), is of little use, for it republishes excellent essays that have been republished more than once already: Trilling, Wilson, Penn Warren, Levin, Baker, Spilka, Plimpton, Cowley, Kazin. The only new essay by John Hollander is of little value. Bloom's brief introduction suggests, among other things, that Hemingway's style came from Walt Whitman. I doubt it.

c. **General Essays.**   Essays that draw on a writer's lifework are slow to read, difficult to synopsize, and thesis-driven. In searching for pervasive patterns that substantiate their theses, such articles, by their very nature, must gloss over entire works, omitting much and ignoring contradictory data. They also tend to identify the author with his characters as progressively older extensions of himself: a dangerous and fallacious idea. Robert D. Young's "Hemingway's Suicide in His Works" (*HemR* 4,ii:24–30) attacks his perception of Phil Young's death wish theory in Hemingway's fiction. R. Young argues that Hemingway's awareness of death gave piquance to his pursuit of life: a fiesta approach to living under the volcano. Order, courage, endurance, work, duty, and love are Hemingway's bastions "against the eternal death which he felt was inevitable." When the fiesta ended, when he would no longer drink, love, or write well, Hemingway killed himself. Well, yes and no. Jake's fiesta attitude doesn't make his life any better or hold back the night. Nor does Harry Morgan, who embodies all the above virtues, find much fiesta in his depression-era life.

Robert P. Lamb attempts an even more metaphysical view of the canon in his "Eternity's Artifice: Time and Transcendence in the Works of Ernest Hemingway" (*HemR* 4,ii:42–52). Using Wallace Stevens and Yeats as touchstones, Lamb links Hemingway with other modernists in his vain struggle "not to fall from mythic time into history; who, having fallen, sought to transcend the historical process by both the themes and especially the structure of his prose" only to be overwhelmed by the nothingness. Learning that history is unavoidable, Hemingway saw that "moments of ecstasy" could transcend time—the matador facing the bull is the strongest example. For the writer that same moment comes when his prose transcends time—the perfect sentence. Irony, indirection, and discipline allow Hemingway to pursue his art, says Lamb, through *For Whom the Bell Tolls*. After that, irony fails him and the remainder of his work is a "morass of self-pity and despair." Perhaps, but Jake Barnes, filled with irony, is not saved by it, and Colonel Cantwell is working in another dimension of time than Lamb wants to consider. Both Young and Lamb would have profited, perhaps, from reading more of what has already been written about Hemingway.

Robert Gajdusek finds cutting away and shedding of significant appendages a pervasive theme in Hemingway's fiction ("Purgation/ Debridement as Therapy/Aesthetics," *HemR* 4,ii:12–17). In a quick overview of the canon Gajdusek finds numerous examples of purgation that control or focus the fiction: Jake Barnes's missing phallus; the gangrened leg at Kilimanjaro; the cesarean birth in the Indian camp; Harry Morgan's missing arm. This obsession with purgation Gajdusek links to American literature's inability "to accept the imperfect or compromising part of the self."

Michael Harper tries a Marxian overview of Hemingway in his "Men Without Politics? Hemingway's Social Consciousness" (*NOR* 12,i:15–26). The overwritten introduction beats a few dead horses (early reviews; Edmund Wilson; Lionel Trilling) to show that earlier readers missed the economic point. Then Harper does an excellent Marxian interpretation of several stories, including "Light of the World" and "Homage to Switzerland." Harper ignores *To Have and Have Not*, picks the easy shots in *The Sun*, but reaches some interesting conclusions, not the least of which is Hemingway's ultimately conservative position. James H. Justus published a well-written essay, "Hemingway and Faulkner: Vision and Repudiation" (*KR* 7,iv:1–14), that has some lovely generalizations but nothing new to say to experienced Hemingway watchers.

In an essay that defies categories, "Hemingway the Hunter and Steinbeck the Farmer" (*MQR* 24:440–60), Jackson Benson, with his customary finesse and agility, brings together for comparison our modernist extrovert Hemingway with the introverted Steinbeck. Because Benson has devoted a good deal of his life to both writers, the results are interesting and well written. With a sharp eye for similarities in background, family, milieu, and ideals, Benson carefully charts out the differences between the two writers, particularly Hemingway's talent for publicizing himself and Steinbeck's gift for anonymity and self-effacement: two faces of the American experience and the American novel.

d. **Essays on Specific Works: Fitzgerald.**   The inordinate attention paid to *The Great Gatsby* in recent years continued through 1985, due, in part, to the Bruccoli essay collection which followed on the heels of the Donaldson collection (see *ALS 1984*). Without denying *Gatsby*'s stature, I would suggest that the novel, like a covey of quail, has been overhunted to the point where some self-imposed restrictions may be necessary. As Richard Anderson points out in "Gatsby's Long Shadow" (*New Essays*, pp. 15–40), in 1974 the novel was required reading in 2,400 colleges and had annual sales of 300,000 copies. Because we write about what we teach, we write about *Gatsby*. Anderson surveys "the ways the author and the novel have impressed themselves on the general public; sales figures; academic-scholarly activity, and . . . the responses on other writers in their own work." His overwhelming evidence tells us what we intuitively knew: *Gatsby* has become a "permanent presence in American culture." Kenneth E. Eble reaches a similar conclusion in his essay "*The Great Gatsby* and the Great American Novel" (*New Essays*, pp. 79–100). Eble rightly maintains that the novel "illuminates the American past and present . . . the light and dark of American experience." Eble's essay might have been more effective had he avoided the red herring of the Great American Novel. His cogent discussion of Fitzgerald's artistic intentions, style, structure, and revisions has, as Eble realizes, little to do with the mythical G.A.N. We can all agree finally that *Gatsby* is both great and an American novel, but there was no argument on those points to begin with.

In "Money, Love, and Aspiration in *The Great Gatsby*" (*New Essays*, pp. 41–57) Roger Lewis tries to resolve an inherent paradox: the pursuit of ideal beauty via the crassness of money. Focusing on the novel's doubleness (double views, double attitudes, double values), Lewis shows that the corrupt cannot attain the ideal, nor can dollars buy integrity. Still he insists that *Gatsby*'s unique contribution is seeing the acquisition of love and money as part of the same dream. This synthesis is less convincing than the definition of the conflict itself.

George Garrett, a gifted writer less inhibited by the critical canon than the scholars, wrote what may be the most sensible essay of the year: "Fire and Freshness: A Matter of Style in *The Great Gatsby*" (*New Essays*, pp. 101–16). With the eye of an accomplished historical novelist, Garrett understands the importance of context: *Gatsby* is not contemporary fiction, but a product of 1925. Using the word "style" in its broadest sense, Garrett reminds us that Fitzgerald is rooted in a particular American time and place, a society that disappeared in 1929, a world as foreign to us as Elizabethan England. The novel remains vibrant due to form and style: Fitzgerald's ability to create tension through structure and his ability to write in several styles as the situation demands.

John Rohrkemper's "The Allusive Past: Historical Perspective in *The Great Gatsby*" (*CollL* 12:153–62) surely overstates his case when he calls the novel "the richest meditation on American history to appear in our fiction." (So rich that the early readers missed the point completely.) The historical references abound a good deal less than Rohrkemper would have us believe. He does very well with Dan Cody as part Dan Boone and part William Cody; he does even better with the differences between Jimmy Gatz's list and his prototype Ben Franklin's list. But it is a gnat-straining exercise to translate the eyes of Dr. T. J. Eckle/berg into Thomas Jefferson's Disgusting/City.

Further straining the outer edges of our belief is Glenn Settle's argument in "Fitzgerald's Daisy: The Siren Voice" (*AL* 57:115–24) that Daisy's voice lures men to their doom just as the classical Sirens did. No argument that Daisy's voice attracts all men. No argument that Gatsby is doomed once he makes Daisy the centerpiece of his life. But Sirens lure men away from their appointed sea rounds. When Settle says, "It is a possibility . . . that Jay Gatsby . . . is on an epic seafaring quest when he meets Daisy," the air thickens with gnats. Settle is far better in demonstrating the Siren-voice effect on Nick Carraway than on Gatsby.

In "Fitzgerald's Use of American Architectural Styles in *The Great Gatsby*" (*AmerS* 25:91–102) Curtis Dahl argues that the specific styles of Fitzgerald's buildings "embody basic aspects of his characters." The analysis and accompanying pictures work best on Gatsby's "Chateauesque Style" and Buchanan's "Georgian Colonial Revival" mansions. Dahl is best on architectural detail and history; weakest on connecting the style with the man. In forcing himself beyond what has already been said about the Gatsby house and Gatsby himself, Dahl suggests Hawthorne's *House of the Seven Gables* and Poe's "Fall of the House of Usher" as Gothic models Fitzgerald had in mind: a bridge too far.

Just when I was certain there was nothing new to say about *Gatsby*, I read what is probably the best article of the year: M. A. Klug's "Horns of Manichaeus: The Conflict of Art and Experience in *The Great Gatsby* and *The Sun Also Rises* (*ELWIU* 12:111–23). Both writers, says Klug, assert "immortal order in the face of universal disintegration." Their art was a defense against the entropy of reality. In both novels disintegration and death are manifest in the body of a woman, and the minor characters affirm and define the real. In both novels major characters are artists (Gatsby and Romero) who create their imagined selves, play out their roles before an audience, and dedicate their creative act to a woman. The two narrators "are prototypes of the failed artist . . . [living] in an agony of consciousness between the dream of order and the resignation to chaos." The philosophical bent of the essay does not summarize easily or, in my case, well, but it should not be missed.

Nor, probably, should Gerry Brenner's amusing "A Letter to Nick Carraway: Fifty Years After" (*MQR* 23:196–206) in which Jordan Baker Rittenhouse (married, two daughters, widowed) writes Nick (never married, retired head of True Value Hardware) a scathing review of his novel. Jordan takes Nick to task for making himself look better than he was, for moral hypocrisy, and for being an accessory to Gatsby's murder (Nick knew what sort of man Wilson was; Nick didn't have to go to work that day). But buried within her letter is the interesting charge that Nick's real problem is his hatred of women. The evidence: his gallery of contemptible women.

The relationship between Zelda Fitzgerald's *Save Me the Waltz* and her husband's *Tender Is the Night* is examined in detail by Sarah B. Fryer's "Nicole Warren Diver and Alabama Beggs Knight: Women on the Threshold of Freedom" (*MFS* 31:318–25). In charting the similarities and differences between the two works, Fryer makes a strong feminist argument for a more sensitive reading of both novels and for a more understanding attitude toward Zelda. But what should we make of "Doctor Diver and General Grant in Fitzgerald's *Tender Is the Night* (*NMAL* 8,Item 16)? Robert Wexelblatt finds four references to Grant, two of which bracket the novel at opening and close. But it's difficult to agree with his conclusion that what "is said of Dick Diver can also be said of Ulysses Grant, that it was their world which blew itself up in the war—different worlds perhaps, and wars, but similar explosions with similar consequences." Nothing short of a Civil War history can explain what is wrong with that conclusion.

Fitzgerald's short stories have never received the attention they deserve. This year is no different, except that the small attention was paid by good people. Alice Hall Petry ("The Picture(s) of Paula Legendre: Fitzgerald's 'The Rich Boy,'" *SSF* 22:232–34) in her consistently sound manner points out a misreading of the Fitzgerald story: the first picture is real; the second is only in Anson's mind, a figment of his guilt. E. R. Hagemann takes Fitzgerald rightly to task for his blooming errors of rhetoric, syntax, and sense in "Should Scott Fitzgerald be Absolved for the Sins of 'Absolution'?" (*JML* 12:169–74). Without apologies Hagemann lists and analyzes the effects of Fitzgerald's numerous writing blunders: "'maudlin exultation,' an emotional impossibility." From misspelled Latin to garbled outbursts of gorgeous rhetoric, the gaffes mount up. (A "sirocco" in summertime North Dakota?) The bottom line: Hagemann cannot forgive Fitzgerald his sloppiness. Neither can we.

e. Essays on Specific Works: Hemingway. Like *Gatsby*, *The Sun Also Rises* is the Hemingway novel of preference these days, and *Sun* articles proliferate, pushing, at times, our credence to its limits. So much fine, solid work has been done on *The Sun* that revisionist readings are forced to positions whose defense requires more rhetorical dexterity and imagination than the book will bear. For example, Milton A. Cohen's fine essay pursues *The Sun*'s Circe parallels but pushes his thesis so hard that the reader pulls back defensively ("Circe and Her Swine: Domination and Debasement in *The Sun Also Rises*," *ArQ* 41:293–305). Summing up the essential elements of the Circe story, Cohen notes the parallels with Brett's behavior and admits the differences: "control and intent." He shows how the men at Pamplona are debased just as was Odysseus' crew. Well and good. But then because Jake must be Odysseus, Pedro Romero has to be Hermes who brought Odysseus the knowledge to avoid Circe's spell. This conclusion in turn forces Cohen to read the ending as Jake/Odysseus being freed from the spell of Brett/Circe. A good article pushed too far.

Wolfgang Rudat's "Cohn and Romero in the Ring: Sports and Religion in *The Sun Also Rises*" (*ArQ* 41:311–18) is another revisionist view that is strangely distracting due to its organization. Rudat insists that Cohn and Romero have more in common than previously suspected, but what he sees as commonalty can also be seen as ironic parallelism. However, to insist that Romero is, in fact, a Jew and that Cohn has the attributes of the "code hero" who stabilizes Brett's "chaotic life" is to ask too much of the reader. Much of Rudat's analysis is useful, but it is devalued by its extremes.

Jim Hinkle's "What's Funny in *The Sun Also Rises*" (*HemR* 4,ii: 31–41) lists in order of complexity and explains some 60 humorous moments in *The Sun* that readers largely ignore. Many of the jokes are based on wordplay, puns, or irony. Sometimes the characters recognize the joke; at other points only the reader catches the irony. If you have to explain jokes, they lose something, but Hinkle's insistence on Hemingway's humor forces us to see that Jake's irony, the source of many jokes, is a defense against taking the world too seriously.

Trevor McNeely's "War Zone Revisited: Hemingway's Aesthetics and *A Farewell to Arms*" (*SDR* 22,iv:14–38) is an important and frustrating investigation of the love–war duality in that novel. McNeely goes beyond earlier work to argue that Frederic Henry fails as a hero when he falls in love, that reality is "truth" (best seen in war), and that love romanticizes reality, falsifying it. Thus what appears to be idyllic during the Swiss interlude is, in fact, self-destructive for Frederic; having failed the test of courage, Frederic is filled with self-hatred, and his true attitude toward love is negative. Despite his unnecessary linking of author and character, McNeely's long arguments (badly summarized here) demand attention.

In what should have been a much better essay than it is, Todd G. Willy looks at Hemingway's safari genre in "The Covenants of Venery: Political Mythopoeism in Ernest Hemingway's *The* [sic] *Green Hills of Africa*" (*SAQ* 84:141–60). Willy glimpses Theodore Roose-

velt's importance but misses that writer's main influence on Hemingway. Willy also defines the characteristics of the safari genre, drawing on numerous little-known books for his examples. Unfortunately,
Willy has little sympathy with the genre or with *Green Hills* and is
given to rhetorical shots of small-bore variety. He is not familiar with
much of the Hemingway work done in recent and not so recent years.
If he had looked at either book on Hemingway's reading, he might
have rethought his essay. He might also have used the book version of R. O. Stephen's *Hemingway's Nonfiction* rather than the
dissertation.

William Adair's *"For Whom the Bell Tolls* as Family Romance"
(*ArQ* 41:329–37) is badly titled and weakly ended, but it is also an
important article: it sees relationships we've missed. Adair demonstrates the relationship between Robert Jordan's early life and the
drama of the novel: Jordan's father's suicide betrays the family, particularly the son; Jordan's final act resists suicide, sacrificing himself for the guerrilla family. Pablo's betrayal of Jordan parallels the
father's act. Jordan's inability to kill Pablo is the son's inability to
destroy the father. Sometimes the Freud gets a bit thick, but it's an
interesting article.

Patrick Cheney's "Hemingway and Christian Epic: The Bible in
For Whom the Bell Tolls" (*PLL* 21:170–91) puts more emphasis on
biblical allusions than on epic machinery, but he does a thorough job
of locating the numerous biblical echoes in the novel. Sometimes he
pushes too hard and too far: Jordan's death as crucifixion doesn't
work—not with Jordan lying flat on his stomach. But just when the
article threatens to go completely around the bend, Cheney brings it
back with the thesis that the biblical parallels are not *imitatio Christi*
but "show how modern man can adapt the *idea* of Christianity to his
own experience, creating a new 'religion of man.'"

In his article "Hemingway's Colonel" (*HemR* 5,i:40–45) George
Monteiro, with his customary precision, makes a strong argument for
the asthetics of *Across the River and into the Trees* being based on
Walter Pater's ideas. Close examination of several key scenes shows
the narrative "is controlled by the Colonel's attempt to bring the
ordering form and intensity of art to quotidian life." In "Hemingway's
'In Another Country' and 'Now I Lay Me'" (*HemR* 5,i:32–39) Jim
Steinke gives a sensitive comparison of these two war stories, so often
linked together by critics. Steinke argues that "Now I Lay Me" is a
Nick Adams story, but that "In Another Country" is "to a large extent

the major's story, told by a narrator who now understands it with a force he never did then." The comparison of the two narrators and of the stories' effects is solidly done. Implicit in the article is the possibility that "In Another Country" does not belong in the Nick Adams canon.

Even more revisionist is the work of Frank Scafella, " 'I and the Abyss': Emerson, Hemingway, and the Modern Vision of Death" (*HemR* 4,ii:2–6), who is trying to make us see the narrator of Hemingway's stories as a separate persona. In this essay he focuses on Nick Adams as the author and narrator of the Nick Adams stories. Nick-the-author is not Nick-the-character, and neither of them is Hemingway, the writer behind both Nicks. Scafella's thesis needs a larger canvas to make its case clearly, but his notion of Hemingway's narrator as separate persona needs the same attention we've lavished on Hawthorne.

In a less ambitious essay Donald Junkins links Hemingway's poetic prose to the precepts of Ezra Pound as found in *The ABC of Reading*. In "Hemingway's Contribution to American Poetry" (*HemR* 4,ii:18–23) Junkins draws on examples from "Cat in the Rain" and "The End of Something" to show that Hemingway's repetition of key words focuses the reader's attention on images, creating "a series of melodic gestures . . . a tone poem based on repetition of archetypal images." Bern Oldsey's note, *"El Pueblo Español*: 'The Capital of the World' " (*SAF* 13:103–10), deals with the influence of the movies and *Grand Hotel* in particular on this little-studied and atypical Hemingway story. Oldsey goes on to show the major theme to be illusion-disillusionment.

This year's Horatio Hemingway award goes to Florence G. Feasley for her essay, "Copywriting and the Prose of Hemingway" (*JQ* 62: 121–26), which poses the question: "can the literature of Ernest Hemingway have anything to say to advertising students and copywriters?" I can't bear to tell you the answer. You'll have to read it for yourself.

North Carolina State University

Part II

11. Literature to 1800

William J. Scheick

This year the outstanding study of colonial American literature is a collection of essays on Puritan poets and poetics. Although the articles in this volume are uneven, they collectively amount to a bold push forward in our appreciation of New England colonial verse. Because of the importance of this book, its contents will be treated in some detail in my following comments.

i. Puritan Poetry

Puritan Poets and Poetics: Seventeenth-Century American Poetry in Theory and Practice (Penn. State), ed. Peter White, includes a section on selected verse genres. General reviews are provided in Robert Secor's "Seventeenth-Century Almanac Verse" (pp. 229–46) and in Harold Jantz's "Baroque Free Verse in New England and Pennsylvania" (pp. 258–73). Robert D. Arner's "Wit, Humor, and Satire in Seventeenth-Century American Poetry" (pp. 274–85) focuses on the poetry of Thomas Morton and Nathaniel Ward; and another outlet for Puritan expression of fun is discussed in Jeffrey Walker's "Anagrams and Acrostics: Puritan Poetic Wit" (pp. 247–85). Whereas these forms of verse appealed to the community, colonial Latin poetry, according to Lawrence Rosenwald in "*Voces Clamantium in Deserto*: Latin Verse of the Puritans" (pp. 303–17), is equivalent to trade jargon, thieves' argot, and sacred priestly language. The special language of meditation interests Ursula Brumm, whose "Meditative Poetry in New England" (pp. 318–36) claims that although contemplative verse was always prevalent, meditative verse specifically designated to prepare the heart was not popular until after the mid-1660s. The year 1660 also represents for my "Tombless Virtue and Hidden Text: New England Puritan Funeral Elegies" (pp. 286–302) a time when several elegies on deceased clergy began to highlight an inward communal turning upon the isolated colonial collective self, which (in contrast to contemporary English elegies) finds no comforting framework of consolation in authority, tradition, or the patterns of society, nature, and art.

The comfort of the divinely sanctioned mythos provided by typology is noted by Karen E. Rowe in "Prophetic Visions: Typology and Colonial American Poetry" (pp. 47–66), and types figure as well in Mason I. Lowance, Jr.'s "Religion in Puritan Poetry: The Doctrine of Accommodation" (pp. 33–46), which explores the Augustinian idea that the divine author directs writers in their use of language and imagery (especially when typological) to reconcile art and truth in verse. That biblical typology was not the only tradition drawn upon by colonial poets is remarked by Cheryl Z. Oreovicz in "Investigating 'the *America* of nature': Alchemy in Early American Poetry" (pp. 99–110). If alchemy maintained a marginal position in the Puritan imagination, so did colonial women; Cheryl Walker's routine "In the Margin: The Image of Women in Early Puritan Poetry" (pp. 111–26) observes that (with the briefly mentioned exception of Edward Taylor) women's work was devalued and made to define male centrality. Walker parrots an earlier study which claimed that whereas deceased women were *generally* seen only as a loss to friends and family, deceased men were considered to be a loss to the church; that these latter men were ministers, not just ordinary male citizens, is an important fact ignored by Walker. Women figure as well in "Puritan Women Poets in America" (pp. 21–32), in which Pattie Cowell catalogs female interest in religion, family, personal attitudes, individual struggles, and the frontier.

Not only these themes, but one colonial woman's hope in a future reality of harmony and oneness, when temporal experiences would eventuate in the fulfillment of divine promises, is the subject of Rosamond R. Rosenmeier's "The Wounds Upon Bathsheba: Anne Bradstreet's Prophetic Art" (pp. 129–46), which also suggests that Bradstreet was a serious, inventive artist who thought of her poems as a means of growing toward a union with Christ. Jeffrey A. Hammond, in "'Make Use of What I Leave in Love': Anne Bradstreet's Didactic Self" (*R&L* 17:11–26), goes further than Rosenmeier in claiming that Bradstreet's poems are at once confessional and didactic; for Hammond, Bradstreet's shifts in mood between rebellion and acceptance are not unconscious, but a deliberate manner designed to indicate to her future readers that their experience of a troubled self unreconciled to divine will is in fact an affirmation of their progress toward redemption. Rosenmeier and Hammond might be correct in thinking that even in her private poems Bradstreet might have had an audience in mind, but Hammond's assertion that Bradstreet's shifts in tone are essentially deliberate does not convince me. Not just a change of tone is involved in such poems as "Upon the Burning of Our House" and "Upon My Son Samuel," but a jarring curtailment of poetic momentum marked by an abrupt interjection of short, choked, and unpoetic lines followed by the dissolution of these works into cant and formulaic submission. The intensity of the poet's voice and the engagement of the poet's presence change with her shift in tone— these are the important facts to note. Moreover, to assume with Hammond that Bradstreet's "purposeful shaping of autobiographical material [is] a means of showing readers how redemption worked in the daily life of the saint" is to attribute to the poet a damning presumption of the very sort she tried to avoid in her recurrent attacks on vanity throughout her prose and poetry.

Controlling youth's vanity was one of the aims of a text for children, explains David H. Watters in " 'I Spoke as a Child': Authority, Metaphor and *The New-England Primer*" (*EAL* 20:193–213). Watters interestingly argues that the text of the *Primer* progresses through various types of imagery (from passive to active in implication) designed to prepare a Puritan child to accept certain root metaphors, especially those pertaining to the authority of a paternal deity and to parentally acceptable expression of the child's voice in words sanctioned by religious tradition.

A recollection of a colonial poet who sometimes assumed the persona of a child in his verse is reported in "Taylor on Taylor: A Family Memoir of Edward Taylor" (*RALS* 12 [1982]:29–42) by Deborah Spangler Koelling; and an updated "memoir" reviewing academic impressions of Taylor is provided by Norman S. Grabo and Jana Wainwright in "Edward Taylor" (*Fifteen American Authors Before 1900*, pp. 439–67). J. Daniel Patterson's "A Reconsideration of Edward Taylor's 'The Preface,' Lines 9–12" (*EAL* 20:64–66) makes clear that Taylor describes the firmament as a locked box (the mortal realm), in which humanity is confined by sin and awaits release by Christ. Rosemary Fithian's " 'Words of My Mouth, Meditations of My Heart': Edward Taylor's *Preparatory Meditations* and the Book of Psalms" (*EAL* 20:89–119) makes clear the important point that Taylor's verse is more indebted to the Davidian model than scholars have been inclined to acknowledge. Similar to the Psalms are Taylor's alternation

between personal and collective voice; his reliance on a poetic structure developing from lament, to supplication, to thanksgiving; and
his use of a persona fond of interrogation, amplification, and antithesis. The language of Taylor's persona also interests Michael Clark,
whose "The Subject of the Text in Early American Literature" (*EAL*
20:120–30) argues that for Taylor phonemes, syntax, and grammar
accomplish what images and metaphors cannot; that is, they establish a connection between the human and the divine. For Taylor,
language fails when it represents or expresses, but succeeds when it is
used discursively, when it situates the individual within a network of
verbal relations.

Clark's "The Honeyed Knot of Puritan Aesthetics" (pp. 67–83), to
return to *Puritan Poets and Poetics*, claims that both Taylor and Bradstreet dramatically cancel the sensible bases of language, a disruption
of the integrity of language as sign that allows for the revelation of
a more ultimate sign. Signs are more what they seem in "Puritan
Iconography: The Art of Edward Taylor's *Gods Determinations*" (pp.
84–98), in which Lynn M. Haims interprets Taylor's long poem as a
drama involving Christ, Satan, and Soul as emblematic characters in
a work divided into four playlike acts, the deliberate roughness of
which registers the poet's aesthetic desires striving against religious
sanction. Taylor's playing a part as if in a drama is the topic of "Edward Taylor, the Acting Poet" (pp. 185–97), in which the late Karl
Keller restates his notion of Taylor as a seeker and desirer who does
not know who he is and enjoys this fact because such ignorance is
freedom.

Apparent ignorance of another kind is noted in Peter White's
"Cannibals and Turks: Benjamin Tompson's Image of the Native
American" (pp. 198–209), an interesting attempt to locate century-old
sources to explain Tompson's failure to depict real Native Americans
in *New Englands Crisis*. That some Puritan poets could see the forest
for the trees as well as for the types is evident in Robert Daly's "The
Danforths: Puritan Poets in the Woods of Arcadia" (pp. 147–57).
Similarly, both spiritual type and worldly reality combine in another
poet's verse: " 'Mutuall Sweet Content': The Love Poetry of John
Saffin" (pp. 175–84) by Kathryn Zabelle Derounian. Not love, but
harshness of tone characterizes *The Day of Doom*, which Alan H.
Pope explores in "Petrus Ramus and Michael Wigglesworth: The
Logic of Poetic Structure" (pp. 210–26) to argue that in the poem
divine refutation of sinners is expressed in carefully structured syl-

logisms; whereas in *Meat Out of the Eater* a gentler voice emerges, one that uses Ramistic logic.

The voice of the past was important to Edward Johnson, who is presented in Jesper Rosenmeier's "To Keep in Memory: The Poetry of Edward Johnson" (pp. 158–74) as someone who felt a sense of loss over the passing of first-generation Puritan divines and who therefore kept covenant with his ancestors through memory, which suggested a coherent past that could keep New England on its sacred mission. That Johnson might be the author of a satiric song is a suggestion first made by Harold Jantz and is now revived in J. A. Leo Lemay's *"New England's Annoyances": America's First Folk Song* (Delaware). This verse burlesques promotional tracts and at the same time satirizes antipromotional literature, Lemay thinks, and it seems to have been meant as an inside joke for New World settlers. Beneath the joke lie real frontier discomforts and, as well, a real patriotic sentiment aimed at retaining colonists. Lemay speculates that the song was written around 1643 as a response to *New Englands First Fruits*. That the poem is written by Johnson is also a matter of speculation, one troubled by stanza 13 (a poke at the Congregationalist practice of exclusion from church membership), which is for me not as easy to explain away as it is for Lemay.

ii. Puritan Prose

Whereas the first American folk song criticizes Congregationalism in passing, Roger Williams' works are painstaking in their objections. Williams' inner life has remained elusive, explains Glenn W. La-Fantasie in "Roger Williams: The Inner and Outer Man" (*CRevAS* 16:375–94), because he thought that his public self was identical to his private self; he maintained a contradictory self-image, combining his role as a man of controversy and as a man of peace, by allowing himself to show outwardly only what he thought was proper in his inner self. Mary Rowlandson too has evaded close scrutiny, but now in "New Light on Mary Rowlandson" (*EAL* 20:24–38) David L. Greene reveals that she was born around 1637 (not 1635), married for a second time, and died on 5 January 1710/11 (not in 1678). Something of the experiences of Samuel Sewall in 1698 is recorded in two of his recently discovered letters. David H. Watters edits "A Letter from Samuel Sewall to His Father" (*NEQ* 58:598–601), in which the Puritan judge combines a matter-of-fact style with millennial sentiments in reporting the news of the day; and Wilson H. Kimnack edits "Note on a Letter: Samuel Sewall to Nehemiah Hobart" (*YULG* 59:152–54), in which the judge remarks problems in the New World but still believes it to be a haven for Protestantism.

Sewall's famous diary is listed in *American Diaries: An Annotated Bibliography of Published American Diaries and Journals, Volume One: Diaries Written from 1492 to 1844* (Gale, 1983) by Laura Arksey, Nancy Pries, and Marcia Reed. So is Cotton Mather's diary, which receives attention in Lawrence Alan Rosenwald's "Cotton Mather as Diarist" (*Prospects* 8[1983]:129–61). Rosenwald discerns three divisions in the diary: the first, in which Mather sees himself as a chosen spokesman entrusted with divine messages; the second, in which (from 1711) he responded to the falsehood of one of the messages by keeping a record of his devices for doing good; the third, in which (from 1724) he transforms his disappointment in trying to do good by now turning to contemplation. Not disappointment so much as frustration characterizes the Mather presented in Mitchell Robert Breitwieser's informed *Cotton Mather and Benjamin Franklin: The Price of Representative Personality* (Cambridge). Breitwieser focuses on what he can see between the lines of Mather's writings, especially *Magnalia Christi Americana*, which evinces a narrative tension between obstinate historical facts and the sacred compositional principles brought to bear on them. In richer detail than ever before Breitwieser discovers an author who wanted the freedom of a self-fathering Sir William Phips; an author who would have preferred not to internalize and suppress the desires of his self in order to accommodate, through sublimation of self in memory, the demands of his culture and ancestors; an author who was ambivalent, on the one hand, in his sense of obligation and allegiance to the past and, on the other hand, in his attraction to the burgeoning independence of mind during the Enlightenment.

This latter attraction is evident in Mather's interest in medical innovation. He and Benjamin Colman might have lacked expertise in medicine, but (as Maxine Van de Wetering reminds us in "A Reconsideration of the Inoculation Controversy" [*NEQ* 58:46–67]) they both were expressing an enlightened position on the issues of human worth and suffering. Mather, like Sewall, was similarly forward-looking not only concerning the black race but also, in a special sense, in their mutual interest in the apocalypse. Although this interest included features imported from England, explains Stephen J. Stein in

"Transatlantic Extensions: Apocalyptic in Early New England" (*The Apocalypse in English Renaissance Thought and Literature* [Manchester, 1984], ed. C. A. Patrides and Joseph Wittreich, pp. 266–98), sometimes (as with Mather) these features were transformed to convey new interpretations.

No interpretations were invited in at least one school text designed to shape character; this slim volume of Latin aphorisms, used between 1671 and 1708, is described by Matthias W. Senger in "The Fate of an Early American Schoolbook: Leonhard Culmann's *Sententiae Pueriles*" (*HLB* 32[1984]:256–73). Not the purpose of texts, but the use of standing type in producing them is remarked by Paul R. Sternberg and John M. Brayer in "A Note on the Printing of the New England Almanacks, 1646–1650" (*PAAS* 94[1984]:156–61).

iii. The South

Both text and pictures interest Marcus B. Simpson, Jr., whose "Copperplate Illustrations in Dr. John Brickell's *Natural History of North-Carolina* (1737): Sources for the Provincial Map, Flora, and Fauna" (*NCHR* 62:119–56) traces sources and concludes that Brickell's text is not entirely plagiarized and that his illustrations, some of which might be original, occasionally show an improvement in accuracy when they are compared with their predecessors. Comparisons of another kind occur in southern colonial humor. In a disappointing essay, "Colonial Humor: Beginning with the Butt" (*Critical Essays on American Humor* [Hall, 1984], ed. William Bedford Clark and W. Craig Turner, pp. 139–54), Robert Micklus points to the work of Nathaniel Ward, Thomas Morton, and William Byrd as examples of primitive humor lampooning others, whereas the writings of Ebenezer Cook and Dr. Alexander Hamilton show increased sophistication in their manifestation of humor aimed at the author himself.

Humor, especially in satire, is a prevalent concern of the contributors to the colonial section of *The History of Southern Literature* (LSU), ed. Louis D. Rubin, Jr., et al. In "The Beginnings" J. A. Leo Lemay focuses particularly on promotional literature and anti-promotional satire, while in his chapter on Captain John Smith, Lemay emphasizes the main themes and concerns of Smith's writings. Concern with satire, together with histories and religious works, informs "Literature in the Eighteenth-Century Colonial South," in which Robert D. Arner reviews rather quickly some of the writings of Robert Beverley, William Stith, Samuel Davies, and Ebenezer Cook. Satire again interests Robert Bain in his chapter on William Byrd of Westover. Not Jefferson's humor, but his struggle in managing his thematic interest in the nature of freedom, on the one hand, and the nature of slavery, on the other hand, in *Notes on the State of Virginia* is remarked with care in Lewis P. Simpson's "The Ideology of Revolution." This new *History* covers much territory in a clear manner and ought to be a handy reference tool for nonspecialists.

iv. Edwards and the Great Awakening

Norman Pettit's 85-page introduction to *The Works of Jonathan Edwards, Volume 7: The Life of David Brainerd* (Yale) succeeds in providing details about Edwards' life in Stockbridge, in defining the Moravian threat to the spread of Congregationalism among Native Americans, and in filling out the facts of Brainerd's life and associations. Less satisfying is Pettit's reticence concerning the glaring peculiarity that Edwards, who claims that Brainerd's diary was put in his hands by Providence, should have had the audacity to "tone down" or to "take great liberties," as Pettit admits, with this divinely sanctioned text. Edwards says he edited the diary "for brevity's sake," but much more is at stake. Pettit says that Edwards "altered what he did not like and omitted what he found unacceptable," and suggests that perhaps Brainerd was too imaginative and desperate for Edwards. Pettit does not report (as I did in 1975) that Edwards' private struggle over the Lord's Supper as practiced in Northampton seems a motivating factor in his editing; but finally the issue is larger than this point as well. Edwards reveals something of himself in his audacious editing of Brainerd's diary, something of that secret inner self of which we hardly get a glimpse anywhere else. Fortunately, Pettit's edition includes all the passages Edwards deleted, and it should not be long before someone probes deeply into the matter of Edwards' silent editing. The importance of this diary in an assessment of Edwards' contribution to later religious thought is argued by Joseph Conforti in "Jonathan Edwards's Most Popular Work: 'The Life of David Brainerd' and Nineteenth-Century Evangelical Culture" (*ChH* 54:188–201); the popular diary, Conforti observes, gave a high-flown definition to true virtue (a radical disinterested benevolence) and thereby gave antebellum America a religious folk hero.

Edwards' influence also concerns Bruce Kuklick, whose *Church-*

men and Philosophers: From Jonathan Edwards to John Dewey (Yale) claims that the divine's emphasis on personal responsibility for depravity was transmitted as a tradition through the New Divinity, the Princeton Orthodoxy, and the New Haven Theology to provide, finally, a framework for John Dewey's thought. Edwards' participation in another tradition, that of the new world aesthetic revolution, is the thesis of "Edwards, Emerson and Beyond: The Hypervisual American Great Awakening"(*MSE* 10:24–45), an elliptical, brusque, and not very original essay in which William E. H. Meyer focuses on Edwards' fascination with sight and light, with salvation by eye alone. Meyer might have written with less hyper self-inflation had he read more scholarship on Edwards and Emerson—James Carse's *Jonathan Edwards and the Visibility of God* (1967), for example, which is treated with other related works in Everett Emerson's sane overview of the field ("Jonathan Edwards," *Fifteen American Authors Before 1900*, pp. 230–49). Future scholars will also need to consider " 'Like Apples of Gold in Pictures of Silver': The Portrait of Wisdom in Jonathan Edwards's Commentary on the Book of Proverbs" (*ChH* 54:324–37), in which Stephen J. Stein demonstrates that Edwards regarded Wisdom, the central figure of Proverbs, as the personification of true virtue, but increasingly he tended to view this figure Christologically as an agent of righteousness and virtue.

　　Edwards' daughter, wrestling with the problem of a self which refused to be utterly dependent upon God alone, speaks her mind in *The Journal of Esther Edwards Burr, 1744–1757* (Yale, 1984), ed. Carol F. Karlsen and Laurie Crumpacker. A greater sense of self-confidence not only informed Esther's thoughts, but also her milieu. One source of this change might have been ethical Common Sense philosophy, which Mark A. Noll ("Common Sense Traditions and American Evangelical Thought" [*AQ* 37:216–38]) discerns as a factor loosening conservative Protestant theology and thereby informing the new sense of human ability to rise to ever-increasing heights of freedom and happiness in mid- and late-18th-century America. Other transformations were beginning as well, including the perception of religious enthusiasm initially as something frightening and then later (by the 19th century) as something compatible to society; this thesis is a strand of the argument of David S. Lovejoy's intelligent *Religious Enthusiasm in the New World: Heresy to Revolution* (Harvard).

　　In the writings of at least one group of religious enthusiasts a relation developed between belief and environment. In "The Evolution

of Quaker Theology and the Unfolding of a Distinctive Quaker Ecological Perspective in Eighteenth-Century America" (*PaH* 52:242–
53) Donald Brooks Kelley discusses the images of change and improvement in the land (as a forthcoming millennial new earth) that
appear as expressions of pride in the works of David Humphreys and
Joel Barlow, and then contrasts these images to those of Quaker
writers, who are more humble and mystical in their sense of a conservative, custodial role in relation to a land which gives evidence of
the benevolence of nature. America's special relation to nature's pro-
fusion attracted the interest of other Pennsylvania authors, who also
believed that a secularized politics of virtue would predetermine the
success of art in America. These writers, as described by David S.
Shields in "The Wits and Poets of Pennsylvania: New Light on the
Rise of Belles Lettres in Provincial Pennsylvania, 1720–1740" (*PMHB*
109:99–143), tended to mythologize Philadelphia as a New Athens of
future peace and to project the eloquence of its authors as a promise
of future glory in American literature and civilization.

v. Franklin, Jefferson, and the Revolutionary Period

Philadelphia served as the background for Franklin's rise to fame in
his autobiography, a work in which Mitchell Robert Breitwieser (*Cotton Mather and Benjamin Franklin*) sees an elaborate concern with
the dynamics of self, which (Breitwieser cogently relates) Franklin
associated with electricity and money; Franklin followed through on
Mather's sublimated resistance and fashioned a self as a conscious
project, first, fully expressed in external works and, second, grounded
in a social context free from the paternal authority of his predecessors,
including his father. However, Franklin believed in an established
authority in the use of English, a belief described by Christopher
Looby in "Phonetics and Politics: Franklin's Alphabet as a Political
Design" (*ECS* 18[1984]:1–34); Franklin wanted to alter the alphabet
toward uniformity in order to standardize speech, halt the process of
linguistic change, and promote social harmony—all of which would
mitigate the effects of commercialism, economic stratification, and
social diversification of many kinds. That Franklin himself became for
his son an authority figure (a despotic father) of the sort he himself
rejected in fashioning his sense of self is the thesis of Willard Randall's
A Little Revenge: Benjamin Franklin and His Son (Little, Brown,
1984). Franklin speaks with the authority of experience in *The Papers*

of Benjamin Franklin, Volume 24: May 1 through September 30, 1777 (Yale, 1984), ed. William B. Willcox, covering the patriot's service as the head of the American delegation to France. Other writings are the principal concern of the critical commentary reviewed by Bruce Granger in "Benjamin Franklin" (*Fifteen American Authors Before 1900*, pp. 250–80).

Authority also interests Joseph Fireoved, whose "Nathaniel Gardner and the *New-England Courant*" (*EAL* 20:214–35) reviews the use of reason, free speech, and wit by a contributor to James Franklin's newspaper in its arguments with influential clergy; and authority interests Douglas L. Wilson, whose "Thomas Jefferson's Early Notebooks" (*WMQ* 42:433–52) revises the dates of these writings and thereby provides clues to Jefferson's formative reading. Breaking with authority concerns Richard K. Matthews in *The Radical Politics of Thomas Jefferson: A Revisionist View* (Kansas, 1984), which argues excessively and polemically the uncertain thesis that Jefferson was not a traditional 18th-century liberal, but was a radical with a pastoral (not agrarian) belief in scientific agriculture, a mode of living on the land that allows one to pursue private and public interests. Land, specifically the Louisiana Purchase, according to Harold Hellenbrand's "Not 'to Destroy But to Fulfil': Jefferson, Indians, and Republican Dispensation" (*ECS* 18:523–49), permitted Jefferson to alter his early belief that the white and red races would soon amalgamate; with the new land he came to accept a much longer time-line for this millennial integration, his vision of which was not informed by fact or served by governmental institutions. The importance of land in Jefferson's thought surfaces again in Hellenbrand's " 'Roads to Happiness': Rhetorical and Philosophical Design in Jefferson's *Notes on the State of Virginia*" (*EAL* 20:3–23), which argues that for Jefferson changeless, stable principles of nature and moral law exist untainted by the agents of history, whereas the human ability to perceive this stasis and to base society on it does mutate; consequently, the rhetoric of *Notes* appears to branch and detour, but actually it conveys a glimpse of the changeless prospect of natural and moral law.

Not Jefferson's rhetoric, but that of a fellow patriot, whose *The Rights of Man* Jefferson admired and endorsed for American publication, to their mutual grief, is a subject treated in Terence Martin's "The Negative Structures of American Literature" (*AL* 57:1–22). Martin detects in Paine's language a negating logic (characteristic of apophatic theology) that is designed to strip away the old to yield, as it were, a blank slate permitting a sense of renewal. A chronological account of Paine's Revolutionary writings as well as the attribution to Paine of *Four Letters on Interesting Subjects* (1776) are provided by A. Owen Aldridge in *Thomas Paine's American Ideology* (Delaware, 1984). Aldridge devotes special attention to *Common Sense*, which in his opinion exhibits an ideological structure, with an ethical basis, even if Paine's principles were not unified. In his search for influences on Paine—including Locke, Rousseau, and Montesquieu—Aldridge is not always convincing, nor is his denial of the influence of religion on Paine's political thought.

The politics of several clerics contemporary to Paine is apparent in the 10 writings (1774–77), replete with typological and millennial notions, collected by David R. Williams in *Revolutionary War Sermons* (Scholars' Facsimiles, 1984). Politics is certainly an issue in Nancy V. Morrow's "The Problem of Slavery in the Polemical Literature of the American Enlightenment" (*EAL* 20:236–55), which reviews how reason and logic, on the one hand, and satire, on the other hand, as well as the idea of compromise were ineffectual tools for forging an abolitionist ideology. Another political work, a poem (1775) written by a black New England minister describing the outlook of the minutemen, is presented by Ruth Bogin in " 'The Battle of Lexington': A Patriotic Ballad By Lemuel Haynes" (*WMQ* 42:499–506). Another poet, who wrote both patriotic and lyrical verse, is defended passionately, ill-temperedly, and unsuccessfully by Richard Nickson, whose "A Plea for Captain Philip Freneau" (*LJHum* 11:11–22) asserts that Freneau's poetry is great because it manifests a wide-ranging spirit and a contemporary cast of mind.

vi. The Early National Period

The career of another poet, also teacher and minister, who with more fervor than finesse celebrated the national heroes behind the securing of American freedom, is reviewed in "George Richards: 'The Best Poet America Ever Produced'" (*EAL* 20:131–55) by Lewis Leary. Leary's interest in another minister, whose selling of his own writings came to occupy him more than preaching, is pursued in *The Book-Peddling Parson: An Account of the Life and Works of Mason Locke Weems* (Algonquin, 1984), which places Weems in a southern tradition of writers who tend but resist full polarization toward fictionalization in their writings.

Folkloric fiction about snakes—e.g., that rattlers have pilot snakes, hypnotize their prey, and lick their victims before swallowing them— is the subject of Richard M. Hurst's "Snakelore Motifs in the Writings of J. Hector St. John de Crèvecoeur and Other Colonial Writers" (*NYFQ* 9 [1984]:55–97). Not serpents, but their wilderness habitat as at once a threat and an asset to the survival of America, receives attention in John Hales's "The Landscape of Tragedy: Crèvecoeur's 'Susquehanna'" (*EAL* 20:39–63). Hale argues that Crèvecoeur's long sketch of a central Pennsylvania village emphasizes a fear articulated at the end of *Letters from an American Farmer*: that the order of American community might be subverted by the potentially destructive malevolence of nature and the degeneration of its human inhabitants.

The wonder of the wilderness, rather than its threat, fascinated William Bartram, who in Larry R. Clarke's "The Quaker Background of William Bartram's View of Nature" (*JHI* 46:435–48) is said to have substituted direct observation for fixed concepts of the laws of nature and to have concluded that his intuitive approach to nature led to a useful and deep understanding of life. If according to Clarke, Bartram did not inhibit his observations by making them conform to Deistic natural laws, the naturalist, according to L. Hugh Moore in "The Aesthetic Theory of William Bartram" (*EAS* 12[1983]:17–35), structured *Travels* around 18th-century concepts of such categories as the beautiful, the sublime, and the picturesque.

vii. Brown and Contemporaries

In *Sensational Designs: The Cultural Work of American Fiction, 1790–1860* (Oxford) Jane Tompkins offers a thoroughly political reading of two of Charles Brockden Brown's romances. For Tompkins *Wieland* presents a post-French Reformationist, negative view of independence that refutes the Jeffersonian Republican faith in the human capacity, through religion and education, to govern without the constraints of an established social order. *Arthur Mervyn*, on the other hand, emphasizes the Federalist values of commerce, marriage, and the exchange of information as rudiments for the new nation, if it is to survive the conditions described in *Wieland*. Tompkins' reading of

Literature to 1800

Wieland is better than that of *Arthur Mervyn*, but the former is marred by her insistence that the earlier romance expresses "a single ideological proposition"; *Wieland*, however, is a multifaceted work conveying many interrelated themes and evincing a broad-based skepticism that in all probability vexes both Republican and Federalist notions. A conservative political reading of Brown, however, appears as well in "Plague and Politics in 1793: *Arthur Mervyn*" (*Criticism* 27:225–46), in which Shirley Samuels argues that Brown's romance teaches Americans what to fear and encourages them to use institutions of social order, especially the family, as a means of countering the related threats of revolution, contagion, and political and sexual infidelity. That these threats relate to Brown's complex social reading of human action, rather than to a Calvinist interpretation of life, is the thesis of Thomas Pribek's "A Note on 'Depravity' in *Wieland*" (*PQ* 64:273–79). The complexity of human behavior, particularly as evidenced in Brown's apparently accurate depiction of place and milieu (change, cosmopolitanism, urbanization, secularism), is the subject of Joseph J. Feeney's "Modernized by 1800: The Portrait of Urban America, Especially Philadelphia, in the Novels of Charles Brockden Brown" (*AmerS* 23[1982]:25–38).

Optimism in response to the modernization of the exemplary new nation, combined with a call for cultural independence, characterizes David Everett's essays for the *Columbian Orator*, which have been collected by Benjamin Franklin V in *Works* (Scholars' Facsimiles, 1983). Some of the contents of another publication are described by E. W. Pitcher in "The Philadelphia *Literary Miscellany* of 1795: Magazine or Serial Anthology?" (*PBSA* 77[1983]:333–35).

Interest in another popular genre of the time, the melodramatic romance, is the subject of Philip Young's "'First American Novel': *The Power of Sympathy*, in Place" (*CollL* 11[1984]:115–24), which I have not seen. Excerpts from such romances as Ann Eliza Schuyler Bleeker's *The History of Maria Kittle* (1791), Susanna Haswell Rowson's *Charlotte* (1794), and Hannah Webster Foster's *The Coquette* (1797) are included in *Hidden Hands: An Anthology of Women Writers, 1790–1870* (Rutgers), ed. Lucy M. Freibert and Barbara A. White, whose book represents a timely asset for studying the literature of the post-Revolution period and whose useful introductory comments are marred only by an unfortunate begging of the question of the artistic merit of the works they have anthologized.

viii. Miscellaneous Studies

Another text worthy of attention is *The Puritans in America: A Narrative Anthology* (Harvard), ed. Alan Heimert and Andrew Delbanco, who have arranged their work chronologically to reflect colonial reactions to historical change or crises. Puritan prose is better represented than poetry, which is not only slighted but which is sometimes denied its aesthetic integrity—for example, the printing of an abbreviated version of Anne Bradstreet's "Contemplations." There are no elegies in the text, nor anything from Michael Wigglesworth's *The Day of Doom*, and very little by Edward Taylor. Indeed the nature of Puritan artistry is ignored not only in the representative selections, but in the otherwise helpful introductions. This anthology, in short, will probably be used profitably more in American studies or history courses than in literature courses. One noteworthy response to this work that emphasizes the degree to which it counters Sacvan Bercovitch's interpretation of Puritan culture is "The Weight of Elijah's Mantle: A New Anthology of American Puritan Writings" (*EAL* 20: 156–63) by Philip F. Gura.

Also useful are Michael S. Montgomery's *American Puritan Studies: An Annotated Bibliography of Dissertations, 1882–1981* (Greenwood, 1984) and Marcus A. McCorison's "Additions and Corrections to 'Vermont Imprints, 1778–1820'" (*PAAS* 94[1984]:343–56). Especially noteworthy is the appearance of *Dictionary of Literary Biography, Volume 39: British Novelists 1660–1800* (DLB 39), ed. Martin C. Battestin; this work, in two parts, should prove to be a valuable resource to anyone interested in the transatlantic roots of early American fiction. That the concept of what constitutes American fiction should be broadened is the thesis of "The Earliest American Novel: Aphra Behn's *Oroonoko*" (*NCF* 38[1984]:384–414), in which William C. Spengemann emphasizes how increasingly the narrator of this romance (1688) becomes the center of attention as she departs from the settled world of English readers and explores an American wilderness derived from her imagination. Although Behn possibly never visited the new world, she is an "American" writer in Spengemann's opinion because of the ambiguity of the tone of her narrative, an ambiguity revealing a typical American tension between traditional authority and newly discovered energies.

Concern with traditional authority certainly appears in the writings of colonial and early national American women authors, 68 of whom are included in *A Dictionary of British and American Women Writers: 1660–1800* (Rowman & Allanheld), ed. Janet Todd. This volume is most welcome because it treats the work of such neglected figures as Hannah Mather Crocker, Hannah Adams, Anna Eliza Bleecker, Deborah Norris Logan, and Mary Jemison, all of whom (among others) were ignored in the three volumes of *Dictionary of Literary Biography* (24, 31, 37) devoted to colonial American literature, excellent reference tools unfortunately marred by insufficient attention to women writers.

As I complete this chapter, my eighth for *ALS*, I ponder two observations possibly pertinent to the extent of the reading and the writing required by this annual task. Perhaps apropos to the amount of writing, there is the cautionary example of Puritan Anne Yale Hopkins, who (John Winthrop reports) "had written many books" which are now all lost and who apparently in the process also lost "her understanding and reason." Perhaps apropos to the amount of reading, there is the unsettling comment by Quaker William Penn that "much reading is an oppression of the mind and extinguishes the natural candle."

University of Texas at Austin

12. 19th-Century Literature

David J. Nordloh

Walt Whitman's notion of permanence amidst change seems particularly appropriate to the scholarly work surveyed in this chapter. Interesting innovations and new perspectives and re- and un- canonizations constantly alter the landscape, even as traditional studies flourish as they always have. The metaphor may be forced, but the sense of productive continuity it conveys is not. Nothing so demonstrates the vitality of American literature as the coexistence of old- fashioned literary history side by side with structuralism, and strong interest in Cooper and Howells as well as in Jewett and Freeman and Chopin.

i. General Studies

The most important and most ambitious publication of the year is *The History of Southern Literature* (LSU), ed. Louis D. Rubin, Jr., et al. Not since Jay B. Hubbell's *The South in American Literature: 1607–1900* (1954) has there been this kind of comprehensive effort. Hubbell's magnificent solitary effort has now been replaced by an editorial team and great numbers of chapter authors, with a resultant unevenness in critical quality at certain points and a certain stridency at others. On the other side, this new history attempts to bring its coverage all the way to the present, rather than stopping at the turn of this century. A simple list of contributing scholars and relevant chapters is impressive: Lewis Leary, "1776–1815" (pp. 68–80); Craig Werner, "The Old South, 1815–1840" (pp. 81–91); Mary Ann Wimsatt, "Antebellum Fiction" (pp. 92–107) and "William Gilmore Simms" (pp. 108–17), and, with Robert L. Phillips, "Antebellum Humor" (pp. 136–56); Rayburn S. Moore, "Antebellum Poetry" (pp. 118–26) and "Poetry of the Late Nineteenth Century" (pp. 188–98); Richard J. Calhoun, "Literary Magazines in the Old South" (pp. 157–63); Lewis P. Simpson, "The Mind of the Antebellum South" (pp.

164–76); Elisabeth Muhlenfeld, "The Civil War and Authorship" (pp. 178–87), with emphasis on Mary Chesnut and other diarists; Thomas Richardson, "Local Color in Louisiana" (pp. 199–208); Merrill Maguire Skaggs, "Varieties of Local Color" (pp. 219–227); and Anne Rowe, "Kate Chopin" (pp. 228–32). Here is the new primer of Southern literature, solid, contemporary, essential.

In *Sensational Designs: The Cultural Work of American Fiction, 1790–1860* (Oxford) Jane Tompkins attempts to redefine rather than identify. Dredging up now very tired issues of high culture and popular culture, and complaining of the "male-dominated scholarly tradition that controls both the canon of American literature . . . and the critical perspective that interprets the canon for society," she proposes a canon comprised of popular works and works by women, selected on the basis of their accessibility to the widest possible audiences. The chief common characteristic of such works is stereotypical character, "instantly recognizable representatives of overlapping racial, sexual, national, ethnic, economic, social, political, and religious categories" which "convey enormous amounts of cultural information in an extremely condensed form." Tompkins demonstrates her thesis in chapters on Cooper, with emphasis on *The Last of the Mohicans*; on Harriet Beecher Stowe; and on the influence of the American Tract Society in the creation of a whole body of work in the sentimental Christian tradition, most notably Susan Warner's *The Wide, Wide World*. Since the titles chosen are already so widely read and so often considered "canonical," Tompkins' argument is mostly redundant—an old non-canon is set up and then knocked down. Still, the readings themselves will provoke interest and discussion, as tough-minded criticism always does.

In *Hard Facts* Philip Fisher defines a provocative and deeply challenging conception of culture and of the function of the novel within it. His introductory premise is that "where culture installs new habits of moral perception, such as the recognition that a child is a person, a black is a person, it accomplishes, as a last step, the forgetting of its own strenuous work so that what are newly learned habits are only remembered as facts"; a culture tends to forget what the alternatives to these "hard facts" had been, how the process of choosing one of them took place. The extension of Fisher's premise in literary terms is that those very elements of individual works which now strike us as weakest—because they are later perceived as such elementary and indisputable truths—may historically have been the strongest, because they represented the authentic "cultural work" of the literature. Chapters on individual authors explore this premise. "Killing a Man: The Historical Novel and the Closing Down of Pre-History," focused on Cooper's *The Deerslayer*, treats the killing off of the Indian in order to free the land. "Making a Thing into a Man: The Sentimental Novel and Slavery" analyzes the justification of slavery in the Jeffersonian world of free and independent yoeman farmers depicted in Stowe's *Uncle Tom's Cabin*.

June Howard's *Form and History in American Literary Naturalism* (No. Car.) applies contemporary literary theory to the old problem of defining Naturalism. Drawing upon the work of Todorov, Lukács, and Culler, Howard proposes that the term is defined by the literature which can be identified by it, and that this literature can be identified by "concepts, types of characterization, and strategies for sequencing narrative and producing closure articulated in a distinctive configuration that bears the marks of that particular historical moment." That distinctive configuration "consists in a group of devices for arranging essentially static material according to a documentary logic." Underneath the jargony theoretical complexity of all this lies the same essential—and still valuable—stuff that V. L. Parrington, Donald Pizer, George Becker, and Charles Child Walcutt have already articulated. The ambition of Howard's study is frustrated by its method: the works studied in the effort to define Naturalism are those which have conventionally been called Naturalistic—among them Norris' *The Octopus, The Pit, Blix*, and *Vandover and the Brute*, Crane's *Maggie* and other Bowery pieces—and so the definition must inevitably be what it has been. Including the work of other writers of the 1890s might have produced contrasts productive of more useful distinctions. Another theoretical book, John Gerlach's *Toward the End: Closure and Structure in the American Short Story* (Alabama), mostly avoids received jargon, sets up its own terms, and discusses issues of ending from the friendly perspective of a writer appreciating writing. Poe is everywhere in Gerlach's study, but there are also intelligent readings of stories by John Neal, Washington Irving, Nathaniel Willis, Thomas Nelson Page, Jewett, and Stephen Crane.

William E. Lenz offers a definition of a personality type rather than of a literary mode in *Fast Talk and Flush Times: The Confidence Man as a Literary Convention* (Missouri). In a fascinating and comprehensive tour of 19th- and early 20th-century texts, Lenz traces the specifically American embodiment of the "archetypal trickster" into the distinctive figure formed out of the conditions of boom-and-bust "flush times" and popular literature and culture. This trickster figure is not mythic but local, not supernatural but self-promoting: his trick is that he seeks and wins confidence, and then betrays it. Lenz's survey includes the work of Parson Weems, Washington Irving, James Kirke Paulding, A. B. Longstreet, Seba Smith, Johnson Jones Hooper, William Gilmore Simms, Joel Chandler Harris, and Charles Chesnut, with a particularly effective look at Howells's *The Leatherwood God* as the end of the line. The book is further enhanced by an impressive list of "texts, tracts, events, and commentaries" dealing with the confidence man.

Elizabeth McKinsey draws upon works by John Neal, George Heriot, Cooper (*The Spy*), Alexander Wilson, and Howells in *Niagara Falls: Icon of the American Sublime* (Cambridge), one of the Cambridge Studies in American Literature and Culture. McKinsey's effort at aesthetic analysis traces through pictorial and literary art, popular culture, and public policy the history of the lure of the place: "Niagara Falls emerges as *the* American icon of the sublime in the early nineteenth century." In other matters of aesthetics Graham Clarke, "Imaging America: Paintings, Pictures and the Poetics of Nineteenth-Century American Landscape" (*Nineteenth-Century American Poetry*, pp. 194–219), outlines the tension created in American art between the "conventions and values of an alien landscape tradition" which is capable of supplying an aesthetic and language equal to America's mythic and literal status on the one hand and a desire to see the new land in a new way on the other. Clarke's survey includes Bryant, Whittier, and Frederick Church (*New England Scenery*, 1851) among others. And William L. Vance, "The Sidelong Glance: Victorian Americans and Baroque Rome" (*NEQ* 58:501–32), treats the curious literary fact of American writers who avoided seeing the "tension between the usable, romantic Rome and the actual Rome." Vance sets out explanations for this blindness to the power of Borromini and Bernini, and mentions in the process Henry Adams, James Russell Lowell, Howells, Timothy Dwight, Francis Marion Crawford, and Henry Blake Fuller.

In concentrating on the law rather than on art Robert A. Ferguson, *Law and Letters in American Culture* (Harvard, 1984) offers a productive overview of ideas that shaped that significant but little explored period between the Great Awakening and the American Renaissance. In some older but revised essays—on Irving and William

Cullen Bryant—and in new ones on Daniel Webster, the Richard
Henry Danas father and son, and Lincoln, Ferguson explores the influence of legal thought and the work of lawyers on literary development. Webster's "subordination of literary expression to republican
principles," for example, though hardly new, made him a specific
target of the writers of the American Renaissance; the Danas, who
"see both the light and the dark in life" but who "see as citizens who
serve the light in a nation of laws," resolved the tension of light and
dark in one way, Emerson and his followers in another; Lincoln, as
political thinker and orator, attempted to reconcile all the sources of
American thought and to serve as peacemaker.

Several volumes treat regional topics. *Upstate Literature: Essays
in Memory of Thomas F. O'Donnell* (Syracuse), ed. Frank Bergmann,
is dedicated to a pioneer in the study of the writers of New York state.
Besides a nice tribute by Edwin H. Cady and reprintings of three of
O'Donnell's essays, the collection includes seven new essays, six of
them relevant here: Perry D. Westbrook, "Writers of the Hudson Val-
ley and the Catskills" (pp. 77–115); Bergmann, "The Meaning of the
Indians and Their Land in Cooper's *The Last of the Mohicans*" (pp.
117–27); Stanton Garner, "The Other Harold Frederic" (pp. 129–41);
Kate H. Winter, "North Country Voices" (pp. 143–64); Lionel D.
Wyld, "The Erie Canal and the Novel" (pp. 165–82); and John M.
Reilly, "Literary Versions of Ethnic History from Upstate New York"
(pp. 183–200). In *The Cavalier in Virginia Fiction* (LSU), Ritchie
Devon Watson, Jr., expands upon William R. Taylor's *Cavalier and
Yankee: The Old South and the American National Character* (1961)
by taking the topic beyond the Civil War while narrowing it to a
single figure *and* to Virginia alone. As a survey, the book can't do full
justice to the opportunity to explore the literary origins of the myth,
its relation to reality, the survival of the myth after the Civil War, the
clash with growing democratic egalitarianism, and the South's reconciliation of that "Cavalier-dominated past" with its historical present.
But it competently discusses works by George Tucker, John Pendleton Kennedy, William Alexander Caruthers, John Esten Cooke,
Thomas Nelson Page, and Mary Johnston among 19th-century writers.
An even more classical perspective on southern writers is provided
by the contributions to *Shakespeare and Southern Writers*. Relevant
essays include Charles S. Watson, "Simms's Use of Shakespearean
Characters" (pp. 13–28); Christina Murphy, "The Artistic Design of
Societal Commitment: Shakespeare and the Poetry of Henry Timrod"

(pp. 29–47); and Thomas Daniel Young, "Lanier and Shakespeare" (pp. 49–61).

In a survey look at women's literature Beverly R. Voloshin, "The Limits of Domesticity: The Female *Bildungsroman* in America, 1820–1870" (*WS* 10[1984]:283–302), examines representative popular fiction of the period in terms of its treatment of women and social organization, and particularly the tension between "idealizations of domesticity and similar, often covert, resistance to it." Particularly in the fiction specified in the title of her essay, women (often orphans) give up hard-won independence in favor of marital security and become both "admired in fashionable society and accepted into it even as they profess to be independent working women." Voloshin thinks this idealized condition "betrays a class bias which prevents it from genuinely offering a new vision of women and social organization." (History has this nasty way of not giving us what we want!) The discussion includes Catharine Sedgwick's *A New-England Tale*, Susan Warner's *The Wide, Wide World*, Maria Susanna Cummins' *The Lamplighter*, and Augusta Jane Evans' *Beulah* and *St. Elmo*.

Other general contributions to the study of women's literature include the biographical essays, brief critical discussions, and preliminary bibliographies in the now-expanded journal *Legacy*, as well as several anthologies. The most accomplished of these, and especially thorough in its combination of introduction, survey of fields and topics, headnotes, and primary and secondary bibliographies of authors represented, is *Hidden Hands: An Anthology of American Women Writers, 1790–1870* (Rutgers), ed. Lucy M. Freibert and Barbara A. White. All of the 20 primary selections, arranged under categories like Melodrama and Early Realism, are excerpts from long fiction, from Tabitha Gilman Tenney's *Female Quixotism* and Salley Barrell Wood's *Dorval* (both 1801) to Martha Finley's *Elsie Dinsmore* (1867). The editors also provide a section of major criticism about women writers. A topical anthology, *Haunted Women: The Best Supernatural Tales by American Women Writers* (Ungar), ed. Alfred Bendixen, collects 13 stories and supplies a predictable introduction on the value of the supernatural in permitting women to explore alternatives to traditional values. Equally narrowly, *Provisions: A Reader from 19th-Century American Women* (Indiana), ed. Judith Fetterley, selects from prose literature for the period 1830 to 1865. The introduction foams along the usual lines—exclusion of women from the canon, the "oppression" that allowed them to deal with oppression itself only indirectly, the inevitably narrow range of female options—but the anthology selections themselves are more interesting. Fetterley includes brief biographical and critical introductions to the selections; these are often so argumentative, so allusive, that basic information—for example, how much of a work is represented by the portion printed here—is buried or missing.

A New Voice for a New People: Midwestern Poetry 1800–1910 (Univ. Press), ed. Bernard F. Engel and Patricia W. Julius, takes an interesting anthology idea but then confuses it. Neither the title nor the introduction indicates whether the focus of the collection is poetry *about* the Midwest or poetry *by* midwesterners. Howells and the Carey sisters and Coates Kinney are here, but so are Longfellow, Bryant, and Margaret Fuller. An anthology of another sort—of good lines—is Arthur Power Dudden, "The Record of Political Humor" (*AQ* 37:50–70), part of a special issue on American humor. Dudden scans the transformation from basic belief in the value of government to the attack on the ideals of democracy and the ability of people to govern themselves. Finley Peter Dunne is most prominent here.

ii. Irving, Cooper, and Their Contemporaries

Albert Von Frank devotes a chapter to Irving in his *The Sacred Game.* Set against his analysis of provincialism as both a form of resistance to traditional culture and an inadequate and incomplete effort to preserve that culture, Von Frank's "Geoffrey Crayon and the Gigantic Race" (pp. 61–78) identifies, particularly with reference to the essay "Roscoe" in *The Sketch Book,* Irving's conservatism and "the conflict he felt between his love of art and his love of home." The topic places Irving in a productive context, albeit an overwritten and at times unnecessarily rhetorical one. Robert Allen Papinchak, " 'The Little Man in Black': The Narrative Mode of America's First Short Story" (*SSF* 22:195–201), describes the mixture of Gothic and German romanticism, of the techniques and structures of both story and essay which characterize Irving's piece. But Papinchak doesn't explain why the discussion is confined to the *first* story. Jeffrey Rubin-Dorsky, "The Value of Storytelling: 'Rip Van Winkle' and 'The Legend of Sleepy Hollow' in the Context of *The Sketch Book*" (*MP* 82:393–406), evaluates the two stories as part of Irving's strategy of using Crayon "to affirm the emotional and psychological value of storytelling." In an ingenious elaboration of stock ideas into a mythic vagueness about literary tradition, Rubin-Dorsky argues that the two stories "reinforce the belief that it was fiction itself, rather than any of the illusions that Crayon invented and then sought to perpetuate, that served as Irving's compensation for the loss of, and the failure to make connections to, the past." And an earlier essay on "Legend," Lloyd M. Daigrepont's "Ichabod Crane: Inglorious Man of Letters" (*EAL* 19[1984]: 68–81), also lacks a convincing basis in cultural history in asserting that "just as Brom saves Sleepy Hollow, Irving saves (for himself, at least) the realm of art and letters. He does so by realizing that the ersatz authors and the pious, common sense detractors of genuine art may be dismissed as easily as Ichabod or the storyteller's challenger."

James Fenimore Cooper's *The Prairie*, edited by James P. Elliott (SUNY), bearing the seal of approval of the CSE, is the latest of the full-scale textual productions of the NEH-funded edition centered at Clark University. Eliott's commentary is so succinct as to be an abstract rather than an essay in laying out the complex textual history, which includes three copy-texts, five different kinds of prepublication materials, five editions, and an autograph revision in an interleaved copy. The disproportion of 117 pages of emendations to only 14 of rejected readings is troublesome, and the editorial treatment will require some study. But I can't fault the continuing productivity of this essential Cooper enterprise. That it is essential is demonstrated by the increasing number of other Cooper publications occurring simultaneous with it. Most prominent of these is the two-volume *The Leatherstocking Tales* (Library of America), with the novels arranged in the order of their original publication. Blake Nevius' name is attached as the Library's authority for the work, but the editors are really James Franklin Beard, Elliott, and their colleagues in "The Writings of James Fenimore Cooper."

Robert Clark has edited *James Fenimore Cooper: New Critical Essays* (Vision), a collection of eight original essays by English, German, and American scholars. The general emphasis of the volume is strongly historical, examining Cooper's writing within the contemporary context and in sum seeing him freshly as an *imaginative* artist turning history into myth and fiction. The authors and essays are Heinz Ickstadt, "Instructing the American Democrat: Cooper and the Concept of Popular Fiction in Jacksonian America" (pp. 15–37); James D. Wallace, "Cultivating an Audience: From *Precaution* to *The Spy*" (pp. 38–54); Eric Cheyfitz, "Literally White, Figuratively Red:

The Frontier of Translation in *The Pioneers*" (pp. 55–95); Charles Swann, "Guns Mean Democracy: *The Pioneers* and the Game Laws" (pp. 96–120); Richard Godden, "Pioneer Properties, or 'What's in a Hut?'" (pp. 121–42); John P. McWilliams, "Red Satan: Cooper and the American Indian Epic" (pp. 143–61); Gordon Brotherston, "*The Prairie* and Cooper's Invention of the West" (pp. 162–86); and Clark's "Rewriting Revolution: Cooper's War of Independence" (pp. 187–205).

Daniel Marder's essay on Cooper in *Exiles at Home: A Story of Literature in Nineteenth Century America* (Univ. Press, 1984), "Cooper: America Is No Place for a Gentleman" (pp. 22–65), is a literary biography focused on life abroad and at home and on the speculations on republicanism and aristocracy those experiences invited. The essay is noteworthy for its nice, brief readings of some of the less-known books. Ross J. Pudaloff, "The Gaze of Power: Cooper's Revision of the Domestic Novel, 1835–1850" (*Genre* 17[1984]:275–96), argues that with *The Monikins* Cooper became disenchanted with America and reshaped the domestic novel—in which he had already asserted that "the character of the democrat could substitute for the blood of the artistocrat"—to now assert that identity is possible only through "disavowal of participation in a democratic political order." William P. Kelly's "Inventing American History: Cooper and the Leatherstocking Tales" (*CUNY English Forum* 1[1984]:259–79) compresses the thesis of Kelly's 1984 book, *Plotting America's Past: Fenimore Cooper and the Leatherstocking Tales*: Cooper's achievement was not a "sharpening sense of an American mythos" or a record of his "mounting alienation from American public life," but rather his record in carefully articulated "structures of thought and feeling" of the special developing pattern of American experience itself. Daryl E. Jones, "Temple in the Promised Land: Old Testament Parallel in Cooper's *The Pioneers*" (*AL* 57:68–78), points out narrative references to Solomon and Ecclesiastes and the equation of Judge Cooper's efforts on behalf of his settlement with the effort of the Israelites to establish a nation, and argues that the novelist was both parodying Templeton's ambition and posing against Natty Bumppo's resistance to historical change the biblical sense that history is an expression of unfathomable divine will. In another essay concentrating on sources and parallels, Benjamin Lease, "America's Shakespeare: Cooper's Brave New World" (*Mythos und Aufklärung*, pp. 143–59), points out images associated with various emotional and intellectual issues derived from the plays. Some of this is Cooper's use of Shakespeare, some of it Lease's inventive correlation.

Calling language the "secret theme," Steven Blakemore argues ingeniously in "Strange Tongues: Cooper's Fiction of Language in *The Last of the Mohicans*" (*EAL* 19[1984]:21–41) that Cooper's manipulation of French and the translated Indian tongues and his presentation of Heyward and Magua as good and bad characters who both manipulate others with words suggest that Cooper "is doubtful about the power of art, the power of language to finally order the discordant tensions of the new world." Paul Rosenzweig answers complaints about the lack of unity in a Cooper novel by proposing in "*The Pathfinder*: The Wilderness Initiation of Mabel Dunham" (*MLQ* 44 [1983]:339–58) that the fault lies in presuming that Natty is the narrative center. Instead, Rosenzweig says, Mabel Dunham "determines the true center of the book; she is the focus not only of the love story but of the adventure story." James Franklin Beard provides a clear text and full transcription of two drafts of the English original of a letter from Cooper to Lafayette, written to support Lafayette's efforts at republicanism in France, in "Cooper, Lafayette, and the French National Budget: A Postscript" (*PAAS* 95:81–99). And Klaus Lubbers mentions Cooper and Robert Montgomery Bird in an overview treatment of "Text as Pretext: Stereotyping the North American Indian" (*Mythos und Aufklärung*, pp. 129–42).

In the only essay about William Gilmore Simms, Miriam J. Shillingsburg draws on her 1969 South Carolina dissertation for "Simms's Last Novel, *The Cub of the Panther*" (*SLJ* 17,ii:108–19), a history of the writing of the novel as well as a discussion of the relevance of fairly unique manuscript material for establishing how Simms worked and of the foci and faults of the novel. A more interesting study, only secondarily about Simms, is John McCardell, "Trent's *Simms*: The Making of a Biography" (*A Master's Due*, pp. 179–203). McCardell connects Charles Dudley Warner's choice of William Peterfield Trent to write the book on Simms in the American Men of Letters series (1892) to Warner's desire for a book with a progressive national rather than a sectional southern perspective.

John Neal, known too commonly for his anonymous praise of himself in the English reviews, gets more appropriate attention in Fritz Fleischmann's " 'A Likeness, Once Acknowledged': John Neal and the 'Idiosyncracies' of Literary History" (*Mythos und Aufklä-*

rung, pp. 161–76), a reading of a Neal story which sets it partly in the context of the current feminist debate and argues that Neal deserves to be installed among the canonized.

iii. Popular Writers of Midcentury

Of the several items treating the Fireside Poets, James H. Justus' comprehensive essay, "The Fireside Poets: Hearthside Values and the Language of Care" (*Nineteenth-Century American Poetry*, pp. 146–65), is the most significant. Surveying topics and vocabularies, Justus describes *how* Bryant, Lowell, Whittier, Longfellow, and Holmes "articulated the values of their culture" and concludes that "the story that these poets tell is not that of the subordination of private purpose to the constituent values that the larger culture endorsed, but of the convergence of personal and public history, of private prerogative and the public weal."

Longfellow is represented by two textual studies by Edward L. Tucker. *The Shaping of Longfellow's* John Endicott: *A Textual History, Including Two Early Versions* (Virginia) supplies the texts and textual apparatus for two earlier forms of a play which finally became part of the *Christus* trilogy, the prose play "The New England Tragedy" and the verse play "Wenlock Christison," neither previously published. Tucker's introduction is an almost too thorough gathering of information about the historical basis, genesis, and composition of the work. He supplies similar textual and critical background in "Longfellow's *The Courtship of Miles Standish*: Some Notes and Two Early Versions" (*SAR*, pp. 285–321), dealing with a work contemporaneous with *John Endicott* and setting out the lighter side of Puritan life. The earlier versions provided here are also hitherto unpublished. In a wonderfully well-written, well-argued essay, E. Miller Budick explores Whittier's reconciliation of belief in immortality with the fact of natural death. "The Immortalizing Power of Imagination: A Reading of Whittier's *Snow-Bound*" (*ESQ* 31:89–99) argues that "the poem identifies the imaginative faculty—the dreaming, remembering part of human consciousness—as a force that can counter the de-imagizing threats of time and change." In a study of fiction rather than poetry Margaret Hallissy, "Poisonous Creature: Holmes's *Elsie Venner*" (*SNNTS* 17:406–19), examines the novel's use of the folkloristic figure of the lamia. Holmes defines the traditional option: the man can remain dispassionate toward the woman as charmer and thus be safe, or risk the experience and in turn risk himself. In *Charles Sealsfield* (WWS 71) Walter Grünzweig provides a brief critical biography of the Czech-born writer whose travel books and novels of the American West were the craze of the 1850s (Longfellow's *Evangeline* drew upon his five-novel cycle *Life in the New World*). And the magazine that best represented such a great number of these writers is the topic of "The Early Years of the *Atlantic Monthly*" (*ATQ* 58:3–30). Ellery Sedgwick III examines the ideological premises of the journal and some of the effects of their application.

The manuscripts of Jones Very are briefly surveyed by Helen R. Deese, "Unpublished and Uncollected Poems of Jones Very" (*ESQ* 30[1984]:154–62). Deese is engaged in a comprehensive edition. David Seed, "Alone with God and Nature: The Poetry of Jones Very and Frederick Goddard Tuckerman" (*Nineteenth-Century American Poetry*, pp. 166–93), sets out a nicely argued comparison of two neglected writers who "embody important directions taken by the New Egland poetic mind in the period 1830 to 1870."

Horatio Alger is finally saved from the fictional melodramatic biography foisted on him by Herbert R. Mayes (*Alger: A Biography without a Hero*, 1928) in *The Lost Life of Horatio Alger, Jr.* (Indiana). Drawing upon thorough research, particularly in the records of the Unitarian church, Gary Scharnhorst, assisted by Jack Bales, sets the record to the facts rather than to the myth. As interesting as that account is Scharnhorst's introductory discussion of the transmission and alteration of Mayes's hoax by other purveyors. Scharnhorst also provides a brief critical perspective in "Dickens and Horatio Alger, Jr." (*Dickens Quarterly* 2:50–53), pointing out Alger's conscious use of Dickens and his vulgarization of Dickensian ideas of success to fit his own didactic purposes.

Much the stronger of two books on Harriet Beecher Stowe is Thomas F. Gossett, Uncle Tom's Cabin *and American Culture* (SMU). Gossett provides a biography of Stowe, with emphasis on early influences; a description of her writing of the book and an analysis of its themes; a survey of reactions to *Uncle Tom's Cabin* in North and South and abroad to the end of the Civil War; a survey of reactions to the play based on the novel during that same period; and a survey of reactions to both book and play to the present time. An interesting selection of illustrations, particularly of scenes and characters from the book, accompanies the text. The weaker book is Moira Davison

Reynolds, *Uncle Tom's Cabin and Mid-Nineteenth Century United States: Pen and Conscience* (McFarland), a collection of chapters on assorted topics—the times, slavery in the times, women and the times, Stowe and the times. Some readers may find the chapter summarizing the plot of the novel useful in an emergency. Reminding us that Stowe also wrote other things, Christopher P. Wilson, "Tempests and Teapots: Harriet Beecher Stowe's *The Minister's Wooing*" (*NEQ* 58: 554–77), proposes somewhat tortuously that the thrust of the novel is not theological but literary, and that Stowe's interest in romance—reflected in her use of the word, her allusion to Shakespeare's *The Tempest*, and the novel's debt to Dickens' *Hard Times*—constitutes a mollifying tendency that makes her vision less effectively reformist, more taken with the "romance" of real life.

Louisa May Alcott is represented by a solid book and two quite effective essays. Charles Strickland, *Victorian Domesticity: Families in the Life and Art of Louisa May Alcott* (Alabama), examines the confused and confusing effects of the conventional conception of domesticity on the one hand and of actual sexual and social distinction and of feminist ideology on the other. In *"Little Women* and the Boy-Book" (*NEQ* 30:384–99) John W. Crowley approaches Alcott's ideological conflicts from the context of a literary tradition. His reading of the process by which Jo March is chastened of her "rebellious impulses" is that, unlike the separatist impulses of the American boy-book tradition, Alcott's character needn't " 'light out for the territory' ": "The glowing sanity of an independent female family allows revolt at the same time that it cherishes home." And Madeleine B. Stern, "Louisa Alcott's Self-Criticism" (*SAR*, pp. 333–82), argues that Alcott's own comments demonstrate her consciousness of literary experimentation in style and language, her sensitivity to reactions to her work, and her professional involvement in all aspects of publication. Stern supports these assertions with excerpts from Stowe's letters and journals and published works, oddly arranged and categorized and not very accessible.

Carol Farley Kessler provides chronology, introduction, selected bibliography, notes, and a few contemporary statements about the novel for a reprint of Elizabeth Stuart Phelps's *The Story of Avis* (Rutgers); Kessler reads the novel as an indictment of those "conditions that block human creativity," with marriage chief among them. And in "Caroline M. Kirkland: Additions to the Canon" (*BRH* 86,

iii[1983–85]:338–46) Audrey Roberts surveys the extant correspondence of one of the first female journalists, establishing among other
things Kirkland's authorship of several anonymously published magazine pieces.

iv. Regionalism and Local Color

In "Sut Lovingood: A Nat'ral Born Durn'd Yarnspinner" (*SLJ* 18:
89–100) Carolyn S. Brown supplies an effective description of the
qualities of the tall tale and of Sut as storyteller while arguing that the
tastelessness of G. W. Harris' "yarns" should be excused by their being
fiction rather than fact. More compelling is the collection of eight essays, focused on several disciplines and oriented primarily toward
folklore, in *Davy Crockett: The Man, the Legend, the Legacy, 1786–
1986*, ed. Michael A. Lofaro (Tenn.). Four pieces hold some literary
interest: Richard Boyd Hauck, "The Man in the Buckskin Hunting
Shirt: Fact and Fiction in the Crockett Story" (pp. 3–20); John Seelye,
"A Well-Wrought Crockett; Or, How the Fakelorists Passed Through
the Credibility Gap and Discovered Kentucky" (pp. 21–45), a revised
and expanded version of the essay which first appeared in *Toward a
New American Literary History* (1980); Lofaro, "The Hidden 'Hero'
of the Nashville Crockett Almanacs" (pp. 46–79); and Catherine L.
Albanese, "Davy Crockett and the Wild Man; Or, the Metaphysics of
the Longue Durée" (pp. 80–101). Edward J. Piacentino, "Another
Chapter in the Literary Relationship of Mark Twain and Joel Chandler Harris" (*MissQ* 38:73–85), speculates unconvincingly that Mark
Twain's boy-books influenced Harris' little-known autobiographical
novel *On the Plantation*. Lee Pederson, "Language in the Uncle
Remus Tales" (*MP* 82:292–98), ascribes to Harris the synthesis in
very consciously manipulated writing of a variety of dialects and of
the literatures associated with them. Edward Eggleston's novels *The
Circuit Rider* and *The Graysons* are among literary works discussed
by Robert Bray, "Camp-Meeting Revivalism and the Idea of Western
Community: Three Generations of Ohio Valley Writers" (*ON* 10
[1984]:257–84).
    Several individual works by Sarah Orne Jewett are the subjects
of essays. Richard G. Carson, "Nature and the Circles of Initiation in
The Country of the Pointed Firs" (*CLQ* 21:154–60), notes the presence of "five distinct circular enclosures which the narrator, carefully
guided, must pass through to reach the 'secret center' she desires to

transcend." Carson likens this mystical and symbolic process to the religious experience described by Teresa of Avila. Kelley Griffith, Jr., "Sylvia as Hero in Sarah Orne Jewett's 'A White Heron'" (*CLQ* 21: 22–27), matches the girl to the hero archetype defined by Joseph Campbell in *The Hero with a Thousand Faces* (1949). Her "quest after a much desired object," in this context, yields not local-color realism but fantasy and a myth of the experience of Jewett and other women with "similar gifts, aspirations, and choices." Edward J. Piacentino, "Local Color and Beyond: The Artistic Dimension of Sarah Orne Jewett's 'The Foreigner'" (*CLQ* 21:92–98), combines the more traditional perspective on Jewett's work with close reading to urge that Mrs. Todd, who tells the story, is a narrator sympathetic to the foreigner in her difference from the community and thus sees her function as "set[ting] the record straight." On the bibliographical front Gwen Lindberg Nagel, "*Sarah Orne Jewett: A Reference Guide*: An Update" (*ALR* 17[1984]:228–63), adds 140 annotated items to the 1978 G. K. Hall volume edited by her and James Nagel.

In *Charlotte Perkins Gilman* (TUSAS 482) Gary Scharnhorst sets out a chronological and thematic analysis representing a more than competent addition to the Twayne series; this Gilman is a professional in letters and ideas rather than a woman revealing her soul through her art, both a poet and a reformer, and a tough-minded intellectual who, "more than any other American of her generation, despised the home." Scharnhorst also supplies the equally impressive *Charlotte Perkins Gilman: A Bibliography* (Scarecrow). The 2,173 primary entries also identify significant replies and continuations of works as well as reviews and principal translations. Other sections include reports on lectures, biographical items, an inventory of manuscripts and related documents, and a selected chronological listing of items discussing Gilman and her ideas and political associations. In an essay on Gilman's best-known story, Conrad Shumaker, "'Too Terribly Good to be Printed': Charlotte Gilman's 'The Yellow Wallpaper'" (*AL* 57:588–99), takes Howells's comment as a starting point for a solid reading of the story, particularly its being a closed but open journal, one not to be read yet addressed to the reader, and acknowledges Howells's implicit understanding of the story's feminist message in including it in *Great Modern American Stories: An Anthology* (1920).

Brent L. Kendrick has edited *The Infant Sphinx: Collected Letters of Mary E. Wilkins Freeman* (Scarecrow), a lavish production despite its typescript facsimile format, with critical and biographical introductions, reproductions of photographs of Freeman and relatives, friends, and residences, full annotation, and index. Kendrick defines his collection as representing all extant letters by Freeman, more than 500 of them in all. But the correspondence is entirely one-sided, with almost no reference made to the exchanges of which these letters were often part. Freeman's *The Wind in the Rose-Bush and Other Tales of the Supernatural* is the subject of "The Haunting Will: The Ghost Stories of Mary Wilkins Freeman" (*CLQ* 21:208–20). Susan Oaks argues that the collection is unified by a tension between self-will and the moral code, reflected in characters who claim acceptance of the code but who yet are haunted by having broken it, often unaware. And a single story is discussed by Beth Wynne Fisken, " 'Unusual' People in a 'Usual Place': 'The Balking of Christopher' by Mary Wilkins Freeman" (*CLQ* 21:99–103), with emphasis on "Emersonian echoes" and the "confident movement between realism and allegory and smooth shifts in point of view."

In other essays on women writers Anne Dalke's " 'Circumstance' and the Creative Woman: Harriet Prescott Spofford" (*ArQ* 41:71–85) is an ambitious but not completely developed potpourri. Dalke discusses Spofford's story as an answer to a Henry James review, a creation which accords with his theories of the goal of fiction but which "challenges his views on the best means of attaining that goal" by offering a female alternative. She also proposes that "Circumstance" is a reworking from a "female perspective" of Poe's fictions of women dying and Hawthorne's "Young Goodman Brown." Sandra A. Zagarell, "The Repossession of a Heritage: Elizabeth Stoddard's *The Morgesons*" (*SAF* 13:44–56), argues extravagantly that the novel which Zagarell has recently edited with Lawrence Buell (see *ALS 1984*) marks Stoddard's "experimental appropriation of narrative traditions," that it "critiques the masculine shape of the *Bildungsroman*," and that it even challenges "the great divide between romanticism and realism." Less spectacularly, Susan K. Harris, "Stoddard's *The Morgesons*: A Contextual Evaluation" (*ESQ* 31:11–22), sets the novel against six other contemporary women's novels to conclude that it "stands out as an iconoclastic attempt to portray a woman's consciousness as she matures from an unruly childhood into responsible adulthood, an attempt that puts Stoddard in the vanguard of nineteenth-century experimental fiction, technically and ideologically."

The local-color fiction of Charles Chesnutt is treated in two essays. Susan Fraiman, "Mother-Daughter Romance in Charles W. Chesnutt's 'Her Virginia Mammy'" (*SSF* 22:443–48), proposes that the story is "narrative alter ego" to Chesnutt's "The Wife of His Youth" in its treatment of racial identity, but that more importantly it is a tale of *female* identity in its concern with generation and gender. The essay could have made its point with less jargon and linguistic tricksiness. Tricksier still is SallyAnn H. Ferguson, " 'Frank Fowler': A Chesnutt Racial Pun" (*SoAR* 50,ii:47–53), proposing that this foul frank(furter; equals phallus) and his father Peter (!) "are labeled sexual foulers" whose presence in *The House Behind the Cedars* signals an inartistic intrusion of Chesnutt's theory of racial separation into the novel.

v. Howells and the Age of Realism

The year saw another reiteration of Howells's importance, with the publication of four books and twice that many essays significantly devoted to him. The most rewarding discussion of the cultural content of the realistic fiction Howells championed is Allen F. Stein's *After the Vows Were Spoken*. In individual chapters on Howells, Kate Chopin, and Robert Herrick, Stein identifies in each author a central idea: Howells used marriage as a source of "many of the most telling instances of how the overwhelming commitment to self . . . might best be overcome"; Chopin took an "exceedingly deterministic vision of the total inability of people either to resist or, more often than not, even understand the deeply rooted impulses that drive them"; and Herrick used marriage as an emblem of his "distaste for an America that he viewed as increasingly corrupt." Kenneth E. Eble's *Old Clemens and W.D.H.: The Story of a Remarkable Friendship* (LSU) is less strenuous but equally compelling, warm and thoroughly humane, a chatty double biography of two unique men at the intersection of their lives, from the first Boston meeting to Howells's painful funeral reminiscence, *My Mark Twain*. In a very different biographical mode, shaped by a Freudian perspective but free of Freudian jargon, John W. Crowley's *The Black Heart's Truth: The Early Career of W. D. Howells* (No. Car.) traces Howells's inner life from the youth about which he said "hell borders hard upon boyhood" to *A Modern Instance*, in the writing of which Howells had a breakdown that Crowley points to as the closest he came to madness. The theme is "the evolution of Howells' 'psychological juggle,' the tactic of psychical self-defence that also became the delimiting means of his art." The study is a fitting culmination to the work on Howells that Crowley has done over the years and skillfully incorporates evidence from the correspondence, the autobiographical writings, and the fiction. Another fitting culmination is *Young Howells and John Brown: Episodes in a Radical Education* (Ohio State), Edwin H. Cady's elegant extended essay. Cady's point is not that John Brown did or did not visit the Howells household, but that "over the initiation of his lifelong exploration of his basic and tropological figure of American fiction . . . Howells set the image of the martyr for liberty, for radical democracy."

In a clever repetition of the axioms Joel Porte, "Manners, Morals, and Mince Pie: Howells' America Revisited" (*Prospects* 10:443–60), focuses on Howells's use in several novels of "New England's notorious propensity for dining on overlarded, undercooked wedges of pie" to "involve us in the enjoyment of moral activity through the medium of a lively awareness of manners." John E. Bassett, "*A Chance Acquaintance*: How Fiction Would Mean" (*NCF* 40:312–26), puts the now-tired conflict of democracy and aristocracy of Howells's early novel into an epistemological stew whose point is that Howells "deploys a surface verisimilitude of the ordinary while actually exploring the meaning of meaning in representational fiction." Fleda Brown Jackson, "The Search for Sermons in Stone: The Pastoral Journey in *A Modern Instance*" (*CLQ* 21:34–44), refers the physical and psychic movement in the novel to the essential function of "pastoral," withdrawal from the sophisticated life to a still place. In *A Modern Instance*, however, this withdrawal—primarily to the country and to instinct—doesn't work, and the two worlds "remain essentially separate and unable to communicate with each other," with disaster as the result. Jackson emphasizes Howells the idealist, for whom the Emersonian Kinney of the novel is a "Pan/Evangelist"; she misses Howells the satirist, for whom he is a kind fool. *A Hazard of New Fortunes* is the focus of Lois Hughson's reading in "From Biography to History: Competing Models for Fiction in James, Howells, and Dos Passos" (*CUNY English Forum* 1[1984]:329–43). Hughson argues that the story of Basil March in the novel is at once incomplete as biography and incompletely incorporated into the narrative history, thus establishing the inability of consciousness to master history. C. A. Erickson analyzes Jere Westover and Jeff Durgin in terms of personality oppositions defined by William James in *Principles of Psychology* and *Pragmatism.* "The Tough and Tender-Minded: W. D. Howells's *The Landlord at Lion's Head* (*SNNTS* 17:383–94) concludes, after a thorough reading shaped by a moral perspective sensitive to Howells's own, that "both [men] have been 'rewarded' with their hearts' desires and neither will realize the hollowness of his 'success.'"

Less ambitiously, William D. Baker, "Ohio's Reaction to William Dean Howells" (*Midamerica* 11[1984]:117–48), surveys the results of a look through midwestern newspapers for reaction to Howells through 1886. Elsa Nettels, "Howells and Mazzini: The Ideal Commonwealth" (*MarkhamR* 14:1–7), belabors the intellectual influence of the Italian patriot on the American Altrurian. Francis Murphy prints two hitherto restricted letters on literary acquaintance gone sour in "The End of a Friendship: Two Unpublished Letters from Twain to Howells about Bret Harte" (*NEQ* 58:87–91). In a final Howells matter, I erroneously asserted in *ALS 1984* that Thomas Wortham's "'The Real Diary of a Boy': Howells in Ohio, 1852–1853" (*ON* 10:3–40) supplies the text of a Howells essay. My witticism went unwitted: though Wortham quotes the title of Howells's essay, he actually transcribes the original diary text.

Diana C. Reep's *Margaret Deland* (TUSAS 479) conveys an effective sense of a writer who *won't* lead the new wave because she pointed to common sense and intelligence and even happy endings as social and fictional solutions. Another series format book, Glenn O. Carey's *Edward Payson Roe* (TUSAS 480), devotes far too much space to the melodramatic and intensely religious *Barriers Burned Away* (1872) to justify the claim that Roe, also a minister and horticulturist, was a novelist for the masses who wrote widely and well. The author speaks mostly for himself in two anthologies. *The Best of George Ade* (Indiana), ed. A. L. Lazarus, also includes an affectionate biographical and barely critical introduction as well as selections from John T. McCutcheon's original illustrations. More ambitiously, *Grandma Never Lived in America: The New Journalism of Abraham Cahan* (Indiana), ed. Moses Rischin, is the first attempt to collect Cahan's earliest work in English. The roughly 175 items, culled from the files of newspapers with which Cahan was associated, include eight original stories and five translations from the Russian. The obvious value of the collection is reduced by Mischin's failure to establish the connection to Tom Wolfe and Norman Mailer which his

subtitle suggests and by the absence of the most rudimentary bibliographical identification of sources, of useful annotation, and of an
index.

Utopian writing of the late 19th century continues to generate
some enthusiasm. In *Dreams and Visions: A Study of American Utopias, 1865–1917* (Greenwood) Charles J. Rooney, Jr., organizes by
ideas rather than by authors, so that Edward Bellamy, King Gillette,
and others less known are scattered everywhere. Rooney's survey
certainly expands our sense of the amount and the variety of the
literature. Many readers will find the annotated primary bibliography
the most significant feature. Kenneth M. Roemer, "Technology, Cor-
poration, and Utopia: Gillette's Unity Regained" (*Technology and
Culture* 26:560–70), introduces the corporate-structured ideas of the
razor blade man.

vi. Crane, Chopin, and the 1890s

The principal discussions of Stephen Crane for the year are essentially
close readings of individual works. Michael D. Warner's "Value,
Agency, and Stephen Crane's 'The Monster'" (*NCF* 40:76–93) is a
case study in the ways Crane constantly "displaces or estranges"
ethical value, an effective instance of Crane's challenge to conventional ways of thinking and feeling. Donald Pizer's "*The Red Badge
of Courage*: Text, Theme, and Form" (*SAQ* 84:302–13) responds to
claims made variously by Hershel Parker, Henry Binder, and Steven
Mailloux that Crane's original manuscript is a better work than the
novel finally published. Pizer finds in the manuscript itself evidence
of Crane's intention to express Henry Fleming's ambivalent nature,
an intention which remained essentially intact throughout the process
of revision and one signaled by his undercutting of the conventional
initiation structure on which the novel is formed. Pizer returns to the
general field of this discussion in "Self-Censorship and Textual Editing," an essay in *Textual Criticism and Literary Interpretation*, ed.
Jerome J. McGann (Chicago, pp. 144–61). There Pizer discusses *Red
Badge*, Norris' *McTeague*, and Dreiser's *Sister Carrie* as examples of
the complex relationship of textual theory and biography to the editing of the novels.

In "*Vandover and the Brute*: The Decisive Experience of Loss"
(*WAL* 19[1984]:3–15) Barbara Hochman contributes yet another
demonstration of the contradiction in Frank Norris between stated in-

tellectual and philosophical concerns and the fictional depiction of experience. She sees the novel as setting out two false propositions— that Vandover is adaptable to change and that he has a horror of boredom. The dramatic action—as distinct from the comments of Vandover himself and of the narrator—demonstrates that he is "definitively shaped" by the loss of his own mother and never adequately recovers from it.

Peggy Skaggs's *Kate Chopin* (TUSAS 485) is fairly typical of the solid features of the series, more broad than deep. Given the little known about Chopin herself, the biographical first chapter is only four pages long. Six of the remaining eight chapters are devoted to the works themselves, all advancing the postulate that Chopin's characters "seem to lack a clear concept of their own roles and purposes in life" and embody her interest in the "search for identity." In those terms, for example, Edna Pontellier chooses to die rather than to live incomplete.

In an essay devoted to *The Awakening* Wayne Batten defines the problem differently. "Illusion and Archetype: The Curious Story of Edna Pontellier" (*SLJ* 18:73–88) describes the heroine as affected by three kinds of illusions, those suggested to her by others, those she creates, and those associated with her by others. Edna's failure, then, consists of her inability to fully confront any of those illusions, or to break through them to reality. In "Techniques of Distancing in the Fiction of Kate Chopin" (*SoSt* 24:69–81) Joyce Coyne Dyer describes the use of prejudice (including stereotyping) and distancing as means to discuss topics like sexuality which might be offensive or dangerous if confronted directly. The discussion of companion stories as contrasting statements on a central idea is particularly good, but the assertion that *The Awakening*, read as a culmination of the earlier fiction, offers the message of the universality of female passion is not sufficiently supported by the narrative facts of the novel or by assertions that stereotyping is sometimes not stereotyping. With Robert Emmett Monroe, Dyer also describes "Texas and Texans in the Fiction of Kate Chopin" (*WAL* 20:3–15). Here too the emphasis is on Chopin's employment of the stereotype, specifically to isolate the more primitive side of human nature.

The Critical Reception of Hamlin Garland 1891–1978, ed. Charles L. P. Silet, Robert E. Welch, and Richard Boudreau (Whitston), assembles 33 representative items and blankets them with introduction, brief headnotes, and—more sensibly than most such collections—full

bibliographical citations. Also included are a 12-page Bibliography
of Further Readings and some useful illustrations. Michael Clark's
"Herbert Spencer, Hamlin Garland, and *Rose of Dutcher's Coolly*"
(*ALR* 17[1984]:203–08) asserts the novelist's debt to the philosopher's ideas, in terms vague rather than specific.

The CSE-approved edition of Harold Frederic's *The Damnation
of Theron Ware or Illumination* (Nebraska), with text established by
Charlyne Dodge and history of the text written by Stanton Garner,
is a mix of precision and indecision. The apparatus sections are long
and thorough, but they perpetuate rather than solve problems. The
title given the text is a crucial example: according to the editors,
Frederic finally decided on *Illumination*, though the text is more
widely known by its other name; the solution is to combine the two
without a separating comma "in order to render the two titles co-
equal, and neither subordinate." The editorial work is better focused
than the history, which wanders too often in its 62-page journey. The
text is a completely eclectic amalgamation of English and American
editions, neither one chosen as copy-text. The same novel, under its
traditional American name, is the focus of Samuel Chase Coale's
"Harold Frederic: Naturalism as Romantic Snarl" (*In Hawthorne's
Shadow*, pp. 46–62). Most readers will need Coale's introductory discussion of Hawthorne's Manichaean vision of light and dark, good
and evil, sinfulness and innocence to fully understand his comparison
of *The Damnation* to *The Scarlet Letter* in structure, image, and idea.
Coale's special innovation is a notion of Frederic's novel "not as an
example of literary naturalism but as the midpoint between Hawthorne's allegories and Faulkner's myths."

Arnold T. Schwab has edited *Americans in the Arts, 1890–1920:
Critiques by James Gibbons Huneker* (AMS Press). The selections
from Huneker's wide-ranging criticism are arranged by the art
(music, drama, literature, visual arts) and under those categories by
roles and issues. The specifically literary nuggets include Huneker's
parody of Stephen Crane's impressionistic style and his alliance with
Howells against "romancers" in fiction.

Issues in poetry of the latter part of the century are among the
essay topics in *American Poetry: Between Tradition and Modernism,
1865–1914*. Reinhold Schiffer's "Small Expectations: Poetry and the
Criticism of Poetry in the *Atlantic Monthly* Between 1890 and 1905"
(pp. 32–54) identifies a policy strongly oriented to tradition and en-
couraging emotionally stilted and stylized work. In "Edmund Clar-

ence Stedman's Aesthetics" (pp. 55–69) Volker Bischoff defines an eclectic traditionalism and strong idealism constituting a "typical manifestation of the genteel tradition." Roland Hagenbüchle's "Abstraction and Desire: Dissolving Contours in the Poetry of Frederick Goddard Tuckerman" (pp. 70–86) articulates the interplay of structure, symbol, and sense in which vagueness constitutes not a tactic of evasion but a functional element expressive of the "ongoing loss of meaning" and of Tuckerman's desire to recover that meaning in poetic form. Wolfgang G. Müller's "Symbolic Motion in Sidney Lanier's Poetry" (pp. 87–104) is better on Lanier's use of syntax to establish kinetic structures than on his contribution to the Symbolist movement. And Dorothy Steiner's "Women Poets in the Twilight Period" (pp. 169–90) is less useful as history or criticism than as a possible way of envisioning a female poetic tradition.

The only notable essay on Henry Adams for the year is John Patrick Diggins' " 'Who Bore the Failure of the Light': Henry Adams and the Crisis of Authority" (*NEQ* 58:165–92). Most of the pronouncements about Adams as the first existential historian and his growing up with a belief in a reasoned morality to an "alien universe that lacked meaning and purpose" are old stuff. The interesting new notion is that he sealed his failure by not admitting the possibility of authority in his own art, where he could have made the rules.

Indiana University

13. Fiction: 1900 to the 1930s

John J. Murphy

Five years ago, when I was collecting material for my first Chapter 13 for *ALS*, David Stouck, from whom I inherited this task, assured me that work on these writers had crested; many of the anniversary celebrations had been concluded, and their ripples would soon disappear. This prediction, however, proved to be inaccurate, especially for Cather and Dreiser, who continue to dominate the period, and, to a lesser degree, for Wharton. Work on London has been a major emphasis, although it has fallen off dramatically this year. In this, my final solo contribution for *ALS*, I have grouped Cather with Dreiser as the major writers of the period, followed by Wharton and, because it is his anniversary year, Lewis. One of the many things I have learned in repeatedly surveying this period is that the entire volume might need restructuring; Cather generating as much critical attention as, say, Dickinson or Fitzgerald becomes a dilemma and a burden for the reviewer occupied with more than a dozen other writers.

i. Willa Cather and Theodore Dreiser

The year's work on Cather divided quite conveniently into attempts to relate her to other writers and traditions, essays on individual works, and, finally, minor miscellaneous pieces. Among the first group, Loretta Wasserman's "The Music of Time: Henri Bergson and Willa Cather" (*AL* 57:226–39) is excellent for its keen insights on *The Professor's House.* Wasserman sees Godfrey St. Peter as excluded from involuntary memory, in what Bergson called spatialized time; "Tom Outland's Story" is seen as offering a way to escape asphyxiation. St. Peter's Jewish son-in-law, Louie Marsellus, is viewed positively as one who allows the past to live in the present. Perhaps exaggerating her complaint that Cather is still neglected, Phyllis Rose, in "The Case of Willa Cather" (*Writing of Women: Essays in a Renaissance*, Wesleyan, pp. 136–52), considers Cather's achievements in lucid style and unfurnished form as modernism at its best. Rose's comments on Cather's taking the "long shot" in characterization by emphasizing the archetypal and eternally human and in bringing realism and naturalism into the realm of the mythic associate her not only with Joyce, Woolf, and Lawrence, but with Henry Moore, Georgia O'Keeffe, and René Magritte. Scriptural dimensions of the frontiering novels and especially of *The Professor's House, My Mortal Enemy, Death Comes for the Archbishop,* and *Shadows on the Rock* is my concern in "Willa Cather and Religion: Highway to the World and Beyond" (*Literature and Belief* 4[1984]:49–68). Detecting echoes from the Grail legend, *The Divine Comedy,* and Goethe's *Faust,* I see Cather as moving from romantic egotism toward self-denial, the models being the Mary of the Annunciation and Christ in Gethsemane. Mary R. Ryder explores a neglected area of Cather in "Prosodic Variations in Willa Cather's Prairie Poems" (*WAL* 20: 223–37), which makes a case for the originality of three prairie poems in *April Twilights.* Ryder analyzes the forms of "Prairie Dawn," "Prairie Spring," and "Going Home" as examples of the growing naturalness of Cather's technique and as reflections of the resolution of her conflict with Nebraska.

Among articles on individual novels are Jean Schwind's "The Benda Illustrations to *My Ántonia:* Cather's 'Silent' Supplement to Jim Burden's Narrative" (*PMLA* 100:51–67) and "Latour's Schismatic Church: The Radical Meaning in the Pictorial Methods of *Death Comes for the Archbishop*" (*SAF* 13:71–88). In the first of these Schwind argues that new countries require new art forms and concepts and that narrator Jim Burden cannot escape conventional dime novel and pastoral views of his experiences with Ántonia. This much is valid, but then Schwind forces the argument that Cather made her own statement, to counteract Jim's distorted one, through the eight sketches she commissioned from W. T. Benda to illustrate her novel, and we are left with the disarming implication that the eight drawings are somehow superior to Cather's text. In treating *Archbishop,* Schwind collapses her valid thesis that Cather's novel depicts an aesthetic conversion from El Greco to Puvis de Chavannes styles (through the developing response of Father Latour to the New Mexico landscape) by stretching it into a theory about rejecting Rome's authority and the doctrine of the Immaculate Conception. What Schwind imagines as Catholic doctrine (Mary's "absolute divinity") would amount to heresy in Rome, and her conclusions about

Latour's rejection of "Rome's ideal woman" are hardly representative of Cather's text. A more mature handling of Cather's New Mexico novel is Merrill Maguire Skaggs's *"Death Comes for the Archbishop*: Cather's Mystery and Manners" (*AL* 57:395–406), which attempts to explain how in this novel Cather could rise from the depths of the pessimism expressed in her previous novel, *My Mortal Enemy*. In theorizing that Cather for the first time successfully combined religion and art in her priest protagonist, Skaggs makes valuable discoveries about the importance of mathematician-philosopher Blaise Pascal to *Archbishop* and offers somewhat confusing if intriguing comments on *My Mortal Enemy*. Skaggs turns her attention to Cather's Quebec novel in "A Good Girl in Her Place: Cather's *Shadows on the Rock*" (*R&L* 17,iii:27–36), which has Cather setting out to disprove the rule that good girls make for insignificant fiction by making Cecile Auclair, her protagonist, the embodiment of cultural continuity and community and by stressing the significance of artificial life-giving order as it struggles with inner tensions and the threat of nature. In "A New Image of Woman: Willa Cather's *O Pioneers!*" (*Currents* 4,i:53–64) Suzanne Carroll traces the developing role of frontier women in fact and fiction as anticipating Cather's heroine Alexandra Bergson, "a beacon of woman's intelligence and strength so long in captivity or deliberately written out of American literature." Minrose C. Gwin's intriguing treatment of the somewhat neglected *Sapphira and the Slave Girl* in *Black and White Women* (pp. 131–49) compares Cather's novel to Faulkner's *Absalom, Absalom!* in inconsistencies of characterization and narrative technique, both novels being reflections of uncertainty about the past. Gwin explains Sapphira's attempts to have her slave girl raped as Cather's attempt "to destroy the female in her own psyche and in her art."

Miscellaneous pieces on Cather include Robert Gregory's "Cather in the Canon" (*MLS* 15,iv:95–101), a somewhat muddled but valuable argument to secure *My Ántonia*'s place in the tradition "because it so relentlessly persists in questioning the success of sublimation and repression." In "Bishop Latour and Professor St. Peter: Cather's Esthetic Intellectuals" (*ArQ* 41:61–70) Margaret Doane distorts Cather's intentions by blaming Latour for not releasing the slave Sada from bondage as she lists some important if obvious parallels between Godfrey St. Peter and the Archbishop: desire and solitude, detachment, intellectualism, dependence on art and religion, male friendship, etc. Finally, two notes from the *Willa Cather Pioneer Memorial*

Newsletter deserve mention: Bruce Baker's "*The Professor's House*: An Early Source" (29:13–14) and Michel Gervaud's "Two Children of the Prairie" (29:2–3). Baker briefly parallels Professor St. Peter's battle against materialism with the similarly doomed struggles of Professor Emerson Graves in the 1902 "genesis" story, "The Professor's Commencement." Gervaud points out similarities between *My Ántonia* and Hamlin Garland's *Boy Life on the Prairie*, and between "A Wagner Matinee" and his "Mrs. Ripley's Trip," concluding that Cather is more universal because more poetic, but that Garland is more documentary.

The year's most significant contribution to Dreiser criticism is Joseph Griffin's *The Small Canvas: An Introduction to Dreiser's Short Stories* (Fairleigh Dickinson), a carefully written and valuable study handling the two collections, *Free and Other Stories* (1918) and *Chains* (1927), and subsequent uncollected stories. Griffin introduces his brief study acknowledging negative reactions to Dreiser as short story writer, indicating the disparity between slick magazine fiction and Dreiser's thematically uncomfortable and verbally dull productions. *Free* demonstrates considerable range and subject matter despite the prevalent theme of entrapment; *Chains* continues the curtailment of freedom theme, while the later "Solution" and "Fine Furniture" reveal a more conventional Dreiser. Griffin's method is briefly but carefully to analyze each of the 31 stories he considers, review other critical estimates, indicate Dreiser's techniques (the development, for example, of his "incremental" style from "The Shining Slave Makers" to "Free"), and, in a final chapter, consider the concerns reflected in the Dreiser canon of this genre. The stories provide a valuable vision of American life while overwhelmingly dealing with man-woman relations, a theme that Griffin further subdivides. Griffin concludes that from a technical perspective "Dreiser's best stories tend to be the interior monologues and stories of omniscient narration"; in subject, "Dreiser's stories deserve to be read because they capture moods and cadences of the American experience that found such articulate expression nowhere else in the short fiction genre."

Defense of Dreiser's artistry colors much of this year's criticism. In " 'And Then Rose for the First Time': Repetition and Doubling in *An American Tragedy*" (*Novel* 19:39–56) Lee Clark Mitchell applauds the accomplishment of Dreiser's craft in illuminating his vision and themes. Mitchell sees character doubling (Clyde/Gilbert and

Clyde/Roberta) and scenic repetition (which weaves together the three books of Dreiser's masterpiece) as contributing to "narrative determinism" in revealing how "the motions of the self are wrenched into shape by an indifferent, and powerfully deterministic, logic." Philip Fisher makes similar claims for Dreiser's mastery of character doubling and scenic repetition and relates them to vision and theme in considering *Sister Carrie* and *An American Tragedy* in *Hard Facts* (pp. 128–78). Fisher's particular concern is Dreiser's theme of developing the self from experience in the city, from without rather than within. Objects, places, clothes, people become avenues to identity in both novels. In each the search for identity leads the protagonist toward extinction of self in the traditional sense. In *Carrie* the route to such extinction is acting; in *Tragedy* the route is murder. Fisher argues for Dreiser as the novelist of the American city, that he defines our city as Cooper defines our wilderness and is comparable as a city novelist to Dickens and Dostoevsky. The artistry of *An American Tragedy* is also stressed by Elizabeth Langland in *Society in the Novel* (No. Car., 1984, pp. 124–46). In contrasting Dreiser's and Zola's sociological naturalism Langland claims that by keeping the reader within a framework of social consequences rather than morals and by allowing his protagonist freedom of feeling within the determinism of society, Dreiser keeps us in sympathy with Clyde. Through artistry rather than polemic or propaganda we realize that American society functions as an "inevitable determinant of individuals' lives. . . ." Shelley Fisher Fishkin examines the contribution of the burly, sometimes lurid world of turn-of-the-century journalism to the art of *An American Tragedy* in *From Fact to Fiction* (pp. 85–134). Fishkin uses letters and trial transcripts to illustrate Dreiser's method and belief "that even a text as panoramic and dense as this one is destined to be incomplete, that life . . . resists containment in the writer's forms."

"Dreiser and the Hostile Critics" (*ON* 10[1984]:307–17) is Richard Lehan's defense of the conflict in Dreiser's fiction between individual instincts and social and religious conventions. Lehan tries to demolish Lionel Trilling's claim in "Reality in America" that Dreiser is "inconsistent" and "inadequate." Like Langland, Lehan credits Dreiser with creating a "purely amoral world and [divorcing] his characters from Christian imperatives. . . ." Dreiser's trilogy, *The Financier, The Titan,* and *The Stoic,* occupies John Vernon in his epilogue to *Money and Fiction* (pp. 194–207), which equates money and power in Cowperwood's story; high finance, like art, involves creating representations of reality rather than reality itself. The connection between art and money concerns Rachel Bowlby as well in *Just Looking: Consumer Culture in Dreiser, Gissing and Zola* (Methuen, pp. 52–65, 118–33), which approaches *The "Genius"* and *Sister Carrie* from the perspective of "new realism" corresponding to new consumer capitalism. The career of Eugene Witla is seen as dramatizing the transformation of art into a cultural enterprise, and Carrie's career becomes an image for others to emulate and envy; material display and consumerism are thus applied to both masculine and feminine careers. John J. Conder in *Naturalism in American Fiction* (pp. 86–117) probes *The Financier, The Titan,* and *The Stoic* as a philosophically coherent unit in which Dreiser solves the dilemma of determinism (human dignity vis-à-vis a universe that proscribes human freedom). Through Bernice Fleming's Brahmanism in *The Stoic*, argues Conder, Dreiser reconciles his humanitarianism and his determinism; after abandoning the Catholicism of his youth, he was forced to seek refuge in the theological form to resolve his dilemma. (See section iv for more on incompatibles in Dreiser.)

Barbara Hochman explores obvious parallels in "Goethe's *Faust*: A Leitmotif in Dreiser's *The 'Genius'*" (*DrN* 16,i:1–12), especially the conflict between stasis and flux, between contentment and restless striving that causes both Faust and Eugene Witla to err. Dreiser is compared to an American contemporary in "The Fate of the Fallen Woman in *Maggie* and *Sister Carrie*," Lawrence E. Hussman's contribution to Pierre L. Horn and Mary Beth Pringle's *The Image of the Prostitute in Modern Literature* (Ungar, 1984, pp. 91–100). Hussman claims that Dreiser's novel is superior to Crane's in exploring the emotions of a fallen woman while rejecting conventional morality in rewarding rather than dooming her. Crane, argues Hussman, accepted conventional morality and found it impossible either to intuit or imagine the thought processes of a prostitute. Dreiser's first novel is also the subject of Stephen C. Brennan's "The Publication of *Sister Carrie*: Old and New Fictions" (*ALR* 18:55–68), which argues convincingly, after thoroughly examining the typescript, the first edition, and later letters, that Dreiser did not succumb to his publisher and editors regarding the revision of his novel. Brennan takes issue with the editors of the Pennsylvania edition (1981) in claiming that Dreiser held out to preserve the integrity of the book's central theme and realism, and that the changes made between typescript and first edition were not without his consent. Rudolf Bader uses the Pennsylvania *Sister Carrie* to argue that Carrie is not essentially passive and that the end is not without hope in "Dreiser's Sister Carrie: More Pupil than Victim" (*IFR* 12:74–78). The novel develops an inarticulate but thinking individual, and the direction is toward "the positive." Dreiser's biographical sketches are the subject of two shorter articles, " 'My Brother Paul' and *Sister Carrie*" (*CRevAS* 16: 411–24) by John P. O'Neill and "Dreiser's Later Sketches" (*DrN* 16,ii:1–13) by Joseph Griffin. O'Neill sees the 1909 sketch of songwriter Paul Dresser, later included in *Twelve Men* (1919), as important in revealing Dreiser's desire for, yet rejection of, the amalgam of big city and small town sentiments expressed in Dresser's popular songs. O'Neill sees *Sister Carrie* as depicting the rejection of family and country values for survival in the city. Griffin singles out the 1934 sketch "Mathewson," of a journalist defeated through supersensitivity, as the best of Dreiser's sketches after *Twelve Men*; he claims that the quality of Dreiser's working in this hybrid biographical-fictional form and in the short story form deteriorated from the mid-'30s. Finally, X. Theodore Barber, in "Drama with a Pointer: The Group Theatre's Production of Piscator's *Case of Clyde Griffiths* (1936)" (*TDR* 28,iv:61–72), traces the development of German playwright Erwin Piscator's Greek tragedy style, leftist adaptation of *An American Tragedy* from its conception through its various productions on the way to New York.

ii. Edith Wharton and Sinclair Lewis

The year's criticism on Wharton is healthy in quantity and quality, with the accent away from narrowing feminist polemics and toward more universal dimensions. Two articles use somewhat broad anthropological canvases to explore Wharton's New York. Mary Ellis Gibson, in "Edith Wharton and the Ethnography of Old New York" (*SAF* 13:57–69), applies the work of Mary Douglas on social environments and the cosmologies they generate to *The House of Mirth, The Custom of the Country*, and *The Age of Innocence*. Gibson sees the first two novels as depicting the challenge of the outsider, as in the "Big Man" system of New Guinea, to a "high classification" social environment of taboos (Lily Bart, for example, is caught between the two camps). *The Age of Innocence*, however, depicts "high classification" society challenged from within, focusing on family and community duty as stabilizing forces. In "Cupid without Bow and Arrow: *The Age of Innocence* and *The Golden Bough*" (*EdWN* 2,i: 2–5) William J. Scheick sees Frazer's work as informing Wharton's work as it did Joyce's and Eliot's. Like her famous contemporaries, Wharton used Frazer ironically in order to show the failure of individual fulfillment in American society. Ellen rather than May is seen as more of a Diana/Artemis figure of renewal of life because May was raised in America. Marriage in Wharton is the emphasis of Allen F. Stein in *After the Vows Were Spoken* (Ohio, pp. 209–77), a thorough if unstartling analysis exploring marriage as entrapment with potentials for painful growth of character or psychological ruin. Several stories ("The Fullness of Life," "The Lamp of Psyche," "Souls Belated," "The Quicksand," and "Joy in the House") and *Ethan Frome* are reviewed as psychological studies. *The House of Mirth*, *The Fruit of the Tree*, *The Custom of the Country*, *Twilight Sleep*, and *Hudson River Bracketed* are discussed as depictions of failed marriages for purposes of social criticism. *The Custom of the Country*, for example, "constitutes no attack on matrimony. . . . Wharton . . . sees the misfortune as ultimately deriving from large failings on the national scene." Finally, and more positively, "The Other Two," "The Letters," and *The Age of Innocence* "detail the sort of moral growth that marriage can inspire." Wharton's French experience occupies Alan W. Bellringer in "Edith Wharton's Use of France" (*YES* 15:109–24), who proves through biographical details and literary accomplishments Wharton's outstanding credentials for writing about France, relates her attitudes to those in W. C. Brownell's *French Traits* (1889), comments on her French-connected fiction (*The Custom of the Country*, "The Recovery," "The Last Asset," *Madame de Treymes*, and *The Reef*), and concludes that these works "have a good deal of marked literary-intellectual interest to offer."

Four essays were devoted exclusively to *The House of Mirth*. Waichee Dimock's "Debasing Exchange: Edith Wharton's *The House of Mirth*" (*PMLA* 100:783–92) is an examination of the debasement of humanity when morality feeds directly into the mechanisms of the marketplace. Lily Bart is seen as ineffectually rejecting such a system in refusing to blackmail Bertha Dorset, and Lawrence Selden is seen as a spectator niggardly conservative in his human relations. In *Gossip* (Knopf, pp. 171–202) Patricia Meyer Spacks places *The House of Mirth* within a context of novels by Gaskell, Trollope, and Eliot in exploring the link between gossip and finance. Spacks sees Wharton's undercutting of Lily and Selden as illustrating the "frequency with which speculation produces misinterpretation" among readers as well as characters. Wharton's undercutting of her heroine and tricking her reader into sentimental responses is Deborah G. Lambert's emphasis in "*The House of Mirth*: Readers Respond" (*TSWL* 4:69–82). Lambert examines negative criticism of the novel against the background of 19th-century women's writing and concludes that through undercutting Wharton increases our awareness of the meanness of the social world she depicts and the impotence of traditional female behavior in it. Finally, Susan Koprince in "The Meaning of Bellomont in *The House of Mirth*" (*EdWN* 2,i:1,5,8) relates the estate to Belmont in *The Merchant of Venice* as the ironic version of a setting for matchmaking and risking all for love.

Summer continues to occupy critics, Barbara A. White seeing it as a seduction novel turned on its head in *Growing Up Female: Adolescent Girlhood in American Fiction* (Greenwood, pp. 47–64). By emphasizing the inner life of the seduced girl, the underside of the plot, Wharton exposes the shrinkage hidden behind what seems an optimistic outcome. Taking issue with this view is Carol Wershoven's "The Divided Conflict of Edith Wharton's *Summer*" (*CLQ* 21:5–10). Wershoven argues that Lawyer Royall's role is a central one, that he is an outsider like Charity, better than his society, and that her marriage to him is positive, "not the incestuous marriage of father and child, . . . but a union of equals, of adults who have grown through confrontation and acceptance of themselves and each other." *The Custom of the Country* is Susan Wolstenholme's concern in "Edith Wharton's Gibson Girl: The Virgin, the Undine, and the Dynamo" (*ALR* 18:92–106), which strains toward significance in examining Wharton's version of the Undine legend as the "missing link" between Henry Adams' concept of the Virgin power source of the old culture and the Dynamo of the new, both of which victimized the woman. Wolstenholme sees Ralph Marvell as caught between these sources and his son Paul as facing a world in which neither seems acceptable. In "Purity and Power in *The Age of Innocence*" (*ALR* 17:153–68) Judith Fryer sees the Pulitzer prize novel and the autobiography, *A Backward Glance*, as springing from the valedictory impulse of fixing images of security, the first of a society, the second of a personality. Fryer then discusses the incompatibility of Newland

Archer and Ellen Olenska, both of whom echo aspects of Wharton herself, due to Archer's inability to breathe in an atmosphere too stimulating for him.

Miscellaneous pieces include "Edith Wharton's Hotels" by Susan Koprince (*MSE* 10:12–23) and John Gerlach's *Toward the End* (pp. 58–60). Koprince catalogs the hotels in the major novels as the antitheses of family unity and tradition generally associated with brownstones; hotels in Wharton are generally reflective of American society's most endemic features: transients and disregard of the past. Gerlach appreciates "Roman Fever" as an excellent example of an untrivial story with a masterful surprise ending binding together the beginning, the middle, and the end while revealing character. Alfred Bendixen gathers "A Guide to Wharton Criticism, 1974–1983" (*EdWN* 2,ii:1–8), which includes annotations ("reviews") by various critics. Finally, Alan Price in "The Making of Edith Wharton's *The Book of the Homeless*" (*PULC* 47:5–21) tells the story of Wharton's 1916 gift book of contributions from contemporaries collected to aid her war charities (aid, after costs, amounted to a mere $1,500).

There has been such little attention paid to Sinclair Lewis in the last several years that the *Modern Fiction Studies'* "Special Issue: Sinclair Lewis" (31,iii:479–616) amounts to a bonanza. In his "Editor's Preface" (pp. 479–93) Martin Light does his best to integrate the variety (in quality and subject) of the nine essays gathered to celebrate "the one hundredth anniversary of the birth of Sinclair Lewis." *Main Street* occupies two critics. In "Pioneers of *Main Street*" (pp. 529–45) James Marshall sees Carol Kennicott's rebellion as suggesting "Lewis' transformation of the mythic pioneer into his allegory of twentieth-century political and personal freedom from the tyranny of Main Street . . . , Carol's passion for nature linking her to the agricultural roots of democratic promise." Such "thematic transvaluation" was suggested to Lewis in Hamlin Garland's *Main-Travelled Roads*, claims Marshall, but literary inspiration in the other direction concerns Robert E. Fleming's "The Influence of *Main Street* on Nella Larsen's *Quicksand*" (pp. 547–53). Lewis' novel is not only the source of the ending of Larsen's 1928 study of a tragically trapped black woman, but Carol Kennicott's sexual attitudes, devoted to betterment, and disillusion parallel those of Helga Crane, Larsen's protagonist.

Lewis' debt to other writers is discussed in several essays in the collection. The influence of Arthur Conan Doyle's detective on the

pure scientist of *Arrowsmith* concerns Robert L. Coard in "Sinclair
Lewis, Max Gottlieb, and Sherlock Holmes" (pp. 565–71). Lewis borrowed not only details for Gottlieb's character but the situations in
which Lewis placed him. Coard includes as evidence explicit references to Holmes in *Arrowsmith* and elsewhere and concludes, "Doyle
was something of a factor in shaping Lewis' literary style and substance." Similarities to *The Divine Comedy* are noticed by Bridget
Puzon in "From Quest to Cure: The Transformation of *Dodsworth*"
(pp. 573–80). Sam Dodsworth is unique among Lewis characters for
his depth and ability to change, whereas Carol and Babbitt "return
to the ways of life they had found lacking from the first. . . ." Puzon
sees Dodsworth's journey as Dantean, associates his wife Fran with
hell and Edith Cortright with Beatrice in guiding him "to Edenic
existence." In another essay Coard establishes Lewis' debt to Wharton
not only for revolt from the village attitudes but for the objects he
satirized, even specific borrowings of plot, character, names, and
titles. In "Edith Wharton's Influence on Sinclair Lewis" (pp. 511–27)
Summer is analyzed as more than the inspiration of *Main Street*; even
Carol's famous walk down Main Street is anticipated in Charity
Royall's trip to Nettleton. Wharton's *The Custom of the Country*
provided the basis for Lewis' Zenith and the cast of characters he
satirized in it. A narrower influence is the concern of Arthur Coleman
in "The Americanization of H. G. Wells: Sinclair Lewis' *Our Mr.
Wrenn*" (pp. 495–501), which sees Lewis' early novel as a combination of two popular Wells novels, *Kipps* and *The History of Mr. Polly*.
Lewis, claims Coleman, "clearly echoes the fundamental Wells thesis
that society has an obligation to provide other alternatives than
misbegotton fantasies for dealing with its institutional imperfections."

Three more or less biographical considerations round out the *MFS*
collection. Bea Knodel's "For Better or for Worse . . ." (pp. 555–63),
in surveying the wives in *Main Street*, *Babbitt*, and *Dodsworth* (including wives not unsatisfied with their marriages, wives humbled by
dependence on husbands or kept childlike by them, and wives with
working brains and no work), singles out Fran Dodsworth as "mini-
mized" by Lewis because patterned after his first wife, Grace Hegger,
and Bea Sorenson in *Main Street*, because unique in her domesticity
and full partnership with her husband. Alcoholism is Roger Forseth's
concern in " 'Alcoholite at the Altar': Sinclair Lewis, Drink, and the
Literary Imagination" (pp. 581–607). *Main Street* is a fully realized
novel because Carol Kennicott, its protagonist, is a fully realized fe-

male character, argues Forseth, but subsequent Lewis work declined
because of his obsession with alcohol and inability to deal honestly
with women and write with emotional conviction. Richard Allan
Davison's "Sinclair Lewis, Charles G. Norris, and Kathleen Norris:
An Early Friendship" (pp. 503–10) claims, for whatever it's worth,
that Lewis' long friendship with the Norrises and theirs with him is a
"tribute to Lewis as a vibrant human being." Excerpts from letters to
Charles Norris indicate, according to Davison, that Lewis had a "keen
eye for the details of writing." This informative collection concludes
with Robert E. Fleming's bibliographical commentary ("Recent Research on Sinclair Lewis," pp. 609–16), which updates his 1980 *Sinclair Lewis: A Reference Guide* (Hall).

iii. Sherwood Anderson, Gertrude Stein, and Ellen Glasgow

Scholarship on Stein has long concentrated on technique, although
the works of Anderson and Glasgow are beginning to emphasize their
technical accomplishments also. Roger J. Bresnahan's "The Village
Grown Up: Sherwood Anderson and Louis Bromfield" (*Midamerica*
12:45–52) is a case in point. Bresnahan sees Anderson's manipulation
of setting in *Winesburg, Ohio* and *Poor White* as illuminating the
narrative and as an "additional character, changing as the narrative
progresses and acting as a foil to the human character." In "Sherwood
Anderson's Unpublished Stories" (*Midamerica* 12:53–58) William
V. Miller finds interest in three of 10 stories in manuscript at the Newberry Library ("Bob," "Fast Woman," and "Brother Earl") for their
underscoring what is "salient and subtle in the best of Anderson's
fiction." Miller speculates as to why these pieces were not published,
concluding that they might have been parts of novels in progress, or
too excessively sexual and autobiographical. In a fascinating, multifaceted essay concerning Anderson's meeting the fiction-writing
daughter of Laura Ingalls Wilder and using her as the source of
his character Rose Frank, "Sherwood Anderson and Rose Wilder
Lane: Source and Method in *Dark Laughter*" (*JML* 12:131–52),
William Holtz comments on Anderson's rejection of notebook realism
in favor of the unrestrained imagination, a Platonic rather than Aristotelian tradition of fiction, making Anderson a latter-day American
transcendentalist. David Stouck plugs Anderson into another "non-
realist" mainstream of American literature in "Sherwood Anderson
and the Postmodern Novel" (*ConL* 26:302–16). Motivated by self-

defense, much like Rose Lane was in her penetration of the well-springs of Anderson's art, Hemingway in *Torrents of Spring* high-lighted important nonrealistic aspects of Anderson's fiction, aspects Anderson attempted to define in "A Story Teller's Story" and which anticipated the works of Hawkes, Barth, Pyncheon, Vonnegut, and others striving to capture the fantastic essence of life. Stouck calls attention to *Dark Laughter, Many Marriages,* and *Winesburg* and is reminded of Gertrude Stein in Anderson's attempt to achieve rhythms of character emotions in sentence structure. In *Toward the End* (pp. 94–100) John Gerlach discusses "Hands" as illustrating Anderson's method of flashbacks dominated by a central image or tableau and as an achievement of closure of form without completion of action. Ray Lewis White provides a calendar, brief descriptions, and photographs of sample pages of the Newberry Library *Winesburg* manuscripts in "The Manuscripts of *Winesburg, Ohio*" (*WE* 11,i:4–10). White notes Anderson's discovery in 1938 of these "lost" manuscripts and con-cludes that they explode Anderson's fabrication that he composed without revision. White comments on the "yellow" first edition of *Winesburg* and three subsequent printings in "*Winesburg, Ohio,* First Printings, Variants and Errors" (*WE* 10,ii:1–3); photographs of the yellow edition and reprints of jacket material are included, as is a table of textual variants and errors in these four printings. Of biographical interest is William A. Sutton's edition of *Letters to Bab: Sherwood Anderson to Marietta D. Finley, 1916–1933* (Illinois). It includes 309 letters Anderson sent to the woman who was his critic, benefactor, comforter, and perhaps more. These letters stopped abruptly when Anderson refused the then Marietta Hahn's request to publish them. It is speculated that she and her psychiatrist husband contemplated a psychological study of Anderson. Finally, in " 'I'm a Fool'—A Source in *Roughing It*" (*SSF* 22:234–37) Wayne W. West-brook suggests that Anderson's inspiration was Twain's anecdote of a retired milk wagon horse frustrating the narrator's attempt to im-press a young lady.

The most interesting of the articles on Stein, Charlotte Melin's "Gertrude Stein and German Letters: Received, Recovered, Revised" (*CLS* 22:497–515), examines Stein's reputation in Germany as mod-ernist personality, as an influence on younger poets after World War II, and as a serious artist after the translation of *The Autobiography of Alice B. Toklas.* Stein's German reception has come full circle, however; in 1981 her early champion Helmut Heissenbuttel revised his estimate of her and claimed that her avant-garde attitudes in literature and break with traditional use of language were destructive. In a less focused general estimate Susan Hastings comments on *The Autobiography of Alice B. Toklas* as well as *Everybody's Autobiography* in "Two of the Weird Sisters: The Eccentricities of Gertrude Stein and Edith Sitwell" (*TSWL* 4:101–23). Hastings associates both writers with Virginia Woolf and discusses Sitwell's autobiography, *Taken Care Of*, as well as autobiographical ramifications of her *Alexander Pope* and *I Live Under a Black Sun*. Both women, she claims, through self-created eccentric legends, challenged traditions and assumed that women approached the world and spoke from a different perspective than men. In "Gertrude Stein: American Librettist" (*CentR* 29:389–99) Paul Cohen argues that the texts of *Four Saints in Three Acts*, *The Mother of Us All*, and *Doctor Faustus Lights the Lights* are among Stein's "most impressive and original creations," that they are innovative in overcoming the conflict in opera between story and music by concentrating meaning in brief bursts and alternating these with less demanding passages, and that they reveal a distinctly American perspective. Stein's technical virtuosity also concerns K. J. Phillips in his note "Ladies' Voices in Donald Barthelme's *The Dead Father* and Gertrude Stein's Dialogues" (*IFR* 12:34–37). Barthelme's novel recalls Stein's "Every Afternoon: A Dialogue" and "Ladies' Voices (Curtain Raiser)," in metamorphosing dialogue into a kind of poetry. Phillips also sees similarities between *Tender Buttons* and the more recent novel in these authors' use of self-referential remarks. In "Bipolar Conflict in Stein's *Melanctha*" (*MLS* 15,ii:55–64) Judith P. Saunders shows how in assigning coarser male traits to her title character and gentle female ones to Jeff Campbell, Stein dramatizes internal conflicts and, by reversing the usual sexual pattern, emphasizes the ludicrousness of one-sidedness in adult characterizations.

Ellen Glasgow's artistry and place in our tradition occupy this year's critics. The most general study is Nancy Walker's "Women Writers and Literary Naturalism: The Case of Ellen Glasgow" (*ALR* 18:133–46), which significantly questions why women novelists are usually left out of discussions of American naturalism. Glasgow, insists Walker, like Chopin and Wharton, made significant contributions to this movement, although the documentary style and focus on lower social classes do not typify her fiction. *The Descendant* and *Phases of an Inferior Planet* demonstrate Glasgow's interest in evolutionary theory, the former depicting a Dreiserian struggle between primitive and civilized natures. The *Southern Quarterly* (23,iv) featured three articles on Glasgow. Phillip D. Atteberry, in "Ellen Glasgow and the Sentimental Novel of Virginia" (pp. 5–14), contends that in *Virginia* (1913) Glasgow came of age as a writer, that previously her compulsion to distance herself from the sentimental novel by attacking it created focus problems in her work. In "The Comic Male: Satire in Ellen Glasgow's Queenborough Trilogy" (pp. 15–26) Kathryn Lee Seidel focuses on male characters in *The Romantic Comedians, They Stooped to Folly,* and *The Sheltered Life* to demonstrate Glasgow's sophistication in using satire to trace the darkening vision of her trilogy. In the first two novels Glasgow employs tender Horatian satire, but in the last havoc and corruption demand bitter Juvenalian satire. Sarah Fryer discusses the impact of passion on human character in the tragic outcome of the Jenny Blair, Eva, and George Birdsong triangle in " 'Love Has Passed Along the Way': Passion and Accident in *The Sheltered Life*" (pp. 27–36). Fryer considers the relationship between Jenny and George the central romance and "story" of the novel. The *Ellen Glasgow Newsletter* makes available two interesting series of Glasgow letters, those to Thomas Ayer of the Richmond Public Library (22:2–4) and those to Allen Tate (23:3–24). The five letters to Ayer concern Glasgow's defense of intellectual freedom during an attempt to censor Lewis' *Elmer Gantry*, which, by the way, she branded a "poor" novel, a "badly written study of crude emotionalism," and "more like a moral tract than a novel." The correspondence with Tate includes 26 letters, dated from 1932 to 1938, from collections at Princeton and Virginia; these are of special interest due to Tate's enthusiastic response to *The Sheltered Life*, which he saluted as her masterpiece, a kind of book different from her others and near perfect in form.

iv. John Dos Passos, Jack London, and Upton Sinclair

It is best to begin this review of Dos Passos scholarship by referring to some delayed items in the Autumn 1983 issue of *Resources for American Literary Study* (13:194–214). Richard S. Kennedy's "John Dos Passos: New Directions in Criticism and Research" calls attention to the availability of new materials. In "Dos Passos: New Possibilities in Biographical Research" (pp. 195–200) Townsend Ludington assesses the state of Dos Passos research while designating the following areas as needing attention: innovative styles and their relationship to Dos Passos personally; the novelist's themes and culture; his painting, poetry, and drama for what they tell us about his fiction; and, finally, insufficiently explored aspects of his life. In "Dos Passos: Some Directions in the Criticism" (pp. 201–06) Linda W. Wagner laments that much study of Dos Passos remains at the introductory, explicative stage, that there have been little or no specialty studies (linguistic, comparative, feminist/structuralist). She wonders if the novelist is too representative for psychological or postmodern treatment, and concludes with a call for his work to be linked to the important theoretical issues of our critical world. Virginia Spencer Carr in "Dos Passos, Painter and Playwright: New Possibilities in Research" (pp. 207–14) sees as a ripe area of study the novelist's contribution to art and drama and the influence on him of the modern movement in Paris.

Shelley Fisher Fishkin devotes a sizable section to Dos Passos in her *From Fact to Fiction* (pp. 165–204), her thesis being that the novelist's experience with nonfiction writing between 1916 and 1930, including his involvement in the Saco-Vanzetti case, contributed to his method in *U.S.A.*, which was to present the reader with conflicting signals and purposes in order to force a direct and clear view of experience rather than be shackled by distorting texts. The influence of nonfiction also concerns Kurt J. Fickert in "The Other Protagonist in Uwe Johnson's *Jahrestage*" (*Monatshefte* 77:151–56), specifically how Dos Passos' trilogy, in its use of the newsreel technique, anticipates the introduction of newspaper articles in the 1970 German novel; also, like Johnson after him, Dos Passos viewed the novel as a reality-establishing vehicle. The limited success of reproducing "reality" is the subject of Brian McHale in "Speaking as a Child in *U.S.A.*: A Problem in the Mimesis of Speech" (*Lang&S* 17 [1984]:351–67), which examines and enumerates with thoroughness the qualities of Dos Passos' child talk and tests this speech against objective linguistic description. In a more general view John J. Conder considers *Manhattan Transfer* as dramatizing a shift in American naturalism from determinism by nature to determinism by society in *Naturalism in American Fiction* (pp. 118–41). Conder sees in Jimmy Herf and Ellen Thatcher the conflict between the socially determined self and the authentic self sacrificed to it (a dual view of the self similar to Henri Bergson's). In "Dos and Hem: A Literary Friendship" (*CentR* 29:163–85) Scott Donaldson compares the two novelists previous to and after their falling out. His revealing angle lies in

evaluating the relationship of each to F. Scott Fitzgerald; with Fitzgerald as with others, Dos Passos' efforts were toward maintaining
friendship, but the friendship pattern for Hemingway "was one of
initial camaraderie, followed by a bitter competitive fissure that did
not admit of healing."

In "The Brainworker: Jack London" (*The Labor of Words* [Geor-
gia, pp. 92–112]) Christopher P. Wilson considers London's career
as reflective of the tension between culture and privilege, and craft
and careerism; he sees *Martin Eden* as a "significant cultural document" in dramatizing the no-man's-land between these poles. Gauging
the conflict between the Victorian parlor and the out-of-doors, London satisfied the tastes of the former with a formula for rendering the
latter. *The Sea-Wolf* is the subject of two essays. Forrest G. Robinson
offers a detailed defense of Maud Brewster in "The Eyes Have It: An
Essay on Jack London's *The Sea-Wolf*" (*ALR* 18:178–95). He concludes that London's heroine is "mature, resourceful, emotionally responsive, shrewd in her assessment and control of her environment,
possessed of great good humor, and determined to survive. In all,
she is easily the most impressive human being to set foot on the
Ghost." Robinson wonders why critics continually misunderstand and
misrepresent Maud: "What is it in our culture, more narrowly, in our
critical prepossessions, that so blinds us?" Adeline R. Tintner's "Jack
London's Use of Joseph Conrad's 'The End of the Tether' in *The Sea-
Wolf*" (*JLN* 17[1984]:61–65) carefully parallels Conrad's and London's depictions of increasing blindness to suggest that London imi-
tated Conrad's story of a good blind sea captain who died with his
ship; she also sees similarities between Van Wyk, the refined planter
friend of Conrad's Captain Whalley, and Wolf Larsen's foil, Van
Weyden.

Christopher Wilson's extensive treatment of Upton Sinclair in
The Labor of Words ("Would-Be Singer: Upton Sinclair," pp. 113–
40) examines the conflict in this novelist between the aristocratic
poet of the ideal and the campaigner for his own careerism: escape
from poverty through literature necessitated entrepreneurialism, then
espousal of the socialist cause became an escape from the isolation
and fatigue of such careerism. Wilson sees *The Journal of Arthur
Stirling*, like *Martin Eden*, as exorcising ideal literary identity and
paving the way for the socialism in *The Jungle*. Ironically, the message of the latter, the exploitation of labor, was distorted by the commercial system that Sinclair had espoused for success. The *Upton*

Sinclair Quarterly reprints a 1940 article by Dreiser on *World's End* (9,ii:3–5) which establishes Sinclair's purpose as campaigning against the exploitation of the public and labor, and laments that this message has been distorted and undermined by the system, that Sinclair had compromised himself by going into politics and dealing with the likes of FDR and Jim Farley. Dreiser's view parallels Wilson's, which sees Sinclair as similarly manipulated by Isaac Marcosson and Frank Doubleday, who diverted the thrust of *The Jungle* to the campaign for meat inspection.

June Howard considers Sinclair with London and Dreiser as reflecting the incompatibles of American naturalism in *Form and History in American Literary Naturalism* (No. Car., pp. 41–50, 51–62, 156–65, and passim). London's *White Fang* emphasizes natural forces while maintaining a concern for social forces: "Weedon Scott's alliance with the Wild invigorates and masculinizes the civilized values and the society he represents." In *Martin Eden* London deals more directly with the issues of class while employing terms that reflect natural forces ("trap," "wild man," "untamed," etc.). Similar tensions, between determinism and human will, are reflected in the protagonist of *Sister Carrie*, whose "passive and dedicated pursuit of her dreams is also an exercise of will that draws her from one level of understanding to another and thus draws her closer to the realm of freedom." Dreiser's vocabulary, his use of terms like "Waif" and "Wisp," and "Forces" and "Tide," reflects human effort as well as determining forces. Howard considers the problem of the spectator as a major antinomy of naturalism. The spectator becomes a sophisticated observer of the Other, caught between empathy and observation. The immobility of the spectator and his tendency toward the documentary calls for certain narrative strategies, like the use of detail to contribute to social phenomena as well as characterization. In *The Jungle* and *King Coal* Sinclair develops the bond among protagonist, narrator, and reader through a form of proletarianization.

v. H. L. Mencken and Others

The most general treatment of Mencken is Edward A. Martin's "On Reading Mencken" (*SR* 93:243–50), which calls attention to the useful overview provided by Mencken's own selection of writings in *A Mencken Chrestomathy* (1949) and by two recent Vintage (Random House) collections: *A Choice of Days* and *The American Scene: A*

Reader. Martin suggests beginning with the autobiographical pieces in *A Choice of Days* (ed. Edward L. Galligan): "*The American Scene* can [then] function as an anthology to illustrate the life that *Days* presents, with the *Chrestomathy* serving as a supplement . . . ." This overview makes two significant points—that Mencken's somewhat overlapping outrage and amusement were aimed at the abuse of language, and that his opinions, even when they bordered on bad taste and unfairness, originated from a positive moral position: "our time of cautionary prose[,] our avoidance of moral perspectives stands in vivid contrast to Mencken's willingness to commit himself . . . to a distinct point of view." A somewhat longer version of Martin's essay appears in *Menckeniana* (91[1984]:1–10).

Several items from past *Menckeniana* numbers deserve comment. In "The Composition and Revision of Mencken's 'Treatise on the Gods'" (88[1983]:9–16) Mary Miller Vass and James L. W. West III analyze the progress of the composition of *Treatise* through the initial 1928–29 composition and the 1945–46 revision by examining surviving manuscripts, typescripts, proofs, and correspondence. The authors conclude that Mencken took pains to polish his style when he was not working against deadlines. An interesting aspect of the analysis is the paralleling of passages from the original and revised versions, which make obvious Mencken's rethinking and toning down his attitude toward Jews. Vass and West stress the need for more exploration of Mencken texts along these lines. Thomas P. Riggio, in "Of the 'Black Horse Cavalry of Humor': Mencken's Contributions to *The Delineator*" (90[1984]:1–5), reprints two early (1910) Mencken spoofs of women's pages for the monthly magazine edited by Dreiser. Riggio notes that before 1911 Dreiser thought of Mencken as a 19th-century-style humorist rather than as either scholar or critic. Mencken's debunking of the American West, eclipsed only by his harsh treatment of the South, is the subject of Gerald Schwartz's "The West as Gauged by H. L. Mencken's *American Mercury*" (89[1984]: 1–11). Mencken encouraged contributions to his magazine, and made some himself, that reduced California to "Moron-Land" and Kansas to a shade above it on the scale of civilization, preferred as western heroes Billy the Kid and Jessie James to Sam Houston, Brigham Young, and John C. Fremont, boosted the Indian at the expense of the Babbitts running the West with their boosterism, and encouraged the contributions of western writers like H. L. Davis, James Stevens, and Louis Adamic.

A similarly sectional stance is taken by H. George Hahn II in "Twilight Reflections: The Hold of Victorian Baltimore on Lizette Woodworth Reese and H. L. Mencken" (*SoQ* 22,iv[1984]:5–21), which makes the point that Mencken, like his poet contemporary, was sensitive to the Baltimore of the last decades of the 19th century, a place of ethnic German neighborhoods and commercial tradition. Hahn provides a brief portrait of August Mencken, H. L.'s father, who bequeathed to his son practical joking and conservative politics. Mencken's letters concern P. J. Wingate in "H. L. Mencken—Man of Letters" (*Menckeniana* 90[1984]:7–12), who marvels at the volume of Mencken's correspondence, estimating that about 200,000 of the letters are still unpublished. Wingate notes that Mencken's letters stress his courtesy and humanity, despite the biting nature of the public man. His helpful sympathy is illustrated in his correspondence with a Catholic nun working on a doctorate at Catholic University of America. Sixteen letters to Mencken's future wife are provided by Marion E. Rodgers in " 'Dear Sara'; Letters to Sara Haardt from H. L. Mencken, 1924" (*Menckeniana* 96:10–16); these record the cementing of their friendship during the months of her developing tuberculosis, which provided Mencken with an opportunity to sympathize with her illness and discuss his own ailments. "The Mencken-Lewis Connection" (*Menckeniana* 95:10–16) concerns Stephen A. Young, who traces the development of the friendship and then its unraveling due to Lewis' antics and, what Mencken considered, inferior productions: "The author of *Babbitt* or an *Elmer Gantry* could be allowed a few antics, however much those antics might violate Mencken's strong sense of propriety. The author of a *Dodsworth* or *Ann Vickers* could not." The influence of Mencken's writings on the author of *Native Son* concerns Charles W. Scruggs's "Finding Out About This Mencken: The Impact of *A Book of Prefaces* on Richard Wright" (*Menckeniana* 95:1–11). Although Wright recorded different versions of his discovery of the Mencken work in *Black Boy*, the preface to *Uncle Tom's Children*, and in a 1938 interview, the constants that emerge are that Wright discovered through Mencken a way to fight with language and shared Mencken's twin themes of "seeking" and "wonder."

Among writers of the South, James Branch Cabell received most attention—two articles in the *Southern Quarterly* (23,ii). Cabell's mixed bag of the magic and the mundane concerns Donald Pizer's analysis of the principal fictions of the vast and diffuse life of Manuel

("The 1920s Fiction of James Branch Cabell: An Essay in Appreciation," pp. 55–74). Pizer comments on the blend of high fantasy and domestic farce in *Jurgen* and *Figures of Earth*, which are explored as his richest work, as "counterparts of the complex whole which is Cabell." Whereas *Jurgen* lightheartedly dramatizes man's inability to achieve the ideal, *Figures of Earth* deals with the artist's refusal to accept things as they are. In the other article, "The Innovative Fantasies of James Branch Cabell" (pp. 75–86), James D. Riemer laments Cabell's neglect during the recent interest in fantasy literature, and then he explores Cabell's unique undercutting of the elements of high fantasy, allowing him "simultaneously to parody high fantasy tradition and to develop his primary themes." The latest issue of *Kalki* (8[1984]) contains two additional considerations. William L. Godshalk, in "Wherein Is Set Forth a Brief Account of Cabell's Early Career, with a Few Even Briefer Comments on Faulkner" (pp. 239–43), quickly covers the same ground as Pizer, after emphasizing the importance of *The Cream of the Jest* (1917) as a fusion of elements separated in Cabell's early career—the comedy of manners and the medieval romance. The "briefer" remarks on Faulkner indicate that he had enjoyed and owned some of Cabell's novels. (Was there a connection?) G. F. Morley-Mower and Joan Powell use Cabell's collected verse, *From the Hidden Way*, to demonstrate his invention of quotations and sources as well as his erroneous and misleading acknowledgment and sloppy use of authentic ones in "Cabell's Mode of Quotation" (pp. 244–52).

Elizabeth Madox Roberts' masterpiece generated only a single consideration this year. In "The Poetry of Space in Elizabeth Madox Roberts' *The Time of Man*" (*SLJ* 18,i:61–72) Anne K. McBride uses phenomenologist Gaston Bachelard's observations in *The Poetics of Space* to analyze the novel as the progressive interaction between sensitive minds (Roberts' as well as heroine Ellen Chesser's) and the common areas of space they encounter. Mississippian Stark Young is the subject of a new Twayne study (TUSAS 463) by John Pilkington. Although Young is best known for his Civil War novel, *So Red the Rose* (1934), which Pilkington sees as one of the best of a cluster of Civil War novels of the 1930s, his other fiction, including *Heaven Trees* (1926), *The Torches of Flare* (1918), and *River House* (1929) are discussed in some detail. *River House* is unusual for its contemporary Mississippi setting, which becomes a symbol for tradition and values. Pilkington does careful work and makes modest claims for his subject, that he "belongs with all those writers who have valued the life of the affections, the harmonious relationships among them, and the importance of beauty and art in the good life."

Once-popular Boston-based novelist Margaret Deland is the subject of another Twayne study (TUSAS 479) by Diana C. Reep, who feels her subject is significant because of a long career of popular successes which reflect the attitudes of her times. Deland was religiously controversial and her first novel, *John Ward, Preacher* (1888), has been compared to Harold Frederic's *The Damnation of Theron Ware*. Similar speculations which see her *The Awakening of Helena Richie* (1906) as indebted to Kate Chopin's masterpiece are discredited by Reep. Deland's other feminist studies include *The Rising Tide* (1916) and *The Vehement Flame* (1922), which explore questions of women's suffrage and education for women. Deland was a moderate on feminist issues and unafraid to treat subjects like divorce, prostitution, and illegitimate pregnancy.

Finally, considerable attention was paid to fabricators of the American West myth, Owen Wister and Zane Grey. Darwin Payne's *Owen Wister: Chronicler of the West, Gentleman of the East* (SMU) is a readable and interesting account of Wister's friendship, travels, and artistic and political ventures; however, it belongs more in the category of American studies than literary criticism. Wister's friends, from Henry James and Theodore Roosevelt to Ernest Hemingway, play parts in this costume drama of literary and political VIPs. Payne concludes the biography by calling his subject an "extraordinary American," which indeed he was. In "The Virginian as Founding Father" (*ArQ* 40[1984]:227–41) Gary Scharnhorst theorizes that Thomas Jefferson and George Washington influenced Wister's conception of the Virginian more than did Andrew Jackson and Teddy Roosevelt. Scharnhorst relates the agrarian sympathies of the hero to Jefferson, and his speculative investments and prosperity to Washington. The *South Dakota Review* (23,iii) offers three essays on Zane Grey, two of them of significance. William Bloodworth's "Zane Grey's Western Eroticism" (pp. 5–14) uses *Wanderer of the Wasteland* and other novels to relate sex to landscape in Grey's fiction. What is evil in the eastern small town or closed-in Ohio frontier becomes natural initiation in the wide-open spaces. Bloodworth recalls that during his own innocence reading Grey was "like having to squirm through a steamy movie scene while Ava Gardner held a kiss against some man's mouth for about ten minutes." John D. Nesbitt, in

"Uncertain Sex in the Sagebrush" (pp. 15–27), credits Grey with less intent in theorizing that his literary orientation in adolescent fiction, Harry Castleman books and Beadle's Dime Library, as well as in Daniel DeFoe and James Fenimore Cooper, left him at cross-purposes with the sexual material in his own work. The sexual identity conflict in *Riders of the Purple Sage* and the handling of passion in *The U.P. Trail* and *To the Last Man* reveal a writer not fully aware of what he has under hand. In "History and Fiction: *To the Last Man*" (pp. 28–32) Edward Loomis suggests that Earle R. Forrest's republished 1836 *Arizona's Dark and Bloody Ground* (Arizona, 1984), a treatment of the Pleasant Valley War (1887–92), be used to assess Grey's earlier fictional treatment of it in his 1922 novel. *Zane Grey: A Photographic Odyssey* (Taylor) is a fascinating collection assembled by the novelist's son Loren. While there are the usual family, group, and personal photographs, there are also first-rate pictures taken during Grey's travels from Nova Scotia to the South Seas. There are many shots of Grey with Hollywood actor friends. But Ava Gardner in a passionate kiss is not among them.

Brigham Young University

14. Fiction: The 1930s to the 1960s

Louis Owens

As seems to have been the case for the last four years, Southerners, Proletarians, and Detectives continue to generate a lot of critical reflection in this period, with O'Connor, Welty, Steinbeck, Hammett, and Chandler leading the pack. Review chapters make strange bedfellows, stranger still this year following the transfer of such figures as Saul Bellow, William Burroughs, Jack Kerouac, and Bernard Malamud from chapter 15 to this chapter. Due to this influx, I've taken the opportunity in this, my last year to write this chapter (for a while at least), to create a new category—"Easterners"—one which, I hope, will accommodate a portion of the new arrivals while complementing the already existing categories here of "Southerners" and "Westerners." Such democratic divisions will, I further hope, nullify any sense of reductive regionalism sometimes attached to such labels. I would also like to seize this final opportunity to offer my apologies to all of those who have been victims of the inevitable omissions and misunderstandings that come with such territories as this chapter.

i. "Art for Humanity's Sake"—Proletarians

a. **James Agee and Others.**   One of the more labor-intensive products appearing this year is Archibald Hanna's *A Mirror for the Nation: An Annotated Bibliography of American Social Fiction, 1901–1950* (Garland). Hanna has put together an impressively thorough list of 3,900 works that fall into this category. Though such annotations as "A black woman in Florida and her three marriages" for Zorah Neale Hurston's *Their Eyes Were Watching God* don't offer much insight to the text, this is the kind of book that will undoubtedly be in every library. A writer of this period who escapes Hanna's wide net is James Agee, the subject of last year's very good biography by Laurence Bergreen, *James Agee: A Life* (*ALS 1984*, p. 268). We have this year a new collection of Agee's nonfiction, *James Agee: Selected Journalism*, edited by Paul Ashdown (Tenn.). Ashdown has gathered the best of Agee's work for *Fortune* and *Time*, including such superb pieces as "Tennessee Valley Authority," "Cockfighting," and "The American Roadside." In a 30-page introduction noteworthy for its informed and clear prose, Ashdown complains rightly that "Agee's journalism, although a considerable portion of the body of his work, is neglected." Though the introduction's attempts to compare Agee with another well-known journalist, Ernest Hemingway, have the flavor of legitimization by association, Ashdown makes a persuasive argument for both the significance and quality of Agee's journalism, an argument certainly supported by the selections included. A more complex undertaking is Paul John Eakin's *Fictions in Autobiography*, an impressive attempt to grapple with what Eakin terms "the vexing issue of factuality" in autobiography focusing on Mary McCarthy, Henry James, and Jean-Paul Sartre. In an extended essay discussing, among other things, McCarthy's "C.Y.E." and "Ask Me No Questions" Eakin concludes that the not-very-secret lesson of McCarthy's autobiographical writing is that "the process of self-discovery is finally inseparable from the art of self-invention." Unfortunately for McCarthy, the inherent attraction of her autobiographical writings pales quickly here beside those of such figures as James and Sartre and even, for this reader, Maxine Hong Kingston, each of whom is taken up by Eakin in subsequent chapters. McCarthy's musings become more accessible still with this year's publication of *Occasional Prose* (Harcourt), a collection of recent lectures, essays, reviews, and miscellaneous pieces that would have benefited from the inclusion of an index. Malcolm Cowley's developmental phase gets a thorough evaluation in James Michael Kempf's excellent study, *The Early Career of Malcolm Cowley: A Humanist Among the Moderns* (LSU). As his title implies, in this well-written and perceptive, if at times adulatory, study Kempf's interest is in the young Cowley as liberal humanist. As we've almost come to expect, 1985 produced still another Malcolm Cowley volume, *The Flower and the Leaf: A Contemporary Record of American Writing Since 1941* (Viking). Edited with an informative introduction by Donald W. Faulkner, this latest volume offers 55 eclectic pieces from brief reviews to major essays. Of additional "proletarian" interest this year is Donald Phelps's *Hearing Out James T. Farrell: Selected Letters* (Smith).

b. **John Steinbeck and John Dos Passos.** The first book-length study of Steinbeck's fiction by a single author in several years, my *John Steinbeck's Re-Vision of America* (Georgia), takes somewhat of an American studies approach as it looks long at Steinbeck's treatment of the American Myth from the early novel *To a God Unknown* through his major fiction to the final novel, *The Winter of Our Discontent.* Steinbeck's fiction, I argue, "represents a lifelong attempt to . . . awaken America to the failure at the heart of the American Dream. . . ." In "John Steinbeck's *The Pastures of Heaven: Illusions of Eden*" (*ArQ* 41:197–213) I contend that this early Steinbeck work must be read with a comprehension of Steinbeck's understanding of and attitude toward "non-teleological thinking." John Ditsky's monograph-length *John Steinbeck: Life, Work, and Criticism,* as part of the Canadian York Press's Authoritative Studies in World Literature, is a concise and valuable work aimed at introducing Steinbeck to students and beginning scholars. Jackson J. Benson follows up last year's monumental biography of Steinbeck (see *ALS 1984,* p. 270) with still another article, "Hemingway the Hunter and Steinbeck the Farmer" (*MQR* 24:441–60), a noncritical essay opposing the worldviews of the two authors and suggesting that in this opposition the two "embodied the fundamental values of the American character." An essay that should stir interest if not a whiff of controversy this year is Stanley Renner's "The Real Woman Inside the Fence in 'The Chrysanthemums'" (*MFS* 31:305–18). Renner argues forcefully that for this story "Steinbeck is undeserving of the feminist acclaim he has received over the last twenty-five years" and that critics have universally misread this story. Elisa Allen, Renner states, is "less a woman imprisoned by men [the accepted reading] than one who secures herself within a fortress of sexual reticence. . . ." Elisa's husband, Henry, rather than thwarting his wife's budding sexuality, is a victim of a castrating female. Though admirable for the energy of its argument, Renner's essay ignores too many critical elements in this story (e.g., the plowed earth waiting for rain, the blood and wine Elisa desires in the end) and is generally rather unconvincing. The *Steinbeck Quarterly* this year is largely taken up with Steinbeck Society matters, offering a handful of reviews of Steinbeck studies and fewer critical essays. Of practical interest is *"The Winter of Our Discontent:* A Critical Survey," by Carol A. Kasparek and edited by John Ditsky (*StQ* 18:20–34), indicating the increasingly positive critical response to Steinbeck's last novel. In "Mary Teller and Sue Bridehead: Birds of a Feather in 'The White Quail' and *Jude the Obscure*" (*StQ* 18:35–45) Stanley Renner argues for thematic similarities between the Steinbeck short story and the Hardy novel, suggesting a conscious borrowing by Steinbeck while defending Steinbeck's "considerable early artistry." A final item worth mentioning this year is Robert S. Hughes, Jr.'s "Steinbeck's Uncollected Stories" (*StQ* 18:79–93), in which Hughes offers quick précis of nine of Steinbeck's undistinguished and thus uncollected fictions. Of much greater practical value to Steinbeck researchers is this year's special issue of *San Jose Studies: The Steinbeck Research Center at San Jose State University: A Descriptive Catalogue*, prepared by Robert H. Woodward (*SJS* 11:i).

John Dos Passos is the subject of an interesting and substantial chapter (pp. 167–204) in Shelley Fisher Fishkin's *From Fact to Fiction*. Fishkin begins with the assertion that "Dos Passos's greatest success as an imaginative writer came when he returned in fiction to subjects, themes, and strategies he had first explored as a journalist." Fishkin goes on to examine *U.S.A.* and build effectively toward the conclusion that with his experiments in narrative "Dos Passos wants to teach his reader how to challenge the authority of the many attractive but misleading 'texts' that surround him." Dos Passos, along with Steinbeck and James T. Farrell—two other writers of this period often accused of naturalistic tendencies—receives oddly brief attention in June Howard's *Form and History in American Literary Naturalism* (No. Car.). A slew of writers of this period come in for critical nods in George Goodin's *The Poetics of Protest*. Among works noticed here are Harriette Arnow's *The Dollmaker*, Erskine Caldwell's *Tobacco Road*, and Robert Cantwell's *Land of Plenty*, as well as works by Dos Passos, Steinbeck, Harvey Fergusson, and Saul Bellow. Getting the most attention among the writers mentioned are Steinbeck and Caldwell. In a few pages (pp. 174–78) Goodin looks at the theme of group resistance in *The Grapes of Wrath*, concluding, along with Steinbeck, that in this novel repression strengthens the repressed. Most interesting here is Goodin's comparison of Steinbeck's Okies with the *cafoni* of Ignazio Silone's *Fontamara*. In a few paragraphs Goodin compares Caldwell's *Tobacco Road* to Steinbeck's *Tortilla Flat* but points out that unlike Steinbeck's novella Caldwell's work "ends with serious suffering." Finally this year, Marcia D. Yarmus considers Steinbeck's fascination with both language and Hispanic culture in "John Steinbeck's Hispanic Onomastic Interests in *The Log from the Sea of Cortez* and *East of Eden*" (*LOS* 12:195–207), a brief essay that nonetheless does important work in this area.

ii. Southerners

a. **General.** Certainly the most monumental production in some time is this year's volume *The History of Southern Literature*, ed. Louis D. Rubin, Jr., et al. (LSU). With a list of contributors that reads like a who's who of authorities on southern writing, this is a book to be taken seriously, but not one to be reviewed here chapter by chapter. As the title suggests, this is the definitive overview of southern writing, an introduction of enormous surface and necessarily little depth. Individual chapters provide introductions to single writers and groups of writers. Rubin's "Thomas Wolfe" (pp. 343–50), for example, offers a rather slight introduction to Wolfe, while James Mellard's "The Fiction of Social Commitment" (pp. 351–56) is a whirlwind gloss of writers from such relative unknowns as Harry Harrison Kroll to such relatively "major" figures as Erskine Caldwell. Other chapters follow suit. Also of wide if less definitive scope is Kathryn Lee Seidel's interesting study *The Southern Belle in the American Novel* (Florida). Seidel considers the blushing belle in a large grouping of southern novels including Margaret Mitchell's *Gone with the Wind*, Caroline Gordon's *The Garden of Adonis* and *Penhally*, and Allen Tate's *The Fathers*.

b. **Robert Penn Warren, the Agrarians, and Others.** Of general interest to followers of the Agrarians will be Thomas W. Cutrer's "Conference on Literature and Reading in the South and Southwest, 1935" (*SoR* 21:260–300), the proceedings of LSU's Agrarian-dominated conference held 10–11 April 1935. Of more critical interest will be William Bedford Clark's brief essay, "Warren's Criticism and the Evolving Self" (*KR* 7:48–53). Clark encourages us to pay careful attention to Warren's criticism, "for it stands as a vital model of how a reader may confront a text in the pursuit of what is (in the last analysis) not so much literary understanding as a measure of self-knowledge." Few will doubt the validity of this argument, though the need for the argument may be questioned. The critical need for such a volume as *Shakespeare and Southern Writers: A Study in Influence*, edited by Philip C. Kolin (Miss.), seems much less obvious. In "Renaissance Men: Shakespeare's Influence on Robert Penn Warren," one of nine

original essays gathered here, Mark Royden Winchell ponders the
Bard's influence upon the poetry and fiction of Renaissance literature
professor Warren. Of slightly more significance are Allen W. Hubsch's
source-hunting piece, "Two Kings and a Jack: The Kipling Factor in
All the King's Men" (*ELN* 22,iv:59–62), which compares Warren's
novel and Rudyard Kipling's *The Man Who Would Be King*; and
Barry Jay Seltser's "Realists, Idealists, and Political Heroism" (*Soundings* 68,i:21–41), which compares *All the King's Men*, Robert Bolt's *A
Man for All Seasons*, and Rolf Hochuth's *The Deputy*. Of considerably
more interest is the intimate picture of this period which became
available in 1985 in *The Southern Mandarins: Letters of Caroline
Gordon to Sally Wood, 1924–1937* (LSU), edited by Sally Wood.
With a genial, authoritative introduction by Andrew Lytle, Wood's
collection of letters provides often fascinating glimpses into the lives
of such Gordon-Tate acquaintances as Robert Penn Warren, Lytle,
Katherine Anne Porter, Malcolm Cowley, Hart Crane, Ford Madox
Ford, and E. E. Cummings. A work received too late for review last
year and well deserving of attention is Rose Ann C. Fraistat's *Caroline
Gordon as Novelist and Woman of Letters* (LSU, 1984), a careful
examination of Gordon's critical writing as well as the novels. More
admiring of and concerned with the use of myth within the novels
than with Gordon as woman of letters, Fraistat concludes that "Gordon's criticism suffers not only from the dogmatic tone but also from
her need to project her own moral and religious viewpoints on the
works she examined." Gordon and Allen Tate come in for lengthy
discussion along with Walker Percy in Robert H. Brinkmeyer, Jr.'s
Three Catholic Writers of the Modern South (Miss.). Brinkmeyer
follows Tate's long groping for religious faith rather inconclusively
through letters and verse, but declares emphatically that while before
her conversion to Catholicism Gordon's work resembles Hemingway's
worldly art, after her conversion "the shape and texture of her art
changed drastically, as she shifted her focus from the secular to the
divine." Shelby Foote's *The Civil War: A Narrative* is the subject of
James M. Cox's ebullience in "Shelby Foote's Civil War" (*SoR* 21:
329–50), an uncritical essay protesting a bit too much that Foote's
three-volume work "is a great work of literature, surely one of the
great works written in this or any other country—a work to rank with
that of Thucydides, Clarendon, Gibbon or Henry Adams." The great
danger, Cox laments, is that Foote's narrative will be lost in the no-
man's-land between history and literature. Also of interest this year

is Steven Youra's impressively thorough essay, "James Agee on Films and the Theater of War" (*FilmC* 10,i:18–31), on Agee, film criticism, and World War II.

c. Flannery O'Connor, Eudora Welty, and Others. Last year Louise Westling published "Demeter and Kore, Southern Style" (*PCP* 19,i–ii:101–07), a discussion of Greek myth in O'Connor's 'A Circle in the Fire'; this year Westling follows impressively with *Sacred Groves and Ravaged Gardens: The Fiction of Eudora Welty, Carson McCullers, and Flannery O'Connor* (Georgia), a careful and provocative study of myth, women's roles, and patriarchy in the fiction of these three southern authors. In *Critical Essays on Flannery O'Connor* (Hall) the editors, Melvin J. Friedman and Beverly Lyon Clark, have collected reviews, reminiscences, and a dozen of the best essays on O'Connor from such critics and writers as John Hawkes, Michel Gresset, and Ronald Schleifer, and provided an effectively annotated bibliography of what the editors consider the most significant O'Connor criticism. Of particular interest to O'Connor fans may be one of the two original pieces in this volume, Irving Malin's brief "Singular Visons: 'The Partridge Festival' " (pp. 180–86), which sees this troubling story as a "celebration" of art's inevitable failure "to capture the invisible, underlying pattern of life. . . ." Friedman provides a much-needed overview of the strained realm of O'Connor criticism in his introduction to this volume, responding to the common question articulated by Robert Coles: "How much more critical attention can a couple of dozen stories and two quite slim novels, however brilliantly and originally crafted, manage to sustain. . . ?" One very useful bit of attention O'Connor's fiction manages to sustain this year is Arthur F. Kinney's *Flannery O'Connor's Library: Resources of Being* (Georgia), an inventory of O'Connor's personal library including notation of O'Connor's marginal linings and underlinings. Among this year's critical essays on O'Connor, Jerry Leath Mills's "Samburan Outside of Toombsboro: Conrad's Influence on 'A Good Man Is Hard To Find' " (*SAQ* 84:186–96) illuminates the influence in matters of "structure, treatment of setting, and conception of character" of Conrad's *Victory* upon O'Connor's story. In a more probing essay, "Anagogical Realism in Flannery O'Connor (*Renascence* 37:80–95), Thomas M. Linehan examines O'Connor's "skyscape," her use of natural imagery of "moon, sun, and woods" to "show the objective spiritual condition of a world redeemed by grace." O'Connor's is a realism of surfaces, Linehan concludes, one through which we can "make religious sense of the world." Sonia Gernes ponders the theme of redemption in a slight piece on O'Connor, "Belief Is the Engine: Faith and the Art of Flannery O'Conner" (*New Catholic World* 228: 162–66), and George Cheatham adds a clarifying note in "Jesus, O'Connor's Artificial Nigger" (*SSF* 22:475–79), in which Cheatham declares that the black statue in "The Artificial Nigger" is "a symbol not only [of] man's innate sin and inevitable suffering but also of his mysterious redemption from sin and suffering through mercy." Of at best curious interest this year is Ruth Fennick's "First Harvest: Flannery O'Connor's 'The Crop'" (*EJ* 74,ii:45–50), in which Fennick suggests that though of inferior quality such early O'Connor stories as "The Crop" lack "the extreme violence, the shockingly grotesque characters, and the somewhat heavy dose of 'redemption through grace'" of the later stories and might therefore make appropriate high school reading. Fennick's essay should lead us to hope that very few high school students are being thus protected. O'Connor also received attention in Lewis A. Lawson's *Another Generation: Southern Fiction Since World War II* (Miss., 1984). Though Lawson makes his comprehensive knowledge of southern fiction as well as his own fine prose style abundantly clear in his preface and introductory chapter, Lawson's essays here on O'Connor and Harriette Arnow don't quite support Thomas Daniel Young's declaration in the foreword that Lawson is "the best reader of difficult . . . [contemporary fiction] alive." In "*Wise Blood* and the Grotesque" (pp. 22–37) Lawson provides a well-written assessment of O'Connor's satire with the deft declaration that in the character of Haze Motes "Miss O'Connor deliberately constructed an oxymoron as character" and by so doing "escaped the danger inherent in using a caricature. . . ." However, in spite of the invocation of Martin Heidegger's *Being and Time* in his chapter on Arnow, "The Knife and the Saw in *The Dollmaker*" (pp. 58–74), in this essay Lawson offers too much summary of this Arnow novel with too little critical insight. Considerably less satisfying still is the reading of O'Connor's "Parker's Back" offered by Carl Ficken in his *God's Story and Modern Literature: Reading Fiction in Community* (Fortress Press). Ficken's analysis seldom rises above the complexity of the first sentence in his O'Connor chapter: "In the fiction of Flannery O'Connor, we find fascinating stories—and some problems." Mary L. Morton probes more difficult territory much more successfully in "Doubling in Flannery O'Connor's Female Characters: Animus and

Anima" (*SoQ* 23,iv:57–63). Morton's thesis is that "O'Connor's stories dramatize the ludicrosity of women who have denied the spirit of femininity, the anima." Such deniers, says Morton, are the "angular, ludicrous" women of O'Connor's fiction. Their doubles, representing the anima, are "fat women of the earth." Morton's approach leads to an excellent reading of "Greenleaf" in particular and to irresistible speculation on my part as to what Morton would do with such a character as fat Hulga in "Good Country People," a story Morton does not discuss. The rebirth of Mrs. May is the subject of another worthwhile essay this year, Richard Giannone's " 'Greenleaf': A Story of Lent" (*SSF* 22:421–29). Other O'Connor essays worthy of note in 1985 include Linda Osborne Payne's "Two Generations of Southern Womanhood in Flannery O'Connor: Mothers, Daughters, Mystery, and Manners" (*MHLS* 8:71–81); Ted R. Spivey's "The Complex Gifts of Flannery O'Connor" (*EAS* 14:49–58), which considers Catholicism and generation gaps; and Joyce C. Dyer's " 'Something' in Flannery O'Connor's *Wise Blood*" (*NConL* 15,v:5–6), which briefly considers "Something." Final incidental O'Connor items to be mentioned are Wilton Beauchamp and David Matchen's "The Cheney-O'Connor Letters" (*PMPA* 9:78–85) and Rainulf A. Stelzmann's "Two Unpublished Letters by Flannery O'Connor" (*XUS* 5,i–ii:49–50).

Southern mythmaking and the oral tradition occupy Carol S. Manning's primary interest in *With Ears Opening Like Morning Glories: Eudora Welty and the Love of Storytelling* (Greenwood). Defending scrutiny of southern regionalism in Welty's fiction, Manning examines what she terms "the narrative reshaping of events" in Welty's South and declares that Welty "proves herself the oral culture's most discriminating admirer and its most incisive critic." Manning has carved out her terrain here in a convincing manner. Naoko Fuwa Thornton builds upon the established critical awareness of myth in Welty's fiction in "Medusa-Perseus Symbolism in Eudora Welty's *The Optimist's Daughter*" (*SoQ* 23,iv:64–76). Although like many myth-hunters Thornton can't resist pushing the quest for allusions a bit too far (drops of nail polish on Judge McKelva's desk are "perhaps the trail of a blood-covered claw defiling this spiritual and intellectual symbol of the McKelva family"), Thornton's search does contribute significantly to our understanding of this short novel. In "Welty's 'The Bride of the Innisfallen' " (*Expl* 43,ii:42–44) Marshall Toman traces the etymology of the word "pavilion" in Welty's story, suggesting that the word "portends the metamorphosis of one of the

story's important characters and signals her allegiance to the Irish
world of freedom and not to the British world of convention." Additional items of critical interest include several by Suzanne Marrs
who has been busy again this year publishing "The Making of *Losing
Battles*: Judge Moody Transformed" (*NMW* 17,ii:47–53), "The Making of *Losing Battles*: Plot Revision" (*SLJ* 18:40–49), "An Annotated
Bibliography of the *Losing Battles* Papers" (*SoQ* 23:116–21), and
"John James Audubon in Fiction and Poetry: Literary Portraits by
Eudora Welty and Robert Penn Warren" (*SoSt* 20:378–83). Also of
interest is Floyd C. Watkins' slight essay "The Journey to Baltimore
in *The Optimist's Daughter*" (MissQ 38:435–39), a look at Becky Mc-
Kelva's journey.

In *Truth and Vision in Katherine Anne Porter's Fiction* (Georgia)
Darlene Harbour Unrue undertakes to provide what she argues
Porter scholarship has thus far failed to provide: "a clear and thorough
answer to questions about Porter's world view and about the relationships among her stories and her novel." Tracing the relationship between illusion and despair through the stories and through a long
chapter on *Ship of Fools*, Unrue succeeds rather well in her quest,
though the frustratingly complex element of Catholicism in Porter's
writing is a point Unrue, unlike Carl Ficken, seems a bit too eager to
sidestep in her discussion. Particularly useful here is Unrue's well-
researched consideration of "Flowering Judas" and "Maria Con-
cepciòn" as well as the general influence of Mexico in Porter's fiction.
In "Granny Weatherall's Dying Moment: Katherine Anne Porter's
Allusions to Emily Dickinson" (*SSF* 22:437–42) David C. Estes
points to allusions in this story to Dickinson poems "Because I could
not stop for Death," "I heard a Fly buzz," and "I've seen a Dying
Eye." Janis P. Stout's "Mr. Hatch's Volubility and Miss Porter's Reserve" (*ELWIU* 12:285–93) considers verbal style in Porter's "Noon
Wine," arguing well the thesis that this style "is for [Porter] an issue
of the utmost seriousness, not only aesthetically and as a matter of
decorum . . . but morally as well." With an eye toward doubling in
the story, Stout studies speech in "Noon Wine" as "the primary index
to character." Also meriting a mention this year is James Walter's
"Revolution and Time: Laura in 'Flowering Judas'" (*Renascence*
38:26–38), an interesting treatment of allegory and alienation in
Porter's story.

In *Growing Up Female: Adolescent Girlhood in American Fiction*
(Greenwood) Barbara A. White sets about to revise the disproportion-

ate critical interest in male adolescence in the American novel, looking for "patterns of experience that hold true for women" in fiction focusing upon adolescence. White offers a corrective to "Feidlerite" readings in her chapter on Carson McCullers, "Loss of Self in Carson McCullers' *The Member of the Wedding*" (pp. 89–111). To those critics who follow Leslie Fiedler's critical line, according to White, the novel's adolescent protagonist, Frankie, resists sexual knowledge because "she is a lesbian or a 'deviate.'" White, on the contrary, sees the almost universally admired Berenice as a negative influence upon the young Frankie, an older example of a woman accepting her diminished role in a male world, and concludes that this novel "is less a novel of initiation into 'acceptance of human limits' than a novel of initiation into acceptance of female limits." Of additional interest may be the *Southern Quarterly*'s special "Louisiana and Film" issue (23:1), with among other essays John R. May's "Louisiana Writers and Film" (pp. 18–31), in which May scans the representation in film of the works of such writers as Robert Penn Warren and Lillian Hellman.

d. **Thomas Wolfe and Erskine Caldwell.** The Thomas Wolfe industry remains much alive this year with the appearance of a new version of Wolfe's play, *Mannerhouse*, ed. Louis D. Rubin, Jr., and John L. Idol, Jr. (LSU). In an introduction explaining the rationale for this new edition, Rubin declares that the play "represents a notable advance in the development of Wolfe's art," and that this work is "strikingly reminiscent—and anticipatory—of Faulkner's *Absalom, Absalom!*" Edward Aswell's controversial revising hand is once again indicted in Idol's "The Text and the Background of the Play," which makes clear the thorough scholarship behind this version of *Mannerhouse*. Wolfe gets to speak in his own voice again this year in *Thomas Wolfe Interviewed, 1929–1938*, ed. Aldo P. Magi and Richard Walser (LSU). The editors have provided introductory notes for the 26 newspaper interviews here, explaining both interviewer and context. John S. Phillipson's *Critical Essays on Thomas Wolfe* extends G. K. Hall's uniformly well-edited Critical Essays On American Literature series with an eclectic gathering of Wolfe essays from the last decade. This collection owes much to the *Thomas Wolfe Review*, with primary consideration naturally enough going to *Look Homeward, Angel* and *Of Time and the River* as well as groupings of critical pieces on the posthumous novels, the plays, and the short fiction. Certainly the most impressive essay in the collection is John Hagan's "Structure, Theme, and Metaphor in Thomas Wolfe's *Look Homeward, Angel*" (pp. 32–47), which first appeared several years ago in *American Literature*, while of less import is "The Gothic Matrix of *Look Homeward, Angel*" (pp. 48–56), one of two essays published here for the first time, in which Darlene H. Unrue offers a brief, rather inconsequential consideration of Gothic elements in the same novel. In the other original essay in this collection, "Thomas Wolfe's Search to Know Brooklyn" (pp. 174–82), Webb Salmon attempts an illumination of the relationship between place, structure, and theme in Wolfe's writing, an attempt that falls somewhat short in these few pages. In "Technique in 'The Child by Tiger': A Portrait of a Mature Artist" (*SCR* 18:83–88) Suzanne Stutman attempts to refute the old charge that "Wolfe's work at its best represents a kind of 'happy accident' accomplished by some miraculous or haphazard circumstance." Stutman contends that "In 'Child by Tiger' Wolfe has fashioned a notable artistic statement about one man's quest for selfhood and mankind's inescapable and tragic humanity." On a final Wolfe note, the *Thomas Wolfe Newsletter* in 1985 again offers substantial critical reflections in several essays: Richard S. Kennedy's "What the Galley Proofs of Wolfe's *Of Time and the River* Tell Us" (ii:1–8), which examines the editing role of John Wheelock; and Mary Aswell Doll's "Searches for the Father" (ii:30–35), which discusses Wolfe's relationship with Edward Aswell. "The Child by Tiger" comes in for more attention in this year's *TWN*, with Delores Washburn's " 'The Child by Tiger' and Students' Innocent Ignorance" (ii:47–52), a discussion of Wolfe's story and the Brownsville riots.

Focusing on a very different kind of southerner in *Erskine Caldwell* (TUSAS 469; 1984), James E. Devlin takes a critical look at a writer he does not admire a great deal, offering the necessary biography as well as critical examinations of Caldwell's major novels. Though praising Caldwell's supreme creations, *Tobacco Road* and *God's Little Acre*, and being critically fair to both works, Devlin concludes that this particular southern writer "is without any question a minor writer, and further, a limited one. Philosophically he is of few ideas and those often inconsistent." Devlin's most damning accusation here and the one most likely to raise hackles is that Caldwell "does not really understand the human beings he writes about. . . ." Marilyn Dorn Staats approaches the aging Caldwell with a very different perspective in "Erskine Caldwell at Eighty-One: An Interview"

(*ArQ* 41:247–57). Caldwell, Staats asserts before beginning her brief, uneventful exchange with the writer, "may yet be recognized as one of the important writers of twentieth-century America."

iii. Expatriates and Émigrés—Vladimir Nabokov and Anaïs Nin

The most entertaining this year because the most Nabokovian of studies in some time is Joann Karges' *Nabokov's Lepidoptera: Genres and Genera* (Ardis). Karges adroitly points to Nabokov's attraction to the "concept of nature's mimicry exceeding its purpose" and goes on to pinpoint lepidopteran allusions and images throughout the novels with prose at times wonderfully evocative of Nabokov himself: "A fritillary fairly common throughout moist areas of temperate North America and ranging into the Rockies . . . is the Cybele (*Speyeria cybele*, the Great-spangled Fritillary)." Less charming but more critically substantial is David Galef's "The Self-Annihilating Artists of *Pale Fire*" (*TCL* 31:421–37). Stressing the self-referential nature of Nabokov's characters, Galef protests that insufficient attention has been paid to poor Hazel Shade who, according to Galef, "functions as an interpretive key, revealing much about Kinbote and his grand extrapolation." This is the most convincing analysis of Hazel and the poltergeist business yet, and one that offers new insight into this much-written-about novel. Of equal interest is John Haegert's "Artist in Exile: The Americanization of Humbert Humbert" (*ELH* 52:777–93), in which Haegert contends that behind the more familiar conflicts in *Lolita* "looms the greatest and most potent of American polarities: the legendary conflict between New World possibilities and Old World sensibilities." Seizing upon Humbert's awareness of the "melodious unity" of children's voices in a scene often noted for its lyrical power, Haegert states that the "true significance" is "preeminently cultural, deriving from Humbert's unfettered awareness, at last, of a native American reality 'unsolipsized' by his émigré imagination." This year's *Nabokovian* is most useful for Stephen Jan Parker's "1984 Nabokov Bibliography" (15:40–56) and most interesting for D. Barton Johnson's "Nabokov and M. Ageyev's *Novel with Cocaine*" (15:11–16), in the latter of which Johnson takes issue with claims that Nabokov may be the real author of that 1930s Russian émigré novel.

Anaïs this year offers several bits of information and reflection upon Anaïs Nin, ranging from Junko Kimura's consideration of Nin and Japanese women writers in "Finding the Inner Self" (3:117–20) to Margaret Miller's "Diary-Keeping and the Young Wife" (3:39–44), a look at sex roles.

iv. Westerners

Complementing this year's publication of *A Cloak of Light* (Harper), the excellent concluding volume of Wright Morris' memoirs, Roy K. Bird's *Wright Morris: Memory and Imagination* (Peter Lang) offers a critically intelligent and informed study of Morris' writing. Though too brief to do serious justice to the astounding range of Morris' work, Bird's study does a perceptive job of applying a contemporary awareness of the self-conscious or self-reflexive novel to Morris' intrusive presence in the text. This is a valuable work worthy of a more polished presentation (read typesetting) than it receives as part of Lang's English Language and Literature series.

A too-neglected westerner receives the full focus of the *South Dakota Review*'s special Wallace Stegner issue this year (23,iv). In a somewhat uneven assortment, essays in this number of *SDR* include such pieces as Wendell Berry's fine reminiscence, "Wallace Stegner and the Great Community" (pp. 10–18); John Milton's "Conversation with Wallace Stegner" (pp. 107–18; reprinted from *SDR* 9:1); James Houston's brief "Wallace Stegner: Universal Truths Rooted in Region" (pp. 6–9); and Melody Graulich's excellent critical assessment of sex roles and myth in "The Guides to Conduct That a Tradition Offers: Wallace Stegner's *Angle of Repose*" (pp. 87–106). Other items in this issue are Edward Loomis' remembrance of teachers past, "Wallace Stegner and Yvor Winters as Teachers" (pp. 19–24) and T. H. Watkins' more lengthy environmental reflection, "Bearing Witness for the Land: The Conservation Career of Wallace Stegner" (pp. 42–57). Another Californian who hasn't suffered from neglect during the past few years is the subject of one noteworthy essay, John A. Mills's study of the absurd in " 'What. What-not.' Absurdity in Saroyan's *The Time of Your Life*" (*MQ* 26:139–59), and a note, Joseph Petite's "Saroyan's 'Laughter' " (*Expl* 43,iii:41–42).

A transplanted westerner continuing to generate interest this year is Mable Dodge Luhan, with a reissue of *Movers and Shakers* (N. Mex.) and a new volume (TUSAS 477), Winifred L. Frazer's *Mabel Dodge Luhan*. As befits its subject and its aim, Frazer's work is a chatty introduction to the belle of Taos, one that attempts to correct a few misconceptions and in the end remains noncommittal about the ultimate value of Luhan's writings. Barbara White in *Growing Up Female* takes a revisionist, feminist look at the fiction of Jean Stafford as well as Carson McCullers and others (see McCullers above). In "Initiation in Jean Stafford's *The Mountain Lion*" (pp. 114–36) White argues very effectively that "the revelation that 'adult men' have the 'real power' is the key to initiation in *The Mountain Lion*." According to White, the male adolescent in the novel, Ralph, "accepts initiation because manhood gives him privileges," while Ralph's sister, Molly, "resists not growth in general, but growth to womanhood, a devalued state." Stafford's eastern connections are the subject of William Leary's interesting piece, "Jean Stafford, Katharine White, and the *New Yorker*" (*SR* 93:584–96).

Max Westbrook blends history, a touch of American Indian mythology, and psychology to take another look at Walter Van Tilburg Clark's novel in "The Indian in the Mirror: Clark's *The Track of the Cat*" (*WAL* 20:17–33). In an essay that would have benefited from a more coherent focus, Westbrook examines "mirrored images of reality"—rational and nonrational realities within the novel. Two other westerners of this period are considered in the Western Writers series this year, Arthur R. Huseboe's *Herbert Krause* (WWS 66) and Merrill Lewis' *Robert Cantwell* (WWS 70). Krause's slight output contributes to the "metaphor of the novel of the West," says Huseboe, both "a new and more intense poetry in the telling of the story of a people, and a powerful evocation of a region in the West that had been neglected in fiction as well as in history." In *Robert Cantwell*, Lewis applies his thorough knowledge of the literature of the West and westering to a well-written treatment of Cantwell's even more slight fictional production as well as Cantwell's nonfiction—a valuable reminder.

David Stouck looks at the defining conventions of one particular kind of western novel in "The Art of the Mountain Man Novel" (*WAL* 20:211–21). Stouck suggests that the art of this novel lies "in the handling of form, in the novel's moral and psychological content, and ultimately in its philosophical vision." Although he goes on to say a few words about such works as A. B. Guthrie's *The Big Sky*, Vardis Fisher's *Mountain Man*, and Harvey Fergusson's *Wolf Song*, Stouck allows serious examination of the art of these novels to remain for another essay on another day. In my essay "The 'Map of the Mind': D'Arcy McNickle and the American Indian Novel" (*WAL* 19:275–

83) I examine the message central to both McNickle's first novel, *The Surrounded* (1936), and his last, posthumous novel, *Wind from an Enemy Sky* (1978). I conclude that between the two works this mixed-blood Indian novelist's message does not change and that, finally, "Few writers have given us darker pictures of the relationship between Indian and white worlds. . . ." In *American Indian Novelists: An Annotated Critical Bibliography* (Garland) Tom Colonnese and I provide brief biographical and extensive annotated bibliographical information for 21 Indian novelists, including such 1930s' writers as McNickle and John Joseph Mathews. Called by *American Indian Culture and Research Journal* "the best work to date on this particular subject" and "a definitive model for critical bibliographies of this sort," *American Indian Novelists* includes entries for fiction, poetry, nonfiction, interviews, and plays.

Still farther west, *The Hollywood Novel and Other Novels About Film, 1912–1982: An Annotated Bibliography* (Garland), by Nancy Brooker-Bowers, provides an impressive deluge of useful information. Though a disappointing number of the entries here simply cite Carolin See's 1963 dissertation, "The Hollywood Novel: An Historical and Critical Study," with no added information, Brooker-Bowers' 694 entries are for the most part briefly and effectively annotated and indexed by title and author.

v. Easterners

Into this year's convenient Easterners category falls Scott Elledge's *E. B. White: A Biography* (Norton, 1984), a volume missed last year and one that serves up all the necessary information with an impressively readable style well suited to its subject. Further biographical information on White appears this year in William Howarth's "E. B. White at the *New Yorker*" (*SR* 93:574–83).

Critical revision is much on Jonathan Wilson's mind in *On Bellow's Planet* (Fairleigh Dickinson). Commencing with the declaration that Saul Bellow's novels "articulate a system, a single vision of the world," Wilson intends to counter here the accepted notion that Bellow is a "life-affirming" novelist. Identifying the "static dialectic" of Bellow's fiction as "oppositions between order and chaos or limitation and freedom, upon whose resolution nothing hangs," Wilson contends that "the irresolvably 'static dialectic' of Bellow's novels would appear to fundamentally contradict the sense of open-ended human possibility that so many critics have discovered in Bellow's fiction." Wilson ignores significant elements in the novels that don't jibe well with this thesis (the abundant, if well-flogged, *Waste Land* allusions, for example), but he offers clear, well-reasoned readings that should provide new stimulus to Bellow followers. Wilson finds a recent Bellow production, *The Dean's December*, to be "the least successful of Bellow's nine novels" and an indication that "its author has lost interest or has a diminished interest in creating fiction," a note sounded also in Seymour Epstein's review-essay, "A Dispassionate December" (*DQ* 19,iv:139–47). In this novel, Epstein concludes, "Bellow restates his humanist position, but with more summarization than passion, more crankiness than intellect." Of Bellow's still more recent collection of short stories, *Him with His Foot in His Mouth*, Epstein suggests that these works "reinforce the view that Saul Bellow may be seen as a social critic in the guise of a fiction writer, or a fiction writer with the single, powerful theme of social criticism." A somewhat fresh slant on *Henderson the Rain King* occupies F. Odun Balgun in "Mythopoeic Quest for the Racial Bridge: *The Radiance of the King* and *Henderson the Rain King*" (*JEthS* 12,iv:19–33). Balogun finds "a revealing unity of ideas in the ways both novelists [Camara Laye and Bellow] employ the form of the mythic quest to expose racist myths" and argues well the point that "both novels create desirable literary myths of racial harmony in order to bridge the racial gap created by undesirable, fallacious racist myths." Ellen Pifer makes a good argument against what she terms the "disproportionate amount of hostile criticism" directed against another Bellow novel in " 'Two Different Speeches': Mystery and Knowledge in *Mr. Sammler's Planet*" (*Mosaic* 18,ii:17–32). Critics such as Alfred Kazin have erred, Pifer says, in assuming that the novel's protagonist "is largely devoid of psychological conflict." On the contrary, Pifer finds Sammler's psyche to be at war with itself, divided between "two modes of consciousness, the analytic and the intuitive." *Mr. Sammler's Planet* also comes in for scrutiny in Alan L. Berger's *Crisis and Covenant: The Holocaust in American Jewish Fiction* (SUNY). Beginning with the assumption that "Covenantal thinking appears to have been rediscovered . . . as the appropriate response to catastrophe" since the Holocaust, Berger examines fictional responses in the work of Bellow and Malamud among others. *Mr. Sammler's Planet*, Berger declares, is Bellow's "most direct engagement with the Holocaust," with Artur Sammler's reactions throughout the novel "those of a survivor." In a

phrase currently loaded with unfortunate ideological baggage, Berger
calls this novel "above all an indictment of secular humanism." In
considerations of Bernard Malamud's stories "The Lady of the Lake"
and "The German Refugee" and Malamud's novels *The Assistant* and
The Fixer, Berger continues to provide analysis with a very narrow
focus. Finally, it seems sufficient to say that the *Saul Bellow Journal*
continues to make itself indispensable to Bellow students and critics
with a cornucopia of information and critical reflection ranging from
such substantial articles as Ted R. Spivey's "Death, Love, and the Rebirth of Language in Saul Bellow's Fiction" (4:5–18) and Ada Aharoni's "*The Victim*: Freedom of Choice" (4:33–44) to such eminently
useful pieces as Gloria L. Cronin's "Selected Annotated Bibliography
for 1981" (4:58–70). Jeffrey Helterman does an admirable job of
making Bernard Malamud understandable in *Understanding Bernard
Malamud,* part of the University of South Carolina's Understanding
Contemporary American Literature series. Aimed, according to series
editor Matthew J. Bruccoli, at "students as well as good nonacademic
readers," Helterman's book very neatly introduces readers to the
mythological structures of Malamud's novels while keeping Malamud's text on a very approachable level. This is the kind of book
beginning literature students will be relieved to discover.

In an effort to "preempt some of the thanatography" that should
be expected following Djuna Barnes's death, Lawrence R. Schehr, in
"Djuna Barnes's *Nightwood*: Dismantling the Folds" (*Style* 19:36–
49), makes an attempt at deconstruction of Barnes's novel. "Before
reading *Nightwood* as a reflection," Schehr suggests, "be it of a public
(societal) or a private world, we should look at the ways in which
the world has been constructed, not brought to life, but to writing."
Schehr's approach, one which works very well, is to consider the
novel's unusual first half as "a text followed by something that is, in
part, an attempt to make sense of various strands and kinds of characterization and semiosis by means of the imposition of plot—rationali-
zation—on language." Thanatography this is not.

vi. Iconoclasts and Innovators

Hollywood's favorite iconoclast receives the most impressive attention this year in Robert Emmet Long's *Nathanael West* in Ungar's
Literature and Life series. Long provides the standard biography,
selecting as his springboard what he terms West's "deeply ambiguous

identity." Though the search for influences reaches a point of diminishing returns here (e.g., Cabell, Pound, Eliot, Dostoyevsky, Gide, Flaubert, Baudelaire, Huysmans, the Dadaists, Picasso, Max Ernst, etc., for *The Dream Life of Balso Snell*), Long's readings are critically intelligent and well informed. This is a useful introduction to West's fiction. Of more practical use still is Steven H. Gale's *S. J. Perelman: An Annotated Bibliography* (Garland), with 1,130 entries arranged in categories of Novel, Collections, Plays, Films, Television Scripts, Sound Recordings, Articles/Short Stories, Incidental Pieces and Reprints, Letters, and a Chronological Index to Perelman's Writing. Gale is thorough, including secondary sources and selected book, film, and play reviews. In spite of the valuable labors performed here, the evidence compiled does not support Gales's introductory claim that "in terms of popularity, longevity, amount and variety of output . . . technical virtuosity, and influence on other writers, Perelman is certainly one of the most important authors in the history of American literature."

More radically innovative is the subject of David Porush's *The Soft Machine: Cybernetic Fiction* (Methuen). Taking off in a great leap forward from Hugh Kenner's *The Counterfeiters*, Porush's study examines a battery of contemporary writers from Kurt Vonnegut, Jr., and William Burroughs to Pynchon, Barth, Beckett, and Donald Barthelme. After defining his terrain exceptionally well in three introductory chapters, "The Metaphor of the Machine," "Roussel's Device for the Perfection of Fiction," and "Cybernetics and Literature," Porush looks at Vonnegut and Burroughs in one chapter, declaring that "the denaturing of language's genetic code indicated in the lacunae, typographical shouting, scatology, introduction of chance and centrifugal imagery of Burroughs' work are all not so much methods for creating and engendering as they are a sort of underground resistance, a disarming of the control implied in any order, any system, including language's natural one, from within." Escape from "the restrictions of naming and representation," from "the coercion and violence of all word and image" in Burroughs' fiction is also the focus of another of the outstanding essays in this area this year, Robin Lydenberg's "Notes from the Orifice: Language and the Body in William Burroughs" (*ConL* 26:55–73). In contradiction to critics who have sought to label Burroughs a metaphorical writer, Lydenberg finds the "pattern revealed in the names and anecdotes of *Naked Lunch*" to be "essentially the pattern of metonymy." Human relationships rather than language in Paul Bowles's fiction, from the '40s to the '80s, is the subject of Linda W. Wagner's "Paul Bowles and the Characterization of Women" (*Crit* 27,i:15–24). Beginning with an affirmation of Johannes Bertens' observation that Bowles is a writer concerned with relationships, Wagner goes on to put together a solid case for change in Bowles's characterization of women and male-female relationships, particularly in the later works such as *Midnight Mass* and *Points in Time*.

Jack Kerouac receives sterling attention this year in John Clellon Holmes's *Gone in October: Last Reflections on Jack Kerouac* (Boise, Idaho: Limberlost Press). Though disappointingly brief—under a hundred pages—Holmes's reflections are among the finest thus far on this particular Beat. *Moody Street Irregulars*, the Jack Kerouac newsletter, turns its attention to Kerouac and popular/jazz music this year, with such tidbits as Alex Albright's "Van Morrison and Kerouac" (*MSI* 15:25) and Kevin Ring's "The Golden Juke Box" (*MSI* 15:23–24). Finally, Umberto D'Alessandro's "The Lost Soul of Northport: Jack Kerouac" (*Confrontation* 30–31:49–52) contributes a few reflections on Kerouac's relation to Northport, while Fred W. McDarrah's *Kerouac and Friends: A Beat Generation Album* (Morrow) collects more than 300 pages of familiar photographs and writings for something resembling a Kerouac retrospective. Iconoclastic J. D. Salinger gets less significant attention than does Kerouac, with such minor essays as Thomas Feeny's "The Possible Influence of J. D. Salinger's *The Catcher in the Rye* upon Lorenza Mazzetti's *Con Rabbia*" (*Neohelicon* 12, ii:35–46), and David Piwinski's "Salinger's 'De Daumier-Smith's Blue Period': Pseudonym as Cryptogram" (*NConL* 15,v:3–4). Giving more import to Salinger criticism this year, however, is Hubert Zapf's application of the theories of Tzvetan Todorov in "Logical Action in *The Catcher in the Rye*" (*CollL* 12:226–71), an excellent essay I wished had been developed still further.

Horror and sci-fi innovators H. P. Lovecraft and Ray Bradbury get noticed very briefly this year in Albert Wendland's *Science, Myth, and the Fictional Creation of Alien Worlds* (UMI Research Press). Wendland allows Lovecraft the slightest of glances but spends a few pages arguing that Bradbury's *The Martian Chronicles* present a Mars that is "less an objectified mirror of Earth culture than an escape-hatch to an old-fashioned American dream. . . ." Lovecraft comes in for additional attention in a pair of essay collections this year. In *Supernatural Fiction Writers: Fantasy and Horror, 2*, edited by Everett

Franklin Bleiler (Scribner's) Donald R. Burleson offers brief commentary upon ancient life cycles and character in Lovecraft's fiction (pp. 853–59), while in *Death and the Serpent: Immortality in Science Fiction,* edited by Carl B. Yoke and Donald M. Hassler (Greenwood), John McInnis' "H. P. Lovecraft's Immortal Culture" (pp. 125–34) discusses intellectual immortality with a focus upon *The Dunwich Horror.* Oddly coupled here, even James Thurber gets notices in *Supernatural Fiction Writers* with Erich S. Rupprecht's note on reality and fantasy in "James Thurber" (pp. 827–31). Also sure to be of some interest to Thurber fans is Melvin Maddocks' much lighter "James Thurber and the Hazards of Humor" (*SR* 93:597–601).

vii. Detectives

This is another pretty good year for hard-boiled writers, beginning with the second edition of John M. Reilly's *Twentieth-Century Crime and Mystery Writers* (St. Martin's), winner of the 1980 Edgar Allan Poe Award and the genre's one indispensable reference work. David Geherin's *The American Private Eye: The Image in Fiction* (Ungar) also covers a wide swath of the genre, introducing the neophyte reader in this field to more than two dozen writers, from John Carroll Daly and Dashiell Hammett in the early years, through the pulps, to Michael Collins in contemporary times. While tracing the development of hard-boiled detective fiction from times of *Waste Land*-induced disillusionment to the present, Geherin offers little innovative commentary but provides a valuable overview. Dwarfing Geherin's study in breadth of ambition is Robert A. Baker and Michael T. Neitzel's *Private Eyes: One Hundred and One Knights: A Survey of American Detective Fiction, 1922–1984* (Bowling Green). The authors even transcend the promise of their title here and follow the introductory survey of the first 101 fictional private eyes with an appendix quickly noting and as quickly dismissing 100 more. With admirable modesty, Baker and Neitzel begin their chapter on Hammett and Chandler with the admission that "so much has been written about them [Hammett and Chandler] that little we could add in the way of facts and literary commentary would be novel or enlightening." With this in mind, the authors proceed to put together a valuable book, an indispensable item for hard-boiled addicts who seek awareness of all the good and bad stuff out there. An impressive work obtained too late for review last year is Stefano Tani's *The Doomed*

Detective: The Contribution of the Detective Novel to Postmodern American and Italian Fiction (So.Ill., 1984). Though most of Tani's study falls outside the boundaries of 1930s to 1960s fiction, being devoted primarily to postmodern writers, his excellent introduction and first chapter merit attention here for their intelligent and well-researched discussions of the literary history and influence of this genre. A work dealing perceptively with such writers as Edgar Allan Poe, Hammett, Chandler, Umberto Eco, Thomas Pynchon, and Vladimir Nabokov in the same critical breath is of rare value. Nabokov's *Pale Fire*, says Tani, "anticipates in terms of anti-detective themes and techniques" the work of both Italo Calvino and Pynchon. Kinbote, in *Pale Fire*, according to Tani, "is an anti-detective, a distorter of the text and not a 'maker of meaning'" (see also *ALS 1984*, pp. 60–61, 297).

In one of the best critical studies of a single author in this genre to date, *Private Investigations: The Novels of Dashiell Hammett* (So. Ill.), Sinda Gregory covers all the familiar ground but argues convincingly for Hammett's originality and difference. Gregory claims that "there is a complex substructure in each of Hammett's novels that operates symbolically, metaphysically, and metafictionally," and goes on to provide an excellent examination of these substructures. Though "metafiction" as a buzzword is certainly becoming a little frayed, this book applies the idea in a refreshingly new area. James M. Cain continues his posthumous career with still another novel, *The Enchanted Isle* (Mysterious Press), appearing in 1985 along with David Madden's second book-length study of this hard-boiled novelist, *Cain's Craft* (Scarecrow). It is a pleasure to have a critical talent such as Madden's focused once again on Cain, a novelist not often embraced by the critical establishment, and Madden, perhaps of necessity, takes the opportunity to try to sort out the very meaning of "popular novelist." The book's approach is heavily comparative as Madden considers first the tough guys of the '30s—Cain, Horace McCoy, and B. Traven—and then goes on to consider Cain and the movies, Cain and Camus, Cain and Wright Morris. Of particular interest should be Madden's chapter first attempting to grapple with the concept of popular culture and then offering a detailed comparison between Morris' *Love Among the Cannibals* and Cain's *Serenade*. Madden concludes that "a carefully articulated and soundly based popular aesthetics may well force a revision of the aesthetics of serious fiction." Robert G. Porfirio registers his dissatisfaction with the Bob

Rafelson-directed movie version of Cain's *The Postman Always Rings Twice* in "Whatever Happened to the Film Noir?" (*LFQ* 13:102–10). This latest attempt, says Porfirio, is "less compelling even than the earlier [1946] version and . . . less effective in capturing the mood of the book."

The Armchair Detective this year casts only one significant glance at the '30s, with J. O. Tate's "The Longest Goodbye: Raymond Chandler and the Poetry of Alcohol" (18:393–406). With much comparison to F. Scott Fitzgerald, Tate takes a long look at *The Long Goodbye*, declaring that this novel "is Chandler's most revealing because it is his most personal work." The poetics of this novel, Tate argues, depends upon "the alcoholic identification" that informs the novelist's theme and style.

Clues this year offers several things of value, beginning with Keith Newlin's "Raymond Chandler: A Critical and Biographical Bibliography (6,ii:61–72). Among critical analyses, most significant is Annica Leenhouts' " 'Taking What's Coming to You': Dashiell Hammett's *The Glass Key*" (6,ii:73–84), in which Leenhout argues that in the protagonist of this novel, Ned Beaumont, "Hammett created a character who did not live by the code of the private investigator as we have come to know it" and that in doing so "Hammett turned *The Glass Key* away from the safe paths of the established detective story to head for new and altogether less reassuring territory." A good essay, Leenhouts' piece would have benefited from somewhat more detailed discussion of just what that "less reassuring territory" was. Also of interest is W. Russel Gray's "The 'Eyes' Have It: Reflections on the Private Detective as Hero" (6,ii:27–39), an essay that takes a shot at debunking the myth of the private eye but ends rather limply by declaring these heroes to be "the stuff of enduring popular legends."

University of New Mexico

15. Fiction: The 1960s to the Present

Jerome Klinkowitz

This appears to have been a quietly productive year for scholarship
in that most volatile field of current fiction. The combination of major
single-author works on Barthelme, Hawkes, Gass, and Elkin plus
significant commentaries on their own art by some of these same
figures set a rather dignified tone for the period, with no critics feeling
the need to launch an aesthetic revolution or lead colleagues into a
battle of the books. However, all is not quiet on the American front,
since several significant essays sought to establish new taxonomies for
understanding contemporary fiction—and behind these suggested
categories lurk the same dichotomies of tradition versus innovation,
humanism versus deconstruction, and modern versus postmodern
which have set the terms for previous debates.

i. General Studies

A curious sense of peace distinguishes the collected critical essays of
that most rambunctious of fictionists, Ronald Sukenick. His *In Form:
Digressions on the Act of Fiction* (So. Ill.) includes commentary on
his own work and that of William H. Gass, Gilbert Sorrentino, Steve
Katz, and the person he sees as a common ancestor, Henry Miller.
"Henry Miller is for American novelists what Whitman is for American poets," Sukenick suggests in his appraisal of the present scene.
"The source of his vitality is the current that began flowing when he
reconnected our art with experience." That art is not about experience
but is more experience becomes Sukenick's theme in essays which relate contemporary fiction to Continental theory, film, and the mysticism of Carlos Castaneda. Comfortable and confident with this sense
of the experiential, Sukenick can review his colleagues with an eye
toward the compositional effect of their work, avoiding most of the
philosophical skirmishes which raise so much dust and resolve so few
issues. A key to Sukenick's confidence is found in his "Up From the

Garret: Success Then and Now" (*NYTBR* 27 Jan. 3:30–31), where he
identifies the myth of the alienated, unrewarded artist as "always a
middle-class soap opera."

William H. Gass's third collection of literary essays, *Habitations
of the Word* (Simon & Schuster), addresses the other side of Sukenick's concern: that of representation and the war for reality, as Gass's
central piece puts it, which considers the contemporary novel's problem as "a fact-infested form" in struggle with design. Gass, Doris
Betts, Wright Morris, Donald Barthelme, Max Apple, John Irving,
George Garrett, and Lee Smith continue this discussion in Allen Wier
and Don Hendrie, Jr.'s *Voicelust* (Nebraska). Barthelme's "Not-
Knowing" (pp. 37–50), which also appears in *GaR* 39:509–22, answers complaints that postmodern fiction by himself, Hawkes, Gass,
Robert Coover, and others "has turned its back on the world" with
the gentle reminder that "Art is a true account of the activity of mind."

Critics, however, feel that there are other activities at work in
fiction. Terence Martin's important essay, "The Negative Structures
of American Literature" (*AL* 57:1–22), sees in our literature "an
impulse to cancel institutions and practices that have developed in
society so that one might celebrate a genuine point of beginning—
with its attendant hope and promise for the future"; among Martin's
contemporary examples are the collisions with a restricting environment in Ken Kesey's *One Flew Over the Cuckoo's Nest*, the satirical
ability to create a character from scratch in Jerzy Kosinski's *Being
There*, and the sense of the Vietnam conflict as a negative definition
in Philip Caputo's *A Rumor of War*. Elizabeth Long finds in *The
American Dream and the Popular American Novel* (Routledge) that
changes in attitudes toward success have led to the disappearance in
fiction of the entrepreneurial world and its ethos; society is in disarray,
its basic values being rethought, and novels which might have once
celebrated the American dream now tend to view self-fulfillment as a
goal. James Dickey's *Deliverance*, Joseph Heller's *Something Happened*, and John Updike's *Rabbit Is Rich* help form a new best-seller
mold in which success is questioned and often results in a new vulner-
ability.

If critics are to be believed, the work of an artist's mind is less of
a compositional affair than a psychological or psychiatric matter.
Samuel Chase Coale uses terms from the 19th-century romance to explore a wide range of current writers; *In Hawthorne's Shadow* traces
evidence of the form in "Cheever's dark corners, Oates's breathless

prose, and Didion's chantlike style of incantation," and most apparently in the "episodic tableaux" of John Gardner's *The Sunlight Dialogues*. Cheever's Manichaean dualism welcomes the stylization of romance, the techniques of which open up his narrative to the marvelous. Updike's Calvinism demands a "terrible insistence upon the actualities of life," yet a certain innocence in art softens the dualism here. To cross this dualistic abyss, Gardner builds a bridge to the pastoral; significantly, Oates and Didion will not take it, as their Manichaean vision overwhelms all else in favor of a sense of "black hole dread" and a posture of "staring into the abyss." Among the innovative fictionists Coale finds a Manichaean vision even more pure, with the result that their fiction seems even less real.

David Punter and David Porush turn directly to the mind as an explanation for the shape of current fiction. Punter's *The Hidden Script: Writing and the Unconscious* (Routledge) describes Kurt Vonnegut as one of "The Cheerfully Demented" (pp. 78–93); his writing holds together the poles of high technology and human eccentricity, commerce and love, and patterning and inconsequence (*Breakfast of Champions* exploring the way the estrangement of power strips away signification, *Wampeters, Foma & Granfalloons* finding key images around which anxieties coalesce, and *The Sirens of Titan* sorting through layers of only apparent control). Punter also praises Robert Coover's talent in "Morris in Chains" for dissolving narrative sequence into discursive oppositions, and admires Donald Barthelme's ability in "The Balloon" to adjust our perception so that fantasy can become acceptable. In *The Soft Machine: Cybernetic Fiction* (Methuen) Porush finds that artificial intelligence provides the basis for new imagery in the work of these same writers plus that of Barth, Pynchon, and Joseph McElroy. Vonnegut's career spans the range of reactions to cybernetics, from initial paranoia to an eventual employment of its principles in the act of fictive communication itself. It takes someone like Barthelme, however, to write "the consummate cybernetic fiction," in which the text becomes a self-questioning machine. Barth's *Letters* and *Giles Goat-Boy* thematicize such virtual "computer generation" of novels, while Pynchon views metaphor itself as a machine capable of producing texts. Porush's study thus explains the essential form of postmodern fiction; Ronald Weber's *Seeing Earth: Responses to Space Exploration* (Ohio) does not, preferring to deal with Vonnegut on the level of plot summary and with Bellow, Mailer, Michener, Updike, and Tom Wolfe as writers who have touched on space travel as a theme which fits Weber's thesis that we still care more about life on earth than in space. Bellow and Updike view such explorations as ironic commentaries on the "messiness" of our own planet, while Michener considers the affair an example of how technological capacity exceeds the public's mood for it. Mailer's *Of a Fire on the Moon* chooses its subject because it is "the hardest story of them all," and thus is more about Mailer's writing than about space; Wolfe's *The Right Stuff* draws readers back into the humanly familiar via the "old fashioned" concepts of fighter-jocks and test pilots.

Thematic concerns and interpretive theses thus shape the taxonomies of contemporary fiction more than most readers might like. A host of minor studies and certain aspects of larger investigations touch upon the subject with greater success. "The Aesthetics of Doubt in Recent Fiction" (*DQ* 20,i:89–106), which Arthur M. Saltzman also includes as a chapter in his *The Fiction of William Gass: The Consolation of Language* (So. Ill.), proposes that polar aesthetics do characterize the current scene, from John Gardner's wish "to address the world" to Gass's desire "to plant a new object in it." At fault in all that follows from this debate is the common misapprehension that equates literary realism and reality. "Lack of concern" in postmodern fiction is not an issue, given an appreciation of how "language tarnishes our experience of the world," the understanding of which constitutes postmodernism's first axiom. Alice A. Jardine agrees, and her *Gynesis: Configurations of Woman and Modernity* (Cornell) puts Pynchon in perspective (his *V.* represents rather than constitutes a new aesthetic space) and shows how Walter Abish's "Crossing the Great Void" leaves all representation (including maps, memory, and mimesis) behind. Vonnegut and Barth transcend thematic limitations to create new forms, Douglas Robinson suggests in *American Apocalypses*. *Cat's Cradle* provides a prophetic lesson by entertaining an apocalypse of apocalypses, while *Giles Goat-Boy* directs the reader "away from the eternalizing movement of apocalyptic visions" and so undermines the sense of absolutism which such visions might otherwise have. One of Robinson's most interesting observations is that those critics who reject this approach to apocalypse also reject the work of Barth, Vonnegut, Coover, and Pynchon.

Form itself merits attention in John Gerlach's *Toward the End*. He finds that Coover's "The Babysitter" plays traditions against innovations which alter the story's shape, allowing internal contradictions to arise which allow the "real ending" to be "*all* of the endings." Barthelme and Gass, however, are minimal in their use of closure signals, to the point of rejecting narrative itself and highlighting the intransience of their stories. A surprising experiment is found in John Cheever's "Artemis, the Honest Well Digger," where all elements work away from rather than toward the story's end, a successful counterstrategy to anticipated closure patterns. Most of the writers discussed so far are surveyed by John Shea in "Modernist Precursors of Block Form" (*JML* 12:297–310), but to the point that Joyce, Kafka, Stein, and Yeats significantly foreshadowed their technique. Shea's study depends upon a disruption of "conventional readerly practice," and today's innovators certainly join their modernist precursors in that attempt; but what follows from that disruption is surely more than the lyrical spatialization of narrative that Shea (following Joseph Frank) insists it must be. Similar gestures toward readerly expectations which are in fact critical assumptions are made by Philip Fisher in *Hard Facts: Setting and Form in the American Novel* (Oxford) and by Shelley Fisher Fishkin in *From Fact to Fiction: Journalism and Imaginative Writing in America* (Hopkins), but their positions are more readily defended. Fisher argues that popular forms serve to mass details and set new directions; instead of simply responding to and exploiting patterns of culture more responsibly established by high art, journalistic parafictions by Mailer, Styron, and others privilege certain expectations by suspending ordinary conditions, preferring to concentrate "on the moment itself with its grotesque or brutal details," shifting the point of view from the victim to the oppressor (a style which invites the success of Jerzy Kosinski in *The Painted Bird* and *Steps*). When acts are without consequences the reader can see, the writer creates "a pornography of the events of violence in which the reader is invited into the pleasures of pure phenomenal action—the point of view of the oppressor." Fishkin extends this analysis to the point of E. L. Doctorow's argument that there are no longer any differences between fiction and nonfiction—that "there is only narrative." She finds polar opposites in Mailer and John Hersey, the former mixing fact and fiction while the latter strives to keep them distinct. Fishkin regrets the prominence of those writers who purvey "fabrifact," because they play upon the reader's confidence in presumed fact to make the job of what is essentially fiction writing easier. The

New Journalism, in her view, is thus a readerly (and not a writerly) problem. Mas'ud Zavarzadeh, however, believes the reader's real problem is still with fiction, as narratives "resist fitting into the prevailing models of intelligibility and thus interrogate the areas of understanding (and ideologies) into which the reader's transcodings aim to integrate them." His "The Semiotics of the Foreseen: Modes of Narrative Intelligibility in (Contemporary) Fiction" (*PoT* 6:607–26) argues that

> when the reader encounters a (problem) text such as Donald Barthelme's "The Sentence" . . . he does not recuperate the text in terms of such cultural, philosophical concepts as "identity," "chronology," and "causality," nor does he resort to the codes of a literary genre such as the "short story." Instead, Barthelme's text is first read and made (or not made) intelligible as a "narrative" (in terms of a repertoire of narratives available to the reader), and only afterwards (and if found intelligible as narrative) will the reader seek ways to "motivate" the narrative's features.

The widest-ranging overviews continue to employ literary history and fictive theory in their assessments. New Zealander Michael Morrissey shows how his country's current fiction shares the beliefs and practices of the American innovators in *The New Fiction* (Auckland West: Lindon); Morrissey's 61-page introduction is especially helpful for incorporating American developments within worldwide patterns. In "American Fictions: The Mega-Novel" (*Conjunctions* 7:248–60) Frederick R. Karl evaluates what Thomas LeClair has elsewhere called "the novel of excess" as a form paralleling Abstract Expressionism in painting and the aleatory in music; its "oceanic . . . vibrations are waves of indeterminate force" and its "uncertain mass" is "a response to postwar America as an indeterminate, problematic, unfixed place"—hence the sprawling monsters of Pynchon, Barth, Gaddis, Gass, and McElroy. Yet "merely to write a lot of words, as Mailer did in *Ancient Evenings* . . . is not necessarily to write a Mega-Novel," since the key is that for this form there are "never enough" words. My own *Literary Subversions: New American Fiction and the Practice of Criticism* (So. Ill.) suggests that while a polemical imperative distinguishes the novels of John Barth, Ishmael Reed, and John Irving, a distinct lyricism pervades the work of John Updike,

Grace Paley, and Robley Wilson; John Gardner, Thomas McGuane, and Richard Yates invite the reader to meditate, while Jerzy Kosinski, Dan Wakefield, and Thomas Glynn require a more personal act of witness.

Scholarship of the contemporary cannot ignore the operations of publishers, but the *DLB: Yearbook 1985* (Gale) as edited by Jean W. Ross displays several alarming trends. This annual's value grows thinner as its high-priced ($88.00) content is bulked up with over half of its 437 pages devoted to self-serving articles by editors appreciating their ephemeral projects and secretaries reading minutes of the club. Its yearly reviews (of drama, poetry, fiction, and "literary biography") are undistinguished rambles among best-seller lists and playbills with no real sense of order, and the individual essays on noteworthy contemporaries too often degenerate into press-agentry. Ross herself (pp. 328–32) details Frederick Barthelme's rise from the deterioration of the late 1960s/early 1970s New York art scene into the more lucrative world of M.F.A. writing workshops, yet she is unwilling to critique his mastery of a superficial hipness. Carl R. Shirley throws objectivity to the winds when in his essay on Jamake Highwater (pp. 359–66) he glosses over the 1984 attack on this writer's claim to Native American blood and announces that the author "has read and approved" all biographical material published here. Shirley's own analysis is limited to that of appreciative wonder: "The year 1969 proved to be a turning point in his life. In October, when Indians invaded Alcatraz island in San Francisco Bay and claimed it was rightfully their property, Highwater's thoughts and writings focused on his heritage." A third critic responsive to the cash register's ring in a writer's career is Mark Busby, whose assessments of William Kennedy (pp. 387–94) are limited to generic statements about a "writer's dream," his "struggle," his ability to write "significant novels about realistic characters," and his talent for combining "a journalist's eye for detail" and "a novelist's feel for plot." This latest *DLB Yearbook* could have been written by publishers' publicists themselves; its editorial policy of allowing the authors under study to approve all material is a poor recommendation for the objectivity and soundness of its critical scholarship. A much better contribution is editor Richard Peabody's *Mavericks: Nine Independent Publishers* (Washington, D.C.: Paycock); George Braziller, Maurice Girodias, David Godine, James Laughlin, John Martin, James Boyer May, Barney Rosset, Alan Swallow, and Noel Young have edited and published a significant number of important American fiction writers, and their histories and comments shed new light on the field.

ii. Cynthia Ozick, Norman Mailer, and Philip Roth

Cynthia Ozick's emergence as a spokesperson for "traditional values" in fiction is documented by Elaine M. Kauvar in "An Interview with Cynthia Ozick" (*ConL* 26:375–401) and in "Cynthia Ozick's Book of Creation: *Puttermesser and Xanthippe*" (*ConL* 26:40–54). Though published afterward, Kauvar's interview in fact sets the stage for her judgments about Ozick's fiction: that literature must evaluate and interpret the world instead of constructing golem-like closed systems.

Norman Mailer's personality continues to dominate discussions of his art. Steven G. Kellman appreciates how defying authority and making love can be metaphors for the literary experience; chapter four, "Nocturnal Combat with Norman Mailer" (pp. 63–72) of his *Loving Reading: Erotics of the Text* (Shoe String) finds such successes in Mailer's *Armies of the Night*, in which the author creates a "dense verbal artifact"—one more example of how self-awareness can generate a text. Peter Manso's collage of taped interviews with Mailer and various associates, *Mailer: His Life and Times* (Simon & Schuster), makes most sense when Mailer discusses the images of himself he has created; too much of what others say is random gossip.

Philip Roth continues to inspire the best criticism among Jewish-American writers of his generation. Jeffrey Berman devotes a full chapter of *The Talking Cure: Literary Representations of Psychoanalysis* (NYU) to "Philip Roth's Psychoanalysts" (pp. 239–69), a group of secondary characters to whom Roth pays tribute by refusing to render as caricatures or mythic figures, using them instead as spokesmen for a view of controllable reality their artist-figure patients do not share. A profitable comparison is drawn by George J. Searles in *The Fiction of Philip Roth and John Updike* (So. Ill.): that while each writer's aims and methods may be similar, their contrasting ethnic backgrounds make Roth's critique of his culture seem more controversial.

iii. Walker Percy and Other Southerners

Although the lion's share of attention this year went to Percy, two good overviews of the region's contemporary fiction will be of help to readers. Thomas Daniel Young contributes "A Second Generation of Novelists" (pp. 466–69) to Louis D. Rubin, Jr.'s *The History of Southern Literature* (LSU), explaining how Doris Betts's fiction reflects the change in racial relations over the past two decades and how Anne Tyler's work shifts attention to a society no longer bound by traditional practices and values. In *Metamorphoses of the Raven* Jefferson Humphries shows how the tradition of loss and mourning subverts traditional devices (which derive from a mode of victory, not defeat). Reynolds Price puts odd language in the mouths of simple characters to suggest the friction between the underworld and the surface; John Kennedy Toole creates a protagonist who "might easily have been the author of *On Moral Fiction,* believing just as firmly as John Gardner in the pure anteriority of moral values and the depravity and inferiority of the present (literary) world in which he lives"; and Barry Hannah presents characters who kill because they cannot articulate their beliefs. As a sidelight, readers can ponder Samuel Chase Coale's belief in "Styron's Disguises: A Provisional Rebel in Christian Masquerade" (*Crit* 26,ii:57–66) that "in Styron's world, we are really in Poe country," a land this author "remains trapped within."

Rubin's *The History of Southern Literature* includes Lewis A. Lawson's "John Barth" (pp. 516–18), in which this native of Maryland's Eastern Shore is regarded as not being very southern at all (due to his lack of interest in detail and his attention to the past only so that his characters may dismiss it). In the case of "Reynolds Price" (pp. 519–22) Michael Kreyling finds that the towering presence of Faulkner and of "the Negro question" leave the author little room to maneuver. "Madison Jones" (pp. 523–26) has a most indelible southern sense of vision growing darker all the time, reflecting an empty life in a region devoid of redemptive memory, according to M. E. Bradford. Forecasting "The Future of Southern Writing" (pp. 578–88), Donald R. Noble suspects that Barry Hannah will continue to treat the old and new together with no ordering vision except optimism, and that Harry Crews will allow no unwarranted optimism whatsoever as he probes the world of violence, death, and disorder; Cormac McCarthy may be the only promising "outlaw," but the future is open for women novelists who wish to explore their gender in fiction. A more likely trend is discussed by Monroe K. Spears in "George Garrett and the Historical Novel" (*VQR* 61:262–76), where the "imaginary past" of such works is justified as a "communal product" based not on the limited scope of one's own imagination "but on the productions, fictional and real, of many people's minds."

Walker Percy's philosophical problems are solved better in his novels than in his essays, Patricia Lewis Poteat argues in *Walker Percy and the Old Modern Age: Reflections on Language, Argument, and the Telling of Stories* (LSU). His conceptual vision blurs and his style and vocabulary lose their narrative edge as his assault on the Cartesian view of self abandons the intentionality of storytelling; he is best at treating characters in predicaments, worst at explaining his theories of mankind (an "empty house of philosophy" discovered by Binx in *The Moviegoer*). In "Walker Percy's *Lancelot*: The Shakespearean Threads" (*Shakespeare and Southern Writers*, pp. 159–72) J. Madison Bell finds a similar disjunction between the essayist's sympathy with the postmodern condition and the novelist's determination to be "quite an 'old-fashioned' novelist by the standards of amoral, meaningless-is-meaning postmodernists" as evidenced by his multilayered allusions to Shakespeare. Robert H. Brinkmeyer, Jr., sees a happier blend in *Three Catholic Writers of the Modern South* (Miss.), suggesting that with the collapse of the Stoic tradition at the end of the 19th century Catholicism offers Percy a stable worldview and provides him with a "job" as a professional philosopher who succeeds when he mines his own experience, merging philosophy and fiction. For Brinkmeyer, Percy's faith is the key, since it gives direction and meaning to Percy's work which a simple existentialist reading fails to do. To Rubin's *The History of Southern Literature* Lewis A. Lawson contributes the thought (pp. 505–09) that the roots of Percy's fiction are found in his need to construct values after the suicides of his grandfather and father; as a novelist, Percy functions as a diagnostic and prescribing physician. Gary M. Ciuba adds his own belief that it is all a matter of apocalypse; "The Omega Factor: Apocalyptic Visions in Walker Percy's *Lancelot*" (*AL* 57:98–112) reminds us that basic to such visions are the patterns of judgment, catastrophe, and renewal which Lancelot seeks to follow but at which only Percival succeeds (as "a bearer of good news, the embodiment of the gospel"). That Percy is making a judgment about the failure of Beat counterculture in his first novel is the surprising but well-argued conclusion of Brooke Horvath in "*The Moviegoer*: The Reel and the Unreal" (pp. 131–51) as collected in editor Rudi Horemans' *Beat Indeed!* (Antwerp, Belgium: Exa); moviegoing contaminates Binx, making him forget that "wonder-producing breaks can occur only against a backdrop of everydayness," a lesson also missed by the counterculture revolutionaries of Percy's era. Percy's remarkable prominence as an interview subject is documented by editors Lewis A. Lawson and Victor S. Kramer in their *Conversations with Walker Percy* (Miss.), an indexed collection which ranges from 1961 through 1983 and across national boundaries to include worthwhile talks in foreign periodicals. The editors' previously unpublished interview (pp. 309–20) covers Percy's meeting with Thomas Merton and his thoughts on the influence of *The Seven Storey Mountain* on his own emergence from "Columbia University agnosticism."

iv. John Updike and John Cheever

George J. Searles's *The Fiction of Philip Roth and John Updike* (So. Ill.) makes the case that Roth and Updike are each "novelists of manners," the substance of their work coming from an artful observation of the nuances of social lives within their groups. Although Searles details interesting features in Updike's work (such as its clear anti-materialistic basis), his originality lies in the new light this comparison sheds on Roth, who is rarely read in such terms. A significant deepening in our understanding of Updike is facilitated by Donald J. Greiner in *Adultery in the American Novel. Couples* and *Marry Me* are important novels which dramatize the marriage of innocence and knowledge, announcing that the transgression of these realms is not as problematic or ambiguous as Hawthorne and James believed. Updike shows his Hawthornian side in *A Month of Sundays*, where sexual transgression prompts a more religious form of guilt, just as the Jamesian social aspect of Updike's work appears in the two "couples" novels; as an individual writer, Updike finds a happy equilibrium between the two. Margaret M. Hallissy follows these same instincts in "Marriage, Morality and Maturity in Updike's *Marry Me*" (*Renascence* 37:96–106), but concludes that Jerry Conant is facing his own mortality; Hallissy sorts through the novel's three alternative endings and selects the one which fits her own moral belief, that "Earthbound man must accept the finitude of choice in one lifetime." A crucially important interpretation is advanced by Kathleen Lathrop's "*The Coup*: John Updike's Modernist Masterpiece" (*MFS* 31: 249–62), that this novel demonstrates Updike's success with form and content beyond the limits of his usual style. His protagonist reverses the archetypal journey of Western heroes, yet cannot change the course of history; Updike's method of "double juxtaposition" keeps

288 Fiction: The 1960s to the Present

the text in multiple focus, as styles of the realistic and absurd, first-
and third-person narrative voices, and American and African memories create a mode of ambivalence that enhances Updike's art.

John Cheever assumes Joycean proportions in M. M. Liberman's
"Stasis, Story, and Anti-Story" (*GaR* 39:527–33), an essay which
explores "stasis" as a center and "epiphany" as an important nuance
of theme in "The Fourth Alarm"; as a pastiche of the postmodern anti-
story, Cheever's work is "Joycean twice removed." John Callaway's
"Interview with John Cheever" (*Story Quarterly* 19:13–36) catches
the author in autobiographical and even confessional moments, with
the best times of all devoted to the rhythms of life of a creative storyteller, especially his responsiveness to periods of light and rain.

v. Realists New and Old

The biggest controversy in 1985 was how to name the style of fiction
popularized by Raymond Carver, Ann Beattie, Bobbie Ann Mason,
and others. A central document in this search is the special issue of
Mississippi Review (nos. 40–41), guest-edited by Kim A. Herzinger.
His "Introduction: On the New Fiction" (pp. 7–22) coins the term
"Minimalist Fiction," after considering other suggestions such as
Dirty Realism, New Realism, Pop Realism, Post-Alcoholic Blue-Collar
Minimalist Hyperrealism, Designer Realism, and TV Fiction. The
most accurate term might well be "M.F.A. Workshop Modern," since
the style described has been taught by and flourishes in such institu-
tions. The issue's most valuable contribution is Larry McCaffery and
Sinda Gregory's "An Interview with Raymond Carver" (pp. 62–82),
though there is some merit in Joe David Bellamy's speculation in "A
Downpour of Literary Republicanism" (pp. 31–39) that editor Gordon Lish may have created the whole phenomenon. In "Ann Beattie's
Implications" (pp. 90–94) William S. Wilson notes how the author's
deliberately flat style "is a method of not implicating the rest of
literature in her fiction," while Diane Stevenson's "Minimalist Fiction
and Critical Doctrine" (pp. 83–89) claims these writers merely popularize a humanist reading of modernism. When it comes to Carver,
William L. Stull agrees, but insists that such a response is positive;
his "Beyond Hopelessness: Another Side of Raymond Carver" (*PQ*
84,i:1–15) praises the author for creating another *Winesburg, Ohio*
and lets few paragraphs pass without mentioning Carver in comparison with Joyce, Anderson, Balzac, or Henry James. Another writer

interested in exploring "the moment" is studied by Thomas E. Kennedy in "This Intersection Time: The Fiction of Gordon Weaver" (*HC* 22,i:1–11); the key names dropped here are T. S. Eliot and Sinclair Lewis. Is it any wonder why these authors are so popular in English departments?

The humanities professors' favorite remains John Gardner. Contributors to editor Jeff Henderson's *Thor's Hammer: Essays on John Gardner* (Conway: Univ. of Central Ark. Press), faced with critiquing an admittedly messianic author, at times produce a hagiography, but several essayists manage to keep their subject under control. In *"On Moral Fiction*: The Embattled John Gardner" (pp. 135–46) Carol MacCurdy admits that "Gardner's creativity appears stymied following the critical controversy. His stance on moral fiction seems to have rigidified his storytelling and hurt the magic of his fable." Leonard C. Butts adds that *Mickelsson's Ghosts* shows Gardner trying to move the realistic elements of his work closer to the fabulative ("The Circle Complete?: Reiteration or Resolution in *Mickelsson's Ghosts*," pp. 181–93); and John M. Howell makes an important biographical correlation in "The Wound and the Albatross: John Gardner's Apprenticeship" (pp. 1–16). The best overall understanding of this writer's work comes once again from Robert A. Morace, whose "John Gardner and His Reviewers" (pp. 17–31) establishes that the greatest controversies surrounding Gardner's fiction were generated on the critics' side of the table. As Morace concludes, Gardner's reviewers often feel that his works have been read "because they are more humane, more ambitious, and more searching than the writings of most contemporary writers. The most difficult task facing Gardner's critics may very well be to prove or refute this rather sweeping but nonetheless pervasive claim."

Beyond the controversies of the minimalists and moralists, realism offers little that is new. Lawrence Grobel's *Conversations with Capote* (NAL Books) offers only cocktail party chatter, while Neal Bowers' *James Dickey: The Poet as Pitchman* (Missouri) interprets *Deliverance* simply as a factor in Dickey's developing interest in the narrative poem; a more specific understanding is expressed by John Jolly in "Drew Ballinger as 'Sacrificial God' in James Dickey's *Deliverance*" (*SCR* 17,ii:102–07) regarding the employment of ancient sacrificial cults. Doctorow's critical reputation is enhanced in the Contemporary Writers series volume, *E. L. Doctorow*, by Paul Levine (Methuen), a treatment which emphasizes the demystification of

history in favor of imaginative truth; a more rigorous study of narratology by Geoffrey Galt Harpham in "E. L. Doctorow and the
Technology of Narrative" (*PMLA* 100:81–95) shows the author developing from a critique of coercive forms to a celebration of open
possibilities. Because the women in *Mysteries of Winterthurn* are not
acknowledged for their capabilities, Cara Chell believes Joyce Carol
Oates considers their ghostliness a feminist characteristic ("Un-
Tricking the Eye: Joyce Carol Oates and the Feminist Ghost Story,"
ArQ 41,i:5–23). William J. Scheick's "Memory in Larry Woiwode's
Novels" (*NDQ* 52:29–40) outlines memory's role as a balancing device which blends imagination and reality; the essentially factual
nature of both memory and memory's art prohibits any chance to
"contain life" within art. A similar conclusion is reached by Stuart
Johnson in "Extraphilosophical Instigations in Don DeLillo's *Running
Dog*" (*ConL* 26:74–90), that the better part of one's art is what one
will never possess, which means the world will remain an essentially
unfamiliar place. How the Vietnam War provides the most compelling
metaphor for this circumstance is detailed by Owen W. Gilman, Jr., in
"Ward Just's Vietnam: Where Word and Deed Did Not Meet" (*SAQ*
84:356–67).

vi. Joseph Heller, Ken Kesey, Kurt Vonnegut, and Richard Brautigan

George Goodin makes valid use of *Catch-22* and *One Flew Over the
Cuckoo's Nest* in *The Poetics of Protest*. The protagonist of each novel
is a pseudovictim, Yossarian's invulnerability having been achieved
via absurdity and McMurphy's confrontation with Big Nurse testing
the conventional power structure of protagonist-antagonist relationships. Pseudovictimhood is a valuable device, since it reveals the
nature of pseudopower.

The uneven nature of Kurt Vonnegut's fiction published since
Slaughterhouse-Five concerns Charles Berryman in "After the Fall:
Kurt Vonnegut" (*Crit* 26:96–102). This important essay makes a few
historical errors, misdating the novel in question by a year and confusing the time of Vonnegut's sister's death (1959) with the year
Vonnegut described it in a novel (1976), but its thesis is eminently
sound: that a nightmare of crime and guilt informs all five of his
novels from *Slaughterhouse-Five* through *Deadeye Dick*. During this
period in his artistic development "Vonnegut uses history to support

[his] personal narrative which in turn reinforces the fiction," leading to a retelling of the same story in a futile attempt to exorcise the ghost of culpability. When he faces this psychological drama honestly, his novels are successes (*Slaughterhouse-Five, Jailbird*, and *Deadeye Dick*); but when he represses it, the failures of *Breakfast of Champions* and *Slapstick* are the result.

Richard Brautigan's untimely death (by his own hand) in 1984 prompted many biographical and critical retrospectives, two of which contain important information. The best by far is Lawrence Wright's "The Life and Death of Richard Brautigan" (*Rolling Stone* 11 Apr.: 30–31,34,36,38,40,59,61), which traces his development from childhood influences, through a period of apprenticeship during the last years of the Beats, to his 1960s fame and 1970s deterioration. Of interest because of its collage of quoted material from professional associates is Peter Manso and Michael McClure's "Brautigan's Wake" (*Vanity Fair*, May:26–68,112–16), though the piece is marred by its recurrent tendency to blame the victim for the misfortune which killed him. An ironically titled essay by Brooke Horvath, "Richard Brautigan's Search for Control over Death" (*AL* 57:434–55), speaks for the survival of this author's work. "To free themselves from the anxieties of death," Horvath explains, "Brautigan's heroes seek to control the life that awakens it, seek the know-how of dominating life through self-imposed restraints upon life and self," a pattern which defines the narrative structure of the first four novels. Horvath concludes that Brautigan's work matured as a critique of the 1960s, which is evident in *The Tokyo-Montana Express*, but cautions that Brautigan was less interested in castigation than in control, and that his deepest concern is with characters "who find they must dissociate themselves from a culture that both throws death constantly in their paths and fails to give it meaning."

vii. John Barth, John Hawkes, and Thomas Pynchon

The John Barth number of *DeltaES* (No. 21), reviewed by Marc Chénetier in the Foreign Scholarship section of this year's *ALS*, deserves special notice, both for its own value and for the complementary role Continental theory plays in Deborah A. Woolley's important stateside essay, "Empty 'Text,' Fecund Voice: Self-Reflexivity in Barth's *Lost in the Funhouse*" (*ConL* 26:460–81). Woolley reviews the "heroism" of free textual play as presented by Sollers, Barthes,

Derrida, and Federman and finds that "it obscures the double nature
of all fiction, including self-reflexive fiction." Barth's collection of
stories demonstrates that two essential tensions cannot be dissolved
successfully: "the linguistic tension between reference and self-
reference, and the narrative tension between mimesis and poesis."
Denying these tensions makes postmodern fiction seem empty and
nihilistic; exploiting them, as Barth does, "deepens our appreciation
of the constructive uses of narrative reflexivity." In *Portraits of the
Artist in Contemporary Fiction* (Nebraska) Lee T. Lemon agrees
with this interpretation of Barth's "funhouse," adding that we deal
with reality via our distortions of it, and that patterns are needed for
art to do its imitative job. The author himself conducts a worthwhile
conversation with George Plimpton in "The Art of Fiction LXXXVI:
John Barth" (*ParisR* 95:144–59), covering significant biographical
points and the different things Barth had in mind when he started his
various novels.

The best of recent insights are found in *Understanding John
Hawkes* (So. Car.) by Donald J. Greiner, whose sharply pointed
analyses appreciate how Hawkes has sought at all stages to expand
fiction beyond the conventional bounds of plot, character, setting,
and theme. He challenges the reader to read actively, both on the
surface of technique and within the depths of the psyche. Like
Hawkes's popular readers, Greiner prefers the lyrically humorous affirmation of *Second Skin*, but the more serious business of Hawkes's
subsequent "triad" of novels dealing with the interpenetration of
death and sexuality is given full and fair treatment.

Only two significant essays on Thomas Pynchon were published
elsewhere than *PNotes*, a clear sign that Khachig Tölölyan and John
Krafft's journal, now in its seventh year, remains the best repository
of scholarship on this demanding author. Richard Pearce ranges
deeply into Modernism to justify "Pynchon's Endings" (*Novel* 18:
145–53), not just that of modern physics but the literary Modernism
of Joyce; reading *V*.'s "Epilogue" as parody keeps the system open,
just as the ending to *The Crying of Lot 49* frustrates even the choice
between seriousness and folly; *Gravity's Rainbow* concludes in a manner fitting Heisenberg's uncertainty principle, yet still forcing us to
examine our choices (however superfluous they may be). Arnold Cassola plays an intriguing game with "Pynchon, *V*., and the Malta Connection" (*JML* 12:311–25), surmising that the author may be in-

verting his own biographical history in the novel's plot. *PNotes* no. 15 is distinguished by Pierre-Yves Petillon's "Thomas Pynchon and Aleatory Space" (pp. 3–46), an essay which suggests the extent to which *Gravity's Rainbow* is an outgrowth of the mystique which produced Mailer's *Of a Fire on the Moon*. Issue no. 16 features David Marriott's "Moviegoing" (pp. 46–77) in which the work of filmmakers Orson Welles, Jean Cocteau, and Monte Hellman provide an analogy for Pynchon's refusal to fulfill expectations, preferring to "astonish" us with a self-apparent use of convention instead. Background information more substantial than Cassola's historical speculations are provided by Steven Weisenburger in "Pynchon's Hereros: A Textual and Bibliographical Note" (pp. 37–45) and by David Seed in "Further Notes and Sources for *Gravity's Rainbow*" (pp. 25–36).

viii. Ronald Sukenick, Steve Katz, Raymond Federman, Walter Abish, and Gilbert Sorrentino

Reversing a trend of the last several years, the central core of serious innovation was not well served in 1985 by major studies published by leading university presses. Sukenick, Katz, Federman, Abish, and Sorrentino, whose work has been served individually by remarkably adept critiques in years previous, suffer egregiously at the hand of Charles Russell in *Poets, Prophets, and Revolutionaries: The Literary Avant-garde from Rimbaud through Postmodernism* (Oxford). Russell has serious claims to make for the Modernist avant-garde, but his attempt to extend his thesis (directed toward social implications) into contemporary times forces him to misread Abish as "a tautological fabulist," Sorrentino as a patternist of the absence of meaning, and Katz, Federman, and Sukenick as watered-down versions of William S. Burroughs. Such disservice to understanding is regrettable in well-intentioned, curious critics who may balk at some of these writers' axioms, but to force deliberate misreadings in the service of a tailored-to-conservative-tastes thesis is an abomination. William E. Lenz takes the same approach in "From the New Country to the Twentieth Century" (pp. 185–204), the concluding chapter to his *Fast Talk and Flush Times: The Confidence Man as a Literary Convention* (Missouri). Sorrentino's *Mulligan Stew* is (negatively) misinterpreted as a narrative about the world rather than as a fictive commentary on other texts, all as a way of justifying the conclusion that "in much

twentieth-century American fiction, the norm is often the bizarre or
the abnormal, and individuals do not appear to fit conventional pre-
conceptions of behavior and motivation." Lenz believes that the postmodernists incorporate the world in their fiction in a way in which
Twain and Melville do not; he feels they are dedicated to making the
absurd appear normal, and that "as modern fictional characters confront a norm that has no respect for individual identity and that
threatens to destroy the self altogether, the confidence man as a convention loses his particular advantage and recedes from prominence."
As with Russell's book, Lenz's study employs knee-jerk reactions
against the contemporary as a way of eliciting agreement with a thesis
about more settled historical periods of literature, which is a shabby
way to criticize indeed. Russell accomplishes his task by ignoring
contemporary scholarship in general; Lenz closes his bibliography of
"current" criticism with works by Ihab Hassan (1961), Richard Boyd
Hauck (1973), and Max Schulz (1973). The reputations of the university presses of Oxford and Missouri will be disgraced by having
published such ill-informed and wrongly argued books.

Much better accounts of Walter Abish and Gilbert Sorrentino
come from less eminent quarters, where there is no pressure to enhance one's own earlier period by degrading the contemporary. Dieter
Saalmann provides an exceptionally helpful analysis in "Walter
Abish's *How German Is It*: Language and the Crisis of Human Behavior" (*Crit* 26:105–21); there has been an "epistemological re-
orientation of avant-garde literature" which has placed the articulation of the text's meaning squarely on the reader's own shoulders:
"The crisis of human behavior and values fictionalized in this work
becomes significant only to the extent that the literary consumer feels
persuaded to formulate his personal position apropos of the interdependence of private morality and public affairs instead of relying on
the false security of expressed essence," a view which not only corrects Russell's misreading of the contemporary avant-garde but which
moderates Woolley's argument about John Barth (see *vii* above).
Menu, a new periodical edited by George Myers, Jr., and published
by the Lunchroom Press (P.O. Box 36027, Grosse Pointe Farms, MI
48236), features in its first number the informative "Mr. Sorrentino's
Neighborhood" (pp. 3–7,10) by Kenneth Warren, who finds Sorrentino weaving his fiction from certain textural resources of voice—from
Brooklyn sandlots through editorial Manhattan to memories of voices
from the past.

ix. Donald Barthelme, Robert Coover, William H. Gass, Stanley Elkin, and William Gaddis

Wayne B. Stengel's *The Shape of Art in the Short Stories of Donald Barthelme* (LSU) organizes Barthelme's stories according to the ways they handle themes of identity, dialogue, society, and objects (physical or artistic): by play, epistemology, repetition, and creation respectively. Much previous criticism has been distracted from formal concerns by Barthelme's satiric treatments of supposedly real-life subjects, but Stengel shows that (like the artists of the 1960s scene he emerged from) this author wants form to dominate content and believes that "the dramatization of the artist's personality in his art may constitute a large part of a work's style." The striving of this Barthelme persona "to remake the world" not only characterizes the majority of his stories, but is a unifying element which explains his "buoyant optimism and gaiety," something the satirically and parodistically oriented critics misunderstand.

"Robert Coover, the Imaginative Self, and the 'Tyrant Other'" (*PLL* 21:192–209) by Robert A. Morace draws a picture of another writer with quite different intentions and means. Coover does attempt to construct a meaningful universe, but turns more directly to "the creative and liberating possibilities of the human imagination"; when characters surrender to mythic structures, Coover signals that all is lost, for such is to be helpless before "the Other." Peter Nelson elicits comments on his working methods from the author in "An Interview with Robert Coover" (*Telescope* 4,i:23–28); now linked to Brown University's main frame computer, he can expand the preparatory stages of his fiction by being able to recall all his jottings (a novel such as *The Public Burning* is evidence of "a tremendous amount of preparatory materials adding up to a few lines of text"). Yet there is no danger of computers and word processors undermining the oral forms of storytelling, as those forms were compromised centuries ago by conventional book technology.

The first books on two close friends (and closely associated figures), Arthur M. Saltzman's *The Fiction of William Gass: The Consolation of Language* (So. Ill.) and Peter J. Bailey's *Reading Stanley Elkin* (Illinois), are happily sound contributions to our understanding of not just these writers but of their period and its style in general. Saltzman is careful to distinguish Gass's work not just from his obvious polar opposite, John Gardner ("Gardner wants to address the world; Gass seeks to plant a new object in it"), but from the complementary yet significantly different achievements of his fellow innovative fictionists, not all of whom are as comfortable with the indeterminacy which breeds literary art. "Our daily apprehension of the world is refracted by a complex system of preconceived attitudes and connotations which accompanies our language," a situation which instead of leading to despair rouses this author's creative resources as he takes advantage of "the freedom to invent by advancing his art without resorting to self-delusion about the world's existence." Bailey's study, incorporating ideas shared in the Elkin issue of *DeltaES* (No. 20) reviewed in the Foreign Scholarship section of this volume, highlights a similar use of language in which "the aggression of syntax and metaphor" becomes a subject and theme for fiction. The special value of *Reading Stanley Elkin* is that Bailey can advocate what Elkin does without denigrating what other writers do (or do not do), a talent too few contemporary critics share. One factor in Bailey's analysis, that Elkin's special use of language is evident even in his earliest works, is confirmed by the only recent availability of this material in the collection *Early Elkin* (Flint, Mich.: Bamberger Books), which includes some historical prefatory comments from Elkin himself.

Robert A. Martin provides a useful schema in "The Five Recognitions of William Gaddis" (*NConL* 15,i:3–5); the five levels in *The Recognitions* are recognition itself, acknowledgment or admission, an entitlement to consideration, the revelation of character nuances, and approval or sanction.

x. Max Apple, Michael Ondaatje, and Thomas McGuane

Alan Wilde undertakes a thorough study of *The Oranging of America* and *Free Agents* in "Dayanu: Max Apple and the Ethics of Sufficiency" (*ConL* 26:254–85), showing that the contents of Apple's latter collection deliberately confound all efforts to set thematic patterns and strategies of organization, an achievement which resists the traditional dichotomies of Western thought; the resulting "midfiction" plays both sides of the issue, observing and participating at the same time.

Barry Maxwell takes on the "Surrealistic Aspects of Michael Ondaatje's *Coming Through Slaughter*" (*Mosaic* 18,iii:101–15) and decides that this postmodern collagist draws his "explosive junctions" from the methods of Max Ernst, Man Ray, and André Breton. How-

ever, the traditionally Surrealistic "madness that one locks up" is transformed by Ondaatje into "the madness that locks one up."

The best piece in years on Thomas McGuane turns out to be Sinda
Gregory and Larry McCaffery's "The Art of Fiction LXXXIX: Thomas
McGuane" (*ParR* 97:34–71). Researched and organized with the
care of a scholarly essay, this interview examines the development of
McGuane's career from his initial counterculturalism through a period
of fast-track high life to the author's present circumstances as a Montana rancher drawing the materials of his fiction from neo-western
life. McGuane is questioned on the thematic and technical links between his earlier and more recent novels, most interestingly the air-
craft fuselage which shelters one protagonist and haunts another,
each as an image of a lost father. Twain's *Life on the Mississippi* is
described as a special influence on McGuane's concern for "the preoccupation with process and mechanics and 'doingness' that has been
a part of American literature from the beginning."

xi. Subgenres

a. **Science Fiction, Fantasy, and Horror.** As these fields boast their
own superb reviews of scholarship, one need note here only the most
prominent trends. Chief among them is Robert Scholes's continued
interest in SF; chapter 6, "The Left Hand of Difference" (pp. 111–28),
is an important part of his *Textual Power* (Yale), using Ursula Le-
Guin's *The Left Hand of Darkness* to show how the binary classification systems dominant in our culture for the past 3,000 years now
yield to the quest for a genuine sense of the knowledge of "other" as
a way of building a bridge across difference. Also worthy of special
note is Don D. Elgin's *The Comedy of the Fantastic: Ecological Perspectives on the Fantasy Novel* (Greenwood), which is based thematically on the ecological philosophy informing Joseph Meekers'
The Comedy of Survival. Meeker's book, published in 1974, presents
an agenda which Elgin fears may estrange us from the world as
easily as it adapts us to it.

Starmont House (Mercer Island, WA) has dedicated itself to covering every aspect of horror writer Stephen King. The best essay in
editor Darrell Schweitzer's *Discovering Modern Horror Fiction* is
"Stephen King as an Epic Writer" (pp. 56–67) by Ben P. Indick;
Marshall B. Tymn's bibliography of scholarship on the subject concludes the volume. That King's oeuvre and various identities are al-

most too much to handle is demonstrated by four additional books Starmont feels compelled to publish: *Discovering Stephen King* (essays edited by Darrell Schweitzer), *The Many Facets of Stephen King* (Michael R. Collings), *The Shorter Works of Stephen King* (coauthored by Collings and David Engebretson) and Collings' investigation of the author's pseudonymous fiction, *Stephen King as Richard Bachman*. And all this is simply for his fiction—in additional books Collings reviews his films (*The Films of Stephen King*) and his life as public spectacle (*The Stephen King Phenomenon*). Since prosaic overkill is a necessary dimension of King's own work, such a critical program can hardly be faulted for its overblown approach. Heavily historical and oriented toward matters of plot, these works will certainly serve King's fans, and occasional attention to structural matters makes them of use to critics. But a more rigorously synthesized approach would make things easier.

b. **Fiction by Women with Gender as an Issue.**   For their *Contemporary American Women Writers: Narrative Strategies* (Kentucky), editors Catherine Rainwater and William J. Scheick have commissioned essays on Ann Beattie, Grace Paley, Annie Dillard, Marge Piercy, Ann Redmon, Cynthia Ozick, Anne Tyler, Alice Walker, Toni Morrison, and Maxine Hong Kingston. Of special value to the readers of this chapter are Carolyn Porter's "Ann Beattie—The Art of the Missing" (pp. 9–25), Ronald Schleifer's "Grace Paley—Chaste Compactness" (pp. 31–48), Scheick's "Annie Dillard—Narrative Fringe" (pp. 51–64), and Elaine Tuttle Hansen's "Marge Piercy: The Double Narrative Structure of *Small Changes*" (pp. 210–29). Beattie's narrative method pursues a metonymic unraveling which adds detail to details; her *The Burning House* locates a new focus in the first person and allows metaphors to grow. Paley's womanly concern for the ordinary surface of things opposes the "totalized meaning" we might fraudulently seek in depth; she rightly favors a "more spacious conception of life," and her endings favor a sense of the ongoing over the "melodrama of closure." Dillard's narrative strategy balances time and eternity, yielding a new comprehension of the world where language would otherwise falter. Piercy shows how even women narrators can assume the dominant discourse of the oppressor's language; open endings encourage alternative ways of understanding.

Marilyn Yalom's *Maternity, Mortality, and the Literature of Madness* (Penn. State) finds that Sylvia Plath's *The Bell Jar* is constructed on the bedrock of existential experiences and employs the "gendered expression of mental disease" when dealing with parental relationships; the five women of Maxine Hong Kingston's *The Woman Warrior* span the range of positive and negative possibilities. In "Sylvia Plath's Specialness in Her Short Stories" (*JNT* 15:1–14) Linda W. Wagner agrees that the author was "culpable" when it came to letting "painful subjectivity" be her real theme; the stories of *Johnny Panic and the Bible of Dreams* and those unpublished stories housed at Indiana University's Lilly Library reveal the alternate successes and failures produced by the tension between "her visualization of her 'place' in the world, and the location she demanded to occupy," a dichotomy which Plath had to learn to exploit for narrative possibilities. One writer's suspicious view of feminist fiction is explored in the "Interview with Helen Yglesias" conducted by Karla Hammond in *Story Quarterly* 19:51–64. Another's support of activist policies is detailed in "A Conversation with Grace Paley" (*MassR* 26:606–14), compiled from a panel discussion with Peter Marchant and Mary Elsie Robertson, as edited by Marchant and Earl Ingersoll. An important writer deserving of more attention, Francine Prose, is exceptionally well critiqued in the sketch by Nancy H. Evans in *Contemporary Authors* (112:402–03). Evans details how "magic, spells, and prophetic dreams" help Prose explore regions beyond the reach of conventional realism; unusual events, mysterious ills, and the business of allegory and tale-telling are the technical resources of her fiction, which extends tradition by exploiting nativistic techniques.

c. **Native American Fiction.** Too many critics in this field favor caution over imagination by restricting their efforts to two fine but already adequately studied writers, N. Scott Momaday and Leslie Silko. Matthias Schubnell's *N. Scott Momaday: The Cultural and Literary Background* (Oklahoma) is an admirable work of scholarship, especially because it broadens our understanding of Momaday as an artist growing out of the broad tradition of literary modernism and not just that of nativistic culture. But for far too many years a representative issue of a journal such as *MELUS* will devote its Native American attention to Momaday, Silko, occasionally James Welch, and rarely anyone else. *WAL* has a much better record, this year including Sanford E. Marovitz's superb "The Entropic World of the Washo: Fatality and Self-Deception in *Rabbit Boss*" (*WAL* 19:219–30) on Thomas Sanchez's important novel (studied here for its narrative structure); and Louis Owens's equally well-written and researched "The 'Map of the Mind': D'Arcy McNickle and the American Indian Novel" (*WAL* 19:275–83), which examines *Wind From an Enemy Sky*. For their innovatively critical efforts, Marovitz and Owens deserve special praise. No specialist in any area is exempt from the temptation to add a secure line to one's vita with the umpteenth essay on Flannery O'Connor, John Barth, or N. Scott Momaday, as opposed to risking one's merit raise by undertaking the first piece on Bobbie Ann Mason, Michael Stephens, or an as-yet undiscovered Native American author. But as nonspecialists look into these fields, we wonder: are there really no other worthwhile novelists writing?

University of Northern Iowa

16. Poetry: 1900 to the 1940s

Timothy A. Hunt

i. Stevens

This year produced a bumper crop of Stevens criticism, much of it concerned with the later poems and much of it revisionary with Bloom, Riddel, and Vendler cast as the rather heterogeneous orthodoxy. One volume sure to provoke discussion is *Wallace Stevens: The Poetics of Modernism* (Cambridge) edited by Albert Gelpi. In "Stevens and Williams: The Epistemology of Modernism" (pp. 3–23) Gelpi summarizes the parallel but finally different ways these two attempted to reclaim "imagination" as the central value after the decay of "the Romantic ideology" into "aestheticism." In "Stevens without Epistemology" (pp. 24–40) Gerald L. Bruns contends we are now primarily interested in language as a social or ideological question and argues that approaching Stevens with this question, rather than Stevens' own concern for language as an epistemological problem, reveals that Stevens used language to keep the "experience of otherness from happening" and to transform "public dialogue and social interchange into private meditation." To Bruns, Stevens' repression of the dialogical in favor of the monological is what links him with earlier French poetry and sets him aside from Emerson, Thoreau, and Williams. Marjorie Perloff's "Revolving in Crystal: The Supreme Fiction and the Impasse of Modernist Lyric" (pp. 41–64) also examines how historical frames can, or ought, to shape readings, but her concern is with Stevens' work in its own moment rather than ours. Bloom, Riddel, and others, she claims, have paid insufficient attention to the fact that "Notes toward a Supreme Fiction" was written during World War II, and suggests we should be more concerned with "not just *how* meanings are created in the poem but *why*" and especially why one would want to join the self to major man at a time such as this. By contrast, Charles Altieri's "Why Stevens Must be Abstract, or What a Poet Can Learn from Painting" (pp. 86–118) argues that Stevens' transactions of idea and material world, subject and object, create a field of reading that is finally communally significant even if it fails to address the specifically social or political. Altieri argues that Stevens is not escapist, that his desire for nobility needs to be taken seriously, and that Stevens' abstraction finally "adds a principle for extending the life of the deep subject into the flux of the quotidian." Like Perloff though, Altieri criticizes typical Stevens' criticism but for its tendency to "translate [late] Stevens back into the pure thematics of Idealist critics or their materialist opponents." The collection's other essays are all useful, though likely to provoke less debate than Bruns's, Perloff's, and Altieri's pieces. In "Effects of an Analogy: Wallace Stevens and Painting" (pp. 65–85) Bonnie Costello suggests Stevens saw painting as an alternative to his work's "rhetoricity and discursiveness" but avoided "copy[ing] the effects of painting." Alan Golding argues for Zukofsky's interest in Stevens' sound and verbal play in spite of Zukofsky's Objectivist orientation in his "The 'Community of Elements' in Wallace Stevens and Louis Zukofsky" (pp. 121–40). And Michael Davidson's "Notes beyond the *Notes*: Wallace Stevens and Contemporary Poetics" (pp. 141–60) sketches Stevens' impact on contemporary poets as different as Dorn, Kelly, and Spicer.

Stevens' poetics was a popular topic this year. In "Singing in Chaos: Wallace Stevens and Three or Four Ideas" (*AL* 57:240–62) David H. Helsa examines various readings of "The Snow Man" to show they reflect a 17th-century "sensationalist epistemology" rather than "the epistemological tradition founded—or resuscitated—by William James," which Helsa claims the poem actually reflects. Helsa then follows out Stevens' "effort to be a philosophical realist for whom the ideas which inform his poetry are 'unsponsored' by the holy." Helsa's history of ideas approach offers common sense and a fresh perspective. In contrast to Helsa, Steven Shaviro argues that Stevens' work, at least the late work, is beyond sources and the Western philosophical tradition. In " 'That Which Is Always Beginning': Stevens's Poetry of Affirmation" (*PMLA* 100:220–33) Shaviro sees the later poetry as "no longer concerned with formal and linguistic innovation or with the familiar dualisms of subject and object and of mind and external world." The work thus resists both "thematic and phenomenological modes of description" because it is outside "the totalizing limitations of Western culture." Shaviro's reading of the late work is neither deconstructionist nor phenomenological, though it has affinities to both. The result is a difficult though challenging essay that testifies yet again to the difficult mode of late Stevens. Robert R.

Tompkins' "Stevens and Zen: The Boundless Reality of the Imagination" (*WSJ* 9:26–39) takes a somewhat less successful approach to some of the same issues. Eleanor Cook also deals with late Stevens in her witty and suggestive "Directions in Reading Wallace Stevens: Up, Down, Across," pp. 298–309, in *Lyric Poetry: Beyond New Criticism*, ed. Chaviva Hosek and Patricia Parker (Cornell). She examines "An Ordinary Evening in New Haven" as an "anti-apocalyptic" poem that is yet not simply the opposite of the apocalyptic and suggests it emphasizes neither the upward motion of comedy nor the downward of tragedy but is rather "a poem of acrossness" dealing with the "commonplace" of here and now. Another study of the same poem is Wolhee Choe's "Stevens' 'An Ordinary Evening in New Haven': The Mind and the Poetic Sequence" (*Lang&S* 18:277–92) which claims the "late philosophical poems" explore a five-stage "perceptual transformation." Choe couples this transformation with what she defines as the poem's two primary syntactic patterns to project a structural schema for it and concludes the poem is "a quintessentially realized philosophical poem." The reading is probably too pat to satisfy many Stevensians but does suggest how analyzing Stevens' syntactical strategies can contribute to analysis of the poem's other dimensions. In addition to these studies J. Hillis Miller offers an updated version of his 1976 essay, "Stevens' Rock and Criticism as Cure" (pp. 390–422) in his *The Linguistic Moment* (Princeton), and devotes pp. 3–15 to a briefer discussion of, primarily, the way "The Man with the Blue Guitar" exemplifies Stevens' intertwining of the three primary views of poetry in the Western tradition. Miller, of course, properly deconstructs his own appeal to origins.

Several biographical studies also appeared this year, most importantly Milton J. Bates's *Wallace Stevens: A Mythology of Self* (Calif.). Although Bates states his study is an examination of the ways "one poet transcended biography by transforming it into fables of identity" and not a "biography," the book does examine the biographical and social materials of those transformations and is finally more an interpretation of Stevens than of Stevens' poems. The earlier part of the book, some of it originally in journals, is perhaps the strongest. Bates examines Stevens' response to Harvard and his courtship of Elsie Moll, coupling milieux and close attention to Stevens' journal and letters to provide a sense of how Stevens viewed what it meant to write (publicly and privately) and to identify how these gestures and roles figure in his early poems. The book is correspondingly less

successful in later stretches because Stevens' own private documents
are less open as Stevens, perhaps, became more aware of the sources
and implications of his poses—often covering them in his correspondence and only disclosing them fully (however obliquely and if
there) in the poems themselves. In the earlier work the personae
seem the product of self and circumstance, while in the later they
seem the product of the poems themselves. Oddly, in these later sections Bates pays less attention to the historical background he used so
successfully early on, and Stevens becomes both foreground and background. Perloff (see above) might have wanted to ask if the impact of
the 1917 draft on the Greenwich Village set is worth analysis, why
not the events of the early 1940s? Still, this is a valuable book and
one that will also be of real help to, as Bates terms it, "students in
and out of the university whose interest and good will have been
balked by the difficulties of Stevens' poetry and the sometimes more
formidable difficulties of Stevens' criticism." In "Wallace Stevens
and the Strength of the Harvard Reaction" (*NEQ* 58:27–48) Alan
Filreis uses the "liberal reform" carried out by Harvard president
Charles W. Eliot and the reaction against it by Santayana and others
to reach essentially the same conclusions as Bates about the conflict
Stevens felt between the careerist goals of his father and his desire to
be a poet. In "Wallace Stevens: Toward a Biography" (*Raritan* 4,iii:
42–65) Joan Richardson gives a more detailed reading of Stevens'
letters to Elsie Moll from the months preceding their marriage. She
suggests Stevens later used these letters as source material for the
Harmonium poems and sees in the letters evidence that Stevens' disappointment in his marriage largely stemmed from his own failures,
not his wife's, and that these failures, traceable in part to his childhood, also help explain the dynamic of his poetry and its importance
to him.

Several studies this year focus specifically on aspects of the history
of Stevens criticism. David Butt's "Wallace Stevens and 'Willful Nonsense'" (*SoRA* 18:279–97) finds Yvor Winters' criticism of Stevens
marred by its use of paraphrase as an approach while praising R. P.
Blackmur for his attention to "Stevens' textual experiments." Butt
then explores how more recent models for the relation of syntax and
meaning can extend Blackmur's approach. In "Concepts of Irony
in Wallace Stevens' Early Critics" (*WSJ* 9:85–97) Melita Schaum
claims the early critical reception of Stevens had less to do with the
argument over French vs. American aesthetics and more with the

debate between figures like Untermeyer and Aiken over "humanism" and "aestheticism." Schaum argues this debate shaped the way critics of the late teens and early twenties responded to Stevens' irony and verbal play. Lynda R. Goldstein chooses a bit more contemporary target in "Harold Bloom's 'Notes' Toward Self-Canonization" (*WSJ* 9:101–17). She sees Bloom's writing as, finally, a somewhat desperate and patriarchal attempt to demonstrate his own "triumph over oblivion, not Stevens'." Charles Doyle's *Wallace Stevens: The Critical Heritage* (Routledge) compiles representative newspaper and magazine reviews of Stevens' original collections. Those wishing to trace the reception of Stevens' work before it became the property of academic journals will want to inspect this useful anthology. The selection is ample, representative, and thoughtful and the notes informative. Doyle's own introduction nicely links the periodical reviews to the few, but important, more extensive studies of Stevens that appeared during the poet's lifetime but which are beyond his collection's scope. Harold Bloom also offers an anthology of criticism this season, *Wallace Stevens* (Chelsea House). Unlike the Doyle anthology, this volume is composed of academic pieces by such Stevensian stalwarts as Miller, Hollander, and Bloom himself. Bloom's introduction is the only new piece in the volume, though several of the essays are available only in festschriften or studies not devoted exclusively to Stevens. The introduction, cast as an appreciation, is a useful introduction to Bloom's approach to Stevens, though readers of the same mind as Goldstein will find his comments on the authors of his own anthology of interest.

Studies of Stevens' materials and strategies for working with them include Barbara M. Fisher's "Ambiguous Birds and Quizzical Messengers: Parody as Stevens' Double Agent" (*WSJ* 9:3–14). Fisher advances Villon as the source for "Le Monocle de Mon Oncle's" opening quotation and suggests why the basis of Stevens' parodies often involve "a point of (Christian) doctrine with erotic overtones." In "Imaginative Origins: 'Peter Quince at the Clavier' and Henry James" (*WSJ* 8:22–27) Daniel Mark Fogel points to Henry James's piece on *The Tempest* for "a remarkably parallel trope" to Stevens'. And Alden R. Turner claims blues music and the "reality" of folk expression was an important starting point for "The Man with the Blue Guitar" in "Wallace Stevens: 'The Man with the *Blues* Guitar'" (*WSJ* 9:46–51). Glauco Cambon's "Wallace Stevens's Dialogue with Dante," pp. 102–27, in *Dante Among the Moderns,* ed. Stuart Y. Mc-

Dougal (No. Car.), admits that Stevens makes fewer direct allusions than the other modernists to Dante but contends that Stevens' "use of thematic cues . . . defines Stevens's responsiveness to Dante" and shows that Dante was "an archetype for his imagination." On the topic of painting, art historian Dorothea Beard interprets Stevens' color symbolism and links his "visual sense" to the Fauvists' " 'liberation' of color from the object," in her "A Modern *Ut Pictura Poesis*: The Legacy of Fauve Color and the Poetry of Wallace Stevens" (*WSJ* 8:3–17). Martha Strom's "Wallace Stevens's Earthy Anecdotes" (*NEQ* 58:421–41) argues Stevens' early work is, like Williams', "preoccupied with the relationship between art and locale" and that various of Stevens poems are correctives or answers to Williams' poems. And in his brief "Stevens' 'The Silver Plough-Boy': A Step Beyond Imagism" (*NMAL* 9:item 2) Kenneth E. Gadomski reads this poem as an example of Stevens' revision of Pound's Imagist program.

Although not intended as a study of Stevens' material, Rajeev S. Patke's *The Long Poems of Wallace Stevens: An Interpretative Study* (Cambridge) offers "a selective collation or concordance" of Stevens' materials and typical gestures in the belief that Stevens' difficulty stems from "his habit of continual, often unconscious, self-reference." Patke suggests that the long poems form their own "history" and that, in the context of this history, Stevens' "allusions are [not] irretrievably obscure or his thought ineffably complex." Patke is most successful with poems like "The Comedian as the Letter C," which can be made to fit a somewhat allegorical or didactic reading, but less so with more improvisational pieces like "The Man with the Blue Guitar," where the referential is suppressed in favor of the metaphorical. Charles Berger in *Forms of Farewell: The Late Poetry of Wallace Stevens* (Wis.) covers some of the same sequences as Patke, though Berger is typically more successful at tracing the movement of the poems and their psychological coherence. Berger's reading, for instance, of the early sections of "The Auroras of Autumn" is particularly strong, but his emphasis on following the poems as they unfold also means the initial and larger thematic issues that begin his study get somewhat lost. Berger may not have quite provided "a plot" for Stevens' final decade, but his book will be useful in the dialogue to establish such a plot. The final Stevens book to be mentioned actually appeared in 1984. In *The Transparent Lyric: Reading and Meaning in the Poetry of Stevens and Williams* (Princeton) David Walker suggests the "rhetorical stance" of Romantic poetry places the reader in a secondary and passive position attending to the poet's essentially prior, completed, and mediated experience. Walker contends Stevens and Williams instead developed models where the poem is "contiguous with reality" and where the act of reading "imitates the process of thinking." At times, though, it is difficult to tell whether Walker means that the reader sees directly through to the poet without the fictionality of a speaking voice or whether he means that the reader experiences the poem as if it has no poet behind (or prior to) it. In his theoretical discussions he seems to suggest the latter model, though his interesting discussions of individual poems more often reflect the former. Still, Walker usefully illustrates the dangers of losing the play in Stevens in treating his lyrics as philosophical commentaries, and, in the third of the book dealing with Williams, offers an interesting discussion of Williams' late lyrics.

Another essay that should be mentioned is Mary Nyquist's "Musing on Susanna's Music," pp. 310–27, in *Lyric Poetry: Beyond New Criticism* (cited above). Nyquist offers a feminist deconstruction of "Peter Quince," arguing critics have imputed a nonexistent thematic unity to the poem and thereby paid insufficient attention to its vocal shifts and treatment of the Susanna legend. Nyquist's reading reveals the poem's "autoeroticism" and the way it " 'preserves as in a vial' the violated Susanna whose 'music' has mothered the verbal artifact that contains her." Joy Pohl offers a less elaborate feminist note in her " 'Sunday Morning': Stevens' Equivocal Lyric" (*WSJ* 8:83–86), which suggests critics have been right to see the poem as a "dialectic" but have too simply privileged the humanism of the male speaker and thereby missed the poem's "equivocation."

ii. Williams

The question of whether Williams' poetic is primarily a visual or an oral one remains a lively topic this year. In *William Carlos Williams and the Meanings of Measure* (Yale) Stephen Cushman examines both Williams' actual prosodic practice and his broader, more polemical use of the term "measure." Cushman is most successful in his first two chapters where he details the visual basis of Williams' actual practice. Cushman isolates and defines Williams' method of counterpointing lineation and sentence patterns and his use of typography to control the motion of the poems and offers a clear, precise analysis of these devices along with a system for describing their functioning in the poems. By basing much of his study on the empirical evidence of the poems, Cushman establishes that visual form is a real and important element of Williams' actual technical practice. Whether those who attend to Williams' own claims for the variable foot will agree that this largely rules out an oral basis to Williams' practice remains to be seen, but future evaluations of an oral basis to Williams' prosody will have to respond to Cushman's demonstration. Although not concerned primarily with prosody, James Paul Gee's "The Structure of Perception in the Poetry of William Carlos Williams: A Stylistic Analysis" (*PoT* 6:375–97) offers a detailed linguistic analysis of three early lyrics to show that visual and oral patterns interact with perceptual and linguistic patterns to create poems which are neither "fictive discourses" nor "like paintings" but which use "the sequentiality of language to essentially non-discursive ends, to create, indeed like painting, an art of showing, not telling or saying." Like Gee, though for different reasons, Lois Bar-yaacov also finds in Williams a blending of oral and visual prosodies. In " 'The Desert Music': An American Form" (*CP* 18:85–102) she sees the two both deriving from the poem's "semantic rhythm" which takes the form of alternate approaches to, flights from, and dances with "the world other than self." And finally, Linda Funkhouser and Daniel C. O'Connell, in " 'Measure' in William Carlos Williams' Poetry: Evidence from His Readings" (*JML* 12: 34–60), conclude that recordings of Williams reading his own poems emphasize, largely, the "idiom and rhythm of speech" rather than the visual measures of lineation or stanzaic patterns and produce detailed measurements (using acoustical devices) of the rate, relative stress patterns, and pauses in Williams' performances to back their claim. Although not specifically about prosody, those interested in Williams and poetics will not want to miss J. Hillis Miller's Williams chapter in his *The Linguistic Moment* (Princeton) (pp. 349–89). Miller offers a reading of "Young Sycamore" and a discussion of *Spring and All* to clarify Williams' poetic and its implications for understanding Williams and his place in the tradition. The chapter does not lend itself to paraphrase, but will certainly do nothing to lessen Miller's reputation as a reader of Williams.

Williams' interest in painting was also discussed widely this year. The best such piece, Dickran Tashjian's "Seeing Through Williams: The Opacity of Duchamp's Ready Mades," appeared in *WCW & Others* (pp. 35–47), a volume published by the Harry Ransom Humanities Research Center (Austin, Tex.) that collects two newer pieces along with the center's four 1983 Williams Centenary Lectures. Tashjian offers an analysis of Williams' encounters with Duchamp and his work and combines this with a subtle reading of Williams' aesthetic in the years following World War I and with useful critiques of J. Hillis Miller's and Henry Sayre's earlier discussions of this connection. Peter Halter's "Expression in Color: The Theory of Wassily Kandinsky and the Poetry of William Carlos Williams" (*SPELL* 2:137–53) and Michael Oren's "Williams and Gris: A Borrowed Aesthetic" (*ConL* 24:197–211) also examine painting and Williams' earlier work, while Stephen C. Behrendt's "Community Relations: The Roles of Artist and Audience in William Carlos Williams's *Pictures from Breughel*" (*AmerP* 2,ii:30–52) considers the later. Halter uses Williams' likely familiarity with Kandinsky's theories to argue for Williams' expressionistic use of color, and Oren explores the relevance of Juan Gris to *January, a novelette,* suggesting that the aesthetic of the piece derives from the example of Gris, even though it actually contradicts Gris's position and is probably closer to the Purists. While Tashjian, Halter, and Oren are interested in the ways Williams' aesthetic may have been shaped by the examples of painters, Behrendt is more concerned with how paintings function as "*occasions*" for Williams' writing. He suggests Breughel's paintings were "neither strictly models for nor parallels to Williams's poems" and details the ways the poems depart from the canvases (and at times even seem to be occasioned by canvases other than those by Breughel) to argue Williams sought to force the reader to complete the text in his or her own creative act of reading, remembering, looking, and comparing paintings and poems. Albert Cook's chapter "William Carlos Williams: Ideas and Things," in his *Figural Choice in Poetry and Art* (New England; pp. 124–48), more generally explores the painterly interaction of "delineation" and "figuration" in Williams' poems and argues Williams developed "a literary proto-Cubism" flexible enough to serve "through the qualities of words themselves, as a literary post-Impressionism, Cezanne merged into Braque."

In addition to such tried and true topics as Williams' prosody and his involvement with painting, this year's work also stresses a newer concern: Williams' portrayal of women and his sense of the feminine. In "Purloined Letters: William Carlos Williams and 'Cress'" (*WCWR* 11,ii:5–15) Sandra M. Gilbert examines the role of the Cress letters in *Paterson* and concludes that Williams, in spite of his "evidently proto-feminist sympathies," was, finally, threatened by the figure of

the "woman of letters." To Gilbert, *Paterson* finally "reinforce[s] traditional gender hierarchies" in spite of its "avant-garde aspirations."
In contrast, Stephen Tapscott's "Williams, Sappho, and the Woman-
as-Other" (*WCWR* 11,ii:30–44) suggests Williams' decision to write
in the voice of the woman poet Corydon in *Paterson* 4.1, even though
begun satirically, led him to discover "the similarity between Corydon's desire and his own" and that from this and his subsequent work
with Sappho he "reconceive[d] . . . female sexuality" and realized he
could not "co-opt [women's] otherness with phallic sexuality." To
Tapscott this shift also helps explain the "more spoken forms" of the
late poems, his shift from a modernist to a postmodernist aesthetic.
Joan Nay's position in "William Carlos Williams and the Singular
Woman" (*WCWR* 11,ii:45–54) is closer to Gilbert's than Tapscott's;
but her claim that what first appears "as [Williams'] detailed admiration of women" ends up on closer examination to be "something far
more critical of their nature" is weakened by what seems at times
reductively and restrictively programmatic readings of the poems.
In "Mother Tongue, Mother Muse: *Yes, Mrs. Williams* (*WCWR* 11,
ii:61–83) Kerry Driscoll argues this late Williams' text has been in-
correctly viewed as a simple memoir when it is actually another of
Williams' experiments (with roots in *Kora in Hell*). Driscoll reads
it as an exploration of "the complex interpersonal dynamic of the
mother-son relationship," and the essay offers useful advice on the
roots of the "two divergent strains of sublimity" in Williams and his
use of "conversation" as a stylistic and structural device. Women in
Williams' plays are the focus of two essays in a special Williams' issue
of *Sagetrieb*. In "The Outrage of *Many Loves*" (*Sagetrieb* 3,ii:63–70)
Linda W. Wagner examines the role of Alise and suggests the play's
unapologetic treatment of blue-collar life may have caused the initial
resistance to it. Theodora R. Graham is also concerned with Williams'
attempt to portray the woman's side of a difficult relationship. Her
"Myra's Emergence in William Carlos Williams' *A Dream of Love*"
(*Sagetrieb* 3,ii:71–79) traces the way Myra is able "to reestablish
her dignity." Graham also claims Williams' treatment of Myra is psychologically richer and "more dramatically consistent" in the play's
second version.

Williams' dealings with his contemporaries was also a popular
topic this year. In "Competitive Giants: Satiric Bedrock in Book One
of William Carlos Williams' *Paterson* (*JML* 12:237–60) Kathleen D.
Matthews argues Williams shaped his materials into a covert and

intricately allegorical satire of his modernist competitors using a method inspired by Quevedo's *El Perro y la Calentura.* The internal evidence may, finally, be insufficient to justify the full reading she suggests, yet several items from Williams' earlier drafts and various coincidences she notes means her case cannot be dismissed out of hand. Jay Grover-Rogoff's "Hart Crane's Presence in *Paterson* (*WCWR* 11, i:20–29) sees the Corydon episode, unlike Tapscott, as a parody of Crane's "diction and technique" and offers an alternative to Paul Mariani's reading of the section's "allegory." John M. Slatin's contribution to *WCW & Others,* "American Beauty: William Carlos Williams and Marianne Moore" (pp. 49–73), compares the impact of *The Waste Land* on the work of these two friends and competitors and then indicates why Moore's work "devolve[d] into self-parody" after the mid-1930s while Williams' continued to evolve. And in the same volume Kurt Heinzelman's "Williams and Stevens: The Vanishing-Point of Resemblance" (pp. 85–113) is an interesting complement to Gelpi's essay on the same topic (see above). Heinzelman offers readings of some of the same poems but with less of an eye to how the contrast between these two "friends" exemplifies modernist aesthetics and with more attention to the way each used his rivalry "to affirm and to reconfirm the way [each] created." Finally, *WCW & Others* offers Neil Baldwin's "The Letters of William Carlos Williams to Louis Zukofsky: A Chronicle of Trust and Difficulty" (pp. 115–27). Baldwin traces Zukofsky's role as Williams' friend and editor and details how Williams' struggle to appreciate Zukofsky's work helped him reconsider his own sense of poetic measure. Patricia Willis contributes new information in her "William Carlos Williams, Marianne Moore, and *The Dial*" (*Sagetrieb* 3,ii:49–59), and Eleanor Berry in "The Williams-Oppen Connection" (*Sagetrieb* 3,ii:99–116) analyzes the formal similarities in the practice of these two while suggesting that finally, "Oppen, like Stevens, is a more philosophical poet than Williams."

Source studies and studies of Williams' interest in history this year include Gale C. Schricker's interesting "The Case of 'Cress': Implications of Allusion in *Paterson*" (*WCWR* 11,ii:16–29). Instead of the feminist issues, Schricker explores the character's name and signature phrase, "la votre C," as part of *Paterson*'s allusions to Chaucer's *Troylus and Criseyde* and finds that Williams uses the parallel both for thematic purposes in the poem itself and as a means to prosecute his long-standing argument with Eliot and the method of *The Waste*

Land. In "Williams' Homage to Keats in *A Voyage to Pagany*
(*WCWR* 11,i:6–12) Stephen Hahn claims "the echoes of Keats's poetry in *A Voyage to Pagany* help to establish the thematic resonance of
the novel" and that reading it "as an allegory of Williams' development as a writer . . . is to realize how deeply Keats influenced Williams." And in "History and Culture in 'The American Background'"
(*WCWR* 11,i:13–19) Dickran Tashjian considers the shift in Williams' sense of culture and what it meant to write history between *In
the American Grain* (1925) and "The American Background" (1934)
and finds that, while the earlier book had rejected culture in favor of
the new, " 'The American Background' offered the possibility of a
synthesis."

Published originally in 1957 and out of print for some time, John
C. Thirlwall's edition of *The Selected Letters of William Carlos
Williams* has now been reissued in an inexpensive New Directions
edition, and New Directions has also issued James E. B. Breslin's compilation of Williams documents: *Something to Say: William Carlos
Williams on Younger Poets,* which includes previously unpublished
material and pieces that appeared in various hard-to-find little magazines along with Breslin's introduction, "The Presence of Williams in
Contemporary Poetry" (pp. 5–37). Breslin suggests why Williams
became an increasingly important figure for young poets and details
Williams' skill as a catalyst while admitting Williams was not always
a shrewd talent scout or a disinterested one. Those interested in the
double-edged problem of how poets find their voice and their audience will find Breslin's introduction and these documents of use. The
other book on Williams this year is Marilyn Kallet's *Honest Simplicity in William Carlos Williams' "Asphodel, That Greeny Flower"*
(LSU). Kallet clearly has a great deal of empathy with the late Williams as she compellingly describes his battle against failing health to
write this poem of reconciliation, but Kallet offers little real analysis,
and her discussion is too often repetitive. Although she deals with
manuscript materials, Kallet's discussion is finally more an appreciation of the poem than a reading of it. And finally Bruce Robbins'
"Modernism and Professionalism: The Case of William Carlos Williams" (*SPELL* 2:191–205) delineates how "the professionalization of
literary criticism" initially established Eliot while ignoring Williams
and then how professionalized assumptions may still be distorting
our perceptions of Williams even though his work is widely accepted

in the academy. Because of its title and place of publication this essay may not receive the attention it deserves.

iii. Bogan, H.D., Amy Lowell, Loy, Moore

After years of relative neglect, H.D. and her work have now become the focus of sustained exploration. In "Re-membering the Mother: A Reading of H.D.'s *Trilogy*" (*Poesis* 6,iii–iv:40–55) Albert Gelpi details H.D.'s successive "identification" with "the male scribes of antiquity," the "Virgin Scribe," and the "Virgin Mother" to create a text that is "perhaps the closest a woman poet has come to claiming the prophetic representativeness of *Leaves of Grass*." In "H.D. and the Origins of Imagism" (*Sagetrieb* 4,i:73–97) Cyrena N. Pondrom examines the early work of H.D., Pound, and Aldington and concludes that a careful check of the dates of its composition and its nature shows H.D.'s work actually "appears to have been the catalyst" to Pound's articulation of the principles of Imagism and that "Pound's practice and his theory rapidly changed in an effort to demonstrate [H.D.'s] ideas of poetic form." Susan Stanford Friedman's "Palimpsest of Origins in H.D.'s Career" (*Poesis* 6,iii–iv:56–73) also explores H.D.'s dealings with Pound but uses her autobiographical novel *Her* (1927) to clarify the dynamics of the triangular affair between H.D., Pound, and Frances Gregg. In Friedman's reading, the novel blends "erotics and poetics" as H.D. reaches out for the expanded sense of reference possible in narrative while simultaneously "recast[ing] Pound's poems about her to break their power to name her identity." Nora Crow Jaffe's " 'She herself is the writing': Language and Sexual Identity in H.D." (*L&M* 4:86–111) analyzes H.D.'s analysis with Freud through *Tribute to Freud* and other texts. The issue of influence in the poetry of women is addressed in Alicia Ostriker's "What Do Women (Poets) Want?: Marianne Moore and H.D. as Poetic Ancestresses" (*Poesis* 6,iii–iv:1–9). Ostriker suggests, as a counter to Bloom's Oedipal model, that women desire "strong mothers" and that the myth that expresses this transaction is that of Demeter and Kore. She sees H.D. and Moore as complimentary "strong mothers" in the way their work embodies "sheer excellence," "a critique" of patriarchal culture, and "the promise of alternative vision." And finally this year brings two new installments of Robert Duncan's ongoing meditation: "From the H.D. Book, Part II, Chapter 5" (*Sagetrieb* 4,ii–iii:39–85) and "H.D. Book:

Book II, Chapter 6" (*SoR* 21:26–48) along with his "H.D.'s Challenge" (*Poesis* 6,iii–iv:21–34).

In "Throwing the Scarecrows from the Garden" (*Parnassus* 12, ii–13,i:45–60) Tess Gallagher argues against "the newest wave of resistance to Moore's poetry" by those feminists who condescend to her for not being sufficiently feminist. Margaret Holley's "Marianne Moore and the Capacity for Change: the Shape of a Career" (*Poesis* 6,iii–iv:10–20) is another useful essay. She points out that Moore's *The Complete Poems* is incomplete and unchronological and argues for approaching "Moore's career as an ongoing endeavor [of eight phases] . . . each phase with its characteristic verse forms and ethical tasks." And in "Unmasking and Masking Stevens' Aesthetic: Moore's Reviews of Stevens" (*WSJ* 9:40–45) Celeste Goodridge suggests Moore in her reviews of Wallace Stevens used "multiple masks" and imitation to indicate "the way in which he 'is beyond fathoming' " while still praising his aesthetic.

Elizabeth Frank's *Louise Bogan: A Portrait* (Knopf) is a thoroughly researched, well-written biography that presents as detailed a life of Bogan as we are ever likely to have. Frank traces Bogan's unfortunate childhood, the conflicts of her adult life, and how those conflicts carried over into Bogan's writing in spite of its lack of explicit autobiographical reference. Frank's research has already helped shape one essay, "Knowledge Puffeth Up" by Donna Dorian (*Parnassus* 12,ii–13,i:144–59), which sees "Medusa," "Cassandra," and "The Sleeping Fury" as poems "transform[ing] those complicated feelings toward her mother [detailed by Frank] into a public, lyric poetry." Mary DeShazer offers somewhat different readings in "My Scourge, My Sister" (pp. 92–104) in *Coming to Light: American Women Poets in the Twentieth Century* (ed. Diane Wood Middlebrook and Marilyn Yalom, Michigan). DeShazer examines Bogan's "fascination with a demonic muse" and reads poems like "Medusa" as dramatic struggles with the muse as " 'monster' " and as expressing the particular significance of "silence" for modern women poets. In the same volume Carolyn Burke seeks to contextualize and recover Mina Loy in "The New Poetry and the New Woman: Mina Loy" (pp. 37–57). Burke details Loy's interest in the work of such figures as Margaret Sanger and shows how the popular press viewed free verse, sexual experimentation, and radical politics as simply different facets of the same phenomenon. Richard Benvenuto also offers a revisionary portrait in *Amy Lowell* (Twayne). Benvenuto recounts Lowell's lonely but aristocratic upbringing and her late turn to poetry. He points out that most accounts of Lowell's feud with Pound derive from Pound and offers an account that makes her actions, reactions, and claims in the literary wars more plausible and defensible. Finally, Benvenuto suggests her actual achievement (along with her limits) as a poet and critic.

iv. Crane, Cummings, Frost

Relatively little was published on these three figures this year, but *Splendid Failure: Hart Crane and the Making of* The Bridge by Edward Brunner (Illinois) is a study that merits attention. Brunner combines biographical, historical, and textual information to clarify the evolution of Crane's poems, and along the way suggests how the tone and aim of various pieces have come to be distorted by the false assumptions and expectations readers bring to them. The book's core is an account of the drafting of the major sections of *The Bridge* in 1926. Brunner argues that the work of 1926 departed radically from Crane's initial plans for the poem and that reading the sections in their order of composition reveals "an impressive poem . . . free of the confusion created by Crane's own [later] assemblage" when he expanded and reordered the poem for its eventual publication. Brunner sees "the 1926 sequence" as "a personal or a lyrical epic, a self-analytical 'Song of Myself.' " At times Brunner seems to believe that Crane's passages must work aesthetically and thematically so long as a rationale derived from context can be found, but if Brunner's readings will necessarily be debated and challenged, his scholarship will also necessarily force a fresh look at a number of Crane's texts. One debate in the making is already implicit between Brunner's reading of *The Bridge*'s composition and Margaret Dickie's in "The Backward Flight of *The Bridge*" (*AL* 57:79–97). As Dickie sees it, Crane wrote the final section of *The Bridge* first and made both it and the first section, which was written next, a vision of wholeness, while Brunner stresses the alterations that resulted in "Atlantis" and reads "Proem" as a model of the conflicts developed in the 1926 work. In Dickie's reading of these two sections, "Crane made the intervening sections . . . not only unnecessary but impossible to write" because the poem in "mov[ing] toward origins . . . either appropriated them for the end or it denied their validity, and either one of these strategies destroys not only the idea of progress but the possibility of long form."

As a result, the poem "must deny history" even though the speaker of the poem knows that to do so is "a lie." While Dickie and Brunner approach the textual evidence somewhat differently, Jennifer Krauss in " 'Times Square to Columbus Circle': The Dual Format of Hart Crane's *Bridge*" (*ELWIU* 12:273–83) largely skips over it. She claims that Crane's marginal commentary in *The Bridge* constitutes a "second verse strand," a poem unto itself, which encircles the text and "posits a self-regenerative mythic world" that "renders" the main text "provisional and inadequate" while "posit[ing] a new perfect text." Brunner's discussion of how and when the marginal commentary came into the poem does not destroy Krauss's claim but does call it into question.

Frost scholars will be interested in Roger D. Sell's edition of "In an Art Factory" and "The Guardeen," which appear under the title "Two Unpublished Plays" (*MR* 26:265–340). Laurence Perrine's "Misreadings of Frost's 'The Silken Tent' " (*NMAL* 9:item 3) points out the mistake various critics have made in attributing "capriciousness" to the tent even though "Frost specifically locates it in 'summer air.' " And on a more general level, Jerry McGuire's "The Discourse of the Two Cheeks: Robert Frost's Concept of 'Colloquiality' " (*AmerP* 3,ii:34–50) explores the " 'relational' " poetics Frost developed to replace "the 'objective' and subjective poetics that had preceded him." To McGuire, Frost's use of "colloquiality" to transform "the problematic of language and subjectivity" places him more fully in the modernist tradition than has been recognized, and by undervaluing this dialogic dimension, critics have misread and wrongly dismissed poems such as "West-Running Brook." In "Robert Frost and the Nature of Narrative" (*NER* 8,i:70–78) Vereen Bell suggests that the "tension between knowledge and regret" in Frost "is apparent . . . in the complex interplay in his narratives between simple description on the one hand and metaphorical or parabolic complexity on the other" and that this is Frost's way of "do[ing] justice both to the claims of passing time in the world and to claims of the ordering mind." Richard Wakefield's *Robert Frost and the Opposing Lights of the Hour* (Peter Lang) includes several interesting readings as it discusses the way Frost's voice and his attitudes toward nature, society, and love result in poems that allow us to experience and test the boundaries of the self and make ourselves in the process. Of less interest is Rachel Hadas' *Form, Cycle, Infinity: Landscape Imagery in the Poetry of Robert Frost and George Seferis* (Bucknell).

In "Poetry, Grammar, and Epistemology: The Order of Prenominal Modifiers in the Poetry of E. E. Cummings" (*Lang&S* 18:64–91) Richard D. Cureton finds that Cummings' use of "polyadjectival noun phrases" is aesthetically successful when Cummings violates the expected order of "prenominal modifiers" to draw the reader into the poem's process of perception. The Italian scholar Marcello Pagnini argues for significant parallels between Cummings' project and the Russian Cubofuturists in "The Case of Cummings" (*PoT* 6:357–73). And Barbara Seidman in " 'Patronize Your Neighborhood Wake-Up-And Dreamery': E. E. Cummings and the Cinematic Imagination" (*LFQ* 13:10–21) shows that Cummings' attitude toward film is more complex than suggested and shows how his parody film script, "A Pair of Jacks," suggests "his interest in film's experimental possibilities and his awareness of the cinematic innovations of the Dadaists and Surrealists." Among discussion of specific poems, Ann R. Morris' "Cummings' 'A Man Who Had Fallen Among Thieves' " (*Expl* 43,iii: 37–39) sees the poem as an allusion to the Crucifixion, not the story of the Good Samaritan, and sees this as an indication Cummings "was writing poems with a religious message" some years earlier than has been thought, and Guy Rotella's "Cummings' 'Kind)' and Whitman's Astronomer" (*CP* 18:39–46) argues that Cummings' poem is modeled on "When I Heard the Learn'd Astronomer."

v. Others

Work on E. A. Robinson was limited to four brief essays this year. In "Recovering E. A. R. and the Narrative of Talk" (*NER* 8,i:62–69) Robert McDowell claims Robinson's long poems, including the seldom-read "Merlin" and "Lancelot," "represent some of the finest American dramatic moments ever written." More modestly, George S. Lensing's "E. A. Robinson: The Sad, Wry Poet" (pp. 122–35) in *American Poetry* asserts that Robinson's blending of the colloquial and formal, his speechlike pentameter, and his skillful placement of isolated detail blend with his tone and vision to make him, finally, a "modern" and one whose best poems, though brief and few in number, "will survive." While Lensing projects Robinson forward against Yeats, Frost, and others, Ronald Primeau looks in the other direction. In "Robinson and Browning Revisited: 'Man Against the Sky' and Childe Roland" (*CollL* 12:222–32) he compares Browning's poem and Robinson's as versions of Bloom's internalized quest romance.

Owen W. Gilman's *"Merlin:* E. A. Robinson's Debt to Emerson" (*CLQ* 21:134–41) is also concerned with sources. Gilman suggests Emerson's "Merlin I" and "Merlin II" "provided Robinson with an aesthetic foundation for his own use of the Merlin legend."

In "The Background of Lindsay's 'The Chinese Nightingale'" (*WIRS* 8,i:70–80) John C. Ward shows that Vachel Lindsay actually had a great deal of information about the Orient from his sister and her husband, Chinese missionaries, and plausibly suggests that the poem merits reconsideration. In a second piece, "Vachel Lindsay Is 'Lying Low'" (*CollL* 12:233–45), Ward addresses more directly the reasons Lindsay is little taught and attempts to rebut them. Also concerned with reviving Lindsay's reputation, Marc Chénetier's "Vachel Lindsay: Modernity and Modernism" (pp. 197–207) in *American Poetry* points to Lindsay's prescience and the way his work anticipated recent interest in such matters as the new orality of the electronic media, the study of pop culture, and the affirmation of ethnicity. Chénetier also sees Lindsay as a pioneering, if intuitive and isolated, semiotician, a "more or less conscious pioneer of formalism and an exponent of the materiality of the sign." If Ward and Chénetier are to have their hopes fulfilled, a large part of the credit will be due to Spoon River Poetry Press and Dennis Camp, who have joined forces to produce *The Poetry of Vachel Lindsay,* a three-volume edition that presents Lindsay's work in order of composition along with reproductions of his drawings. Earlier editions have been incomplete, textually corrupt, and arranged thematically. The new edition makes serious study of Lindsay a much more viable option. Camp's edition lacks a complete apparatus and his brief comments on Lindsay's work habits and the earlier pattern of publication suggest the poems will merit further textual scrutiny, but the Spoon River edition clearly supersedes the *Collected Poems* of 1925.

Two of this year's four Robinson Jeffers pieces treat his late and unpopular *The Double Axe.* Patrick Murphy's "Robinson Jeffers' Macabre and Darkly Marvelous Double Axe" (*WAL* 20:195–209) views the two narratives, "The Love and the Hate" and "The Inhumanist," of that volume as a single poem of "two contrasting halves" tied together by Jeffers' use of a "negative fantasy of abjection" in the first and a "positive fantasy of mythopoeia" in the second. Murphy's account of the "mixture of psychoanalytic and mythic symbolism" in "The Love and the Hate" is particularly effective. Mark Jarman, in "Robinson Jeffers: 'The Love and the Hate'" (*NER*

8,i:90–97), stresses instead Jeffers' skill as a storyteller and his emphasis on character and motivation. Where Murphy sees the main character, Hoult, as an inverted Christ, Jarman suggests he is a kind of Hamlet. And where Murphy stresses the complementary nature of the volume's two narratives, Jarman stresses "The Love and the Hate" as an independent narrative, "one of Jeffers' best." Robert Brophy's "Robinson Jeffers" (*WAL* 20:133–50) is a much more general piece prepared for the forthcoming *A Literary History of the West* and printed as part of a special "sampler" issue of *Western American Literature*. Brophy's chapter is a graceful and balanced overview of Jeffers and his career that includes material not generally available elsewhere. Also John Elder's book, *Imagining the Earth: Poetry and the Vision of Nature* (Illinois), opens with a chapter, "The Covenant of Loss" (pp. 7–23), that reads several of Jeffers' shorter poems against Wordsworth and Eliot to support his claim that "Jeffers is one of the most important precursors of contemporary nature poetry, especially in his radical critique of Western civilization."

Modern Southern poetry is amply covered in *The History of Southern Literature* (ed. Louis D. Rubin et al., LSU). In "The New Poetry" (pp. 315–18) Mark Royden Winchell describes the work of such "non-Fugitive Southerners" as William Alexander Percy, Beatrice Witte Ravenel, and John Gould Fletcher and suggests their "efforts should provide greater appreciation of the heterogeneity of modern Southern poetry." In "The Fugitives: Ransom, Davidson, Tate" (pp. 319–32) Thomas Daniel Young traces the history of this group, including Merrill Moore and John Peale Bishop, while sketching its poetic achievements. Young also considers Ransom's, Tate's, and Brooks's role in the New Criticism and the impact of Brooks and Warren as writers of textbooks in "Editors and Critics" (pp. 407–14) and adds a brief sketch of "The Agrarians" (pp. 429–35). Young has also joined with George Core to edit *Selected Letters of John Crowe Ransom* (LSU). The edition's 250 letters represent two-thirds of the Ransom letters known to have survived, the majority to literary colleagues, particularly Allen Tate. Ransom is also the primary focus of Kelsie B. Harder's "Southern Formalism and Shakespeare: Ransom on the Sonnets" in *Shakespeare and Southern Writers*, pp. 125–36. Harder uses Ransom's preference for the metaphysical poetry of Donne to explain his negative view of the sonnets in spite of his circle's high regard for Shakespeare. Jeffrey J. Folks examines "Allen Tate and the Victorians" (*SoAR* 50,ii:55–66) and suggests that "despite his frequent repudiation of all things Victorian, Tate's project of transforming modern poetics is bound up with his fascination with those metaphysical dilemmas that are dramatized in Victorian poetry." And in "Vergil, Allen Tate, and the Analogy of Experience" (*CML* 5,ii:87–98) Susan Ford Wiltshire explores Tate's rediscovery of Virgil in 1932 and the three "major poems" and novel that rediscovery generated.

Classical parallels are also at issue in David H. Porter's "MacLeish's *Herakles* and Wilder's *Alcestiad*" (*CJ* 80:145–50). Porter contends that Archibald MacLeish's play, though not entirely successful, shows the poet's understanding of the function of myth in the classical plays. Karen Alkalay-Gut contributes the year's only two pieces on Adelaide Crapsey. In "Death, Order, and Poetry: 'The Presentation Copy' of Adelaide Crapsey" (*AL* 57:263–89) she reads the collection Crapsey prepared shortly before her death as a purposeful sequence meant to reflect the poet's "growing awareness" of death and concludes that the tubercular Crapsey did not think of her poems as an "immortalization of the self" but as an urn "containing poetic ashes of life." In her second piece Alkalay-Gut offers a reading of "To the Dead in the Grave-Yard under my Window" (*Expl* 43,ii:25–28). In "A Basis for Criticism: The Literary Essays of Conrad Aiken" (*MQ* 26:425–45) Gregory Waters presents a critical biography of Aiken as a critic, tracing his development from a philosophical critic (influenced by Santayana) to a critic whose sense of poetry's source and function owed something to Freud to a critic concerned with "consciousness" as "our supreme gift." Also Michael Castro offers a chapter, "The Indian as a Symbol: Vachel Lindsay, Hart Crane, and William Carlos Williams" (pp. 47–69), in his book *Interpreting the Indian: Twentieth-Century Poets and the Native American* (N. Mex.).

Finally, readers of this chapter will want to note two books that appeared this year: Gorham Munson's *The Awakening Twenties: A Memoir-History of a Literary Period* (LSU) and William and Anne Rich Pratt's translation of René Taupin's classic 1929 study, *The Influence of French Symbolism on Modern American Poetry* (AMS Press). Munson's study, prepared for publication by his widow, deals only intermittently with the poets of this chapter but does detail his interactions with Crane and Frost. It also gives a good sense of the vitality and importance of the different little magazines in this period and reminds us of the importance of Waldo Frank, Stieglitz, and others in focusing a version of a "new" art that was American and rooted in Whitman rather than in European culture. In contrast, Taupin's study was a seminal source for those interested in American modernism as an outgrowth of European traditions and offers detailed discussions of both minor and major figures. Many discussions over the years have drawn on Taupin's research, and this translation will make this standard study available to a generation of students increasingly unable to read it in the original.

Indiana University–Purdue University Fort Wayne

17. Poetry: The 1940s to the Present

Lee Bartlett

i. Groundwork

This is my sixth year writing on contemporary poetry criticism for *ALS* and, for a time at least, my last. Interestingly, one of the first books I reviewed in my 1980 chapter was Helen Vendler's *Part of Nature, Part of Us,* and now I find myself beginning this year's chapter with mention of her anthology, *The Harvard Book of Contemporary American Poetry* (Harvard). This is not a pleasure; in fact, if this were most any other anthology edited by a critic whose presence was less emphatic than Vendler's in our literary landscape, or published by a less venerable press, I'd simply disregard the book. But, after all, this is *Helen Vendler's Harvard* selection, and in my mind it charts a rather reactionary and one-dimensional territory. While Vendler's collection of *contemporary* writing contains selections by Wallace Stevens (born *1879*), Theodore Roethke, and Elizabeth Bishop, there is nothing by Ezra Pound, William Carlos Williams, H.D., George Oppen, Louis Zukofsky, Charles Reznikoff, Denise Levertov, Charles Olson, Robert Duncan, or Robert Creeley. Rather than such obscure writers as Edward Dorn, Diane Wakoski, Clayton Eshleman, or Michael Palmer, Vendler's canon of the contemporary offers us Frank Bidart, Amy Clampitt, and Rita Dove. There are two obvious answers to the enigma of this book, though neither finally holds. Is it possible Vendler simply doesn't know the work of the writers she shuns? Of course not. Then, perhaps the anthology is meant, like Donald Allen's 1960 *The New American Poetry* (Grove), to offer a countertradition to the prevailing mode, calling attention to work not generally regarded. Yet Vendler's poets for the most part are all well-published and winners of major awards. We can read Vendler's selections only as a glaring reminder that the split sensibility American poetry has suffered (especially in terms of university canon formation) since at least Emerson and Poe is as disconcertingly wide in 1985 as it was 25 years ago. Vendler's actual selections (save those by

Gary Snyder) are first-rate, but without a supplemental volume covering our major modernist and contemporary poets, this book is inappropriate for classroom use.

A second anthology to appear this year, *Singular Voices: American Poetry Today* (Avon), is edited by Stephen Berg, editor of the *American Poetry Review*. While the collection's format is not new, it remains engaging—here, 31 poets offer new poems with "self-interpretive essays." Berg's canon includes primarily (if not exclusively) writers who appear rather regularly in *APR*, including Marvin Bell, Robert Bly, Hayden Carruth, Jorie Grahm, Donald Hall, Galway Kinnell, Stanley Plumly, William Stafford, Gerald Stern, C. K. Williams, and others. The commentaries are in the main brief, but telling—Robert Bly: "I write prose poems when I long for intimacy"; Stanley Plumly: "The life in detail, the small moment, the texture of a thing . . . is where the poetry is"; Robert Penn Warren: "I find that many poems have a germ in a recollection"—and to that extent the volume is recommended. Like Vendler's, however, Berg's choice seems to imply a not-so-hidden agenda. In his preface he maintains that this gathering offers "a wealth of original voices," which is fair enough; and yet there is generally a unanimity as to the nature of the poem running through most of these writers—faith in the possibility of the lyric voice, for example, and an acceptance of referentiality as a given—which belies the seemingly inclusive subtitle, "American Poetry Today." Berg tries to anticipate this objection in his "editor's note" by mentioning that another editor might have included Ginsberg, Creeley, Oppen, and Duncan (to which we might add the names of any number of innovative writers), but he develops this exclusion no further than to plead, like Vendler, "personal taste." Of course, any editor must be allowed his or her taste, but with figures of the stature and power of Vendler and Berg, with Harvard and *APR* behind them, mere pleading is at the least unsatisfying.

Robert von Hallberg's *American Poetry and Culture, 1945–1980* (Harvard) provides a fascinating examination of work by Robert Creeley, John Ashbery, James Merrill, Robert Lowell, Edward Dorn, and many others in terms of its relationship to postwar American culture and politics. Following an opening chapter on "audience and canon" (which describes the current "stable audience" for poetry, convention, and the nature of major and minor poetry), von Hallberg ranges through systems analysis, "travel poetry" and "monument" poems, irony, class, political poetry, and "pop culture," all with the notion of showing "that many of the best poets of the last forty years have written with fascination for the ideas, experiences, and even institutions that seemed central to the country." A useful, intelligent, and highly readable study.

Beyond *American Poetry and Culture*, this year saw no attempts to describe the range of current American poetry as ambitious as last year's studies by James Breslin, Charles Altieri, and Alan Williamson, though a number of interesting gatherings of essays did far more than simply mark time. Two volumes paid particular attention to postwar verse, Peter Stitt's *The World's Hieroglyphic Beauty* (Georgia) and Dave Smith's *Local Assays: On Contemporary Poetry* (Illinois). Stitt is one of our most perspicacious reviewers of mainstream contemporary poetry (for years reviewing regularly for the *Georgia Review*), and his volume makes use of Ekbert Fass's *Towards a New American Poetics* methodology. Having conducted over the past two decades classic interviews with Richard Wilbur, William Stafford, Louis Simpson, James Wright, and Robert Penn Warren, here Stitt reprints the conversations, each prefaced by a substantial critical essay. While each essay/interview combination is more or less self-contained, in his introduction Stitt argues that a thread runs through all five, that each of his poets "loves the physical world to such a degree that they sense within it some transcendent meaning, some hovering aura of belief." Each shares a "movement that proceeds from the concrete toward the abstract, from the physical toward the spiritual, from the body toward the mind." As a critic, Stitt is engaged, reading usefully through each writer's corpus. It is as an interviewer, however, that in this book he excels, drawing from Wilbur, Stafford, Simpson, Wright, and Warren articulate and extended commentary on their own practice, as well as that of their contemporaries.

Poet Dave Smith's *Local Assays* divides into four parts, each offering a different way into one aspect or another of recent poetry, though the subtitle, "On Contemporary American Poetry," is perhaps a bit misleading. In his preface Smith admits that his concerns are "limited, disjointed, personal, and lacking a singular thesis," and in fact the ground he covers is similar to Stitt's; that is, he shows no interest in work outside the rather limiting narrative, referential mode, what we have come to speak of as the "workshop" poem. Still, he is an intelligent reader, and his nine essays on individual poets (two each on Robert Penn Warren and Richard Hugo, James Wright, May Swenson, Louis Simpson, Sylvia Plath, and James Dickey) isolate several important themes. His "Notes on Responsibility and the Teaching of Creative Writing" will be of particular interest to any number of us involved even peripherally in this activity; there, Smith tellingly calls Warren "the finest living American poet."

There are a few critics we are drawn to not only for insight into their particular enthusiasm of the moment but also for the sheer joy of watching their intelligence worry this text or that. Certainly Hugh Kenner is an example, and Harold Bloom. For our area, Marjorie Perloff is quickly joining their ranks. This year's *The Dance of the Intellect: Studies in the Poetry of the Pound Tradition* (Cambridge), in gathering 10 essays which explore "questions of structure, mode, and genre," serves as an important corrective to the Stitt and Smith books. Here we don't find yet more meditations on Wilbur and Warren, but rather discussions of work by George Oppen and Louis Zukofsky, John Cage and David Antin, Ron Silliman and Charles Bernstein, Gertrude Stein and Edward Dorn. Three pieces in particular will be of interest to readers of this chapter: "Beckett and the New Poetry," which examines the nature of "prose" verse; "Postmodernism and the Impasse of Lyric," an informed response to Christopher Clausen; and "The Word as Such," an important extended review of major language poet texts, as well as an analysis of a few of their general concerns. Certainly one of the most compelling and spirited volumes to appear this year, this collection continues the project begun by Perloff in *The Poetics of Indeterminacy*, examination of the "other" (dare we yet say primary?) tradition in American poetry.

Two more collections of essays of interest this year include William Carlos Williams' *Something to Say* (New Directions) and Robert Pack's *Affirming Limits* (Mass.). In editing Williams' essays, reviews, and introductions on younger poets, James E. B. Breslin gathers pieces on figures ranging from Louis Zukofsky, Kenneth Patchen, and Kenneth Rexroth to Robert Lowell, Allen Ginsberg, and Karl Shapiro. While a few of these pieces are ephemeral, Williams is of course always perceptive, and often lyrical in his praise. Pack's book collects a dozen previously published essays on writers from Shakespeare to Stevens, including five semiautobiographical pieces on subjects like "lyric narration" and "fatal desire." Also of interest is *Writing in a Nuclear Age* (New England), edited by Jim Schley, a collection of poetry, fiction, and essays by Galway Kinnell, Denise Levertov, Maxine Kumin, and many others as a gesture against the nuclear menace.

Last year Mary Kinzie's "The Rhapsodic Fallacy" (*Salmagundi*

65:63–80), followed by responses by Terence Diggory and Charles Molesworth, argued that "contemporary poetry suffers from dryness, prosaism, and imaginative commonplace," that the notion that the aim of poetry as apotheosis, "an ecstatic and unmediated self-consumption in the moment of perception and feeling," has run bare. The debate continued (*Salmagundi* 67:134–63) with responses by Paul Breslin, Alan Shapiro, Stephen Yenser, Marjorie Perloff, Julia Randall, and Bonnie Costello, with Kinzie's rejoinder. As we'd expect, all these pieces are intelligent and articulate, though again Perloff has the most perceptive response. Finding some merit in Kinzie's "decline-and-fall theory" (the two critics find little of value in many of the same poets), she goes on to point out that Kinzie's discussion both limits itself to certain "poetic tics" (thus neglecting any experimental or innovative work, for example) and offers no "alternative model." Yet another response comes from Clayton Eshleman (*Sulfur* 13:153–57); taking a similar exception, Eshleman accuses Kinzie of "a willful exclusion and a presentation of insignificant contemporary poems as representative of the state of the art." When, he asks appropriately, "will critics like Kinzie, Harold Bloom, and Helen Vendler start writing on poetry that knows more than they do?"

John Elder's *Imagining the Earth: Poetry and the Vision of Nature* (Illinois) examines "the attentiveness to nature distinguishing today's American poetry," discussing work by Gary Snyder, William Everson, A. R. Ammons, Denise Levertov, Wendell Berry, and Robert Pack. Section one of his study deals directly with "the relation between attentiveness to nature and alienation from the tradition"; the second "investigates the ways in which inner and outer landscapes inform and sustain one another"; section three examines attempts by current poets to assimilate "scientific insights," thus carrying out "a crucial realignment of Western tradition." Elder defines his territory carefully, chooses key texts, and writes lucidly; a thoroughly satisfying analysis of a major emphasis of our verse. Another interesting, specialized volume is Michael North's *The Final Sculpture: Public Monuments and Modern Poets* (Cornell). Following extended studies of W. B. Yeats and Ezra Pound in terms of the architecture of the monument, North devotes section to Wallace Stevens, John Berryman, and Robert Lowell (Berryman sees in Saint-Gaudens' monument the "irreconcilable conflict" between worship and love, while Lowell is "a contemporary graveyard poet.") Yet another focused volume is Ronald Weber's brief *Seeing Earth: Literary Responses to Space Exploration*

(Ohio), which mentions lunar work by Paul Blackburn, James Dickey, and Adrienne Rich, among others.

Much has been written on the influence of Chinese literature on American poets from Walt Whitman to Ezra Pound to Gary Snyder. Sanehide Kodama's *American Poetry and Japanese Culture* (Archon, 1984), however, devotes a chapter to the influence of Nippon on Kenneth Rexroth, and a second to Richard Wright, Richard Wilbur, Allen Ginsberg, Gary Snyder and their romance with the Far East. Although much of the biographical material won't be new to most American readers, Kodama's readings are sensitive, and undoubtedly his own knowledge of Japanese history, society, and literature brings much of use to the discussion.

Hispanic poetry gets much attention this year, the focus of two full-length studies. *Chicano Literature: A Reference Guide* (Greenwood), ed. Julio A. Martinez and Francisco A Lomeli, provides a concise and useful overview of Chicano poetry, with an emphasis on postwar verse. More specifically, Marta Ester Sanchez's *Contemporary Chicana Poetry: A Critical Approach to an Emerging Literature* (Calif.), despite the very real limitation of discussing poets who have published relatively little, importantly attempts to "contribute to an emerging body of literature that traditionally has had no voice in dominant academic discourse." Individual chapters on Alma Villanueva, Lorna Dee Cervantes, Lucha Corpi, and Bernice Zamora are prefaced by an interesting analysis of "gender, ethnicity, and silence" in current Chicana poetry in which Sanchez defines this body of work "as a poetry of conflict and struggle." Additionally, discussion of access to publication and distribution (as well as the oral over against the written tradition) obviously has relevance beyond the specific Chicana writers analyzed.

Three other volumes, while not exactly focused on work in our area, will undoubtedly be of interest to readers of this chapter. Donald Wesling's *The New Poetries* (Bucknell) is an extremely detailed analysis of modern prosody, with mention of David Antin, John Berryman, Robert Duncan, Stanley Kunitz, Charles Olson, Karl Shapiro, Ron Silliman, Louis Zukofsky, and others. In *Poets, Prophets, & Revolutionaries* (Oxford) Charles Russell discusses Rimbaud, the Italian Futurists, Dada, Surrealism, Russian Futurism, Brecht, and a number of contemporary American writers in an effort to define the avant-garde and "postmodernism." Further, Anthony Thwaite's *Poetry Today* (Longman) serves as an interesting brief guide to current British poetry (including discussion of Ted Hughes and Sylvia Plath, "Movement" and "Group" and "pop" poets, and experimental poets), with reference to Charles Olson, Robert Creeley, and Gary Snyder. Additionally, the University of California Press this year reprinted Jerome Rothenberg's seminal (and long out-of-print) anthology, *Technicians of the Sacred*, in an updated edition. This "range of poetries from Africa, America, Asia, Europe, and Oceana," first published in 1968, introduced many of us to ethnopoetics; this second edition contains work and translations by Robert Bly, Clark Coolidge, Robert Duncan, George Economou, Clayton Eshleman, Robert Kelly, George Oppen, and Diane Wakoski, among many others.

In "Person and Personae: The Other 'I' " (*AmerP* 3,i:2–23) David Wojahn attempts to examine the fact that "American poets appear to be adopting the highly simplistic notion that their poems are either pure autobiography . . . or pure fictional invention." Ranging through work by Linda Gregg, Weldon Kees, John Berryman, and Fernando Pessoa, Wojahn argues for a return to "the search for our lost identity." Donald Hall, William Matthews, Stanley Plumly, and James Laughlin are a few of the poets who contribute appreciations to an "Ezra Pound Symposium" in *Field* (33:5–70), while in "The Contemporary of Our Grandchildren: Pound's Influence" (Bornstein, *Ezra Pound Among the Poets*, Chicago) Marjorie Perloff argues that of Pound's many contributions to current verse, his "new conception of the poem as 'the tale of the tribe' that no longer privileges lyric over narrative," incorporates "the contemporary and the archaic, economics and myth, the everyday and the elevated" has been the most crucial (with reference to Allen Ginsberg, Louis Zukofsky, and Jerome Rothenberg). In "Fresh Frozen Fenix: Random Notes on the Sublime, the Beautiful, and the Ugly in the Postmodern Era" (*NLH* 16:417–25) Nathaniel Tarn interestingly meditates the "coincidence" of modernism/postmodernism. Translator and editor Reginald Gibbons writes on "Poetic Form and the Translator" (*CritI* 11,iv:654–71), arguing that "the task of translating a poem should be the most practical exercise in reading it," with reference to Ezra Pound, Roman Jakobson, and others.

Julie H. Wosk's "The Distancing Effect of Technology in 20th Century Poetry and Painting" (*SJS* 11,ii:22–41) offers an interesting discussion of the effect of "machines such as the airplane bomber" on modern art, with reference to Randall Jarrell, Denise Levertov, Galway Kinnell, James Dickey, and others. Janis P. Stout briefly examines

"Fretting Not: Multiple Traditions of the Sonnet in the Twentieth Century" (*CP* 18,i–ii:21–35). Taking Gerard Manley Hopkins and E. A. Robinson as illustrations of two "contrasting major strains" of the sonnet in our age, Stout makes reference to Karl Shapiro, John Berryman, Robert Lowell, and others. The same issue of *CP* includes a fascinating history of *"The Floating Bear* and the Poetry Wars of the 1960s" (pp. 1–18) by Kennith L. Simmons. Retracing much of what Alan Golding has offered in his "A History of American Poetry Anthologies" (see *ALS 1984*, p. 366) Simmons usefully outlines the life of LeRoi Jones and Diane Di Prima's influential journal as an attempt to define a "community." James Applewhite's "Children in Contemporary Poetry" (*SCR* 17,ii:66–71) briefly discusses "the child-figure-as-redemptive possibility": Lowell and Jarrell continue the "disillusioned Freudian portrait of the child," while for Roethke "the child seems to offer a model of cleansed perception." Finally, in "Faith of a Poet: A Reminiscence" (*Poesis* 7,i:1–7) Willis Barnstone meditates on his sense that "for the poet whose faith is gone or weak or on pause, the effect is sterility."

The work of Ron Silliman is the focus of an issue of *The Difficulties* (2,ii), edited by Tom Beckett. Following a selection of Silliman's writing, Beckett provides a substantial interview, ranging from discussion of Silliman's long poems to political questions; Larry Eigner, Hannah Weiner, Bruce Andrews, Rae Armantrout, David Bromige, Robert Grenier, Alan Davies, and others contribute poems and comments, while Charles Bernstein offers an interesting analysis of Silliman's "narrating narration." The issue closes with a bibliography. Andrei Codrescu's *Exquisite Corpse: A Monthly of Books and Ideas* (LSU) continues to offer with each issue brief polemical pieces on any number of issues. To list all of these would require far too much space here, but two of particular interest include Rodger Kamenetz's "Jew-Hating in American Poetry" (3:9–10) and Paul Green's "Cambridge: British Small Press" report (3:11–12). Thoroughly entertaining and highly recommended.

A few new reference works of note. Louis D. Rubin, Jr.'s *The History of Southern Literature* (LSU) provides a number of short essays on southern poetry: James H. Justus' "Poets After Midcentury" looks at a number of poets (including Donald Justice and Jonathan Williams) in an attempt to describe the "diversity of the contemporary Southern aesthetic sensibility"; William Harmon reads Randall

Jarrell as part of a generation inhabiting "an age of contraction and consolidation"; for Richard J. Calhoun, James Dickey is at his best "a superb craftsman"; Harmon closes with a brief piece on A. R. Ammons' "pervasive, persistent influences" of North Carolina. Gale continues its generally first-rate Dictionary of Literary Biography series with *Afro-American Poets Since 1955* (volume 41), edited by Trudier Harris and Thadious M. Davis. Of interest to all readers of this chapter, this volume collects biographical/bibliographical essays by various contributors on 51 contemporary black American poets, including Jayne Cortez, Michael S. Harper, and Eugene B. Redmond (though inexplicably Ishmael Reed is excluded). Lloyd Davis continues his roster, *Contemporary American Poetry: A Checklist, Second Series, 1973–1983* (Scarecrow), listing over 5,000 volumes by poets from Kathryn Aal to Martha Zweig.

ii. A Kind of Field

a. **George Oppen, Charles Reznikoff, Louis Zukofsky, Carl Rakosi, Lorine Niedecker.** Michael Heller's *Convection's Net of Branches: Essays on the Objectivist Poets and Poetry* (Illinois) is the first book-length study of these poets. As might be expected, it usefully attempts to define the aesthetic and historical territory, then follows with two chapters on Louis Zukofsky (whose "three notions of sincerity, objectification, and rested tonality were to become the parameters by which Objectivist poetry was to be defined"), and a chapter each on Carl Rakosi (who explores "the ground between intercommunication and divination"), Lorine Niedecker (whose work was "an attempt to render the music of the personal occasion"), Charles Reznikoff (whose seeming "absence of style" makes him appear the most "objective" of the group), and George Oppen (a poetry "marked by an awareness of the human effort"). A clear and concise exposition. Norman M. Finkelstein's "What Was Objectivism . . ." (*AmerP* 2,iii:51–63) covers the same subject. Taking off from the notion that "one means of evaluating contemporary poetry—that is, of making canonical judgments—depends on gauging the extent and quality of the poem's engagement" with historical forces, Finkelstein argues that in Objectivist poetry "the privileged moment seems to be derived not from an interior impulse but an exterior object . . . of perception itself." Extended reference to Oppen and Zukofsky.

Ironwood follows last year's fine Robert Duncan issue this year
with a special number devoted to George Oppen. Of first importance
is the selection of previously unpublished poems, prose, and letters
by Oppen (many of which are drawn into a "daybook" by Michael
Davidson from the papers of the Oppen Collection housed in the
Archive for New Poetry at the University of California, San Diego).
The wealth of essays which follows includes Philip Booth's "George
and Mary in Maine," Robert Hass's "tribute" to Oppen, Marie Syrkin's
"Meetings with Charles Reznikoff," Michael Heller's discussion of
the late poems, Alan Golding's "Politics and Style: Oppen's Discrete
Series," Sharon Olds's "George & Mary Oppen," Jeremy Hooker's ex-
tended analysis of "Of Being Numerous," Charles Sharpe's exami-
nation of Oppen's "world intact," Cid Corman's brief memory of the
poet, Shirley Kaufman's "Thoughts About 'Disasters,'" John Taggart's discussion of *Seascape: Needle's Eye*, Robert Pinsky's look at
"The Undertaking," Hilda Morley's "A Language of New York,"
Marjorie Perloff's discussion of "Of Being Numerous," Hugh Kenner's
"Disconnected Numerousness," Louise Glück's "The Art of George
Oppen," Charles Bernstein's brief discussion of "Of Being Numerous,"
Jack Marshall's "On George Oppen's Poetry," John Taggart's interesting discussion of "Oppen and the Anthologies," Burton Hatlen's extended analysis of "Of Being Numerous" (certainly the most developed piece in the collection), Peter Weltner's discussion of the last
poems, and an Oppen interview with David McAleavy. Ranks with
the Oppen volume edited by Burton Hatlen (see *ALS 1981*, p. 35b)
as a benchmark in Objectivist studies.

Michele Leggott carefully reads the later Zukofsky in "'See How
the Roses Burn!' The Epigraph of Zukofsky's *80 Flowers*" (*Sagetrieb*
4,i:115–36), concluding that the epigraph offers "a meditation . . . on
making" and concealment, while in "Charles Reznikoff's Privately-
Printed Way" (pp. 139–44) Robert Franciosi discusses that poet's
relationship with Harriet Monroe and *Poetry* as a microcosm of his
larger insistence on "consistent private publication."

b. Charles Olson, Edward Dorn, Denise Levertov. George Butterick continues his project of bringing Olson's work into print with
"The Collected Poems of Charles Olson: 1950–57" (*Sulfur* 12:75–95),
gathering over a dozen previously unpublished poems from the Olson
Archive. Mark Karlins' "The Primacy of Source: The Derivative

Poetics of Charles Olson's *The Maximus Poems* (Vol. I)" (*Sagetrieb* 4,i:33–60) argues that Olson "continues the tradition" of Pound's and Olson's "derivative poetics," while eliminating the first's "egocentric" and classical vision, and the second's "anecdotalness." Closely examining use of quotation and allusion in *Maximus*, a process which is sourced in the poet's reading, Karlins argues that "the origin for Olson's position as a derivative poet is finally a belief that man simply is derivative," that attempts at originality are futile. Gerald Burns reads Olson's "The K" (*Sagetrieb* 4,i:109–13) as a "lyric remark" in which "wisps of allusion . . . reinforce the local, immediate sense."

"You know," Olson said of his student and friend Edward Dorn in his 1966 NET interview, "he's so goddamn good!" This year, *Internal Resistances: The Poetry of Edward Dorn* (Calif.), ed. Donald Wesling, offered six solid essays (two published previously) on the full range of Dorn's work, confirming Olson's judgment. In his introduction Wesling clearly outlines what each of the essayists seems to imply, that like Olson and Creeley, Dorn is "nomadic and marginal in the circumstances of personality and publishing and yet central in his presumption to American culture." Michael Davidson (pp. 113–49) reads Slinger as allegory, in which the "space of the poem is the West in its largest sense," while William J. Lockwood (pp. 150–207) focuses on the recognition that the long poem "is predominantly grounded in the mode of song and that the mode of song is grounded in Dorn's sense of 'intensity' (in-tensity) of places." These pieces are bracketed by Wesling's discussion (pp. 13–44) of the short poetry in terms of Dorn's "morality of attention," Robert von Hallberg's examination (pp. 45–86) of the poet's "spirited" "accidentalism," Paul Dressman's look at Dorn and the American Indian (pp. 87–112), and Alan Golding's valiant attempt (pp. 208–34) at making Dorn's latest minimalist work seem somehow interesting. A first-rate collection— one of the better books in our area in some time.

Of these writers, Denise Levertov has always been the most politically engaged, and that seems to be a focus of critics this year. Sandra M. Gilbert discusses the political dimension of Levertov's poetry (see sect. iv), and Paul A. Lacey's "The Poetry of Political Anguish" (*Sagetrieb* 4,i:61–71) covers some of the same ground. Looking closely at *To Stay Alive* ("her most significant exploration of political themes in her poetry"), Lacey convincingly argues that there at least the poet has managed to fuse the didactic and the lyrical, to "integrate reportage and documentary into lyrical form." Levertov is interviewed by Lorrie Smith, with specific reference to her political poetry, this year in *MQR* (24,iv:597–604).

iii. The Middle Generation

a. **Robert Lowell, Randall Jarrell.** Aspects of Robert Lowell's life continue to interest his readers. Kathleen Spivack, who in the late '50s was one of the poet's students at Boston University, reminisces about Lowell's relationships with fellow students Sylvia Plath, George Starbuck, and Anne Sexton, as well as describing a "typical" Lowell writing workshop and his Romantics seminar (*Ironwood* 25:76–92). In "Pity the Monster? Reflections on a Biography of Robert Lowell" (*CritQ* 27,iii:53–62) Edward Neill takes issue with Helen Vendler's review of the Ian Hamilton biography in which she senses that the book doesn't "in any direct way" illuminate the poetry; Neill looks closely at various Lowell drafts provided by Hamilton, arguing that this material "adds hugely to the stock" of understanding. Katharine T. Wallingford's "Robert Lowell's Poetry of Repetition" (*AL* 57:424–33) uses Freud's sense of "working through" trauma to explain Lowell's repetition of the rebellion motif as a working out of the poet's guilt for striking his father in an argument. Influence and relationship occupy Steven Gould Axelrod and Bruce Michelson this year. In "Robert Lowell and Hopkins" (*TCL* 31:55–69) Axelrod argues that Lowell's enthusiasm for Hopkins went through three stages: imitation, revision, and parody (in which "the poet finally seeks to free his poetry from the bounds of influence through a mastery of a style that dismisses the style"). Michelson's "Randall Jarrell and Robert Lowell: The Making of *Lord Weary's Castle*" (*ConL* 26:402–25) reads through a number of Jarrell's letters to Lowell to conclude that Lowell's second collection "owes a heavy debt to the way Jarrell expressed himself about the book in its formative stages."

Jarrell himself is well served this year with the appearance of *Randall Jarrell's Letters* (Houghton Mifflin), edited by Mary Jarrell, assisted by Stuart Wright. The first letter is dated 1935, to Robert Penn Warren, the last 30 years later, to Adrienne Rich; in between we have numerous extended missives to John Berryman, Robert Lowell, Elizabeth Bishop, his two wives, Edmund Wilson, Peter Taylor, Hannah Arendt, and many others. Throughout Mary Jarrell provides a running biographical commentary, always usefully setting the context and explaining obscure references. A major contribution to both the study of Jarrell and other poets of his generation, as well as an immensely readable gathering.

b. **Elizabeth Bishop, Theodore Roethke, Stanley Kunitz, J. V. Cunningham, Donald Justice, John Hollander.** Last year Bishop scholarship was extensive; this year it was not, though Lee Edelman's reading of Bishop's "In the Waiting Room," "The Geography of Gender" (*ConL* 26:179–96), is of interest, as it examines the poem's "literality." Further, in "Prodigal Years: Elizabeth Bishop and Robert Lowell" (*Grand Street* 3,i:115–35) David Kalstone looks at the relationship between the two poets, while in "The Wildness of Elizabeth Bishop" (*SR* 93,i:95–115) Patricia B. Wallace discusses the poet's treatment of the self.

In "Theodore Roethke As Meditative Poet: An Analysis of 'Meditations of an Old Woman' " (*SLitI* 18,i:49–63) Ann T. Foster argues that Roethke "employs contemplation to attain a consciousness of the Absolute immanent in the natural world" in that he "considers the creative act a form of meditation." Foster offers an analysis of "Meditations" as an "existential rendering of the initial steps of the mystic way: Awakening, Purification, and Illumination of the Self." Michael Paul Novak's "Love and Influence: Louise Bogan, Rolfe Humphries, and Theodore Roethke" (*KR* 7,iii:9–20) discusses "the two most important relationships in Roethke's young life," whom he needed but surpassed, while in " 'You're My Toughest Mentor': William Carlos Williams and Theodore Roethke (1940–42)" (*JML* 12:332–44) Robert Kusch refers to a number of Williams' letters to Roethke as he traces the poet's "building upon Williams' image of what he can become."

Poet Gregory Orr's book-length *Stanley Kunitz: An Introduction to the Poetry* (Columbia) is an extended and thoroughgoing primer. Following a foreword by John Unterecker and a detailed biographical "chronology," Orr attempts through a close analysis of Kunitz's 50 years of work as a dramatic lyricist to rescue the poet from "critical neglect": "the themes of identity and of the self's quest for autonomy and intensity of being emerge as the principal constellations in which each fine poem is a separate star." In "Seedcorn and Windfall"(*Antaeus* 55:76–84) Kunitz himself gives us what appear to be notebook meditations on a variety of subjects.

J. V. Cunningham is the object of a "Special Section: A Tribute"

(*ChiR* 35,i:4–32); Robert Pinsky reprints an appreciation of the poet's work as "brilliant, portably brief, with a dazzling formal precision and an unmistakable depth of fire," while other contributions come from W. S. DiPiero, Thom Gunn, Raymond Oliver, Alan Shapiro, and Kenneth Fields. In " 'Musical Possibilities': Music, Memory, and Composition in the Poetry of Donald Justice" (*CP* 18,i–ii:57–66) Mary Gosselink De Jong points out that Justice's "commitment to the appropriate form" is sourced in his early interest in music, especially the piano. Finally, John Hollander is interviewed by J. D. McClatchy for the *Paris Review* "Art of Poetry" series (97:140–61).

iv. The Autochthonic Spirit

a. **Robert Duncan.** Robert Duncan's first commercially published book in almost two decades, *Groundwork: Before the War*, appeared last year, and it was startling in both its reach and its lyricism. This year Duncan was awarded the first National Poetry Award (that he didn't win the Pulitzer prize was, at best, disgusting), and a number of first-rate critical pieces appeared. *Sagetrieb* devoted a 350-page special issue to Duncan's work (4,ii–iii), which will stand alongside *Scales of the Marvellous* (New Directions, 1979) and the *Ironwood* Duncan issue (22) as an important piece of a major ongoing critical assessment of perhaps our finest poet. The first section of the volume contains poems/tributes to the poet by Robert Creeley, Robert Kelly, Thom Gunn, and others. The second ("the vortex") offers over a hundred pages of Duncan's prose: part II, chapter 5 of the *H.D. Book*; an interview with Duncan by Michael Andre Bernstein and Burton Hatlen (an extended piece, covering the influence of Pound, Williams, Stein, Zukofsky, and others); nine letters from Duncan to William Everson from 1940 and after, along with other Duncan documents, which I edited. In "The Excerner" (Part III) Michael Andre Bernstein discusses "Talent and the Individual Tradition"; Joseph G. Kronick, Duncan's interest in myth and his association with the Mother; Norman Finkelstein, Duncan's and Jack Spicer's sense of poetic composition; R. S. Hamilton, Duncan's debts to Pound and H.D.; and De Villo Sloan's fascinating discussion of the language poets and the "San Francisco Bay Area Poetry War" (though exactly what place this article has in the collection is beyond me, save the geographical). In Part IV Carl D. Esbjornson explicates Duncan's *Caesar's Gate*, George F. Butterick offers "A First Reading" of

Groundwork, and Thomas Gardner examines *Passages* 1–12. At only $8.95 ($6.00 for subscribers) one of the best critical bargains of the decade.

Rather surprisingly, given its seeming lack of interest in innovative work, the *Southern Review* also offers a Duncan symposium of sorts this year, and again it is quite valuable. Rodger Kamenetz leads off with an interesting interview with Duncan, focusing on the place of the Jewish tradition in his work. Next comes Book II, chapter 6 of the ongoing *H.D. Book*, followed by Duncan's moving "After a Long Illness." Thomas Parkinson's extended review of *Groundwork* closes out the feature; here, Parkinson warns that while Duncan has affinities with Coleridge, Whitman, Pound, and Williams, he is not easily classified. For Parkinson, *Groundwork* "grows from the body and its being in the universe and returns through language to the body in its finest articulations. . . . Only greed would ask for more."

A lively "Writers Interview Writers" discussion between Duncan and Michael McClure (*Conjunctions* 7:69–86) ranges through Duncan's poetry, the nematode, Milton, Jackson Pollock, Structuralism, and Donald Allen's *New American Poetry* anthology. The same issue contains an informative review of *Groundwork* (261–67) by Kenneth Irby.

b. **Kenneth Rexroth, William Everson, Jack Spicer.** Kenneth Rexroth's abbreviated diary—apparently his first and only such record—kept in 1969 as he taught at the University of California, Santa Barbara, makes for pleasant reading (*Conjunctions* 8:62–80), with comments on domestic life, the Japanese, current reading, and a variety of other subjects. In *The Maze in the Mind and the World: Labyrinths in Modern Literature* (Whitson) Donald Gutierrez offers two readings of Rexroth's poetry: the first examines the poet's love poetry as "projecting a mythopoeic world of love that Rexroth . . . once inhabited but which is now poignantly inaccessible" as well as a world of "intense exaltation of the beloved"; the second reads Rexroth's nature poetry as "a context for love and sex, an inspiration to contemplation, a stabilizing contrast to the overwhelming corruption of 20th century societies and experience."

My *William Everson* (WWS 67) is intended as an introduction to the life and work of the California poet who for 18 years was Brother Antoninus. The pamphlet charts the development of Everson's aesthetic through his early years in the California Central Valley, his experiences as a conscientious objector during World War II, his conversion to Catholicism, his two decades spent as a Dominican religious, his reentry into secular life, and the four women around whom each of his major phases revolved. In "Ghostwriting the Text: Translation and the Poetics of Jack Spicer" (*ConL* 26:426–42) Lori Chamberlain reads *After Lorca* as a prefiguration of what Spicer "later calls a 'poetics of dictation,'" a poetics which "calls into question both romantic notions of the self-sufficient or expressive self and symbolist notions of the poet's egoless, vatic function."

iv. Dream of a Common Language

Two first-rate volumes on women's writing appeared this year. In *Coming to Light* (Michigan), edited by Diane Wood Middlebrook and Marilyn Yalom, 15 papers presented at the 1982 Stanford University conference on women's poetry form a very fine collection. Bracketed between Middlebrook's preface and Patricia Klindienst Joplin's epilogue, we have Mary DeShazer on Louise Bogan; David Kalstone on Elizabeth Bishop and Marianne Moore; Joanne Feit Diehl on Elizabeth Bishop; John Felstiner on Denise Levertov; Sandra M. Gilbert, Yalom, and Barbara Antonia Clarke Mossberg on Sylvia Plath (the implication of three essays on Plath being, I suppose, that she holds a central place in the imagination of the conference planners); Middlebrook on Anne Sexton; Andrea Benton Rushing on Lucille Clifton; Paula Gunn Allen on American Indian women's writing; Susan Stanford Friedman on H. D. and Adrienne Rich; with additional essays by Alicia Ostriker, Carolyn Burke, Ulla E. Dydo, and Albert Gelpi. Wide-ranging, learned, and enthusiastic, this volume is an important contribution to both an understanding of a major body of American poetry and feminist criticism.

A single issue of *Parnassus* (12,ii–13,i) provides an important 600-page collection of women's poetry and commentary. Just a few of the poetry contributors include May Swenson, Audre Lorde, Lorine Niedecker, Adrienne Rich, Paula Gunn Allen, Colette Inez, Sonia Sanchez, and Cynthia Macdonald. In a series of extended reviews Donna Dorian examines work by Louise Bogan, Patricia Storaler by Elizabeth Bishop; Diane Middlebrook by Anne Sexton; Sven Birkerts on May Swenson; Vickie Karp by Cynthia Macdonald and Tess Gallagher; Brad Crenshaw by Maxine Kumin; Laurence Goldstein by

Diane Ackerman; William Logan by Vickie Hearne, Mary Jo Salter, and Amy Clampitt; Christopher Benfey by Molly Peacock; and Calvin Hernton by Toi Derricotte, Brenda Maries Osbey, Thulani Davis, Colleen McElroy, Cheryl Clarke, and Rita Dove. In essays proper, Alicia Ostriker discusses "Being Nobody Together: Duplicity, Identity, and Women's Poetry" (Dickinson is a primary source for contemporary women's poetry; "the single most common issue is the issue of identity"); Robert Bertholf's "Lorine Niedecker: A Portrait of a Poet" examines the poet's life and work in terms of Dickinson, Zukofsky, and other influences; in "Adrienne Rich and Lesbian/Feminist Poetry" Catharine Stimpson traces the poet's emergence during the '70s as a major lesbian poet; Calvin Bedient's "Oh, Plath" briefly examines Sylvia Plath's romantic rage, while Marjorie Perloff's "Icon of the Fifties" admits that while the critic cannot make "a strong case of Plath's work on the grounds of postmodern poetics," she remains intrigued; in "Revolutionary Love: Denise Levertov and the Poetics of Politics" Sandra M. Gilbert argues that the poet's "most revolutionary gesture is probably her persistent articulation of joy." Additionally, Herbert Leibowitz offers "Exploding Myths," an interview with Sonia Sanchez.

Another volume which deserves mention (received too late to be included in last year's chapter) is Jean Gould's *Modern American Women Poets* (Dodd, Mead, 1984), a collection of readable biographical and critical essays on 18 writers: Muriel Rukeyser, Denise Levertov, Elizabeth Bishop, Sylvia Plath, Anne Sexton, Adrienne Rich, Audre Lorde, Marge Piercy, Nikki Giovanni, and others. A companion volume to Gould's 1980 *American Women Poets*, this volume offers in its critical judgments and surprising wealth of biographical detail a fine introduction to postwar poetry by women, closing with a useful bibliography of both primary and secondary work.

Karen Alkalay-Gut's "Form and the Feminist Revolution in Poetry" (*Poesis* 7,i:35–53) looks at form and technique of a number of women poets (including Adrienne Rich and Marilyn Hacker), arguing that such ideas as democratization of language, "rejection of 'artificial' literary devices," and "toleration of ambiguity," among other possibilities, earmark "major formal innovations among feminists." While Alkalay-Gut's discussion of individual poems is often enlightening, her general thesis certainly can, and obviously does, apply to scores of male poets in this century as well. Another essay on this topic is needed. Alkalay-Gut usefully reads Adrienne Rich's "An Unsaid Word" (*Expl* 43:53–56) as a "parallel" to Shakespeare's "Sonnet 94."

As mentioned above, Sylvia Plath continues to hold a seminal place in contemporary women's writing. Paul Alexander collects a number of very good pieces on Plath in *Ariel Ascending* (Harper): Helen Vendler's "An Intractable Metal" (on the *Collected Poems*); Stanley Plumly's "What Ceremony of Words" ("a poetry of constant preparation for the next move"); Joyce Carol Oates's discussion of Plath's "cultural significance," with emphasis on the "artfully constructed" lyric/tragic "I"; John Frederick Nims's careful examination of Plath's prosody; and other essays by Barbara Hardy, Mary Lynn Broe, Katha Pollitt, Elizabeth Hardwick, Rosellen Brown, Howard Moss, Robert Scholes, Vance Bourjaily, Ted Hughes, Grace Schulman, Anne Sexton, A. Alvarez, and Aurelia S. Plath on the poetry, the fiction, the journals, and the life. As most of these pieces have been published before, the collection is no real critical advance in Plath studies, yet as a general guide to the full range of the poet's work *Ariel Ascending* can be highly recommended. Steven Gould Axelrod's "The Mirror and the Shadow: Plath's Poetics of Self-Doubt" (*ConL* 26:286–301) examines the poet's "images of incapacity"—specifically mirrors and shadows—with reference to James Frazer, Otto Rank, and Sigmund Freud, and their sense of the double. In "The Dread of Sylvia Plath" (*Poesis* 7,i:8–22) Dannie Abse continues the attempt to demystify the poet's death, arguing that her "talent was extraordinary," and often more detached than her suicide would have us believe.

Anne Sexton continues to live in Plath's shadow, though this year Steven E. Colburn has gathered Anne Sexton's selected essays, interviews, and other prose in *No Evil Star* (Michigan). Here we have Sexton's memoirs of Robert Lowell and Plath, her thoughts on readings, comment on her poem "Some Foreign Letters," and eight interviews with Harry Moore; Patricia Marx; Barbara Kevles; Brigitte Weeks; Lois Ames; William Heyen and Al Poulin; Maxine Kumin, Elaine Showalter, and Carol Smith; and Gregory Fitz Gerald. A useful selection, though an index would be helpful.

v. A Complex of Occasions

a. **James Dickey.**   James Dickey was the focus this year of quite a bit of critical energy, including two book-length studies. In *Under-*

standing James Dickey (So. Car.) Ronald Baughman offers a student's guide to the range of the poet's work, focusing on a threefold movement of "confrontation, reordering, and renewal" of the Self; discussion of the individual volumes of poetry from *Into the Stone* to *Puella, Deliverence,* and Dickey's criticism, concluding with a bibliography. Neal Bowers' *James Dickey: The Poet as Pitchman* (Missouri) reads through a number of poems by a writer who has "publicized himself and promoted his work more actively" than probably any other American poet in our century. Three engaging chapters—"Selling the Poet," "Selling the Poem," and "Selling God"—offer a new and thought-provoking approach to a sometimes fascinating and often outrageous American con artist par excellence.

The *James Dickey Newsletter* (2,i) offered a number of interesting pieces this year. In "Steering to the Morning Land" A. Gordon Van Ness III examines "the poet's redemptive vision" in *The Zodiac;* "Appalachia: Myth and Reality" provides a panel discussion with Dickey, Boyd Lewis, Paul Hemphill, Terry Kay, and Floyd C. Watkins; Marion Hodge reads "Dover: Believing in Kings" as "the most psychologically complex" of Dickey's poems; Robert C. Covel continues his Dickey checklist. Harold Bloom's "James Dickey: From 'The Other' through *The Early Motion*" (*SoR* 21:63–78) judges the poet to be "a heroic celebrator . . . of the American self proper, which demands victory"; here, Bloom engages Dickey's "counter-song of otherness," a song whose "origin is guilt, and guilt ostensibly of being a substitute or replacement for a brother dead before one was born." In "The Predator, the Prey, and the Poet" (*SLitI* 18,i:47–65) Nelson Hathcock sees Dickey as a Romantic, reading "The Heaven of Animals" as a poem in which "exclusion creates the subliminal lament"; here, the poet "envies the power of blood and claw—the elemental, instinctive act." Finally, Floyd C. Watkins' "Three Georgia Mountain Poets" (*SCR* 18,i:99–113) looks at Dickey's "mountain poems" as those of a "sojourner in the high altitudes," as opposed to the more accurate sense of place found in Byron Herbert Reece and Frank Manley.

b. **Andrew Glaze, John Ashbery, A. R. Ammons, James Wright, Robert Bly.** William Doreski's *Earth That Sings: On the Poetry of Andrew Glaze* (Houston: Ford-Brown) anthologizes a number of Glaze's poems from 1966 to the present, along with a brief memoir by the poet, "On Growing Up in Alabama." The volume's opening essay,

Carol Kiler's "To Dance Out Despair," offers a good preface to the range of the poet's work, his "persistent interest" in "citizen poetry"; Stephen Ford Brown interviews Glaze as a "quiet revolutionary"; in "The Poet as Dancer" Robert Wilkinson argues that Glaze makes us see the integrity "of even the most apparently degraded creature or thing"; Doreski's "The Urban Voice of Andrew Glaze," Theodore Haddin's "Expanding the View," and a good bibliography close out this interesting and provocative study.

John Ashbery's *Selected Poems* (Viking) appeared this year, and *American Poetry* offered two good articles on his work. The first, "Expressionism Not Wholly Abstract" (2,ii:53–70) by Albert Cook, argues that Ashbery's poetry "fuses Andre Breton's program of openness to unconscious experience with Marcel Duchamp's anti-art stratagem of self-obfuscation and unresolvable contradiction"; further, here Cook relates Ashbery's work to that of Eliot, Dickinson, Pierre Reverdy, and others. In "Psychic Geometry: John Ashbery's Prose Poems" (3,i:24–42) S. H. Miller examines *Three Poems* as "the elaboration of the mind's activity," bodied forth in an "analytic prose poem" wherein the poet "is able to articulate the perception of his own being as decentered, as fragmentary and multiple." In "Some Notes on the Obscurity of John Ashbery" (*Pembroke Mag.* 16[1984]: 49–60) David Rigsbee very interestingly uses "Self-Portrait in a Convex Mirror" to address the question of supposed obscurity in Ashbery, answering such charges as "anti-lyricism" and "excessive self-referentiality." In "The Alcatraz Effect: Belief and Postmodernity" (*SubStance* 13,i:71–84) Andrew Ross uses "Self-Portrait in a Convex Mirror" to discuss the relationship of representation to belief in postmodern art. Herman Rapaport's "Deconstructing Apocalyptic Rhetoric: Ashbery, Derrida, Blancot" (*Criticism* 27:387–400) offers an analysis of the apocalyptic tone of postmodern style in terms of current literary theory, while in "Finding What Will Suffice: John Ashbery's A Wave (*MLN* 100:1044–79) Joan Dayan compares Ashbery's poem to work by Whitman, Rimbaud, and Wordsworth.

The romanticism of A. R. Ammons is the subject of Donald H. Reiman's "A. R. Ammons: Ecological Naturalism and the Romantic Tradition" (*TCL* 31:22–51). Here, Reiman discusses Ammons as a poet of "unself-conscious Nature," one whose "ecological naturalism" brings him "to the point where its spirit approximates that of the supernaturalism of his childhood heritage." In "Relationship and Change" (*AmerP* 3,i:43–55) Victoria Frenkel Harris reads James

Wright's "Blue Teal's Mother" and Robert Bly's "With Pale Women
in Maryland" as attempts to "lay to rest the barriers between the
critic and the poet" as the "authority of objectivism and rationalism
relents before the rarer qualities of imagination and intuition." William H. Robertson provides the second part of his Robert Bly checklist, this time focusing on the poet's contributions to periodicals from
1954 to 1984 (*BB* 41:81–95).

**c. Daniel Hoffman, Robert Peters, Galway Kinnell, W. S. Merwin,
and Others.** Lewis Turco's explication of Daniel Hoffman's "As I
Was Going to Saint Ives" (*Poesis* 7,i:54–58) pays close attention to
the poem's prosody, while Russell T. Harrison's "An Analysis of
Charles Bukowski's 'fire station'" (*CP* 18,i–ii:67–83) usefully suggests that like much of Bukowski's work the poem is perhaps more
subtle and complex than it appears on first reading. In the third of her
"neglected poets" pieces (*AmerP* 2,ii:71–78) Diane Wakoski regards
Robert Peters as a poet in the Whitman tradition, one who in his later
poetry has set out to work "with the taboo in our basic erotic instincts" in order to recover the source of creativity. Ronald K. Giles
reads William Stafford's "Traveling Through the Dark" (*Expl* 43:44–
45) as a poem of dramatic reflection.

Andrew Hudgins' " 'One and Zero Walk Off Together': Dualism
in Galway Kinnell's *The Book of Nightmares*" (*AmerP* 3,i:56–71)
argues that at the center of Kinnell's book-length poem is a split between the "rational mind," which believes life ends with death, and
the "irrational mind," which "intuits a mystical oneness in death"; a
close reading of an important and powerful poem. In "The Singing
of Mortal Lives: The Poetry of Galway Kinnell" (*DQ* 19,iii:83–93)
Richard Stamelman opens with a short piece on Kinnell as "a poet of
the physical world" who "confronts death and dying," then follows
with an interview with the poet. Thomas B. Byers discusses W. S.
Merwin's prose in "The Peace in the Middle of the Floor" (*MLQ* 44:
65–79) as "a parallel enactment . . . of Merwin's over-all project," the
recognition that "self-consciousness alienates us from the harmony of
difference in which all things exist." In "A Miracle of Human Close-
ness" (*Pembroke Mag.* 17:95–98) Sister Bernetta Quinn, O.S.F., reads
a few poems from David Ray's *The Touched Life*, while in the same
issue (pp. 7–13) Fred Chappell seeks to introduce the work of Ronald
H. Bayes, specifically the *Umapine* tetralogy.

d. **Talking Poetry.** At their best, interviews not only make for pleasurable reading but provide us with new ways into a poet's work. The entire issue of *Costerus* (vol. 50) is devoted to "Conversations with Contemporary American Writers," conducted by Sanford Pinsker, and including Josephine Miles, Gerald Stern, Stephen Dunn, Etheridge Knight, and William Stafford; Pinsker is an able and knowledgeable interviewer, and it is a shame that this collection will be difficult to find in this country. Jonathan Williams and Ronald Johnson engagingly discuss a variety of subjects—including the Objectivists, music, and hiking—in "Nearly Twenty Questions" (*Conjunctions* 7:225–38). Michael Palmer talks about his work, intertextuality, and Wittgenstein in "A Conversation" (*AmerP* 3,i:72–88), part of a series of discussions with poets and creative writing students which I will publish as a collection next year. Clayton Eshleman takes part in another of these encounters, with subjects ranging from translation to revision, in *Another Chicago Magazine* (12:168–85). David Wojahn and Lynda Hull speak with Denis Johnson in "The Kind of Light I'm Seeing" (*Ironwood* 25:31–44), while Kim Addonizio and John High speak with Carolyn Forchè about her aesthetic, specific poems, and her politics (*Five Fingers Review* 3:116–31). Anne Waldman talks with Mark Hillringhouse about her work, influences, Naropa, and New York Poets in *AmerP* (2,iii:75–89), Jonathan Holden with Brenda DeMartini (*MissR* 8,ii:35–41), Charles Wright with Elizabeth McBride (*OhR* 34:32–41), Joel Oppenheimer with William Sylvester (*Credences* 3,iii:69–76), Robert Kelly with Dennis Barone (*Credences* 3,iii:100–122), and Maxine Kumin with Diana Hume George (*Poesis* 6,ii:1–18).

In my 1982 chapter I mentioned that some of the material I encounter in preparing this survey each year is superficial and/or redundant, written most probably with an eye too close to the rail of tenure and promotion. And yet, looking back through the scholarship on contemporary poetry over the first half of this decade (about 300 books and another 750 articles), while we still obviously need to open up the canon, I am astounded at the number of really first-rate critical projects we've seen: the birth of *Sagetrieb, Conjunctions,* and *Sulfur* magazines, among others; Olson's full *Maximus,* along with Creeley's, Plath's, and Ginsberg's collected poetry; volumes in the Man and Poet series (Orono, Me.) on Louis Zukofsky, George Oppen, and Charles Reznikoff; the multivolume collected Olson/Creeley letters; James E. Miller's *The American Quest for a Supreme Fiction,* Cary Nelson's

Our First Last Poets, Marjorie Perloff's *The Poetics of Indeterminacy* and *The Dance of the Intellect,* Laszlo K. Gefin's *Ideogram: History of a Poetic Method;* M. L. Rosenthal and Sally M. Gall's *The Modern Poetic Sequence;* Stephen Fredman's *Poet's Prose;* Bruce Andrews and Charles Bernstein's *The L=A=N=G=U=A=G=E Book;* James E. B. Breslin's *From Modern to Contemporary;* Charles Altieri's *Self and Sensibility in Contemporary Poetry;* Donald Hall's "Poets on Poetry" series; model biographies of John Berryman and Robert Lowell. While writers like Robert Kelly, Robert Duncan, Nathaniel Tarn, Diane Wakoski, Robert Creeley, and so many others continue to be relatively neglected in at least the more mainstream (and thus available) academic journals, these enterprises have been a gift.

University of New Mexico

18. Drama

Walter J. Meserve

"D'you think a fool can stand alone and shake the deep foundations o' the world? Out o' my way, presumptuous man!" and with these words the archbishop rises in full "majesty and strength," thoroughly intimidating the recalcitrant Boss in Edward Sheldon's 1911 play. With slight regard either for the archbishop's anger or St. Augustine's warning, "presumptuous man" continues to be so, particularly as he (or she) as a critic assesses a writer's work or theorizes about the genre that absorbs his interest. As time passes, the writing style of the essayist seems to become increasingly adulterated with that most intimate personal pronoun as well as those conscious assertions of self-importance that were once scrupulously avoided by most serious writers not exercising their talents in a preface or a familiar essay. Such personalizing writing habits, once reserved for the most revered scholars, are now quite common, extending from works of professional critics through the academic ranks to teaching assistants. It is perhaps, alas, a sign of the times.

i. Reference Works

The most useful popular reference book published this year is *Contemporary Theatre, Film & Television*, volume 2 (Gale), edited by Monica M. O'Donnell. Replacing *Who's Who in the Theatre*, 17th ed., as a biographical guide to performers, directors, writers, critics, etc., volume 1 appeared in 1984 and with this second volume the reference work now includes some 1,800 biographies and 500 photographs plus a cumulative index. Not all entries are complete, however, and some identify very minor personalities, but playwrights are included. George Bryan's *Stage Lives* (Greenwood) is a bibliography and index to theatrical biographies published in English and can be extremely valuable for the theater and drama historian. Part I, Section A includes an annotated listing of 126 theatrical biographies of actors, managers, and playwrights, complete with tables of contents and illustrations. Section B is an annotated listing of 28 nontheatrical biographies, such as Hamlin Garland's *Roadside Meetings* in which Garland comments on a number of actors and playwrights. Section C simply lists 2,597 individual biographies and autobiographies. Part II provides an index and necrology through 1984. The bias of the volume, unfortunately, is toward English "stage lives." Americans in general and American playwrights in particular are slighted.

In order to provide a record of the language of the theater as it has been and is still used in books, articles, and conversation from the 6th century B.C. to the present day, Joel Trapido has edited *An International Dictionary of Theatre Language* (Greenwood). For some 10,000 entries in English and 5,000 more in 60 foreign languages, Trapido and a host of contributors provide a literal meaning and definitions. The Asian coverage is particularly good as Trapido, retired from the University of Hawaii, considers just about everything from A-lamp to Zuoerqian (pinyin) or tso erh ch'ien (Wade-Giles transliteration). *The Encyclopedia of the New York Stage, 1920–1930*, 2 vols. (Greenwood) is another monumental reference work. Samuel L. Leiter, editor-in-chief, purports to provide a description of every legitimate theater production in New York during the 1920s. Each entry gives title, category, author, theater, opening date, length of run, and director, designer, and producer. In addition to comments and criticisms which, unfortunately, lack sources for the quotations, there is a broad range of listings arranged according to subject matter, language, theaters, sources for each play, or seasonal statistics—all of which is made available through the glory or curse of our computer age. Leiter ends his work with a useful bibliography and indexes of names and titles. A new work by a well-known publisher, *Critical Survey of Drama* (Salem), maintains the usual form and standards of this creator of multivolume library reference works.

Like the volumes reviewed above, *Selected Theatre Criticism, Volume I: 1900–1919* (Scarecrow), ed. Anthony Slide, gives the reader only the opportunity to search out plays by American authors. Just as many literary critics still find few American dramatists worthy of their concentration, most theater historians and reviewers view the American theater almost completely in terms of the work of foreign playwrights. Slide reprints selected reviews—many by Channing Pollock and James Metcalfe—of more than 200 original New York productions of dramas, musicals, or revues. Of the few American plays reviewed are one by Rachael Crothers, three by Clyde Fitch, and one by Edward Sheldon, *The Boss*. For another collection of reviews, James Fenton selected his material from a distinctively different point of view. *You Were Marvelous: Theatre Reviews from the Sunday Times* (Topsfield, Mass.: Merrimack Publishers' Circle) is much more closely related to theater than to drama. An academic orientation to theater and drama, plays and players, is presented in Charles A. Carpenter's "Modern Drama Studies: An Annual Bibliography" (*MD* 28:223–327), always a reliable and admired resource, which lists 166 entries under Section B: Americans.

Among reference works for aspiring playwrights and teachers of aspiring playwrights there is a new work entitled *The Playwright's Handbook* (NAL) by Frank Pike and Thomas G. Dunn, who advocate the workshop approach in which playwrights collaborate with actors, directors, and designers. Although certainly not a novel concept in America, the workshop idea has attracted considerable attention with a younger generation of would-be playwrights. *The Playwright's Companion, 1986* (Nashville, Ind.: Feedback Theatrebooks), ed. Mollie Ann Meserve, is an annual submission guide to playwriting contests and to theaters that produce original plays. This issue includes an introduction on submission etiquette, detailed information on more than 550 theaters, contests and programs, plus *Shtetl Tales*, a new play by Rachel F. Urist. The *Dramatists Sourcebook, 1985–86*, (TCG), ed. M. Elizabeth Osborn, provides information on some 200 TCG theaters and 90 playwriting contests, plus production, publication, and developmental or financial support details for playwrights. There is also a revealing essay of advice by the artistic directors of five theaters entitled "The American Theatre Is a Writer's Theatre" which, though idealistic in its concept, is argued with compelling enthusiasm.

ii. Histories

The most recent scholar to attempt a critical assessment of modern American drama is C. W. E. Bigsby, an Englishman whose noteworthy accomplishments in numerous essays and books, clear writing style, and perceptive mind underscore his growing reputation as a major historian of theater and drama in America. In *A Critical Introduction to Twentieth Century American Drama*, vol. 1, 1900–1940 (Cambridge, 1982) he traces the more sophisticated development of

Drama

modern American drama through the activities of major little theaters and selected playwrights. Volume 2: *Tennessee Williams, Arthur Miller, Edward Albee* (1984) concentrates upon the achievements of these three distinguished playwrights. In his third and final volume, *Beyond Broadway*, Bigsby emphasizes the theater more than the drama and pays particular attention to the Performance Theatre, the Living Theater, and the Open Theatre. He also shows his interest in such theatrical entrepreneurs as Robert Wilson, Richard Foreman, and Lee Brewer. The two playwrights he considers in detail are Sam Shepard and David Mamet, but as he concludes his volume, he turns once again to those theaters he terms "committed"—San Francisco Mime Troup, El Teatro Campesino, Black Theatre, Gay Theatre, American Indian Theatre, and Women's Theatre.

In *America's Musical Stage: Two Hundred Years of Musical Theatre* (Greenwood) Julian Mates provides a chronological survey with a lot of factual information but rather little analysis. His history section is particularly readable, but he uses few contemporary sources and relies heavily on his earlier and excellent work concerned with musical theater before 1800. Mates's chatty and informal style and his tendency to relate earlier works to the musicals of the 1950s suggest the problems serious scholars will have with his work. They will miss in particular much of America's rich heritage from the 19th-century stage—the opera, burlesque, vaudeville, comedy, and the contributions of Ned Harrigan, none of which is afforded adequate commentary in this volume. It is, of course, truly difficult to do justice to this subject in a single volume. Gerald Bordman has allowed himself greater latitude with his several volumes on musical theater. The latest, *American Musical Revue: From* The Passing Show *to* Sugar Babies (Oxford), concentrates on the innumerable skits, songs, dance numbers, and chorus lines that flooded American stages during the first half of the 20th century.

A new paperback edition of Brooks Atkinson's *Broadway* (Proscenium) completes the broader historical interpretations this year, although three works provide historical approaches to lesser aspects of American drama and theater. John W. Frick's *New York's First Theatrical Center, The Rialto at Union Square* (UMI) takes a minor aspect of a larger issue and argues the importance of Union Square in American theater life from 1870 to 1900. Using this physical location as a focus, Frick discusses the Academy of Music, the Union Square Theatre, two 14th Street theaters, and the Hippotheatron. The information is sometimes interesting, but the work has slight value as history or as a discussion of theater art. On a more modern topic, defined as political, prowoman, and didactic, Elizabeth J. Natalle writes about *Feminist Theatre: A Study in Persuasion* (Scarecrow). Concerned with "the rhetorical nature of feminist theatre," Natalle ardently and aggressively adopts an argument for plays that speak to women and function as a persuasive bolstering of feminist beliefs. Robert Skloot once again pursues his objective relative to the historic Jewish Holocaust by attempting to understand the events of a generation through an analysis of Ben Hecht's pageant—"*We Will Never Die*: The Success and Failure of a Holocaust Pageant" (*TJ* 37:167–80). Against a well-documented background of events, Skloot tries to relate Hecht's artistic endeavors to the political reality.

iii. Theory and Criticism

What is theater? How does one approach the study of theater, define it, or criticize it? Where does the drama fit in? Is "the play the thing"? Or is it the actor? Or the director? These are the questions that occasionally stimulate discussion, to be answered in different ways by different people at different times in history. In an essay entitled "The Play's the Thing—A Polemic" (*PerfAJ* 26–27:160–62) Colette Brooks argues a popular approach. Opposed to the dull teaching of a play as a set literary text, she sees the playwright as only "one element" of a "theatrical ensemble" which may create a "sense of imaginative movement through the work." Such an approach either to teaching or producing a play, however, can bring the problems that Gerald Rabkin envisions—but without providing solutions—in "Is There a Text on This Stage?" (*PerfAJ* 26–27:142–59). Concerned with the argument of authorship vs. interpretation, as illustrated by the recent activities of Arthur Miller and Samuel Beckett, Rabkin suggests that if interpretation is the key to production, there are many rules to be considered.

Vera Pistotnik attempts to isolate and compare the value of a "stage history" of a play to its critical assessment. In an essay entitled "Toward a Redefinition of Dramatic Genre and Stage History" (*MD* 28:677–87) she questions the argument that "the requirements and effects of staging" enhance one's understanding of a play or form a necessary part of literary criticism. Instead, she sees the recent proliferation of stage histories as a beginning step toward social history and in the process dismisses another recent approach to the study of drama—semiotics—as severely limiting the potential for theater appreciation. From the opposite point of view, Marvin Carlson, in "Semiotics and Nonsemiotics in Performance" (*MD* 28:70–76), not only argues the vital importance of the study of semiotics in the theater but steadfastly contends that there is no such thing as "non-semiotics" in performance. Obviously, critics of the drama and theater are unlikely ever to agree—nor should they. In addition, it is an ill-defined career they follow. "Theatre Criticism: The Elusive Object, the Fading Craft" (*PerfAJ* 26–27:133–41), according to Gordon Rogoff, needs higher standards and a tradition of artistry. He decries the elitists and those who curry popular favor as well as the critics who fail to respect all aspects of the theater and search for fads such as the current emphasis upon the director. The power of the critic, Rogoff contends, rests upon the gift of language, and, he argues, there should be a literature of dramatic criticism. When that criticism has been lacking there have been other means employed to judge plays, such as the one explained by David K. Rod in "Trial By Jury: An Alternative Form of Theatrical Censorship in New York, 1921–1925" (*ThS* 26:47–61). This essay describes this experimental form of censorship or criticism used by New York from the production of Avery Hopwood's *The Demi-Virgin* to O'Neill's *Desire Under the Elms*.

In *Is the Theatre Still Dying?* (Greenwood) Eric Salmon assumes the affectation of a critic whose wandering thoughts disintegrate into two-and-a-half-page paragraphs and a tendency toward "sermonizing" which he readily admits. Of the 12 chapters in his book, six have appeared in print previously. After his first chapter, "An Attempt at Perfection," an argument which strikes one as fine, sensible, and well stated, Salmon's perceptive comments become increasingly lost in a tangle of tangential observations on Shaw, Synge, and Shakespeare. The same unnecessary garrulousness detracts from his discussion of *American Buffalo, Children of a Lesser God*, and *A Soldier's Play* in his chapter on "Three American Plays." In general, he answers his title question affirmatively, although some of his discussion contradicts this conclusion. Herbert Blau is another critic whose ego seems to determine his discussions, sometimes to the great benefit of his readers. *Take Up the Bodies*, which he first published in 1982, is now available in paperback. Bruce A. McConachie uses the writings of another historian and critic, Oscar Brockett, as a stepping-stone to promote his own theories. His essay, "Toward a Postpositivist Theatre History" (*TJ* 37:456–86), also depends to a marked degree upon the "dramatistic-logological" theories of Kenneth Burke. Understanding the theater as a social event, McConachie argues against the theater historian who emphasizes the need for factual evidence. Instead, he insists that a "play must be understood within the context of actors and audiences pursuing their own purposes in the midst of a social historical situation" (p. 477).

Between Theater and Anthropology (Penn.) is Richard Schechner's most recent and most thoughtful book on performance theory. After an introduction by the late Victor Turner, who was impressed by Schechner's egocentric observations, Schechner outlines six points of contact between theater and anthropology. Having discovered Asia some dozen or more years ago and now completely enamored of it, Schechner, more coherently than most theorists, recognizes the value of Asian theater. With particular reference to Indian theater, for example, he comments perceptively on Restored Behavior as a major characteristic of performance. Although some of his explanations appear to be simply reminiscences of his experiences in India, he uses the Ramlila of Ramnagar very effectively to illustrate a "theatrical-religious-political-social-event." His concluding chapter on "Love, Sex and Performance Theory" is somehow depressing, ugly, and sadistic, and his discussion of a production of Genet's *Balcony* seems pointless, but his attempt to compare the training of the Indian Kathakali actor and the Japanese Noh actor with the Euro-American performers suggests a direction in his concern for theater and dramas that may well have an effect upon future American theater productions.

iv. The 19th Century

Although the 19th century seems to appeal more to the historians and reviewers of theatrical eccentricities than to the critics of American plays, a number of researchers have found interest in John Augustus Stone's *Metamora*, William Wells Brown's *The Escape*, Joaquin Miller's *The Danites*, and Steele Mackaye's *Marriage*. Two of these articles are among the best written this year. B. Donald Grosse's "Edwin Forrest, *Metamora* and the Indian Removal Act of 1830" (*TJ* 37:181–91) argues that the Indian Removal Act, the politics of the times, and subsequent white-Indian hostilities had a direct effect upon the success of this play, which emphasized both the "red Devil" and noble savage aspects of Metamora. Julia Curtis traces the public reaction to a dramatization of one of George Lippard's novels staged by Francis C. Wemyss: "Philadelphia in an Uproar: *The Monks of Monk Hall, 1844*" (*ThHS* 5:41–47). The dramatization, entitled *The Quaker City*, so outraged the elite of Philadelphia who found themselves satirized on stage that the play was withdrawn. *My Chains Fall Off: William Wells Brown, Fugitive Abolitionist* (Univ. Press) by L. H. Whelchel, Jr., is a disappointing and brief volume that attempts to present Brown from a religious point of view. The author provides a brief plot of Brown's play, *The Escape*, and quotes some sentimental lines.

The conflict between the theater and the church prompts Claudia D. Johnson's essay about "The Theatre's Qualified Victory in an Old War" (*ThS* 25[1984]:193–209). The essay ebbs and flows with miscellaneous information concerning the effect of the disappearance of the third tier by 1860, the reaction against actors after the assassination of Lincoln, and the furor in 1871 over the burial of an actor, George Holland, of New York, an event which created and named the "Little Church Around the Corner." Johnson concludes her historical argument with the plea, widely recognized by 1900, for a "Christian theatre." Levi Darmon Phillips' description of Arthur McKee Rankin's *The Danites, 1877–1881*: Prime Example of the American Touring Process" (*ThS* 25[1984]:225–47) is a particularly well-documented argument showing the dominance of the combination system during these years. Kathleen A. McLennan is the author of another excellent essay, this one entitled "Woman's Place: *Marriage* in America's Gilded Age" (*TJ* 37:345–56). Through her careful analysis of MacKaye's play, McLennan shows the playwright's revolt against the traditional role of woman in 19th-century melodrama in a play that becomes a critique on the social structure of the Gilded Age and its progression toward social determinism. In yet another essay on theater at Dartmouth College, Professor Emeritus Henry B. Williams discusses the coming of age of theater of Dartmouth in "The Revival of Drama and the Birth of the Dartmouth Dramatic Club: 1885–1900" (*DCLB* 26: 2–22). One potentially interesting discovery is of a production at the commencement of 1893 of a play entitled *The American Fascination*. Unfortunately, neither the script nor the name of the author has survived.

v. Drama and Theater: Economics and Politics

Theatre for Working-Class Audiences in the United States, 1830–1980 (Greenwood), ed. Bruce A. McConachie and Daniel Friedman, includes an introduction in which the editors explain their sociological approach, focusing attention upon a dialectic between actors and spectators, and describing the type of theater that emerges from such a relationship. Of the 13 essays in the volume, four have been previously published. There is an excellent bibliography. McConachie's "The Theatre of the Mob: Apocalyptic Melodrama and Preindustrial Riots in Antebellum New York" (pp. 17–46) reveals excellent research as he details the violence on American stages and in America's streets in an attempt to equate the terror of the melodramas to the fervor of the numerous strikes. It is an interesting idea but a difficult comparison to argue convincingly. In "The Plebeian Movement: Theatre and Working-Class Life in Late Nineteenth Century Pittsburgh" (pp. 47–60) Francis G. Couvares illustrates plebeian theater with Bartley Campbell's *The Lower Million* which (set in Pittsburgh) dramatizes events of the riots of 1877; otherwise, there are few references to plays. In "German-American Socialist Workers' Theater, 1877–1900" Carol Poore discusses only an anonymous play called *Die Nihilestes* to any measurable extent. "Let Them Be Amused: The Industrial Drama Movement, 1910–1929" (pp. 97–110), a particularly well-researched and imaginatively conceived essay by Hiroko Tsuchiya, provides fascinating material on the little-known propagandistic efforts of American industry. Other essays in this collection treat the Workers' Laboratory Theatre, the Federal Theatre Project's search for an audience, the farmworkers' theater, plays about auto workers' strikes, and a review of working-class theater in America.

Theatres of the Left, 1880–1935: Workers' Theatre Movements in Britain and America (Routledge) by Raphael Samuel, Ewan MacColl, and Stuart Cosgrove is another book on propaganda theater. Although mainly concerned with theater in Britain, the writers provide a well-documented history of the Workers' Theatre Movement, a chapter on "The Political Stage in the United States," and the texts of four plays: *Art Is a Weapon,* 1931; *Fifteen Minute Red Revue,* 1932; *Newsboy,* 1934; and *Waiting for Lefty,* 1935. It is perhaps appropriate to note here that Gerald Weales's excellent 1971 book entitled *Clifford Odets—Playwright* is now available in paperback as *Odets: The*

Playwright (Methuen), part of the Methuen Modern Theater Profiles.

For the tenth anniversary issue of the *Performing Arts Journal*, Eric Bentley prepared "Writing for a Political Theatre" (*PerfAJ* 26–27:45–58). Questioning the place of propaganda in the theater as well as the value of docudrama in which reporting and invention appear to merge, he finds a happy solution in his own *Are You Now or Have You Ever Been*. Mixing politics and dramatic criticism in his usual adroit fashion, Bentley declares that bad propaganda drama is bad theater just as good propaganda drama is good theater. Ira A. Levine treats the topic of propaganda in the theater with all the passion of a believer in *Left-Wing Dramatic Theory in the American Theatre* (UMI Research Press). In his given time span of 1911 to 1939 Levine uncovers a patchwork of disparate opinions that he assesses more through a discussion of plays than by a clear presentation of theories. His first chapter, covering "The Prewar Perspective on Social Drama" in which he comments on the work of Emma Goldman, Sheldon Cheney, and Archibald Henderson, is one of the best in the volume. The chapter on dramatic theory in the 1920s includes a perceptive analysis of *Gods of the Lightning*, which illustrates the writer's interest in play analysis. The third chapter ends with a discussion of John Howard Lawson's theories, which he appropriately terms "revolutionary realism," although by declaring that the phrase had not been previously used Levine shows his ignorance of the Chinese antecedents of his topic. His concern, in fact, is exclusively with Russian theory, to which he refers frequently in his text. Consequently, he successfully negotiates the "Dramatic Aesthetics of the Popular Front (1936–1939)" and concludes with a discussion of the languishing revolutionary theater, which he summarizes with considerable skill.

vi. Eugene O'Neill

As in past years, critics of Eugene O'Neill were again, active. The most significant book is Virginia Floyd's latest work for which she had access to the O'Neill notebooks at Yale: *The Plays of Eugene O'Neill* (Ungar). This is Floyd's praiseworthy attempt to make students aware of O'Neill's achievements. Her introduction clearly reveals her thoughtful understanding of her subject and her dedication to helping others appreciate her own enthusiasm. Floyd's task is, of course, considerable as she explores and explains the O'Neill canon: from O'Neill's early plays through his experimental plays and his "self" plays to his final "Great Plays." It is all carefully and sensitively presented, all sifted through the author's perceptive understanding and bolstered by numerous illuminating references to the notebooks. Judith E. Barlow's *Final Acts: The Creation of Three Late O'Neill Plays* (Georgia) treats *The Iceman Cometh, Long Day's Journey into Night,* and *Moon for the Misbegotten,* which she analyzes from a knowledge of O'Neill's early notes, his outlines and scenarios, and his finished manuscripts. Essentially, she considers the "composition process"—origins, sources, character models, parallels with other plays, manuscript revisions, changes, and omissions. As she determines when O'Neill's revisions took place and what his successive drafts accomplished, Barlow sees similar patterns of revision emerge. An intelligently detailed study, this book helps explain the artistry of America's still best-known dramatist.

Two other books from a year past also add to O'Neill scholarship. Margaret Loftus Renald's *The Eugene O'Neill Companion* (Greenwood, 1984), helpful to general readers and scholars alike, attempts to give a full synopsis and brief analysis of every complete O'Neill play. Appendixes provide chronological production information, the details of film and other performance adaptations, an assessment of O'Neill's theory and practices, and a useful bibliography. In *The German Reception of America's First Dramatist* (Peter Lang, 1984) Ward B. Lewis recognizes O'Neill as the first significant American dramatist but suggests that his borrowings from Europe render him rather old-fashioned. Although O'Neill remains a classic author with a favored position in German theater repertory, the height of his popularity, reached in the mid-1960s, is beginning to diminish as other American dramatists appear.

The most interesting article on O'Neill this year was Gary Jay Williams' "Turned Down in Providence: O'Neill's Debut Reexamined" (*TJ* 37:155–66). Carefully researched and sensitively written, the essay explores the facts versus the legend in terms of the early O'Neill play that was produced at the Provincetown—*Bound East for Cardiff.* As a sidelight on this theater and the group O'Neill penetrated, Robert K. Sarlos writes about "George Cram (Jig) Cook: An American Devotee of Dionysos" (*JAC* 8:47–52) with a special emphasis upon *The Athenian Women* and Cook's life as a "Greek Thoreau." Sarlos praises Cook as "an inspirer and intoxicator of others" and includes three pictures with his essay. Michael Selman's "Past, Present and Future Converged: The Place of *More Stately*

Mansions in the Eugene O'Neill Canon" (*MD* 28:553–62) wanders vaguely around a pretentious topic on which the author repeats well-publicized ideas and appears excited to recognize *More Stately Mansions* as an O'Neill play. Robert E. Fleming's "O'Neill's *The Hairy Ape* As a Source for *Native Son*" (*CLAJ* 28:434–43) compares Yank and Bigger Thomas, the images of the ape throughout the play and novel, May Dalton and Mildred Douglas, and the authors' interest in communism. It is a thin issue, however, and the essay does not help "answer some of the questions about Wright's treatment of his literary materials."

The Eugene O'Neill Newsletter now appears to have a significant place among the numerous yearly contributions to O'Neill scholarship. With its brief essays it once seemed esoteric and somewhat frivolous. The essays remain brief, but they are now occasionally linked by a theme, and when they are not, they generally stand alone as insightful observations by people with considerable knowledge of the O'Neill canon. Essentially, the newsletter allows major scholars as well as younger scholars an opportunity to pass on a thought, an anecdote, or an experience that might not see print otherwise or, at least, not so quickly. The essays in the Spring issue were mainly concerned with drinking, drugs, and family problems—in O'Neill's plays and his life. In "Drinking and Drunkenness in *The Iceman Cometh*: A Response to Mary McCarthy" (9:3–12) Steven F. Bloom takes issue with an early review by McCarthy, arguing well that O'Neill did show drunkenness realistically. "A Family Disease" (9: 12–14), as briefly explained by Gloria Dibble Pond, was alcoholism. Robert Einenkel describes "Long Day's Journey Toward Separation: The Mary–Edmund Struggle" (9:14–23) as a great personal tragedy, "an awesome theatrical moment." "Ella O'Neill's Addiction" (9:24–26) is again outlined by Stephen A. Black. In "O'Neill's First Wife Defamed" (9:26–29) Louis Schaffer gives some pertinent information to retrieve that damaged reputation from further spurious defamation. Finally, in the Spring issue, George C. White provides a fascinating narrative of his recent experience with *Anna Christie* in China—"Directing O'Neill in China" (9:29–36).

The seven essays in the Summer-Fall number of the *Eugene O'Neill Newsletter* were more eclectically chosen and most are of little consequence—an esoteric wordplay on "closure" and "enclosure" in *More Stately Mansions*, more comments on the stone image in *Desire Under the Elms*, a lighthearted and nonsensical comparison of

She Stoops to Conquer and *Long Day's Journey into Night*, a desperate attempt to show that O'Neill did not invent Irish-American types. Michael Manheim repeats a number of well-known observations in "Eugene O'Neill: America's National Playwright" (9:17–23). Much more exciting and rewarding for the O'Neill enthusiast or scholar are Donald Gallup's chronology and description of "The Eugene O'Neill Collection at Yale" (9:3–11) and Travis Bogard's well-expressed observations on O'Neill in California—"Eugene O'Neill in the West" (9: 11–16). The Winter issue again has a focus as three critics explore the major productions of *The Iceman Cometh*, the particular adulterations of the text for the Theatre Guild Production in 1946, and the 1985 production in Washington, D.C., directed by Jose Quintero: William Hanley, "*The Iceman Cometh* and the Critics—1946, 1956, 1973" (9:5–10), Gary Vena, "Chipping of *The Iceman*: The Text and the 1946 Theatre Guild Production" (9:11–17), and "Recreating a Myth: *The Iceman Cometh* in Washington, 1985" (9:17–23) by Sheila Hickey Garvey.

vii. Scattered Shots: Black Drama, Wilder, Saroyan, Miller, Albee

Beginning with the work of black dramatists during the 1920s, such as Willis Richardson, Eulalie Spence, and Randolph Edmonds, and plays by Ridgely Torrence, O'Neill, and Paul Green, Freda L. Scott discusses the impact of the Harlem Renaissance in "Black Drama and the Harlem Renaissance" (*TJ* 37:426–39). Scott also shows how plays by both blacks and whites created on Broadway a divergence of thought about blacks. Through a discussion of the efforts of more recent black playwrights and the debate over a distinctive black American aesthetic, Scott defines a basic truth in those black plays which created a beginning statement about blacks for future generations.

In "Thornton Wilder: Broadway Production History" (*ThHS* 5: 57–71) Martin Blank provides a quick look at Wilder's experiences on Broadway from 1932 to 1955. John W. Kirk and Ralph B. Bellas' *The Art of Directing* (Wadsworth) has a chapter on "Analyses: Discovering the Play's Structure," in which there is a thorough analysis of William Saroyan's *Hello Out There* (pp. 39–57) and a reprint of the play (pp. 195–211).

In "History and Other Spectres in Arthur Miller's *The Crucible*"

(*MD* 28:535–52) E. Miller Budick gives detailed attention to what he terms the "drama's theological issues" and argues that the author's concern for morality underscores the play's "historical consciousness and historical knowledge." Budick finds at the heart of the play a moral arrogance which he feels is basic to the American temperament. Miller, he states, writes historical drama to help readers and viewers understand the changing nature of morality. Someday it will probably be acknowledged that Edward Albee has subjected himself to the wit as well as the simpering of more interviewers than any of his peers. Add to this number a sensitive and well-balanced interview on a rather expanded basis created by the Dramatists Guild and moderated by Terrence McNally—"Conversations with Edward Albee" (*DGQ* 22,ii:12–23). Albee covers a variety of subjects—his first play, his work with Alan Schneider, his interest in directing his own plays, the Playwrights Unit, and the problems following the production of *Lolita* and his later plays, particularly *The Man Who Had Three Arms*. In his usual pleasant fashion Albee tells a lot about himself and at no time with greater insight than in his condemnation of the concept of "developing plays" as "nonsense."

viii. Tennessee Williams

The Tennessee Williams bandwagon is currently and deservedly attracting attention around the world. Harlow Robinson ("From Broadway to Gorky Street," *AmTh* 1,ix:12–17,40–41) reports that Williams' plays, once banned in Russia along with other American plays, have had eight recent productions in Moscow. "The western play of today is primarily American," writes Robinson, who allows the most space to the reception of Williams' plays. It is also significant that Twayne Publishers, ever interested in the marketplace, has published a paperback edition of the 1978 version of Signi L. Falk's *Tennessee Williams* (TUSAS 10, 1978), one of the best early books on Williams. Another alert publisher offers *Tennessee Williams on File* (Methuen), compiled by Catherine M. Arnott. This is the first book on an American in this series, now numbering six titles and introduced by Simon Trussler, created to present selected contemporary comments on a dramatist's plays as well as the dramatist's own views about his work and world. With well-chosen selections, informative comments, and slight but choice bibliographies, the series appears to suggest excellence. In this instance the documents and the approach praise Williams as one of two outstanding American dramatists. The thin paperback volume provides a brief chronology; basic information on 70 plays and screenplays (published and not published) from *Moony's Kid Don't Cry* (1934) to *Something Cloudy, Something Clear* (1981); a guide to nondramatic work; comments on his works; and a bibliography. The basic information on each play includes original production details, publication data, a synopsis and critical response. Although the reviews provide only a representative taste (excerpts from six on *Glass Menagerie*, for example), Williams' own comments, taken largely from his letters, suggest a personal view of his work and attitudes that distinguishes the flavor and adds to the value of the volume.

There is something about Tennessee Williams the man, a feeling that lingers in his work, that tempts critics to psychoanalyze him rather than limit themselves to literary or dramatic criticism. Undoubtedly, books such as Donald Windham's *As If . . . : A Personal View of Tennessee Williams* (New York: Sandy Campbell) encourage such activities, but critics need little encouragement. "The Circle Closed: A Psychological Reading of *The Glass Menagerie* and *The Two Character Play*" (*MD* 28:517–34) is R. B. Parker's attempt to interpret the plays through a knowledge of the dramatist's life, particularly his relationship with his sister Rose. Parker also defends Williams' therapeutic use of theater/drama as an "introversion." Robert Bray simply asserts that Williams' drama is "largely misunderstood." His solution involves the recurring theme of the emphasis of the past upon the present in "The Burden of the Past in the Plays of Tennessee Williams" (pp. 1–9) which appears in *The Many Forms of Drama* (Univ. Press), ed. Karelisa V. Hartigan.

ix. Feminism in the Drama

Eventually, this heading will become less popularly distinctive as the concepts involved become integrated with other aspects of drama and theater, an integration that is already occurring with black drama. The issue of Rosemary K. Curb's "Pre-Feminism in the Black Revolutionary Drama of Sonia Sanchez" (pp. 19–29)—in *The Many Forms of Drama*—exploits the abuse of black women by black men. Curb defines her approach in terms of feminism but is also aware of the broader social issue in her discussion of such late '60s plays as *The Bronx Is Next, Sister Son/Ji* and *Uh, Uh; But How Do It Free Us?* Steven R. Carter describes a similar problem—man's oppression of wom-en—in "Images of Men in Lorraine Hansberry's Writing" (*BALF* 19: 160–62). Carter argues that Hansberry created sympathetic male pro-tagonists, such as Walter Lee, Sydney Brustein, and the main char-acter of *Les Blancs* who are caught in a web of male supremacy and whose situations bring harm to women and to themselves. In "Wom-en/Text/Theatre" (*PerfAJ* 26–27:185–90) Gayle Austin complains of the lack of power among women playwrights early in this century and, as one-time literary manager of the Women's Project of the American Place Theatre, advocates workshop dramas in which she sees a blend of writer and performer. "Banish decorum," she writes, "bust barriers," but her rhetoric overwhelms the issue. "Women's Work" (*AmTh* 2,v:10–15) gives two contemporary women play-wrights, Tina Howe and Maria Irene Fornes, opportunity to explain why they write differently from male dramatists. Admittedly, scholars have a painful tendency to attempt catalogs and lists, divisions of thought and labor, and sentences involving a series of at least three items. Just as Aristotle discusses tragedy and comedy and Chinese historians divide their plays into civil and military, critics may some-day discuss good and bad plays and find little value in identifying the gender or race of the dramatist.

x. Sondheim, Simon, Shepard, and Mamet

The Landmark Symposiums organized by the Dramatists Guild de-serve much better publicity among scholars than they have yet at-tracted, although the dialogue of each symposium is published in the *Dramatists Guild Quarterly*. "Landmark Symposium: *West Side Story*" (*DGQ* 22,iii:11–25) provides a thoroughly fascinating remi-niscence by Leonard Bernstein, Arthur Laurents, Stephen Sondheim, and Jerome Robbins on the way this musical was started and de-veloped. Presumably, each person inspired and challenged the others as the cooperative venture took shape. Linda Winer, "Sondheim in His Own Words" (*AmTh* 2,ii:10–15,42), interviewed Sondheim on the subject of musical theater. The "Landmark Symposium: *Barefoot in the Park* (*DGQ* 21,iv:10,16–32) included Mike Nichols, Mildred Natwick, Elizabeth Ashley, and Neil Simon. Again the symposium format stimulated the telling of some interesting anecdotes and pro-duced a modicum of peripheral commentary as memories conflicted and fears of the past, now lost, were refocused. "Neil Simon and the

Play" (*DGQ* 21,iv:11–16) by Dale Ramsey provides commentary on the symposium as well as an interview, allowing Simon to express some of his feelings—his desire to be alone, writing, for example.

There were two books on the inimitable Sam Shepard this year. Don Shewey's *Sam Shepard* (Dell) is essentially popular propaganda for a star-playwright, actor, and screenwriter. Lacking notes or sources, the book purports to explore "the life, the loves behind the legend of a true American original." Vivian M. Patraka and Mark Siegel in *Sam Shepard* (WWS 69) concentrate upon themes and motifs in Shepard's plays and forsake commentary on technique to focus on Shepard's objectives. After relating Shepard to the West, they discuss the disintegration of American life that his plays dramatize—the distortion of the human community, the false heroes and idols, the failure of home and family—and conclude that Shepard as dramatist must exorcise the evils of American life. The volume on *David Mamet* (Methuen) by C. W. E. Bigsby is the first book-length study of Mamet and the first American playwright in Methuen's Contemporary Writers series. Based on articles in print and two interviews with Mamet, the study identifies Mamet as a "poet of loss" and attempts to illuminate his works as well as the artistic, social, and moral assumptions on which they rest. With his customary insight, Bigsby works other Chicago writers—Veblen, Fuller—into his assessment of the Mamet canon from *Lifeboat* to *Glengarry Glen Ross*. Throughout, Bigsby emphasizes Mamet's sense of loss and catalogs him as a faultfinder for American society.

xi. The Theater and Its Plays

The purpose of those whose works are noted in this essay is generally to enlighten the reader, although some writers apparently aspire also to influence. In any event, the materials which inspire their research and their judgments—the plays and the performances—in many instances are readily available. This situation, however, is not always true: American publishers have never felt that there was much of a reading public for plays. One new collection to challenge that conception, *Coming to Terms: American Plays & the Vietnam War* (TCG) includes *Streamers* by David Rabe, *Botticelli* by Terrence McNally, *How I Got That Story* by Amlin Gray, *Medal of Honor Rag* by Tom Cole, *Moonchildren* by Michael Weller, *Still Life* by Emily Mann, and *Strange Snow* by Steven Metcalfe. The introduction by James

Reston, Jr., which first appeared in *American Theatre* (2,ii:16–19), stresses the importance of lessons to be learned from these plays and urges theaters to let these voices be heard.

It is not usually difficult to know exactly where to draw the line with most books written about American screenwriters, but when a major American dramatic critic undertakes to write about the movies he enjoys, attention should be paid. So it should be–to Gerald Weales's *Canned Goods As Caviar* (Chicago). This eclectic view of American film comedies of the 1930s offers no systematic approach, merely the intelligent and delightful response of a youthful lover who repudiates his nostalgia with a scholarly vigor while acknowledging the charm of inauthenticity in anecdotes. Discussing the aspects that attracted him to a dozen films from *City Lights* (1931) to *Destry Rides Again* (1939), Weales stimulates a thoughtful interest. *The Best of Rob Wagner's Script* (Scarecrow) has been edited by Anthony Slide. *Script*, a journal of two-page articles, was published in Beverly Hills from 1929 to 1949 and included a fascinating variety of essays by an equally fascinating group of people. There is "What's Wrong with Musical Pictures" (pp. 9–13) by Sigmund Romberg, several essays by William Saroyan including "Or Leave a Kiss Within the Cup" (pp. 144–46), and "Charlie Chaplin's First Story" (pp. 27–30), "Rhythm" (pp. 80–82), and "The Fool" (pp. 134–37)–all by Charlie Chaplin. Eddie Cantor wrote "I Like to Remember" (pp. 111–13) and "Comics and the War" (pp. 113–15), and Ben Hecht contributed a skit entitled "The Common Man" (pp. 117–30). It is a pleasing book to read.

"The Sake of Argument: A New American National Theater" (*Theater* 16,iii:7–10) strikes a recurring note among theater critics. This essay by D. W. King comments in some detail, and hopefully, on the American National Theater, the complexities of its organization, and the power of Peter Sellars. Another kind of national attitude becomes apparent in Jan Stuart's "Stars and Stripes Forever" (*AmTh* 2,i: 12–18). The questions posed–What have we come to? What have we come from?–are answered with reference to Peter Parnell's *Romance Language*, Michael Weller's *The Ballad of Soapy Smith*, and John Guare's Lydie Breeze tetralogy. From these and others, a host of panoramic plays, the author tries to bring the past into the present–to learn from the past and be free. Lastly, there is Gerald Weales's "American Theatre Watch, 1984–1985" (*GaR* 39:619–28), always a good concluding item for this essay. Although Simon's *Biloxi*

Blues won the Tony, Weales found it old stuff, army clichés. He liked Rabe's *Hurly Burly* better. Only these two plays recovered their investments. August Wilson's *Ma Rainey's Black Bottom* was a good play about blacks getting back at whites; but Weales found both William Hoffman's play about AIDS, *As Is*, and *The Normal Heart*, Larry Kramer's agitprop against Mayor Koch, despairingly sentimental. Like many others, Weales was disappointed in *Harrigan 'n Hart*, which died in a week, and saw only clichés in *Quilters*. This was not a great year for new plays in America, but a few critical essays and a number of reference works and scholarly books do deserve the shelf space.

Indiana University

19. Black Literature

John M. Reilly

The distinction of this chapter lies in the fact that besides reviewing scholarship it also records a field's process of self-definition. There has been cross-fertilization from the seeds of feminism and Continental theory brightening everyone's garden, but looking back at the reports I have written since 1979 I am most pleased to see how rapidly Afro-Americanists have framed their discipline by posing the problems of theory, literary history, and interpretation in light of the special setting and historical materials of black American culture. Once again, then, I am able to write as much about what the year's work proposes as I do about what it has accomplished.

i. Bibliography, Reference Works

Indicating that "Studies in Afro-American Literature: An Annual Annotated Bibliography" has been institutionalized as a regular feature of his journal, Charles H. Rowell has joined with William Lyne to produce the entry for 1984 (*Callaloo* 8:630–60). The form remains the one Rowell chose for annotated listings in *Obsidian* and that Marcellus Blount continued in last year's renewal of the project, so the 178 items are classed by genre or reference to individual authors. Annotations are uniformly sound, entries cross-referenced and indexed. While the listings do not yet include primary works, as Blount thought might be possible—however daunting the prospect of compiling them—references to dissertations reinforce the impression a user derives of trends and fashions in criticism. A restricted compilation by Janet Sims-Wood, "African-American Women Writers: A Selected Listing of Masters Theses and Doctoral Dissertations" (*Sage* 2,i:69–70), may or may not become a regular offering, but in the meantime identifies recent work done in the universities on one of the most active subfields of Black Studies.

Selected Black American, African, and Caribbean Authors: A Bio-

Bibliography by James A. Page and Joe Min Roh (Libraries Unlimited) is a revised and expanded edition of Page's 1977 volume. The 632 alphabetically arranged entries, most of them American, include a biographical note, listings of writings divided into fiction and nonfiction, sidelights, and notice of resources consulted. The volume includes an occupations index for entrants and a title index. The editors consulted notable teachers and critics in choosing their subjects, but seem not to have asked them to check the editorial copy. As a result, categories are confusing (some of Darwin Turner's editorial work is identified as fiction, as is everybody's poetry and drama), entries are sometimes inexplicably selective (*Cane* is the only publication listed for Toomer; the entry for Frederick Douglass includes the standard scholarly edition, but the one for Booker T. Washington does not), and there are obvious misattributions (such as the inclusion of a book titled *Farthings Fortunes* among works of Richard Wright). This is a book to be used only with caution.

By contrast, *Carter G. Woodson: A Bio-Bibliography* by Sister Anthony Scally (Greenwood) is a highly dependable resource. Biographical information is presented in a 20-page sketch and a chronology, while the heart of the book consists of more than 800 entries, chronologically listed and arranged in sections devoted to books, which includes those Woodson jointly authored and edited, and their reviews; articles and reviews contributed by Woodson to *JNH* and *Negro History Bulletin*; selections from his works appearing in books and periodicals and secondary treatments in theses, dissertations, and newspapers. Suggestive of the thoroughness of Scally's work are the annotations leading a reader through the topics of each of the books or articles and the appended notes she provides about manuscript collections.

Memorializing and inviting imitation of the example of cooperation among Suffolk University, the Boston African American Historical Site, and that city's Museum of Afro-American History, Edward Clark's *Black Writers in New England, A Bibliography, with Biographical Notes, of Books by and About Afro-American Writers Associated with New England in the "Collection of Afro-American Literature"* (Boston: National Park Service) reports on the 200 writers represented in the total collection of 3,500 titles by their own 625 books and another 125 books written about the authors with a New England connection. Clark began the collection in 1971 with the intention of providing a resource for study in a central city location;

therefore, generous inclusiveness rather than rarity of publications has been the guiding principle. Writers are listed alphabetically with a biographical note and publication data for works by and about the author. Since teaching, studying, or residing briefly in New England qualifies writers for inclusion just as much as nativity, the lists include many prominent figures. A concluding section of the book identifies 80 writers appropriate for the collection but not yet represented in it. Let us hope the energy displayed by the curators will soon repair the omissions.

Another regionally focused bibliography is Jerry W. Ward, Jr.'s "Selected Bibliography for the Study of Southern Black Literature in the Twentieth Century" (*SoQ* 23,ii:94–115), which serves as a guide to primary and secondary sources published from 1970 to 1982. Intending to supplement Darwin T. Turner's *Afro-American Writers* (1970) and to amplify the listings in Richard Barksdale and Keneth Kinnamon's anthology *Black Writers of America* (1972), Ward arranges his new items according to the model of Turner's work. George Hill guest editing issues of *BB* is responsible for updating key author bibliographies and reprinting the originals. For John Edgar Tidwell and John Wright's "Alain Locke: A Comprehensive Bibliography" originally published in *Callaloo* (1981), Hill adds 30 secondary sources, half of them articles (42:95–104); and to the bibliography produced by Xavier Nicholas on Robert Hayden for *Obsidian* (1981 and 1982), he adds titles from *World Order*, a publication of the Baha'i Trust, along with recent books about Hayden, memorial items, articles, and obituaries (42:140–53).

Acknowledging the insuperable value of Herbert Aptheker's *Annotated Bibliography of the Writings of W. E. B. Du Bois* (1973), William L. Andrews presents his "Checklist of Du Bois's Autobiographical Writings" with the aim of stimulating work in an area still understudied (*W. E. B. Du Bois*, pp. 226–30). Besides the four major books of Du Bois's autobiography, Andrews gives a representative sample of some 59 briefer memoirs, travel sketches, and essays published between 1886 and the 1960s. Andrews' critical challenge can be seen in his reminder that the narrative "I" was characteristic for most of Du Bois's work as editor and commentator also.

Articles from the testimonial issue of *Callaloo* for Larry Neal, ed. Kimberly Benston, will be discussed later, but here two complementary versions of a Neal bibliography by Eleanor Traylor must be noted. The first is " 'And the Resurrection, Let It Be Complete': The

Achievement of Larry Neal (A Biobibliography of a Critical Imagination)" (8:36–69). An appreciation, meditation, and summation studded with quotations from Neal, this article beautifully weaves references to Neal's writing and notes on his reading into an exposition of the conjunction of ethics and aesthetics that made Neal a herald of transition in the 1960s. Here Traylor elevates the genre of bio-bibliography to the level of imaginative criticism. Her second contribution to the celebration of Neal is constructed on more conventional lines as "An Annotated Bibliography of the Works of Larry (Lawrence Paul) Neal" (8:265–73). Subdividing the works into reviews; essays of social and cultural analysis and aesthetic theory; literary history, theory, and criticism; short fiction; poetry; drama; and editorships, Traylor documents the breadth of Neal's interests and the numerous forms of his influence on contemporaries.

All the bibliographies included in *Contemporary American Women Writers* are described by the volume's editors as compilations in anticipation of further work by other hands; thus, they serve as guides to further reading rather than definitive listings. Elizabeth Fifer's "A Bibliography of Writings by Alice Walker" (pp. 165–71) gives the first U.S. edition of books, and in recording short stories, poems, and articles indicates reprintings as well as inclusion in Walker's collections. The bibliography is completed by listings of reviews and miscellaneous items. A footnote by Fifer acknowledges the aid of Susan Kirschner, who last year published a checklist of Walker's nonfiction in *BALF* that surpasses this one by including publications after Fifer's cutoff date of early 1983. Curtis Martin's "A Bibliography of Writings by Toni Morrison" (pp. 205–07) is also limited by reason of an early cutoff date. His latest entry is dated 1981. Beyond that, though, it is spare because of a decision to omit the numerous interviews in which Morrison speaks provocatively on the art of fiction and its relationship in her case to black culture.

The impressive editorial work of Thadious M. Davis and Trudier Harris on last year's *DLB* volume devoted to Afro-American fiction writers is matched this year by their compilations of *Afro-American Writers After 1955: Dramatists and Prose Writers* and *Afro-American Poets Since 1955* (DLB 38 and 41). The work on dramatists and prose writers includes 35 entries of varying length depending upon the dimensions of an author's canon. Predictably there are sizable essays on Amiri Baraka (by Floyd Gaffney), Ed Bullins (by Leslie Sanders), Alice Childress (by Trudier Harris), June Jordan (by Peter B. Erickson), and Adrienne Kennedy (by Margaret B. Wilkerson); but the volume is equally valuable for its inclusion of essays about Albert Murray (by Elizabeth Schultz), Marvin X (by Lorenzo Thomas), Samm-Art Williams (by Trudier Harris), and Paul Carter Harrison (by Steven Carter). In the interests of helping to define their literary period the editors also reprint six informative essays on black theater, its organization and aesthetics. Presumably to signal priority of responsibility, the title page of the poets' volume lists Harris before Davis, but in any case this collection of 51 entries with its coverage of poets who came of age during the 1960s and 1970s gives a strong sense of the variety of program and practice among writers too often grouped as though they spoke with a single voice. Nearly all the entrants can be said to be in midcareer, and some of the writers belong in the category of "new." Many of the writers included in these splendid volumes have published most of their work in small magazines or had it produced in local theaters. Making them accessible through dependable survey essays and checklists that recover elusive publication data constitutes a major service to Afro-American literary study.

ii. General Studies, Literary History

I must trust that readers will feel that "better late than never" is sufficient commentary on my belated notice of *Blues, Ideology, and Afro-American Literature: A Vernacular Theory* by Houston A. Baker, Jr. (Chicago, 1984), for this exemplary volume will influence critical discussion and very likely help define the pattern of theory for a considerable time. The portions of the book treating "generational shifts" that formed the basis of Baker's critique of "reconstructionist" critics in *BALF* (1981), his reading of Dunbar's *Sport of the Gods* as a discourse on the fallibility of the habits of thought embodied in the Plantation Tradition that also appeared in 1981, and his 1983 *PMLA* article investigating the substratum of commerce and exposing the metacommentary on the issue of folk art/literary art in Ralph Ellison's Trueblood episode have been previously noted in *ALS*. Amplified and incorporated into a perspective that roots the ideology of form in the material conditions of slavery and its legacy, the previous writings now become the flesh of a paradigm for studying those "moments of discourse," figured by the blues as the matrix and code of cultural signifying, when narrators negotiate the economics of slavery. Noting in the first chapter how the language of Olaudah Equiano and Frederick Douglass privileges economic terms while pursuing a theme of the transformation of property into humanity, Baker describes a bonding that threads its way through the increasingly differentiated texts of later black writers. While the inscription of economic contours within these texts represents a process of appropriating literature to black experience, the secondary discourse of literary historians remains oblivious to it. So, then, a study of criticism follows as a necessary challenge to the assumptions of traditional literary history Baker believes are antipathetic to an Afro-American outlook. Against this background of critical dialogue and its limitations, Baker uses his third chapter to present innovative readings of Dunbar and Ellison and a penetrating study of Richard Wright's nullification of apparently fixed genres in order to project his radical vision in a determinedly nonbourgeois art. *Blues, Ideology, and Afro-American Literature* will earn praise deservedly for its intelligent interpretations, including one that yields the best study of the history of black criticism that we have, and for morphology that serves criticism by suggesting engaging subjects for further work—all aided by Baker's persuasive, artful style.

Another critic of engaging style and deserved repute for the outlook his style manifests is Henry Louis Gates, Jr. Readers will know of the instructive disputes Gates and Baker have, but they should also be aware of the commonality of purpose their works show. As it happens, Gates's "Writing 'Race' and the Difference It Makes," which serves as his introduction to the issue of *CritI* (12:1–20) he guest edited, also mounts a challenge to conventional literary history in the observation that as race has been bracketed in the 20th century on the assumption that Judeo-Christian and Greco-Roman culture is the source of values, the trope of race has remained an invisible factor denominating "the other" sub rosa. Gates has room for little more than announcement of an agenda to deconstruct the hidden relations of power inhering in the academic usage of race, but he uses his space to rehearse the Kantian conflation of reason with color that made it axiomatic to say blacks could not write since they could not reason, and to identify the inception of Anglo-African literature as a response to the allegation of the absence of black reason and writing.

A literary history fully cognizant of the politics of race will be alert to problems like those announced in "Minority Writers: The Struggle for Authenticity and Authority" by Muriel Schulz (*Language and Power*, pp. 206–17), who gives a compact statement of such matters as the inevitably political writing required to alter traditional stereotypes that have covertly enforced ideological ends and the difficulty of achieving authority for texts when acceptance of minority literacy requires the consent of a dominating group that monopolizes power to designate what is important and true. Some of the difficulties Schulz outlines arise within the group, others out of writers' need to reject Western, white, male culture while remaining free of its values. In an attempt to codify the modes of response in those circumstances Berndt Ostendorf writes "Literary Acculturation: What Makes Ethnic Literature Ethnic?" (*Callaloo* 8:577–86). Establishing "ethnicity" as an agonistic term implying duality of identity and conflict, Ostendorf surveys categories and types of ethnic literature in the manner of a reference book article.

A convenient source for detailing the charge that conventional American history misrepresents the reality of black experience comes to hand in William L. Van Deburg's *Slavery and Race in American Popular Culture* (Wisconsin, 1984). Van Deburg examines white literature in tracing the hardening of stereotypes and black literature in terms of challenges to stereotypes, but the bulk of the study is devoted to the writings of historians, black and white, in conflict over interpretations of slavery. The book is solidly grounded but hardly optimistic about the power of unaided persuasion to transform the nation's dominant culture.

Literary texts struggling to counter misrepresentation of Afro-American culture form the body of study for Carole McAlpine Watson, whose *Prologue: The Novels of Black American Women, 1891–1965* (Greenwood) identifies 64 novels, all listed chronologically in appendixes with a chart of themes and topics and an annotated bibliography providing the plot for 59. The main body of the book classifies 58 of the novels into three periods with illustrative examples discussed in each. Watson characterizes the period from 1891 to 1920 as devoted to racial uplift with a focus on religious behavior and a call for flawless morality. Among her exhibits are Frances Harper's *Iola Leroy* and Pauline Hopkins' *Contending Forces*, the first an overly moral work, the second a melodramatic but forceful protest challenging the benevolent view of slavery. For 1921 to 1945, illustrated by works of Jessie Fauset and Zora Neale Hurston, group-centered issues such as middle-class values and self-help themes are the immediate didactic concerns. A major shift appears to Watson to mark the works of 1946 to 1965: integration replacing nationalism turns the attention of novelists to what keeps the races apart, and the focus is increasingly individualistic in such examples as Ann Petry's *The Street* and *The Narrows*, Paule Marshall's *Brown Girl, Brownstones*, Kristin Hunter's *God Bless the Child*, and Mary E. Vroman's *Esther*. To round out her study, Watson compares black women's writing to the American "mainstream," finding that a consistent tone of political urgency (incidentally setting apart the women's writing from the Harlem Renaissance) and the retention of romance for didactic purpose are chief traits. Watson's book compiles the data to set a tradition, as well as periods in its development, but the intense concentration on themes leaves the impression that art is largely message.

In "Trajectories of Self-Definition: Placing Contemporary Afro-American Women's Fiction" (*Conjuring*, pp. 233–48), an essay also included in her collected writings (*Black Feminist Criticism*, pp. 171–86), Barbara Christian posits study on the principle that the development of fiction mirrors the relations of sexism and racism, thus confirming the idea expressed in her book on women novelists (*ALS 1980*). Besides their writing against stereotype, the new essay notes also an apparent belief among earlier writers that black women would lose important aspects of themselves if they achieved the feminine norm of American culture. That tension survives as Zora Neale Hurston introduces a language for exploration of the self and Gwendolyn Brooks's *Maud Martha* intensifies the emphasis on self-definition. Inevitably even the black community threatens the autonomy of self, so rebellious women appear tentatively in writing by Paule Marshall, Toni Morrison, and Alice Walker, though a community of black sisters resolves that conflict and relaxes the conflict over white norms. Christian sees the fruits of the history she tells in the group of contemporary writers introducing new complexity to literary forms directly expressive of female culture. In reconnoitering the ground for literary history of women's fiction Susan Willis' "Black Women Writers: Taking a Critical Perspective" (*Making a Difference*, pp. 211–37) eschews themes for what Willis terms "central concerns" generating the dynamics of texts. She appraises concerns—community, journey, and sensuality vs. sexuality—with the lens of Marxist critical method: thus, she sees writers problematizing the notion of community in order to resist the tendency of bourgeois fiction to mirror social fragmentation in its portrayal of isolated individuals; interested in journey not simply because it is a structuring device but because it is a metaphor for the arrival of consciousness integral to the unfolding of history; and representing women's free companionships and households as a way of suggesting alternatives to the sexual repression induced by capitalism and race hatred.

Defining a women's tradition also forms the agenda for Marjorie Pryse and Hortense J. Spillers in their edited collection, *Conjuring.* The compilation of 15 pieces (10 of them printed for the first time and noted later in this report) is introduced by Pryse's "Zora Neale Hurston, Alice Walker, and the 'Ancient Power' of Black Women" (pp. 1–24) and concluded by Spillers' "Afterword—Cross-Current, Discontinuities: Black Women's Fiction" (pp. 249–61). Pryse's verification of tradition centers on the problem of literary authority. Not until Chesnutt, she says, does a black writer locate some other source than God for creativity. For Chesnutt it was the magic of black folk life. Enlarging upon that, Hurston also broke the connection between authority and patriarchal power, becoming a second founder of black literature and rooting its unique female strand in the framework of women's friendship. Though it remains an outline, Pryse's essay suggestively combines interests seen in other critics' approaches. For her part, Spillers indicates reasons for serious modification of any simple linear description of lineage, since she sees the female tradition as "a matrix of discontinuities that partially articulate various periods of consciousness in the history of an African-American people." The most serious of these discontinuities are Hurston's rejecting the power of necessity found in Nella Larsen and Jessie Fauset and Ann Petry's replacement of genetic determinism with environmentalism. The strength of Spillers' approach lies in her attention to "epistemic procedure," a matter that in time must find accommodation in the methodology of literary history with the themes that concern Watson or Christian, the treatment of authority that interests Pryse, and the sensitive awareness of the effect of material experience shown by Willis.

Meanwhile, an emerging literary history must also make room for detailed consideration of the modes of writing fiction. A comprehensive effort to address that need appears in the contention by Keith E. Byerman's *Fingering the Jagged Grain: Tradition and Form in Recent Black Fiction* (Georgia) that folklore provides black writers an alternative form of discourse challenging the authority of closed, conventional systems of representation. *Invisible Man*—with its opposition of the concrete particulars of discontinuous reality to the abstract, idealized, or fixed schemes of ideologues—serves as Byerman's

model of literature he denominates as black because of its constel-
lation of technical characteristics associated with folk literature rather
than for the social fact of race. Taking the folk elements to include
subjects, the received forms they have been given, ways of seeing, and
a worldview of "organicism," Byerman gives well-informed formalist
readings for works by Toni Cade Bambara, Alice Walker, Gayl Jones,
Toni Morrison, Ishmael Reed, and Clarence Major. Though he an-
nounces reluctance about relating texts to an historical context, Byerman acknowledges that social issues inhere in the forms of literature,
and his book deserves attentive reading because this willingness to
modify a strict formalist approach has led him to treat black literature
according to its own differentiated cultural sources.

   The feminist insight that gender significantly mediates racial and
cultural experience has been a root cause of valuable critical study of
the works of black female writers. But critics have been reluctant to
follow the lead of some political figures and invert that insight to make
the proposition that the experiences one has because of gender are
historically primary. Minrose C. Gwin's *Black and White Women of
the Old South* does much to explain that reluctance. Gwin aptly uses
the image from *Absalom, Absalom!* of Rosa Coldfield's haunting confrontation with Clytie in a sisterhood of interconnection and rejection
as a refrain throughout her well-conceived study of a century of both
black and white literature, for the relationships she explores are pe-
culiarly charged. Investigating the polemics of *Uncle Tom's Cabin*
and Mary H. Eastman's proslavery response in *Aunt Phillis's Cabin*,
Gwin finds the subtext of stock figures, including black stereotypes, is
the same, while her examination of narratives by female slaves in
conjunction with autobiographies by white mistresses yields important contrasts. The earlier slave narratives assume control over a painful past by rendering portraits of sadistic mistresses now power-
less to challenge the memory. For their part, the white women's life
writings desexualize slave women into selfless stereotypes feeding the
narcissistic image the whites have of themselves as objects of devotion. The sharp contrast slackens in the writing of black women
who were youngsters during the Civil War, and in Gwin's treatment
of 20th-century literature featuring Margaret Walker's *Jubilee* she
finds evidence of conciliatory gesture, though on the whole it is by
action of black authors, since novels by whites make no effort to enter
slave women's minds. The intrinsic interest of taking biracial female

experience as a mode of entry into the ambiguities of the literature of the South can hardly be exaggerated, and the regular citation of references to studies of power relationships and sexuality along with Gwin's intelligent willingness to use psychological tools for analyzing language indicates the possibility of the literature confirming broader cultural investigations as well. The value of pursuing the topic of bi-racial friendships beyond regional setting can be seen in Elizabeth Schultz's "Out of the Woods and into the World: A Study of Inter-racial Friendships between Women in American Novels" (*Conjuring*, pp. 67–85). Schultz has done excellent comparative work previously on such topics as community and family in black and white fiction (*ALS* 1979, 1980). Now her point of contrast is the white male novelists' mythic invocation of black-white male bonding. The paucity of friendships of black and white women is startling. Al Young's *Who Is Angelina?* stands alone as a work by a male (black or white) who examines a continuing friendship; in white women's novels the friend-ships do not survive the conclusion of the story; while in the fiction of black women there are by Schultz's count only four exceptions to the rule that friendships are interrupted by power plays on the part of white women. Of course, the reason for the differences lies in the effect of the social order that works to suppress the impulse to imagine sisterhood.

Described as work-in-progress, Phyllis R. Klotman's " 'Tearing a Hole in History': Lynching as Theme and Motif" (*BALF* 19:55–63) threads historical references through an exposition of the thematic and technically varying treatments of lynching by 10 black writers. Though she adds examples to those cited by Trudier Harris in *Exor-cizing Blackness* (1984), Klotman's study when complete seems un-likely to alter the picture. Harris and Klotman show literary portrayal of lynching and its ritual enactment as predominantly a feature of the male critique of racism. That women have addressed racism differ-ently is the occasion for Hazel V. Carby's revisionary essay in literary periodizing. Echoing a phrase of Frances Watkins Harper in her title, " 'On the Threshold of Woman's Era': Lynching, Empire and Sexual-ity in Black Feminist Theory" (*CritI* 12:262–77), Carby describes how such Afro-American women intellectuals as Anna Julia Cooper, Ida B. Wells, and Pauline Hopkins theorized about patriarchal and racial power in a period usually associated with the male genius of Du Bois and Booker T. Washington. The broad approach of these writers, as-

sisted in their work by the forum offered by the National Association
of Colored Women, linked imperialism, sexual politics, and internal
colonialism. Wells exposed both lynching and rape as means of social
control founded on sexual ideology, Cooper espoused education as a
means to self-determination, and Hopkins sought to use the historical
knowledge favored by all of these intellectuals to shift the debate on
racial degradation from the biological image of mixed blood to a political consideration of patriarchal power. Adducing the example of
writers who demystified the issue of race, Carby adds an important
facet to the representation of black response to violence, and since
her approach derives from the recognition that history is differentially
experienced, she illustrates how new theory can reconstruct historiographical method as well as the history it produces. Yet differentiation
is far from being uniformly gender-based. Betty J. Overton's "Black
Women Preachers: A Literary View (SoQ 23,iii:157–66) cites por-
trayals of women clergy in Langston Hughes, James Baldwin, Claude
Brown, Ann Shockley, and Kristin Hunter, showing that they are all
presented as grounding their ministry in emotionalism and reaping
suffering implicitly attributed to their having dared to take on a male
role. That the one-sided and unforgiving view results from an un-
questioned sexism derived from American examples and incorporated
into Afro-American culture seems clear to Overton, who says that in
African societies the place of women in leadership and religion is
more prominent than in the West.

A good brief outline of one writer's intellectual history, "More
Stately Mansions: New Negro Movements and Langston Hughes'
Literary Theory" by Wilson Jeremiah Moses (LHRev 4:40–46), distinguishes between an "old" New Negro Movement comprising the
work of 19th-century nationalists, Du Bois, and Marcus Garvey that
left an artistic legacy of "monumentalism" evident in the paintings of
Aaron Douglass and the writings of J. A. Rogers and a "new" New
Negro Movement espousing modernistic primitivism and belief in
proletarian folk wisdom. Despite his appreciation of preceding generations, Hughes like most Harlem-based writers of the 1920s was
generally unsympathetic to the monumental works of the past and
reveled in avant-garde modernism. Hughes's sense, despite a constant concern about escape from traditionalism, led him in the 1960s
to counsel newer New Black artists against further rejection of the
past. The lesson Moses draws from this story of continuity obscured
is that "ideology adapts to the shape of its container and takes on the

qualities of the environment in which it thrives," a cautionary point
of value to literary critics equally with writers.

"Southern Standard-Bearers in the New Negro Renaissance," an
overview essay contributed by Thadious M. Davis to *The History of
Southern Literature* (pp. 291–313), seeks on the one hand to restore
a role for the masses in the cultural movement of the 1920s by indicating that after all it was southerners who made folk culture available
to the Talented Tenth, and on the other hand to argue through discussion of the careers of Georgia Douglas Johnson, Anne Spencer, and
active writers in South Carolina and Mississippi that the "renaissance"
was not limited to Harlem. Both arguments form cogent parts of a
survey that discusses the mechanisms of the literary movement and
proposes a lineage of major and minor figures. Literary language and
critical suppositions are the focus for Aderemi Bamikunle in "The
Harlem Renaissance and White Critical Tradition" (*CLAJ* 29:33–51).
A Nigerian critic trained in America, Bamikunle clear-sightedly appraises the effort to create "high culture" as the result of generations
of subordination of black writing to white standards. Perhaps it is the
knowledge of a similar situation in the production of African writing that encourages Bamikunle to challenge commonplaces about the
Harlem Renaissance, as in the assertion that a motive of the period
was repudiation of the folk past, but whatever dispute a reader may
have with portions of this essay will be incidental compared to its
value as concrete application for discourse theory in the study of
period formation.

Lee Greene has provocative remarks to make about canon and
transition within the post-Renaissance period in "Black Novelists and
Novels, 1930–1950" (*The History of Southern Literature*, pp. 383–
98). The story of the early 1930s is largely one of affirmation of black
culture with a focus on ethnicity rather than sociology, but pride of
place goes to George Wylie Henderson, not Zora Neale Hurston, for
according to Greene it is *Ollie Miss* that bridges the span in evolution
of technique between *Cane* and *Invisible Man*. Social realism joins
with folk realism in *These Low Grounds* by Waters Edward Turpin
and *River George* by George Washington Lee, but on the whole the
Great Depression is seldom a focus in southern novels which take the
recent or remote past as their settings—until the late 1930s and 1940s,
when migrants to industrial cities offer a new subject. The suggestions
for historical reconsideration are completed by Greene's declaration
that Saunders Redding's *Stranger and Alone*, employing the figure of

the educator, second only to the preacher as an institutional figure in black culture, is a bridge in the development of psychological complexity between *Native Son* and *Invisible Man*.

Sigmund Ro claims the experience and example of the Third World as a major source for repudiation of the aesthetic of protest—which he characterizes with Wright's phrase "Negro as American's metaphor" in his " 'Desecrators' and 'Necromancers': Black American Writers and Critics in the Nineteen-Sixties and the Third World Perspective" (*Callaloo* 8:563–76). A contribution to a special collection of European criticism ("Recent Essays from Europe," Fall issue of *Callaloo* ed. Robert B. Stepto and Vera M. Kutzinski), Ro's excellent study in period formation describes the transformation of rage and celebration, twin impulses of earlier black literature, into a new variety of writing stripped of frustration and need to affirm essential Americanness. While much that Ro says has long been familiar, the historical perspective inherent in the scheme of decolonizing aesthetics he takes from Third World history underpins the detail with a theory of considerable use for defining the operations of literary history as distinct from relating its substance. A type of resistance new black literary history encounters becomes evident in Josef Jarab's "Black Aesthetic: A Cultural or a Political Concept?" (*Callaloo* 8:587–93), which is critical of the misunderstanding of history fostered by critics in the Black Arts Movement. An appropriate response should be that Jarab is himself insufficiently appreciative of historical circumstances surrounding literary manifestos. Such circumstances as they appeared in the 1960s are developed in Houston A. Baker, Jr.'s "Critical Change and Blues Continuity: An Essay on the Criticism of Larry Neal" (*Callaloo* 8:70–84). Baker characterizes the work of Neal, a leading player in the movement discussed by Ro and Jarab, as the worrying of an Ellisonian line, so that the Black Aesthetic project could take account of the function of vibrant Afro-American cultural forms while shying away from Ellison's emphasis on craft. For his purpose Neal constructed an activist nationalism that evoked Richard Wright to legitimate the project with a past, while declaring that creativity must be placed in the reach of the people by a theater where audience, popular taste, and Ellisonian genius could be wed. In Baker's version of literary history Neal eventually admitted Ellison into his pantheon when his cultural projects required him to confront the techniques of world literature. According to Baker's story of commonality briefly disguised, the difference between Ellison and Neal turned on the one seeing the blues analogous to European folk art and the other seeing the blues originating in African conditions.

Mance Williams states that he was impelled to write *Black Theatre in the 1960s and 1970s: A Historical-Critical Analysis of the Movement* (Greenwood) because of the limited and sometimes negative approaches of critics to the productions that represented the acme of Black Aesthetic theory and practice. Williams singles out the group of one-act plays produced in New York under the title *Black Quartet* in 1969 as a point of inception, describing the productions as revolutionary in their Black Power politics, antithetical aesthetic, and effort to tap audience participation in line with the tradition of black call-and-response. In the introduction to his book Williams specifies the need for a multiple approach to his subject, so analysis of the historical conditions for Black Consciousness accompanies his accounts of theatrical companies, discussion of producers, and survey of black theater since the 1930s. The book, thus, touches on a wealth of topics, including a chapter on "non-polemical structuralists," and concludes with a levelheaded discussion of a movement in search of audiences.

For her part Trudier Harris is also very well aware of the politics of literary change, but necessarily more attentive to regional groupings in "Black Writers in a Changed Landscape, Since 1950" (*The History of Southern Literature*, pp. 566–77), an essay that describes the need felt by southern writers to respond to the Civil Rights movement while withstanding the rhetorical demands of the Black Arts writers based in the North. Among those Harris singles out are Alice Walker, whose *Meridian* is the best treatment of the psychological impact of the Civil Rights movement; Albert Murray, who celebrates the culture intrinsic to the black community; and Robert Dean Pharr, whose work shows that southern writers can sometimes be less concerned to react to whites than the Black Arts authors. Conceived in part at least as a corrective to criticism that has had no time for the South, Harris' survey attempts to show the richness of indigenous work and the support which new journals and theater give the region's black writing. Blyden Jackson's "The Black Academy and Southern Literature" (*The History of Southern Literature*, pp. 600–605) provides the background for these later regional developments in its brief history of black higher education, and especially the role of the great humanistic teachers who conveyed a lasting love of literature to

their students and organized themselves as the College Language
Association, whose journal remains a dependable guide to attitudinal
developments in the black South.

Clyde Taylor takes Richard Wright's "Blueprint for Negro Writing" (1937) as a prophetic document whose dreams he finds nearly all
fulfilled in "Black Writing as Immanent Humanism" (*SoR* 21:790–
800). The causes of this accomplishment he locates in the recovery of
Africa, the pugnacious break with white standards in the 1960s, and
the womanist energy in literature—unanticipated by Wright, but
evincing a deeply humanist attack on all forms of domination. Taylor
concludes that now no writing can match the breadth of vision evident
in Afro-America's literature.

iii. Fiction

a. **Founders of Black Fiction.**   Taking five literary motifs originally
noted in reference to the slave narrative by J. Noel Heermance in his
study of William Wells Brown (1969), Richard O. Lewis pursues
them through the three versions of *Clotelle* and the narrative of *My
Southern Home* in "Literary Conventions in the Novels of William
Wells Brown" (*CLAJ* 29:129–56). The most vivid of the motifs, "mistaken identity," Lewis classifies in terms of the variety of disguises and
incidents of role-playing that appear in the novels. While his discussion is often derivative of earlier studies, such as Jules Zanger's on
the "tragic octoroon," Lewis' elaborated discussion of the functions
served by each device contributes detail about the degree to which
early black formal writing was shaped by the need to address suppositions of the white audience. Charles Hackenberry's coverage of
symmetrical characterization and mulattoes in "Meaning and Models: The Uses of Characterization in Chesnutt's *The Marrow of Tradition* and *Mandy Oxendine*" (*ALR* 17[1984]:193–202) makes a related point while amplifying the generally accepted view of the
failure of Charles W. Chesnutt's formal novels: devising characters
on the black side of the color line to generate belief in black humanity,
Chesnutt, despite investment of his own self-image in the fiction, cannot successfully provide authoritative answers to the social issues that
inform his plots. When he adapted traditions arising within Afro-
American culture, however, Chesnutt was able to cancel and debunk
the contemporary social outlook that denied narrative authority to his

conventional romances; thus, Bill Christophersen's "Conjurin' the White Folks: Charles Chesnutt's Other 'Julius' Tales" (*ALR* 18:208–18) examines the ways seven stories recently collected in Sylvia Lyons Render's edition of the short fiction expose the violence under the sentimental plantation myth, rebut racist views of survival of the fittest, and generally work to make white readers see from alternative vantage points. The Aesopian wit and structural inventiveness of the frame story is given a brilliant exposition by John Edgar Wideman in "Charles Chesnutt and the WPA Narratives: The Oral and Literate Roots of Afro-American Literature" (*The Slave's Narrative*, pp. 59–78). Reading the story "A Deep Sleeper" as a ritualized struggle between the white narrator and the vulnerable black storyteller for personal space and territory, Wideman's exercise in narratology reveals the technical genius of the stock of stories, surviving in the 20th-century WPA collections, that subvert the literary conventions commonly used to mock black life.

All of the items compiled by William L. Andrews for *W. E. B. Du Bois* emphasize literature. Those written specifically for the volume are Bernard W. Bell's "W. E. B. Du Bois's Struggle to Reconcile Folk and High Art" (pp. 106–22), which explains that devotion to the mission of racial uplift included beliefs that folk art, providing a window into the souls of the people, is the foundation of national high art and that the role of the artist is to transform unrestrained expression into something more studied; and Nellie McKay's presentation in "W. E. B. Du Bois: The Black Women in His Writings—Selected Fictional and Autobiographical Portraits" (pp. 230–52) of the break with contemporary convention that allowed Du Bois to express his deep sympathy and admiration for black women by projecting them as morally superior figures central to the action of his narratives and, thus, important role models for himself and his audience. According to the deconstructions of Anthony Appiah's "The Uncompleted Argument: Du Bois and the Illusion of Race" (*CritI* 12:21–37), the leader's conception of race was much less satisfactorily concluded than his ideas on art and the role of women. Appiah's argument, which deserves careful reading for the relevance it has to the reasoning of anyone seeking to negate the scientism of the illegitimate category of race, holds that while Du Bois attempted to use "race" as a metonym for culture, he was unable to escape the term's latent capacity to biologize difference. A conscious contradiction in Du Bois's thought provides the subject of Manning Marable's "The Black Faith of W. E. B. Du Bois: Sociocultural and Political Dimensions of Black Religion" (*SoQ* 23,iii:15–33). Biographical evidence of Du Bois's experiences with the *nommo* (essence), music, and frenzy of the southern black church and wide citation of his research and published works supports Marable's representation of a version of the double-consciousness that allowed Du Bois to be agnostic toward the religion of the white world and expressive of a love of God inside the color line.

The happenstance of publication dates evidently prohibited Roger Whitlow from consulting Gloria T. Hull's edition of Alice Dunbar-Nelson's diary while preparing "Alice Dunbar-Nelson: New Orleans Writer" (*Regionalism and the Female Imagination*, pp. 109–25), but he was able to use Eugene Wesley Metcalf's unpublished 1973 dissertation on the letters of Alice and her husband Paul Laurence Dunbar for biographical information to shore up this outline for recovery of the publications of an author critically eclipsed by the fame of the man to whom she was married four years. Concentrating his attention on the volumes of short stories, the first of which was published when the author was 20, Whitlow identifies themes of unrequited love, quietly tragic heroism, women's rights, and Creole portraits in tales he views as melodramatic and slight.

It is safe to predict that before long there will probably be further articles on Dunbar-Nelson probing the pattern of her career more deeply, just as Claudia Tate aims to do for another early writer in "Pauline Hopkins: Our Literary Foremother" (*Conjuring*, pp. 53–66). Though Hopkins was a contemporary of Chesnutt who also believed that fiction could be a vehicle for racial advancement, she has, according to Tate, received such inadequate treatment that it is necessary to summarize plots of the unread novels and list the themes she explored in modes shared with 19th-century white women authors. At first, injustice to blacks is central to the domestic, sentimental romances, but gradually Hopkins narrowed her scope, perhaps indicating the frustration she shared with other black writers employing popular conventions.

James Weldon Johnson does not need recovery, but the issue of thematic intent in his best-known work evidently remains clouded by the old problem of audience response to black novels written during the nadir of American race relations. Howard Faulkner opens "James

Weldon Johnson's Portrait of the Artist as Invisible Man" (*BALF* 19: 147–51) with discussion of continued critical resistance to the irony of *Autobiography of An Ex-Colored Man*, even though its significance has been argued regularly at least since Robert E. Fleming wrote about it in 1971. Faulkner admits how hard it is for readers to detach themselves from the thoughts of a narrator who is an articulate artist but proceeds to show the series of contrasts between incidents and the protagonist's response that signify deliberate repression and self-effacement. Susan J. Koprince's contribution to a description of Johnson's worldview in "Femininity and the Harlem Experience: A Note on James Weldon Johnson" (*CLAJ* 29:52–56) consists in observation of the images of women as temptresses and saintly mothers in *God's Trombones* and assertion that the archetypes express a persistent dichotomy of sensual and spiritual reappearing in *Black Manhattan*.

b. Novelists in the Era of the "New Negro."   Two of this year's articles on Jean Toomer address the anomalous circumstance of *Cane's* reputation as an expression of the spirit of the Harlem Renaissance though its author denied the persistent attribution to him of black identity. In "Looking Behind *Cane*" (*SoR* 21:682–94) David Bradley recalls being deeply moved at seeing how Toomer's technique engaged emotion and wondering how a writer could accept so completely in his work what he repudiated in his life. With sympathy deriving from his own sense of being out of step with the politics of race in 1970 when he first read Toomer, Bradley answers his question by charging that critics and publicists misread and misrepresented the man who strove for fusion rather than exclusivity and, thus, drove him to resist classification as Negro. Rudolph P. Byrd in "Jean Toomer and the Afro-American Literary Tradition" (*Callaloo* 8:310–19) shares Bradley's estimate that Toomer, as a matter of fact, was not really central to the New Negro movement and agrees that critics have made the declaration of Toomer's racial identity for him, but rather than representing Toomer as the victim of literary or racial politics, Byrd is content to state that one criterion for inclusion in the black literary tradition ought to be an author's declaration of identity. Absent that, let Toomer go. Maria Isabel Caldeira's "Jean Toomer's *Cane*: The Anxiety of the Modern Artist" (*Callaloo* 8:544–50) confines her biographical approach to the text where she reads a conflict between the artist's search for wholeness, which Toomer emphasized by drawing attention to the intended circularity of the book, and the Afro-American experience of double-consciousness resulting in a fragmentary literary form. Kabnis figures as the prototypical modern artist sharing Toomer's dilemma. Regardless of the outcome of biographical study of Toomer, there will always be occasion for such investigations of technique and racial drama as that undertaken by Alain Solard in "Myth and Narrative Fiction in *Cane*: 'Blood-Burning Moon'" (*Callaloo* 8:551–62), which analyzes imagery based upon folk beliefs combining with the pictorial texture of setting and the sound of language to render characters locked in ambivalent relationships to black life.

The reevaluation of Jessie Fauset begun by Carolyn Sylvander (*ALS 1981*, pp. 394–95) drew attention to the psychology of characters faced with society's color mania. Now Deborah E. McDowell ably continues discussion in "The Neglected Dimension of Jessie Redmon Fauset" (*Conjuring*, pp. 86–104), an essay that discusses such self-conscious strategies as the use of inverted fairy-tale patterns that lead the protagonist of Fauset's manners fiction to find her happy ending in the realization of black culture, not a rich prince. McDowell urges readers to see the works in a context of publishers' hostility to controversial topics that required Fauset to adopt protective coloration for her stories and at times to retreat to a system of traditional values. "A Question of Power or, the Rear Guard Faces Front," McDowell's introduction to a new reprint of *Plum Bun* (London: Pandora Press, pp. ix–xxiv), expands upon the idea of covert themes by explaining how the apparent novel of passing, if carefully read for discordant notes, shows itself to be a critique of the fantasy of passing and a transformation of conventions to point up their deficiencies.

The critical aim of uncovering subversive subtexts is adopted also by Priscilla Ramsey in "Freeze the Day: A Feminist Reading of Nella Larsen's *Quicksand* and *Passing*" (*Afro-Americans in New York Life and History* [Buffalo, N.Y.] 9,i:27–41). Ramsey counters the jibes at Larsen's naive assimilationism by arguing that her novels illuminate the shallow patterns imposed by men on women's thrust for political power. Robert E. Fleming offers support for such a reading by studying "The Influence of *Main Street* on Nella Larsen's *Quicksand*" (*MFS* 31:547–53). Acknowledging earlier discussion of parallels between Larsen's book and Henry James's *Portrait of a Lady* by Mary M. Lay (1977), Fleming argues for seeing a break from James's model and adoption of features of Carol Kennicott's life to represent the way disillusion with reform follows upon disillusion with a husband in whom the female protagonist had submerged her own identity.

As a later section of this report will make clear, Zora Neale Hurston now holds the repute of parent for a women's tradition in black fiction; yet she also retains importance to the period of the "New Negro" because of techniques and subjects related to the informal program of the writers who self-consciously came of age in the 1920s. Barbara Johnson's "Thresholds of Difference: Structures of Address in Zora Neale Hurston" (*CritI* 12:278–89), focusing on two essays and *Mules and Men*, explains how Hurston's ironic tone undercuts conventional suppositions and supports a stance on the border between inside/outside interactions of black/white. In part, Johnson's essay is further development of her treatment of Hurston's double voicing in fiction (*ALS 1984*), but its demonstration that Hurston's narrative practices show that "questions of difference and identity are always a function of a specific interlocutionary situation" gives suggestive direction for reading all of Hurston's canon including the problematic autobiography. Claire Crabtree's "The Confluence of Folklore, Feminism and Black Self-Determination in Zora Neale Hurston's *Their Eyes Were Watching God*" (*SLJ* 17,ii:54–66) provides an examination of the techniques of framing, dialect, gaming, and portrayal of community consciousness that clarifies how the authentic folk manner by which the narrative claims authority is transformed into self-reflexive art. Crabtree's description of achieved synthesis is a welcome elaboration of the practical issues so often deflected in abstract discussion of folk art vs. high art. An alternative example of synthetic interpretation is found in Donald R. Marks's "Sex, Violence, and Organic Consciousness in Zora Neale Hurston's *Their Eyes Were Watching God* (*BALF* 19:152–57). Diagramming the novel according to the grouping of Janie's four sexual relationships into those of passion and those of control, each marked by distinct tropes and sign structures, Marks contends that Janie like Hurston can neither come to terms with the violence of heterosexual passion nor endorse the image of a society that makes nonviolent heterosexuality possible. As a result, the novel is ideologically stymied. The organicist vision of passionate relationship that Hurston romanticizes can exist at the end only in solitary consciousness. The final article on Hurston properly belonging in this section of the report is Ruthe T. Sheffey's "Zora Neale Hurston's *Moses, Man of the Mountain*: A Fictionalized Manifesto on the Imperatives of Leadership" (*CLAJ* 29:206–20), which investigates folk roots and the techniques of audience appeal to explain how Hurston exploited the place Moses holds in the Afro-American imagination because of his apparent kinship to black preachers.

c. **The Age of Wright.** The outstanding publishing event in Wright studies for this year is the appearance of Michel Fabre's *The World of Richard Wright* (Miss.), which includes the early story "Superstition" (1931), a selection of verse from the period when Wright was best known as a left-wing poet, two new essays by Fabre, and 12 of the pieces he has previously published. One of the new essays, "Wright's South" (pp. 77–92), surveys the canon to show how Wright rejected the South that denied him the opportunity to replicate Faulkner's creation of a comprehensive fictional representation, yet compulsively returned to telling how the South had shaped him. His treatment of the South varied from the obliteration of culture in the story of *Black Boy* to later adoption of a global idea of racial heritage with each variation figuring as part of an archetypal quest for freedom that recalls the motive of the fugitive slave narratives. In its essentials Fabre's portrait of the southern Wright agrees with Blyden Jackson's "Richard Wright" (*The History of Southern Literature*, pp. 443–49), which in Jackson's characteristically felicitous style sums up Wright as an author whose subject was always the South and whose skill as a writer can be seen in the creation of an epic-sized character in a book that "altered the terms of the dialogue about color endemic to America." Fabre's other new essay, "Wright, Negritude, and African Writing" (pp. 192–213), offers a narrative about Wright's cautious approach to African culture, the persons who encouraged his distrust of lyrical African literature and suspicion of intellectuals from the Francophone countries, and his adoption of a role as representative of the English-speaking members of the diaspora and mediator in their disputes—all of this directed by an interest in Africa that was more political than literary.

Obviously the book to which Blyden Jackson ascribes the effect of changing American racial dialogue is *Native Son*, and so it is natural that such a study as George Goodin's *The Poetics of Protest* should examine the classic novel. Goodin's approach, indebted to Kenneth Burke's model of the writing act, assumes that each type of protagonist generates a different structure. The subgroup to which he assigns *Native Son* is the flawed victim who internalizes his source of oppression. In the case of Bigger Thomas it is individualism that produces

his conviction that human relations are a matter of one person dominating others. Up to this point Goodin's analysis can find wide support among other critics, but as he proceeds to charge that the text
contains too little explanation of how Bigger came to be and that at
the end of his story he desperately tries to find meaning in his murders
because he is more confused than ever, Goodin goes pretty far afield.
Not that one must agree with precedent critics, but a reader suspects
that here an interest in the validity of the hypothesis about typical
structures of protest fiction is more important than the specific dynamics of Wright's text. It might be expected that a source study
would be another opportunity for pushing a thesis at the expense of
detail, and of course it is, but not when the study is as controlled as
Robert E. Fleming's "O'Neill's *The Hairy Ape* as a Source for *Native
Son*" (*CLAJ* 28:434–43), which establishes congruity of character
conception and elements of surreal setting not on grounds of imitation
but instead with the observation that Wright was a professional
author naturally willing to study craft wherever he found it.

The detective story element is the prime subject of Lynn Beach
Sadler's study of Wright's venture into Freudianism and the "race-
less" novel. The title "Richard Wright's *Savage Holiday*: The Criminal
Mind Its Own Best Detective" (*JoPL* 1,ii:61–72) states the thesis
Sadler develops through readings of the ingenious play of names and
image chains and analysis of the unfolding of Erskine Fowler's psychology. "The Sociolinguistics of Underground Blues" by Keith Gilyard (*BALF* 19:158–59) aims to develop Houston Baker's reading of
"The Man Who Lived Underground" in his new book by examining
the inability of Fred Daniels to validate his experience in language
others can accept. The well-taken point also serves to aid Gilyard's
other announced purpose of contributing to the portrayal of Wright's
ability as a symbolist.

To move his subject out of the shadow of Wright, Bernard W. Bell
in "Ann Petry's Demythologizing of American Culture and Afro-
American Character" (*Conjuring*, pp. 105–15) discusses the ways
Petry builds sympathy for Lutie Johnson in *The Street* and explores
the importance of time and place for white and black characters in
her later works. Bell is correct in saying Petry's characters differ
significantly from Wright's, and Chester Himes's, in their lack of
pathology, but he overstates his case in the claim that this difference
shows Petry going beyond the naturalism he believes remained
Wright's mode. Among the matters Bell considers are myths dear

to white culture. Such myths are also of interest to Marjorie Pryse in " 'Pattern Against the Sky': Deism and Motherhood in Ann Petry's *The Street*" (*Conjuring*, pp. 116–31). The article works satisfactorily enough in asserting that the larger forces of racist environment in the novel are personalized in the white Chandler family and in its positing a set of alternative forces in black characters connected to their own traditions, but Pryse also wishes to introduce deism as context for it all. That I fail to grasp.

Among Afro-American expatriate writers William Gardner Smith holds fascination because of early accomplishments and the fact that he made a career abroad from the age of 24 until he died at 47. Some of the curiosity will now be satisfied by *Portrait of an Expatriate: William Gardner Smith* by LeRoy S. Hodges, Jr. (Greenwood), a noninterpretive biography that uses extensive interviews with Smith's family and friends, FBI files, letters, and other documentary sources to establish the facts of his career. Hodges summarizes each of Smith's five books, discusses their composition, and includes a bibliography of primary and secondary materials.

d. **Post-Protest Fiction.**   Barbara Christian's "Nuance and the Novella: A Study of Gwendolyn Brooks's *Maud Martha*" (*Black Feminist Criticism*, pp. 127–41) addresses the causes for the lack of critical attention since *Maud Martha*'s publication in 1953. While the inward-looking focus on the ordinary experiences of a woman neither tragic nor domineering can explain why this short novel once seemed slight, it is time to recognize that the apparently trivial concerns of Maud Martha are sources in personal life for the literary and social movements of the 1960s, deserving such analysis as Christian offers for the techniques of distillation by image and rhythmic sound which structure the book's vignette architecture. In " 'An Order of Constancy,': Notes on Brooks and the Feminine" (*CentR* 29:223–48) Hortense J. Spillers goes further and persuasively claims that the customary topics of the female landscape are less the subject of the novel than is the power of imaginative play in Maud's consciousness, broadening our understanding of what is heroic, establishing a synonymity of the feminine and the imagination, and allowing us to see that a narrative lacking structure other than that provided by the shadings of consciousness demonstrates a woman's freedom.

Ralph Ellison's famous remark about a writer's freedom to choose ancestors even if relatives are inevitable proves to be a profound description of the process of creating modernist prose in Robert G. O'Meally's "The Rules of Magic: Hemingway as Ellison's 'Ancestor' " (*SoR* 21:751–69). By O'Meally's account, Ellison once related Hemingway's understated, allusive style to jazz and the stoicism of his heroes to the blues. During this period Ellison's attempt to equal the ancestral sentence structure can be heard in the cadences of contributions to the *New Masses*. Briefly Ellison became disturbed about Hemingway's narrowness, especially the lack of statement about blacks, but by the time he was writing *Invisible Man* had returned to his original view with the result that his protagonist appears to be a cousin of Nick Adams engaged in a struggle for meaning through episodes O'Meally contends are often akin to Hemingwayesque confrontations of reality. Since styles of modernism, which are O'Meally's concern, arise as responses to experiences perceived as uniquely new, his essay might well be read in conjunction with Daniel B. Weber's "Metropolitan Freedom and Restraint in Ellison's *Invisible Man*" (*CollL* 12:163–75), for Weber uses Georg Simmel's idea that intellectuality is developed by modern people to preserve their subjectivity against the overwhelming power of metropolitan life in order to elucidate the compounded problem of self-education faced by Ellison's narrator undergoing initiation into the life of New York City. Both experience and the style of its representation are the subject of Michel Fabre's analysis of "The Narrator/Narratee Relationship in *Invisible Man*" (*Callaloo* 8:535–43). Examining the prologue to show the narrator's expectation that his auditor shares a specialized knowledge of Western culture and the devices which point to the listener's responses, Fabre elicits the shape of a suggested drama between a black claimant for the equality due his humanity and a modern Everyman embodying the consensus of white Americans. Besides offering new entry through narratology into the dynamics of the novel, Fabre's reading of verbal situation and gesture also reestablishes for the novel a militancy that criticism of the 1970s overlooked.

With an essay treating an equation of imagery associated with women and the South (*ALS 1983*), Trudier Harris initiated a discussion that promised to link a range of themes in the works of James Baldwin. Now with *Black Women in the Fiction of James Baldwin* (Tenn.) she shows that consideration of female characters and their progression provides a way into all the texts of the writer who for 30 years has been publishing investigations of love in human relationships. Even though most of Baldwin's female characters are scarred by guilt, are assigned to traditional roles in which they support males, and, except for *Beale Street*, are presented in the narrations of males, Harris' detailed analyses of the novels reveals that paradoxically these women become memorable precisely because they are usually in the position of seeing to others' needs. In summary this sounds like decided conservatism, and Harris would hardly deny that; still her study reveals evidence of Baldwin's projection of autobiographical problems such as ambivalence about an oppressive stepfather, a record of his intellectual biography as he increasingly places women along with men outside the church, and the chance to see his bold concern with such themes as incest. Harris correctly points out that among black male writers Baldwin is the most consistently interested in portrayal of black women, even as his works show that he believes men and women are most at peace with each other when they are out of each other's presence or resolve their conflicts in a platonic relationship. Challenge to "influential" interpretations is the stated aim of Michael Clark in "James Baldwin's 'Sonny's Blues': Childhood, Light and Art" (*CLAJ* 29:197–205). According to Clark, it is the formal artistry of overall structures rather than the received view of Baldwin's aesthetics stressing expressive moments that distinguishes his most famous story. His demonstration consists in notation of the metaphor of childhood supported throughout the story by images of light and darkness. This successfully describes a fusion of complex elements in the story, though it does not necessarily contradict longstanding descriptions of blues aesthetic in Baldwin's work. Sigmund Ro's analysis of Baldwin's story is secondary to his use of it to characterize a literary period in "The Black Musician as Literary Hero: Baldwin's 'Sonny's Blues' and Kelley's 'Cry for Me'" (*Rage and Celebration*, pp. 9–43), which shrewdly observes that literary historians must look for the premise in fiction ultimately located in the extraliterary reality of a writer's culture, and the formal component most immediately revelatory is characterization. On these grounds he finds Sonny articulating a story of submission to Western values in familiar existentialist categories, while Kelley's similarly framed story shows transition to a mythically resonant characterization repudiating individualism and resolving middle-class uneasiness with the folk past.

I am tempted to say that Charles H. Rowell's "The Quarters: Ernest Gaines and the Sense of Place" (*SoR* 21:733–50) does for the Louisiana writer what Malcolm Cowley's essay in the *Portable Faulk-*

ner does for the Mississippian, but the evocative writing about St. Raphael Parish so effectively summons the feel of physical and social experience in the quarters, so convincingly demonstrates that the landscape is the basis and correlative of Afro-American culture that finally I have to decline the comparison to other criticism and say simply that Rowell's essay amounts to immersion in Gaines's South.

"Toward the Post-Protest Novel: The Fiction of John A. Williams" by Sigmund Ro (*Rage and Celebration*, pp. 85–112) continues the effort seen in his other essays to present the paradigm of the 1960s. By Ro's reckoning Williams lends himself especially well to the purpose since before 1963 he wrote in the framework of traditional protest writing. After that date he bent and stretched the fictional medium of representational realism so that fantasy in the service of a revisionist historical view would reveal the surreal logic of persistent racism and exultantly address a black audience in celebration of the will to survive. What gives each of Ro's efforts at period definition persuasive force, and the essay on Williams above all, is the sensitive reading of particulars of the texts.

To date there has been so little criticism of Amiri Baraka's fiction that we welcome Ikenna Dieke's "Sadeanism: Baraka, Sexuality, and the Perverse Imagination in *The System of Dante's Hell*" (*BALF* 19: 163–66) for its enunciation of such principal elements as ritualization of sexual villainy and symbolization of sacral sexuality, the first of which Baraka views as avoidance of reality, and the second as affirmation in his "psychodrama of erotic turbulence." John Wideman, another author of innovative fiction, should fare well in criticism as the popular reissues of his works during the last year circulate. Meanwhile, there is the treatment of voice and tale in "Going Back Home: The Literary Development of John Edgar Wideman" by James W. Coleman (*CLAJ* 28:326–43), who attributes the recent use of stream of consciousness and development of a family history to Wideman's need to find a sustaining myth to overcome the sterility of the world he presented in *The Lynchers* (1973); and Jacqueline Berben's "Beyond Discourse: The Unspoken versus Words in the Fiction of John Edgar Wideman" (*Callaloo* 8:525–34) that describes the network of psychological and verbal subterfuges making the ability to deal with truth and recognition of nonverbal forms of sincerity the tests of success in Wideman's representation of the ghetto.

In her essay "The Wise Witches: Black Women Mentors in the Fiction of Octavia E. Butler" (*Conjuring*, pp. 203–15) Thelma J.

Shinn speculates that Butler writes science fiction because its mytho-poesis grants freedom for imaging of change and ambiguity. More particularly, Shinn discusses the use of female archetypes. Seth Mc-Evoy's *Samuel R. Delany* (Ungar, 1984) might be faulted for critical awkwardness, as it has been in a review by Mary Kay Bray (*BALF* 19:171–72), and given approval for frankness, as it was by Jerome Klinkowitz in last year's *ALS*. In the context of innovative black fiction it deserves attention because Delany's generous help to McEvoy provides the book engaging anecdotes and quotations illuminating the writer's concern with feminism and his experimental projects.

e. **New Women's Writing.** Trying to detect in Paule Marshall's first novel the theme of heritage that marks her later *Praise Song for the Widow*, Eugenia Collier has written "Selina's Journey Home: From Alienation to Unity in Paule Marshall's *Brown Girl, Brownstones*" (*Obsidian* 8 [1982],ii–iii:6–19). There can be no objection to Collier's description of Selina's alienation and the accents of loneliness mark-ing rejection of her father and the negative vision she has of Bajan womanhood, but reading the ending of the novel when Selina pursues her own independent way, disillusioned about white society and re-jecting the help of her immigrant community, as a positive synthesis of heritage and self is questionable. Hortense J. Spillers' "*Chosen Place, Timeless People*: Some Figurations on the New World" (*Con-juring*, pp. 151–75) offers a vocabulary for studying Marshall—that of Kenneth Burke and Roland Barthes—rather than new interpretations of the text. Unloading the freight of design and structure, Spillers ex-plains the socioeconomic matrices generated by a complex system of figuration. The literal matter of language and culture provides sub-stance for Velma Pollard's "Cultural Connections in Paule Marshall's *Praise Song for the Widow*" (*WLWE* 25:285–98). Pollard is confident that Marshall uses linguistic research, but more than that too, to ex-plore what Edward Brathwaite calls the "submarine unity" of the African diaspora. The term applies to the echoing sound of relatives' voices Avey hears in the West Indies, the old man who becomes a link to the gods, like Legba invoked in voodoo, and the distinctly non-Western ritual of cleansing and baptism Avey undergoes. This display of the rich texture of reference in the novel shows how Mar-shall validates Avey's eventual consciousness of African heritage.

The authors of the first book on Toni Morrison are Bessie W. Jones and Audrey L. Vinson, whose volume *The World of Toni Morrison:*

Explorations in Literary Criticism (Dubuque, Iowa: Kendall/Hunt)
consists of nine discrete essays, independently written by one or the
other author, together with an interview of Morrison. Opening the
book after a brief introduction (pp. 1–6) in which she describes the
works as "metaphors of escape which visually and aurally transport
characters out of the confines of reality into freeing ideals," Vinson's
"The Other World of Toni Morrison" (pp. 7–21) discusses the meta-
realism of absurdity and grotesques that graphically represent attitudes and social statements. Jones's "Ironic Use of Fairy Tale Motifs
in *The Bluest Eye*" (pp. 25–34) notes the contrasts between make-
believe and real worlds advanced in Morrison's caricature and parody.
"Vacant Places: Setting in the Novels of Toni Morrison" by Vinson
(pp. 37–46) attempts to develop archetypal patterns of dual worlds,
pitting blacks in *Song of Solomon* against the norms of whites. The
remaining essays focus on individual novels. In its construction
around explication of modes and motifs, its coupling of heavy reference to "classic" Western texts with discussion of the unique circumstances of black American life, and its provision of open-ended study
questions appended to each essay, the book bears the marks of orientation toward a pedagogy of masterpieces that will "mainstream" a
major black writer. Since the essays display a uniformly high level of
intelligence in their readings and have the virtue of concision besides,
they are likely to advance that aim.

Madonne M. Miner's "Lady No Longer Sings the Blues: Rape,
Madness, and Silence in *The Bluest Eye*" (*Conjuring*, pp. 176–91)
also adopts the tactic of legitimating a text through reference to classical parallels and discusses the myths of Philomela and Persephone,
the latter in its redaction by Phyllis Chesler (1973), to show that the
story of Pecola shares with the myths a blueprint of female fate plus
a psychological significance given by Morrison to the importance of
seeing and being seen in identity formation. Victoria Middleton's
look at a life that by deliberate extravagance becomes heroic in "*Sula*:
An Experimental Life" (*CLAJ* 28:367–81) again taps mythology to
represent Sula as Promethean in imaginatively re-creating the world
that tries to restrict her to a submissive female role. "The Scary Face
of the Self: An Analysis of the Character of Sula in Toni Morrison's
Sula" by Naana Banyiwa-Horne (*Sage* 2,i:28–31) agrees that Sula
suprarealistically shows a problematic dimension of the feminine
psyche existing in all people, joining that description to elaboration
on the idea that Sula and Nel are separate faces of the same being, a

Hyde and Jekyll. Josie P. Campbell's "To Sing the Song, To Tell the Tale: A Study of Toni Morrison and Simone Schwarz-Bart" (*CLS* 22:394–412) takes the structural view of myth in the work of Joseph Campbell as the basis for a comparative study of the personal and ethnohistorical dimensions of the journeys to self-discovery in *Song of Solomon, Tar Baby*, and two novels of the Guadeloupe writer. Such motifs as orphanage, naming, and flight together with images of cosmic and natural reality embedded in the narrative are the shared features of the texts.

Because of past literary politics, one becomes uneasy with the eagerness of critics to "universalize" black literature. For Morrison a corrective is needed, much as it has been required in studies of Ellison before her, to caution critics not to mirror in their interpretations the subjugation of Afro-America that historically has been a practice of the dominant Euro-American culture. The best critical theory noted in these annual reports provides suggestive direction, and for the case of Morrison "Recitation to the Griot: Storytelling and Learning in Toni Morrison's *Song of Solomon*" by Joseph T. Skerrett, Jr. (*Conjuring*, pp. 192–202), gives the model for practical criticism. Declaring that images of folk processes informing Afro-American life, especially images of folk communication, characterize Morrison's work, Skerrett shows how stories and storytelling through the agency of Pilate, a literary descendant from Hurston and Ellison, envelop Milkman and pose the riddle of the song whose solution requires his reentry into the folk world. The dramatic ending of the novel and the trope for Morrison's art, thus, occurs when Milkman gives the retrieved song to Pilate in a recitation completing the lessons of his griot. Valerie Smith's "The Quest for and Discovery of Identity in Toni Morrison's *Song of Solomon*" (*SoR* 21:721–32), excellent in its own right, complements Skerrett's essay by demonstrating the centrality of linguistic community in all of Morrison's fiction to the questions posed about personal alienation, scapegoating, and group membership; therefore as Milkman binds familial to personal history in present life he shows that "assuming identity is . . . a communal gesture."

Narratology, introduced as a method for investigation of black literature in the essays by Wideman on Chestnutt and Fabre on Ellison, takes center stage in Chiara Spallino's "*Song of Solomon*: An Adventure in Structure" (*Calaloo* 8:510–24) where the methodology of Vladimir Propp, Gérard Genette, and also Northrop Frye are given a virtuoso performance. The schematic identifying 35 kernels of fable and the diagrams of the two parts of the narrative distinguish a discourse of the past (other people's time) from the narration of Milkman's time and show how the components of the mythic are gradually foregrounded. If narratology becomes more common in black criticism, the issue of the startling ahistoricism of its abstract schemes will have to be faced (is this "universalism" with a new face?), but for now it can be appreciated for the rigor of its premise that meaning and reality are artful constructions by communities of audience and author.

The best-expressed generalizing statement on Morrison for the year is Linda W. Wagner's "Toni Morrison: Master of Narrative" (*Contemporary American Women Writers*, pp. 191–205). Wagner's evaluative thesis maintains that Morrison's "inspired self-consciousness" effectively nullifies any sense of the "anxiety of authorship" we have recently learned to associate with women writers in the male commercial publishing world. In support, Wagner singles out in each of the four novels elements of craft and structure—all of them insightfully and soundly described—showing Morrison's writing confidently entering new arenas with every publication.

In "Black Matrilineage: The Case of Alice Walker and Zora Neale Hurston" (*Signs* 11:4–26) Dianne F. Sadoff also takes up Sandra M. Gilbert and Susan Gubar's concept of the "anxiety of authorship" along with Harold Bloom's "anxiety of influence." As Gilbert and Gubar revised Bloom's idea to account for women's alienation from the male canon, Sadoff proposes to recast the theory to account for black women's greater need for matrilineage and their simultaneous tendency to suppress their ambivalence about it. In Walker she finds a virtual invention of Hurston intended to validate her own enterprise, yet an ambivalence about using the South in her fiction that appears to rewrite Hurston's anxiety about separation from a rural past. Sadoff's lengthy consideration of Hurston's writings provides a wealth of data about ambiguous self-representation in *Dust Tracks on a Road* and the covering over of subversive rage at males in *Their Eyes Were Watching God*. The latter point she finds repeated by Walker in *The Color Purple*. Though she does not pursue matrilineage into other writers, Sadoff presumably disagrees with Wagner's thesis on Morrison, for she suggests that her investigation gives reason to test the idea of an anxiety-free matrilineage on such a text as *Sula*. Alma S. Freeman's interest in writers' relationships in

"Zora Neale Hurston and Alice Walker: A Spiritual Kinship" (*Sage* 2,i:37–40) concentrates on textual congruity, such as the insertion of voodoo practice from *Mules and Men* in Walker's "The Revenge of Hannah Kembuss," and similarities between the characters of Janie Crawford and Meridian Hill. Susan Willis relates Walker's use of anecdotes as basic narrative units to the effort to create a viable literary language, but "Alice Walker's Women" (*NOR* 12:33–41) is devoted mostly to exposition of antitheses between autonomous self-hood and the demands of bourgeois class interests manifest in the academic community of *Meridian* and the pressures of sexism and racism evident in all of Walker's works. A return to the people is the imperative for female growth in Walker's work as it is throughout the black female tradition. "Alice Walker's Celebration of Self in Southern Generations" by Thadious M. Davis (*Women Writers of the Contemporary South,* pp. 39–53) rounds out the idea of generational continuity in black women's writing by discussing Walker's evident sympathy for the older women who carry the legacy of survival and the weight she gives to the issue of familial identity.

In the course of her argument Willis mentions that *The Color Purple* suggests what a nonsexist, nonracist society might be like. Frank W. Shelton's "Alienation and Integration in Alice Walker's *The Color Purple*" (*CLAJ* 28:382–92) is a full treatment of the utopian moment envisioned by that novel's picture of the emergence of disalienated relationships between the sexes, among women, between people and nature, and people and God. "*The Color Purple*: Revisions and *Redefinitions*" by Mae G. Henderson (*Sage* 2,i:14–18) offers a discussion of how such community is accomplished by Celie through writing that becomes the means of structuring her identity. The importance given to writing attests both to the search for power through literacy underlying Afro-American writing since slave narratives and the functional importance of the epistolary genre traditionally associated with women's writing. Elizabeth Fifer elaborates the latter point in "The Dialect and Letters of *The Color Purple*" (*Contemporary American Women Writers,* pp. 155–65) where she explores the function of dialect as a literary mask controlling the reader's response and revealing the power to create reality as Celie's letters progress from simple reports to extended scenarios. Fifer maintains that Walker's epistolary technique embodies the rise of a feminist consciousness, but surely Henderson's suggestion that the broader

impulse to empowerment through literacy must also be recalled so
that the book can be fully historicized.

"Patches: Quilts and Community in Alice Walker's 'Everyday
Use' " by Houston A. Baker, Jr., and Charlotte Pierce-Baker (*SoR* 21:
706–20) tells us that the patchwork quilt as a European female
tradition transmuted into black women's folk art is "a signal instance
of a patterned wholeness in the African diaspora," a vernacular representation as it were of lives conducted in the margins. So quilts as a
sign of communal bonding open a fascinating interpretive window,
which the Bakers peer through to see a story of conflict over the value
of heritage privileging a woman's craft as a mode of confronting
chaos. That Walker sees quiltmaking as a model of her own craft
can be seen in other criticism, such as Barbara Christian's essay on
the artist as wayward (*ALS 1981*). That sewing continues to image
human bonding for Walker can be proved by *The Color Purple*.

f. General Criticism of Fiction. Among the articles in a special issue
of *Sage* on women's writings are Bell Hooks's "Black Women Writing:
Creating More Space" (2,i:44–46), which presents a black development of Virginia Woolf's famous remarks; and "Mothering and Healing in Recent Black Women's Fiction" by Carole Boyce Davies (2,i:
41–43), who adds detail to the observation of women writers' concern
with community by noting instances of healers who mother characters
to whom they are not biologically related.

Chikwenye Okonjo Ogunyemi's "Womanism: The Dynamics of
the Contemporary Black Female Novel in English" (*Signs* 11:63–80)
centers the difference between black feminism and white upon the
fact that in the white world patriarchy relates to world power while
in the black world it is more a domestic matter since white patriarchy
is the ultimate oppressor. In support of the argument Ogunyemi
cites examples of the hostility seen in black women's portrayal of
white women, a response in part to white women terming their condition slavery and espousing as classics of liberation such works as
Jane Eyre in which female triumph is expressly white.

Drawing upon his work assembling the collection of black literature by writers associated with New England, Edward Clark writes
"Boston Black and White: The Voice of Fiction" (*BALF* 19:83–89).
Amply descriptive of the racially distinct cities of Boston appearing
in seven novels by black writers, Clark's essay uses the dichotomy to

show the illusory appeal of the white side of the city, the security characters find in the black region, and the conflicts between the two ways of life in works published from 1900 to 1971.

iv. Poetry

a. **Foundations.** Klaus Ensslen sets "The Status of Black Poetry from 1865 to 1914" (*American Poetry*, pp. 136–68) against the background of the nostalgic Plantation Tradition and the buffoonery of minstrel shows that monopolized popular imagery of blacks in the later 19th century. On this uncertain literary ground many poets continued to write in the vein of polemical protest shaped by abolitionism or embodied didacticism in stately romantic verse. By Ensslen's evaluation the inability of these poets to come to terms with the conditions of a national literary audience and market is associated with their detachment from black oral literature. So the field was open to Paul Laurence Dunbar who first among blacks found it possible to consider himself a professional poet and whose career, therefore, gave him scope to clarify the issues of standard and dialect language, audience, and the function of black poetry. This is not to say Ensslen believes Dunbar resolved the issues, for he sees contention not fusion in Dunbar's two strands of standard English and dialect verse, with the first marked by technical versatility but also a patchwork of conventions, abstractions, and personal perspective, while it is in dialect that Dunbar concretely realizes his own code of dramatized gestures. The judgment concurs with other Dunbar criticism, such as Peter Revell's TUSAS volume (*ALS 1979*), but one doesn't look for dispute on that point any more than one expects treatment of Dunbar's works apart from their historical context. The attraction of Ensslen's study, then, lies not in novelty but in its development of a view of Dunbar's poetry as a system partly defensive, partly celebratory of black life, and partly composed of self-referential imagery.

The rapprochement of poetry and the style of popular performance that Ensslen sees in Dunbar has its 20th-century breakthrough in the period of the New Negro and the prolific output of blues poetry by Langston Hughes, paralleled almost immediately by Sterling A. Brown's adaptation of song forms and naturalized dialect, and later manifest in the performance poems of the Black Arts poets. The apparent ease of Hughes's writing, and possibly its mass also, have led to perfunctory commentary on his genius and criticism limited to the play of techniques in individual poems. If the preview of Arnold Rampersad's forthcoming biography in "The Origins of Poetry in Langston Hughes" (*SoR* 21:695–705) is a fair sample, that situation should soon be changed. Posing the question of how an aspiring author of verses becomes a poet, which happened for Hughes in "The Negro Speaks of Rivers" as it had for Keats with "On First Looking into Chapman's Homer," Rampersad imaginatively extracts a psychological drama from two well-known incidents of illness Hughes describes in his autobiography, one associated with the visit to his father in Mexico in 1919, the other developing as he was banished 11 years later by the patron he called "Godmother." These events were a challenge to the childlike self and amorphous poetic consciousness Hughes considered his authentic self. Contending with the challenges, Hughes drew upon a depth of commitment to blacks, thereby evoking defensive will and energizing his poetic consciousness with the materials for concrete art. The interpretation is plausible, but definitiveness is less important than the fact that Rampersad constructs a gateway to Hughes's interior life that promises to found criticism on a full portrayal of the poet's experience. Aaron D. Gresson's "Beyond Selves Deferred: Langston Hughes' Style and Psychology of Black Selfhood" (*LHRev* 4:47–54) sees the poet resisting narcissism while appraising the problem of the self and the collective. The point relates to Rampersad's suggestive biographical outline, as does Sherley Anne Williams' notation of an overly critical outlook toward his peers in "Langston Hughes and the Negro Renaissance" (*LHRev* 4: 37–39).

Steppingstones, a still irregularly published journal, alternates its literary issues with special tributes including one dated Winter 1984 on Langston Hughes. Among the testimonial poetry and prose are two critical essays. One by James L. de Jongh, "Langston Hughes and the Motif of Black Harlem in Africana Poetry" (pp. 33–44), neatly describes the legendary landscape of Harlem portending the authority of black cultural assertion for all of the 20th-century literary movements of the diaspora and credits Hughes with responsibility for much of its mythic power as well as effective resolution of the duality between the abstract vision of soul and actuality in works like "Jazzonia" by use of the pattern of call-and-response. Though the creative tension collapsed in Hughes's work of the 1940s, Francophone and Lusophone poets inspired by his example sustained his vision, and Hughes himself later restored the imagistic credibility of Harlem to such effect that it became prophetic for Afro-American poets of the 1960s. The second critical contribution, Vaughana Macy's "The Politics and Poetry of Langston Hughes's Last Work: *The Panther and the Lash*" (pp. 63–72), recounts conflicting reviews and seeks to clarify Hughes's purpose by showing how he revives the Marxist politics of his earlier poetry and address to the American Writers Congress in 1935. The Fall issue of *LHRev* amplifies the international perspective on Hughes with an essay on his translations and several on appearances of his work in other languages. "And Bid Him Translate: Langston Hughes' Translations of Poetry from French" by Alfred J. Guillaume, Jr. (4:1–8), describes the 13 translations, reprinted side by side with their originals (4:9–23) as approximate imitations sometimes insufficiently accurate. The remaining papers discuss translation of Hughes by other hands and include Harry Jones's "Simple Speaks Danish" (4:24–26) on the effect of dialect in conveying cultural outlook; Reginald Kearney's "Langston Hughes in Japanese Translation" (4:27–29) about the problems encountered in making Hughes available to Japanese readers who are acquainted with their nation's meticulous scholarship on Hughes; and Soi-Daniel W. Brown's "'Black Orpheus': Langston Hughes' Reception in German Translation (An Overview)" (4:30–38).

Joanne V. Gabbin had a major job of work cut out for her in writing the first full-length study of an author who pioneered a major development in black poetry, laid a foundation for criticism with some of the earliest surveys and discussions of black creativity in American life, and continues to this day to be an important influence in the community of black writing. Titled *Sterling A. Brown: Building the Black Aesthetic Tradition* (Greenwood), Gabbin's book covers it all in a first-rate way. Portraying Brown biographically as the product of a proud, accomplished black middle-class milieu, she traces a career of involvement with other black academicians whose accomplishments Brown matched by designing a study of literature, in published books and reviews, that shows the treatment of blacks in literature. Recognizing that Brown might best be characterized as the founder of Afro-American modernism, Gabbin studies the black vernacular traditions and Anglo-American materials he mined for his distinctive "portraitures" and poetic diction. With its analysis of Brown's artful syntheses and its incorporation of prior scholarship Gabbin's book becomes an indispensable source.

b. **Black Modernists.** Robert M. Farnsworth caps the research already responsible for an edition of *A Gallery of Harlem Portraits* (*ALS 1979*) and a collection of the "Caviar and Cabbage" columns (*ALS 1982*) with a full-length biography, *Melvin B. Tolson, 1898– 1966: Plain Talk and Poetic Prophecy* (Missouri, 1984). Farnsworth's extensive research in primary sources permits him to draw an affecting picture of Tolson's career as a teacher, but since after all the work is a literary biography it centers on such issues as the problem of audience faced by a poet with populist and Marxist convictions who chooses to write in a complex fashion. Consideration of all published and unpublished works along with close readings that elicit evidence, for example, of the reworking of *A Gallery of Harlem Portraits* into *Harlem Gallery* lend substance to discussion of Tolson's manner of writing. The weight of evidence from Tolson's own remarks indicates he conceived his audience running vertically into the future more than horizontally toward all potential readers of the present, and Farnsworth handles reputation, including the exchange of letters between Tolson and Allen Tate leading to Tate's disconcerting preface to *Libretto for the Republic of Liberia*, in well-informed reviews of critical debate that he never hesitates to join. A genuinely critical biography, this work is definitive.

I must again reach back to 1984 to report two books on Robert Hayden. The first of these, Fred M. Fetrow's *Robert Hayden* (TUSAS 471), skillfully handles technical features such as the use of voices and line structures in measuring Hayden's success in objectifying feelling, in dramatic qualities, and in the processes of revision. In contrast to many other volumes in the Twayne series which use biography as expository framework, Fetrow's tends to read the poems as further evidence for the biography developed by his series of interviews with Hayden. The second book on Hayden, John Hatcher's *From the Auroral Darkness: The Life and Poetry of Robert Hayden* (Oxford: George Ronald, 1984), was first commissioned by the Association for Studies on the Baha'i Faith, a fact that bears upon Hatcher's detection of a Baha'i concept of history in *Words in the Mourning Time* and his defense of Hayden against charges of downplaying his black identity by citing the principles of abstinence from politics and the expansive vision of brotherhood that are fundamental to the faith Hayden adopted in 1943. Hatcher writes the synopsis of biography in the first part of his book according to a plot of Hayden progressively overcoming the disorientation of his foster parentage, a heavy workload in his teaching career, and the attack he suffered at the Fisk Writers' Conference in 1966 from Tolson and others. Then stressing the continuity of experiment with repeated themes and refinement of the allusive surface of Hayden's poems, he proceeds to a chronological survey, volume by volume, that includes excellent readings. Finally, he presents a study of the shaping of poetic form that will arouse dispute, for while Hatcher reasonably discusses how Hayden distanced himself from the emotion of his poetry and the poems from his personality, in the manner recommended by New Criticism, the place of Afro-American language and identity appears minimally in the account of Hayden's construction of an intricate art of poetic perception and illumination. To be sure, the Baha'i faith has never before Hatcher appeared so integral to Hayden's writing, but in repairing critical omission he creates the need for others to restore the balance. Such recovery of Hayden's Afro-American interest will be helped by Reginald Gibbons' "Robert Hayden in the 1940s" (*TriQ* 62:177–86), which introduces and publishes for the first time three untitled poems from *The Black Spear* (1942) treating racial discrimination, and Fritz Oehlschlaeger's "Robert Hayden's Meditations on Art: The Final Sequence of *Words in the Mourning Time*" (*BALF* 19:115–19), which considers the poet's use of allusion and imagery to contemplate the value of art in a period that saw the deaths of Martin Luther King, Jr., and Robert Kennedy.

c. **Black Arts Poets, Contemporaries, and Postmodernists.** Following the format of testimonials to deceased contemporaries, the issue of *Callaloo* edited by Kimberly W. Benston on Larry Neal includes, besides pieces noted elsewhere in this report, an editorial introduction (8:5–7) noting Neal's instigation of publications and attributing his influence to a "capacity to materialize his theoretic arguments in sudden myth"; a notable interview with Neal conducted by Charles H. Rowell in 1974; examples of Neal's creative writing; appraisals and recollections including one by his collaborator Amiri Baraka (8:248–56), who calls Neal the spiritual leader of their movement. Among the critical statements, Stephen E. Henderson's essay "Take Two—Larry Neal and the Blues God: Aspects of the Poetry" (8:215–39) is notably comprehensive. Writing out of deep knowledge of the Black Arts Movement and acute sensitivity to the patterns of black poetry, Henderson explores the techniques and structures of *Black Boogaloo* and the self-conscious revisions Neal made in the poems that "cross over" into the second volume, *Hoodoo Hollerin' Bebop Ghosts*. The result is a lucid treatment of evolving poetics and practice substantiating the claim that such a poem as "Don't Say Goodbye to the Porkpie Hat" reprinted in the special issue represents a major conceptualization and "quantum jump in the ideology and iconography of Afro-American cultural history."

Taking as his subject a poet who has been given some of the most intelligent as well as purblind criticism, William J. Harris in *The Poetry and Poetics of Amiri Baraka: The Jazz Aesthetic* (Missouri) gives an authoritative exposition of the sources and literary consequences of positions adopted by Baraka in the 1960s and traces his relationship to literary milieu with sensible recognition that dispositions and ideas are mediated for a poet by technical choices. In previous criticism Lloyd W. Brown explains Baraka by his antipathy to the mainstream (*ALS 1980*) and W. D. E. Andrews sees his poetic practice growing from historical and psychological experience (*ALS 1982*). Harris takes the tack of showing how Baraka learned to write and think about poetry from the examples of projectivism and William Carlos Williams' orality, but learned from jazz how to transform and "signify" on his influences, in effect committing parricide to make room for a black writing. Beyond this explanatory scheme Harris' analyses of jazzified poetry offer suggestive directions for reading Baraka. He notes, for example, not only the kinship of Baraka's achieved oral style to the performances of James Brown but also warns that the "I" of the poems is not so much a persona as a person in the poems and that surrealism amounts to a way of magnifying reality to create sociopolitical allegories. In the end, Harris' thesis comes down to declaration that Baraka had to re-create himself as an engaged, black poet when he discerned that the postmoderns failed to mount a truly radical ethical or political challenge to the racial status quo. Given the evidence Harris summons, his thesis is likely to prevail.

Amiri Baraka: The Kaleidoscopic Torch, an unnumbered *Steppingstones* tribute issued in 1985, includes a section of Harris' book and five items pertaining to critical interpretation of Baraka's poetic writing. "Aesthetic Theory: Imamu Amiri Baraka" by Norris B. Clark (pp. 41–60) rightly claims that controversy over the poems since *Target Study* centers on racial and political content rather than the techniques which are alterations of Baraka's avant-garde conventions of the 1950s designed to support a shift from egocentric to ethnocentric content. Entering the controversy himself, Clark judges the newer poems failures on several counts, the most damning of which are that Marxism-Leninism is simply not germane to most black Americans and Baraka's antithesis of European and African culture does not acknowledge the syncretic forms emergent in Afro-America. In the end, Clark's appraisal reverts to the dogmatic manner he originally censures. Conventional views about engaged writing are the object of Joe Weixlmann's scorn in "Critics' Jaws, Genres' Bellies, and Amiri Baraka" (pp. 176–81), an essay dissecting the biases in the "academically stylish putdowns" evident in reviews of Baraka's work by Darryl Pinckney and Henry Louis Gates along with the dismissal of later writings in Henry C. Lacey's book on Baraka (*ALS 1981*). For his part, Khaliquzzaman Elias in "Amiri Baraka: The Poet of Action" (pp. 61–74) enthusiastically endorses the practice of open propaganda and adjudges Baraka realistic and politically sound in his calls for a new political party and eventual repudiation of the mystic implications of a racially based program. "Theme and Variations: The Early Poetics of Amiri Baraka and Jay Wright" by A. L. Nielsen (pp. 116–26) limns the conjunctions and variety of black postmodernism in his analysis of the intertextual relationships of Wright's "Variations on a Theme by LeRoi Jones" to "Way Out West" and "A Poem for Willie Best." Finally, Arnold Rampersad brings to bear his biographical research in "Amiri Baraka and Langston Hughes" (pp. 135–43) to relate the story of succession emplotted by personal admiration between two poets devoted to the people's culture and incidents of disagreement about the content of nationalism.

Priscilla R. Ramsey's "Transcendence: The Poetry of Maya Angelou" (*Current Bibliography on African Affairs* 17,ii:139–53) likens the poetry to Angelou's continuing autobiography in its glorification of life and sensuality as a fortress against despair. Reading political poems for irony, self-defining ones for their adaptation of a collective "I," and love poems for intimate confession, Ramsey shows Angelou to be a practitioner in the full range of contemporary black verse and herself a critic with a keen eye for the psychodynamics of verse.

d. General Criticism of Poetry.   Calvin Hernton's "The Tradition" (*Parnassus* 13:518–50) is a long review-article meriting notice as a model for explaining and judging black women's poetry in relation to the experience of a community of writers. Quoting generously from Toi Derricotte, Brenda Osbey, Thulani Davis, Colleen McElroy, Cheryl Clarke, and Rita Dove—all of them representative of a new generation of poets—Hernton places their practice against the ground of oral poetics reaching in tradition back through the writing of Georgia Douglas Johnson and Gwendolyn Bennett to Sojourner Truth and Frances Watkins Harper, while illustrating their diversification in dealing with elements of women's lives in women's terms. Expressing high appreciation of the humanism he sees in these poets, Hernton makes a case not just broadly but with the detail that invites readers of the review to go beyond it and read the poems.

v. Drama

Aside from Mance Williams' book on new black theater, noted as a contribution to literary history in this report, publications on drama did not bulk large in 1985. William J. Mahar touches on the subject by using printed stage texts to argue in "Black English in Early Blackface Minstrelsy: A New Interpretation of the Sources of Minstrel Show Dialect" (*AQ* 37:260–85) that for at least the first 40 years the stage dialect of Negro impersonators was taken from either Black English Vernacular, West African Pidgin English, or Plantation Creole. Adding that a blackface foil represented a means for criticizing white society, he also claims that the shows were more than racially oriented entertainment.

Doris E. Abramson looks at works written by black authors in the early 20th century in "Angelina Weld Grimke, Mary T. Burrill, Georgia Douglas Johnson, and Marita O. Bonner: An Analysis of Their Plays" (*Sage* 2,i:9–13) to indicate the themes of these middle-class writers. Grimke's *Rachel*, a propaganda play on refusal of motherhood as response to a world of prejudice, was the only one produced on stage. The others, also didactic works, on such matters as birth control, poverty, and in Bonner's case an allegory of revolution against white devils, appeared in magazines.

Anthony Barthelemy uses "Mother, Sister, Wife: A Dramatic Perspective" (*SoR* 21:770–89) to relate an intertextual debate on the characterization of women. Initiated by Theodore Ward's presentation of his hero in *Big White Fog* (1938) surrounded by flawed females, the debate was joined by Lorraine Hansberry's representation of strong, positive females moving toward bourgeois America rather than Ward's socialism in *Raisin in the Sun* (1959), a work displaying similarities to Ward's play in structure and plot. Again employing plot similarities, Joseph Walker's *The River Niger* (1973) revises Hansberry with a revolutionary lesson directed toward males alone, while women are shown strong only when men need them to be. Commenting on gender portrayal, Steven R. Carter's "Images of Men in Lorraine Hansberry's Writing" (*BALF* 19:160–62) draws attention to the attractive figure of Walter Lee Younger, Jr., in *Raisin* and moderate instances of male chauvinism in other plays that Carter sees as more effective feminism than if the males were total villains.

"Larry Neal/The Genesis of Vision" by the playwright Paul Carter Harrison (*Callaloo* 8:170–94) comments on Neal's *The Glorious Monster in the Belly of the Horn* published in the same issue (pp. 87–169). Harrison re-creates the circumstances of the play in the black world of art, labels it an authentic, that is, hip rather than hep creation of theater, and explicates the work. The detail of Harrison's discussion of aesthetics and dramaturgy does not lend itself readily to summary, but don't let the generality of my notice of his essay forestall careful reading of the essay for the insights of a practiced inventor of black drama. "Ghosts, Monsters, and Magic: The Ritual Drama of Larry Neal" by Mae G. Henderson (*Callaloo* 8:195–214) can be more easily described as a study of Neal's conjoining of Western and non-Western elements to shape an Afro-American cosmology, specifically in adaptation of the African belief that the dead are spiritual forces influencing the living. The cosmology informs *Glorious Monster's* demonstration of the restorative powers of community, while Neal's *In an Upstate Motel* deploys Dantesque imagery and a theme of entrapment echoing Sartre's *No Exit* to show the destruction awaiting individuals severed from the black community.

E. San Juan, Jr.'s "Amiri Baraka, Revolutionary Playwright" (*Steppingstones*, pp. 151–56) offers a gloss on *What Was the Role of the Lone Ranger to the Means of Production?* explaining the structure of polarized characters and giving a political explication in terms of materialist class analysis.

vi. Slave Narratives and Autobiography

The expanding use of slave narratives in literary studies has been signaled in recent years by the appearance of articles applying a variety of methods to describe the interpretive power of writing by fugitive and ex-slaves and by the publication of a collection of original essays edited by John Sekora and Darwin T. Turner (*ALS 1983*). Adding to the body of work in 1985, *The Slave's Narrative*, eds. Charles T. Davis and Henry Louis Gates, Jr., provides a sample of 10 contemporary reviews published between 1750 and 1861 and includes newly published studies among the seven discussions of slave narratives as history and eight essays of literary criticism. The bibliographies of 106 book-length narratives from 1760 to 1865 and 35 "Narratives of African Muslims in Antebellum America," the latter compiled by Allan Austin, complement the checklist of criticism prepared by Gregory S. Sojka for the Sekora-Turner volume. Acknowledging the principle that led historians of black America to pioneer in the use of slave narratives, Davis and Gates argue in their introduction, "The Language of Slavery" (pp. xi–xxxiv), that the narratives have identical documentary value as other accounts of slavery. Beyond that, as products of narrators who write themselves into being, they first express the motive of black literature.

Although the essays by Paul Edwards and Susan Willis are beyond the coverage of this survey, because their subjects are texts written in England and Cuba rather than on the North American continent, their analyses have a methodological value that should not be overlooked. In the case of Edwards' "Three West African Writers of the 1780s" (*The Slave's Narrative*, pp. 175–98) the contribution lies in intelligent apprehension of the authenticity of texts. The contribution by Willis entitled "Crushed Geraniums: Juan Francisco Manzano and the Language of Slavery" (*The Slave's Narrative*, pp. 199–224) elaborates the apparently obvious principle that the position of the narrator is the key to understanding the narrative into a useful interpretive framework by investigating the perspectives resulting from authors' movement into modes of free labor, use of Christian concepts, and adoption of abolitionist purpose. Similarly, Wilfred D. Samuels in "Disguised Voice in *The Interesting Narrative of Olaudah Equiano, or Gustavus Vassa, The African*" (*BALF* 19:64–69) provides an object lesson in skilled interpretation by using the tools of hermeneutics to discern an implied characterization of the self.

Study of North American slave narrators continues to emphasize Frederick Douglass to very good ends. C. Peter Ripley's "The Autobiographical Writings of Frederick Douglass" (*SoSt* 24:5–29) uses published correspondence and reviews to relate the debate about credentials surrounding publication of the 1845 narrative, the split between Douglass and the Garrisonians that becomes evident with the 1855 autobiography, and Douglass' experiences with publishers and reviewers as he wrote the 1881 life story with an eye to posterity. John Sekora in "Comprehending Slavery: Language and Personal History in Douglass' *Narrative* of 1845" (*CLAJ* 29:157–70) takes up such contextual details to argue that because the personal history of slavery was written at the intersection of abolitionists' and proslavery agents' efforts to define Douglass, the book is not so much a black recollection engaging memory, that is, a true autobiography, but a form resulting as Douglass negotiated against his sponsors' prescriptions for control of his text. Focusing on one of the consequences, "Reconciling Public and Private in Frederick Douglass' *Narrative*" (*AL* 57:549–69) by Donald B. Gibson studies the balance of unique individual experience and a public perspective stressing representative qualities. Gibson seeks evidence of the strategy both in localized style and overall structure, a procedure that yields an excellent reading that reveals, for example, the theme of controlled aggression in the crucial scene with Covey. Bernd Ostendorf's "Violence and Freedom: The Covey Episode in Frederick Douglass' Autobiography" (*Mythos und Aufklärung*, pp. 257–70) concurs with Gibson's analysis in seeing the *Narrative* as an odyssey of consciousness with the Covey episode as its paradigmatic core but in doing so stresses the witness to violence that turns life writing into testimony about the structural violence of slavery and the instrumental violence recommended for political opposition to slavery.

In *The Mind of Frederick Douglass* (No. Car., 1984) Waldo E. Martin, Jr., solves the problem of writing an intellectual biography of a man whose ideas he characterizes as more often representative than original by shaping the results of primary source research into a narrative that uses the framework of psychological interpretation to vivify the significance his ideas held for Douglass and employs a detailed, lively writing style to reanimate the debates that were crucial to him as a man, leader, and ex-slave. Originally a dissertation evidently designed not to supplant but to supplement previous biographies, Martin's book shows Douglass responding to the familiar influences of Protestantism, the Enlightenment, and Romanticism with a philosophy of social reform that needed revolutionary structural changes to achieve its goals of equality and freedom but rested content with the liberalism Douglass shared with many of his contemporaries.

While Esther Terry's main purpose in "Sojourner Truth and Frederick Douglass in Florence, Massachusetts" (*MR* 26:425–44) is to describe Truth apart from the symbol she became for Harriet Beecher Stowe as The Libyan Sibyl, she also adds insight into Douglass' mind by recounting his uneasiness about her and reprinting his "What I Found at the Northampton Association," which describes Truth as "a genuine specimen of the uncultured negro." As for Truth herself, Terry relates her life in New Paltz, New York, and the subsequent calling that led her to become a "God-inspired party" working with religious force and conviction from her home at the utopian socialist community in Florence. L. H. Whelchel, Jr., treats another contemporary in *My Chains Fell Off: William Wells Brown, Fugitive Abolitionist* (Univ. Press). A summary rather than a work in interpretation, the book draws on published primary and secondary sources to present the arguments Brown used in his writings to correct impressions of black inferiority.

Minrose C. Gwin's "Green-Eyed Monsters of the Slaveocrary: Jealous Mistresses in Two Slave Narratives" (*Conjuring*, pp. 39–52) expands the discussion of her book on "the peculiar sisterhood" to a consideration of sexual rivalry and the inversion of the convention of True Womanhood that marks descriptions of slave mistresses by Harriet Jacobs and Elizabeth Keckley. Frances Smith Foster in "Adding Color and Contour to Early American Self-Portraiture: Autobiographical Writings of Afro-American Women" (*Conjuring*, pp. 25–38) reminds us that not all black writers of the 19th century were slaves or southern, and in illustration of their diversity discusses the spiritual autobiography of Jarena Lee, the travel writing of Mrs. Nancy Prince, and the autobiographical novel by Harriet Wilson, *Our Nig*. According to Foster, the selves in these writings are uniquely individualized, varying significantly from the two-dimensional women of slave narratives and the conventionalized "True Woman" of romances.

Still, the slave narratives retain priority as a source for literary tradition. Charles H. Nichols gives his account of its production by attending to the formation of genre in "The Slave Narrators and the Picaresque Mode: Archetypes for Modern Black Personae" (*The Slave's Narrative*, pp. 283–98). Nichols identifies the triumph of victims behind a mask the corrupt society forces them to adapt as the dominant trait of the genre. The double vision and the stratagems for survival that constitute its leitmotifs remain durable in later black life writings such as *Black Boy* and carry over into increasingly complex fictional constructions. The larger culture of which literature forms a part occupies Melvin Dixon whose "Singing Swords: The Literary Legacy of Slavery" (*The Slave's Narrative*, pp. 298–317) sees the Bible as a store of myth and history available to syncretism as the slaves established "an active contemporary apocalypse in the realm of their own daily experience." By this account, Christianity was less a matter of belief than an instrument of communication whose images of pilgrimage and conversion afforded philosophical tenets of mobility with which the slaves constructed a culture for progression into freedom.

Though the interviews with former slaves conducted by WPA workers in the 1930s have so far proved of more interest to historians than to students of written texts, this wealth of material deserves the attention of critics and literary historians because of its intrinsic interest as storytelling and for the entry it offers to culture. Perhaps notice of three essays here will help encourage broader attention. Sterling A. Brown wrote his memorandum "On Dialect Usage" (*The Slave's Narrative*, pp. 37–39) in 1936 to proscribe editorializing, "artistic" introductions, and racist terminology employed by white interviewers. In the course of declaring that truth to idiom is more important to capture than pronunciation Brown also tells us something about literary rendition of dialect. Paul D. Escott, who analyzed 2,500 interviews for his *Slavery Remembered*, tells us in "The Art and Science of Reading WPA Slave Narratives" (*The Slave's Narrative*, pp. 40–48) how formality of address and racial etiquette can be used to measure rapport between interviewers and informants and that quantitative analysis of differences in the objective conditions of slavery has led him to see that class divisions in the slave community were overshadowed by a sense of brotherhood. Again there are implications for literature, as there are in Norman R. Yetman's "Ex-Slave Interviews and the Historiography of Slavery" (*AQ* 36[1984]:181–210) that recounts the process of collecting interviews and, in assessing their value to recent slavery studies, shows how they have encouraged recognition of the creativity of slave culture.

Report of the study of 20th-century autobiography must stress the edition by Gloria T. Hull of *Give Us Each Day: The Diary of Alice Dunbar-Nelson* (Norton, 1984). An active writer even though she failed to get a novel published and could not produce screenplays that suited the studios, Dunbar-Nelson kept her diary during a 10-year period when her life was in flux. Hull's editorial apparatus includes an outline of the life, a description of manuscripts, notes explaining lapses in the entries, and illuminating discussion of what the diary reveals about the life and society of its well-connected author. All in all a very fine job and a useful source of information about a circle of middle-class black women deserving historical attention.

Four of this year's articles on *Black Boy* are written against the background of prevailing interpretations. Yoshinobu Hakutani enters the dialogue in "Creation of the Self in Richard Wright's *Black Boy*" (*BALF* 19:70–75) by contending with critics who find the autobiography too personal and overdrawn. Hakutani responds to the charge by arguing that the sentiments expressed as young Wright's are not totally his own but represent the voiceless boys of the South describing their environment in a book that also contains a second story of precocity and innate rebellion refuting the impression that racism must doom its objects. "An Apprenticeship to Life and Art: Narrative Design in Wright's *Black Boy*" by John O. Hodges (*CLAJ* 38:415–33) characterizes Wright's structure as a journey from innocence to experience proceeding through sections devoted to the household, the black community, and the white world with the whole narrative related in the distinct voices of a young Wright experiencing and a mature Wright interpreting events. The objective of Wright's design, Hodges says, is to retrace his own steps for self-understanding and to pronounce judgment on southern white society. With the latter purpose Hodges also addresses Wright's alleged isolation and agrees with Hakutani that there is an attempt to achieve closer identification with the voiceless. In "I Do Believe Him Though I Know He Lies: Lying as Genre and Metaphor in Richard Wright's *Black Boy*" (*PSt* 8:172–87) Timothy Dow Adams advances the familiar premise that the book is an imaginative creation in order to argue that the whole work is marked by a repeated pattern of misrepresentation designed to advance Wright's theme that his environment "conspired to prevent him from hearing the truth, speaking the truth, or even being believed unless he lied." Janice Thaddeus speaks to the mismatch of the conclusion to the body of the narrative in "The Metamorphosis of Richard Wright's *Black Boy*" (*AL* 57:199–214). She frames her discussion with an interesting distinction between a defined autobiography such as Frederick Douglass' that moves to a plateau and an open autobiography that continues searching, but in explaining the incongruity of the six-page conclusion that briefly changes *Black Boy* from open to defined she has nothing new to add by way of explanation. The fifth article relating to Wright, Linda Peterson's "Repetition and Metaphor in the Early Stages of Composing" (*CCC* 36:429–43), takes the seven drafts he made in composing an interview statement on *Black Boy* to illustrate the difference between generative stages in which the writer attempts to discover thought and the editorial revisions necessary to consolidate it.

Sigmund Ro uses Addison Gayle's "The Son of My Father" and Amiri Baraka's "Heretics" in "The 'Negro to Black Conversion' in Contemporary Afro-American Autobiography" (*Rage and Celebration*, pp. 69–84) in order to illustrate the archetypal motif developed by 1960s writers intent upon projecting their personal stories as moral parables. Yusef A. Salaam's "The Autobiography of LeRoi Jones/ Amiri Baraka" (*Steppingstones*, pp. 145–49) gives special notice to the power of self-criticism that accompanies the themes of racial affiliation and political changes in Baraka's recently published life story. Going well beyond the summary manner of a reviewer, Clyde Taylor in "Black Culture Is Modern Art, II: *The Autobiography*" (*Steppingstones*, pp. 167–74) perceives the gropings for self-definition of a youth poised in an urban setting between the folk lessons of the slavery past and "gimmick progress." Through hip speech—a variety of modern poetry—and a reading of black musical forms as intense as Marx's reading of economics, Baraka found the codes that became the basis of his sociology; thus, Taylor describes the emergence of the postmodernism that denominates Baraka's place as a major black writer.

State University of New York at Albany

20. Themes, Topics, Criticism

Michael J. Hoffman

The number of books published in 1985 that were relevant to this chapter will not be reflected in the text because my allotted space permits me to write about only half of those sent me for review. That statement suggests, however, just how much activity there now is in theory and its application to American literature. American literary scholarship is indeed a growth industry, which may or may not be a good thing. As usual, the quality of the books was mixed, but enough of value were published to give one confidence about the profession.

I shall continue to use the format established last year, with one minor variation: in the discussion of American literature I shall include those books with a women's studies orientation that deal directly with American texts to reflect the increasing concern among feminist scholars with the history of American literature. The following are, in order, the topics covered by this chapter: American literature, women's studies, modernism, theory of fiction, and literary theory. Within each section I shall treat the books in alphabetical order by author.

i. American Literature

Cleanth Brooks's short book, *The Language of the American South* (Georgia), was first given as the Mercer University Lamar Memorial Lectures (No. 28). An obvious labor of love, it reminds us that Brooks began his career as a student of language. The book clearly displays its origins as a lecture series in its informal tone and in the relative absence of scholarly apparatus. Its three chapters explore the origins of the language ("Where It Came From"); the penchant for educated southerners to use elaborate diction and classical allusions ("The Language of the Gentry and the Folk"); and what the book jacket calls the "earthbound eloquence" of farmers and the folk ("The Language in the Present Day"). A good, well-written introduction to these ma-

terials, it is more impressionistic than analytical, and readers wishing
to explore the subject in depth should look elsewhere.

Chapters from Samuel Chase Coale's *In Hawthorne's Shadow:
American Romance from Melville to Mailer* (Kentucky) will probably
be covered elsewhere, but I should like briefly to mention this modest
book, which studies the tradition in American romance that emanates
from Hawthorne's work. Coale defines the "radical dualism" of Hawthorne in his opening chapter to show how this became a tradition for
American romancers. Some of his authors are Faulkner, Styron, Updike, Cheever, Oates, and Didion, and he includes information obtained through interviews. This useful work contains good readings
of individual novels, but the definition developed does not really advance our theoretical understanding of the American romance.

A collection of Malcolm Cowley's essays and reviews appears in
*The Flower and the Leaf: A Contemporary Record of American Writ-
ing Since 1941* (Viking Penguin), ed. Donald W. Faulkner. Selected
from Cowley's journalism, these pieces focus mostly on major writers
and topics. They do not contain definitive readings, but when read as
a whole, they do provide a good overview of the period. Always literate and rarely partisan, the essays are ordered by topics and, within
the topics, by chronology. Faulkner's introduction is a good retrospective on the latter part of Cowley's career.

One realizes how long Cowley has been around when one reads
James Michael Kempf's *The Early Career of Malcolm Cowley* (LSU),
a biographical study that ends with the 1920s. This highly detailed
book is a good exposition, and, although brief, it seems complete. I
should have preferred to stay with Cowley for a longer period, but
because he is ultimately most important as a representative figure,
the factual knowledge we learn about the period gives us a valuable
context for the literary history of the '20s.

Margo Culley's *One Day at a Time: The Diary Literature of
American Women from 1764 to the Present* (Feminist Press at CUNY)
contains excerpts from the diary literature of "ordinary" American
women of the past three centuries. None of the writers is particularly
well known to literature; the choices are of women with careers and
those who were primarily homemakers, designed to suggest the variety of roles played by American women from many social levels and
geographical regions and to change our awareness of women in our
history. The book has a good introduction and useful scholarly ap-

paratus, including headnotes about each author. Many selections are quite eloquent, and my only complaint is that some are too short.

Another anthology of women's writings is *Provisions: A Reader from 19th-Century American Women* (Indiana), ed. Judith Fetterley and focusing on prose writers between 1830 and 1865. The familiar names of Harriet Beecher Stowe, Lydia Sigourney, and Rebecca Harding Davis are here, along with many others who have become more familiar in recent years but still remain largely unread except by scholars. Many of these were the most popular novelists of their time, more well known in fact than Hawthorne or Melville or Poe. Fetterley's selections are excellent—not only representative, but interesting in and of themselves, and her introduction is thorough and enjoyable, connecting neatly with the major works by Philip Fisher and Jane Tompkins that I shall be discussing shortly as well as with other anthologies also discussed in this section.

In *Hard Facts: Setting and Form in the American Novel* (Oxford) Philip Fisher writes about the popular novel because he believes it is the form that most closely connects the fictional imagination with the hard facts of society. The popular novel more than the "art" novel can deal directly with such hard facts because, as a form for the present, it transforms actuality through the Freudian sequence of "recognition, repetition, and working through" (p. 7). Fisher focuses on three major "popular" authors, none of whom consciously tried to write works of "high art": Cooper, Stowe, and Dreiser.

The hard facts on which Fisher concentrates are these: "the killing of the Indians, which gave a 'clear land' where a 'new world' might be built [*The Pathfinder*]; the slavery that was a moral and rational outrage in a society picturing itself in Jeffersonian terms as a nation of free and independent yeoman farmers [*Uncle Tom's Cabin*]; and, finally, the severe evacuation and objectification of the self that followed from the economic and future-oriented world of capitalism and the city [*Sister Carrie* and *An American Tragedy*]" (p. 5). Each writer intuitively understands the contradictions embodied in society's attempts to deal with these contradictions, and each uses a popular formulaic genre that enables him or her to express the problem. Whether through the historical novel or the sentimental novel, or by combining the bildungsroman with the "novel of society," the "cultural work" of these authors is a "process by which the unimaginable becomes, finally, the obvious. It is the ordinariness of Cooper

and Stowe and Dreiser that permits them a transforming power unavailable to the 'genius' of Melville, Dickinson, or James who, for all
of their extraordinary and dense *uniqueness*, were unable to bring
about the work of the cultural present" (p. 8). We usually consider
the makers of high art to be the ones who most engage the present,
and it is disconcerting to read an assertion that the opposite is true.
I find it intriguing to contemplate such a deconstructive reversal,
and I find much merit in it. But I think it misses the point about Melville, Dickinson, and James, whose symbolic techniques may well explore the present even more profoundly—though indirectly.

Nonetheless, Fisher does make it possible for us to read "popular"
authors with a seriousness that was not always possible during a
time of high modernist consciousness and an accompanying criticism
that responded primarily to stylistic tropes rather than larger rhetorical forms. As Fisher points out, the intention of these authors is the
opposite of the " 'defamiliarization' or 'estrangement' that the Russian formalist Shklovsky proposed as the central act of culture. Making familiar or making ordinary is the radical 'work' done by popular
forms" (p. 19). Fisher proposes many suggestive insights, such as how
conventions of sentimentality make us feel the moral proposition of
Uncle Tom's Cabin more powerfully, and how such novels become
"anti-ironic in exactly the degree that the modern ironic form is anti-
sentimental" (p. 99). Or how there are no characters in Dreiser's city
novel, because "for a man inside the city his self is not inside his body
but around him, outside the body" (p. 134); and how *An American
Tragedy* contains not "the slightest trace of society, as that word is
understood in nineteenth-century novels. Instead there are worlds,
like the world of the Green-Davidson Hotel, the social world of the
Griffiths, the world of condemned prisoners at the penitentiary, the
shabby rural world Roberta comes from, the sexually languid world
of the girls who work for Clyde" (p. 141). This book forces one to
rethink many things. I wish, however, that it had a concluding chapter
to bring its thesis into focus once again.

A less ambitious but still engaging work is *From Fact to Fiction:
Journalism & Imaginative Writing in America* (Hopkins) by Shelley
Fisher Fishkin, which studies how journalistic careers shaped the
work of five major American writers. The book focuses on a key
volume by each writer to discuss the journalistic experiences that
played a role in its development. These are Whitman's 1855 *Leaves
of Grass*, Twain's *Huck Finn*, Dreiser's *An American Tragedy*, Hem-

ingway's *For Whom the Bell Tolls,* and Dos Passos' *USA.* While not primarily theoretical, Fisher's work is analytic and scholarly. Most of us have told our classes that being journalists affected these authors; but Fishkin supports such impressions with convincing evidence.

Another collection by 19th-century American women has been edited by Lucy M. Freibert and Barbara A. White, in *Hidden Hands: An Anthology of American Women Writers, 1790–1870* (Rutgers), part of the Douglass Series on Women's Lives and the Meaning of Gender. This book overlaps somewhat with Fetterley's, but many authors are different. The editors use such categories as "Early Didacticism," "Melodrama," "Frontier Romance," "Later Didacticism," and "Polemic." Because so many names are unfamiliar, snippets of their writings may be enough to introduce them and perhaps to interest a press in publishing individual works. I, for instance, had never read Maria Cummins' *The Lamplighter,* one of the 19th century's most popular novels and the model for James Joyce's wonderful parody in the Gerty McDowell chapter ("Nausicaa") of *Ulysses.* In reading the selection in *Hidden Hands,* I discover that Joyce's parody is sensationally accurate, and the giveaway to readers in the know is that *The Lamplighter's* main character is also named Gerty. Yet nowhere in the commentary is there any mention of Joyce's use of Cummins' novel (I read the prefatory materials three times and checked the index.). Surely that book's chief claim to any recent fame rests on Joyce's parody, and that usage will color any contemporary reader's response. Why then is Joyce not mentioned? Did the editors not know? And if they did, how could they have chosen to ignore it?

Donald J. Greiner's *Adultery in the American Novel: Updike, James, and Hawthorne* (So. Car.) studies the use of adultery as a theme in American fiction. The study begins with Updike, using his work as a norm, then looks back to James and Hawthorne. I believe it would have been more effective to stay with chronology, because the use of Updike's work as a trope forces Greiner to choose fictional examples that lack the mythic dimension of those in Hawthorne and James. What better tropes to use in reading Updike's than *The Scarlet Letter* and *The Golden Bowl?* Even so, the book works on the descriptive level, and its comments on Updike are valuable.

Remembering America: A Sampler of the WPA American Guide Series (Columbia) was edited by Archie Hobson, with introductions by Bill Stott. Most of these guidebooks are available only in rare book stores. While it is good to have some access to these documents,

I must question the decision that gives us such bits and pieces. In less than 400 pages the book contains more than 500 (!) thematically arranged selections, of which only a few are longer than a paragraph. This attractive volume contains pleasant graphics, and the introduction is informative; but I was hungry for more. I hope another publisher will produce a selection of lengthier excerpts.

Readers of *ALS* who know *The Rise of American Philosophy* will want to read Bruce Kuklick's *Churchmen and Philosophers: From Jonathan Edwards to John Dewey* (Yale), which studies the influence of Jonathan Edwards on American philosophical thought. Kuklick believes that there are strong continuities between early American theological thought and the development of "scientific" philosophy which culminated in the work of such writers as Dewey. The book deals with all the major centers of American thought during the Colonial period and after, including Yale, Princeton, Brown, and Williams, as well as Harvard. Many influential thinkers, such as Edwards and James McCosh and Francis Bowen, were in fact college presidents, which suggests the sources of the ethically based college curriculum that was dominant in the era before the research university. The book contains a number of wonderful old photographs.

I shall discuss William E. Lenz's *Fast Talk & Flush Times: The Confidence Man as a Literary Convention* (Missouri) only briefly because its contents will be covered in other chapters. This book makes a respectable contribution to the growing literature on the confidence man. It deals mostly with 19th-century works, although the final chapter connects the tradition to our own century. The book is historically oriented rather than critical or analytical, and its scholarship seems up-to-date. I still believe the best book on the subject to be Gary Lindberg's *The Confidence Man in American Literature* (*ALS 1982*).

A minor figure of the period, Gorham Munson, is the author of *The Awakening Twenties: A Memoir-History of a Literary Period* (LSU), published posthumously. Munson does not overly romanticize that decade. He says, "I will venture the remark that if the word for the Yellow Nineties is pretty *infantilism*, the word for the Twenties is arrogant *juvenility*. Perhaps that is why I cannot, in the manner of several chroniclers of the early jazz age, review my immersion in it with romantic regret over time's passing. The period was something to be outgrown" (p. 169). Munson is better at recollecting events and telling about little magazines than he is in assessing or analyzing complex personalities. The most interesting sections are on Hart Crane and A. R. Orage, a follower of Gurdjieff, although it is difficult for most contemporary readers to be terribly concerned about Orage. Munson settles some old scores, particularly with Matthew Josephson, and one virtue of the book is that—unlike most memoirs of that decade—it covers primarily the American scene. The book's rhetoric seems to be a mix of the scholarly and personal, but the book would have been more interesting had Munson decided on one or the other.

Douglas Robinson's *American Apocalypses: The Image of the End of the World in American Literature* (Hopkins), a revisionary hermeneutical study, is the best book I know on the apocalypse in American literature. The author uses the theological and philosophical meanings of both hermeneutics and the apocalypse, and the impact of this knowledge is displayed in the range of reference and sinewy reasoning of this erudite book. Robinson claims that "The American Dream as European Dream was fundamentally a Protestant dream of historical apocalypse—a dream of a transformation *of* history *in* history that would consummate and so give meaning *to* history" (p. 2). If apocalyptic ideology is therefore concerned with "historical transformation," it is "fundamental to American literature" (p. 3).

Robinson believes that "the importance of the image of the end of the world in American literature is not at all formal, as many critics have argued, but ideological; not structural but *relational* . . . never a merely formal pattern in an American work but the author's interpretive stance on the future of the world and on the past of the text, its relation both to history as con-text and to previous apocalypses as pre-text" (p. 7). Robinson's strategy is "to place [him]self hermeneutically between texts, to read texts in assertive intertextual relation . . ." (p. 13). He posits American literature as being basically Romantic, with Emerson as the apocalyptic hermeneutist, the model for those who follow his lead and the target for those whose apocalypse is more negative. Within the Emersonian intertext, it is the negative voice to which Robinson gives the most attention, with Poe the author who receives the most space and *Moby-Dick* seen as the strongest apocalyptic narrative in our literature. Robinson treats works throughout the span of American literature.

We now hear much talk about the new literary history and the need to revise our attitudes toward the literary past. Major efforts are being sponsored by the university presses at Cambridge (ed. Sacvan Bercovitch) and Columbia (ed. Emory Elliott) to revise our interpretations of the entire range of American literature, with both projects intending to use new theories of literary historical interpretation. However, before the appearance of the Cambridge and Columbia histories we have *The History of Southern Literature* (LSU), edited by Louis D. Rubin, Jr., Blyden Jackson, Rayburn S. Moore, Lewis P. Simpson, and Thomas Daniel Young, all of them senior figures in that field. This large-scale collective effort, organized in the manner of the *Literary History of the United States* (ed. Spiller et al.) and the proposed Columbia history, contains short chapters on southern topics and authors, each done by an individual.

Many writers are included who were not covered by Jay Hubbell. The scholarship is thorough, and for this the editors should be commended, although as with most many-authored works, the quality does vary. What I find most problematic about this otherwise admirable book is that it really does not project a clear vision of how such a history ought to be written; there is hardly any theoretical overview. As a result, the book's coherence comes primarily from the order in which the chapters are printed and not from any belief that literary history is shaped by certain forces and in certain ways. As a result, one does not come away with a coherent sense of southern literature. I believe the book will be useful primarily as a reference work, available to teachers who need to bone up for a class or to refresh shaky memories.

Brief mention goes to Howard P. Segal's *Technological Utopianism in American Culture* (Chicago), which studies the relation between the development of American technology between 1883 and 1933 and the ideology of technology expressed in utopian writings of that period. While the books about which Segal writes are only peripherally related to traditional literary concerns (Bellamy's *Looking Backward* is a rare exception), the study is an excellent overview of the cultural forces related to the rise of technocratic and technological ideologies, and it introduces readers to a number of writers and titles of which they have probably never heard. Segal also provides good insights into why utopia eventually gave way to dystopia, and he distinguishes well between American utopias and other national varieties.

Richard Slotkin's new book, *The Fatal Environment: The Myth of the Frontier in the Age of Industrialization, 1800–1890* (Atheneum), arrived too late for me to read through, but I do want to commend it to *ALS* readers who know the author's *Regeneration Through Vio-*

lence (*ALS 1973*). *The Fatal Environment* presents the story of how the frontier myth was developed from the earliest parts of the 19th century until the 1890 census and the "closing" of the frontier. This compendious work attempts to write the definitive study of the frontier in our cultural experience, and it covers much of the ground of earlier works but in much more detail and in the spirit of the new historiography. Slotkin is informed throughout by a comprehensive theory of myth and how it is developed, not only as a trope but as a historical necessity.

Jane Tompkins' *Sensational Designs: The Cultural Work of American Fiction, 1790–1860* (Oxford) is, along with Fisher's *Hard Facts*, one of the important works of the year. Like *Hard Facts* it focuses on how works of literature express dominating cultural needs, but in this case Tompkins focuses on how these needs and forces act in concert to create a "canon." Tompkins "sees literary texts not as works of art embodying enduring themes in complex forms, but as attempts to redefine the social order" (p. xi). She attempts to set aside modernist assumptions about psychological complexity and moral ambiguity to show what certain novels held in common with other contemporary examples of the same genre, including formulaic ways of presenting their materials.

Were Tompkins content with pointing out, as does Fisher, how fictional formulas express deep-seated cultural needs, the book would not be controversial. But she claims that our value judgments about works of the past are determined almost totally by convention; that we judge from within a modernist perspective and therefore overvalue those works that meet modernist criteria, and also that many past works met the criteria of an existent elite and have continued to be overvalued since that time. *Moby-Dick* might be an example of the former type of work; *The Scarlet Letter* the latter. For instance, Tompkins believes we read works like Hawthorne's novel because from the start they have met the conditions for being taken seriously by "literary" people. Because such conditions continue to be operant, we continue to value *The Scarlet Letter*. Such are the reasons that lie behind Hawthorne's original and continued establishment as an important author. These arguments seem both brilliant and wrongheaded, but in any argument about literary value judgments it is as easy to prove one side as the other, depending on what you believe at the start.

Because contemporary readers inevitably apply modernist criteria,

Tompkins believes we are unable to appreciate such popular genres as "sentimental" and fantasy adventure novels. She is probably correct. Her excellent readings of such novelists as Brown, Cooper, Stowe, and Warner show how their works met contemporary political and cultural needs. Tompkins demonstrates how we must recapture the consciousness of a past age in order to read works that might well have been taken more seriously when they were published than many books we now assign in American literature courses or write about in scholarly journals. This claim is obviously valid, and Tompkins shows how serious historical scholarship can enable us to read many works that would escape a contemporary sensibility. Nonetheless, it will be hard for most readers to accept the claim that works by these authors, because they meet Tompkins' historical criteria, are as "good" as or better than works in the traditional canon. In stating her case so extremely, Tompkins has probably done herself a disservice, even though her argument is often convincing. I found myself fighting with this book from beginning to end, but it was worth the fight because it contains some of the best arguments I know on the conventionality of canon formation.

J. A. Ward's *American Silences: The Realism of James Agee, Walker Evans, and Edward Hopper* (LSU) is a solid, modest book that explores connections among three realist artists from different genres. These artists worked against the dominant realist tradition of a "culture that exaggerated the importance of speed, noise, and chaotic movement" (p. 12). These are artists of silence, a claim that can be corroborated by a look at Hopper's paintings or Evans' photographs. Ward's concept of realism is essentialist rather than one of surfaces. He traces a tradition that runs from Poe, Melville, James, and Adams, through Anderson and Hemingway to Agee. There is an excellent chapter on the latter author, and much good material on the relationship between Agee and Walker Evans, who collaborated on *Let Us Now Praise Famous Men.*

I shall close this section with brief discussion of two books that use an American Studies focus. Ronald Weber's *Seeing Earth: Literary Responses to Space Exploration* (Ohio) studies how writers in various genres have responded to space exploration. Dividing the subject thematically rather than generically, he has discovered an amazing number of references to space exploration in such writers as Updike, Mailer, Bellow, Kesey, Carl Sagan, and Oriana Fallaci. Although this brief, erudite book is weighty with reference, its interpretations are more journalistic than scholarly. For those interested in the topic it is a solid, well-written introduction.

In what the press release claims to be the "first book to be written on female adolescence in American literature," *Growing Up Female: Adolescent Girlhood in American Fiction* (Greenwood), Barbara A. White shows that female adolescence played a major role in American fiction in much the same way it did with teenage boys. Part of the Contributions in Women's Studies series, this book is mostly about American fiction of the current century, with chapters on Edith Wharton, Ruth Suckow, Carson McCullers, and Jean Stafford. The scholarship is thorough, and the approach is a conventional thematic one. A first-rate bibliography will help anyone who wants to go on with the subject.

ii. Women's Studies

I begin this section with mention of Josephine Donovan's *Feminist Theory: The Intellectual Traditions of American Feminism* (Ungar), which focuses on feminism as primarily a political movement. Each chapter takes a prominent topic—e.g., Marx, Freud, Existentialism, "The New Feminist Moral Vision"—reviews the intellectual history and explains the basic principles, then talks about the present tradition in relation to feminist concerns; but the book does not focus much on literary matters. The bibliography, for instance, does not mention Gilbert and Gubar or Showalter. Virginia Woolf is discussed primarily in light of *A Room of One's Own* and *Three Guineas*, and the literary figure discussed most prominently is Simone de Beauvoir.

Another introductory text that surveys feminist studies is a cooperative effort entitled *Feminist Scholarship: Kindling in the Groves of Academe* (Illinois). The names on the title page are Ellen Carol DuBois, Gail Paradise Kelly, Elizabeth Lapovsky Kennedy, Carolyn W. Korsmeyer, and Lillian S. Robinson, with each chapter written collectively. This book is more academic than Donovan's, with each section examining the impact of feminist scholarship on a scholarly discipline. The text is designed to introduce feminist perspectives and materials to students in women's studies programs, and for that purpose I recommend it. My only hesitation stems from a certain dryness in the language, understandable in a book written by a committee.

More focused on a single field is *Making a Difference: Feminist Literary Criticism* (Methuen), ed. Gayle Greene and Coppelia Kahn,

a collection of essays in the New Accents series written by a number
of critics prominent in feminist literary circles. While this collection
is not as schematically organized as some others, many of the individual essays are very good, and the excellent introduction, "Feminist Scholarship and the Social Construction of Women," ties the collection together well. I especially recommend the following essays:
Ann Rosalind Jones, "Inscribing Feminity: French Theories of the
Feminine" (pp. 80–112); Cora Kaplan, "Pandora's Box: Subjectivity,
Class and Sexuality in Socialist Feminist Criticism" (pp. 146–76); and
Bonnie Zimmerman, "What Has Never Been: An Overview of Lesbian
Feminist Criticism" (pp. 177–210).

The major feminist text of 1985 is *The Norton Anthology of Literature by Women: The Tradition in English,* ed. Sandra M. Gilbert
and Susan Gubar. As much an event as a book, this collection has
been reviewed widely as a major attempt to establish a feminist canon
of writings in English by women. It has been praised and attacked,
often on the same ground, frequently polemically. As a result, the
book has become a political document, a weather vane for determining one's ideological orientation. Because they have been prominent
for so long, Gilbert and Gubar have come for some radical feminists
to represent merely an establishment point of view; for others they
remain, along with most feminist criticism, on the fringe of academic
respectability. What I wish to do is describe briefly what I think they
are trying to do and then suggest the book's relevance for students of
American literature.

The collection attempts to define "the exuberant variety yet strong
continuity of the literature that English-speaking women have produced between the fourteenth century and the present" (p. xxvii).
The editors quote from *A Room of One's Own,* Virginia Woolf's thesis
that women's books "continue each other," and through such interactions create a tradition of women's writing "which, for several
centuries, has coexisted with, revised, and influenced male literary
models" (p. xxvii). Furthermore, the editors believe that conventional
periodization does not "suit women's literary history." They divide
women's literary history in English into the following periods: "1)
Literature of the Middle Ages and the Renaissance; 2) Literature of
the Seventeenth and Eighteenth Centuries; 3) Literature of the Nineteenth Century; 4) Turn-of-the-Century Literature; 5) Modernist
Literature; 6) Contemporary Literature" (p. xxviii). Such divisions

seem to make sense, although it is also the case that such a "tradition" will have to be measured against the usual literary periods.

Any attempt to define or assert a tradition is inherently problematic. It involves selecting in and selecting out, and it involves establishing a principle for doing both. I wish the editors had been more explicit about their principles of selection, because what I have to say now comes more from inference than from direct statements I could locate. The principle that seems inherent in the selection process is that the writings chosen focus primarily on problems of gender, on the problems of being female in a patriarchal society, or, in the more contemporary texts, on the assertion of feminist values. Some negative reviews have complained that the "best" works of particular authors are often not included and that women writers less concerned than others with matters of gender have been omitted. I think these assertions are true, but I'm not sure that the complaints have merit. The editors have not claimed to be making judgments purely on belletristic grounds. They posit that there is a female tradition in writing and they try to represent it. In my judgment they should have been more explicit about the particular constitution of that tradition, but they may have been advised against doing that by the Norton editors. After all, another famous Norton anthology posited "an American tradition in literature," an assertion that in its own way seems arbitrary. But I believe it is better to have an intellectually justifiable principle than simply to rely on personal taste.

This anthology will establish, more than any work of theory, the parameters of a tradition in women's writing. It displays a variety of forms, including such full-length works as *Jane Eyre*, Chopin's *The Awakening*, and Toni Morrison's *The Bluest Eye*, as well as a number of racial and ethnic backgrounds. As one might expect, there are also many fresh authors and titles. Any course in literature in English by women will do well to use such an anthology as a core text. Given all the pressures that must have plagued the editors in producing so sensitive a document, Gilbert and Gubar have done remarkably well. I shall be interested to see what changes they choose to make when constructing the next edition.

Toril Moi's *Sexual/Textual Politics: Feminist Literary Theory* (Methuen) is a brief introduction to the field. Marxist in orientation, it is organized successively around Anglo-American and French feminist criticism, with brief expositions of some leading figures in each.

The chapters are constructed as both summary and criticism, but Moi contributes few theoretical statements of her own. As a result, this solid, unexciting book is useful as an introduction but is not for the advanced student.

I shall close this section by discussing briefly a volume of essays that explore the field of feminist studies: *For Alma Mater: Theory and Practice in Feminist Scholarship* (Illinois), ed. Paula A. Treichler, Cheris Kramarae, and Beth Stafford. Emanating from a conference held at the University of Illinois, the collection is organized into the following sections: (1) On Women and the Academy; (2) On Language; (3) On Boundaries; (4) On Methodologies; (5) On the Body; (6) On the Relationship between the Personal and the Professional; and (7) On Resources. Most of the essays are written by scholars at the beginning or middle of their careers, and the collective quality is higher than one usually finds in such books. It is therefore a good companion volume to the summaries that appear in *Feminist Scholarship: Kindling in the Groves of Academe*, mentioned earlier.

iii. Modernism

Books on modernism continue to appear with great frequency, although none has yet satisfied this reader in explaining that complex literary and artistic phenomenon. Linda Hutcheon's *A Theory of Parody: The Teachings of Twentieth-Century Art Forms* (Methuen) studies a leading mode of modern art. A brief inductive study of literature, architecture, painting, and music, it attempts to let works of art define the theory of parody, although the book also relies heavily on other critics and theorists. Hutcheon has been strongly influenced by Bakhtin's concepts of intertextuality and the carnivalesque in claiming dominance for parody in modern culture. "Parody," she says, "is related to burlesque, travesty, pastiche, plagiarism, quotation, and allusion, but remains distinct from them. It shares with them a restriction of focus: its repetition is always of another discursive text. The ethos of that act of repetition can vary, but its 'target' is always intramural in this sense" (p. 43). The book's heavy reliance on secondary sources prevents it from making a really original contribution, but it lays out well the parameters within which parodic modernist forms might be studied.

In *Prophets of Extremity: Nietzsche, Heidegger, Foucault, Derrida* (Calif.) Allen Megill studies a sequence in Western thought that extends from Nietzsche to Derrida. Focusing on the former as its crucial central figure, the book posits that philosopher as having set the agenda for advanced thought in our time and as having put forth the visionary critiques of culture with which other thinkers have had to come to terms. Given the complexity of the topic, the book is a lucid example of the history of ideas at a very high level. While it is hardly a substitute for the original thinkers, the book makes a number of essential points about how contemporary thought developed within a modernist consciousness.

This year's most extraordinary polemic is Charles Newman's *The Post-Modern Aura: The Act of Fiction in an Age of Inflation* (Northwestern), a lively book-length essay that works from the following distinction: "Post-Modernism is defined by the confusion which comes from bringing forth the dogmatic aesthetic techniques of Modernism against an entirely unprecedented form of production, transmission and administration of knowledge, a system no less binding because it is unstructured (what Hans Enzensberger calls 'the Consciousness Industry'). Modernism in its heroic phase is a retrospective revolt against a retrograde mechanical industrialism. Post-Modernism is an ahistorical rebellion without heroes against a blindly innovative information society" (p. 10). Heavily influenced by economic metaphors, Newman is familiar with both the publishing industry and the academic marketplace. With a high level of erudition, he posits postmodernism as not having a style per se as much as a superabundance of styles and points of view. A novelist himself, Newman writes with high moral urgency, but his book ultimately lacks a conclusion. Even so, it contains a deeply disturbing look at contemporary American intellectual culture.

Ricardo J. Quinones' *Mapping Literary Modernism: Time and Development* (Princeton), a sequel to *The Renaissance Discovery of Time*, draws parallels between the innovative forces behind the first breakthrough into the "modern" with those behind the more recent breakthrough into modernism. The author focuses first on time and then on the historical development of the modernist tradition, in which space and time are seen to exist relative to one another. Quinones' major writers include Nietzsche, Lawrence, Woolf, Joyce, Eliot, Yeats, and Mann. His strategy is to list the characteristics of modernism and then show how each author fits them. The problem is that such typologies are infinitely expandable, urging you to list different characteristics from those suggested, thus reducing theory formation to listmaking. What I miss in this book is an overall theory that explains modernism from within a larger perspective, not simply from the point of view of conventional markers like time or space. Building on the earlier work of Renato Poggioli and Matei Calinescu, Charles Russell has written a distinguished book on the avant-garde: *Poets, Prophets, & Revolutionaries: The Literary Avant-garde from Rimbaud through Postmodernism* (Oxford). Russell distinguishes between modernist and avant-garde writers and artists according to their political and social behavior. "In every case," he claims, "avant-garde writers and artists are more extreme, more radical in their behavior and in their aesthetic and ultimately political vision than are the modernists. . . . But for all avant-garde writers, the basis of personal and collective vision and the agent of social change is the aesthetic activism of literary innovation" (p. ix). The avant-garde is political because it is both self-consciously modern and explicitly critical of contemporary values. Avant-garde artists attempt to create new social roles in an effort to transform society, believing that through radical art forms and language they can bring to birth new states of consciousness and activity. The early parts of the book present excellent historical and theoretical perspectives on modernism and the avant-garde, and the book is informed philosophically. There are excellent chapters on the Italian Futurists, the Surrealists, and the Dadaists, and Postmodernism. Individual writers on whom Russell focuses include Rimbaud, Apollinaire, Mayakovsky, and Brecht.

Sanford Schwartz's *The Matrix of Modernism: Pound, Eliot, & Early 20th-Century Thought* (Princeton) is a well-written study of the philosophical backgrounds of modernist thought and their place in the writings of Pound and Eliot. What Schwartz has to say about the two poets will be covered elsewhere, but I should like to comment on his theory of the transition into modernism. Schwartz describes the crucial tension during this period as one "between abstraction and experience" (p. 10), a phenomenon he locates historically: "At the turn of the century, the human sciences were undergoing a global shift from the developmental (or 'before-and-after') paradigms of the nineteenth century to the structural (or 'surface-and-depth') paradigms of the twentieth. This turn from genetic to structural modes of explanation is evident in certain transitional works that display both sets of paradigms" (p. 5), his examples being Frazer's *Golden Bough* and Freud's *Totem and Taboo*. Schwartz is also eloquent in describing the shift in narrative from representation to presentation: "the modern artist no longer *represents* a preexisting reality but *presents* a new set of relations, a 'model,' through which to order the world anew" (p. 102).

I conclude this section with brief mention of Walter J. Slatoff's *The Look of Distance: Reflections on Suffering & Sympathy in Modern Literature—Auden to Agee, Whitman to Woolf* (Ohio State). This personal book is concerned with whether literature and similar humanistic values are genuinely viable in a world such as ours, particularly with the presence of so much human suffering. Slatoff focuses on the theme of suffering in a number of 20th-century writers, poets as well as novelists, discussing the authors' lives and their works. The book is organized topically, with good readings of a number of individual works, such as Greene's *The Heart of the Matter*, Agee's *Let Us Now Praise Famous Men*, and Conrad's *The Secret Agent*.

iv. Theory of Fiction

In this brief section I shall review four books that focus on the theory of fiction, a field sufficiently distinct from the rest of theory that I believe it should be treated separately. The first is Mieke Bal's *Narratology: Introduction to the Theory of Narrative* (Toronto), trans. Christine Van Boheemen. This book reminds me of Gerard Genette's *Narrative Discourse*, because of its highly schematic structuralist approach to narrative theory. Bal's approach is more linguistically based, however, focusing on sentences as exemplary units, whereas Genette is concerned with the larger narrative structures in novels. Unfortunately, I find Bal to be interested in classification almost to a fault, and a great deal of the book is given over to a series of dry lists. Bal is himself aware of the dangers in his technique (p. 46), but this self-awareness does not keep his book from seeming tedious, particularly because it makes insufficient reference to specific works of narrative.

A more substantial, less technical book is *Reading for the Plot: Design and Intention in Narrative* (Knopf) by Peter Brooks, which claims that plot is basic both to reading and to making sense of experience. Brooks distinguishes between the structuralist and classificatory functions of "narratology" and his own concern "with how narratives work on us, as readers, to create models of understanding, and with why we need and want such shaping orders" (p. xiii). Plot, he says, "is the logic and dynamic of narrative, and narrative itself a form of understanding and explanation" (p. 10). Freudian theory is Brooks's basic model for the experience of reading, and telling one's tale to the analyst is analogous to the relationship of writer and reader. Repetition is basic to the transferential relationships of both analysand/analyst and writer/reader.

The closer that modern novels get to mirroring the repetition compulsion, as it is defined in Freud's *Beyond the Pleasure Principle*, the more difficulty the modern novelist has in ending a novel, because modernist storytelling mirrors psychic necessity. With the 19th-century's discovery of the unconscious, and that period's concern with deviance, comes the emphasis in precursors of the modernist novel with such matters as dreams, outlaws, and prostitutes. Brooks supports his theories with excellent readings of Dickens, Flaubert, Conrad, and Faulkner. This gracefully written, erudite book ends with the following observation about the necessity for narrative in human life: "Narrative is one of the ways in which we speak, one of the large categories in which we think. Plot is its thread of design and its active shaping force, the product of our refusal to allow temporality to be meaningless, our stubborn insistence on making meaning in the world and in our lives" (p. 323).

Mary Ann Caws in *Reading Frames in Modern Fiction* (Princeton) posits the theory that certain episodes, scenes, or passages are heightened in novels by various "framing" techniques. "First, . . . in the most widely read and enduring narratives, certain passages stand out in relief from the flow of the prose and create, in so standing, different expectations and different effects. . . . Second, these noticeable passages often enable the intrusion of another genre into the narrative text by appropriate means. . . . Third, . . . the principal texts of modernism emphasize the very idea of framing as it calls attention, above all, to itself, and to the frames rather than what they include" (p. xi). In an opening chapter that also reminds me of Genette, Caws gives a structural taxonomy of various framing techniques. These include such concepts as Architectural Design, Focus, Verbal Repetition, Double Insetting and Developing Object, Inset Turns, and Super-Positioning, all of them explained at some length and then exemplified in the extended readings that make up the rest of the book. Caws presents many good analyses of framing structures in Austen, James, Proust, and Woolf, and I find particularly convincing her developed assertion that in modernist works the frame itself becomes the principal focus of attention.

After reading books that are heavy with theory it is a relief to discuss a book that uses a common-sense approach to one of the thornier problems in fiction. Baruch Hochman in *Character in Literature* (Cornell) uses such an approach to develop reasons why we need to discuss character when talking about literature, even though such a common-sense notion as the existence of character has been ruled out of order by postmodernist thinking. Hochman claims that "if character is to be dealt with at all as an element in its own right, it must be dealt with as an aspect of the surface structure of the text. . . . That is, character in literature, as we ordinarily think of it, is generated by the words that point to structured sequences of events within the work" (p. 31). Hochman goes on to claim that in fact "characters do not in themselves *constitute* character; they *signify* it. . . . They, like everything else in the text, exist meaningfully only insofar as they come to exist in our consciousness" (p. 32).

What occurs in our analyses of literary characters is that they connect with our preexisting notions of what constitutes the reality of another person in actual life, what Hochman calls "the integral unity of our conception of people and of how they operate. . . . In my view, even the clues that we take in and use to construct an image of a person are virtually identical in literature and in life" (p. 36). It is the very selectivity of our knowledge of characters in texts that gives us the sense that we know them so well. With the analogy we draw between real people and characters, along with the unified concept of humanity that we carry in our heads, we often feel "we know them better than we know real people" (p. 62). And we often do, precisely because even though we know fewer details about them, the ones we do know are significant. The style of this sensible, useful book is engaging, and the text is replete with solid examples from many fictional texts.

v. Literary Theory

So many works of literary theory were published during 1985 that I must limit my coverage to those books I believe will have lasting general importance. I shall begin by briefly mentioning two new translations of works by Roland Barthes. The first is *The Grain of the Voice: Interviews 1962–1980* (Hill & Wang), trans. Linda Coverdale. The interviews cover the span of Barthes' career and chart his rise to eminence as writer and critic. Reading through them is a good way to track Barthes' major concerns as they evolve through his works, from

Writing Degree Zero to *On Racine* to *S/Z* to *The Empire of Signs* to *A Lover's Discourse*, and the interviews show Barthes at his most accessible. Although intellectual, he is philosophically unsystematic; he is self-centered about his own concerns and sensuous in his approach to ideas and language. In these conversations he explains many of his key concepts, such as his theory of semiology and his concept of codes, as well as his playful puns on *jouer/jouir*.

The second work, also published by Hill & Wang, is *The Responsibility of Forms: Critical Essays on Music, Art, and Representation*, trans. Richard Howard. Many of these are published in English for the first time, although five appeared in *Image-Music-Text* (1977). There is a variety of topics here, from photography to the Greek theater to painting and music, most of them wittily turned to show the polymath's mind at work. Each essay describes and defines the discourse contained in its subject.

A number of interesting books assess the impact of deconstruction. I begin with *Rhetoric and Form: Deconstruction at Yale* (Oklahoma), eds. Robert Con Davis and Ronald Schleifer, a collection that grew out of the Oklahoma Conference on Contemporary Genre Theory and the Yale School, held 31 May to 1 June 1984. The contributors include members of the Yale faculty and critics of the "Yale School," including J. Hillis Miller, Geoffrey Hartman, Barbara Johnson, Christopher Norris, and the two editors. The quality here is high, and the editors' introduction effectively sets the Yale School in context. I especially recommend J. Hillis Miller, "The Search for Grounds in Literary Study"; Barbara Foley, "The Politics of Deconstruction"; Robert Con Davis, "Error at Yale: Geoffrey Hartman, Psychoanalysis, and Deconstruction"; and Christopher Norris, "Some Versions of Rhetoric: Empson and de Man."

An important book is the translation of Shoshana Felman's *Writing and Madness (Literature/Philosophy/Psychoanalysis)* (Cornell), by Martha Noel Evans and Felman with the assistance of Brian Massumi. First published in French in 1978, this book studies the interrelationship of madness and literature, and what each tells us about the other, in order to define the "rhetoric of madness." In her theoretical chapters Felman focuses on the copious modern discourse about madness and what this fact implies. "To say that madness has indeed become our commonplace is thus to say that madness in the contemporary world points to the radical ambiguity of the inside and the

outside, insofar as this ambiguity escapes the speaking subjects . . .
our entire era . . . has become subsumed within the space of madness.
No discourse about madness can now know whether it is inside or
outside of the madness it discusses" (pp. 13–14).

The bulk of *Writing and Madness* is concerned with reading texts
that define that ambiguous space, and the writers with whom Felman
concerns herself include Michel Foucault, Gustave Flaubert, Jacques
Lacan, and Henry James. Also published here is Felman's celebrated
essay on *The Turn of the Screw*. Felman's reflections on what it means
to discuss madness contain a number of excellent insights. For instance: *"To talk about madness* is always, in fact, *to deny it*. However
one represents madness to oneself or others, to represent madness is
always, consciously or unconsciously, to play out the *scene* of the
denial of *one's own* madness" (p. 252—Felman's italics). Finally, I
find quite convincing Felman's own contribution to the contemporary
discussion on why and how certain texts resist interpretation: "The
more a text is 'mad'—the more, in other words, it resists interpretation—the more the specific modes of its resistance to reading constitute
its 'subject' and its literariness. What literature recounts in each text
is precisely *the specificity of its resistance to our reading*" (p. 254—
Felman's italics).

Howard Felperin's *Beyond Deconstruction: The Uses and Abuses
of Literary Theory* (Oxford) is a metatheoretical work that examines
various critical schools, particularly deconstruction, with an eye
toward establishing a critical understanding of their strengths and
weaknesses, as well as their prospects for leaving us with something
lasting. The book assumes familiarity with the critical texts it discusses. Felperin's tone is skeptical and polemical in support of his
assumption that there is no firm truth in any critical position and that
all critical positions are built in an infinite series on the deconstructed
ruins of previous schools. The author's style lends itself to quotation,
as in his statement that "Marxist criticism is prevented by the necessary pretensions of its own discourse to the extra-historical univocality
of scientific discourse from fully recognizing the metaphorical nature,
the rhetoricity or fictiveness, of its own claim to having its referential
resting-point in history" (p. 69).

Felperin finds irony in the fact that while deconstruction has cut
the ground from under logocentric readings of texts, it has also created
an enormous amount of work for critics, who can read all the clas-

sic texts anew in order to deconstruct them. For Felperin the "anxiety
of deconstruction" lies in the concern that it might turn out to be "an
empty technology of the text, like its old rival, structuralist poetics"
(p. 141). In order to avoid this result, many "critics are now beginning
to write *from within theory*—the present book is just one example—
against the institutionalization of theory, including that of deconstructive theory" (p. 145—my italics). Felperin concludes that deconstruction should now be used "contextually" with any other critical tools
one wishes in order continuously to find the cruxes and aporias in
texts. In service of such contextual readings the "great classic texts"
will remain, continuing "to repay so richly each historical construction
and deconstruction they attract" (p. 223). I think I agree with that
assertion, but it seems vaguely unsatisfying after so much polemical
sophistication.

    Another metatheoretical work is Michael Fischer's *Does Decon-
struction Make Any Difference?* (Indiana), which sees deconstruction
as an ultimately conservative, though revisionist, school of criticism,
ironically preserving the institutions it seems most designed to subvert. Deconstruction deals with the "marginality of literature" by
"infecting both knowledge and politics with what deconstructionists
see as the self-nullifying groundlessness of literary works" (p. 31).
Fischer begins by examining Matthew Arnold's, then Northrop Frye's,
defenses of literature's special place in the realm of knowledge. He
then examines the revisionary attempts of deconstructionist critics to
demonstrate indeterminacy of meaning in all texts, literary and
other, and he attempts to place deconstruction within "the currently
troubled state of academic literary study" (p. 110).

    Fischer's conclusion is that "the academic establishment has not
collapsed before revisionist criticism; it has scarcely trembled" (p.
92). He states further that "the often noted assimilation of deconstruction by the university thus does not indicate the tolerance of self-
destructiveness of the university but the docility of deconstruction"
(p. 125). While deconstruction might well be accused of docility, the
statement strikes me as a bit naive, because it underestimates the
power of large institutions—in this case, the institution of literary
study—to absorb (co-opt) even its most powerful enemies and make
them allies. Criticism that comes from within the academy is always
easy to absorb.

    I should now like to mention a few books by and about the late
Michel Foucault, including the *Foucault Reader* (Pantheon), ed.

Paul Rabinow, which contains excerpts from books as well as a few previously unpublished pieces. The editor's introduction is a helpful entrée into the writings. The second volume of *The History of Sexuality*, entitled *The Use of Pleasure* (Pantheon), has been published in Robert Hurley's translation. Foucault's desire is to explore the ways in which sexual experience became a matter of moral concern. He uses the Greeks to explore "how, why, and in what forms was sexuality constituted as a moral domain? Why [was] this ethical concern . . . so persistent despite its varying forms and intensity" (p. 10)?

The texts Foucault uses are those "written for the purpose of offering rules, opinions, and advice on how to behave as one should: 'practical' texts, which are themselves objects of a 'practice' in that they were designed to be read, learned, reflected upon, and tested out, and they were intended to constitute the eventual framework of everyday conduct" (pp. 12–13). Foucault uses those texts to examine "why the four great domains of relations in which it seemed that a free man in classical societies was able to develop and display his activity without encountering any major prohibition, were precisely the locuses of an intense problematization of sexual practice" (p. 24). The areas to which he refers are the "body," the "wife," "boys," and "truth." I am exploring the beginnings of Foucault's argument at length because what is special about this book is not so much the conclusions he draws as the fascinating ways he sets up his discourse and the particular questions he chooses to ask. I look forward to publication of the next volume.

Foucault is also the subject of two brief books. Mark Poster's *Foucault, Marxism & History: Mode of Production versus Mode of Information* (Polity Press) studies Foucault's most recent works and uses them to develop a theory of history. Poster demonstrates Foucault's development out of Sartre and relates his theories to Marxist and neo-Marxist theories of production. Poster's most important development out of Foucault is the latter's notion of a "mode of information" as the principal driving force behind power in the world. John Rajchman in *Michel Foucault: The Freedom of Philosophy* (Columbia) takes Foucault more seriously as a philosopher than others have. A philosopher himself, Rajchman treats Foucault's ideas topically and thematically, and his opening chapter, "The Ends of Modernism," places Foucault squarely in a context that evolved from the great early 20th-century masters.

Another work that attempts to apply modern theory to university

438 Themes, Topics, Criticism

teaching and the literature curriculum is *Criticism in the University* (Northwestern), ed. Gerald Graff and Reginald Gibbons, the Tri-Quarterly Series No. 1 on Criticism and Culture. This collection of essays is concerned with the role of criticism in culture, the university, and teaching, and it is dominated by a belief that current critical trends have gone too far. This is not to say that the book expresses only one point of view. In fact, there are a variety of viewpoints, and the quality of the essays is mixed; but the book makes a good start in the direction of absorbing the theory revolution, and I suspect that we shall be seeing many more such books in the next few years. I especially recommend the following essays: Wallace Douglas, "Accidental Institution: On the Origin of Modern Language Study" (pp. 35–61); Gerald Graff, "The University and the Prevention of Culture" (pp. 62–82); Gene H. Bell-Villada, "Criticism and the State (Political and Otherwise) of the Americas" (pp. 124–44); and William H. Pritchard, "English Studies, Now and Then" (pp. 198–206).

Frank Kermode's small book, *Forms of Attention* (Chicago), the Wellek Library Lectures, explores the nature of the "canon," a matter about which Kermode has written in *The Classic*. In *Forms of Attention* Kermode discusses the ways classic works of art become part of a canon. He explores how Botticelli's paintings, once considered unimportant, have become part of the High Renaissance canon. With *Hamlet* he examines a classic that has always been a classic, putting that text through a deconstructionist reading to show how resilient it has always been to the latest analytic technique. Kermode states that a classic "must be assumed to have permanent value and, which is really the same thing, perpetual modernity" (p. 62). His conclusion is similar to Howard Felperin's in that he will accept all forms of revisionary interpretation of classic works. "What is not good is anything whatever that might destroy the objects valued or their value, or divert from them the special forms of attention they have been accorded" (p. 92). Classic texts will always outlive their critics.

In *History & Criticism* (Cornell) Dominick LaCapra, himself a historian, has collected a series of essays applying theory to historical matters in the manner of Hayden White. He asks basic questions about the nature of discourse in all humanistic disciplines, and, like White, he sees historical discourse from within the context of rhetoric. His essay, "Rhetoric and History," is a highly accessible discussion of contemporary discourse. Most of these papers were given as talks, and they have the easy flow of an oral presentation; but they are also quite substantial and they have much to offer students of literature. I especially recommend "Writing the History of Criticism Now?" (pp. 95–114) and "History and the Novel" (pp. 115–34).

Brief mention goes to Floyd Merrell's *Deconstruction Reframed* (Purdue), a historical survey that traces deconstruction from its origins in Peircean semiotics through the work of Derrida. This is a synthetic work which traces the development of deconstruction through modern science and the work of people like Kurt Gödel to modernist authors like Samuel Beckett who are engaged in a similar enterprise. Merrell's style has a pleasant clarity, but I miss the critical sensibility of Megill's *Prophets of Extremity* which covers some of the same ground.

Christopher Norris' *The Contest of Faculties: Philosophy and Theory After Deconstruction* (Methuen) is another collection of essays by that prolific author, most of them deconstructive readings of texts more philosophical than literary. Norris resists the assumption that all texts, whether philosophical or not, are simply to be read rhetorically. "This is why," he writes, "these essays refuse the Rortyan option of collapsing philosophy into literary criticism, or a version of literary criticism which excludes 'theory' as just one more effort to smuggle philosophy in by the back door. . . . Rather, it is to argue that deconstructive theory has uncovered certain problematic aspects of philosophy which can now be thought through in more rigorous fashion *without* losing sight of philosophy's distinctive concerns" (pp. 10–11). Norris' sinewy writing is theoretically exacting but clear, and he uses elegant rhetorical tools on critics and thinkers such as de Man, Husserl, Roger Scruton, and Richard Rorty. Norris does his analytical work with such care and so much range that he avoids the deadening effect that so often emanates from critics criticizing critics. All these essays are good, but for me the most interesting, original piece is "Suspended Sentences: Textual Theory and the Law," which studies the developing interest among theorists in a rhetorical analysis of the law.

Daniel T. O'Hara's *The Romance of Interpretation: Visionary Criticism from Pater to de Man* (Columbia) studies modern criticism as a quest tradition established by the great Romantic writers. The author asserts that "the Romantic internalization of the quest-pattern has been ironically exposed by and used to produce many now 'clas-

sic' modern texts, whether of literary or philosophical origins. . . .
Thanks to Northrop Frye and Harold Bloom . . . , the romance of
interpretation has been carried into literary criticism, not only as a
theme to be discovered (or exposed) in poetic texts, but also as a principle of construction animating critical texts and entire careers" (p.
97). O'Hara follows this theme through extended analyses of Pater,
Bloom, Hartman, Frye, and de Man. Although no chapter is written
directly on him, Nietzsche is in fact the guiding revisionary intellect
behind this study. O'Hara quite convincingly demonstrates how literary critics and theorists participate in the same vital tradition as poets
and novelists.

Textual Power: Literary Theory and the Teaching of English
(Yale) by Robert Scholes is another attempt to relate the enterprise
of theory to university teaching. As always, Scholes is a good explainer
of difficult concepts, and his early theoretical chapters, while not
highly original, synthesize many critical perspectives into good common sense. In laying out the paradoxes apparent in contemporary
theory, Scholes talks first about the invidious distinction traditionally
made between "literature and non-literature" and between "the production and consumption of texts." He stresses the fact that a middle-
class society like ours "privileges the consuming class over the producing class" (p. 5). He then discusses how we no longer privilege
works of art as a form of "secular scripture," which he attributes to
a "loss of faith in the universality of human nature and a corresponding loss of faith in the universal wisdom of the authors of literary
texts" (p. 13).

This is not all bad, however, because Scholes believes that poetry's
loss of a privileged position has helped us escape that invidious distinction between literature and non-literature. Once we understand
that all forms of language are equally subject to critical scrutiny, we
can begin, through a literary education, to give our students the
ability to deal critically with an electronic society dominated by mass
communications. "In an age of manipulation," Scholes writes, "when
our students are in dire need of critical strength to resist the continuing assaults of all the media, the worst thing we can do is to foster in
them an attitude of reverence before texts" (p. 16). He proposes that
we organize our "pedagogical goal in terms of three related skills,
which I will call reading, interpretation, and criticism" (p. 21). Such
teaching must not be narrowly linguistic or belletristic, but should

proceed from a deep knowledge of the surrounding culture, for "in order to teach the interpretation of a literary text, we must be prepared to teach the cultural text as well" (p. 33). An understanding of how texts work will teach us that "we neither capture nor create the world with our texts, but interact with it. Human language intervenes in a world that has already intervened in language" (p. 111–12). The less interesting parts of the book occur later, particularly when Scholes engages in an unproductive polemic with Stanley Fish; but, though uneven, *Textual Power* is the most interesting attempt yet to develop a post-structuralist pedagogy.

I conclude this section with brief mention of two books. The first is Henry Staten's *Wittgenstein and Derrida* (Nebraska). This is basically a study of Derrida; but through a close look at the French philosopher, Staten convincingly shows how Wittgenstein was really engaged in the work of deconstruction in his *Philosophical Investigations*. Gregory L .Ulmer in *Applied Grammatology: Post(e)-Pedagogy from Jacques Derrida to Joseph Beuys* (Hopkins) is also developing a pedagogy from deconstruction. Ulmer focuses on the third, "applied" phase of grammatology, or what Derrida calls the "science of writing," in his search for a new humanistic pedagogy. He uses the late, playful Derrida of *Glas, Truth in Painting*, and *The Post Card* as the source for his own playfulness, and what emerges is a work interesting in its own right that connects deconstruction with recent movements in the plastic arts. Most readers will find, however, that the "pedagogy" proposed is not yet applicable to their own teaching situations.

vi. Conclusion

Post-structuralist theory has by now been widely absorbed into academic practice in both literary theory and pedagogy. Critics of post-structuralism are no longer simply those who are unsympathetic to deconstruction or reader-response theory; they arise from within the movement itself. The most interesting trend in the books I have read this year is the lively discussion about where all the interest in theory has taken us. It is too early to say that we are at the end of this particular age of theory, but reassessments like the current one most often do occur at the end of a process. I believe that what we have learned from theory will manifest itself in the new ways we read texts and, most important, in the ways we convey that knowledge to our students. In its time the New Criticism changed most of our strategies for reading and teaching poetry and fiction. I now look forward to examining the ways in which similar pedagogical strategies develop out of post-structuralist theory. Stay tuned.

University of California, Davis

21. Foreign Scholarship

i. East European Contributions

F. Lyra

In the Soviet Union the most important contribution in 1985 was *Istoki i formirovanie amerikanskoi natsionalnoi literatury. XVII–XVIII vv.* [*The Beginnings and Formation of American National Literature: 17th and 18th Centuries*] (Moscow: "Nauka"), a collection of 14 essays, including Ya. N. Zasurskii's "Introduction" (pp. 3–16). The substance of the collection merits a listing of the studies: A. V. Vashchenko, " 'Indeiskaya Amerika' i literatura SSHA kolonialnogo perioda" ["Indian America" and the Literature of the United States of the Colonial Period] (pp. 17–44), A. A. Dolinin, "U istokov amerikanskoy kultury: 'kartina mira' v literature kolonii Novoi Anglii XVII veka" [At the sources of American Culture: "The Image of the World" in the Colonial Literature of New England] (pp. 45–86), V. T. Oleinik, "Tvorchestvo Enn Bredstrit [Anne Bradstreet's Work] (pp. 87–121), M. M. Koreneva, "Tvorchestvo E. Teilora i puritanskaya traditsiya" [E. Taylor's Work and the Puritan Tradition] (pp. 122–49), V. T. Oleinik, "Formirovanie zhanra anagramy-elegii v poezii Novoi Anglii XVII veka" [The Development of the Anagram-Elegy in the Poetry of 17th-Century New England] (pp. 150–59), T. L. Morozova, "O natsionalnom svoebrazii amerikanskogo Prosveshcheniya" [On the National Singularity of the American Enlightenment] (pp. 160–85), E. A. Stetsenko, "T. Dzhefferson i literatura amerikanskogo Yuga" [T. Jefferson and Southern Literature of the 17th and 18th Centuries] (pp. 186–231), E. A. Stetsenko, "T. Pein i problemy Prosveshcheniya" [Thomas Paine and the Problems of Enlightenment] (pp. 232–60), A. M. Zverev, "Poet amerikanskoi revolutsii. Tvorchestvo Filipa Freno i problema sentimentalizma v literature SSHA" [The Poet of the American Revolution: Philip Freneau's Work and the Problem of Sentimentalism in the Literature of the United States] (pp. 261–79), E. M. Apenko and E. V. Lazareva, "Rol' satiricheskikh serii i nravoopisatel'nykh esse XVIII veka v formirovanii khudozhestvennoi prozy SSHA" [The Role of Satire Series and the Moral Essay in the Development of American Artistic Prose] (pp. 279–306), A. M. Shemyakin, "Vozniknovenie i formirovanie zhanra romana v amerikanskoi literature" [The Emergence and Development of the American Novel] (pp. 307–39), A. M. Shemyakin, "Khudozhestvennoe svoeobraze romanov Tcharlza Brokdena Brauna" [The Artistic Originality of Charles Brockden Brown's Novels] (pp. 340–61), and S. A. Tchakovskii, "Vozniknovenie negrityanskoi literatury" [The Emergence of Negro Literature] (pp. 362–83).

The essays differ considerably in method and degree of penetration. Some are descriptive and surveylike; others, analytical and evaluative. All reveal good knowledge of the colonials and their culture, although specialists in early American literature will find no revelations, but they will appreciate the fresh interpretations of some of the familiar subjects and the largely unconventional distribution of emphasis. One is almost relieved, for instance, for not finding in the collection a separate article on Benjamin Franklin, though T. L. Morozova devotes a few pages to him (pp. 177–83). She finds hardly any reasons to criticize Franklin. Morozova's high opinion of him prompts her to almost excuse "the bourgeois aspects of his worldliness" and to assume the attitude of an apologist defending him against "the unjust attacks" of the romantics and D. H. Lawrence. Even Brian M. Barbour's views expressed in his "*The Great Gatsby* and the American Past" (*ALS 1973*, p. 167), which she mistakenly identifies as "Franklin and Emerson," arouses her indignation. Franklin's detractors will be astonished by her high praise of *Poor Richard's Almanac*. Morozova, however, makes a valid point, her exaggerations notwithstanding: "The Franklinian *Almanac* contains a leading idea and a leading protagonist. He already reflects the traits of a national character. . . . *Poor Richard's Almanac* lies at the roots of the so called plebeian (low-brow) tradition in the literature of the United States," and she discerns an analogy between the collective wisdom of the *Almanac* derived from many nations and the ethnic heterogeneity of the American nation.

Vashchenko's opening essay reflects the growing desire to begin the history of American literature with a discussion of the Indian heritage. The author examines the subject in terms of "three types of interaction of 'Indian America' and the European settlers." These are the negative perception, the positive perception, the latent contacts between both races, by which he means the influence of the Indian upon the American mind, and the convergence and integration of the other side's values and forms of expression. Vashchenko does not pretend to be comprehensive in treating the topic. The shortcomings of his study, such as, for example, the one-sided considerations of types one and two, or the gaps in the knowledge of the early Indian imagination are inherent in the subject.

Such gaps do not impede the study of the Puritan mind. Supported with seven densely printed pages of footnotes and annotations, Dolinin's article is an impressive achievement revealing a thorough grasp of the chief traits of that mind as disclosed in the Puritans' writings and the key concepts with which it has been described and interpreted by others. Basically, his approach to Puritan culture, weltanschauung, and imagination is in line with the historiography of Perry Miller, Ursula Brumm—though Dolinin seems to be unaware of her work—and Sacvan Bercovitch, but he slightly modifies it in a stimulating way by occasional recourse to Russian and European studies and by stressing "the two-fold heritage" of the Puritan intellect: the renaissance and the baroque.

This heritage, Oleinik suggests, was shared only partly by Anne Bradstreet. "She does not at all belong to the pleiad of 'dark' poets of the baroque." Oleinik presents a captivating interpretation of her poetry. In the first place, his attitude toward Anne Bradstreet is free of the condescending tone that marks some past criticism. His admiration for her character and work is grounded in a close reading of all her poems in a wide context. Oleinik corrects certain errors which, in his opinion, some American scholars are guilty of. For example, he convincingly argues against those who "contrast her earlier, the 'larned' poems, with the 'mature' ones." These scholars "do not catch the internal wholeness" of her poetry. "What is more serious," says Oleinik further on, "the negative attitude of some scholars toward the poet's early work may give evidence of complete ignorance of the singular role which Bradstreet's poetry played in the literary history of the United States, the formation of professional poetry of New England." Her *Tenth Muse* "is a collection of 'pure' poetry." Oleinik succeeds in distracting our attention from the acknowledged weaknesses of her poetry by emphasizing her intellectual prowess and broad interests, for instance, in history. He provides a fresh approach to the "Contemplations" and to "A Dialogue Between Old England and New." He explains her political conservatism and critical attitude toward the New England administration. Commenting upon Anne Bradstreet's attachment to European culture, however, Oleinik overemphasizes the cultural and spiritual separatism of New England. He does not neglect to point out that she was a Puritan and a Calvinist, but assigns only secondary importance to her religious beliefs.

Predictably, Maya Koreneva pays some attention to Edward Taylor's baroque style and insists—not quite credibly—on his originality, demonstrating his uniqueness within the context of American Puritan literary culture. Koreneva discerns in Taylor's poetry the reflection of "a profound" internal drama, but she does not explain it satisfactorily. In contrast to other interpretations, she almost neglects to discuss Taylor as a religious poet, although she presents an excellent précis of "God's Determination." As a matter of fact, with the exception of Dolinin and Morozova, the contributors tend to simplify or lose sight of the religious quality of the early American mind. What we also miss in both Oleinik's and Koreneva's essays is why Soviet readers should read Bradstreet's and Taylor's poetry.

Apart from Stetsenko's piece, the volume contains little else on the literature of the South. He devotes several pages to John Smith, half of the article to Jefferson, and the rest to a cursory glance at Robert Beverley, William Byrd (who gets less space than the former), Hugh Jones, William Stith, and some minor writers. In discussing Jefferson, Stetsenko takes the opportunity to make a few useful observations on the art of letter writing in 18th-century America. On the whole, however, for the Soviet scholar Richard Beale Davis and J. A. Leo Lemay may have toiled in vain.

In view of the Soviet scholars' extensive application of broad historiographical categories, such as renaissance, baroque, rationalism, enlightenment, and others, the absence of "classicism" and "neoclassicism" seems to be a deficiency that is due to the omission of 18th-century American poetry and poetics. The Connecticut Wits, for example, are mentioned only in passing. But the scholars make frequent references to and use of "sentimentalism," which, of course, has relevance for the study of the early novel. The beginnings of American fiction have been comprehensively presented by Shemyakin, who also contributed an excellent survey of Charles Brockden Brown's work, paying special attention to the original qualities of the novelist. In his contribution Zverev supports his theoretical deliberations with a pertinent discussion of Freneau as a sentimentalist. Zverev shows why Freneau can be called both a "revolutionary" and a "sentimental" poet. Due cognizance is also given to the essay in

18th-century America, but Apenko and Lazarova's article on the topic does not supersede B. Granger's or M. Christadler's studies.

Appropriately enough, the book concludes with a survey of early black literature. Tchakovskii's interpretation of Phillis Wheatley's poems does not strike us as original. His calling her "the second most important (after Anne Bradstreet) American poetess in the seventeenth and eighteenth centuries" cannot be questioned, but putting her beside Philip Freneau as "a pioneer of 'the American theme'" is not credible.

Only a few studies of 19th-century American literature appeared. T. T. Alunin explored a familiar theme in Melville's *Israel Potter*, "Romanticheskii bunt Germana Melvilla protiv eticheskoi doktrine Bendzhamina Franklina: 'Izrael Potter'" [Herman Melville's Romantic Rebellion Against Benjamin Franklin's Ethic Doctrine: *Israel Potter* (*Uchen. Zap. Tart. Unita*, vyp. 698:20–27), and N. I. Nakaznyuk wrote about *Pierre*: "Romanticheskiya ironiya kak kontseptualno-stilicheskoe nachalo v romane G. Melvilla 'P'er'" [Romantic Irony as a Conceptual-Stylistic Principle in H. Melville's novel *Pierre*], pp. 46–56 in *Problemy metoda i poetiki v zarubezhnykh literaturakh XIX–XX vekov* [Problems of Method and Poetics in Foreign Literatures of the 19th and 20th Centuries] (Perm). Unfortunately, I had no access to either the former or the latter, which, incidentally, also contains an article on Hemingway by A. B. Murza, "Ob evolutsii struktury povestvovaniya v romanakh E.Khemingueya" [On the Evolution of Narrative Structure in E. Hemingway's Novels], pp. 126–35.

The Hungarian scholar Aladár Sarbu addressed himself to a philosophic question in "Melville, Our Contemporary" (*ALASH* 27,iii–iv: 295–306).[1] The title of his article, Sarbu acknowledges, was inspired by Jan Kott's *Shakespeare, Our Contemporary* (but not by his attitude, unless in a negative manner). Sarbu's essay deals with weighty dichotomic themes: "the interaction between the personal and the social" (*Typee, Omoo, Mardi*), "appearance and reality" (*Moby-Dick*), "freedom, morality, and necessity" as corresponding to "innocence, nature, morality" and "depravity, civilization, necessity" ("Bartleby, the Scrivener" and *Billy Budd, Sailor*). The themes are persuasively argued, though too laconically.

The fiction of the 19th century and the beginning of the 20th at-

1. The Hungarian material in the present report has been procured for me by Zoltán Abádi-Nagy.

tracted a number of scholars. In a well-established tradition of commemorating anniversaries, the Soviet literary milieu celebrated Mark Twain's 150th birthday with a spate of publications preceded in 1984 by Russian editions of *The American Claimant* and *The Innocents Abroad*, followed this year with a volume containing *The Gilded Age* and a number of tales, a collection of satires, and a tome of essays, articles, pamphlets, *Dary tsivilizatsii* [*Gifts of Civilization*] (Moscow: Progress), some of them published in Russian translation for the first time, with commentaries and an introduction by A. Zverev, who presents a sound characterization of Twain's "aggressive laughter," warning the reader not to take Twain's pessimistic views of man and the future literally, and saying why. These translated works have been complemented by commemorative articles in various journals and a second edition of Abel' I. Startsev's book, *Mark Tven i Amerika* [*Mark Twain and America*] (Moscow: Sovetskii Pisatel'); the first edition was published in 1963. Startsev's monograph is addressed to readers unacquainted with the writer's life and work, which he interprets primarily in terms of Twain's quarrel with bourgeois America. Although aware of Twain's weaknesses and prejudices, Statsev is not bothered by them. He is mainly concerned with tracing the evolution of Twain as a literary artist, social thinker, and ideologist. On the literary level such an approach leads him to see Twain's artistic life as a development toward the ideal work, the creation of "a critical-realistic social novel." Twain never managed to bring it off, although "in the late period of his life, he made various attempts at reaching the goal" and came close to it with *Pudd'nhead Wilson*. According to Startsev, the evolution of Twain's social and philosophical thinking reached its peak in "Knights of Labor—The New Dynasty." Ultimately Startsev comes close to raising Twain to the status of an apocalyptic prophet. "Much that Twain only expected in the life of his country became later reality in full view of mankind in the disgraceful intervention of the United States in Vietnam, in the immense political Watergate scandals, in the unprecedented militarization and imperialistic claims of the United States to world domination in subsequent years."

In "Mark Twain i Rossiya" [Mark Twain and Russia] (*VLit* 10: 191–204) V. Aleksandrov rehearses what is already known to anybody closely interested in Twain's life: his visit to Russia as a correspondent of the *Alta California*, his meeting with Turgenev in 1879 brought about by Hjalmar Boyesen, who had met Twain in 1874, the Gorky incident. He also describes the writer's contact with S. Stepnyak-Kravchinski, whom he met through William Dean Howells. Twain was acquainted with the anarchist's writings, which inspired him to write the satire "The Czar's Soliloquy."

Twain's contemporaries, Howells and Henry James, were studied selectively by a Soviet and Hungarian scholar. Unfortunately, I was unable to obtain O. Ya. Marchenko's "Tipy abzatsev i ikh stilicheskaya znachimost' v proze G. Dzheimsa: Na materiale romanov 'Posly,' 'Kryl'ya golubki,' novelly 'Zver v v chashche'" [Types of Paragraphs and Their Stylistic Significance in H. James's Prose: On the Material of the Novels *The Ambassadors, The Wings of the Dove,* and the Tale "The Beast in the Jungle"] (*IAT* 3:77–83). The title promises original substance. By contrast, Aladár Sarbu's "Romance, Novel and the Businessman: Aspects of Realism in the Work of Howells and James" (*AUSBSPM* 15[1984]:85–100) suggests conventional contents. In fact, it is an original piece of scholarship that provides a fresh perception of both writers' work, though Sarbu brings to bear his analytical power on only *The Hazard of New Fortunes* and *The Golden Bowl,* but the theoretical premises and the evaluative comparison of both novels are treated extensively. Sarbu's vivid style and the occasional volleys at some luminaries in the field make delightful and, more importantly, instructive reading.

Sarbu's contribution is complemented by Charlotte Kretzoi, "Observing and/or Making Observations: Vision and Method in American Fiction at the Turn of the Century" (*AUSBSPM* 15[1984]:67–83). Hers is a successfully integrated intellectual and literary study of the significance of Darwin and Spencer in American fiction of that period. Kretzoi demonstrates the important role of John Fiske in the assimilation of naturalism among American writers. "Spencer and Fiske in interpreting evolution provided American writers with a rich mine of contradictory ideas . . . making it possible for both writers to create tragic tensions." By way of illustrating the ways the authors absorbed evolutionary thinking creatively, she presents succinct discussions of Norris' *McTeague* and *Vandover and the Brute,* London's *Martin Eden,* and Dreiser's *The "Genius."* Since she asserts that "exact observation without explicit judgment"—in her view the most positive results of the influence of evolutionary theory on American writing—"was easier to do . . . in shorter literary forms and genres," it is a pity she illustrates the statement with an all too brief discussion of London's "The Law of Life" only.

Since no studies of American poetry and prose of the pre-World War II period have come to my attention, it is appropriate to begin with Krystyna Wilkoszewska's *O krytyce T. S. Eliota* [*On T. S. Eliot's Criticism*] (Krakow: Uniwersytet Jagiellonski). Claiming to fill a gap in Eliot scholarship, Wilkoszewska cogently reviews Eliot's aesthetic opinions, especially his set of criteria for judging literary works of art, his interest in the creative process, the aesthetic experience, and reception of poetry. She deserves credit for having avoided yet another survey of the relationship between his critical views and poetry. Wilkoszewska, however, does not elaborate her observation that much of Eliot's aesthetic thinking was incongruent with certain principles of the New Criticism. Her study would have gained in value if she, herself a specialist in aesthetics, had offered a critical opinion on her subject's aesthetic views.

Considerable attention was given to the short story. In the Soviet Union Valentina I. Oleneva has produced yet another book on the genre in American literature: *Modernitskaya novella SSHA. 60-70-e gody* [The Modernist Short Story: The '60s and '70s] (Kiev: Naukova Dumka). Her repeated protestations of adherence to realism coupled with a negative attitude toward modernism as understood by Soviet scholars prompt the reader to wonder why she has undertaken to write the book, since "discoveries in the field of twentieth-century American literature were made primarily by realism," which, she says, "has even affected such talented writers as Joyce, Proust, Eliot, Kafka." The three chapters that make up the book strongly imply thematic incongruity: "Faces and Masks: On the Concept of Character and the Literary Hero" (pp. 11–85), "Short Stories and Fragments" (pp. 86–245), "In Place of Conclusions: The Realistic Short Story" (Cheever, John Gardner, Capote) (pp. 246–94), but the contents of the whole, by a little stretch of the reader's imagination, attains dialectical unity. In the first chapter, to prove the scope of the "destruction" of the classical short story, Oleneva goes back to *The Decameron*, devoting 16 pages to Boccaccio's work, then leaps forward to the 1950s to start an extensive discussion of the ideological, cultural, and literary background preparatory to the main part of the book. What follows in the second chapter is first a 10-page passage of reflections on various opinions of American contemporary writers viewed in the light of modernism and realism, and then a miniature monograph on Barth's short prose, poetics, and ideology presented in critical perspective with references to Soviet American and other scholars. Her critical discussion of Barth's short fiction is balanced and includes extensive summaries of individual works (pp. 95–161). Barth's work, says Oleneva, has little value for the Soviet reader, however, if only because "his exploration of everyday reality is sterile, his implements and attitudes mechanical." Oleneva devotes 50 pages to Donald Barthelme, whose black humor and absurdity do not prevent her, or the Soviet literary establishment for that matter, to regard his short fiction with sympathetic interest. The Soviets' response to J. P. Donleavy's short fiction is even more favorable, though "his work manifests modernist tendencies." But Oleneva makes short shrift with his prose by allowing him only 13 pages (pp. 212–24). Turning direction abruptly, she charges at Susan Sontag, condemning her for "leftist [*levatskii*] doctrinairism and nihilism." (There is no English word to convey the repugnant connotation of the expression *levatskii*), for her adherence to modernism, her "primitive language. She apparently has chosen such a style to demonstrate her break with modernist elitism. But the style only evinces that her modernist pretensions reached a dead-end." Thomas Pynchon is the last of the modernists Valentina Oleneva examines (pp. 229–44). His fiction is subjected to objective reading, appreciated for its romantic and scientific elements. The final chapter of the book serves as a kind of counterpoint to show the variety of the contemporary American short story and to drive home the crucial lesson: neither modernist nor postmodernist trends succeeded in decreasing realism in the fiction of the '60s and '70s. Of the three authors whose work she surveys in the chapter—John Cheever, John Gardner, and Truman Capote—Gardner is the best representative of today's American literature. He "manifests and maintains the interdependence of art and reality, the dialectic unity of the world."

In addition to Valentina Oleneva's book two other Soviet scholars made brief contributions to the study of the short story. E. T. Kumskova examined "Zhanrovoe svoeobraze novelistiki Flanneri O'Konnor" [Genre Originality of Flannery O'Connor's Short Stories] in *Literaturnye proizvedenia XVIII–XIX vekov v istoricheskom i kulturnom kontekste* [The Literature of the 18th–20th Centuries in Historical and Cultural Context] (Moscow,) pp. 137–47. M. Landor's informative "Malaya proza u svoikh granits. (Zapadnye razkazchiki o tradytsii russkogo rasskaza)" [Western Story Tellers in the Tradition of the Russian Story] (*VLit* 8:64–95) contains extensive references to American authors who were influenced by Russian short fiction writers, especially Gogol and Chekhov. In contrast to the study of the impact of the Russian novel, the influence of Russian short fiction has not been adequately explored, Landor asserts authoritatively.

To conclude the survey of Soviet scholars' contributions, we should give notice to a few additional publications. N. E. Znamenskaya presents a valuable, albeit brief, discussion of selected contemporary American historical novels in "Istoricheskii personazh i istoricheskii kolorit v sovremmenom romane SSHA" [The Historical Character and the Historical Color in the Contemporary American Novel] (*VMU* 4:28–34). Znamenskaya concentrates mainly on Gore Vidal's novels of the '70s, contrasting his and some other authors' work with 19th-century American historical romances, pointing out the "psychologism," "de-heroization" of protagonists and "the destruction of stereotypes." A. C. Mulyarchik's "Realizm v poslevoennom romane SSHA" [Realism in the Postwar American Novel] (*Problemy Amerikanistiki* 3:260–80) provokes no comment. In " 'Ya vybirayu put' Lenina': sud'ba Linkol'na Steffensa" [I Choose Lenin's Path: Lincoln Steffens' Destiny] (*Novaya i Noveishaya Istoriya* 6:71–92), a thoroughly researched article, B. A. Gilenson shows how Steffens' *Autobiography* persuaded many American writers and intellectuals to take up procommunist positions.

No year passes without some attention to Hemingway. I have already mentioned A. B. Murza's article; another contribution, though not available for comment, was I. N. K. Krylova's "K voprosu o sposobakh vyrazheniya podteksta v sbornike rasskazov E. Khemingueya 'Muzhchini bez zhenshchin' " [On the Question of Expressing Implied Meaning in E. Hemingway's Collection of Stories *Men Without Women* (*Analiz stilei Zarub. Khudozh. i Nauch. Lit.* 4:89–96).

In "Teodor Draizer—pisatel', kommunist" [Theodore Dreiser—Writer, Communist] (*Novaya i Noveishaya Istoriya* 2:127–43) S. E. Ivan'ko claims that Dreiser has not been known well enough as a friend of the Soviet Union and as a fighter against fascism and war.

A. Nikolyukin, an authority on American-Russian relations, produced two publications in this area. "Lev Tolstoy i Amerika ego vremeni" [Leo Tolstoy and America of His Times] (*VLit* 10:131–55) answers in great detail the question with which he opens his article: "Why did Americans discover Tolstoy earlier than Western Europeans?" Not Flaubert, but Eugene Schuyler was the first to introduce

the Russian writer to the West. I was unable to get hold of Nikolyukin's other piece, "Russkaya klassika i amerikanskie pisateli" [The
Russian Classics and American Writers] (*Literaturnaya Ucheba* 2:
176–82).

In Poland this year's most important work on American literature
was in the field of the short story as it was practiced by Katherine
Anne Porter. Maciej Holota's *Wzorce krotkiej prozy narracyjnej Ka-
tarzyny Anny Porter* [*Patterns of Katherine Anne Porter's Short Narrative Prose*] (Lublin: Uniwersytet Marii Curie-Sklodowskiej), though
narrow in scope, reveals a deep insight into Porter's art. If Warren
French's observation (*ALS 1973*, p. 243) holds, which indeed seems
to be the case, that "Katherine Anne Porter still awaits discovery,"
then Holota's book is a significant step toward that goal. Although he
is mainly concerned with the formal aspects, he has managed to integrate the aesthetic, the thematic, and the ideological values of the
writer's short fiction in an exemplary fashion. No scholar interested
in Porter's work will want to miss Holota's study. Regretfully, it is in
Polish, but the extensive bibliography of 205 items and 59 pages of
footnotes, many of them containing extensive comments, will be useful to scholars ignorant of Polish.

The Poles' growing interest in contemporary American literature
is reflected in two useful monographs on as many writers, both published in a series entitled *Classics of the XXth Century* under the expert editorship of Lech Budrecki, an outstanding critic and authority
on American 19th- and 20th-century literature. One is on *John Barth*
(Warsaw: Czytelnik) by Slawomir Magala, the other on *James Baldwin* (Warsaw: Czytelnik) by Waclaw Sadkowski. The series assures
a uniform structure of the books. Each contains a comprehensive
survey of the respective authors' work, samples of opinions of both
Polish and American critics, chronologies, and lists of Polish translations. Magala, who translated *The Sot-Weed Factor*, comes close
to exalting Barth. A more critical attitude would have provided the
Polish reader with a better perspective on his achievement, although
Magala shows him in the context of contemporary American prose. It
is to the critic's credit to wonder whether Barth's work will remain
immune to literary fashions; as of now, "it has survived the first trial
of time and criticism." Sadkowski's book is more objective. Since
seven of Baldwin's books have been translated into Polish, Sadkowski
was able to deal with general issues rather than review the work in

detail. It is worthwhile to note that the critic has succeeded in accounting for Baldwin's artistic decline during the last two decades.

It is only fitting that Peter Egri's excellent contributions to the study of American drama should by themselves fill our drama review. His authority in the field exceeds my competence, and since one of his two studies noted here is in English I feel absolved from reviewing "Novel in the Drama: Eugene O'Neill: More Stately Mansions" (*ALASH* 26,iii–iv:339–64). The other contribution is in Hungarian; the translation of the title has been provided by Zoltán Abádi-Nagy, "Lukács György rejtett drámaelmélete és az amerikai dráma fejlödése" [George Lukács' Hidden Theory of Drama and the Development of American Drama], pp. 29–38 in *Lukács György irodalomelmélete* [*The Literary Theory of George Lukács*] (Pécs). This is the proceedings volume of a symposium held in Pécs to mark the centennial year of Lukács' birth.

University of Warsaw

ii. French Contributions

Marc Chénetier

Research in American Literature goes on unabated in France this year, even though lots of energy was directed to translation. A tremendous upsurge in translation of American literature is noticeable these days, both in fiction and poetry, in book form and in a host of periodical publications. Not that this constitutes the essential activity of French critics, needless to say, but the success of American studies has been such in the last 10 to 15 years that there is a growing demand on the part of publishers for academic presentations of new translations and for these translations themselves, more and more often involving critics and specialists of the field. As this happens at a time when literature has a more and more difficult time faring in university curricula—and not especially American; as a matter of fact, American literature does relatively well at a time when pragmatic preoccupations tend to make students commit themselves to something other than the humanities—this year's production is not quite as plentiful as in previous years. This, however may also be due to the documented fact that many books are in preparation, short-circuiting such other tasks as articles and bibliographies. Fewer, thicker, but also further apart seems to be the motto.

a. **Colonial America.** Even though it does not deal with literature *stricto sensu*, Jean Pierre Martin's thesis should be mentioned here, to begin with. *Philosophie, politique et idéologie chez Roger Williams (1607–1683)* (Aix: Presses de l'Université de Provence) is now available in book form. Jean Béranger edited the special issue (Fall 1984) of *Early American Literature* dedicated to European views of the subject, a fact I failed to mention last year. He also published in 1985 "Images de l'immigration et des migrations intérieures dans le *Voyage dans la Haute Pennsylvanie et dans l'Etat de New York* (1801) de Michel Guillaume Jean de Crèvecoeur" (*Annales du CRAA*, no. 10, Séminaires 1984).

b. **19th Century.** Michel Granger, in "Le paysage intermédiaire de Henry D. Thoreau" (*RFEA* 26:359–72), shows that for the sake of his survival economy, Thoreau transformed the ordinary landscape of the Concord woods into a significant scenery and tried to make believe in an adventure on the frontier but that he in fact became more deeply rooted in his native land and arranged a narcissistic place for withdrawal and expansion. Thoreau's description of the landscape offers a model of an ideal life, out of society, in a paradoxical intermediate space that reconciles primeval nature and culture.

Incidentally, the *Revue Française d'Etudes Américaines*, on the occasion of its tenth anniversary, has changed its format and now accommodates a few articles unrelated to its central theme; also one issue a year will be an open issue, the journal now being published four times a year instead of three.

Jean-Jacques Mayoux' beautiful *Vivants Piliers*, out of print for many years, has been reissued by Lettres Nouvelles (Paris); one can read with pleasure again his essays on Melville, Hawthorne, and James, alongside pieces that bear on English literature. Roger Asselineau, in "Hawthorne in France" (*HSN* 11,ii:1–6), reviews Hawthorne scholarship in this country since 1963.

Major work on Poe is forthcoming in France, under the pen of Henri Justin and Claude Richard, two distinguished specialists in the field. Claude Delarue's essay *Edgar Poe* (Paris: Balland) takes a novelistic tack to present Poe's "long crime against himself." An imaginative book, it tries to give a sense of Poe's destiny from within. Two shorter articles complement Poe studies: Bertrand Rougé's "Irony and Ventriloquy: Notes Toward an Interpretation of Edgar Allan Poe's 'Thou Art the Man'" (*Interface*, pp. 21–30) and Alexis

Briant's "Poe et la mer" (*Actes du Colloque sur la Mer*, Brest: Université de Bretagne Occidentale, pp. 59–74).

James is once again the center of interest for numerous scholars. Catherine Vieilledent contributed "'L'honnête femme n'a pas de roman': le vulgaire et le romanesque chez Henry James" (*JSSE* 5:94–107), as well as "Representation and Reproduction: A Reading of Henry James's 'The Real Thing,'" (*Interface*, pp. 31–50). A special issue (no. 222) of the *Magazine Littéraire* was also devoted to James with a chronology by Raymond Bellour and brief contributions by Evelyne Labbé ("L'art de la représentation," pp. 25–26), Jean Perrot ("Une Inconnue sur le Tapis," pp. 27–29), Diane de Margerie ("Au féminin," pp. 30–31), Christine Jordis ("La soeur de mon âme," pp. 32–33), Laurette Véza ("Du droit d'aînesse," p. 34), Jean Pavans ("Italie aimée," p. 40). The "dossier" closes on four unpublished letters and a bibliography.

Hubert Teyssandier, for his part, gave "De Balzac à James: la vision de Paris dans *The Ambassadors*, de Henry James" to *CVE* (21: 51–62) and "L'image de Venise dans *The Wings of the Dove*" to the *Annales Littéraires de l'Université de Besançon* (Paris: Les Belles Lettres, pp. 69–82).

c. **Drama.** Geneviève Fabre's "El Teatro Campesino: mythes de la dépossession et de la filiation, rites du sacrifice et de la libération" (*Les Minorités Hispaniques en Amérique du Nord*, ed. Jean Cazemajou, Presses Universitaires de Bordeaux, pp. 133–50) is an offshoot of her book on black American drama published in the United States last year, with a clearer focus on the thematics of El Teatro Campesino.

The only other important contribution to drama studies this year is a special issue of *Coup de Théatre* (Dijon, no. 5) on Tennessee Williams, whose *Cat on a Hot Tin Roof* was on the syllabus of Agrégation this year. Claude Coulon gave the issue its frame with a chronology (pp. 5–16), a panoramic view ("Evolution comparée du théâtre américain à l'époque de Tennessee Williams," pp. 17–22) and a selective bibliography (pp. 89–96), as well as an article entitled, predictably enough, "Le jeu de l'amour et de la mort" (pp. 23–28), in which he explores the play's major themes. Liliane Kerjan's "La chatte sur un toit brûlant: l'endroit du décor" (pp. 29–44) deals with considerations of space, setting, the central scenic motifs, wardrobe, lighting, and colors from the clearly stated descriptions to his style and dramatic metaphors, and, further, to Peter Brook's staging of the play. Danièle Pitavy-Souques, in "Au soir de la fête: notes sur l'espace dans *Cat on a Hot Tin Roof*" (pp. 45–54), argues that the dramatic strength of the play rests on its various explorations of space used to stage the two poles of the play, namely, Big Daddy's birthday party and the battle for the plantation, i.e., celebration and money. Homosexuality as disease is the theme of Colette Gerbaud's "Famille et Homosexualité dans *Cat on a Hot Tin Roof*" (pp. 55–70). The issue involved here, she says, is nothing less than the family continuation, jeopardized by Brick Pollitt's homosexual tendencies. As for François Pitavy, his "Le jeu du mot et de la chose" (pp. 79–88) explores Williams' work as exploring the play (in the theatrical and mechanical senses of the term) of words and things.

d. **Poetry.** A "dossier" on contemporary American poetry was prepared by Pierre Joris and inserted in *Jungle* (Paris; no. 8), introducing several contemporary poets to the French public, an enterprise soon to be prolonged by a bilingual anthology of contemporary American poetry in two volumes now being prepared by *DeltaES*. Two articles written for the new edition of *Encyclopaedia Universalis* complete this set of attempts at introducing American poetry to a wider French audience: my essay, "Le renouveau de la poésie américaine" (pp. 391–93), followed by Jacques Roubaud's "L'essor de la poésie américaine contemporaine" (pp. 393–94). One sign, among many, of renewed interest in today's American poetry is the publication of "William Bronk, 'Les gardes de vie: six poèmes' edited and presented by A. Suberchicot" in *Nulle Part* (Paris; 5:27–33).

Moving back to the 19th century, two articles are worth noticing: Jules Zanger's "'The Premature Elegy': Bryant's 'The Prairies' as Political Poem" (*Interface*, pp. 13–20) and Roger Asselineau's "Les toujours vertes Feuilles d'herbe de Walt Whitman: quelques publications récentes" (*EA* 28:282–87).

My two volume (1,196-page) study of the aesthetics of Vachel Lindsay's poetry is now available in book form from the Atelier de Reproduction des Thèses de Lille (*L'Obsession des Signes: l'Esthétique de Vachel Lindsay: prose, poèmes et dessins*). In it I propose a new vision of a poet best known for his sound and, studying the integral corpus of Lindsay work available, suggest that the poet is mostly a visual and visionary one, one whose "imperial eye" compels him to relate shapes and unify them into a private cosmology from which every single item of his work derives. I also prepared a dossier on Vachel Lindsay for *Poésie 85* (Paris; 9:75–92), a general presentation of the poet, iconographic documents, and the first translation in French of "The Golden Whales of California."

Monique Lojkine-Morelec's *T. S. Eliot: Essai sur la genèse d'une écriture* (Paris: Klincksieck) must soon become a work of reference for Eliot studies. Ten years in preparation, this book is a study of the mythical space where Eliot's poetry constitutes itself. The work of dream and the conscious work of an artist engaged in a double quest, aesthetic and spiritual, that presents itself as the reconquest of a tradition, Eliot's poetry intertextually feeds on all great mythical texts. Circe, Narcissus, Artemis, the Christian tiger are all there. They find their way to a fusion with the great Shakespearean themes by means of the works of Joyce, Flaubert, Mallarmé. A devouring orality is transmuted into the myth of the all-conquering word. This rigorous piece of work relies on poetics and syntactic, rhetorical, and metaphoric analysis but does not for all that forget the imaginary and ideological dimensions of a corpus both published and unpublished; this is by all means one of the most important books to date on the subject.

e. **Early and Mid-20th-Century Fiction.** A special issue of *Europe* (Paris) dealt with Gertrude Stein this year, but it has not reached me at the time of this writing. Hemingway's resistance to metaphor is explored by John Atherton in the second issue of *GRAAT*. His "The Itinerary and the Postcard: Minimal Strategies in *The Sun Also Rises*" (pp. 1–24) explores the geographies of Paris and Spanish towns in the novel to show that such resistance can "be seen as a denial of the responsibility for narrating, a desire to shift it *elsewhere*," that Jake, the narrator, "simply follows in the footsteps of Jake, the guide." Several other articles deal with this period, from very diverse points of view. J. Michel Gervaud's "La France dans l'oeuvre de Willa Cather," ("L'Amérique et l'Europe: réalités et représentations," *Actes du GRENA*:1:153–66) deals with Willa Cather's francophilia; Marie-Christine Cunci's "Sinclair Lewis et Edward Hopper: objets d'art et d'utilité dans la chambre claire" (*Les Cahiers d'Inter-Textes*, Fontenay-aux-Roses: Publications du Centre de Recherche Inter-Textes Arts et Littératures Modernes, 1:96–125), in a volume dedicated to intermedia research, studies the kinship that exists between writing and painting; and in "Les biographies de *42nd Parallel*: miroirs d'une idéologie?" (*Essais sur l'Idéologie,* Centre de recherches et d'études anglophones, Univ. de Grenoble III, 1:155–66) Patricia Bleu endeavors to track down ideological components in Dos Passos' "biographies." Bleuette Pion's "Un autre détour: l'emprunt à une langue étrangère dans certains romans américains de 1910 à 1950" (*GRAAT* 2:73–84), banking on Nietzsche's vision of Aristotle's metaphor, studies the views of the "New Southwest" in novels and short stories of the first half of the century insofar as they are informed by foreign expressions.

But the most important contribution in the period this year is doubtless Claire Bruyère's *Sherwood Anderson: l'impuissance créatrice* (Paris: Klincksieck). The author mostly aims at modifying an image and sharing a discovery. Veering away from chronology, she presents the internal coherence of Anderson's works, a coherence that has to do with an obsession, his feeling of powerlessness which enables her to explain simultaneously the genesis of the artist, his formal investigations, his themes, and his vision of America. For Anderson, she argues, powerlessness becomes creative as soon as it generates a form that feigns doubt, anxiety, paralysis, a near aphasia, in front of an equivocal or unsayable reality. Organized in four parts ("The Paradoxes of Art," "Disorder," "Immaturity," "Powerlessness and Flight") and followed by an impressive set of bibliographical notes, this book is the single most important work on the question ever published in France and a fundamental contribution to Anderson studies the world over.

From Anderson to Faulkner is, naturally, a short distance, and the traditional abundance of Faulknerian output is not gainsaid this year. Ann Lecercle's "The Chink and the Chip: l'agonie du 'je' et le problème de l'énonciation dans *As I Lay Dying*" (*Fabula* 5:9–30) proposes a theory to account for the phenomenon of internal fading to which the principal narrative voices of *As I Lay Dying* are periodically prone and which makes of "madness" not so much the theme as the very system of enunciation of this work. "The eclipse, eviction and ultimate expulsion of the ostensible subject of enunciation" leads one to reinterpret the title in terms of the aphanisis of the subject as such: "as (the) 'I' lay dying." Closely related thematically one to the other are two articles by André Bleikasten: "'Cet affreux goût d'encre': Emma Bovary's Ghost in *Sanctuary*" (*Intertextuality in Faulkner,* pp. 26–56) and "Terror and Nausea: Bodies in *Sanctuary*" (*FJ* 1:17–29). But Bleikasten, still at work on the second volume of

La Pléiade's edition of Faulkner's works, also found time for a brief note on Faulkner's tales ("Vingt-cinq nouvelles de Faulkner," *QL* 452:9–10) and an interesting piece on another writer, "The Heresy of Flannery O'Connor," in *Critical Essays on Flannery O'Connor*, eds. Melvin J. Friedman and Beverly L. Clark (Hall), pp. 138–58. *Intertextuality in Faulkner* is the result of a seminar on the question organized at the Ecole Normale Supérieure in 1982, on the fringes of the Paris Conference of the European Association for American Studies.

François Pitavy contributed two chapters in similar collective endeavors: " 'Anything but earth': The Disastrous and Necessary Sartoris Game," in Arthur F. Kinney, *Critical Essays on William Faulkner: The Sartoris Family* (Hall), pp. 267–73, and "The Narrative Voice and Function of Shreve: Remarks on the Production of Meaning in *Absalom, Absalom!*" (in Elisabeth Muhlenfeld, *William Faulkner's* Absalom, Absalom!: *A Critical Casebook*, Garland, 1984, pp. 189–206). Also to be noted in this section are Jean Rouberol's "Southwestern Humor and Faulkner's View of Man" (*WiF* 7:38–46) and a related study by Michel Bandry, " 'Cabin-road': John Faulkner's Lafayette County" (*Interface*, pp. 71–80).

f. **Contemporary Fiction.** One article of a general nature deals with contemporary American fiction this year: my "Charting Contemporary American Fiction: A View from Abroad" (*NLH* 16:653–69) explores the theoretical and methodological problems encountered by whomever would chart the literary history of the present, discusses the validity of "categories," and makes a number of empirical suggestions for such enterprises. I also authored a portrait of Jerome Charyn for *Contreciel* (Paris; 10:2–5) and an article on Richard Brautigan for *Encyclopaedia Universalis* ("Universalia," pp. 548–49).

A couple of publications also put out special issues dealing with contemporary American fiction. *La Quinzaine Littéraire* (no. 439) contains articles on Walter Abish (p. 8) and John Gardner (p. 10) by Evelyne Pieiller, Raymond Carver by Claude Richard (p. 9), as well as a review of William Styron by George-Michel Sarrotte (p. 13), my presentation of the Fiction Collective (p. 12), and sundry overviews. This issue was published on the day of contemporary American literature in Paris, May 4, 1985, attended by over 500 people. Philippe Jaworski wrote the presentation of this issue and edited the final issue of *Bas de Casse* (no. 7), the second to be dedicated to "Fictions d'Amérique." It contains translations of stories by Walter Abish, Raymond Carver, Guy Davenport, William Kotzwinkle, Stephen Millhauser, and Grace Paley as well as my own general introduction (pp. 5–10).

"Ville dans la brume: perspectives littéraires de San Francisco" (*RANAM* 18:299–313) is an attempt by Georgiana Colvile to sum up the California city's literary importance in the preceding three decades, from Ginsberg's *Howl* to Pynchon's *The Crying of Lot 49*. The latter book is the focus of an extremely sophisticated study by Michel Turpin in *GRAAT* no. 2: "Thomas Pynchon: *The Crying of Lot 49*: Comment l'esprit vient au lecteur" (pp. 117–38). In *RANAM* 18 Colvile brings together "Two I(s)-Landed Anti-Heroes: Cendrars's Dan Yack and Hawkes's Skipper" (pp. 213–21), while Georges Gary, in the second part dealing with the city in American culture, describes "Les multiples visages de la ville dans trois romans de Walker Percy" (pp. 271–80). Simone Vauthier wrote an article on Leon Rooke, the first to be published in France: "Dangerous Crossing: A Reading of Leon Rooke's 'The Birth Control King of Upper Volta'" (*JSSE* 4:109–39).

In an issue of *Fabula* (no. 6) entitled "La Part de l'Objet" two articles were published on contemporary authors to illustrate the presence of material things in the written texts and analyze their treatment. One is Michel Turpin's "La peinture dans les mots: réflexions sur *Pictures of Fidelman*, de Bernard Malamud" (pp. 37–52). It asks how art can relate to its object and asserts that in *Pictures of Fidelman* Malamud ventures a paradoxical solution through his own practice. "He sets out to gradually blur the assumed clearcut distinction between writing and its object, so that doubt takes hold of the reader's mind, forcing him to reconsider his own position," a vision Turpin already had in the back of his mind when writing his article on Pynchon. Here, he affirms, through fragmentation, writing becomes an object and the object invades the writing. Such, to a certain extent, is the conclusion of Annie Mouyen's "Les mots et les choses ou les paradoxes du collectionneur dans *The Floating Opera* de John Barth" (pp. 139–50), inasmuch as her study of Barth's book indicates that Todd Andrews is obsessed by objects and behaves toward them as a collector would; simultaneously, the reader is forced to consider Andrews' narrative as a collection of words he has to decipher.

The *Revue Française d'Etudes Américaines* gave no. 23 to Jean Rouberol under whose guest-editorship "the American South" was

looked into. In this issue Ben Forkner contributed a very useful panorama of "Contemporary Stories of the American South" (pp. 51–62).
Elsewhere, in a post-face to his and Armand Himy's translation of
Eudora Welty's *A Curtain of Green* (*L'Homme Pétrifié*, Paris: Flam-
marion), Michel Gresset gives interesting views on "the serious writer"
and presents with his usual acumen the works and figure of Welty.

Finally, the two issues of *DeltaES* for 1985 gathered essays on John
Barth (no. 21) and Stanley Elkin (no. 20). I edited the Stanley Elkin
issue in collaboration with members of the René Tadlov Research
group in Contemporary American Literature (Maison des Sciences de
l'Homme de Paris), which group gathers contributions of French and
American scholars. Among French contributions are my introduction
(pp. 1–10) and my interview with Stanley Elkin (pp. 15–36); Maurice
Couturier's essay on *George Mills* ("How to make an ectoplasm
schmooze," pp. 73–92); Laurent Danon-Boileau's linguistic analysis
of the first paragraphs of "The Condominium" in *Searches and Seizures* ("Déclinaison du non," pp. 111–26); Françoise Sammarcelli's
"Comparaison et Intériorité dans *Searches and Seizures*" (pp. 127–
48), where the failure to communicate is linked with the metaphorical
system of the text; a long, half-practical, half-theoretical article by
Yves Abrioux on language and the body ("Animal et Etre parlant:
The Making of Ashenden,'" pp. 149–80); and my "Organisme, or-
ganicisme et écriture dans *Searches and Seizures*" (pp. 181–206) in
which physical details are related to structure and to a vision of language. A selective but up-to-date bibliography follows (pp. 207–14).

The John Barth issue of *DeltaES* was guest-edited by Nancy
Blake. It includes three French contributions, among which is Blake's
"Fiction as Screen Memory" (pp. 95–104), a short text on *Lost in the
Funhouse* where she uses the stories to make a number of psychoanalytical points. Claude Richard's "The Character of Fiction as
Physical System: Quantity and Quality in *The Floating Opera*" (pp.
17–30) takes an epistemological entry into the text and Françoise
Sammarcelli's "La chambre aux échos: notes sur l'intertextualité
restrreinte dans *Letters*" (pp. 105–25) is an offshoot of her work in
progress on the more general problem of intertextuality in Barth's
work.

g. Ethnic Literature.　　As usual, the work of Michel Fabre on black
literature dominates this year's production. Nos. 20 and 21 of his
AFRAM Newsletter (Paris III) were published, and his book (*La*

Rive Noire: de Harlem à la Seine (Paris: Editions Lieu Commun) made headlines in France since it is mostly concerned with the experience and history of black American émigrés in Paris. Fabre was also responsible for the special issue on black literature in North America published by *Notre Librairie* (Paris). Besides a general piece on "Littérature Afro-Américaine" meant to complement the new edition of *Encyclopaedia Universalis* (Paris; pp. 396–98), Fabre also contributed a book on his favorite author (*The World of Richard Wright* [Miss.]) and an interesting chapter in *Soleil Eclaté* (eds. J. Leiner and Gunter Narr, Tubingen): "Du mouvement Nouveau Noir à la Négritude Césairienne" (pp. 149–59).

Other contributions to black literary studies this year include Jean Cazemajou's "L'autobiographie de Maya Angelou: itinéraires d'une pionnière du mouvement des droits civiques" (*Annales du CRAA*, no. 10, pp. 57–70) and Claude Julien's " 'The Eye that cannot/will not see': Location and Intertextuality in Jean Toomer's 'Becky' " (*JSSE* 5:85–102).

The rise in Latino studies is perceptible on this side of the Atlantic too. A most useful panorama of Chicano literature was published as a chapter in a book dealing with wider issues (Juan Bruce-Novoa: "Chicano Literary Production, 1960–80," in *Les Minorités Hispaniques en Amérique du Nord (1960–80)*, ed. Jean Cazemajou, Presses Universitaires de Bordeaux, pp. 115–32), a book in which also appeared a literary piece by Marcienne Rocard, "From Alienation to Self-Assertion in *Famous All Over Town* (1983) by Dany Santiago" (pp. 151–62), as well as a groundbreaking article by Michel Fabre, "Race et hispanité à travers la littérature nuyoricaine" (pp. 199–214). In the same area Fabre also gave a piece to *Etudes inter-ethniques* (7 [1984]:73–86): "Dialectique de l'émigration et du retour au pays dans la littérature porto-ricaine contemporaine."

h. Science Fiction and the Fantastic. A special issue of *Caliban* (22) was entirely composed of articles on "L'esthétique de la Science-Fiction." It has unfortunately not reached me at this time, and I am only able to report that its table of contents includes a presentation by Gérard Cordesse, an article by Jacques Goimard entitled "La Science-Fiction est-elle étrange?," Hélène Greven-Borde's "Science-Fiction et discours didactique: la problématique du voyage dans trois oeuvres d'Ursula Le Guin," "Science et esthétique: la science-fiction et l'espace einsteinien" by Denise Terrel, and an article on Ray Bradbury by

Claudine Verley, "Etude narrative et thématique de *The Pedestrian*: le cycle rompu."

Finally, Jean Marigny's massive thesis, *Le Vampire dans la Littérature Anglo-Saxonne*, is now available in book form (Paris: Didier). Several chapters deal with the vampire in American literature, even though the essential part of the book deals with British sources. Chapter 3 has a section on "le vampire aux Etats-Unis" (p. 71) and chapter 4 another, covering 1900 to 1950 (pp. 155–79). Throughout, however, American examples abound, and links are established with science fiction on a systematic basis.

Université d'Orléans

iii. German Contributions

Rolf Meyn

In contrast to previous years, German scholars distributed their interest more evenly between 18th-, 19th-, and 20th-century American literature in 1985. This development is largely due to the publication of a bulky festschrift, *Mythos und Aufklärung*. Book-length studies dealing with special themes through decades or even centuries were at least as numerous as the year before. On the whole, classic American literature was paid more attention to than in previous years.

a. **Literary Criticism and Theory: Comparative Studies.** This chapter will have to begin with the biggest endeavor, Harmut Lutz's "*Indianer und Native Americans": Zur sozial–und literaturhistorischen Vermittlung eines Stereotyps* (Hildesheim: Georg Olms), a *Habilitationsschrift*. It consists of four parts: (1) a historical survey of Euroamerican–Indian relations, ranging from the first Viking settlements to our times, (2) an exploration of literary stereotypes from captivity narratives and frontier romances to modern picaresque Indian novels by white authors and semianthropological fiction, (3) the genesis of stereotypes in Germany from Renaissance times to the present, to a great extent shaped by the influence of the French Enlightenment, James Fenimore Cooper, and the painter George Catlin and (4) the negative influence of the German trivial writer Karl May and his near-fascist successor Fritz Steuben (alias Ehrhard Wittek). Because of their unbroken popularity, Lutz holds, both May and Steuben exert a dangerous influence, for the former indulged in colonial-imperialist escapist fantasies, whereas the latter glorified strong leadership and racist ideas. An appendix discussing questionnaires developed by Lutz and some of his colleagues at the University of Osnabrück for both West Germany and the United States and their results concludes this 538-page study. There is no doubt that it is the most comprehensive study on the American Indian that has been published in Germany in recent years. But because of its wide scope, even a work of this length can only set up priorities. Lutz's historical survey covers all the essentials, but his discussion of Indian stereotypes in German and American novels of the 19th and 20th centuries must necessarily remain very eclectic. The underlying structure of Lutz's book is a basic opposition he sees running through the literary treatment of the Indian from the discovery of America to the present: on the one hand, a negative stereotype (the Indian as cruel barbarian, of inferior race and obstacle to civilization) on the other hand, the Indian as hero (though nevertheless a member of a doomed race). The latter stereotype stems largely from the "noble savage image" of the romantic era. In recent times, Lutz observes, anthropological interest has partly succeeded in establishing a more objective view of the Indian's way of life, though in the United States as well as in Germany a deplorable ignorance of the Indian's real situation prevails. In today's Germany cliché Indians play a considerable role in the entertainment industry, in advertising business, but also as figureheads of antitechnological campaigns. In all these functions their diverse roles reflect German conditions, not American ones.

The strong interest of German scholars in utopian fiction in the last decades definitely reached a climax with a three-volume collection of essays: Wilhelm Vosskamp, ed., *Utopieforschung. Interdisziplinäre Studien zur neuzeitlichen Utopie* (Frankfurt: Suhrkamp). A more expensive hardcover edition was already published in 1982 (Stuttgart: Metzler). Although the collection provides for a good survey (utopian thinking is pursued into history, philosophy, sociology, and literature), students of American literature will surely be a bit disappointed. Of interest for them will be only a review-essay by Hans Ulrich Seeber and Walter Bachem (I:143–91) commenting on recent German efforts to deal with British and American utopian fiction, Peter Boerner's "Utopia in der Neuen Welt: Von europäischen Träumen zum American Dream" (II:358–74), in which American utopian thinking is traced back to the European expectation of a Golden Land, and finally Hans Ulrich Seeber's "Thomas Morus'

Utopia (1516) und Edward Bellamys *Looking Backward* (1888): Ein funktionsgeschichtlicher Vergleich" (III:357–77). Seeber poignantly points out that in contrast to More's *Utopia* Bellamy evokes a closed system of society that by its machinelike organization and central planning contradicts the author's hypothesis of a constant evolution.

b. **Literary History.** Bernd Engler's excellent dissertation, *"Die amerikanische Ode": Gattungsgeschichtliche Untersuchungen* (Paderborn: Ferdinand Schöningh), deserves to be mentioned first. A study of this kind dealing with the American ode from the beginning to the present has not been published so far, because the ode has met with only marginal interest. As Engler lucidly shows, the ode before 1776 began as predominantly an academic exercise in stylistics (John Trumbull, Philip Freneau). The genre quickly gained importance during the struggle for independence, however. The political ode in the United States developed a tradition of its own; it became a medium of revolutionary thinking and something like a mass product, in contrast to England where political odes remained part of an aristocratic literary business. In America it was considered the only literary form to bestow a frame of dignity upon public celebrations of military victories or commemorations. In other words, it became an established form of public poetry within a political framework. At the same time another strand of tradition continued in the United States as well as in England: the ode dealing with abstract themes— e.g., Ralph Waldo Emerson's "Ode to Beauty." Engler discerns four stages in the history of the American ode; they also illustrate a change of function: in the patriotic odes at the time of the American Revolution, hymnic affirmation prevails. After 1860 the odes of commemoration also include elegiac laments of transitoriness. Furthermore, a skeptical counterimage to the hymnic worldview is clearly visible in the odes of Henry Timrod, James Russell Lowell, and Bayard Taylor. The "centennial odes" around 1876 are strikingly different from those by William Cullen Bryant and John Greenleaf Whittier, and Timrod, Lowell, and Taylor are marked by an even greater contrast between elegy and paean. Laments over the loss of theological certainty and doubt about the validity of earlier hopes are only thinly veiled by a subdued affirmation at the end of most odes. From the turn of the century on, the ode critical of progress and civilization becomes the dominant form. The two strands—political odes and those devoted to abstract values—often overlap, as Allen Tate's "Ode to the Confederate Dead" amply illustrates. As regards the purely political ode, Engler sees in it more continuity from the 18th century to the 20th century than in the ode on abstract values, which is more open to variations. The author illustrates this by concise interpretations of odes by Robert Penn Warren, Robert Lowell, Tate, William Dunbar, Peter Viereck, and Frank O'Hara. On the whole, Engler claims, there is a close affinity between the ode and the epic long poem in American poetry. This is one of the great achievements in Engler's study: the ode is never explored as an isolated phenomenon but as a part of American poetry, and it is always carefully distinguished from the works of such a hymnic poet as Walt Whitman.

Literary history of the last 25 years is covered in Eberhard Kreutzer's *Habilitationsschrift New York in der zeitgenössischen Erzählliteratur* (Heidelberg: Carl Winter). Kreutzer discusses all the recognized writers that have made New York either the main theme or an important background in their novels, that is, more than 40 writers from Renata Adler, William Gaddis, and Herbert Gold to James Herlihy, James Purdy, Charles Wright, and Sol Yurick. The main trends in the literary treatment of New York from Jacob Riis and William Dean Howells to post-World War II literature is briefly but by no means superficially dealt with. Kreutzer tackles this wealth of material not from a purely literary point of view, but from a historical, sociological, and geographical one as well, emphasizing that New York does not only reflect typical developments in urban America, but is at the same time a "unique territorial experience of enormous compactness and complexity." Kreutzer assumes that the authors' attitudes toward New York and their literary reflections of it are determined by social factors such as regional and ethnic origin, education, vocation, social status, and position in public life, but also by psychological reactions to the overwhelming city, e.g., rejection, identity crisis, or mixed feelings of depression and fascination. In his analysis of the narrative transmission Kreutzer goes far beyond the criteria established by Blanche Gelfant. He assesses his material from what he calls "socio-topographical concepts," that is, peculiarities of city neighborhoods like downtown Manhattan, Greenwich Village, the Lower East Side, Upper West Side, Central Park, etc. The "dimension of city verticals," denoting both underground fantasies that end in apocalyptic visions and the bottom of the social ladder, is applied to the works of Bellow, Gaddis, Baldwin, Cheever, Pynchon, and Blechmann. New York as a metropolis in contrast to rural areas as background of a young man's initiation into urban life is exemplified in the novels of Kerouac, Goodman, and Salinger. New York as "Fun City" or playground of comic vision is tracked in the novels of Gold and Donleavy, whereas Kreutzer deals with New York as a melting pot and cosmopolis in connection with Bellow, Wallant, Baldwin, and Malamud and with a special emphasis on the theme of Jewish-Black conflicts. In this chapter, "Naked City," the author focuses on social misery as depicted by Warren Miller and Hubert Selby, both of whom he sees in the tradition of Stephen Crane. Postmodern writers like Gaddis, Pynchon, and Barthelme take most of a chapter called " 'Unreal City': The Fantastic Foregrounding of a Cultural Metropolis." Kreutzer claims that these novelists still exploit Eliot's Waste Land leitmotif and link it to the topos of the sensitive artists lost in New York—a tradition he traces back to Wolfe and Dos Passos. Kreutzer concludes that shortly after 1960 New York as a literary subject both qualitatively and quantitatively became a central metaphor of American reality. In 1963 and 1964 numerous novels were published in which New York, if not the real protagonist, became at least the all-embracing setting. Also striking are technical innovations and thematic varieties. Fantastic distortion, satire, and neorealism are equally prominent. Kreutzer, however, is opposed to putting too much emphasis on the novelty of this generation of writers. James, Howells, Crane, Dreiser, Henry Adams, and Wharton, he reminds us, created their novels from the viewpoint of disillusioned urbanity; their works display the same tendencies that still guide the authors of the 1960s. It is only understandable that Kreutzer is not able to cover New York's impact on the 40-odd writers and their novels in equal breadth. His strategy is to analyze intensively several novels he thinks the most significant within the frames of his criteria and point to other works marginally. In spite of these restrictions I daresay that Kreutzer's book surpasses all previous studies on New York as a literary shaping force, both in America and in Germany.

To the book-length overviews of theater and drama in America from the beginnings to the present that were published in the last years, another collection of essays was added in the form of a festschrift. In Manfred Siebald and Horst Immel, eds., *Amerikanisierung des Dramas und Dramatisierung Amerikas: Studien zu Ehren von Hans Helmcke* (Frankfurt: Lang) the focus of the 16 contributions is both on the development of drama and theater under national aspects in the United States and in Canada and on the literary relations be-

tween America and Europe. Peter Erlebach's essay "Die Situation des
Dramas in Amerika im 17. und 18. Jahrhundert" (pp. 9–22) and that
of Horst Immel, "Vom Lesedrama zum Bühnenweihspiel: Die amerikanische Revolution im amerikanischen Drama des 18. Jahrhunderts"
(pp. 23–38) contain some interesting aspects of the beginnings of
American drama. Nineteenth-century drama is dealt with in four
contributions. They are Klaus Lubbers' "Der 'King Philip'-Stoff und
John Augustus Stones *Metamora*: Bemerkungen zur Rolle des In-
dianers in der amerikanischen Mythographie des frühen 19. Jahrhunderts" (pp. 39–54), Manfred Siebald's "The Christian Slave: Harriet Beecher Stowes Dramatisierung von *Uncle Tom's Cabin*" (pp.
55–71), Heinz Kosok's "Dion Boucicaults 'amerikanische' Dramen:
Zum Problem der Abgrenzung von National-literaturen in englischer
Sprache" (pp. 73–90), and Dieter Küster's "James A. Hernes *Shore
Acres* als Beispiele des frühen Realismus in amerikanischen Drama"
(pp. 91–113). Two essays are devoted to 20th-century black drama;
they are Renate von Bardeleben's "Leroi Jones/Amiri Barakas *Dutch-
man*: das Drama des schwarzen Baudelaire" (pp. 194–206) and Jürgen
Koepel's "Loften Mitchell, *Tell Pharao*: Ein Zeugnis afro-amerikani-
schen Theaterlebens in den sechziger Jahren" (pp. 207–17). Uwe
Bruhns's essay, "Geschichte im amerikanischen Drama: Die Darstel-
lung der 'Black Rebellion' bei Randolph Edmonds, Paul Peters and
Clifford Mason" (pp. 139–59), examines the subgenre of historical
drama. Klaus Lanzinger in his "Faustadaptionen bei Thomas Wolfe"
(pp. 131–38) turns to a writer and playwright who had his hey-
day in German scholarship in the first two decades after World War
II. Eugene O'Neill and Edward Albee are as popular as ever, as Wolfgang Müller's "Der Bewusstseinsstrom im Roman und auf der Bühne:
James Joyces *Ulysses* und Eugene O'Neills *Strange Interlude*" (pp.
115–29) and Franz Schulz's "Amerikakritik in Edward Albees *The
American Dream*" (pp. 173–93) testify. Such divergent contributions
as Frieder Busch's "*Arsenic and Old Lace*: Eine schwarze Komödie"
(pp. 161–72), Heiner Bus's "*The Ecstasy of Rita Joe* (1967): Die
Rolle der Sängerin in George Rygas Theaterstück" (pp. 219–35),
Horst Priessnitz's "'. . . fragments, of the house of Usher': David
Campton's *Usher* and Stephen Berkhoff's *The Fall of the House of
Usher*" (pp. 237–50), and Winfried Herget's "Transformation als Spie-
lart des amerikanischen Theaters der Gegenwart" (pp. 251–71) conclude a collection of essays that partly stays on main-traveled roads
and partly is decidedly off the beaten track. All in all, the Helmcke

festschrift is a useful supplement to books on the American drama
published over the last years in Germany.

c. **Colonial Literature.** Hans Galinsky in " 'I cannot join with the
multitude'—Daniel Gookin (1612–87), Critical Historian of Indian-
English Relations" (*Mythos und Aufklärung*, pp. 21–54), examines a
chapter of Puritan-Indian relations that has often been overlooked.
For him, Gookin's sympathy for the Indians, albeit Christianized, even
in the face of the "traumatic event of King Philip's War," puts this
Puritan historian into the same rank as an earlier protester and critic
of European-Indian relations, the Spaniard Father Bartholomé de las
Casas (1474–1566), had been promoted to long ago. Whereas Galinsky is more inclined toward history, Alfred Weber follows with a
contribution concerned with problems of genre. In his "die Anfänge
des kurzen Erzählens im Amerika des 17. und 18. Jahrhunderts: Die
'Providences' der amerikanischen Puritaner" (pp. 55–70) he contradicts those scholars who still echo Fred Lewis Pattee's thesis (1923)
that the American short story began with Washington Irving's *The
Sketch Book* (1819). Oral traditions, argues Weber, have been of
great influence on American narrative genres since earliest times.
Therefore, any history of the American short story ought to begin
with Increase Mather's collection of "Illustrious Providences" (1684),
especially since Mather in his foreword shows a keen awareness of the
problems of presentation. Cotton Mather, in his *Magnalia Christi
Americana* (1702), followed in his father's footsteps. Indian captivity
stories became another important variant of the "Providences" with
a typical structure, beginning with the Indian ambush, the cruel
march through the wilderness into captivity, the exile in an Indian
wigwam or in Canada, and finally the dramatic return. Whether in
the form of "sea-deliverances" or captivity stories, the "Providences"
are documents of Puritan life and narrative forms that influenced even
Edgar Allan Poe. Dorothea Steiner in her essay "Anne Bradstreet—
Poet of Communication" (*ArAA* 10:137–53) is dissatisfied with the
neglect with which Bradstreet has been treated as an innovator of
poetry, a poetry of communication. Steiner sees her as a "joint product
of a new secularism . . . based on Humanist thought and Renaissance
culture" and a "new orthodoxy" that led to a Puritan theocracy in the
New World. Yet, though Bradstreet felt heavily indebted to Thomas
Dudley, Sir Philip Sidney, and Du Bartas, she militantly defended
her human right to self-expression. This, claims Steiner, is Anne Brad-

street's supreme achievement. She saw herself as mother and writer, and from this position entered a dialogue with her world, sometimes from a wider political and religious viewpoint of the Old World, sometimes with various partners of her everyday life. Writing to Bradstreet was an act of communication, an attempt to share the experience of her autonomous self with the people around her.

An important contribution to Puritan studies I hadn't had time to look into earlier is a collection of essays, *Studies in New England Puritanism*, ed. Winfried Herget (Frankfurt: Lang 1983), the result of papers delivered at a symposium on "Issues in Puritan Studies" at the University of Mainz in 1981. Like the essays discussed above, they analyze texts in their historical context and with regard to form and function. Hans Galinsky in his " 'Now I understand by experience': Kolonialer Frühpuritanismus aus der Sicht von Lechford und Gorton" (pp. 9–34) unearths two lesser-known successors and allies of Thomas Morton. Lechford, Galinsky stresses, attempted to write a balanced account of life in New England, but he became very critical whenever his Anglican views clashed with religious matters in Congregationalist New England. Samuel Gorton's enemy was also early colonial Puritanism, yet his vision was far more apocalyptic. Galinsky comes up with an interesting comparison: Gorton, as a defender of the "simple heart," bears a close resemblance to another baroque figure, the German Simplicius Simplicissimus (1668). Peter Wagner in "The Jeremiad and Social Reality in Mid-Seventeenth-Century New England" (pp. 35–48) joins Sacvan Bercovitch by claiming that the jeremiad, though the clergy used this form of rhetoric to achieve quite different aims, provided the settlers with a sense of purpose and even filled them with pride by frequently associating biblical Israel with 17th-century New England.

Edgar Kleinen in his "The Half-Way Covenant: Problems of the Demographic Approach" (pp. 49–70) cautiously questions the demographic approach employed by Robert G. Pope in *The Half-Way Covenant* (1969). Pope's thesis "that the half-way covenant was introduced in response to a decrease in full covenants," Kleinen argues, has to be supported by at least a greater variety of data from a larger number of communities. Hans-Joachim Lang in "The Strategic Unity of Cotton Mather's *Wonders of the Invisible World*" (pp. 71–97) is amazed that so far hardly any critic has tried to discuss the problem of unity in Mather's work. Lang starts out from two different concepts—that of the "subjective unity," which is rooted in Mather's de-

fense of the trials; and the "strategic unity," which is a consequence
of the book's political purpose and religious indoctrinating. Taking
into account the major interpretations of *Wonders of the Invisible
World* of the last two centuries, Lang comes to the conclusion that
"the essential crime prosecuted was not witchcraft at all but noncon-
formity." Mather bracketed witchcraft, murder, and conspiracy. He
also frequently pointed to similar occurrences in Europe—sure signs
that for him there was more at stake than just witchcraft in Salem.
Ultimately, Lang holds, *Wonders of the Invisible World* must be
understood as a piece of political writing conceived in times that
were crisis-ridden in the eyes of many contemporaries. Gaby Steinbach's essay, " 'Thou shalt not suffer a witch to live' (Exodus 22:18)—
Girardian Theory and Salem Witchcraft" (pp. 99–111), is concerned
with roughly the same theme. Applying René Girard's theory of ritual
and its prominent figure of a "victim-surrogate" to the incidents in
Salem, Steinbach speculates that the preachings of Samuel Parris, who
saw himself surrounded by traitors, might have contributed to a psy-
chosis that kindled the witch hunts. Although Steinbach's analysis of
the historical situation in Salem is interesting enough, the fact remains
that most of the accused were not social outsiders predestined for
their roles of "surrogate-victims" but respectable members of the
community.

Winfried Herget in his "Writing after the Ministers: The Significance of Sermon Notes" (pp. 113–38) deals with the custom of taking
notes of Puritan sermons. It has always been well known but has
hardly evoked any scholarship so far. Herget points to the fact that
more than 5,000 notations of sermons preached in the Boston area between 1670 and 1700 are extant in various New England libraries.
Hitherto largely neglected, they are nevertheless an indispensable
source. In "The Art of Puritan Meditation in New England" (pp. 139–
67) Ursula Brumm sees Thomas Hooker as the outstanding Puritan
theorist on the role of meditation, which for her played as large a role
in Protestant traditions as in the writings of Ignatius of Loyola and
other Counter-Reformation writers. Much of Michael Wigglesworth's
poetry, but above all Edward Taylor and his "Preparatory Meditations," illustrate how deeply American Puritan poetry was infused by
a passionate meditative intensity.

Introspection instead of meditation is the theme of Renate von
Bardeleben's "Formen autobiographischer Prosa im puritanischen
Schrifttum" (pp. 169–98). In her examination of various forms of

autobiographical writing, e.g., personal narratives, travel reports, diaries, and conversion accounts, von Bardeleben comes to the conclusion that this kind of literature was invariably an instrument of self-examination, of ordering the Puritan experience for personal benefit, and as a spiritual legacy for the children. The final goal, of course, remained the salvation of the soul. Gustav H. Blanke concludes the collection with his far-flung essay, "Puritan Contributions to the Rhetoric of America's World Mission" (pp. 199–231). Blanke singles out Thomas Lechford (1641) as an early observer of what he calls the "American brag," a rhetoric mixed up of "colonial pretentiousness and spiritual arrogance." Lechford, like several of his contemporaries, saw that reality lagged far behind rhetoric in New England. This fact, however, did not prevent Puritan ministers from becoming mythographers of God's covenant with His "New American Israel." They began what generations later turned into America's world mission. Blanke is not opposed to this development, for "all great nations have developed a sense of mission and have invented a rhetoric to support it."

All in all, *Studies in New England Puritanism* is an impressive collection of essays covering a vast scope of Puritan literature. Since most of the contributions are in English, it should attract many American scholars.

d. **Nineteenth-Century Literature.** Our overview of essays on 19th-century literature ought to begin with Fritz Fleischmann's " 'A Likeness, Once Acknowledged': John Neal and the 'Ideosyncracies' of Literary History" (*Mythos und Aufklärung*, pp. 161–76). Fleischmann continues Lang's trailblazing efforts of long ago to resuscitate the art and works of John Neal. The author concentrates on "Ideosyncracies," a tale about the madness of patriarchy, which he thinks one of Neal's most mature complex stories. Fleischmann convincingly shows that this story can be understood only in the light of Neal's campaign for women's rights. Neal's more famous contemporary, James Fenimore Cooper, is assessed in Benjamin Lease's "America's Shakespeare: Coopers's Brave New World" (*Mythos und Aufklärung*, pp. 143–60). Cooper, Lease reminds us, was deeply influenced by Shakespeare. The Natty Bumppo of *The Pioneers*, for example, is modeled after King Lear, and *The Water-Witch* can be interpreted properly only if one keeps in mind that it is a novelistic version of *The Tempest*. Cooper is also discussed in Klaus Lubbers' "Text as Pretext: Stereotyping the North American Indian" (*Mythos und Aufklärung*, pp. 129–42). Lubbers follows the development of stereotyping from John Cotton through Hugh Henry Brackenridge to Timothy Flint and Theodore Roosevelt. The largest space, however, is devoted to Cooper and his rival, Robert Montgomery Bird. Lubbers clearly shows that Cooper approved the removal of the Indians in the early 19th century and could glorify them only after having pushed them into the past. Like nearly all his contemporaries, he saw hope for them only if they joined the march of civilization. Other artists were equally unable to avoid clichés and stereotypes. The sculptor Horatio Greenough's famous neoclassical "Rescue Group" of 1839 expresses the same attitude toward the supremacy of "white" civilization and the heroic frontiersman over his "barbarian" opponents.

A famous example of 19th-century black literature is scrutinized in Bernd Ostendorf's "Violence and Freedom: The Covey Episode in Frederick Douglass' *Autobiography*" (*Mythos und Aufklärung*, pp. 257–70). Ostendorf believes the Covey episode to be "the paradigmatic core" of Douglass' life story because the narrator resorts to violence as the last means to escape the violence enacted upon him. This, surmises Ostendorf, is "an act of American self-liberation," an "act of self-acceptance as a black and as an American."

Herman Melville enjoyed quite a lot of attention in *Mythos und Aufklärung*, in contrast to Hawthorne, who is only marginally mentioned. Olaf Hansen's "Melvilles skeptischer Gnostizimus" (pp. 177–93) is based on the premise that nearly all of Melville's works are marked by a "stoic gnosticism," with the possible exception of *Billy Budd*. Hansen attributes this gnosticism not so much to Melville's personality, but to the "cosmological doubt" of his time, the results of a growing economic complexity that man was unable to look through and a religious and existential insecurity after the collapse of Puritan typological thinking. Thus man, and especially the sensitive Melville, experienced a growing alienation in the world. Above all, *Moby-Dick*, *The Confidence-Man*, and "Bartleby the Scrivener" testify to Melville's gnostic "doubt and even despair." Gerhard Hoffmann follows suit with "The Mythical Experience and the Crisis of Symbolic Thinking: Melville's *Moby Dick* at the Cross-Roads" (*Mythos und Aufklärung*, pp. 195–225). According to Hoffmann, Melville anticipated the modern mythic perspective, especially in its function of a substitute to conceptual and clear-cut answers to existential questions. Disillusionment with established religions and with empirical reality led to a renaissance of myth or, rather, mythic-analogical forms of experience as integrating powers. After briefly analyzing mythic thinking in contemporary writers and Melville's earlier works, Hoffmann turns to *Moby-Dick* in which the crisis of symbolic thinking becomes most obvious. Ishmael is unable to cope with the symbols of the infinite, and Ahab despairs of the lack of symbolic moral reference. Only the certainty of the ultimate subjectivity of all symbolic thinking remains. Manfred Pütz in his "Typologie and Historischer Roman: Zum skeptischen Geschichtsbild von Herman Melvilles *Israel Potter*" (*Mythos und Aufklärung*, pp. 227–50) compares the original version of Potter's autobiography with Melville's novel and discovers in the latter a wealth of allusions to both the Old Testament and secular historical types, suggesting a structure that is completely missing in the former. Pütz claims that Melville's Israel Potter is a complex figure, representing, among other types, Israel's exile in Egypt, the Wandering Jew, the biblical Jacob, the Prodigal Son, a "plebeian Lear or Oedipus," and even Christ. Other prominent figures in the novel—Benjamin Franklin, Ethan Allen, John Paul Jones, and King George III—are also characterized with the help of a network of references to historical or biblical persons. Their stories arouse expectations in the reader that are not fulfilled. In other words, legends are turned into their opposite. The debunking of the historical telos leaves a historical landscape devoid of any signpost. In this respect, Melville's *Israel Potter* is closer to the 20th century than to Scott's tradition of the historical novel.

Melville also looms large in Dietmar Haack's "Der kurze Traum vom Paradies: Südseebilder in der amerikanischen Literatur des 19. Jahrhunderts" (*Mythos und Aufklärung*, pp. 271–98). Haack starts out from the fascination the South Sea Islands exerted on the minds of Europeans and Americans from the times of Bougainville and Cook to the end of the 19th century when Mark Twain, Henry Adams, and Jack London wrote about it as an almost vanished earthly paradise. In the eyes of Haack, Melville's *Typee* and *Omoo* form a sequence. In the first book the author perpetuates the strange mixture of South Sea motifs, desires, and realistic details as had been established by Chateaubriand, Marryat, and their lesser contemporaries. Yet even in *Typee*, Melville wavers between hope and resignation, between romantic primitivism and a harsh criticism of Western civilization. In *Omoo* arcadian-idyllic scenes recede in favor of matter-of-fact descriptions. Haack emphatically contradicts those critics who think this travelogue Melville's most hilarious and light-hearted book. Whereas in *Typee* the reader can still find some vague hope for the survival of a golden dream of an earthly paradise, *Omoo* is predominantly a testament of utter disillusionment. That is also the tenor of later South Sea observers, e.g., Charles Warren Stoddard and Mark Twain. Henry Adams is the only writer who seems to retain some of the romantic views of the Bougainville era. Yet Adams becomes also the first modern historian of a degenerating South Sea world.

Equally broad in scope and concerned with another classic writer is Uwe Böker's "Scott, Dickens and die indianischen Legenden in Mark Twains *Life on the Mississippi*" (*Amst* 30:59–73). This essay is another attempt to explain Twain's criticism of Sir Walter Scott and the inclusion of three Indian legends in *Life on the Mississippi*. Böker's theory is that Twain might have got his notion to attack Scott and the Indians in his book by reading Dickens' *American Notes* for a comment on Cairo. Böker concedes, of course, that it was not Dickens alone who triggered Twain's hostility toward Scott and the Indians. Twain, until the last 20 years of his life, was a staunch believer in the progress of American civilization, and in his eyes both the conservative South with its cavalier ethos and the Indians were impediments to it.

The last 19th-century writer to be discussed in *Mythos und Aufklärung* is Henry James, whose vision of history in the last phase of his career Heinz Ickstadt explores in "'The Salt That Saves': Fiction and History in the Late Work of Henry James" (pp. 299–320). Focusing on *The Golden Bowl* (1904), the unfinished novels, and the unfinished autobiography, Ickstadt holds that the fiction James had written before was sustained by a "myth of civilization," implying a code of manners, a system of social relations, and a teleology. James, like other upper-class intellectuals, hoped that the expanding economy in America at the turn of the century would be followed by a flowering of art and culture. Yet, though sometimes James was confident that he as a writer could use his power of imagination to help civilization develop in the hoped-for direction, works like *The Golden Bowl* and *The American Scene* nevertheless demonstrate that he, like Henry Adams, sensed dissolution, waste, and entropy behind all rampant optimism.

Our survey of 19th-century scholarship should fittingly end with Hans-Joachim Lang's book *Poeten und Pointen: Zur amerikanischen Erzählung des 19. Jahrhunderts* (Erlangen: Palm and Enke). It contains nearly all the scholar's essays on 19th-century American short stories written over a period of 25 years, ranging from Washington Irving to Henry James's "The Turn of the Screw." Among them, there is also a German translation of Lang's "How Ambiguous Is Hawthorne?" that was included in A. N. Kaul's edition of critical essays more than two decades ago (1964). Lang, I must hasten to add, does not like the term "short story." In his introductory chapter, he even pokes fun at those critics—German and American alike—who still try to arrive at some final definition of this genre. Poe, Hawthorne, Melville, and James, whether they write shorter or longer fiction, are for Lang "Artists of the Beautiful," and that has always remained this German scholar's highest criterion in regard to the classic American writers. The main part of the book begins with an analysis of prose narratives published in the *Atlantic Souvenir* from 1826 to 1832 in order to illuminate the situation of short fiction between Irving and Poe. Lang discovers that, though the market was dominated by Miss Sedgwick and James Kirke Paulding plus many amateurish productions, the ground was nevertheless prepared for a short story in the tradition of Poe or Hawthorne. Then Lang turns to Hawthorne's story "The Hollow of the Three Hills" and his technique of ambiguity. This is continued in another chapter devoted to four more ambiguous tales, "Young Goodman Brown," "The Minister's Black Veil," "The Birthmark," and "Rappaccini's Daughter." A shorter chapter on "The Artist of the Beautiful" concludes the Hawthorne part of the book. As for Melville, two essays are concerned with "Benito Cereno" and one with the influence of Hawthorne and Poe on "The Bell Tower." An analysis of Henry James's "The Turn of the Screw" and a short epilogue on the ends and means of narrating closes a book that in spite of the temporal differences of its chapters always remains remarkably consistent. This is a consequence of Lang's own critical practice: he is never content with just rendering his interpretation, however original it may be. His approach toward a literary work of art is always by way of its reception, both in its time and throughout history. Only then is he willing to come up with his version, which always rests on two pillars—the aesthetic and the sociological.

e. **20th-Century Literature.**   Another collective endeavor stands out here. It is Günter Ahrends and Hans Ulrich Seeber, eds., *Englische und amerikanische Naturdichtung im 20. Jahrhundert* (Tübingen: Gunter Narr). The book is not a comparative study, as the title might suggest. The first part, edited by Seeber, contains essays on British nature poetry, while the second part, edited by Ahrends, is made up of 10 essays by different authors on American nature poetry, so that each part could have been published independently. In the section on American poetry some coherence is achieved by Ahrends's introductory "Wandlungen in der Naturkonzeption in der amerikanischen Lyrik des 20. Jahrhunderts" (pp. 215–34) and Armin Geraths's concluding "Natur und Spontanität. Zur Ästhetik der Kunstlosigkeit in der amerikanischen Lyrik des 20. Jahrhunderts" (pp. 370–95). Ahrends sees two different concepts of nature at work, which he illustrates by Howard Nemerov's "Elegy for a Nature Poet" (1962) and Richard Wilbur's "Advice to a Prophet" (1961). In the first poem nature appears as an independent force, which is a blunt negation of the romantic concept of nature as the manifestation of a divine plan; in the second a return to a romantic view of literature is obvious. According to Ahrends, Carl Sandburg, Edwin Arlington Robinson, Robinson Jeffers, Robert Frost, Theodore Roethke, Richard Eberhart, Allen Ginsberg, Charles Olson, and Gary Snyder can be classified as "modern romantics," though some of them display an ambivalent attitude toward nature. Conversely, an antiromantic view of nature dominates the poetry of Hilda Doolittle, Robert Lowell, and Archibald MacLeish. Marianne Moore, William Carlos Williams, and Wallace Stevens occupy a position somewhere in the middle. Armin Geraths traces spontaneity as "natural expression" back to Poe and Emerson. Poe, the mediator of European romanticism, commented sarcastically on the transformation of trivial everyday phenomena by private emotions in the poetry of Wordsworth. Emerson, on the other hand, got lost in his various attempts to find a final definition of nature and discovered that he had come across only a "system of approximations" instead. But his disciple Whitman, promulgator of democratic aesthetics, returned to a naive concept of nature and declared himself for the principle of spontaneity, which was also a professed aesthetics of artlessness. This position left a deep impact on the American poetry that followed. Geraths then turns to Whitman's successors in the 20th century, among whom he includes Hart Crane, Jack Kerouac, Allen Ginsberg, and Gary Snyder, but also Rock and Pop artists like Bob Dylan, Frank Zappa, and Patti Smith. Geraths knows, of course, that the avant-garde can be defined only in opposition to Whitman, and some of the other contributors are of the same opinion.

Heinrich F. Plett in " 'A heap of broken images': Bilder des Kultur-verfalls in T. S. Eliots *The Waste Land*" (pp. 235–59) sees paradises and deserts as an opposition that forms the "symbolic topography of *The Waste Land.*" Within this binary structure nature very often serves as an analogue to culture. Paradises turn out as pseudo-paradises, having mostly negative connotations, e.g., the Garden Gethsemane or the Hyacinth garden in which the paralyzed speaker is unable to act as he wished he could. Pastoral landscapes, Plett argues, are places of a thwarted initiation into a higher state of being in Eliot's poetry. They are not as bad as deserts or cities, yet they are also part of his negative world. Eliot's counterpart, Robert Frost, is discussed in Waldemar Zacharasiewicz's "Die moderne amerikanische Naturdichtung und die pastorale Tradition: Robert Frost" (pp. 260–77). The author points to the fact that Frost was influenced by the Greek and Roman pastoral tradition, not by 19th-century poetry with its idealizing bucolic texts. Like the classic pastoral poets, Frost created eclogues that were in close touch with reality. The contrast between countryside and city remains as strong as with the Roman poets. Frost never creates idealized types, but often emotionally disturbed or queer people suffering from their isolation. In this respect, he goes far beyond John Greenleaf Whittier and Bayard Taylor. Zacharasiewicz thinks Frost's position in American poetry secure. In times of suburban extension at the cost of nature and an increasing ecological consciousness Frost's voice will continue to be heard.

Kuno Schumann in his "Kontaktaufnahmen: Imagistische Dichtung und Natur" (pp. 278–93) is less sure in regard to the Imagists. As modern poets, they did not try to cultivate nature as a whole. They were against an excessive use of symbols and called for directness and a focus on the object itself. Schumann then turns to Hilda Doolittle to demonstrate that imagism, because of its insistence on the moment and the corresponding brevity of its poetry, is only of limited significance within the context of nature poetry. Reinhold Schiffer in "*Natura povera*: Natur und Grossstadt in der Lyrik Charles Reznikoffs" (pp. 294–302) takes up a poet that, in Germany at least, has hardly ever been mentioned. Nature in the city of New York, Schiffer succinctly shows, may be only a minor theme in Reznikoff's poetry, but it is an important one, for it demonstrates his credo that concentration on small objects leads to the discovery of beauty. Günter Ahrends' " 'Not to copy nature': Die Naturlyrik von Marianne Moore und William Carlos Williams im Spiegel von poetologischer Reflexion und romantischer Tradition" (pp. 303–20) assumes that both poets conceived texts characterized by a combination of poetological reflection and representation of nature. Moore understood imagination as the creator of an aesthetic order that structures reality. This also goes for Williams, who, more than Moore, refused to subordinate the imaginative world of the poet to nature, as Romantics like Wordsworth and Coleridge had always demanded.

Wallace Stevens is a different case, as Wolfgang Riehle in "Die Naturlyrik von Wallace Stevens" (pp. 321–34) demonstrates. He discovers close affinities with the symbolists, yet also sees vital differences. Stevens often started out from what he understood as "reality," but then turned it into art or new reality, which, however, was only valid at a given moment. Natural phenomena were often fragmented, torn out of their context and transformed into imaginative and fictional elements. Rather abruptly then follows Eberhard Kreutzer's "Zur Aktualität zeitgenössischer Naturdichtung: Gary Snyder und der ökologische Imperativ" (pp. 335–52). Kreutzer finds the basis of Snyder's poetry in the poet's visionary experience of nature and Robinson Jeffers' "lyrical model," which confronted a timeless world of elementary forces with the artificiality of civilization's progress on the California coast. In addition, Snyder identifies himself with the working class, which for him is exploited like the nature around him. Zen Buddhism provides him with a congenial perspective: a frugal, spiritual life in close contact with nature. For Kreutzer, Snyder surpasses most of the contemporary poets by the richness of his vision, which is sustained by Far Eastern mysticism, American Indian myths, social criticism, regionalistic and ecological engagement, and scientific arguments.

Reinhold Schiffer's "Ist Adam ein Löwe? Bilder aus der nichtmenschlichen Natur als Vorbilder menschlicher Natürlichkeit in der postmodernen amerikanischen Lyrik" (pp. 353–69) is the last essay before Geraths' summary mentioned above. Schiffer claims that postmodern American poetry is looking for a radically new way that leads to the equation of human and nonhuman existence. He illuminates this thesis by pointing to Michael McClure's preaching of animalistic sexuality in both his essays and poetry, to images of plants and animals in many of Anne Sexton's and Susan Griffin's poems, and to the role of demonized nature in the poetry of Denise Levertov. All in all, one can safely surmise that *Englische und amerikanische Naturdich-tung*, though by no means exhaustive, will become indispensable in German university libraries.

Also concerned with modern American poetry is Harald Mesch's "Von der Repräsentation zur Präsentation: Asymbolische Tendenzen in der amerikanischen Dichtung, Kunst und Musik nach 1950" (*ArAA* 10:207–32), doubtless a by-product of his *Habilitationsschrift*, which I discussed last year (*ALS 1984*, pp. 505–06). Mesch's thesis is that, since the neo-avant-garde transcends the limits of modernist aesthetics, that is, Heidegger's "metaphysical conception of language," a new understanding of art and the language of poetry since 1950 is necessary. Mesch sees William Carlos Williams as one of the trailblazers of anti-symbolism that belongs to the essentials of the neo-avant-garde and pop art, an antisymbolism he traces back through Ezra Pound, William James, Ralph Waldo Emerson, to the Puritans—the tradition of striving for immediacy of experience, unhampered by metaphysical thinking. According to Mesch, postmodern artists refuse to accept semanticizing bipolarity because it can end only in a loss of reality in language and to a growing alienation of man in his world. Thus, Mesch claims, age-old antagonism between life and art, mind and body can be dissolved.

In comparison to previous years, fiction found fewer proponents. Karl E. Keiner's dissertation, *Die Funktion des Reichtums im Erzähl-werk von F. Scott Fitzgerald* (Frankfurt: Lang), takes up a writer who has always fascinated German students and scholars alike. In a way the study tells us why, for the emphasis is again on Fitzgerald's symbolistic treatment of the American Dream and wealth. This is not to say that Keiner is repetitive: his analysis of wealth as a shaping force on figures, space, and time in Fitzgerald's work provides us with some valuable insights. Also typical of a widespread scholarly interest in Germany is Susanne Opfermann's dissertation, "Der Mythos der Neuen Welt im amerikanischen Europaroman *The Marble Faun, For Whom the Bell Tolls, A Fable*" (Erlangen: Palm and Enke). Although with *The Marble Faun* 19th-century literature comes under scrutiny, the appropriate place to discuss it is here. Opfermann employs the three novels to illustrate the "myth of the New World," which for her means America's sincere belief in a "second start in history," after Europe missed its chance, a thesis she adopts from R. W. B. Lewis' *The American Adam*. She concedes that the three writers were well

aware of the discrepancy between myth and American reality. Hawthorne, however, did not question America's moral superiority, although he was aware of the incompatibility of American innocence
with art, which always demands sensuality. In contrast to his previous
works, Hemingway in *For Whom the Bell Tolls* returns to the traditional myth of America. The protagonist, Robert Jordan, repeatedly
defines his partisanship in Spain by his allegiance to a national creed
and the tradition of commitment for a just cause. For Faulkner, there
does not exist a big difference between America and Europe. Both
continents are guilt-ridden and equally distant from a truly human
world as envisioned by Jesus Christ. Yet mankind can be saved by a
return to the values of American dream; this is, so Opfermann holds,
Faulkner's message in *A Fable*. Hemingway and Faulkner are also
lumped together in Dieter Meindl's "Hemingway and Faulkner:
Companions in Modernism" (*Mythos und Aufklärung*, pp. 375–98).
Here, however, the emphasis is on style. Meindl sees the prose of both
authors dominated by the "imagery of stasis," though they structured
their works differently. But in spite of their stylistic differences they
shared the urge not to imitate but to arrest the motion of life.

Two of Faulkner's southern contemporaries are assessed by Waldemar Zacharasiewicz in "The Sense of Place in Southern Fiction by
Eudora Welty and Flannery O'Connor" (*ArAA* 10:189–206). He
praises Erskine Caldwell for having ended the literature of celebration of traditional values and for helping to promote a concept of
the "grotesque" characterizing Southern fiction. Welty and O'Connor,
however, refused to be taken in by this new tradition, although they
shared with Caldwell a sociological interest in a closely observed region. Their firm grip on the social and physical reality of a specific
geographical region vitalized their art.

John Cheever has not met the interest he deserves in Germany.
Günter Ahrends' "'Adonis in Amerika': Zur Funktion transformierter
Mythen in den Kurzgeschichten von John Cheever" (*Anglia* 103:336–
64) is an attempt to make up for this deficit. Ahrends believes that
Cheever fell back on Greek myths because for him modern man's
alienation was a result of the inaccessibility of his past. Besides,
myths, skillfully incorporated, always stress the universality of a
writer's message. A dissertation I didn't have time to read last year
but which ought to be mentioned is Renate Hof's *Das Spiel des 'unreliable narrator.' Aspekte unglaubwürdigen Erzählens im Werk von
Wladimir Nabokov* (München: Wilhelm Fink, 1984). Hof under-

stands Nabokov's novels as games "endlessly repeating themselves, constructed by the wizard and magician Nabokov." His games are antirealistic; they reflect the freedom of the individual consciousness. The unrealiable narrator becomes a rule of the game, his playful freedom and imagination almost monomaniac. While it is possible to differentiate between various levels of communication in *Lolita*, this is impossible in the case of *Transparent Things* and *Pale Fire*. There is no privileged position from which to correct the various narrative voices. To be arrested in one's own fiction is, of course, a source of comedy. It stops being comic, however, when a figure like Humbert Humbert becomes aware of it and experiences his own self-consciousness as forced upon him. Like several other of Nabokov's characters, he desperately tries to keep his balance, knowing that we force our own fictions on reality to produce a self-created absurdity. Hof's dissertation is without doubt one of the better studies of this writer.

Gerhard Hoffmann's long essay, "Comedy and Parody in John Barth's Fiction" (*Amst* 30:235–78), is based on the assumption that Barth's work is nothing less than "the exemplification of the postmodern concepts of comedy and parody and their interrelation." Hoffmann believes Barth's work to be marked by the experience of entropy, caused mainly by loss of metaphysical meaning and a general decline of culture. He then proceeds to define three concepts of comedy in Barth's work: the traditional comedy with its hierarchy of values, the reversal with its emphasis on the debased, and a third type that blurs the difference between "norm-obedience" and "norm-Violation." Space, time, character, action, and event are carefully analyzed in terms of their significance for comedy and parody.

This year's survey should fittingly end with Klaus Poenicke's "Liquidations: 'Blockade' and 'Flooding' in Some Postmodern Texts" (*Mythos und Aufklärung*, pp. 433-54), an essay that is in itself a comprehensive analysis of an important tendency in postmodern writing: the dam-bursting release of creative energies in many texts. Poenicke's "hermeneutics of excess," rooted in the "dimensions of unlimited wish fulfillment" in our consumerist society, seems to be a useful strategy to come to terms with much of postmodern literature. His model interpretation of some texts clearly proves this.

Universität Hamburg

iv. Japanese Contributions

Keiko Beppu

In our report for *ALS 1983* (p. 492) we read: "despite the professed interest in and enthusiasm for American women writers and poets, they received little critical attention in 1983. . . . And substantial studies on women writers . . . are yet to be written." That modest prediction seems to have been fulfilled during the past two years by the collaboration of our scholars. In 1984 there appeared *Contemporary American Women Writers and Their Subconscious Worlds* (Kyoto: Minerva), *Heroines in American Literature* (Liebel Shuppan), a historical survey of American heroines from Hester to Blanche Du Bois, and *Women and American Literature* (Yashio Shuppan). Further illustration of such academic pursuit in 1985 is the publication of two books on women writers and/or women in American writings: *Gendai America Bungaku no Joseizo* [*The Images of Women in Contemporary American Literature*] ed. Misako Koike and Eriko Hara (Keisoshobo)[1] and my own edition, *America Bungaku ni okeru Joseizo: Tsukurareta Kao to Tsukkuta Kao* [*What Manner of Woman in American Literature: Portraits and Self-Portraits*] (Yumishobo). These recent contributions by Japanese women scholars signify that feminist literary criticism and other new critical approaches to American literature have become a common practice with professors and students of American literature in this country.

Another salient feature of Japanese scholarship for 1985, as might be expected, is a phenomenal publication of books and articles dealing with 19th-century American writers. Of special import among such achievements is a significant addition to Dickinson scholarship, which may account for our interest in American women writers and also for the prospective centennial in 1986 of the poet's death. Aside from two book-length studies of the poet completed in 1985, two books of translation deserve mention here: Thomas H. Johnson's *The Life of Emily Dickinson* by Toshikazu Niikura and Hiroko Uno (Kokubunsha) and Mordecai Marcus' *Cliff's Notes Emily Dickinson: Selected Poems* by Minoru Hirooka (Osaka: Osaka Kyoikutosho). Serialization of textual readings of Dickinson's poems in *EigoS* by Takao Furukawa (130:439–41, 497–99, 548–50, 597–99) is still an-

1. When no place of publication is indicated, the place is Tokyo.

other indication of the critical reception the 19th-century poet enjoys in this country.

Likewise, our scholarly activities for 1985 are accentuated by two other literary commemorations: *EigoS* featured articles on Ezra Pound in celebration of the centennial of the poet's birth (131,viii) and on Mark Twain in commemoration of the hundredth year of the publication of *The Adventures of Huckleberry Finn* (131, x). These and other individual accomplishments for 1985 are grouped for the present review as follows: general studies; 19th-century fiction and poetry; 20th-century fiction; contemporary literature—fiction, drama, and poetry; American studies. Articles here examined are restricted, as usual, to those published in our major journals: *EigoS*, *SALit*, and *SELit*.

Studies in American literature on themes like home, religion, woman or "the self-made" man, the city or the garden, examined in historical perspective, constitute an academic venture popular among our scholars. Important works produced in 1985 in this category are the aforementioned *What Manner of Woman in American Literature*; *America Bungaku to New York* [*Literary New York*] ed. Nobunao Matsuyama (Nan'un-do); and Nozomu Yagyu's *Eibei Bungaku ni miru Gendaijin no Ishiki no Henyo* [*Changes in Modern Consciousness and Anglo-American Writers*] (Jordan-sha).

What Manner of Woman is a report on the symposium held at the annual convention of the American Literature Society of Japan in 1982. The book examines historically the images of women created by men *and* women novelists; for this purpose the following five pairs of novelists are chosen to represent the five phases of American literary history: Charles Brockden Brown vs. Susanna Rowson and Hannah Foster; Melville vs. Harriet Beecher Stowe with reference to Hawthorne; James vs. Kate Chopin; Hemingway vs. Anaïs Nin; John Updike vs. Joyce Carol Oates. The selection of the authors remains controversial; yet overall it serves the objective of the book clarifying the difference between self-portraits made by women and portraits rendered by *the other*. A sample conclusion is the portraits of women by men register little change throughout, whereas those by women undergo a considerable evolution from Charlotte Temple to Oates's Elena Howe. Such inference is, however, open for discussion, since the contributors and the editor-author are all women. The essay on Rowson and Foster is probably the first of its kind to appear in this country, introducing these neglected but interesting writers. Like *What Manner of Woman, Literary New York* is a report on the symposium at the Kyoto American Studies Seminar in 1982. The book consists of 15 essays on various American writers and poets whose literary careers are fostered by the most fabulous of American cities, one that has played a decisive role in the formation of the nation's literature. The introductory chapter, "The City and American Literature" (pp. 13–34) by Hisao Kanaseki, is counterbalanced by Irving Howe's "The City and Literature" (pp. 283–304). "What *is* New York to American writers?" or "How does the city exert its influence on the American imagination"—these questions are answered in the essays contributed on such diverse American authors as Melville, Whitman, Howells, James, Crane, Fitzgerald, Dos Passos, Malamud, Bellow, Kerouac, Baldwin, and Capote. Read with the other *Literary New York: A History and Guide* by Susan Edmiston and Linda Cirino (1976), our *Literary New York* gives a reader the impression that the city is indeed the sole progenitor of American literature.

Nozomu Yagyu's *Changes in Modern Consciousness and Anglo-American Writers* is the extensively revised version of the same author's *Literature without God*, which went through many printings. Yagyu's introduction is a succinct summary on vicissitudes the Christian faith has suffered in changing the American cultural milieu. The critic then examines the Puritan frame of mind in Hawthorne's *The Scarlet Letter*; traces its secularized form called "the American Dream" and its disillusionment demonstrated in the works by Dreiser, Steinbeck, and Arthur Miller, until declining American faith, divine and secular, reaches its nadir in the ethics of nihilism in Hemingway and his world. To counter such a tendency, Yagyu introduces William Faulkner, whose characters retain, so he believes, some residue of Puritan tradition inherited from Hawthorne. Yagyu's analysis of *Light in August* or *The Sound and the Fury* (pp. 153–94) draws heavily upon former scholarship; yet given the scheme of the book, his ultimate assessment of the giant of 20th-century American literature sounds only valid. Also of interest is his discussion of T. S. Eliot, which leads to the concluding chapter, "Religiosity and Contemporary Writers." Yagyu's contention that the death of God has brought about the death of language and that atheism not only affects modern consciousness but also its means of communication (p. 314) rings a bell in many who are deeply concerned with similar problems. All three books surveyed above constitute a multifaceted literary history of the

United States. They explore evolutions in the meaning of potent cultural symbols—woman, city, God, and the like—and how they have changed from 19th-century through contemporary America.

Richard Chase once made it explicit in *The American Novel and Its Tradition* (1957) that the American novel as opposed to the English novel was formed during the 19th century. Hence our persistent involvements with 19th-century American novelists. Impressive is a checklist of book-length studies produced in 1985 that fall in this group of our scholarly achievements: Masayuki Sakamoto's *Sabaku no Umi: Melville o Yomu* [*The Watery Desert: Studies in Herman Melville*] (Kenkyusha); Eiichi Fujita's *Henry James no Aimaisei* [*The Ambiguity of Henry James*] (Osaka: Sogensha); Kazuko Ashihara's *Henry James Ronkoh* [*Essays on Henry James*] (Hokuseido); Hachiro Kayashima's *Emily Dickinson no Sekai* [*The World of Emily Dickinson*] (Nan'un-do); and Katsuhiko Inada's *Emily Dickinson: Tengoku Kakutoku no Strategy* [*Emily Dickinson: Strategies for Immortality*] (Kinseido).

The Watery Desert is an ambitious attempt to come to terms with Melville's quest for truth. It consists of 12 chapters plus an introduction and epilogue, with a chronology and an annotated bibliography (pp. 354–468); the entire work runs close to 500 pages, twice as long as a usual book-length study. A noted scholar with books on Hawthorne, Emerson, and other American Renaissance writers behind him, Sakamoto offers long and often meandering monologues on Melvillean heroes. Cross-references to preceding or subsequent chapters hinder the flow of his argument. Moreover, frequent references to Emerson and Whitman made in an attempt to distinguish Melville from the transcendentalists are strained. Comparison and contrast turn out to be compulsory rather than inevitable.

The title, *The Watery Desert*, is suggested by W. H. Auden's *The Enchafed Flood* (1951), where both the sea and the desert are the symbol of freedom and solitude, yet with a vital difference between the two. For Auden the sea is "the Alpha of existence," which means "potential life," while the desert is the end of the world (of life), "the Omega of life." Sakamoto applies this ambivalent nature of the sea and the desert to his reading of Melville's works. *The Watery Desert* is an elaboration of Sakamoto's thesis that the Melvillean hero, whose prototype is Ishmael, is a traveler who becomes engaged in an epistemological journey in search of the elusive phantom of life. Which sounds familiar enough. The motif of quest/journey recurs in Japa-

nese scholarship on the novelist; Tatsuo Kambara's *Herman Melville,
Solitary Pilgrim* (*ALS 1975*) and Ginsaku Sugiura's *Herman Melville:
The Doomed Voyager* (*ALS 1981*) readily come to mind. Likewise,
Sakamoto's contention that the metaphysical journey dramatized in
Melville's works parallels that of the author is again true enough. So
such declaration as Ishmael's voyage out into the ocean ends in
Clarel's wandering in the desert implies that Ishmael's pursuit after
"the ungraspable phantom of life" becomes a failed quest. So is Melville's journey in search of truth. And Sakamoto's gigantic volume
in turn becomes as elusive as that "phantom of life" that Taji, Ishmael,
and other Melville heroes pursue.

For all the negative factors mentioned above, we commend just
the same the critic's sheer intellectual energy, which has made completion of the ambitious task possible. The chapter on *The Confidence-
Man* (pp. 308–64) is a judicious commentary on the novel; and the
annotated bibliography is carefully compiled and useful to Melville
scholars in this country. Thus, as *The Watery Desert* shows, Melville
presents us no end of critical problems.

Among the articles written on the novelist in 1985 the following
deserves brief comment here: Michiko Shimokohbe's "Reading/Writ-
ing in 'Benito Cereno'" (*SALit* 22:19–32) exemplifies a new critical
approach to the story and is a pungent reading of Melville's novella.
For Shimokohbe, "Benito Cereno" is what Roland Barthes terms
"polysemic space," where reading equals producing one's own meaning from the text, which equals writing. Here we may also recall
two essays on Melville and New York included in *Literary New York*
(pp. 35–50, pp. 51–70); and another discussion in *What Manner of
Woman*, which explores Melville's women characters in *Pierre* (pp.
46–58).

Fujita's *The Ambiguity of Henry James* takes up four of James's
"puzzlers": "The Lesson of the Master," "The Figure in the Carpet,"
"The Turn of the Screw," and *The Sacred Fount*. Fujita puts his finger
on the crux of James criticism that Jamesian ambiguity necessitates a
new literary theory. Yet curiously enough, no reference is made either
to Wolfgang Iser's discussion of "The Figure in the Carpet" in *The Act
of Reading* (1978) or to any other relevant recent scholarship. The
critic's observation that the ambiguity of James is conducive to multiple interpretations of his stories (p. 31) becomes self-contradictory
in the strongly personal and dogmatic reading presented. So, contrary

to what the title promises, no new light is shed on the nature of Jamesian ambiguity. Instead, supplemented with a fair amount of excerpts from each of the texts discussed, *The Ambiguity of Henry James* claims its raison d'être in a modest way as a James reader for Japanese college students.

Studies in Henry James by Kazuko Ashihara is a collection of numerous essays formerly published in various academic journals over a period of 20 years. It is a fruit of her long commitment to the master, redolent with a sense of wonder and awe the author has experienced in reading James's works. Following general remarks on the characteristics of James's novels, the second chapter discusses individual works: *The Ambassadors, The Wings of the Dove, The Golden Bowl,* and "The Turn of the Screw." The third chapter consists of essays on James's style, particularly during his major phase. The last chapter gives us comparative studies on James, George Eliot, and Hawthorne, a reiteration of obvious former scholarship.

Ashihara's discussion of James's later style in the third chapter is worthy of special comment here. Using Seymour Chatman's *The Later Style of Henry James* (1971), Ian Watt, or Richard Bridgeman, her analyses of James's *The Golden Bowl* or *The Wings of the Dove* (pp. 202–24), provided with apt illustrations from the texts, are valuable exercises in stylistics. As studies of this kind are scarce—with the exception of Hisayoshi Watanabe's book, *The Language of Henry James* (*ALS 1978*, p. 478)—Ashihara's essays on James's style are an important addition to James scholarship in Japan.

As mentioned, Emily Dickinson received considerable critical attention in 1985. Like Ashihara's or a few other books surveyed here, Hachiro Kayashima's *The World of Emily Dickinson* is an anthology of his own essays previously published in academic journals. Kayashima's aim is to present the poet's inner world, through examination of her poetry, as a battleground where the poet's Puritan heritage, transcendental ideas of her time, and an onslaught of new science and technology clash. But the author falls short of attaining his objective, and *The World of Emily Dickinson* remains an unaffected exploration of the poet's inner turmoil.

Inada's thesis in *Emily Dickinson: Strategies for Immortality* is: Dickinson employs various rhetorical strategies in her poetry to attain immortality, which is carefully developed through analysis and appreciation of some 160 Dickinson poems. The book demonstrates constant oscillations Dickinson experienced between bliss and despair. Indeed, as Dickinson writes in one of her poems (338): "Would not the fun/ Look too expensive!/ Would not the jest—/ Have crawled too far!"

Of special interest to foreign readers are the final two chapters of the book, which read Dickinson's poems in relation to Japanese haiku; a good illustration of such a reading is the juxtaposition of Bashō, the master haiku poet, and Dickinson (pp. 296–302). It is well known that haiku inspired not a few modern American poets at the turn of the century; Dickinson seems to have employed the "short form," by mere coincidence, in an isolated place and time. What is salutary about these chapters and the book in general is Inada's critical detachment, which enables him to show a clear divergence between haiku and an apparently similar cryptic form that Dickinson's poetry takes. Likewise, the same critical discretion is observed in his comparison of Dickinson and a Japanese Christian poet, Jyukichi Yagi (1898–1927); the juxtaposition again clarifies the cultural differences between the two poets who shared the same religious faith and similar tactics in the practice of their art.

Finally, as Inada admits in the preface, his interpretation of Dickinson's poetry is strongly influenced by his own religious (supposedly Christian) and cultural (Japanese) background (pp. iii–iv). In this sense *Emily Dickinson: Strategies for Immortality* is Inada's "personal Dickinson." As has been mentioned earlier, the serialization of textual readings of Dickinson's poems in *EigoS* by Takao Furukawa is an excellent accompaniment to these Dickinson studies because, when all is told, we necessarily return to the text itself.

Along with the above-examined book-length studies, the current year produced a great number of articles on 19th-century American writers. Limited space permits me to mention only the following titles of some significance. *EigoS* prepared a special number on *The Adventures of Huckleberry Finn* on the centennial of the book's publication (131, x). The issue includes Toshio Watanabe's "A Century of *Huckleberry Finn* studies"; Kenichi Akao's "Humor in *Huckleberry Finn*"; Takeo Hamamoto's "*Huck Finn* and the Blacks," a reassessment of Ralph Ellison's critique of the novel; Takeshi Morita's "Modernism and *Huck Finn*"; and Takaki Hiraishi's "Huck Finn as a Writer." Another article on Twain worthy of note here is Kayoko Fujimori's "Huckleberry Finn and the Confidence Men: What the

Inside Story Suggests" (*SALit* 22:49–60). Fujimori argues that the
King and the Duke episode could be titled "The Misadventures of the
Con Men," and these confidence men are nothing but the shadows of
Huck.

Japanese scholarship on Hawthorne, a favorite among our scholars, was meager in 1985. Of such, the following deserve mention here:
the chapter in *Changes in Modern Consciousness and Anglo-American
Writers* (pp. 37–73) and Fumio Ano's "Hawthorne and Poison"
(*EigoS* 131:117–19), an influence study of Hawthorne's "Rappaccini's
Daughter" on the Russian writer Fyodor Kuzmich Sologub's short
story, "Otravlemny Sad." Articles on other 19th-century writers are
Tsuyoshi Tanaka's "Henry Adams and Nirvana" (*EigoS* 130:582–84),
concerning the bronze statue in Rock Creek Cemetery in which
Adams saw the convergence of East and West, and Shoko Itoh's
"Gnostic Apocalypse in Edgar Allan Poe" written in English (*SALit*
22:1–17).

In contrast to the prodigious amount of Japanese scholarship on
19th-century American writers, our scholarly accomplishments in
20th-century American literature was scant. Only one book-length
study in this third group appeared in 1985: Satoshi Tatsumi's *Hemingway to Warera no Jidai: Hyozan Riron no Kaimei* [*Hemingway and
Our Time: Iceberg Theory Explained*] (Kyoto: Koyoshobo). Like
his work on Hawthorne (*ALS 1983*), Tatsumi's *Hemingway and Our
Time* is a curious monograph of the 20th-century novelist as a Nietz-
schean philosopher, in which the author concludes that Hemingway is
Hawthorne's and Melville's spiritual offspring (pp. 12–16). Also, as
in the case of Tatsumi's book on Hawthorne, the second half of the
book contains his translation of Hemingway's *In Our Time*, exclusive
of chapters 6–10 (pp. 153–246).

Articles and essays worth at least mention in this category are the
chapter on Hemingway in Yagyu's *Changes in Modern Consciousness
and Anglo-American Writers* (pp. 125–52), seems to converge with
Tatsumi's conclusions in his *Hemingway and Our Time*; also the chapter on Hemingway and Anaïs Nin in *What Manner of Woman* technically falls in this group. Similarly, the essays on Fitzgerald and
Dos Passos included in *Literary New York* and Yagyu's discussion of
Faulkner in his *Changes in Modern Consciousness* count among our
achievements on 20th-century American novelists. Other single articles in this group produced in 1985 are Margaret Mitsutani's "Viktor

Frankl and F. Scott Fitzgerald" (*EigoS* 131:242–45) and Ikuko Fujihira's study on Faulkner, "The Seer's Crystal Ball: The Horsethief
Episode in *A Fable*," available in English (*SALit* 22:77–94).

Due to the many translations of contemporary American writers,
newer American literature has been well received by Japanese readers as well as by scholars. (To name a few important titles published
in 1985: Toni Morrison's *Tar Baby*, Alice Walker's *The Color Purple*,
E. L. Doctorow's *The Book of Daniel*.) Contrary to what might be
expected from our interest in their writings, however, *The Images of
Women in Contemporary American Literature* is the sole book-length
study produced in 1985. This book is somewhat similar in its scheme
to *What Manner of Woman in American Literature*. It is an anthology
of essays written by women critics, the first half given to the images
of women in novels and plays by men: Eugene O'Neill, Tennessee
Williams, John Barth, Ken Kesey, and John Updike; the second half
is devoted to discussions of women characters portrayed by women
writers: Anne Sexton, Toni Morrison, Margaret Atwood, Cynthia
Ozick, and Anne Beattie. As is often the case with anthologies of this
kind, much remains to be desired as to the selection of the authors
treated; the variety of novelists, playwrights, and poets chosen in
this book, however, well represents the sociocultural and religious
structure peculiar to contemporary American society. It offers us an
epitome of the contemporary American literary scene. Furthermore,
each discussion functions as an independent essay on a specific contemporary American writer, like the chapters in *Literary New York*.

Among numerous articles on contemporary American writers, the
following deserve mention: Naoto Sugiyama's "Point of View in
Eudora Welty's *The Golden Apples* (*SALit* 22:95–107); Hideaki
Hatayama's "The Structure and Its Meaning of John Barth's *Letters*"
(*SALit* 22:111–22); Hiroshi Narazaki's "William Gaddis and His Confidence Men: Between Modernism and Post-Modernism" (*EigoS*
130:574–78); Hideo Kotake's "The Motif of the Child in Kurt Vonnegut's Novels" (*SELit* 62:241–52). As has been stated, *EigoS* featured articles on Ezra Pound in celebration of the centennial of the
poet's birth: Sanehide Kodama's report on the International Ezra
Pound Conference held at the University of Maine (May, 1985) is a
quick rundown of Pound scholarship; and an interview between
Toshikazu Niikura and Yukinobu Kagiya illuminates the chaotic universe of Pound's poetry, which is synonymous with Wallace Stevens'
"Great disorder is order"; another interesting article on contemporary

poets is Akio Gotoh's "Berryman and Lowell—Poets Possessed by Muse" (*EigoS* 130:532–33, 594–96).

The interdisciplinary approach to American literature is now indeed a major academic field of studies in this country. Two books of interest appeared in 1985: Koji Oi's *Frontier no Yukue: Seikimatsu America no Kiki to Sozo* [*The Frontier Closed: Crisis and the American Imagination at the Fin du Siècle*] (Kaibunsha); and Shunsuke Kamei's *Huckleberry Finn wa Ima: America Bunka no Yume* [*Huckleberry Finn Now: The Heroes in America*] (Kodansha). The authors of these works are noted scholars and prolific critics of American culture and literature and well-known to readers of *ALS*. *The Frontier Closed* is a collection of essays previously published in various books and journals over the past five years. Oi's historic-histo-literary perspective derives from Parrington's, Leo Marx's, and D. W. Noble's monumental scholarship. With his critical position constant from his book on Hawthorne (1974) onward, the reader can rest assured as to where his argument leads. Here, Oi explores shifting relations the American imagination has borne to the myth of "the New World Garden," which apparently disappeared after the Civil War. Drastic transformations brought about in various fields of life in America by the industrialization and urbanization of the country caused an impending sense of anxiety and fear concerning the national identity, which the critic calls "Crisis" at the end of the 19th century.

As the subtitle shows, Oi attempts to show how that American crisis was reflected in popular novels written between 1880 to 1910. The writers treated, with the exception of William Dean Howells, are such then-popular writers of fiction (but seldom discussed among critics of American literature) as Ignatius Donnelly, Frank L. Baum, Owen Wister, and Lincoln Steffens. *The Frontier Closed* is a rich resource book on these writers, and consequently our horizon on American literature expands into an area outside the canon. It is doubtful, however, whether the book will do what Leslie Fiedler once called "opening the canon."

Oi's dilemma results from his double-barreled critical stance, which tries to do justice to his materials (resourceful and fine) as works of art and to treat them as mere critical tools to illustrate the book's ultimate thesis. And as the critic himself acknowledges, Howells suffers most from such treatment. For the chapters on Howells (pp. 73–162) that cover more than one-third of the book may as well belong, with other 19th-century American writers, to the

494 Foreign Scholarship

third group in the present review. Still, Oi's discussion of Howells's *A Modern Instance* (pp. 114–38), the most recent essay included, is a penetrating analysis of the novel that articulates the sense of anxiety "the dean of American literature" felt at the end of the century.

Shunsuke Kamei's *Huckleberry Finn Now: The Heroes in America* is a collection of essays and sketches published in our major newspapers, literary magazines, and journals from 1979 to 1985. Like other books by the same author (see *ALS 1979*), *Huckleberry Finn Now* is a readable, informative, and funny critique of American culture. Expert on the comparative literature and culture of the two countries, Kamei's critical position is clearly cross-cultural. Like *The Frontier Closed*, Kamei's book pursues the theme of the American Dream. The difference in tone between the two, however, is great. The author of *The Frontier Closed* is concerned with the ambivalence inherent in the myth of America, whereas Kamei transcends such an enigma (being ever aware of its presence) and is enthused with the exuberance of creative energies that the popular American imagination generates. Kamei contends that America has created a rich literature in pursuit of its national hero—the dream American people dream incarnate; fantasies of the people thus share with the American literary imagination the one and same sap and root. Hence the author counts Huck Finn as the archetypal American whose descendants constitute a strange alloy—Tarzan, Marilyn Monroe, and even Jim Jones of People's Temple together with the heroes of Sherwood Anderson, Salinger, Bellow, and Kerouac.

Through its history, the traditional hero in America (Natty Bumppo and his likes) has changed into antihero, then superhero of science fiction and fantasy, and finally into a facetious middle-aged man of contemporary films. The transformation is generally regarded negatively as a descending curve—as Man's Fall from innocence. On the contrary here, Kamei sees the phenomenon as the sign of a sturdy America's coming of age and its eventual maturity, therefore an occasion for celebration, which surely reflects the critic's vantage point as an outsider of the culture analyzed. In this respect, *Huckleberry Finn Now* is, to borrow Tony Tanner's title, another *Reign of Wonder*; both share a spectator's detachment and curiosity. Kamei's prose flows smoothly, and whatever pessimism he might detect in America and its people, he sets it aside, and, à la Autolycus, "for the life to come" he and his American heroes "sleep out the thought of it." And seriously the title essay, "Huckleberry Finn Now" (pp. 215–41), and the book as a whole are this versatile scholar's tribute—like the articles in the special number of *EigoS*—to the centennial of the publication of Twain's masterpiece.

In conclusion, it seems that this review of Japanese scholarship on American literature for 1985 has witnessed as ever the diversity of our scholars' interest in American writings of various periods and genre. Like American poetry, which Louis Simpson once characterized, our scholarly explorations in American literature must also contend with: "Rubber, coal, uranium, moons, poems."

Kobe College

v. Scandinavian Contributions

Mona Pers

Scandinavian research in the field of American literature this year has been centered in Norway and Sweden, where four books and a dozen articles were published. Most of them deal with modern prose works, but a handful of the articles are about poetry, traditional as well as modern.

In his essay, "The Growth of Regionalism in the Early Poetry of the American Northwest" (*SN* 57:191–202), Lars Nordström contends that not until about two decades into the 20th century did the Pacific Northwest feel "the stirrings of a more substantial literary awakening." It was initiated by Colonel E. Hofer, who through his poetry magazine, *The Lariat,* created a forum for "Western literature." Nordström describes the impact and evaluates the importance of this conservative publication in relation to subsequent contending centers of literary activities, such as the manifesto *Status Rerum, The Frontier, The Outlander,* and *The Literary Monthly,* all of them predominantly regionalist. Then follows a discussion of what the term regionalism implies in the Northwest, how it relates to "local color," and in what ways it is mirrored in three anthologies of Northwest poetry published in the 1930s. In summing up, Nordström suggests that the early Northwest regionalist movement be regarded as consisting of three major aspects: it was frontier- and nature-oriented, concerned with the traits distinguishing the region; it is documentary, objective, realistic, and factual in tone, its style simple and direct, its form traditional, its mood narrative and descriptive; it was a self-conscious

movement, fighting for cultural independence by creating its own out-
lets centered upon small literary magazines. Nordström's factual and
compactly written essay is a promising foretaste of his forthcoming
book-length study of Northwest poetry.

Gunnar Larsson's "Rosens mönster–fågelsången. Om Ezra Pounds
Canto LXXV" [The Rose Pattern and the Bird Song] (*Artes* 10,ii:75–
80) is also a factual and tightly written essay, which in a few pages
manages to account for the origin of the many name references in
Pound's cryptic seven-line poem, "a short episode loaded with private
memory associations." It also makes a courageous attempt to explain
the intricate connection between the poem and the adjunct musical
score, which is at least six times as long as the text. Larsson offers
some suggestions as to how Pound might have imagined the performance of this canto set to music.

Hardly a year goes by without something being written in Sweden
about T. S. Eliot. Of the two essays on Eliot published this year one
deals with two poems that have not to my knowledge been attended
to before in Scandinavia. The aim of Clive K. R. Cressy's "T. S. Eliot's
'The Burnt Dancer,' 'The Death of Saint Narcissus,' and Mysticism"
(*MSpr* 79:209–21) is to show how the influence of Dante and mysticism is evident in Eliot's work at a much earlier stage than has hitherto been assumed. To this end Cressy pays special attention to the
way Eliot uses his literary sources in the two poems and to such
structural and thematic characteristics as are common to all the saints'
poems. Cressy reaches the conclusion that the two poems subjected to
his examination anticipate by more than 20 years the theme of saint-
hood and martyrdom in *Murder in the Cathedral* and the theme of
sin and expiation in *The Family Reunion*.

The second essay on Eliot is a well-balanced five-part study, " 'The
Waste Land' as Modernist Discourse" (*OL* 40:244–57), where Gerald
Doherty offers an illuminating structural analysis of the poem, applying the distinctions between readerly and writerly texts established by Roland Barthes in *The Pleasure of Text*. Doherty demonstrates why, in Barthesian terms, "The Waste Land" is an exemplary
modernist text: "in each section (or subsection) of the poem a text
that invites a 'readerly' reading with an autonomous (male) speaker,
a coherent system of referents, clearly articulated spatio-temporal
alignments and a settled site for the reader is followed by one which
invites a 'writerly' reading, one with multiple (female) voices, ambiguous referents, fragmented sequences and a destabilized site for

the reader." Doherty shows how at certain key points a Barthesian "third-term" emerges and "the conventional bond between signifier and signified is abolished and the sign becomes empty."

Doherty's lucid style of writing makes it easy for the reader to follow his argument. This same tribute cannot be paid to H. W. Fawkner, whose contrived language makes things more difficult than they need be. With "The Intricate Evasions of As. Wallace Stevens *à pic*" included in *Papers on Language and Literature*, ed. Sven Bäckman and Göran Kjellmer (Göteborg, pp. 138–52), Fawkner challenges other critics' straightforward acceptance of the theory Stevens developed in *The Necessary Angel* concerning the reality/imagination duality by claiming that "it is possible to find a much more vital clue to the essential structure of the poems and to the essential structure of Stevens's entire work." Fawkner has selected "An Ordinary Evening in New Haven" to prove the soundness of his proposition that "there is an internal rift between contraceptualization and ecstasy" in Stevens' work. "The theory of poetry is denied by the poetry," according to Fawkner.

This interest in exploring the relations between a writer's theories of literature and his artistic practice is shared by Per Winther, who begins *The Art of John Gardner: Instruction and Exploration* (Oslo) by investigating the philosophical and theoretical foundations of the novelist's approach to literature. Because it provides valuable clues to the author's artistic practice, Winther considers *On Moral Fiction* to be the "obvious starting point for a study of Gardner's theoretically developed views on the role and nature of art." The aspects of Gardner's art that Winther focuses on are the narrative and authorial voice, the experimentation with genre, the collage technique, and the dialectical method, which in his opinion is that of thesis, antithesis, and synthesis, where Gardner sets up "literary experiments" by juxtaposing contrary ideas or principles "to see what truths may issue from the ideational conflict." Winther maintains that Gardner in developing his collage technique "explores certain systemic semantic relationships between text and source," and to illustrate what he means, Winther makes effective use of "The King's Indian" as a case study. His contention that Gardner's collage technique and his "penchant for testing ideas or values, through counterpoise, are the most distinct figures in the carpet of his fiction" is supported by extensive evidence.

To measure one part of a writer's production against another is also the concern of Hans H. Skei. *William Faulkner: The Novelist as*

Short Story Writer (Oslo) may be considered a companion volume to
Skei's *William Faulkner: The Short Story Career* (Oslo, 1981), the
biographical and textual facts of which form the basis for the present
study. More than twice as long, the present book still closely follows
the structure of the earlier one. Thus Skei discusses, with varying
emphasis on formal and thematic significance, the texts in chronological order according to their place in what he terms the four periods of Faulkner's short story career: 1919–27, 1928–32, 1933–41, and
1942–62. The stated goal of the book is to demonstrate the importance
of the short stories in the author's total production through "a composite but structured presentation of Faulkner's short story universe."
Skei's comparative analyses reveal that the novel-story relationship is
insignificant in the early years but remarkably close later on. The
aspect of this relationship that interests him most is "the question of
the type of material and its narrative handling in story and novel,"
i.e., the role of the narrator and the relationship between the story
recounted and the discourse in which it is told. Although Skei acknowledges that Faulkner is a novelist first and that this fact has
greatly influenced his short stories, his study shows that Faulkner's
short stories also influenced and even made up some of his novels.
Skei therefore suggests we regard Faulkner as novelist *and* short story
writer.

Joyce Carol Oates, the novelist and short story writer, is like
Faulkner a recurrent feature in Scandinavian literary research and
criticism. In "Joyce Carol Oates: Passion and Madness, Moderne
Amerika" (*Vinduet* 39,iv:32–38), Kristin Hoel uses three Oates novels,
Angel of Light, *Bellefleur*, and *Solstice*, to illustrate why she considers "passion and madness" to be key words covering the main
themes in Oates's oeuvre. The aim of Monica Loeb's "Henry James
and Joyce Carol Oates: 'The Turn of the Screw' Times Two" (*AmerSS*
17:1–9) is to establish which elements from the "original" story inspired the contemporary writer "to create a 'marriage' or an 'infidelity.'" She decides that there are numerous parallels between the
two stories as regards date, setting, theme, subject, character, mood,
points of view, and style, which leads her to the conclusion that
Oates's "version" is more of a "marriage" than an "infidelity."

Four other female writers have been submitted to comparative
studies. Both Inger-Anita Markussen's essay, "To Syn på kvinnefrig-
jøring. Fay Weldon: *Praxis* og Marilyn French: *Kvinner*" and Toril

Hanssen's "Kunst som kampmiddel. Svarte kvinneliga forfattere i USA: Alice Walker og Toni Cade Bambara" are chapters in *Oppbrudd. Skrivende kvinner over hela verden* [*Breaking Up: Women Writing All Over the World*]. (Oslo). Markussen's entry offers a comparison of the themes, tone, and style in *Praxis* and *The Women's Room*; Hanssen's focuses on three novels—Walker's *Meridian* and *The Color Purple* and Bambara's *The Salt Eaters*. Her analysis shows that the two writers, although they express it differently, share a strong belief in art and man's possibilities to survive and develop. Markussen and Hanssen have both applied a feminist approach to their material. To a lesser extent this is true of Victoria Maubrey-Rose, who in *The Anti-Representational Response: Gertrude Stein's Lucy Church Amiably* (Uppsala) valiantly attempts to close in on Stein's inaccessible novel "through semantic and linguistic aspects of feminist, schizophasic, and avant-garde discourse taken from Marxist and post-structuralist literary discourse," an approach that takes Rose almost half the book to explain and justify. The aim of the study seems to be a demonstration of how Stein's use of language and landscape is "a refusal of the Phallic signifier, of phallogocentric discourse," and a rejection of traditional narrative representation, including the limitations of metaphor. It is Rose's contention that events in Stein's private life and her response to the period she lived in conspired to her "negation through language of the text as a means to representation." Rose's discovery that there is an "abyss" in the novel between the author's desire to attain the "thing-in-itself" and its actual production challenged her to undertake the formidable task of analyzing, through various ideational constructs, that nebulous abyss.

There is a growing fascination with methodological experimentation among literary scholars in Scandinavia. Åsebrit Sundquist's *Pocohontas & Co.—The Fictional American Indian Woman in Nineteenth Century Literature: A Study of Method* (Oslo) is primarily a report on "the outcome of an investigation relying on some methodological innovations intended to yield more reliable conclusions" than those based on the traditional motley of individual critics. She has used what she calls the "Questionnaire-Computer" and "List" methods, both described thoroughly in the beginning of the book, which contains no less than 186 tables clarifying scores of characteristics pertaining to Indian women, some comparing them to Indian men and white women. Although not all the information she has processed seems of central interest, Sundquist's study makes good her claim that "a quantitative analysis of literature can support and enrich a traditional analysis."

This year a newly awakened interest in Native American literature seems to have superseded our interest in immigrant literature. In "Mythic Realism in Native American Literature" (*AmerSS* 17:65–73) Bo Schöler attempts to answer the question, "What makes Native American literature different from other American literature?" He suggests that it is primarily the "malleability or creative flux of things." Since this is what constitutes "the foundation upon which most Native American writers base their thought on writing and being," it lies at the heart of what Schöler terms "mythic realism." He has wisely chosen for analysis Leslie Silko's well-known novel *Ceremony*, an excellent example of "malleability of reality," to illustrate his point. Schöler's interest in Native American literature is further documented by " 'I would save the cat': An Interview with Ralph Salisbury" (*AmerSS* 17:27–34), focusing on the poetic theories and practice of this writer and professor of literature, who is part eastern Cherokee, part Irish, and part English.

A few words about Helge Normann Nilsen's "Irene as Moral Norm: A Note on Malamud's *The Tenants*" (*AmerSS* 17:23–26) will close this report. In his short article Nilsen argues against the generally accepted critical view that Irene is "an all-too human female character." He also refutes the femme fatale notion that in this novel "it is the woman who fails the man" by insisting that "Malamud's novel presents a clear example of female love and tolerance in the midst of a fictional world dominated by egotism and hatred."

University College at Västerås, Sweden

22. General Reference Works

J. Albert Robbins

As our readers know, we generally notice major author and genre bibliographies in appropriate *ALS* chapters. Thus we are left in this mop-up chapter with a miscellaneous bag of titles—more miscellaneous this year, it seems, than usual.

The most important of the lot for 1985 is the Modern Language Association's *MLA Style Manual* designed for doctoral students and established scholars. (The *MLA Handbook for Writers of Research Papers* [see *ALS 1984*, pp. 577–78] is addressed to undergraduates.) It was, however, in this undergraduate *Handbook* (2nd edition, 1984) that the MLA first laid out the scheme of parenthetical documentation. But even before that—the chronology of all this becomes confusing—*PMLA* initiated parenthetical documentation in its May 1982 issue. (For the MLA's account of the history of all this, see *PMLA* 97[1982]:307–08.) If you were wondering, the journal *American Literature* has not converted to parenthetical documentation.

This 271-page *Manual* codifies much of what publishing scholars have been practicing for many years, but introduces such new topics as the revised copyright law and the question of fair use (pp. 32–42); libel (pp. 40–41); anonymous submission of articles to journals (pp. 89–90); nonsexist language (p. 2); new publishing techniques (p. 30); aspects of writing for publication and seeing a piece through the press (pp. 12–27).

Frederic G. Cassidy, chief editor, and a large staff of specialists and informants have published the *Dictionary of Regional English* (DARE), vol. 1, consisting of a detailed introduction and the letters A–C (Belknap). It has the usual apparatus of the historical dictionary plus something new (to me, at least)—computer-generated usage maps. It will be a welcome new resource on Americanisms. And it invites browsing. Anyone might guess the meaning of "Abe Lincoln fence" (split-rail fence), but do you know what an "Abe Lincoln bug" once was in Georgia? (A harlequin cabbage bug, which has a bad odor and taste.) How about "cut a gut"? (To make a mistake.) "Bunny-in-the monk"? (A game of marbles.) "Bung fodder"? (Toilet paper or substitute therefor.)

There are two works on children's literature. The first is rather elementary in scope, for the editors, Alethea K. Helbig and Agnes Regan Perkins, in *Dictionary of American Children's Fiction, 1859–1959; Books of Recognized Merit* (Greenwood), include only titles which have won awards or citations. They provide career sketches of authors and in title entries summarize plots and describe works. More professional is *American Writers for Children before 1900* (DLB 42), ed. Glenn E. Estes, a companion volume to John Cech's *American Writers for Children, 1900–1960* (DLB 22, 1983). The range is from "Now I lay me down to sleep" (the *New England Primer*, 1727) to Eugene Field's "Little Boy Blue" (1892)—a rich period of classics by Louisa May Alcott, Thomas Bailey Aldrich, "Peter Parley," Joel Chandler Harris, Clement Clarke Moore, George W. Peck, and others.

We do not normally notice anthologies, but I should note that Donald Hall has edited the first edition of *The Oxford Book of Children's Verse in America*—companion volume to *The Oxford Book of Children's Verse* (the qualifying adjective "British" is presumed).

A welcome guide to the subject is Roger O. Rock's *The Native American in American Literature: A Selectively Annotated Bibliography* (Greenwood), intended to augment existing guides to the bibliographical literature in both its phases: writing about Native Americans (pp. 56–98) and writing by Native Americans (pp. 99–182).

The Greenwood Press has published *Chicano Literature, A Reference Guide*, ed. Julio A. Martinez and Francisco A. Lomeli. They call it "the first reference guide to the creative writers, periods, and genres of Chicano literature." The editors also provide articles on theater, poetry, the novel, history of Chicano literature and criticism, Chicano children's literature, and Chicano philosophy.

Two publishers issued reference works on supernatural and science fiction. E. F. Bleiler has edited *Supernatural Fiction Writers: Fantasy and Horror* (2 vols., Scribner's), with sections on French and German authors of the genre, a large section on British writers, and a somewhat smaller one on American. There are eight to 10 double-column page essays on authors ranging from Irving and Poe to such living practitioners as Harlan Ellison, Ursula Le Guin, and Richard

Matheson. Scribner's published Bleiler's companion volume, *Science Fiction Writers*, in 1982. It is a more volatile area which editors Marshall B. Tymn and Mike Ashley try to bring under bibliographical control in *Science Fiction, Fantasy, and Weird Fiction Magazines* (Greenwood). In this fat, 970-page volume, the entries record publication history, location sources, index sources, and provide short descriptive essays on what, not too long ago, we considered subliterary and ephemeral materials unworthy of academic study.

A directory of *Contemporary Poets*, 4th edition, ed. James Vinson and D. L. Fitzpatrick (St. Martin's), updates the lives and careers of some 800 major living poets writing in English. It summarizes biography, lists publications, includes a signed essay, and, when available, adds a poet's own comments on the craft of poetry. There are a title list of poems cited, an appendix on major postwar poets who have died, notes on poetic movements, and a selective list of poetry anthologies since 1960.

The second volume of *Contemporary Authors: Autobiography Series* (Gale) contains memoirs by 13 American authors, foremost being John Ciardi, Cid Corman, and Jean-Claude van Itallie.

With *American Newspaper Journalists, 1690–1872* (DLB 43), editor Perry J. Ashley has, in four volumes, concluded a chronicle of national journalists from the beginning to the mid-20th century. Of the 66 journalists in this volume only three are of literary interest—Benjamin Franklin, Philip Freneau, and William Cullen Bryant.

The DLB *Yearbook 1984* follows what is now an established pattern, publishing materials which are proper yearbook matter (the year's book awards, for example, well over 100 for writing of all kinds); obituaries and necrology for the year; best-seller lists; four essays on the year in literary biography, drama, poetry, and fiction, and materials which are not. Among the latter are useful essays which might have appeared in professional journals: interviews, a series on small presses and on research archives, and an essay on "A Contemporary Fluorescence of Chicano Literature" by Carl R. Shirley (pp. 7–16). The *Yearbook* is also a place where new DLB biographical entries are added and occasionally old ones updated.

Author Index

Abbott, Philip, 17–18
Abramson, Doris E., 407
Abrioux, Yves, 462
Abse, Dannie, 340
Achtert, Walter S., 501
Ackroyd, Peter, 135
Adair, William, 185
Adams, Stephen, 79
Adams, Timothy Dow, 413
Addonizio, Kim, 344
Aharoni, Ada, 270
Ahlstrom, Sydney E., 7
Ahluwalia, Harsharan Singh, 77
Ahrends, Günter, 477–78, 479–80, 482
Aithal, S. Krishnamoorthy, 79
Akao, Kenichi, 490
Akiyama, Masayuki, 106
Albanese, Catherine L., 218
Albert, Walter, 45
Albright, Alex, 272
Albright, Daniel, 129
Aldridge, A. Owen, 200
Aleksandrov, V., 447
Alexander, John, 126
Alexander, Paul, 340
Alkalay-Gut, Karen, 320, 339–40
Allen, Paula Gunn, 338
Altieri, Charles, 126, 301–02
Alunin, T. T., 447
Alvarez, A., 340
Ames, Lois, 340
Anderson, Douglas, 97
Anderson, Richard, 180
Andrews, William L., 369, 383
Ano, Fumio, 491
Antczak, Frederick J., 95
Apenko, E. M., 443
Appiah, Anthony, 383
Applewhite, James, 330
Arac, Jonathan, 9, 94
Arksey, Laura, 194
Arner, Robert D., 189, 195–96
Arnott, Catherine M., 360
Aschkenasy, Nehama, 113

Ashdown, Paul, 254
Ashihara, Kazuko, 487, 489
Ashley, Mike, 503
Ashley, Perry J., 503
Aspiz, Harold, 70, 73
Asselineau, Roger, 30, 97, 455, 457
Atherton, John, 458
Atkinson, Brooks, 350
Atteberry, Phillip D., 243
Austin, Allan, 409
Austin, Gayle, 362
Autrey, Max L., 39–40
Axelrod, Steven Gould, 334, 340

Bachem, Walter, 465
Bachinger, Katrina, 85
Bacigalupo, Massimo, 123, 132
Bäckman, Sven, 497
Bader, Rudolf, 235
Baginski, Thomas, 41
Bailey, Peter J., 295, 296
Bain, Robert, 196
Baker, Bruce, 232
Baker, Houston A., Jr., 371–72, 380–81,
    399
Baker, Robert A., 273
Baker, William, 134
Baker, William D., 90, 223
Bal, Mieke, 431
Balbert, Peter, 130
Baldick, Chris, 145
Baldwin, Neil, 311
Bales, Jack, 216
Bales, Kent, 33–34
Balgun, F. Odun, 269
Bamikunle, Aderemi, 379
Bandry, Michel, 460
Bandy, W. T., 70, 72, 73
Banyiwa-Horne, Naana, 395
Bar-yaacov, Lois, 308
Baraka, Amiri, 404
Barber, X. Theodore, 235
Barbera, Jack, 166
Barker, Jonathan, 143

Barlow, Judith E., 357
Barnstone, Willis, 330
Barone, Dennis, 344
Barthelemy, Anthony, 407
Bartlett, Lee, 124, 336, 337–38, 344
Bassett, John E., 96, 222
Bates, Milton J., 303–04
Batten, Wayne, 225
Battestin, Martin C., 203
Baughman, Ronald, 341
Baumann, Walter, 133
Baym, Nina, 29–30
Beacham, Walton, 45
Beard, Dorothea, 306
Beard, James Franklin, 212, 214
Beauchamp, Wilton, 261
Beckett, Tom, 330
Bedient, Calvin, 339
Behrendt, Stephen C., 309
Beidler, Peter G., 119
Bell, Bernard W., 97, 383, 389
Bell, Ian F. A., 12–13, 20, 112–13,
    114–15, 127, 139–40
Bell, J. Madison, 286
Bell, Michael Davitt, 31, 99–100
Bell, Millicent, 63, 105, 110, 112, 115–
    16
Bell, Vereen, 316
Bell-Villada, Gene H., 438
Bellamy, Joe David, 288
Bellas, Ralph B., 359
Bellour, Raymond, 456
Bellringer, Alan W., 116, 236
Bender, Eileen T., 161
Bendixen, Alfred, 210, 238
Benevento, Joseph J., 78
Benfey, Christopher, 339
Bennett, Ken, 167
Bensick, Carol Marie, 32–33, 38
Benson, Jackson J., 180, 255
Benston, Kimberly W., 369, 404
Bentley, Eric, 356
Benvenuto, Richard, 314–15
Beppu, Keiko, 484, 491
Béranger, Jean, 455
Berben, Jacqueline, 393
Bercovitch, Sacvan, vii, 77, 421
Berg, Stephen, 140, 324
Berger, Alan L., 269–70
Berger, Charles, 306
Bergmann, Frank, 209
Bergreen, Laurence, 253
Berman, Jeffrey, 144, 284

Bernstein, Charles, 127, 330, 332
Bernstein, Michael André, 127, 130,
    336
Berrett, Anthony J., 97
Berry, Eleanor, 311
Berry, Wendell, 266
Berryman, Charles, 290–91
Bertholf, Robert, 339
Bickman, Martin, 62–63
Biddle, Jeff E., 100
Bidley, Martin, 155, 161
Bigsby, C. W. E., 349–50, 363
Bird, Roy K., 266
Birkerts, Sven, 338
Bischoff, Volker, 227
Bishop, George, 118
Bishop, Jonathan, 141–42
Björk, Lennart A., 107
Black, Stephen A., 358
Blair, Walter, 92
Blake, Nancy, 159, 163, 462
Blakemore, Steven, 214
Blanck, Jacob, 44
Blanding, Thomas, 5
Blank, Martin, 359
Blanke, Gustav H., 473
Blanshard, Brand, 135
Blasing, Mutlu Konuk, 11
Blau, Herbert, 352
Bleikasten, André, 158, 160–61, 459–
    60
Bleiler, Everett Franklin, 272–73, 502–
    03
Bleu, Patricia, 458–59
Bloodworth, William, 250
Bloom, Harold, 50, 178, 305, 341
Bloom, Steven F., 358
Blotner, Joseph, 147, 151, 154
Bluestein, Gene, 65
Boerner, Peter, 465
Boewe, Mary, 100
Bogard, Travis, 359
Bogardus, Ralph F., 109–10
Bogin, Ruth, 200
Böker, Uwe, 476
Bonner, Willard H., 16–17
Booth, Philip, 332
Booty, John E., 142
Bordman, Gerald, 350
Bornstein, George, 124, 128
Borsten, Orin, 149
Boudreau, Richard, 225
Bourjaily, Vance, 340

Bouyssou, Roland, 143
Bowers, Neal, 289, 341
Bowlby, Rachel, 234
Bradbury, Nicola, 112
Bradford, M. E., 285
Bradley, David, 385
Brady, Kristin, 37
Branch, Edgar M., 90, 95, 96
Branch, Watson, 61
Brand, Dana, 52, 53, 79
Brashear, Lucy, 84
Braswell, Mary Flowers, 168
Bray, Mary Kay, 394
Bray, Robert, 218, 361
Brayer, John M., 195
Breitwieser, Mitchell Robert, 194, 198
Brennan, Stephen C., 234-35
Brenner, Gerry, 182
Breslin, James E. B., 312, 326
Breslin, Paul, 327
Bresnahan, Roger J., 240
Briant, Alexis, 456
Brinkmeyer, Robert H., Jr., 258, 286
Brodsky, Louis Daniel, 149, 151
Broe, Mary Lynn, 340
Brooker, Jewel Spears, 137
Brooker-Bowers, Nancy, 268
Brooks, Cleanth, 145, 153, 154, 156, 160, 415
Brooks, Colette, 351
Brooks, Peter, 106, 431-32
Brophy, Robert, 319
Brotherston, Gordon, 213
Brown, Calvin S., 154, 163, 166
Brown, Carolyn S., 218
Brown, Dennis, 127
Brown, Rosellen, 340
Brown, Soi-Daniel W., 402
Brown, Stephen Ford, 342
Brown, Sterling A., 412
Bruccoli, Matthew J., 178
Bruce-Novoa, Juan, 463
Bruhn, Uwe, 469
Brumm, Ursula, 189, 472
Brunner, Edward, 315
Bruns, Gerald L., 301
Bruyère, Claire, 459
Bryan, George, 347-48
Bryant, John, 68
Buck, Heather, 142
Buckler, William E., 107
Budd, John, 116
Budd, Louis J., 93, 94-95, 99

Budick, E. Miller, 82, 215, 360
Budrecki, Lech, 453
Bunting, Basil, 140
Burduck, Michael, 45
Burke, Carolyn, 314, 338
Burke, William M., 142
Burkholder, Robert E., 3-4
Burleson, Donald R., 273
Burns, Gerald, 333
Burt, John, 29
Bus, Heiner, 469
Busby, Mark, 283
Busch, Frieder, 469
Bush, Ronald, 128, 138, 139
Bush, Sargent, Jr., 20-21
Butt, David, 304
Butterick, George F., 332, 336
Butts, Leonard C., 289
Byerman, Keith E., 375-76
Byers, Thomas B., 343
Byrd, Rudolph P., 385

Cady, Edwin H., 209, 222
Cady, Joseph, 75
Caldeira, Maria Isabel, 385-86
Calder, Jenni, 113
Calhoun, Richard J., 205, 331
Callaway, John, 288
Cambon, Glauco, 305-06
Cameron, Kenneth Walter, 26
Cameron, Sharon, 3, 15-16
Camp, Dennis, 318
Campbell, Josie P., 396
Cantor, Eddie, 364
Capellan, Angel, 176-77
Caramello, Charles, 114
Carby, Hazel V., 377-78
Carey, Glenn O., 223
Carey, Jonathan S., 7
Carlson, Marvin, 352
Carlson, Susan, 119-20
Carlson, Thomas C., 48
Carothers, James B., 151, 166
Carpenter, Charles A., 349
Carr, Virginia Spencer, 244
Carroll, Suzanne, 231
Carson, Richard G., 218-19
Carter, Everett, 98
Carter, Steven R., 361-62, 371, 408
Carton, Evan, 9, 27-28, 49-50, 82
Cascardi, Anthony J., 10-11
Casillo, Robert, 128, 131, 133
Cassidy, Frederic G., 501

Cassola, Arnold, 292
Castro, Michael, 320
Cavitch, David, 71
Caws, Mary Ann, 112, 432
Cayley, John, 132
Cazemajou, Jean, 456, 463
Cech, John, 502
Chamberlain, Lori, 338
Chambers, Ross, 52
Chaplin, Charlie, 364
Chappell, Fred, 343
Cheatham, George, 260
Chell, Cara, 290
Chénetier, Marc, 318, 457–58, 460, 462
Cheney, Patrick, 185
Cherrin, Bonnie D., 169–70
Chesler, Phyllis, 395
Cheyfitz, Eric, 212
Chiari, Joseph, 135
Childs, John Steven, 144
Choe, Wolhee, 303
Christian, Barbara, 374, 390
Christophersen, Bill, 383
Ciuba, Gary M., 286
Clark, Beverly Lyon, 259, 460
Clark, Edward, 368–69, 399–400
Clark, Michael, 192, 226, 392
Clark, Norris B., 405–06
Clark, Robert, 212–13
Clark, William Bedford, 195, 257
Clarke, Graham, 208
Clarke, Larry R., 201
Clements, Patricia, 138
Coale, Samuel Chase, 26, 27, 155, 226, 278–79, 285, 416
Coard, Robert L., 238–39
Codrescu, Andrei, 330
Coffler, Gail, 57–58, 68
Cohen, Milton A., 183–84
Cohen, Paul, 242
Cohen, Philip, 158
Colacurcio, Michael J., 31, 32
Colburn, Steven E., 340
Coleman, Arthur, 239
Coleman, Elizabeth, 121
Coleman, James W., 393
Collier, Eugenia, 394
Collings, Michael R., 298
Colonnese, Tom, 268
Colvile, Georgiana, 461
Conder, John J., 234, 244
Conforti, Joseph, 196
Conley, Timothy Kevin, 155–56

Connors, Marie, 166
Conron, John, 11
Cook, Albert, 309, 342
Cook, Eleanor, 303
Cookson, William, 131
Cooper, Michele F., 133
Cordesse, Gérard, 463
Core, George, 319
Cork, Richard, 124
Corman, Cid, 332
Cosgrove, Stuart, 355
Costa, Richard Hauer, 108
Costello, Bonnie, 302, 327
Coulon, Claude, 456
Couturier, Maurice, 462
Couvares, Francis G., 355
Covel, Robert C., 341
Cowell, Pattie, 190
Cox, Dianne, 160
Cox, Don Richard, 113
Cox, James M., 258
Crabtree, Claire, 387
Craft, Robert, 144
Crasnow, Ellman, 112
Crawford, Robert, 138
Crenshaw, Brad, 338
Cressy, Clive K. R., 496
Cronin, Gloria L., 270
Cross, Mary, 117
Crowley, J. Donald, 98–99
Crowley, John W., 217, 221–22
Crumpacker, Laurie, 197
Cuddy, Lois A., 86
Culley, Margo, 416
Culver, Stuart, 112
Cunci, Marie-Christine, 458
Curb, Rosemary K., 361
Cureton, Richard D., 317
Current-García, Eugene, 38, 48–49
Curtis, Julia, 354
Cushman, Stephen, 307–08
Cutrer, Thomas W., 257

Dahl, Curtis, 182
Daigrepont, Lloyd M., 212
Dale, Peter, 138, 142
D'Alessandro, Umberto, 272
Dalke, Anne French, 75–76, 85, 220
Daly, Robert, 192
Dameron, J. Lasley, 14
Danon-Boileau, Laurent, 462
Dasenbrock, Reed Way, 126
Davenport, Edward, 144

Davidson, Clifford, 143
Davidson, Harriet, 136
Davidson, Michael, 302, 332, 333
Davie, Donald, 127, 134
Davies, Carole Boyce, 399
Davis, Charles T., 409
Davis, Mary E., 155
Davis, Robert Con, 434
Davis, Thadious M., 331, 370–71, 379, 398
Davison, Richard Allan, 240
Day, William Patrick, 54
Dayan, Joan, 342
Deese, Helen R., 216
De Jong, Mary Gosselink, 336
de Jongh, James L., 401
Delano, Sterling F., 5
Delarue, Claude, 455
Delbanco, Andrew, 203
de Margerie, Diane, 456
DeMartini, Brenda, 344
Derounian, Kathryn Zabelle, 192
DeShazer, Mary, 314, 338
Devlin, James E., 264
Dickie, Margaret, 315–16
Diehl, Joanne Feit, 338
Dieke, Ikenna, 393
Diggins, John Patrick, 227
Diggory, Terence, 327
Dimino, Andrea, 157
Dimock, Wai-chee, 236
DiPiero, W. S., 336
Ditsky, John, 255
Dixon, Melvin, 412
Doane, Margaret, 231
Dodge, Charlyne, 226
Doherty, Gerald, 496–97
Dolinin, A. A., 443, 445
Dolis, John, 36
Doll, Mary Aswell, 264
Dolmetsch, Carl, 101–02
Donaldson, Scott, 171, 244–45
Donoghue, Denis, 141
Donohue, Agnes McNeill, 26–27
Donovan, Josephine, 425
Doreski, William, 19, 341–42
Dorian, Donna, 314, 338
Doudna, Martin K., 41, 77
Douglas, Keith, 139
Douglas, Wallace, 438
Douglass, Paul, 142–43
Downey, Sr. Charlotte, 84
Doyle, Charles, 305

Doyle, N. Ann, 172
Dressman, Paul, 333
Driscoll, Kerry, 310
Dryden, Edgar A., 66–67
Duban, James, 22–23
Dubie, Norman, 133
DuBois, Ellen Carol, 425
Dudden, Arthur Power, 211
Duncan, Robert, 313–14
Dunn, Margaret, 164
Dunn, Thomas G., 349
Durant, Alan, 127
du Sautoy, Peter, 135
Dydo, Ulla L., 338
Dyer, Joyce Coyne, 225, 261

Eager, Gerald, 105–06
Eakin, Paul John, 254
Eaves, T. C. Duncan, 132
Eberwein, Jane Donahue, 83
Eble, Kenneth E., 91, 180, 221
Edel, Leon, 104, 118
Edelman, Lee, 335
Edwards, Betty, 12
Edwards, Paul, 409
Egan, Kenneth V., 22
Egri, Peter, 454
Einenkel, Robert, 358
Eitner, Walter H., 70
Elder, John, 319, 327
Elgin, Don D., 297
Elias, Khaliquzzaman, 406
Eliot, Valerie, 135–36
Elledge, Scott, 268
Elliott, Emory, vii, 421
Elliott, James P., 212
Ellis, James, 119
Ellmann, Maud, 112
Emerson, Everett, 89–90, 93, 197
Empson, William, 135
Engebretson, David, 298
Engel, Bernard F., 211
Engel, Leonard W., 54
Engler, Balz, 112
Engler, Bernd, 466–67
Ensslen, Klaus, 400
Epstein, Seymour, 269
Erickson, C. A., 222–23
Erickson, Peter B., 370–71
Erkkila, Betsy, 73–74, 81, 87
Erlebach, Peter, 469
Esbjornson, Carl D., 336
Escott, Paul D., 412

Eshleman, Clayton, 327
Eshuis, Enny de Boer, 114
Estes, David C., 262
Estes, Glenn E., 502
Evans, Nancy H., 299
Evans, Walter, 66

Fabiny, Tibor, 130–31
Fabre, Geneviève, 456
Fabre, Michel, 388, 391, 462–63
Falk, Signi L., 360
Farnsworth, Robert M., 403
Fass, Ekbert, 325
Faulkner, Donald W., 254, 416
Faulkner, Howard, 384–85
Fawkner, H. W., 497
Fay, Stephanie, 38–39
Feasley, Florence G., 186
Feder, Lillian, 128
Feeney, Joseph J., 202
Feeny, Thomas, 272
Feldstein, Richard, 159
Felman, Shoshana, 434–35
Felperin, Howard, 435–36
Felstiner, John, 338
Fennick, Ruth, 260
Fenton, James, 349
Ferguson, Robert A., 208–09
Ferguson, SallyAnn H., 221
Fetrow, Fred M., 403
Fetterley, Judith, 210–11, 417
Ficken, Carl, 260
Fickert, Kurt J., 244
Fields, Kenneth, 336
Fifer, Elizabeth, 370, 398
Filreis, Alan, 304
Finkelstein, Norman M., 331, 336
Fireoved, Joseph, 199
Fischer, Michael, 436
Fischer, Victor, 92
Fisher, Barbara M., 305
Fisher, Benjamin Franklin, IV, 45
Fisher, Philip, 206–07, 233, 281, 417–18
Fishkin, Shelley Fisher, 73, 94, 233, 244, 256, 281–82, 418–19
Fisken, Beth Wynne, 220
Fithian, Rosemary, 191
Fitz Gerald, Gregory, 340
Fitzgerald, Norma M., 85
Fitzpatrick, D. L., 503
Fleck, Richard, 17
Fleischmann, Fritz, 214–15, 473

Fleming, Robert E., 238, 240, 358, 386–87, 389
Flower, Dean, 105
Floyd, Virginia, 356–57
Fogel, Daniel Mark, 305
Foley, Barbara, 434
Foley, Brian, 65
Folks, Jeffrey J., 319–20
Folsom, Ed, 70, 79, 130
Forkner, Ben, 452
Forseth, Roger, 239–40
Foster, Ann T., 335
Foster, Frances Smith, 411
Fournier, Michael, 132–33
Fowler, Doreen, 149, 154
Fowlie, Wallace, 135
Fox, Peggy L., 124
Fraiman, Susan, 221
Fraistat, Rose Ann C., 258
Franciosi, Robert, 141, 332
Frank, Elizabeth, 314
Frank, Frederick S., 45–46
Frank, Joseph, 281
Frank, Perry, 98
Frank, Stuart M., 60
Franklin, Benjamin, V, 202
Franklin, Rosemary F., 39
Frazer, Winifred L., 165, 266
Freed, Richard C., 34
Freedman, Florence Bernstein, 71
Freeman, Alma S., 397–98
Freibert, Lucy M., 202, 210, 419
Frick, John W., 350–51
Friedman, Alan Warren, 153
Friedman, Donald, 355
Friedman, Melvin J., 259, 460
Friedman, Susan Stanford, 313, 338
Froula, Christine, 129
Fry, Christopher, 135
Fryer, Judith, 237–38
Fryer, Sarah B., 182–83, 243
Fujihira, Ikuko, 492
Fujimori, Kayoko, 490–91
Fujita, Eiichi, 487, 488
Fulkerson, Tahita, 142
Fuller, Roy, 138
Funkhouser, Linda, 308
Furbank, P. N., 125, 139
Furnas, J. C., 97
Furukawa, Takao, 484, 490

Gabbin, Joanne V., 402
Gabler, Janet A., 115

Gadomski, Kenneth E., 306
Gaffney, Floyd, 370
Gajdusek, Robert, 179
Gale, Steven H., 271
Calef, David, 265
Galinsky, Hans, 470, 471
Gallagher, Tess, 314
Gallup, Donald, 47, 123–24, 134, 359
Gardner, Thomas, 337
Gargano, James, 55
Garner, Stanton, 58, 209, 226
Garrett, George, 181
Garvey, Sheila Hickey, 359
Gaskell, Ronald, 138
Gates, Henry Louis, Jr., 372, 409
Gee, James Paul, 308
Geherin, David, 273
Gelpi, Albert, 301, 313, 338
George, Diana Hume, 344
Gerath, Armin, 478
Gerbaud, Colette, 457
Gerlach, John, 167, 207, 238, 241, 280–81
Gernes, Sonia, 260
Gervaud, J. Michel, 232, 458
Giannone, Richard, 261
Gibaldi, Joseph, 501
Gibbons, Gerald, 438
Gibbons, Reginald, 329, 404
Gibson, Donald B., 410
Gibson, Mary Ellis, 235
Giddings, Robert, 93–94, 102
Gilbert, Sandra M., 309–10, 333, 338, 339, 426–27
Gilenson, B. A., 452
Giles, F., 138
Giles, Richard F., 129
Giles, Ronald K., 343
Gillman, Susan K., 100–101
Gilman, Owen W., Jr., 290, 318
Gilmore, Michael T., 13, 20, 28
Gilyard, Keith, 389
Girard, René, 472
Girgus, Sam B., 77–78
Glenn, I. E., 140–41
Glück, Louise, 140, 332
Godden, Richard, 112, 163, 213
Godshalk, William L., 249
Goimard, Jacques, 463
Golding, Alan, 302, 330, 332, 333
Goldstein, Laurence, 338–39
Goldstein, Lynda R., 305
Golemba, Henry, 21

Gollin, Rita K., 17
Goodin, George, 256, 290, 388–89
Goodridge, Celeste, 314
Gordon, David, 132, 133
Gordon, Lyndall, 134
Gossett, Thomas F., 216
Gotoh, Akio, 493
Gougeon, Len, 14–15, 72
Gould, Jean, 339
Grabo, Norman S., 191
Graff, Gerald, 438
Graham, Desmond, 139
Graham, Kenneth W., 46
Graham, Theodora R., 310
Granger, Bruce, 199
Granger, Michel, 21–22, 455
Graulich, Melody, 266
Gray, J. C., 144
Gray, W. Russel, 275
Grearson, Pauline S., 6
Green, Paul, 330
Greenberg, Robert M., 10
Greene, David L., 193
Greene, Gayle, 425–26
Greene, Lee, 379–80
Gregory, Robert, 108, 231
Gregory, Sinda, 274, 288, 297
Greiner, Donald J., 42, 108–09, 287, 292, 419
Gresset, Michel, 150, 153, 161, 462
Gresson, Aaron D., 401
Greven-Borde, Hélène, 463
Grey, Loren, 251
Gribben, Alan, 47, 90, 93, 94
Griffin, Joseph, 232, 235
Griffin, Peter, 171, 172–73
Griffin, Susan M., 117
Griffith, Kelley, Jr., 219
Griffiths, A. Phillips, 117
Grigson, Geoffrey, 135
Grimes, Larry, 177–78
Grimwood, Michael, 155, 167
Grobel, Lawrence, 289
Gross, Harvey, 141
Gross, Robert A., 20
Grosse, B. Donald, 353–54
Grove, James, 94
Grover-Rogoff, Jay, 311
Grünzweig, Walter, 102, 216
Grusin, Richard A., 14
Gubar, Susan, 426–27
Guest, Barbara, 130
Guillaume, Alfred J., Jr., 402

Guinness, Sir Alec, 135
Gunn, Thom, 336
Gura, Philip F., 203
Gutierrez, Donald, 337
Gwin, Minrose C., 162, 231, 376–77, 411

Haack, Dietmar, 475–76
Habegger, Alfred, 105
Habich, Robert D., 6, 23
Hackenberry, Charles, 382
Hadas, Rachel, 316
Haddin, Theodore, 342
Haegert, John, 265
Hagan, John, 264
Hagemann, E. R., 183
Hagenbüchle, Roland, 227
Hahn, H. George, II, 248
Hahn, Stephen, 161, 312
Haims, Lynn M., 192
Hakutani, Yoshinobu, 413
Hale, John, 201
Hall, Donald, 127, 140, 329, 502
Hallissy, Margaret M., 215, 287
Halperin, John, 107
Halter, Peter, 309
Hamamoto, Takeo, 490
Hamblin, Robert W., 149
Hamilton, R. S., 336
Hammond, Jeffrey A., 190–91
Hammond, Karla, 299
Hanley, William, 359
Hanna, Archibald, 253
Hansen, Arlen J., 15
Hansen, Elaine Tuttle, 298
Hansen, Olaf, 474
Hanssen, Toril, 498–99
Hara, Eriko, 484, 492
Harbison, Sherrill, 158
Harder, Kelsie B., 319
Harding, Brian, 11
Hardwick, Elizabeth, 340
Hardy, Barbara, 340
Hargrove, Nancy D., 143
Harmon, William, 330–31
Harper, Michael, 179
Harpham, Geoffrey Galt, 290
Harrington, Gary, 164
Harris, Natalie, 75
Harris, Susan K., 93, 220
Harris, Trudier, 331, 370–71, 381, 391–92
Harris, Victoria Frenkel, 342–43

Harris, William J., 405
Harrison, Paul Carter, 408
Harrison, Robert, 151
Harrison, Russell T., 343
Hartigan, Karelisa V., 361
Hartman, Geoffrey, 434
Hartstein, Arnold M., 64
Hass, Robert, 332
Hassler, Donald M., 273
Hastings, Michael, 135
Hastings, Susan, 242
Hatayama, Hideaki, 492
Hatcher, John, 403–04
Hathcock, Nelson, 341
Hatlen, Burton, 127, 130, 332, 336
Hattenhauer, Darryl, 66
Hauck, Richard Boyd, 218
Hauge, H., 129, 143–44
Hawkins, E. O., 163
Hawkins, Peter S., 137
Haynes, Jane Isbell, 151
Hays, Peter, 176
Heath-Stubbs, John, 138, 142
Hecht, Anthony, 140
Hecht, Ben, 364
Hedeen, Paul M., 159
Heermance, J. Noel, 382
Heimert, Alan, 203
Heinzelman, Kurt, 311
Helbig, Alethea K., 502
Hellenbrand, Harold, 199
Heller, Michael, 331, 332
Helm, Thomas E., 141
Helsa, David H., 302
Helterman, Jeffrey, 270
Henderson, Eric, 68
Henderson, Jeff, 289
Henderson, Mae G., 398, 408
Henderson, Stephen E., 404–05
Hendeson, Archie, 123
Hendrie, Don, Jr., 278
Herget, Winifred, 469, 471, 472
Hermans, Theo, 126
Hernton, Calvin, 339, 406–07
Herrnstadt, Richard L., 7
Herzinger, Kim A., 288
Hesford, Walter, 18–19
Heyen, William, 340
Higdon, David Leon, 109
High, John, 344
Hiles, Jane, 167
Hillringhouse, Mark, 344
Himy, Armand, 462

Hinchliffe, Arnold P., 143
Hinkle, James, 154, 184
Hiraishi, Takaki, 490
Hirooka, Minoru, 484
Hirsch, David H., 113
Hirsch, P. L., 67
Hirst, Robert H., 96
Hlavsa, Virginia V., 153–54
Hlus, Carolyn, 24
Hoag, Ronald Wesley, 61, 161–62
Hobson, Archie, 419
Hochman, Barbara, 224–25, 234
Hochman, Baruch, 433
Hocks, Richard A., 19
Hodge, Marion, 341
Hodges, John O., 413
Hodges, LeRoy S., Jr., 390
Hoel, Kristin, 498
Hof, Renate, 482–83
Hoffmann, Gerhard, 474–75, 483
Hollander, John, 178
Holley, Margaret, 314
Holloway, Patricia Mosco, 143
Holly, Carol, 121–22
Holmes, John Clellon, 272
Holota, Maciej, 453
Holtz, William, 240
Homans, Margaret, 83
Hooker, Jeremy, 332
Hooks, Bell, 399
Hooley, Daniel M., 131
Horemans, Rudi, 286
Horn, Andrew, 48
Horn, Pierre L., 234
Horvath, Brooke, 286, 291
Hosek, Chaviva, 303
Houston, James, 266
Houston, Neal B., 172
Hovanec, Carol P., 66
Hovet, Theodore, 8
Howard, David, 112
Howard, Goldena, 90–91
Howard, June, 207, 246, 256
Howard, Oliver, 90–91
Howarth, William, 268
Howell, John M., 289
Howes, Craig, 53–54
Hubsch, Allen W., 258
Hudgins, Andrew, 343
Hughes, Robert S., Jr., 256
Hughes, Ted, 340
Hughson, Lois, 222
Hull, Gloria T., 384, 412–13

Hull, Lynda, 344
Humphreys, Richard, 126
Humphries, Jefferson, 49, 155, 285
Hurst, Richard M., 201
Huseboe, Arthur R., 267
Hussman, Lawrence E., 234
Hutcheon, Linda, 428

Ickstadt, Heinz, 111, 212, 476
Idol, John L., Jr., 39, 263
Immel, Horst, 468, 469
Inada, Katsuhiko, 487, 489–90
Indick, Ben P., 297
Inge, M. Thomas, 98
Ingersoll, Earl, 299
Irby, Kenneth, 337
Irwin, W. R., 97
Isani, Muktar Ali, 45
Ishii, Michiyo, 158
Itoh, Shoko, 491
Ivan'ko, S. E., 452
Iwamatsu, Hirofumi, 140

Jackson, Blyden, 381–82, 388, 422
Jackson, Fleda Brown, 222
Jacobs, Robert D., 49
Jaffe, Nora Crow, 313
Jang, Gyung-Ryul, 131
Jantz, Harold, 189, 193
Jarab, Josef, 380
Jardine, Alice A., 280
Jarman, Mark, 318–19
Jarrell, Mary, 334
Jaworski, Philippe, 460
Johnson, Anthony L., 141
Johnson, Barbara, 387, 434
Johnson, Claudia D., 354
Johnson, Courtney, 106
Johnson, D. Barton, 265
Johnson, Greg, 83
Johnson, Stuart, 114, 290
Johnson, Susie Paul, 140, 162
Johnson, Thomas H., 80, 484
Jolly, John, 289
Jones, Ann Rosalind, 426
Jones, Bessie W., 394–95
Jones, Buford, 47
Jones, Daryl E., 65, 213
Jones, Harry, 402
Jones, Peter, 117
Jones, Suzanne W., 162
Jones, Vivien, 120–21
Joplin, Patricia Klindienst, 338

Jordis, Christine, 456
Joris, Pierre, 457
Juhasz, Suzanne, 83, 84
Julien, Claude, 463
Julius, Patricia H., 211
Junkins, Donald, 186
Justice, Donald, 131
Justin, Henri, 455
Justus, James H., 180, 215, 330

Kagiya, Yukinobu, 492
Kahn, Coppelia, 425–26
Kahn, Sholom J., 101
Kalinevitch, Karen, 5
Kallet, Marilyn, 312
Kalstone, David, 335, 338
Kamei, Shunsuke, 493, 494–95
Kamenetz, Rodger, 330, 337
Kamuf, Peggy, 33
Kanaseki, Hisao, 486
Kaplan, Cora, 426
Kaplan, Justin, 91
Kappel, Andrew J., 125, 132
Karcher, Carolyn L., 28
Karges, Joann, 265
Karl, Frederick R., 282
Karlins, Mark, 332–33
Karlsen, Carol F., 197
Karp, Vickie, 338
Kasparek, Carol A., 255
Kaufman, Shirley, 332
Kaufman, William, 94
Kauvar, Elaine M., 284
Kavka, Jerome, 125
Kawin, Bruce, 157
Kayashima, Hachiro, 487, 489
Kayman, Martin, 127
Kearney, Reginald, 402
Keesey, Douglas, 108
Keiner, Karl E., 481
Keller, Clifton, 5
Keller, Karl, 192
Kelley, Donald Brooks, 197–98
Kellman, Steven G., 284
Kelly, Gail Paradise, 425
Kelly, Lionel, 127
Kelly, William P., 213
Kemp, Anthony, 47
Kempf, James Michael, 254, 416
Kendrick, Brent L., 219–20
Kennedy, Elizabeth Lapovsky, 425
Kennedy, J. Gerald, 52
Kennedy, Richard S., 243, 264

Kennedy, Thomas E., 289
Kenner, Hugh, 125, 128, 131, 332
Kenner, Mary Anne, 124
Kerjan, Liliane, 456
Kermode, Frank, 438
Kerner, David, 170
Kessler, Carol Farley, 217
Ketterer, David, 47, 51
Kevles, Barbara, 340
Kiler, Carol, 342
Killingsworth, M. Jimmie, 75, 76
Kimball, Jean, 120
Kimnack, Wilson H., 194
Kimpel, Ben D., 132
Kimura, Junko, 265
King, D. W., 364
King, Michael, 130
King, Richard H., 166
Kinneavy, Gerald B., 143
Kinney, Arthur F., 157–59, 259, 460
Kinney, James, 101
Kinzie, Mary, 326–27
Kirk, John W., 359
Kjellmer, Göran, 497
Kleinen, Edgar, 471
Klinkowitz, Jerome, 282–83, 394
Klotman, Phyllis R., 377
Klug, M. A., 182
Knodel, Bea, 239
Kobler, J. F., 177–78
Kock, Christian, 55
Kodama, Sanehide, 328, 492
Koelling, Deborah Spangler, 191
Koepel, Jürgen, 469
Koike, Misako, 484, 492
Kolin, Philip C., 257
Kolodny, Annette, vii, 24
Kopley, Richard, 45, 48
Koprince, Susan J., 237, 238, 385
Koreneva, Maya M., 443, 446
Korn, Marianne, 127
Korsmeyer, Carolyn W., 425
Kosok, Heinz, 469
Kotake, Hideo, 492
Kramarae, Cheris, 428
Kramer, Victor S., 287
Krauss, Jennifer, 316
Krauth, Leland, 93
Kretzoi, Charlotte, 449
Kreutzer, Eberhard, 467–68, 480
Kreyling, Michael, 285
Krieg, Joann Peck, 9, 74–75
Kronick, Joseph G., 336

Krylova, I. N. K., 452
Kuberski, Philip, 132
Kuklick, Bruce, 8, 196–97, 420
Kumin, Maxine, 340
Kumskova, E. T., 451
Kunitz, Stanley, 335
Kusch, Robert, 335
Küster, Dieter, 469
Kutzinski, Vera M., 380

Labbé, Evelyne, 456
LaCapra, Dominick, 438–39
Lacey, Paul A., 333–34
Lackey, Kris, 62
LaFantasie, Glenn W., 193
Lamb, Robert Paul, 75, 179
Lambert, Deborah G., 237
Landor, M., 451–52
Lang, Hans-Joachim, 471–72, 476–77
Langbaum, Robert, 128
Langland, Elizabeth, 107, 233
Lanzinger, Klaus, 469
Larkin, Greg, 132
Larsson, Gunnar, 496
Lathrop, Kathleen, 287–88
Lauber, John, 90
Laughlin, James, 124, 125, 128, 131, 329
Laurence, Dan H., 129
Law, Joe K., 68
Lawson, Lewis A., 260, 285, 286, 287
Lazareva, E. V., 443
Lazarus, A. L., 223
Lazer, Hank, 79
Leahy, Sharon L., 165
Leary, Lewis, 200–201, 205
Leary, William, 267
Lease, Benjamin, 213–14, 473
Leavell, Linda, 142, 143
LeBeau, Bryan F., 23–24
Lecercle, Ann, 459
Lecroy, Douglas, 142
Lee, A. Robert, 68
Leenhouts, Annica, 275
Leggott, Michele, 332
Lehan, Richard, 233
Leibowitz, Herbert, 339
Leigh, John, 128–29
Leiner, J., 463
Leiter, Samuel L., 348
LeMaster, J. R., 92
Lemay, J. A. Leo, 193, 195
Lemon, Lee T., 292

Lensing, George S., 317
Lenz, William E., 95, 207–08, 293–94, 420
Levi, Peter, 144
Levin, Harry, 135
Levine, Ira A., 356
Levine, Paul, 289
Lewis, Merrill, 267
Lewis, Richard O., 382
Lewis, Roger, 181
Lewis, Ward B., 357
Leyda, Jay, 58–59
Liberman, M. M., 288
Light, Martin, 238
Linares, Andres, 125
Lindberg, Kathryne V., 126
Lindberg-Seyersted, Brita, 123
Linehan, Thomas M., 259–60
Link, Franz, 131
Lish, Gordon, 288
Little, Matthew, 121, 133
Litz, A. Walton, 128, 130, 134
Ljungquist, Kent P., 54
Lockwood, William J., 333
Loeb, Monica, 498
Lofaro, Michael A., 218
Logan, William, 339
Lojkine-Morelec, Monique, 143, 458
Lomeli, Francisco A., 328, 502
Long, E. Hudson, 92
Long, Elizabeth, 278
Long, Robert Emmet, 270–71
Longenbach, James, 129, 136
Longsworth, Polly, 82
Looby, Christopher, 198
Loomis, Edward, 251, 266
Lovejoy, David S., 197
Lowrance, Mason I., Jr., 190
Lubbers, Klaus, 469, 473–74
Ludington, Townsend, 243–44
Lutz, Harmut, 464–65
Lydenberg, Robin, 271
Lyne, William, 367
Lynn, Kenneth, 171
Lytle, Andrew, 258

McAleavy, David, 332
McBride, Anne K., 249
McBride, Elizabeth, 344
McCaffery, Larry, 288, 297
McCardell, John, 214
McClatchy, J. D., 336
McClave, Heather, 137

McClure, Michael, 291
MacColl, Ewan, 355
McConachie, Bruce A., 352–53, 355
McConahay, Mary Davidson, 19
McCool, Campbell, 149
McCorison, Marcus A., 203
MacCurdy, Carol, 289
McDarrah, Fred W., 272
McDougal, Stuart Y., 128, 138, 305–06
McDowell, Colin, 129
McDowell, Deborah E., 386
McDowell, Robert, 317
McEvoy, Seth, 394
McGann, Jerome J., 224
McGee, Patrick, 164
McGuire, Jerry, 316
McHale, Brian, 244
McHaney, Thomas L., 140, 153
McInnis, John, 273
McIntosh, James, 35–36
MacKay, Carol Hanbery, 36–37
McKay, Janet Holmgren, 100
McKay, Nellie, 383
McKinsey, Elizabeth, 24, 40, 208
McLarty, Chester A., 151
McLennan, Kathleen A., 354
McNally, Terrence, 360
McNamara, Eugene, 141
McNeely, Trevor, 184
MacVean, Jean, 144
McWilliams, John P., 213
Macy, Vaughana, 402
Madden, David, 274
Maddocks, Melvin, 273
Magala, Slawomir, 453
Magi, Aldo P., 263
Mahar, William J., 407
Mahoney, Dennis J., 101
Mailloux, Steven, 100
Makin, Peter, 132
Malin, Irving, 259
Manheim, Michael, 359
Manning, Carol S., 261
Manso, Peter, 284, 291
Maqbool, Aziz, 103
Marable, Manning, 384
Marchant, Peter, 299
Marchenko, O. Ya., 449
Marcus, Mordecai, 484
Marcus, Phillip L., 130
Marder, Daniel, 213
Margolis, Anne T., 110–11

Marigny, Jean, 464
Marks, Donald R., 387
Markussen, Inger-Anita, 498–99
Marovitz, Sanford E., 299, 300
Marriott, David, 293
Marrs, Suzanne, 262
Marshall, Jack, 332
Marshall, James, 238
Martin, Curtis, 370
Martin, Edward A., 246–47
Martin, Jean Pierre, 455
Martin, John Stephen, 4, 14, 40–41
Martin, Luther H., 34
Martin, Robert A., 296
Martin, Robert K., 115
Martin, Terence, 199–200, 278
Martin, W. R., 175–76
Martin, Waldo E., Jr., 410
Martin, Wendy, 86
Martinez, Julio A., 328, 502
Marx, Leo, 493
Marx, Patricia, 340
Massa, Ann, 139
Massey, Alan, 142
Matchen, David, 261
Materer, Timothy, 123, 129
Mates, Julian, 350
Matsui, Midori, 140
Matsuyama, Nobunao, 485
Matthews, John T., 151, 155
Matthews, Kathleen D., 310–11
Matthews, Richard K., 199
Matthews, William, 131, 329
Maubrey-Rose, Victoria, 499
Maxfield-Miller, Elizabeth, 4–5
Maxwell, Barry, 296–97
May, John R., 263
Mayoux, Jean-Jacques, 455
Megill, Allen, 428–29
Meindl, Dieter, 482
Melin, Charlotte, 241–42
Mellard, James, 257
Mellow, James, 171
Mercer, Caroline G., 116
Merrell, Floyd, 439
Mesch, Harald, 481
Meserve, Mollie Ann, 349
Metcalf, Eugene Wesley, 384
Meyer, Michael, 17
Meyer, William E. H., 197
Meyers, Jeffrey, 116, **134, 171, 172,**
    173–74

Miall, David S., 118–19
Michaels, Walter Benn, 16, 35
Michelson, Bruce, 334
Mickelsen, David, 164–65
Micklus, Robert, 195
Middlebrook, Diane Wood, 314, 338
Middleton, Victoria, 395
Mikriammos, Philippe, 124
Milder, Robert, 63
Miller, J. Hillis, 303, 308, 434
Miller, Linda, 171–72
Miller, Margaret, 266
Miller, S. H., 342
Miller, William V., 240
Millgate, Michael, 151, 160
Mills, Jerry Leath, 259
Mills, John A., 266
Milne, W. S., 138
Milton, John, 266
Miner, Madonne M., 395
Mishra, R. S., 76
Mitchell, Lee Clark, 100, 232–33
Mitsutani, Margaret, 491–92
Mizruchi, Susan L., 115
Moddelmog, Debra A., 42, 58, 139, 162, 169
Moers, Ellen, 34
Moi, Toril, 427–28
Molesworth, Charles, 327
Monroe, Robert Emmett, 225
Monteiro, George, 5, 85, 97–98, 105, 185
Montes, Catalina, 154
Montgomery, Michael S., 203
Moore, Harry, 340
Moore, L. Hugh, 201
Moore, Margaret B., 40
Moore, Rayburn S., 205, 422
Morace, Robert A., 289, 295
Moreland, Kim, 175
Morita, Takeshi, 490
Morley, Hilda, 332
Morley-Mower, G. F., 249
Morozova, T. L., 443, 444
Morris, Ann R., 317
Morris, Timothy, 14, 85–86
Morrissey, Michael, 282
Morrow, Nancy V., 200
Morse, Jonathan, 143
Mortland, Don, 23
Morton, Mary L., 260–61
Moses, Carol, 66

Moses, Wilson Jeremiah, 378–79
Moss, Howard, 140, 340
Mossberg, Barbara Antonia Clarke, 338
Mott, Wesley T., 5
Mouyen, Annie, 461
Mueller, Lisel, 140
Muhlenfeld, Elisabeth, 206, 460
Muir, Kenneth, 144
Müller, Wolfgang G., 227, 469
Mulyarchik, A. C., 452
Munson, Gorham, 320–21, 420–21
Murphy, Christina, 209
Murphy, Francis, 223
Murphy, John J., 230
Murphy, Michael, 65
Murphy, Patrick, 318
Murray, David, 127
Murray, Henry A., 59
Murza, A. B., 447
Muske, Carol, 133, 140
Myerson, Harvey, 59
Myerson, Joel, 3–4, 6, 17, 24

Nadal, Rafael Martínez, 139
Nagel, Gwen Lindberg, 219
Nagel, James, 93
Nakaznyuk, N. I., 447
Nänny, Max, 127, 141
Narazaki, Hiroshi, 492
Narr, Gunter, 463
Natalle, Elizabeth J., 351
Nathanson, Tenney, 75
Natoli, Joseph, 141
Nay, Joan, 310
Needham, John, 144
Neider, Charles, 91, 92
Neill, Edward, 334
Neitzel, Michael T., 273
Nelles, William, 93
Nelson, Peter, 295
Nesbitt, John D., 250–51
Nettels, Elsa, 223
Nevius, Blake, 212
Newlin, Keith, 275
Newman, Charles, 429
Nibbelink, Herbert, 19
Nicholas, Xavier, 369
Nichols, Charles H., 411
Nickson, Richard, 200
Nielsen, A. L., 406
Niikura, Toshikazu, 492

Nikolyukin, A., 452–53
Nilsen, Helge Normann, 500
Nims, John Frederick, 340
Noble, D. W., 493
Noble, Donald R., 285
Nocera, Gigliola, 19
Nolde, John J., 127
Noll, Mark A., 197
Nordström, Lars, 495–96
Noriega, Ignacio Gracia, 125
Norris, Christopher, 434, 439
North, Michael, 127, 327
Novak, Barbara, 12
Novak, György, 130–31
Novak, Michael Paul, 335
Nye, David E., 66
Nyquist, Mary, 307

Oaks, Susan, 220
Oates, Joyce Carol, 340
Ober, Warren U., 175–76
O'Connell, Daniel C., 308
O'Donnell, Monica M., 347
Oehlschlaeger, Fritz, 404
Ogden, Marlene A., 5
Oggel, L. Terry, 93
Ogunyemi, Chikwenye Okonjo, 399
O'Hara, Daniel T., 439–40
Ohashi, Kenzaburo, 153
Oi, Koji, 493–94
Olds, Sharon, 332
Oldsey, Bern, 186
Oleinik, V. T., 443, 445–46
Oleneva, Valentina, I., 450–51
Oliphant, Dave, 130
Oliver, Raymond, 336
Olney, James, 122
Olpin, Larry R., 81
O'Meally, Robert G., 176, 391
O'Neill, John P., 235
Ono, Kiyoyuki, 153, 160
Onoe, Masaji, 140
Opfermann, Susanne, 481–82
Oppenheim, Lois, 130
Oren, Michael, 309
Oreovicz, Cheryl Z., 190
Orr, Gregory, 335
Ortiz, Fernando, 139
Osborn, M. Elizabeth, 349
Ostendorf, Berndt (Bernd), 373, 410, 474
Ostriker, Alicia, 313, 338, 339

Overton, Betty J., 378
Owens, Louis, 255, 267–68, 300

Pack, Robert, 326
Page, James A., 368
Page, Peter C., 47
Pagnini, Marcello, 317
Papinchak, Robert Allen, 211
Pardo, Jesus, 125
Parker, Herschel, 35
Parker, Patricia, 303
Parker, R. B., 361
Parker, Robert Dale, 152
Parker, Stephen Jan, 265
Parkinson, Thomas, 128, 337
Parrington, Vernon Louis, 493
Patke, Rajeev S., 306
Patraka, Vivian M., 363
Patrides, C. A., 195
Patten, Robert L., 100–101
Patterson, J. Daniel, 191
Patterson, Mark, 13
Paul, Sherman, 22
Payne, Darwin, 250
Payne, Linda Osborne, 261
Peabody, Richard, 283
Peacock, Alan J., 127
Peake, C. H., 159–60
Pearce, Richard, 292
Pearson, Norman Holmes, 25
Peck, Elizabeth, 41
Pederson, Lee, 218
Perkins, Agnes Regan, 502
Perl, Jeffrey M., 137
Perloff, Marjorie, 127, 128, 301, 326, 327, 329, 332, 339
Perrine, Laurence, 167, 316
Perrot, Jean, 456
Peterson, Linda, 413
Petillon, Pierre-Yves, 293
Petite, Joseph, 266
Petronella, Vincent F., 67
Petry, Alice Hall, 176, 183
Pettit, Norman, 196
Phelps, Donald, 254
Phillips, K. J., 153, 242
Phillips, Larry, 171
Phillips, Levi Darmon, 354
Phillips, Robert L., 205
Phillipson, John S., 263
Piacentino, Edward J., 45, 218, 219
Pieiller, Evelyne, 460

Pierce-Baker, Charlotte, 399
Pietsch, Michael, 170
Pifer, Ellen, 269
Pike, Frank, 349
Pilkington, John, 249–50
Pinsker, Sanford, 344
Pinsky, Robert, 140, 332, 336
Pion, Bleuette, 459
Pistotnik, Vera, 351
Pitavy, François L., 157, 164, 457, 460
Pitavy-Souques, Danièle, 457
Pitcher, E. W., 202
Pitcher, Edward W. R., 51
Pitts, Mary E., 23
Piwinski, David, 272
Pizer, Donald, 148, 224, 248–49
Pizzi, Lawrence Z., 165–66
Pladott, Dinnah, 154
Plath, Aurelia S., 340
Plett, Heinrich F., 479
Plimpton, George, 125, 135, 292
Plumly, Stanley, 131, 329, 340
Poenicke, Klaus, 483
Pohl, Joy, 307
Polk, Noel, 147–49, 153, 161, 165–66
Pollard, Velma, 394
Pollin, Burton R., 43–44, 45, 46, 48, 52
Pollitt, Katha, 340
Pond, Gloria Dibble, 358
Pondrom, Cyrena N., 130, 313
Poole, Stan, 93
Poore, Carol, 355
Pope, Alan H., 192–93
Porfirio, Robert G., 274–75
Porte, Joel, 222
Porter, Carolyn, 64, 298
Porter, David H., 320
Porush, David, 271, 279
Posnock, Ross, 106–07
Poster, Mark, 437
Poteat, Patricia Lewis, 286
Poulin, Al, 340
Powell, Joan, 249
Powers, Lyall H., 95–96, 109
Press, Roger C., 62
Preyer, Robert O., 114
Pribeck, Thomas, 40, 65–66, 202
Price, Alan, 238
Price, Kenneth M., 78
Pries, Nancy, 194

Priessnitz, Horst, 469
Primeau, Ronald, 317
Prince, F. T., 137
Pringle, Mary Beth, 234
Pritchard, William H., 438
Pryse, Marjorie, 375, 390
Pudaloff, Ross J., 213
Punter, David, 279
Purcell, Victor, 138
Pütz, Manfred, 475
Putzel, Max, 152
Puzon, Bridget, 239

Quennell, Peter, 135
Quinn, Sr. Bernetta, 343
Quinones, Ricardo J., 136, 429
Quirk, Tom, 29

Rabinow, Paul, 437
Rabkin, Gerald, 351
Raffel, Burton, 125, 136
Ragan, David Paul, 165
Raina, B. N., 85
Raine, Kathleen, 142
Rainer, Michael, 76
Rainwater, Catherine, 298
Rajan, Balachandra, 129, 132, 136–37, 139
Rajchman, John, 437
Rampersad, Arnold, 401, 406
Ramsey, Dale, 362–63
Ramsey, Priscilla R., 386, 406
Randall, Julia, 327
Randall, Willard, 198
Rapaport, Herman, 342
Rashid, Frank D., 84–85
Read, Allen Walker, 142
Redford, Bruce, 120
Reed, Marcia, 194
Reep, Diana C., 223, 250
Reeves, Gareth, 138
Reilly, John E., 47
Reilly, John M., 209, 273
Reiman, Donald H., 342
Reising, Russell J., 129–30
Renald, Margaret Loftus, 357
Render, Sylvia Lyons, 383
Renner, Stanley, 255, 256
Renza, Louis, 50
Reston, James, Jr., 363–64
Reynolds, Larry J., 30–31
Reynolds, Mark, 117

Reynolds, Michael, 171
Reynolds, Michael S., 171
Reynolds, Moira Davison, 216–17
Rhodes, Pamela, 163
Richard, Claude, 455, 460, 462
Richardson, Joan, 304
Richardson, Thomas, 206
Richardson, Thomas C., 97
Richardson, Thomas J., 95
Riehle, Wolfgang, 480
Riemer, James D., 249
Riggio, Thomas P., 247
Rigsbee, David, 342
Ring, Kevin, 272
Ripley, C. Peter, 409
Riquelme, J. P., 144
Rischin, Moses, 223
Ro, Sigmund, 380, 392, 393, 414
Robbins, Bruce, 312
Roberts, Audrey, 218
Robertson, Mary Elsie, 299
Robertson, William H., 343
Robinson, Alan, 126
Robinson, David, 4, 7
Robinson, Douglas, 50–51, 100, 102,
    280, 421
Robinson, Forrest G., 245
Robinson, Harlow, 360
Robinson, Janice S., 130
Robinson, Lillian S., 425
Robinson, Peter, 126
Roby, Kinley E., 143
Rocard, Marcienne, 463
Rock, Roger O., 502
Rod, David K., 352
Rodgers, Marion E., 248
Roemer, Kenneth M., 224
Rogoff, Gordon, 352
Roh, Joe Min, 368
Rohrkemper, John, 181
Romberg, Sigmund, 364
Rood, Karen Lane, 124
Rooney, Charles J., Jr., 224
Rose, Phyllis, 229–30
Rosen, Fred S., 35
Rosenmeier, Jesper, 193
Rosenmeier, Rosamond R., 190
Rosenthal, M. L., 140, 142
Rosenwald, Lawrence Alan, 189, 194
Rosenzweig, Paul, 214
Ross, Andrew, 342
Ross, Jean W., 283

Ross, Stephen M., 159, 162
Rotella, Guy, 79, 317
Roth, Martin, 55–56
Roth, Marty, 60
Rothenberg, Jerome, 329
Roubaud, Jacques, 457
Rouberol, Jean, 156, 460, 461–62
Rougé, Bertrand, 455
Rowe, Anne, 206
Rowe, John Carlos, 16
Rowe, Karen E., 190
Rowell, Charles H., 367, 392–93, 404
Rozsnyai, Bálint, 130–31
Rubin, Louis D., Jr., 94, 195, 205, 257,
    263, 285, 319, 330, 422
Rubin-Dorsky, Jeffrey, 211–12
Rudat, Wolfgang, 184
Ruddick, Nicholas, 55
Rupprecht, Erich S., 273
Rusch, Frederik L., 141
Rushing, Andrea Benton, 338
Russell, Charles, 293, 294, 328, 430
Ryder, Mary R., 230

Saalman, Dieter, 294
Sadkowski, Waclaw, 453
Sadler, Lynn Beach, 389
Sadoff, Dianne F., 397
St. Armand, Barton Levi, 86
Sakamoto, Masayuki, 487–88
Salaam, Yusef A., 414
Saldívar, Ramón, 63–64
Salmon, Eric, 352
Salmon, Webb, 264
Salsbury, Edith, 91
Salska, Agnieszka, 69–70
Saltzman, Arthur M., 280, 295–96
Sammarcelli, Françoise, 462
Samuel, Raphael, 355
Samuels, Shirley, 202
Samuels, Wilfred D., 409
Samway, Patrick, 163
Sanchez, Marta Ester, 328
Sanders, Leslie, 370
San Juan, E., Jr., 408
Sarbu, Aladár, 447, 449
Sarlos, Robert K., 357
Saroyan, William, 364
Sarrotte, George-Michel, 460
Sattelmeyer, Robert, 4, 19, 98–99
Saunders, Brian, 61–62
Saunders, Judith P., 242

Sawicki, Joseph, 97
Sawyer, Richard, 133
Sayre, Robert F., 17
Scafella, Frank, 186
Scally, Sr. Anthony, 368
Schaffer, Louis, 358
Scharnhorst, Gary, 54, 81, 216, 219, 250
Schaum, Melita, 304–05
Schechner, Richard, 353
Schechter, Harold, 42
Schehr, Lawrence R., 270
Scheick, William J., 189–90, 236, 290, 298
Schenkel, Elmar, 55
Scherer, Olga, 163
Schiffer, Reinhold, 226, 479, 480
Schleifer, Ronald, 298, 434
Schley, Jim, 326
Schmitz, Neil, 95, 107–08
Schneider, Daniel J., 108
Schneider, Richard J., 18
Schofield, Edmund, 17
Schöler, Bo, 500
Scholes, James B., 17
Scholes, Robert, 297, 340, 440–41
Schotter, Anne Howland, 137
Schramm, Peter W., 101
Schricker, Gale C., 311
Schubnell, Matthias, 299
Schuchard, Ronald, 137
Schulman, Grace, 340
Schultz, Elizabeth, 371, 377
Schulz, Franz, 469
Schulz, Muriel, 372–73
Schumann, Kuno, 479
Schwab, Arnold T., 226
Schwartz, Gerald, 247
Schwartz, Sanford, 125–26, 136, 430
Schweitzer, Darrell, 297, 298
Schwind, Jean, 80, 230–31
Scott, Freda L., 359
Scruggs, Charles W., 248
Sealts, Merton M., Jr., 9–10
Searles, George J., 284, 287
Secor, Robert, 42, 58, 139, 169, 189
Sedgwick, Ellery, III, 216
See, Fred G., 96
Seeber, Hans Ulrich, 465–66, 477–78
Seed, David, 293
Seelye, John, 92, 98, 218
Segal, Howard P., 422

Seidel, Kathryn Lee, 156, 243, 257
Seidman, Barbara, 317
Sekora, John, 410
Selby, Sara E., 51–52
Sell, Roger D., 316
Selman, Michael, 357–58
Seltser, Barry Jay, 258
Selzer, John L., 165
Sena, Vinod, 139
Senger, Matthias W., 195
Sensibar, Judith L., 140, 152
Settle, Glenn, 181–82
Sewell, David, 99
Sexton, Anne, 340
Shah, Ramesh Chandra, 138
Shaheen, Mohammad Y., 127
Shapiro, Alan, 327, 336
Shapiro, Fred R., 44
Sharma, Jitendra Kumar, 138
Sharp, Richard D., 60
Sharpe, Charles, 332
Sharratt, Bernard, 142
Sharrock, Roger, 134
Shaviro, Steven, 302
Shea, John, 281
Sheffey, Ruthe T., 387–88
Shelton, Frank W., 398
Shemyakin, A. M., 444
Shewey, Don, 363
Shi, David, 8
Shields, David S., 198
Shillingsburg, Miriam J., 90, 214
Shimokohbe, Michiko, 488
Shinn, Thelma J., 393–94
Shirley, Carl R., 283, 503
Showalter, Elaine, 340
Shuffleton, Frank, 6
Shumaker, Conrad, 219
Sibbald, K. M., 139
Sicari, Stephen, 128
Sidnell, M. J., 139
Siebald, Manfred, 468, 469
Siebers, Tobin, 52–53
Sieburth, Richard, 124, 132
Siegel, Mark, 363
Silet, Charles L. P., 225
Silver, Thomas B., 101
Simmons, Kennith L., 330
Simpson, Lewis P., 196, 205, 422
Simpson, Marcus B., Jr., 195
Sims-Wood, Janet, 367
Singh, G., 129

Sisson, C. H., 142
Skaff, William, 126
Skaggs, Merrill Maguire, 206, 231
Skaggs, Peggy, 225
Skei, Hans H., 497-98
Skerrett, Joseph T., Jr., 396
Skinner, John L., 167-68
Skloot, Robert, 351
Slatin, John M., 311
Slatoff, Walter J., 431
Slide, Anthony, 348-49, 364
Sloan, De Villo, 336
Slotkin, Richard, 422-23
Smart, Ninian, 7
Smith, Carol H., 143, 340
Smith, Dave, 325-26
Smith, Frederik N., 160
Smith, Gayle L., 11-12, 63
Smith, Henry Nash, 92
Smith, Janet Adam, 135
Smith, Judy R., 37-38
Smith, L. Neal, 25
Smith, Lorrie, 18, 334
Smith, Stan, 131
Smith, Valerie, 396
Smyers, Virginia L., 44
Sojka, Gregory S., 176, 409
Solard, Alain, 386
Solt, Mary Ellen, 124
Spacks, Patricia Meyer, 236-37
Spallino, Chiara, 396
Spears, Monroe K., 285-86
Spengemann, William C., vii, 203
Spillers, Hortense J., 375, 390, 394
Spivack, Kathleen, 334
Spivey, Ted R., 261, 270
Sri, P. S., 137
Srivastava, S. B., 138
Staats, Marilyn Dorn, 264-65
Stafford, Beth, 428
Stafford, William T., 103
Stamelman, Richard, 343
Stanek, Lou Willett, 102
Stanford, Derek, 137
Staten, Henry, 441
Steele, Jeffrey, 76-77
Stein, Allen F., 221, 236
Stein, Stephen J., 194-95, 197
Steinbach, Gaby, 472
Steiner, Dorothea, 470-71
Steiner, Dorothy, 227
Steinke, Jim, 185
Stelzmann, Rainulf A., 261

Stengel, Wayne B., 295
Stepto, Robert B., 380
Stern, Madeleine B., 217
Sternberg, Paul R., 195
Stessel, Edward, 13
Stetsenko, E. A., 443, 446
Stevenson, Diane, 288
Stevenson, Frank, 133
Stewart, E. Kate, 46-47
Stimpson, Catharine, 339
Stineback, David, 29
Stitt, Peter, 325
Stoicheff, Peter, 133-34
Stokes, Edward, 41-42
Storaler, Patricia, 338
Stott, Bill, 419
Stouck, David, 240-41, 267
Stout, Janis P., 262, 329-30
Strickland, Charles, 217
Strom, Martha, 306
Stuart, Jan, 364
Stull, William L., 288
Stutman, Suzanne, 264
Suberchicot, A., 457
Sugiyama, Naoto, 492
Sullivan, Sheila, 138
Sultan, Stanley, 141, 144
Sundquist, Åsebrit, 499-500
Sundquist, Eric J., 9, 16
Sutton, William A., 241
Swabey, Henry, 125
Swan, Marshall W. S., 5
Swann, Charles, 66, 213
Sweeney, Patricia E., 150
Sylvester, William, 344
Sypher, Wylie, 140
Syrkin, Marie, 332
Szathmary, Louis, 72

Taggart, John, 332
Tallmadge, John, 22
Tanaka, Tsuyoshi, 491
Tani, Stefano, 273-74
Tanner, Tony, 111-12
Tapscott, Stephen, 129, 310
Tarn, Nathaniel, 329
Tashjian, Dickran, 308-09, 312
Tate, Claudia, 384
Tate, J. O., 275
Tatsumi, Satoshi, 491
Taupin, René, 320, 321
Taylor, Clyde, 382, 414
Taylor, Eugene, 59

Tchakovskii, S. A., 444, 447
Telotte, J. P., 119
Tenney, Thomas A., 97, 98
Terrel, Denise, 463
Terrell, C. F., 132
Terry, Esther Alexander, 158, 410–11
Teyssandier, Hubert, 116–17, 456
Thaddeus, Janice, 413
Thirlwall, John C., 312
Thomas, Lorenzo, 371
Thomas, M. Wynn, 13, 76, 78–79
Thompson, Lou, 37
Thomsen, Christen Kold, 66
Thornberry, Robert, 171
Thornton, Naoko Fuwa, 261
Thorpe, Dwayne, 53
Thwaite, Anthony, 328–29
Tidwell, John Edgar, 369
Tintner, Adeline R., 47, 103–04, 107, 118, 175, 245
Todd, Janet, 204
Toman, Marshall, 261
Tomlin, E. W. F., 135
Tompkins, Jane, 201–02, 206, 423–24
Tompkins, Robert R., 302–03
Toolan, Michael, 156
Torgovnick, Marianna, 109
Torsney, Cheryl B., 21
Trahan, Elizabeth W., 104
Trapido, Joel, 348
Traylor, Eleanor, 369–70
Treichler, Paula A., 428
Trotter, David, 133, 136
Trouard, Dawn, 164
Trussler, Simon, 360
Tsuchiya, Hiroko, 355
Tuck, Andrew, 137
Tucker, Edward L., 215
Tucker, John, 127
Tucker, Stephanie, 176
Turco, Lewis, 343
Turner, Alden R., 305
Turner, Arlin, 48
Turner, Victor, 353
Turner, W. Craig, 195
Turpin, Michel, 461
Tymieniecka, Anna-Teresa, 130
Tymn, Marshall B., 297, 503

Ulmer, Gregory L., 441
Unger, Leonard, 137
Unrue, Darlene Harbour, 262, 264
Uscatescu, Jorge, 125

Valenti, Patricia Dunlavy, 39
Vance, William L., 208
Van Cromphout, Gustaaf, 60
Vande Berg, Michael, 79
Van Deburg, William L., 373
Van de Wetering, Maxine, 194
Van Leer, David, 31–32
Van Ness, A. Gordon, III, 341
Vashchenko, A. V., 443, 444–45
Vass, Mary Miller, 247
Vauthier, Simone, 461
Vena, Gary, 359
Vendler, Helen, 323, 340
Verduin, Kathleen, 175
Verley, Claudine, 464
Vernon, John, 233–34
Véza, Laurette, 456
Vickery, Olga, 160
Vieilledent, Catherine, 456
Vineberg, Steve, 110
Vinson, Audrey L., 394–95
Vinson, James, 503
Voloshin, Beverly R., 210
von Bardeleben, Renate, 469, 472–73
Von Frank, Albert J., 8–9, 211
von Hallberg, Robert, 51, 324–25, 333
Vosskamp, Wilhelm, 465

Wade, Stephen, 144
Wagner, Linda W., 244, 272, 299, 310, 397
Wagner, Peter, 471
Wagner, Vern, 113
Wainwright, Jana, 191
Wakefield, Richard, 316
Wakoski, Diane, 343
Walker, Cheryl, 190
Walker, David, 306–07
Walker, Jeffrey, 189
Walker, Nancy, 242–43
Wallace, James D., 212
Wallace, Patricia B., 335
Wallace, Robert K., 59
Wallingford, Katharine T., 334
Walser, Richard, 263
Walter, James, 262
Walther, Y. T., 126
Wangensteen, Sarah D., 116
Ward, J. A., 108, 424
Ward, Jerry W., Jr., 369
Ward, John C., 318
Ward, Jonathan, 129
Ward, Patricia, 60

Warner, Michael D., 224
Warren, Austin, 135
Warren, James Perrin, 76
Warren, Keith, 294
Washburn, Delores, 264
Wasserman, Loretta, 229
Watanabe, Toshio, 490
Waters, Gregory, 320
Watkins, Floyd C., 262, 341
Watkins, T. H., 266
Watson, Carole McAlpine, 373–74
Watson, Charles S., 209
Watson, George, 136
Watson, Ritchie Devon, Jr., 209
Watters, David H., 191, 193–94
Weales, Gerald, 355, 364–65
Weber, Alfred, 470
Weber, Daniel B., 391
Weber, Ronald, 279–80, 327–28, 424–25
Weeks, Brigitte, 340
Wegelin, Christof, 103
Wegener, Larry Edward, 57
Weinblatt, Alan, 137
Weisenburger, Steven, 293
Weiss, Theodore, 140
Weissbourd, Katherine, 105
Weissman, Judith, 113–14
Weixlmann, Joe, 406
Welch, Robert E., 225
Weltner, Peter, 332
Wendland, Albert, 272
Werner, Craig, 205
Werness, Hope B., 80
Wershoven, Carol J., 36, 237
Wesling, Donald, 328, 333
West, James L. W., III, 247
Westbrook, Max, 267
Westbrook, Perry D., 209
Westbrook, Wayne W., 79, 241
Westling, Louise, 259
Whelchel, L. H., Jr., 354, 411
Whitby, Julie, 137
White, Barbara A., 202, 210, 237, 262–63, 267, 419, 425
White, George C., 358
White, Peter, 189, 192
White, Ray Lewis, 241
White, William, 70, 80, 170
Whitford, Kathryn, 81–82
Whitley, John S., 96
Whitlow, Roger, 384
Wideman, John Edgar, 383

Wier, Allen, 278
Wilde, Alan, 296
Wilde, Meta Carpenter, 149
Wilhelm, James J., 124
Wilkerson, Margaret B., 371
Wilkinson, Robert, 342
Wilkoszewska, Krystyna, 450
Willcox, William B., 199
Williams, David R., 200
Williams, Gary Jay, 357
Williams, Henry B., 354
Williams, M. A., 118
Williams, Mance, 381
Williams, Michael, 54–55
Williams, Sherley Anne, 401
Willis, Patricia C., 108, 311
Willis, Susan, 374–75, 398, 409
Willy, Todd G., 184–85
Wilson, Christopher P., 217, 245
Wilson, Douglas L., 199
Wilson, Jonathan, 268
Wilson, Stephen, 127
Wilson, William S., 288
Wiltshire, Susan Ford, 320
Wimsatt, Mary Ann, 205
Winchell, Mark Royden, 258, 319
Windham, Donald, 361
Winer, Linda, 362
Wingate, P. J., 248
Winship, Michael, 44
Winter, Kate H., 209
Winther, Per, 497
Witemeyer, Hugh, 128, 129
Witherell, Elizabeth Hall, 17
Witherington, Paul, 55
Wittreich, Joseph, 195
Wojahn, David, 329, 344
Wolk, Merla, 113
Wolosky, Shira, 87
Wolstenholme, Susan, 237
Wood, Sally, 258
Woodson, Thomas, 25, 26
Woodward, Robert H., 256
Woolley, Deborah A., 291–92, 294
Wortham, Thomas, 223
Wosk, Julie H., 329
Wright, Anne, 141
Wright, Charles, 130
Wright, John, 369
Wright, Lawrence, 291
Wright, Stuart, 334
Wyatt, David, 157
Wyld, Lionel D., 209

Yacobi, Tamar, 118
Yagyu, Nozomu, 485, 486, 491
Yalom, Marilyn, 298–99, 314, 338
Yarmus, Marcia D., 256
Yeager, Freda E., 64–65
Yellin, David G., 166
Yenser, Stephen, 327
Yetman, Norman R., 412
Yoke, Carl B., 273
Young, Philip, 202
Young, Robert D., 178
Young, Stephen A., 248
Young, Thomas Daniel, 210, 260, 285, 319, 422
Youra, Steven, 259

Zacharasiewicz, Waldemar, 479, 482
Zagarell, Sandra A., 220
Zall, P. M., 91–92
Zanger, Jules, 457
Zapf, Hubert, 272
Zasurskii, Ya. N., 443
Zavarzadeh, Mas'ud, 282
Zayed, George, 53
Zigal, Thomas, 130
Zimmerman, Bonnie, 426
Znamenskaya, N. E., 452
Zorzi, Rosella Mamoli, 123
Zverey, A. M., 443, 446–47, 448
Zwarg, Christina, 101

Subject Index

Abish, Walter, 280, 293, 294, 460
Ackerman, Diane, 339
Adams, Henry, 108, 141, 175, 227, 468, 475, 476, 491
Adams, Mary Newbury, 7
Ade, George, 223
Agee, James, 108, 253–54, 259, 424, 431
Ageyev, M., 265
Aiken, Conrad, 320
Albee, Edward, 350, 360, 469
Alcott, A. Bronson, 7, 8,
Alcott, Louisa May, 105, 217
Alger, Horatio, Jr., 216
Allen, Donald, 337
Ammons, A. R., 327, 331, 342
Anderson, Maxwell, 356
Anderson, Sherwood, 240–41, 459, 494
Angelou, Maya, 406, 463
Antin, David, 326
Apollinaire, Guillaume, 430
Apple, Max, 278, 296
Aristotle, 459
Arnold, Matthew, 120, 436
Arnow, Harriette, 256, 260
Ashbery, John, 342
Ashley, Elizabeth, 362
Aswell, Edward, 263, 264
Atwood, Margaret, 492
Audubon, John James, 262
Augustine, Saint, 190
Austen, Jane, 432
Ayer, Thomas, 243

Bachelard, Gaston, 249
Baker, Carlos, 169
Bakhtin, Mikhail, 64, 131
Baldwin, James, 109, 378, 391–92, 453–54, 467, 468
Balzac, Honoré de, 117, 120, 456
Bambara, Toni Cade, 376, 499
Baraka, Amiri (LeRoi Jones), 330, 370, 393, 405–06, 408, 414, 469

Barlow, Joel, 198
Barnes, Djuna, 270
Barth, John, 271, 279, 280, 282, 285, 291–92, 294, 450–51, 453, 461, 462, 483, 492
Barthelme, Donald, 242, 271, 278, 279, 281, 282, 295, 451, 468
Barthelme, Frederick, 283
Barthes, Roland, 291, 394, 433–34, 496
Bartram, William, 201
Baudelaire, Charles, 138
Baum, L. Frank, 493
Baxter, Viola, 123
Bayes, Ronald H., 343
Beattie, Ann, 288, 298, 492
Beckett, Samuel, 161, 271, 326, 351
Beckford, William, 46
Behn, Aphra, 203
Bell, Charles, 39
Bellamy, Edward, 224, 466
Bellow, Saul, 256, 268–70, 279, 280, 467, 468, 494
Bergson, Henri, 126, 136, 229
Berkeley, George, 5
Berkhoff, Stephen, 469
Bernstein, Charles, 326
Bernstein, Leonard, 362
Berry, Wendell, 19, 327
Berryman, John, 327, 493
Besant, Walter, 120
Betts, Doris, 278, 285
Beverley, Robert, 196, 446
Bezzerides, Albert I., 151
Bird, Robert Montgomery, 214, 474
Bishop, Elizabeth, 335, 338
Bishop, John Peale, 319
Blackmur, R. P., 304
Blake, William, 155
Blancot, Maurice, 342
Blechman, Burt, 467
Bloom, Harold, 144, 301, 305, 313, 317, 397, 440
Bly, Robert, 343
Boccaccio, Giovanni, 450

Bogan, Louise, 314, 335, 338
Bolt, Robert, 258
Bonner, Marita O., 407
Borges, Jorge Luis, 78
Boucicault, Dion, 469
Bowen, Francis, 420
Bowles, Paul, 272
Boyesen, Hjalmar, 448
Bradbury, Ray, 272, 463–64
Bradley, Francis Herbert, 126, 136
Bradstreet, Anne, 9, 190–91, 192, 443, 445–46, 470
Brainerd, David, 196
Brautigan, Richard, 291, 460
Braziller, George, 283
Brecht, Bertolt, 328, 430
Breton, André, 296, 342
Brewer, Lee, 350
Brickell, John, 195
Bridges, Robert, 129
Briggs, Charles F., 68
Brockett, Oscar, 352
Bronk, William, 457
Brontë, Charlotte, 427
Brook, Peter, 457
Brooks, Cleanth, 319
Brooks, Gwendolyn, 374, 390
Brown, Charles Brockden, 201–02, 424, 446, 485
Brown, Claude, 378
Brown, John, 222
Brown, Sterling A., 402
Brown, William Wells, 354, 382, 411
Brownell, W. C., 236
Browning, Robert, 106–07, 128, 129, 317
Brownson, Orestes Augustus, 28
Bryant, William Cullen, 208–09, 215, 457, 466, 503
Bukowski, Charles, 343
Bullins, Ed, 370
Bulwer-Lytton, Edward, 165
Burke, Edmund, 53
Burke, Kenneth, 353, 394
Burr, Esther Edwards, 197
Burrill, Mary T., 407
Burroughs, William S., 271, 293
Bushnell, Horace, 8
Butler, Octavia E., 393–94
Byrd, William, 195, 196, 446
Byron, George Gordon, Lord, 49, 53, 155

Cabell, James Branch, 248–49
Cage, John, 19, 326
Cahan, Abraham, 223–24
Cain, James M., 274–75
Caldwell, Erskine, 256, 264–65, 482
Calvin, John, 26–27
Calvino, Italo, 274
Campbell, Bartley, 355
Campbell, Joseph, 219
Campton, David, 469
Camus, Albert, 274
Cantwell, Robert, 256, 267
Capote, Truman, 289, 450, 451
Caputo, Philip, 278
Caruthers, William Alexander, 209
Carver, Raymond, 288, 460
Castaneda, Carlos, 277
Cather, Willa, 229–32, 458
Catlin, George, 464
Cendrars, Blaise, 461
Cernuda, Luis, 139
Cervantes, Lorna Dee, 328
Chandler, Raymond, 66, 274, 275
Channing, W. H., 5, 14–15
Channing, William Ellery, 7
Charyn, Jerome, 460
Chaucer, Geoffrey, 168, 311
Cheever, John, 278–79, 281, 288, 416, 450, 451, 467, 482
Cheney, Brainard, 261
Cheney, Sheldon, 356
Chesnut, Mary, 206
Chesnutt, Charles W., 220–21, 375, 382–83
Childress, Alice, 370
Chopin, Kate, 206, 221, 225, 427, 485
Ciardi, John, 503
Clampitt, Amy, 339
Clark, Walter Van Tilburg, 267
Clarke, Cheryl, 339, 407
Clausen, Christopher, 326
Clifton, Lucille, 338
Coburn, Alvin Langdon, 109–10
Cocteau, Jean, 293
Cole, Tom, 363
Coleridge, Samuel Taylor, 14, 19, 337
Colman, Benjamin, 194
Confucius, 132
Conrad, Joseph, 42, 58, 108, 139, 169, 245, 259, 431, 432
Cook, Ebenezer, 195, 196
Cook, George Cram, 357
Cooke, John Esten, 209

Cooper, Anna Julia, 377–78
Cooper, James Fenimore, 65, 98, 206, 207, 208, 209, 212–14, 417–18, 424, 464, 473–74
Coover, Robert, 278, 279, 280–81, 295
Corman, Cid, 503
Corpi, Lucha, 328
Cowley, Malcolm, 254, 416
Crane, Hart, 311, 315–16, 320, 421, 478
Crane, Stephen, 207, 224, 226, 234, 468
Crapsey, Adelaide, 320
Crèvecoeur, Michel-Guillaume Jean de, 201, 455
Crews, Harry, 285
Crockett, Davy, 218
Crothers, Rachael, 349
Crozier, Eric, 68
Culler, Jonathan, 207
Culmann, Leonhard, 195
Cummings, E. E., 79, 317
Cummins, Maria Susanna, 210, 419
Cunningham, J. V., 335–36

Damashek, Barbara, 365
Dana, Richard Henry, Jr., 209
Dana, Richard Henry, Sr., 209
Danforth, John, 192
Danforth, Samuel (elder), 192
Danforth, Samuel (younger), 192
D'Annunzio, Gabriele, 175
Dante Alighieri, 60–61, 128, 138, 230, 239, 305–06, 496
Darwin, Charles, 449
Daudet, Alphonse, 120
Davidson, Donald, 319
Davies, Samuel, 196
Davis, Rebecca Harding, 417
Davis, Thulani, 339, 407
de Angulo, Jaime, 124
de Beauvoir, Simone, 425
de Born, Bertran, 128
Deland, Margaret, 223, 250
Delany, Samuel R., 394
DeLillo, Don, 290
de Man, Paul, 434, 440
de Maupassant, Guy, 120
Derricotte, Toi, 339, 407
Derrida, Jacques, 85, 292, 342, 428–29, 441
Dewey, John, 197
Di Prima, Diane, 330

Dicey, Edward, 26
Dickens, Charles, 41–42, 47, 65, 98, 100, 216, 217, 432, 476
Dickey, James, 278, 289, 325, 331, 340–41
Dickinson, Emily, 14, 69–70, 80–87, 262, 339, 342, 418, 484, 487, 489–90
Didion, Joan, 279, 416
Dillard, Annie, 19, 298
Dilthey, Wilhelm, 136, 144
Doctorow, E. L., 281, 289–90, 492
Donleavy, J. P., 451, 468
Donne, John, 319
Donnelly, Ignatius, 493
Doolittle, Hilda (H.D.), 130, 313–14, 336, 337, 338, 478, 479
Dorn, Edward, 302, 326, 333
Dos Passos, John, 171, 222, 243–45, 256, 419, 458–59, 468, 491
Doubleday, Frank, 246
Douglas, Mary, 235
Douglass, Aaron, 378
Douglass, Frederick, 372, 409–11, 474
Dove, Rita, 339, 407
Dreiser, Theodore, 224, 232–35, 246, 247, 417–18, 449, 452, 468, 486
Du Bartas, Guillaume, 470
Du Bois, W. E. B., 369, 378, 383–84
Duchamp, Marcel, 308–09, 342
Dudley, Thomas, 470
Dunbar, Paul Laurence, 371, 372, 400
Dunbar, William, 467
Dunbar-Nelson, Alice, 384, 412–13
Duncan, Robert, 130, 336–37
Dunn, Stephen, 344
Dunne, Finley Peter, 211
Dwight, John Sullivan, 5, 6
Dwight, Timothy, 9
Dylan, Bob, 478
Dymond, Jonathan, 22–23

Eastman, Mary H., 376
Eberhart, Richard, 478
Eco, Umberto, 274
Edmonds, Randolph, 359, 469
Edwards, Jonathan, 196–97, 420
Eggleston, Edward, 218
Eliot, George, 41–42, 236
Eliot, T. S., 125, 127, 128, 134–45, 311, 312, 319, 342, 429, 430, 450, 458, 468, 479, 486, 496
Elkin, Stanley, 295, 296, 462

Ellison, Ralph, 176, 371, 372, 379, 380–81, 390–91, 490
Emerson, Ralph Waldo, 3–5, 7–15, 32, 40–41, 51, 65, 72, 78–79, 82, 85–86, 97, 197, 318, 421, 466, 478
Empedocles, 47
Empson, William, 434
Equiano, Olaudah, 372, 409
Erikson, Erik H., 105
Ernst, Max, 296
Eshleman, Clayton, 344
Evans, Augusta Jane, 210
Evans, Walker, 424
Everett, David, 202
Everson, William, 327, 336, 337–38

Farrell, James T., 254, 256
Faulkner, William, 61, 140, 147–68, 180, 231, 249, 416, 432, 459–60, 481–82, 486, 492, 497–98
Fauset, Jessie Redmon, 373, 375, 386
Federman, Raymond, 292, 293
Fergusson, Harvey, 256, 267
Finley, Marietta D., 241
Finley, Martha, 210
Fisher, Vardis, 267
Fiske, John, 449
Fitch, Clyde, 349
FitzGerald, Edward, 141
Fitzgerald, F. Scott, 169, 171, 175, 178, 180–83, 245, 275, 481, 491, 492
Fitzgerald, Zelda, 182–83
Flaubert, Gustave, 120, 158, 161, 432, 435, 459
Fletcher, John Gould, 319
Foote, Shelby, 258
Forbes, Edwin, 72
Forché, Carolyn, 344
Ford, Ford Madox, 123
Foreman, Richard, 350
Forgacs, Reszö, 128
Fornes, Maria Irene, 362
Forrest, Earle R., 251
Forrest, Edwin, 353
Forster, E. M., 68, 139
Foster, Hannah, 485
Foucault, Michel, 428–29, 435, 436–37
Frank, Waldo, 320
Frankl, Viktor, 491–92
Franklin, Benjamin, 194, 198–99, 444, 503

Frazer, Sir James George, 236, 340, 430
Frederic, Harold, 209, 226
Freeman, Mary E. Wilkins, 219–20
French, Marilyn, 498, 499
Freneau, Philip, 200, 443, 446, 466, 503
Freud, Sigmund, 97, 313, 320, 334, 340, 425, 430, 431–32
Frost, Robert, 316, 320, 478, 479
Frye, Northrop, 436, 440
Fuentes, Carlos, 155
Fuller, Blair, 363
Fuller, Margaret, 6–7, 9, 24

Gaddis, William, 282, 296, 467, 468, 492
Gaines, Ernest, 392–93
Gallagher, Tess, 338
García Márquez, Gabriel, 155
Gardner, John, 279, 280, 283, 289, 295–96, 450, 451, 497
Gardner, Nathaniel, 199
Garelli, Jacques, 130
Garland, Hamlin, 78, 225–26, 232, 238
Garrett, George, 278, 285–86
Garrison, William Lloyd, 22
Garvey, Marcus, 378
Gaskell, Elizabeth, 236
Gass, William H., 277, 278, 280, 281, 282, 295–96
Gaudier, Henri, 124
Gayle, Addison, 414
Gilbert, Sandra M., 397
Gillette, King, 224
Gilman, Charlotte Perkins, 219
Ginsberg, Allen, 328, 329, 478
Girodias, Maurice, 283
Glasgow, Ellen, 242–43
Glaze, Andrew, 341–42
Glynn, Thomas, 283
Godine, David, 283
Godwin, Parke, 6
Goethe, Johann Wolfgang von, 230
Gold, Herbert, 468
Goldman, Emma, 356
Goldsmith, Oliver, 359
Goodman, Paul, 468
Gookin, Daniel, 470
Gordon, Caroline, 257, 258
Gorky, Maxim, 448–49
Gorton, Samuel, 471

Gray, Amlin, 363
Green, Paul, 359
Greene, Graham, 431
Gregg, Frances, 313
Grey, Zane, 250–51
Griffin, Susan, 480
Grimke, Angelina Weld, 407
Gris, Juan, 309
Guare, John, 364
Gubar, Susan, 397
Guillén, Jorge, 139
Gurdjieff, George Ivanovich, 421
Guthrie, A. B., 267

Haecker, Theodor, 138
Hale, Emily, 134
Hamilton, Dr. Alexander, 195
Hamilton, Ian, 334
Hammett, Dashiell, 274, 275
Hannah, Barry, 285
Hansberry, Lorraine, 362, 407–08
Harding, Walter, 17
Hardy, Thomas, 107, 256
Harper, Frances, 373
Harris, George Washington, 218
Harris, Joel Chandler, 218
Harris, William Torrey, 8
Harrison, Paul Carter, 371
Harte, Bret, 223
Hartman, Geoffrey, 440
Hawkes, John, 278, 292, 461
Hawthorne, Julian, 48
Hawthorne, Nathaniel, 14, 25–42, 48,
    52, 66, 67, 107, 109, 139, 155, 160,
    182, 220, 226, 278–79, 287, 416,
    419, 477, 481–82, 485, 486, 491
Hayden, Robert, 369, 403–04
Hayne, Paul Hamilton, 72
Haynes, Lemuel, 200
Hayward, John, 135
Hazlitt, William, 60–61
Hearne, Vickie, 339
Hecht, Ben, 351
Hedge, Frederic Henry, 23–24
Heidegger, Martin, 136, 260, 428–29,
    481
Heisenberg, Werner, 292
Heissenbuttel, Helmut, 241
Heller, Joseph, 278, 290
Hellman, Lillian, 109, 263
Hellman, Monte, 293

Hemingway, Ernest, 169–80, 182, 183–
    86, 241, 244–45, 255, 258, 391,
    418–19, 447, 452, 458, 481–82,
    485, 486, 491
Hemphill, Paul, 341
Henderson, Archibald, 356
Henderson, George Wylie, 379
Heraud, John Abraham, 14
Heriot, George, 208
Herne, James A., 469
Herrick, Robert, 221
Hersey, John, 281
Higginson, Thomas Wentworth, 81
Highwater, Jamake, 283
Hinckley, Caroline, 6
Hoar, Elizabeth Sherman, 4–5
Hochuth, Rolf, 258
Hoffman, Daniel, 343
Hoffman, William, 365
Holden, Jonathan, 344
Hollander, John, 336
Holmes, Oliver Wendell, 215–16
Homer, 128
Hooker, Thomas, 472
Hopkins, Gerard Manley, 129, 138,
    330, 334
Hopkins, Pauline, 373, 377–78, 384
Hopper, Edward, 424, 458
Howe, Tina, 362
Howells, William Dean, 91, 120, 208,
    221–23, 449, 468, 493–94, 517
Hubbell, Jay, 422
Hughes, Langston, 378, 400–402, 406
Hughes, Ted, 329
Hugo, Richard, 325
Humphreys, David, 198
Humphries, Rolfe, 335
Huneker, James Gibbons, 226
Hunt, William Holman, 107
Hunter, Kristin, 374, 378
Hurston, Zora Neale, 373, 374, 375,
    387–88, 397–98
Husserl, Edmund, 136

Irving, John, 278, 282
Irving, Washington, 207, 208, 211–12
Iser, Wolfgang, 37, 118
Ivancich, Adriana, 172
Ivory, James, 110

Jackson, Helen Hunt, 81
Jacobs, Harriet, 411
James, Alice, 104

James, Henry, Jr., 95, 103–22, 175–76, 220, 222, 254, 287, 305, 386, 418, 419, 432, 435, 449, 456, 468, 476, 477, 485, 487, 488–89, 498
James, Henry, Sr., 105
James, William, 79, 82, 105, 121, 126, 136, 223
Jarrell, Randall, 330–31, 334–35
Jeffers, Robinson, 318–19, 478, 480
Jefferson, Thomas, 196, 199, 250, 443, 446
Jewett, Sarah Orne, 207, 218–19
Jhabvala, Ruth Prawer, 110
Johnson, Denis, 344
Johnson, Edward, 193
Johnson, Georgia Douglas, 379, 407
Johnson, James Weldon, 384–85
Johnson, Ronald, 344
Johnson, Uwe, 244
Johnston, Mary, 209
Jones, Gayl, 376
Jones, Hugh, 446
Jones, Madison, 285
Jordan, June, 370
Joyce, James, 129, 230, 281, 288, 292, 419, 429, 469
Just, Ward, 290
Justice, Donald, 336

Kafka, Franz, 281
Kandinsky, Wassily, 309
Katz, Steve, 277, 293
Kay, Terry, 341
Keats, John, 18, 312
Keckley, Elizabeth, 411
Kelly, Robert, 302, 344
Kennedy, Adrienne, 371
Kennedy, John Pendleton, 209
Kennedy, William, 283
Kenner, Hugh, 271
Kerouac, Jack, 272, 468, 478, 494
Kesey, Ken, 278, 290, 492
King, Stephen, 297–98
Kingston, Maxine Hong, 254, 298, 299
Kinnell, Galway, 343
Kipling, Rudyard, 258
Kirkland, Caroline M., 217–18
Knight, Etheridge, 344
Kosinski, Jerzy, 278, 281, 283
Kramer, Larry, 365
Krause, Herbert, 267
Kumin, Maxine, 338, 344
Kunitz, Stanley, 335

Lacan, Jacques, 128, 155, 159, 163, 435
Lane, Rose Wilder, 240
Lanier, Sidney, 210, 227
Larsen, Nella, 238, 375, 386–87
Laughlin, James, 283
Laurents, Arthur, 362
Lawrence, D. H., 109, 130, 175, 230, 429
Lawson, John Howard, 356
Laye, Camara, 269
Lechford, Thomas, 471, 473
Lee, George Washington, 379
Lee, Jarena, 411
Le Guin, Ursula K., 297, 463
Levertov, Denise, 327, 333–34, 338, 339, 480
Lewis, Boyd, 341
Lewis, Sinclair, 238–40, 243, 248, 386, 458
Lewis, Wyndham, 123, 126
Lincoln, Abraham, 209
Lindsay, Vachel, 318, 320, 457–58
Li Po, 128
Lippard, George, 354
Locke, Alain, 369
London, Jack, 245, 246, 449, 475, 476
Longfellow, Henry Wadsworth, 215, 216
Lovecraft, H. P., 272
Lowell, Amy, 314–15
Lowell, James Russell, 215, 466
Lowell, Robert, 19, 136, 327, 330, 334, 335, 340, 467, 478, 493
Loy, Mina, 314
Luhan, Mable Dodge, 266–67
Lukács, Georg, 97, 207, 454
Lundkvist, Arthur, 79

McCarthy, Cormac, 285
McCarthy, Mary, 254, 358
McClure, Michael, 337, 480
McCosh, James, 420
McCoy, Horace, 274
McCullers, Carson, 259, 263, 267, 425
Macdonald, Cynthia, 338
McElroy, Colleen, 339, 407
McElroy, Joseph, 279, 282
McGuane, Thomas, 283, 297
MacKaye, Steele, 354
MacLeish, Archibald, 320, 478
McNally, Terrence, 363
McNickle, D'Arcy, 267–68, 300
Magritte, René, 230

Mailer, Norman, 223, 279, 280, 281, 284, 293
Major, Clarence, 376
Malamud, Bernard, 269–70, 461, 468, 500
Mallarmé, Étienne, 155
Mamet, David, 350, 363
Manley, Frank, 341
Mann, Emily, 363
Mann, Mary Peabody, 6
Mann, Thomas, 429
Marcosson, Isaac, 246
Mariani, Paul, 311
Markham, Beryl, 176
Marlowe, Christopher, 141
Marsh, James, 8
Marshall, Paule, 374, 394
Martin, John, 283
Marvin X, 371
Marx, Karl, 425
Mason, Clifford, 469
Masterman, C. F. G., 124
Mather, Cotton, 194, 198, 470, 471–72
Mather, Increase, 470
Mathews, John Joseph, 268
Matthiessen, F. O., 9
May, James Boyer, 283
May, Karl, 464
Mayakovsky, Vladimir, 430
Mazzetti, Lorenza, 272
Mazzini, Giuseppe, 223
Meekers, Joseph, 297
Meinong, Alexius, 136
Melville, Herman, 28, 54, 57–68, 108, 294, 418, 421, 447, 474–76, 477, 485, 487–88, 491
Mencken, H. L., 246–48
Mencken, Sara Haardt, 248
Mengin, Urbain, 104
Merton, Thomas, 287
Merwin, W. S., 130, 343
Metcalf, Evelina, 6
Metcalfe, Steven, 363
Michener, James, 279, 280
Miles, Josephine, 344
Miller, Arthur, 350, 351, 359–60, 486
Miller, Henry, 277
Miller, Joaquin, 354
Miller, Warren, 468
Mills, George, 462
Milton, John, 41, 129, 337
Mitchell, Margaret, 257
Momaday, N. Scott, 299

Monroe, Harriet, 139, 332
Moore, Henry, 230
Moore, Marianne, 108, 311, 313, 314, 338, 478, 479–80
Moore, Merrill, 319
More, Sir Thomas, 465–66
Morris, Wright, 266, 274, 278
Morrison, Toni, 298, 370, 374, 376, 394–97, 427, 492
Morrison, Van, 272
Morton, Thomas, 189, 195
Muir, John, 15, 17
Murphy, Gerald, 172
Murray, Albert, 371, 381

Nabokov, Vladimir, 108, 265, 274, 482–83
Nast, Thomas, 143
Natwick, Mildred, 362
Neal, John, 207, 208, 214–15, 473
Neal, Larry, 369–70, 380–81, 404–05, 408
Nemerov, Howard, 478
Newman, Molly, 365
Nichols, Mike, 362
Niedecker, Lorine, 331, 339
Nietzsche, Friedrich Wilhelm, 126, 136, 143, 428–29, 459, 491
Nin, Anaïs, 265–66, 485, 491
Norris, Charles G., 240
Norris, Frank, 224–25, 449
Norris, Kathleen, 240

Oates, Joyce Carol, 278–79, 290, 416, 485, 498
O'Connor, Flannery, 259–61, 451, 460, 482
O'Connor, William Douglas, 71
Odets, Clifford, 355–56
O'Donnell, Thomas F., 209
O'Hara, Frank, 467
O'Keeffe, Georgia, 230
Olson, Charles, 125, 332–33, 478
Ondaatje, Michael, 296
O'Neill, Ella, 358
O'Neill, Eugene, 356–59, 389, 454, 469, 492
Oppen, George, 311, 326, 331, 332
Oppenheimer, Joel, 344
Orage, A. R., 421
Osbey, Brenda Maries, 339, 407
Osgood, Frances Sargent, 47

Subject Index

Ovid, 128
Ozick, Cynthia, 284, 298, 492

Pack, Robert, 327
Page, Thomas Nelson, 207, 209
Paine, Thomas, 199–200
Paley, Grace, 283, 298, 299
Palmer, Michael, 344
Parnell, Peter, 364
Pater, Walter, 185, 440
Peabody, Elizabeth, 5–6
Peacock, Molly, 339
Percy, Walker, 258, 286–87, 461
Percy, William Alexander, 319
Perelman, S. J., 271
Peters, Paul, 469
Peters, Robert, 343
Petry, Ann, 374, 375, 389–90
Pharr, Robert Dean, 381
Phelps, Elizabeth Stuart, 217
Phips, Sir William, 194
Piercy, Marge, 298
Pinter, Harold, 176
Piscator, Erwin, 235
Plath, Sylvia, 298–99, 325, 329, 334, 338, 339, 340
Poe, Edgar Allan, 41–56, 108, 182, 207, 220, 274, 421, 455–56, 469, 470, 478, 491
Pollock, Jackson, 337
Pope, Alexander, 44
Porter, Katherine Anne, 262, 453
Post, Emily, 140
Pound, Ezra, 123–34, 136, 139, 143, 186, 306, 313, 315, 327, 329, 336, 337, 430, 485, 492, 496
Price, Reynolds, 285
Prince, Nancy, 411
Prose, Francine, 299
Proust, Marcel, 432
Pynchon, Thomas, 271, 274, 279, 280, 282, 292–93, 451, 461, 467, 468

Quevedo, Francisco Gómez de, 311
Quintero, Jose, 359

Rabe, David, 363, 365
Rafelson, Bob, 274–75
Rakoski, Carl, 331
Ramus, Petrus, 192–93
Rank, Otto, 340
Rankin, Arthur McKee, 354
Ransom, John Crowe, 319

Ravenel, Beatrice Witte, 319
Ray, David, 343
Ray, Man, 296
Redding, Saunders, 379
Redmon, Ann, 298
Reece, Byron Herbert, 341
Reed, Ishmael, 282, 376
Reese, Lizette Woodworth, 248
Renan, Joseph Ernest, 133
Reverdy, Pierre, 342
Rexroth, Kenneth, 328, 337
Reznikoff, Charles, 331, 332, 479
Rich, Adrienne, 338, 339, 340
Richards, George, 200
Richardson, Willis, 359
Ricketson, Daniel, 23
Riddel, Joseph, 301
Rimbaud, Arthur, 328, 342, 430
Ripley, George, 5, 6
Robbins, Jerome, 362
Roberts, Elizabeth Madox, 249
Robinson, Edwin Arlington, 317–18, 330, 478
Roe, Edward Payson, 223
Roethke, Theodore, 330, 335, 478
Rogers, J. A., 378
Rooke, Leon, 461
Rosset, Barney, 283
Roth, Philip, 107, 284, 287
Rothenberg, Jerome, 329
Rousseau, Jean-Jacques, 10
Rowlandson, Mary, 193
Rowson, Susanna, 485
Ruskin, John, 60
Ryga, George, 469

Saffin, John, 192
Sainte-Beuve, Charles Augustin, 120
Salinger, J. D., 272, 468, 494
Salisbury, Ralph, 500
Salter, Mary Jo, 339
Sanchez, Sonia, 339, 361
Sanchez, Thomas, 299
Sand, George, 120
Sandburg, Carl, 478
Sanger, Margaret, 314
Santayana, George, 320
Santiago, Dany, 463
Sappho, 310
Saroyan, William, 266, 359
Sartre, Jean-Paul, 155, 254, 408, 425
Saxon, Lyle, 155
Schneider, Alan, 360

Schuyler, Eugene, 452
Schwarz-Bart, Simone, 396
Scott, Ridley, 42
Scott, Sir Walter, 97, 98, 476
Sealsfield, Charles, 216
Sedgwick, Catharine, 210
Seferis, George, 316
Selby, Hubert, 468
Sellars, Peter, 364
Serly, Tibor, 130
Sewall, Samuel, 193–94
Sexton, Anne, 334, 338, 340, 480, 492
Shakespeare, William, 46, 67, 95, 155–56, 209, 210, 214, 217, 237, 257–58, 286, 319
Shaw, George Bernard, 120, 129
Sheldon, Edward, 349
Shelley, Percy Bysshe, 18, 86, 155
Shepard, Sam, 350, 363
Shepard, William Pierce, 128
Shockley, Ann, 378
Showalter, Max, 365
Sidney, Sir Philip, 470
Sienkiewicz, Henryk, 165
Sigourney, Lydia, 417
Silko, Leslie, 299, 500
Silliman, Ron, 326, 330
Simms, William Gilmore, 209, 214
Simon, Neil, 362–63, 364–65
Simpson, Louis, 79, 325
Sinclair, Upton, 245–46
Sitwell, Dame Edith, 242
Smith, John, 195, 446
Smith, Lee, 278
Smith, Patti, 478
Smith, William Gardner, 390
Snyder, Gary, 327, 328, 478
Sollers, Werner, 291
Sologub, Fyodor Kuzmich, 491
Sondheim, Stephen, 362
Sontag, Susan, 451
Sophocles, 162
Sorrentino, Gilbert, 277, 293, 294
Spence, Eulalie, 359
Spencer, Anne, 379
Spencer, Herbert, 226, 449
Spender, Stephen, 125, 135
Spengler, Oswald, 175
Spenser, Edmund, 9
Spicer, Jack, 302, 336, 338
Spofford, Harriet Prescott, 220
Stafford, Jean, 267, 425
Stafford, William, 325, 343, 344

Starbuck, George, 334
Stedman, Edmund Clarence, 226–27
Steffens, Lincoln, 452, 493
Stegner, Wallace, 266
Stein, Gertrude, 241–42, 281, 326, 336, 458, 499
Steinbeck, John, 180, 255–57, 486
Stepnyak-Kravchinski, S., 449
Stern, Gerald, 344
Steuben, Fritz, 464
Stevens, Elsie Moll, 303–04
Stevens, Wallace, 179, 301–07, 311, 314, 327, 478, 480, 497
Stevenson, Robert Louis, 120, 121
Stieglitz, Alfred, 320
Stith, William, 196, 446
Stoddard, Elizabeth, 220
Stone, John Augustus, 353, 469
Stowe, Harriet Beecher, 206, 207, 216–17, 376, 417–18, 424, 469, 485
Styron, William, 281, 285, 416, 460
Suckow, Ruth, 425
Sue, Eugene, 43
Sukenick, Ronald, 277–78, 293
Swallow, Alan, 283
Swenson, May, 325, 338

Taine, Hippolyte, 121
Tate, Allen, 243, 257, 258, 319–20, 403, 466–67
Taylor, Bayard, 466
Taylor, Edward, 190, 191–92, 443, 446, 472
Taylor, Tom, 118
Taylor, William R., 209
Tenney, Tabitha Gilman, 210
Thackeray, William Makepeace, 60
Thompson, John R., 72
Thomson, James, 138
Thoreau, Henry David, 3–5, 8, 15–23, 455
Thurber, James, 273
Tieck, Ludwig, 41
Timrod, Henry, 209, 466
Todorov, Tsvetan, 207, 272
Tolson, Melvin B., 403
Tolstoy, Leo, 33, 452
Tompson, Benjamin, 192
Toole, John Kennedy, 285
Toomer, Jean, 379, 385–86, 463
Torrence, Ridgely, 359
Traven, B., 274
Trent, William Peterfield, 214

Trollope, Anthony, 107, 236
Trumbull, John, 466
Truth, Sojourner, 410–11
Tucker, George, 209
Tuckerman, Frederick Goddard, 216, 227
Turgenev, Ivan, 129, 144, 448
Turner, J. M. W., 59
Turpin, Waters Edward, 379
Twain, Mark, 47, 89–102, 107–08, 218, 221, 223, 241, 294, 297, 418, 448–49, 475, 476, 485, 490–91, 493, 494–95
Tyler, Anne, 285, 298
Tyler, Parker, 124

Updike, John, 42, 155, 278, 279, 280, 282, 284, 287–88, 416, 419, 485, 492
Urist, Rachel F., 349

Van Gogh, Vincent, 80
van Itallie, Jean-Claude, 503
Vargas Llosa, Mario, 155
Veblen, Peter, 363
Veblen, Thorstein, 100
Velázquez, Diego, 106
Vendler, Helen, 301, 334
Very, Jones, 216
Vidal, Gore, 452
Viereck, Peter, 467
Villanueva, Alma, 328
Villon, François, 305
Virgil (Vergil), 138, 320
Vonnegut, Kurt, Jr., 271, 279, 280, 290–91, 492
Vroman, Mary E., 374

Waddell, L. A., 133
Wagner, Rob, 364
Wakefield, Dan, 283
Waldman, Anne, 344
Walker, Alice, 298, 370, 374, 375, 376, 381, 397–99, 492, 499
Walker, Joseph, 408
Walker, Margaret, 376
Wallant, Edward Lewis, 468
Ward, Nathaniel, 189, 195
Ward, Theodore, 407
Warner, Charles Dudley, 214
Warner, Susan, 206, 210, 424
Warren, Robert Penn, 257–58, 262, 263, 319, 325, 326, 467

Washington, George, 250
Watkins, Floyd C., 341
Weaver, Gordon, 289
Webster, Daniel, 209
Weems, Mason Locke, 200–201
Welch, James, 299
Weldon, Fay, 498, 499
Weller, Michael, 363, 364
Welles, Orson, 293
Wells, H. G., 108, 120, 239
Wells, Ida B., 377–78
Welty, Eudora, 259, 261–62, 462, 482, 492
Wemyss, Francis C., 354
West, Dame Rebecca, 135
West, Nathanael, 270–71
Wharton, Edith, 104, 235–38, 239, 425, 468
Wheatley, Phillis, 447
Wheelock, John, 264
White, E. B., 268
White, Katharine, 267
Whitman, Walt, 5, 13, 69–80, 86, 128, 129, 317, 321, 337, 342, 343, 418, 457, 478
Whittier, John Greenleaf, 215, 466
Wideman, John Edgar, 393
Wigglesworth, Michael, 192, 472
Wilbur, Richard, 325, 328, 478
Wilde, Oscar, 144
Wilder, Thornton, 47–48, 320, 359
Williams, John A., 393
Williams, Jonathan, 344
Williams, Roger, 193
Williams, Rose, 361
Williams, Sam-Art, 371
Williams, Tennessee, 350, 360–61, 456–57, 492
Williams, William Carlos, 124, 128, 129, 130, 301, 306, 307–13, 320, 326, 335, 336, 337, 405, 478, 480, 481
Willis, Nathaniel Parker, 26, 207
Wilson, Alexander, 208
Wilson, August, 365
Wilson, Edward, 139
Wilson, Harriet, 411
Wilson, Robert, 350
Wilson, Robley, 283
Winters, Yvor, 266, 304
Winthrop, John, 32
Wister, Owen, 250, 493
Wittgenstein, Ludwig, 344, 441

Woiwode, Larry, 290
Wolfe, Thomas, 263–64, 468, 469
Wolfe, Tom, 223, 279, 280
Wood, Salley Barrell, 210
Woodson, Carter G., 368
Woolf, Virginia, 109, 136, 230, 242, 425, 429, 432
Wordsworth, William, 155, 319, 342, 478
Wright, Charles, 344
Wright, James, 325, 342–43
Wright, Jay, 406
Wright, Richard, 248, 328, 358, 372, 380, 382, 388–89, 413–14, 463

Yagi, Jyukichi, 490
Yates, Richard, 283
Yeats, William Butler, 128, 129, 138, 139, 141, 179, 281, 327, 429
Yglesias, Helen, 299
Young, Al, 377
Young, Noel, 283
Young, Stark, 249–50

Zamora, Bernice, 328
Zappa, Frank, 478
Zola, Émile, 120, 233
Zukofsky, Louis, 302, 311, 326, 329, 331, 332, 336, 339